Visualization and Modeling

k t . turned on . ore

Visualization and Modeling

Edited by

Rae Earnshaw
University of Bradford, UK

John Vince
Bournemouth University, UK

Huw Jones
Middlesex University, UK

ACADEMIC PRESS
San Diego   London   Boston
New York   Sydney   Tokyo   Toronto

This book is printed on acid-free paper.

Academic Press Inc.
525 B Street, Suite 1900, San Diego, California 92101-4495, USA
http://www.apnet.com

Academic Press Limited
24–28 Oval Road, London NW1 7DX, UK
http://www.hbuk.co.uk/ap/

ISBN 0–12–227738–4

A catalogue record for this book is available from the British Library

Typeset by Phoenix Photosetting, Chatham, Kent
Printed in Great Britain at the University Printing House, Cambridge

97 98 99 00 01 02 EB 9 8 7 6 5 4 3 2 1

Contents

Color Plates are located between pp. 46–47.

Contributors

D. B. Arnold, School of Information Systems, University of East Anglia, Norwich NR4 7TJ.

A. Berro, Institut de Recherche en Informatique de Toulouse, Université Paul Sabatier, 118 Route de Narbonne, 31062 Toulouse Cedex, France.

Jack Bresenham, Winthrop University, Rock Hill, SC 29733, USA.

Paul Briggs, Aspect Computing Pty, 290 Glen Osmond Road, Fullarton SA 5063, Australia.

Ken Brodlie, School of Computer Studies, University of Leeds, Leeds LS2 9JT, UK.

Judith R. Brown, ITS Academic, 134A LC, The University of Iowa, Iowa City, IA 52242, USA.

Patrick Callet, Laboratoire Produtique Logistique, Ecole Centrale Paris – Grande Voie des Vignes, 92290 Châtenay-Malabry, France.

Richard Cant, Department of Computing, Faculty of Engineering & Computing, Nottingham Trent University, Burton Street, Nottingham NG1 4BU, UK.

René Caubet, Institut de Recherche en Informatique de Toulouse, Université Paul Sabatier, 118 Route de Narbonne, 31062 Toulouse Cedex, France.

Mark Caulfield-Browne, Department of Mechanical Engineering, PNG University of Technology, Papua New Guinea.

K. J. Clark, Quantisci, Chiltern House, 45 Station Road, Henley-on-Thames, Oxon RG9 1AT, UK.

Dalcidio Moraes Claudio, Instituto de Informática, UFRGS-Universidade Federal do Rio Grande do Sul, Caixa Postal 15064, 91501–970 Porto Alegre, RS, Brazil.

Robert A. Cross, Naval Research Laboratory, Washington, DC 20375, USA.

I. Curington, AVS/UNIRAS Ltd, Montrose House, Chertsey Boulevard, Hanworth Lane, Chertsey, Surrey KT16 9JX, UK.

Laurent Da Dalto, Institut de Recherche en Informatique de Toulouse, Université Paul Sabatier, 118 Route de Narbonne, 31062 Toulouse Cedex, France.

A. M. Day, School of Information Systems, University of East Anglia, Norwich NR4 7TJ, UK.

†Justin J. Doick, Department of Mathematics, University of Essex, Wivenhoe Park, Colchester CO4 3SQ, UK.

Y. Duthen, Institut de Recherche en Informatique de Toulouse, Université Paul Sabatier, 118 Route de Narbonne, 31062 Toulouse Cedex, France.

Rae Earnshaw, Electronic Imaging and Media Communications, University of Bradford, Bradford BD7 1DP, UK.

Eddy Flerackers, Expertise Centre for Digital Media, Limburg University Centre, Wetenschapspark 2, B3590 Diepenbeek, Belgium.

Brian Francis, Centre for Applied Statistics, Fylde College, Lancaster University, Lancaster LA1 4YF, UK.

Carla Maria Dal Sasso Freitas, Instituto de Informática, UFRGS-Universidade Federal do Rio Grande do Sul, Caixa Postal 15064, 91501–970 Porto Alegre, RS, Brazil.

Teruyoshi Fujiwara, Department of Precision Machinery Engineering, University of Tokyo, Hongo 7–3–1, Bunkyo, Tokyo 113, Japan.

Mark Fuller, Lightwork Design Ltd, 60 Clarkehouse Road, Sheffield S10 2LH, UK.

A. Gareau, LISPI/LIGIM, Bâtiment 710, Université Claude Bernard Lyon 1, 43 Bd du 11 Novembre 1918, 69622 Villeurbanne Cedex, France.

Jens Herder, University of Aizu, Tsuruga, Ikki-machi, Aizu-Wakamatsu City, Fukushima 965–80, Japan.

Anthony R. Holt, Department of Mathematics, University of Essex, Wivenhoe Park, Colchester CO4 3SQ, UK.

J. P. Humm, Quantisci, Chiltern House, 45 Station Road, Henley-on-Thames, Oxon RG9 1AT, UK.

Masumi Ibusuki, Fifty Limited Company and Dame Dental Clinic, 1–24–4 Highland, Yokosuka City, Kanagawa 239, Japan.

†Deceased.

Atsumi Imamiya, Department of Electrical Engineering and Computer Science, Yamanashi University, 4–3–11 Takeda, Kofu, Japan 400.

M. D. Impey, Quantisci, Chiltern House, 45 Station Road, Henley-on-Thames, Oxon RG9 1AT, UK.

Mikael Jern, Vice President Technology, AVS/UNIRAS, 15 Blokken, DK 3460 Birkerod, Denmark.

Jean-Pierre Jessel, Institut de Recherche en Informatique de Toulouse, Université Paul Sabatier, 118 Route de Narbonne, 31062 Toulouse Cedex, France.

Huw Jones, Centre for Electronic Arts, Middlesex University, Cat Hill, Barnet EN4 8HT, UK.

Mark W. Jones, Department of Computer Science, University of Wales Swansea, Singleton Park, Swansea SA2 8PP, UK.

Fumihiko Kimura, Department of Precision Machinery Engineering, University of Tokyo, Hongo 7–3–1, Bunkyo, Tokyo 113, Japan.

Shankar Krishnan, Department of Computer Science, University of North Carolina, Chapel Hill, NC 27599, USA.

Subodh Kumar, Department of Computer Science, University of North Carolina, Chapel Hill, NC 27599, USA.

Tosiyasu L. Kunii, University of Aizu, Tsuruga, Ikki-machi, Aizu-Wakamatsu City, Fukushima 965–80, Japan.

Wim Lamotte, Expertise Centre for Digital Media, Limburg University Centre, Wetenschapspark 2, B3590 Diepenbeek, Belgium.

Hervé Luga, Institut de Recherche en Informatique de Toulouse, Université Paul Sabatier, 118 Route de Narbonne, 31062 Toulouse Cedex, France.

Bart MacCarthy, Department of Manufacturing Engineering, University of Nottingham, University Park, Nottingham NG7 2RD, UK.

Dinesh Manocha, Department of Computer Science, University of North Carolina, Chapel Hill, NC 27599, USA.

Isabel Harb Manssour, Instituto de Informática, UFRGS-Universidade Federal do Rio Grande do Sul, Caixa Postal 15064, 91501–970 Porto Alegre, RS, Brazil.

R. Minghim, School of Information Systems, University of East Anglia, Norwich NR4 7TJ, UK and ICMSC-USP, CP 668, 13560 Sao Carlos-SP, Brazil.

Karol Myszkowski, University of Aizu, Tsuruga, Ikki-machi, Aizu-Wakamatsu City, Fukushima 965–80, Japan.

Atul Narkhede, Department of Computer Science, University of North Carolina, Chapel Hill, NC 27599, USA.

Galina Okuneva, University of Aizu, Tsuruga, Ikki-machi, Aizu-Wakamatsu City, Fukushima 965–80, Japan.

R. Pelle, Institut de Recherche en Informatique de Toulouse, Université Paul Sabatier, 118 Route de Narbonne, 31062 Toulouse Cedex, France.

Lawrence J. Rosenblum, Naval Research Laboratory, 4555 Overlook Ave. SW Washington, DC 20375, USA.

S. Shah, Quantisci, Chiltern House, 45 Station Road, Henley-on-Thames, Oxon RG9 1AT, UK.

Paul Shrubsole, Department of Computing, Faculty of Engineering & Computing, Nottingham Trent University, Burton Street, Nottingham NG1 4BU, UK.

Nilo Stolte, Institut de Recherche en Informatique de Toulouse, Université Paul Sabatier, 118 Route de Narbonne, 31062 Toulouse Cedex, France.

Hiromasa Suzuki, Department of Precision Machinery Engineering, University of Tokyo, Hongo 7-3-1, Bunkyo, Tokyo 113, Japan.

Mikio Terasawa, Nihon University, Misaki-cho 1-3-2, Chiyoda-ku, Tokyo, Japan.

A. L. Thomas, School of Engineering, University of Sussex, Falmer, Brighton BN1 9QT, UK.

Andrew Tunbridge, Beal High School, Woodford Bridge Road, Essex, UK

S. M. Turner, School of Environmental Sciences, University of East Anglia, Norwich NR4 7TJ, UK.

D. Vandorpe, LISPI/LIGIM, Bâtiment 710, Université Claude Bernard Lyon 1, 43 Bd du 11 Novembre 1918, 69622 Villeurbanne Cedex, France.

K. van Overveld, Department of Mathematics and Computer Science, Eindhoven University of Technology, PO Box 513, 5600 MB, Eindhoven, The Netherlands.

Frank Van Reeth, Expertise Centre for Digital Media, Limburg University Centre, Wetenschapspark 2, B3590 Diepenbeek, Belgium.

Flávio Rech Wagner, Instituto de Informática, UFRGS-Universidade Federal do Rio Grande do Sul, Caixa Postal 15064, 91501–970 Porto Alegre, RS, Brazil.

M. J. Williams, Quantisci, Chiltern House, 45 Station Road, Henley-on-Thames, Oxon RG9 1AT, UK.

Jason Wood, School of Computer Studies, University of Leeds, Leeds LS2 9JT, UK.

Helen Wright, School of Computer Studies, University of Leeds, Leeds LS2 9JT, UK.

Brian Wyvill, Department of Computer Science, University of Calgary, Calgary, Alberta, Canada T2N 1N4.

Kouji Yoshizaki, Tokyo Gas Corporation, Shibaura 1-16-25, Minato-ku, Tokyo, Japan.

Dong Zhang, Department of Electrical Engineering and Computer Science, Yamanashi University, 4–3–11 Takeda, Kofu, Japan 400.

Introduction

Early computer-generated images were composed from lines drawn on paper or plastic cell, and from this ability to draw lines emerged the subject of computer graphics. From lines and curves came shape and form, which gave rise to perspective line drawings of simple three-dimensional (3D) objects. Immediately, there was a requirement for hidden-line removal algorithms, to remove line segments masked by opaque features. Although the construction of objects from polygons was convenient, planar surfaces could not accurately model objects formed from complex curved surfaces. However, the research work of Coons, Bézier, and De Casteljau revealed mathematical tools for describing parametric surface patches that could be assembled to define a rich variety of smooth continuous surfaces.

Representing an object as a seamless skin of polygons and patches is a convenient and powerful modeling tool, but such a scheme bears little resemblance to the solid objects we handle in the real world. Solid modeling became a reality when it was realized that the mathematical description of certain objects such as cylinders, spheres, cones, toroids, and so on, could be the basis of an alternate modeling scheme. These basic geometric primitives could be organized into complex structures using the Boolean operators *union*, *difference*, and *intersection*. Today, boundary representation and set-theoretic models still play a central role in 3D modeling systems; but they are not ideal for modeling soft and elastic objects, liquids, gases, flames, plants, hair, and the like. Further modeling schemes have had to be developed to cope with these structures. And although geometric modeling has made significant advances in recent years, there are still many outstanding problems, especially in the modeling of organic structures such as skin, flesh, and muscle.

Modeling, however, is still only part of the story in creating virtual objects. We still need to obtain a graphical representation of the model captured on paper or projected onto a screen. The problem of transforming abstract computer models into images has been an exciting era in the field of computer graphics, and has given rise to topics such as illumination models, scan-line renderers, ray tracing, texture mapping, bump mapping, transparency maps, and radiosity. As one might expect, modeling and rendering are closely related. Certain modeling schemes have a preferred rendering technique and result in efficient display times. Given the right processing environment, it is possible to render images in fractions of seconds, making possible real-time graphics. During the last decade, real-time graphics has brought virtual reality systems to the marketplace that enable us to build, see, hear, touch, and interact with a wide variety of virtual worlds.

Numerical data sets, however, are not associated just with 3D geometry; they also can arise from experiments conducted in the real world. For example, weather prediction relies heavily upon sampling temperature and pressure over a specific geographical area, and observing how these distributions change over a period of time. Although such numerical data sets are convenient for computer programs, our understanding of the data is greatly enhanced if they are represented graphically. It is this conversion of numbers into images that has given rise to the subject of computer visualization. Scalar data sets recording temperature or pressure can be visualized using contour plots, histograms, color maps, or height fields, where spatial characteristics help us recognize peaks, troughs, ridges and plateaux. These data sets are not only used to measure a scalar value over a surface, they are also used to record changes throughout a volume of space. Visualizing 3D volumetric data calls for a new set of graphical techniques that permit volumes to be explored visually. Vector data sets recording wind velocities, for example, where a scalar and a direction are encoded, require special techniques to reveal the direction of the datum. This can be represented by an arrowhead in a static picture, but another family of techniques can be used if animation is employed. The movement of particles, for example, is an excellent way of illustrating the magnitude of vector fields.

In the space of 40 years, or so, we have progressed from primitive line drawings to being immersed in stereoscopic, 3D virtual worlds. But what is even more exciting is that this is not the end. Computer modeling and visualization are still in their infancy, and will continue to evolve as we uncover new solutions to some tantalizing problems. Faster computer processors and new display hardware will create new avenues of research and exciting new products.

Today, computer modeling and visualization are still a vital dynamic area of study, and this book provides the reader with a snapshot of what is happening around the world. In all, there are 26 chapters, written by leading experts in their field, and they show how inventive research is still taking us down an exciting road of discovery.

In Chapter 1, Judith Brown discusses the importance of graphic design in scientific visualization, and explores how color and viewpoint can enhance the effectiveness of a visualization. She then reviews seven case studies, highlighting relevant features that influenced the type of visualization employed. Finally, she discusses how the technologies of multimedia and virtual reality are affecting the future development of scientific visualization.

In Chapter 2, Jason Wood and colleagues report on their research into Computer Supported Collaborative Visualization (CSCV). They argue that modern scientific research is rarely undertaken by an individual – it tends to be collaborative. Consequently, they have developed a set of visualization tools that support such collaborative projects.

In Chapter 3, M. D. Impey and colleagues discuss the growing demand for quantitative assessment of the impact of pollutants in the environment, and the need to communicate the results of assessment studies to nonspecialists and decision makers. The chapter focuses on the issues that need to be tackled in designing an integrated and interactive system for modeling subsurface pollutant migration, and describe the design principles which have been adopted in the development of one such application, MACRO-AFFINITY.

In Chapter 4, Isabel Manssour and colleagues report on the architecture and facilities of a visualization system designed to support daily tasks and long-term research conducted by meteorologists at the 8th Meteorological District, in Southern Brazil. They also discuss the results of applying the multiquadratic method to interpolating data for the construction of contour maps.

In Chapter 5, Mark Fuller and Brian Francis describe how recent developments in computer visualization have generated new graphical representations of event history data. The resulting three-dimensional displays are closely related to Lexis plots, and can show the complete complexity of the collected data.

In Chapter 6, Justin Doick and Anthony Holt discuss the advantages and problems inherent in using proprietary software packages in the task of data visualization. In particular, he reports on the progress being made toward a three-dimensional product for the interpretation of weather radar data.

In Chapter 7, A. M. Day and colleagues present a technique for the treatment and formatting of marine time-dependent data for visualization, as well as discussing the utility of a number of techniques for analysis of the resulting data.

In Chapter 8, Adrian Thomas explores a series of interrelated topics concerned with the problem of representing shape in pictures and diagrams. He presents a series of studies concerned with the capture, use, and display of the shape of objects. These range from solid objects at one extreme to continuously varying spatial distributions, such as pollution thresholds in bodies of gas or water, at the other.

In Chapter 9, Laurent Da Dalto and Jean-Pierre Jessel describe a new sampling solution for computing global illumination. The new approach has numerous advantages: low memory and computation costs; greater realism; and increased ease of interaction. The authors describe how their technique is used to create solid-object illumination, shadows on volumes, and direct and indirect shadows.

In Chapter 10, Nilo Stolte and René Caubet compare two rasterization algorithms for implicit surfaces. They also show how implicit surfaces can be visualized in their voxel format with the aid of an octree. This allows for near real-time interaction with quite high-resolution scenes.

In Chapter 11, Subodh Kumar and colleagues describe a system for fast and accurate display of CSG (constructive solid geometry) models. During a preprocessing phase, the B-rep (boundary representation) from the CSG tree is computed, and is used to represent the resulting solid using trimmed spline surfaces. One of the advantages of this technique is that it permits dynamic level of detail.

In Chapter 12, Richard Cant and Paul Shrubsole present a new method of overcoming aliasing problems which result from point-to-point texture mapping. The algorithm deals with transformed pixels in texture space by first building a 'potential' array of the original texture. An average texture intensity is then obtained by traversing around the edges of the transformed pixel and applying a 'potential map' across its boundaries. In conclusion, the authors compare their technique with other well-established techniques.

In Chapter 13, H. Luga and colleagues describe a method for automatically converting objects described by traditional modeling methods (like meshes or NURBS) into an extended algebraic surface one. They also describe an adaptive optimization algorithm based on genetic algorithms. These algorithms, based upon the process of natural selection, need to compute the ability of a proposed solution to solve the problem. They conclude by showing how their technique is successfully applied to a variety of objects.

In Chapter 14, Mark Jones investigates the main techniques for accelerating the volume rendering of 3D regular data. In addition to the description of each method, he gives full details of a new acceleration method which gives 30% to 50% speedup with very little image degradation.

In Chapter 15, Patrick Callet describes a generalization of a model for interference in thin films. The algorithm employs complex refractive indices, and can simulate the behavior of natural light and polarized light with thin films.

In Chapter 16, Huw Jones and colleagues describe a method for modeling the passage of nutrients and energy through the structure of a growing biological model. The model is implemented using parametric L-systems, and allows nutrient and energy levels and environmental features to affect the growing structure.

In Chapter 17, Jack Bresenham describes the exciting technologies behind 3D rapid prototyping. Such systems are able to create 3D physical forms from geometric descriptions, and provide the ultimate visualization of a virtual object.

In Chapter 18, Robert Cross and Lawrence Rosenblum discuss important problems faced in current virtual reality research in its attempts to provide interaction, visual realism, and multimodal immersion. They also examine selected applications to provide a sense of what is achievable today in VR, and the directions in which the field is heading.

In Chapter 19, A. Gareau and D. Vandorpe describe a new approach to special effects in computer animation. Their technique employs autonomous agents for communicating messages between geometric primitives, and they show how sets of particles, edges, and polygons can be used to model rigid objects and natural phenomena.

In Chapter 20, Atsumi Imamiya and Dong Zhang outline a geometric model for describing breaking waves. They show how the shape of the ocean floor, depth of water, and wave refraction influence the final animation. They also consider the issues of breaking spray, and examples of breaking waves in different scenarios.

In Chapter 21, B. L. MacCarthy and M. Caulfield-Browne describe the principles and development of a computer-aided engineering tool for motion specification problems. The technique is particularly useful for high-speed systems and for mechanism design and synthesis. The system, which is called MODUS (motion design using splines), has been developed with a core generation module on which application modules for specific application areas can be built.

In Chapter 22, Horomasa Suzuki and colleagues report on research they have undertaken to develop a system for assisting designers in the visualization of flexible mechanical parts. Their approach allows the capture of features of motion and deformation, with the minimum of computation.

In Chapter 23, Brian Wyvill and Kees van Overveld describe recent research into visualizing and animating implicit and solid models. Their approach is to combine implicit surface modeling (ISM) with constructive solid geometry (CSG) to create BCSO models. They show how such models may be defined and how they are used in animation.

In Chapter 24, Karol Myszkowski and colleagues present work on new visual tools and a related user interface for global articulation simulation, developed for the Intelligent Dental Care System project. The aim of the simulation is the visual representation of characteristics relevant to the chewing process.

In Chapter 25, Mikael Jern discusses human–computer interaction within the context of data visualization. The paper focuses on the visual user interface, component technology, and visual programming. The author also describes the problems of working with large data sets, and how to interact with them in real time.

In Chapter 26, Wim Lamotte and colleagues describe how they exploit asynchronous transfer mode (ATM) to support multimedia applications requiring high communication bandwidth. The authors report on recent results obtained from their VISINET project, and discuss how a local MPEG-1-based Video Retrieval trial is set up over the same ATM network.

1
Visualization and Scientific Applications

Judith R. Brown

1.1 Introduction

Visualization tools and techniques enable scientists to explore their research data, to gain new scientific insight, and to communicate their discoveries to others. Visualization allows the conversion of information that cannot be perceived by the human eye into forms suitable for this most highly developed human sense. As illustrated in reference [1], the importance of visualization as a key component of the research process is now recognized, and researchers consider visualization of their research data to be an essential tool for understanding their research results, sharing these results with their peers, and presenting their science to the general public and to policy makers.

We have experienced a revolution in how we probe and present data. Visualization – combining computer graphics, computation, communication, and interaction – is invaluable for changing data into information, designing products, and supporting complex decision making. This revolution, allowing us to understand realities on a larger scale, has resulted in the need to change laws and policies, such as the United States 1990 guidelines for the Clean Air Act, as described later in this paper. Although early technological breakthroughs were driven by defense, some major advances now are driven by the entertainment industry, and there is an evolution of visual computing in the financial industry.

We can communicate visual information through color, form, and animation, where, as described by Canadian film-maker Norman McLaren, 'Animation is not the art of drawings that move, but of movement that is drawn.' There are some things that we cannot see properly unless they are animated. Some of the scientific techniques for obtaining more information are image processing (changing the pixels in an image in terms of color or through transformations), volume visualization (building a 3D volume from data slices such as those from magnetic resonance imaging scans), and simulation of scientific phenomena based on scientific rules and constraints. This ability to interact rapidly with a simulation during the computation has become increasingly important. The ability for scientists and students to steer their experiments or simulations as they are happening, or to interact with their data in a virtual environment, has become essential for some research and educational applications.

Visualization and Modeling
ISBN 0-12-227738-4

1.2 Effective Design

If the visualizations that we produce are to be informative and effective, we must understand principles of design, how colors interact, and how we perceive visual information. Scientists and visualization specialists at the National Center for Supercomputing Applications (NCSA) have produced some excellent examples of scientific visualization. Since early on, artists and designers have been involved with the scientific visualization. They probe ways to improve design aspects of the data visualization in order to get more information and better understanding from scientific images and animations, as shown in the following examples.

Data for the 1989 animation, 'Study of a Numerically Modeled Severe Storm,' came from a CRAY simulation of a severe thunderstorm across Texas and Oklahoma. This storm spawned a tornado that caused 111 injuries, 7 deaths, and $15 million worth of damage. The simulation and visualization of this storm illustrate air movement and conditions during the storm period, based on actual wind velocity, moisture, temperature, and pressure data. This landmark animation has been shown worldwide and stands as an example of how to present scientific information to the general public and to policy makers in an effective and attention-getting way.

Visualization specialists (Edward Tufte from Yale University and Colleen Bushell, Matthew Arrott, Polly Baker, and Mike McNeil from NCSA) have revisited this thunderstorm animation to try to improve the design of this particular animation, and to develop guidelines for effective visualization design in general, as communicated in reference [5]. They produced guidelines on color and line widths, especially if the image is going to be transferred to video. Principles of design illustrated in these new images include the effective use of color, animation, and annotation. The shadows and the grid were rendered more subtly so that all are still perceptible, although the new images provide more information with less distraction. These new images also feature annotated axes and a timeline with a series of images showing where each image is in the animation sequence. A later version of the animation adds more information by showing two slices from the storm cloud with a new, modified color palette and histograms that show the maximum amount of rainwater at the level of those slices throughout the storm sequence.

1.3 Effective Use of Color

Artists use color to create an emotional effect or to convey a message. Viewing the color in the artistic expression of the Romantic painters or the effects of light, shadows, and other aspects of color used by the Impressionists, leaves little doubt about the power of color. However, color may have a different meaning for each viewer, depending on his or her experiences or culture, or the particular application.

The color of an object varies with its surroundings, the lighting, and the perception of the viewer. The lightwaves that determine the perception of color can be measured, and visible light ranges through the spectrum of red, orange, yellow, green, blue, indigo, and violet. Although the lightwave of length 700 nanometers (nm) is perceived as red, and that of 400 nm is perceived as violet, these colors may be perceived differently by every viewer.

An understanding of elementary physiology helps artists and designers use color effectively. For example, the retinas of our eyes have cones. Chemicals, called photopigments, contained in these cones are sensitive to particular wavelengths of light, therefore causing the sensation of color. Since the cones that contain the photopigment for blue are scarce, making up only 2% of all the cones, our eyes are least sensitive to the color blue (especially for thin lines, text, or small shapes) and to subtle variations in blue. However, because these cones are evenly distributed across the retina (even though they make up only 2% of all the cones), blue is therefore a good color for backgrounds or large areas. For similar reasons, red and green are more effectively placed at the center of an image than at the periphery. Because the cones that contain the photopigments for red and green are concentrated in the center of the retina, the eye is not sensitive to red and green if they are in the visual periphery, especially if they are used for text or small shapes.

The interaction of color is also very interesting. Certain color combinations placed next to each other, such as bright blue and bright yellow, result in blurring or vibrations at the edges where they meet. These vibrations also occur with a combination of intense colors from any two of the red, green, and blue primaries. Color is very deceptive, as discussed in references [2] and [3]. Two different colors can look the same against different backgrounds. Also, a color can look very different, depending on the background color, the adjacent colors, or the size of the area of the color.

Color selection may vary depending on the application, the cultural meaning, or the professional association, as discussed in reference [4]. For example, applications such as three-dimensional modeling need more colors for realistic rendering than do graphs and charts. As a cultural example on the meaning of color, in the United States red traditionally means 'stop' or 'danger,' and white is the traditional wedding color, whereas in China red is the traditional wedding color, and white is a color for funerals. Color can also affect moods, depending on the experiences of the viewer. Color deficiencies, sometimes mistakenly referred to as 'color blindness,' affect some people and prevent them from distinguishing certain colors. About 8% of males and 0.5% of females have a color deficiency that makes it impossible for them to distinguish small color differences, especially with low brightness levels. Viewers may have difficulty distinguishing red from green or differentiating subtle variations of color or grayscale, and older viewers have more difficulty seeing blue.

1.4 Viewing Three Dimensions

When viewing three-dimensional images, you need to understand the images' positions in space. Stereo viewing is thus very important in some applications to provide this depth information, although many people are unable to see stereo images. In virtual reality applications, you need as many depth cues as possible, including sound. Virtual reality is discussed later in this chapter.

PHSColograms (pronounced skol-o-grams) employ a new technique that provides a hardcopy record of virtual environments without the need for special glasses. These digitally produced autostereo hardcopy images use a proprietary technique from (Art)^n Laboratory. The original images can be created from nearly any software capable of creating 3D images, or from digitized photography. After a number of views (usually

13 views) of the 3D object are created, the $(Art)^n$ software combines the views by interleaving strips from the 13 images into one image. This image is viewed through a barrier screen that blocks out 12 of the 13 images at any given viewing angle. Because each of our eyes is at a different viewing angle, we see two views and thus experience a different 3D image as we move to different viewing angles. The term PHSCologram is based on photography, holography, sculpture, and computer graphics. It has been used both as an art form and as a means to understand scientific images. The final high-resolution images range in size (usually 20 inches by 24 inches), and they are mounted on 1/4 inch Plexiglas, backlit in an ordinary lightbox. Plates 1 and 2, illustrate two of the many scientific images that have been produced as virtual photography PHSCologram s.

1.5   Visualization Case Studies

Visualization applications cut across all disciplines and industries. The use of computer graphics to understand data is not dependent on the type of data or how the data was acquired. Here is a sampling of effective uses of visualization techniques.

1.5.1   Lyapunov chaos space

The Lyapunov formula, named after the Russian mathematician Aleksandr M. Lyapunov, tells us how chaotically a system is behaving. At the University of Iowa, this model was extended to three dimensions and run in parallel to test parallel computers around the United States. The resultant beautiful images are a side benefit of the timing tests run on various computers. Plate 3, shows one frame from an animated sequence of flying through the Lyapunov chaos space. At each point in the image, if the system is capable of chaotic behavior, the point is colored black. If the system is stable, the point is colored some shade of a selected color, such as yellow.

1.5.2   Data visualization in numerical simulation of metal casting

University of Iowa researchers illustrate the numerical results from a two-phase simulation of solidification of metal alloys. This solidification simulation shows the fluid flow pattern within the mold, distribution of copper in a copper/aluminum mixture, and temperature ranges within the mold. This application is especially valuable to manufacturers of aluminum products such as Alcoa, so they can see where the alloys are not evenly mixed as they solidify. Plate 4, shows the distribution of solute composition of copper (Cu), ranging from 1% Cu to 6% Cu, in an aluminum/copper mixture. This nonhomogeneity of composition causes defects in the final casting product. The overlaid contour plot illustrates the temperature range from 751 kelvin to 921 kelvin.

1.5.3   Environmental visualization and public policy

The US Environmental Protection Agency (EPA) uses an air-quality model to simulate significant chemical and physical processes responsible for the photochemical production of ozone. These images and animations improve EPA researchers' understanding of the photochemical models. Although the 1990 Clean Air Act set guidelines on when each state had to lower its pollution levels, in some cases visualization of the air pollution source and receptor areas resulted in the discovery of flaws in the guidelines for pollution clean-up. The visualization showed the situation where a state that was the recipient of air pollution from another state had an earlier air pollution clean-up date than the state that was causing the air pollution. This was one example of visualization changing public policy, as the 1990 Clean Air Act legal guidelines had to be changed.

A map of the specific geographic domain is combined with the visualization to provide spatial context for the Regional Oxidant Model (ROM) data sets. Many 2D and 3D visualization techniques are utilized to gain the best information from the simulations. Plate 5, is a two-dimensional example where wind information is illustrated by wind vector representations animated over time. Short vectors in cool colors, such as blue, indicate low speeds. Long vectors and warm colors, such as orange, indicate high speeds. This figure also shows how air pollution moves across state lines.

Visualization helps to clarify what exists or to change the way scientists think. In another example of visualization's effect on policy makers, California pollution studies resulted in a ban on lighter fluid in backyard barbecues in the state of California.

Environmentalists and policy makers gather to discuss future possibilities through scenarios. They are interested in where depositions come from and where they go. As in the case of United States air pollution crossing state lines, air pollution from one country spreads to other countries. The policy makers use computer graphics to see what will happen in the future if certain controls are put on emissions or if nothing is done to curb emissions. For example, by the year 2020, China's emissions will triple from what they were in 1990 if nothing is done. Curbing air pollution nationally or internationally will require cooperation and changes in lifestyles.

1.5.4   Air convection within a room

Plate 6, shows the temperature distribution in a room, along with the air flow pattern and velocity field. In this room model, all the walls are thermally insulated except the left and right walls, which are isothermal at a high temperature and a low temperature, respectively. As the air next to the left wall is heated, it rises and flows across the top of the room while cooling and sinking on the opposite side of the room. This is caused by a buoyancy force due to the density of the air varying with temperature. In Plate 6, the color represents the temperature distribution in the room, and the vectors show the air flow pattern and velocity field.

This computational fluid dynamics (CFD) model was constructed by Dr Jun Ni, Advanced Research Computing Services at The University of Iowa, using PHOENICS software. Execution of this model produced a three-dimensional grid of discrete points at which pressure, temperature, and air flow direction and velocity were computed at a particular point in time. The data from this model was then brought into Data Explorer for visualization by Jun Ni and Tom Halverson.

1.5.5   Knots in 3-space

Dr Jonathan Simon, Mathematics Department, The University of Iowa, researches on knots, simple closed curves in 3-space. If the closed polygon can untwist into a simple loop without breaking, it is an 'unknot.' The knots that are generally studied are smooth or polygonal, and Simon's interests include both knots and unknots, and the 'energy functions' for knots. Energy functions associate a number to a knot that represents how complicated the knot is. The goals are twofold: (1) to gain a better understanding of the collection of all knots, and (2) to model (eventually to understand and predict) the behavior of DNA or other polymers when they form knotted loops (which they do!).

Plate 7, illustrates a tangled unknot as it untangles. Simon has developed an energy function for polygons in space that causes the sticks of the polygon to repel each other, so that the polygon flows from its initial conformation to one in which the energy is minimal. During this process, the sticks of the polygon cannot pass through each other (i.e., a knotted polygon cannot become unknotted or vice versa).

These figures, three frames from an animation of a knot untangling, reveal that a very complicated initial figure is indeed an unknot. The color in these images has no meaning, but it allows us to see better how the knot is entangled. Without a multicolor palette, it is difficult to see which parts of the knot are in the front and which parts are in the back.

1.5.6   Biomechanics of athletic movement

Dr James Hay, Exercise Department, The University of Iowa, collaborates with Computer Science professor Joseph Kearney to use motion capture and computer animation to visualize the motion of elite athletes. As the athlete moves (runs, jumps, etc.) he or she is photographed with two calibrated cine cameras at a rate of 60 frames a second. The locations of 21 points on the athlete's body are identified in each frame, and the three-dimensional locations of joints are recovered through triangulation of the stereo views. Three-dimensional animations are produced with software that is based on the Open Inventor toolkit for interactive modeling. Figures 1.1a–e show frames from the animation of an athlete doing a broad jump. The triple jumper illustrated here is United States athlete Sheila Hudson, and this is the winning triple jump from the last Olympic trials. Visualization was done by Matthew Atherton, Pete Willemsen, and Joseph Kearney.

1.5.7   Hoppers

Although motion for the previous example came from digitization of an actual athlete performing a triple jump, computer-generated figures have been jumping (and hopping, flipping, etc.) in the University of Iowa Computer Science Department for a long time. Professors Joseph Kearney and James Cremer have been investigating constraint-based motion control for the last eight years. In their research and related classes, movements are simulated using a model-based dynamics simulator called Newton that was developed by Cremer at Cornell University. Students dressed the hoppers with geometric models to create animations. Figure 1.2 shows a scene from a 'hopper'

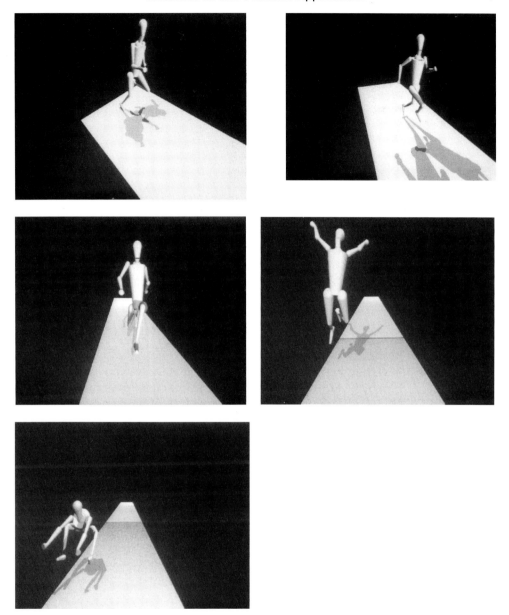

Figure 1.1 Frames from an animation of a runner performing a broad jump. Visualization was done by Matthew Atherton, Pete Willemsen, and Joseph Kearney, Computer Science, University of Iowa. © Joseph Kearney.

baseball game. This corn field scene is a takeoff on the movie 'Field of Dreams,' which was filmed in Iowa. However, in our version, the players and the fans are also stalks of corn. Visualization was done by Joseph Kearney, John Knaack, Kerri Price, Dan Stevenson, Pete Willemsen, and Chien Kok Yang.

Figure 1.2 Hopper from corn video. Visualization was done by Joseph Kearney, John Knaack, Kerri Price, Dan Stevenson, Pete Willemsen, and Chien Kok Yang, Computer Science, University of Iowa. © Joseph Kearney.

1.6   The Edge of Technology

There are many continuing developments in computer graphics, visualization, multimedia, and virtual reality. Futuristic activities in the research laboratories gradually make their way into use in university and industrial production laboratories and eventually into classrooms. Through computer graphics, we can turn vision into creation. High-speed computer networks allow us additional and valuable opportunities to access remote resources and collaborate with our colleagues around the world.

1.6.1   Multimedia for education

At the University of Iowa's Second Look Computing, a New Media center, rich multimedia experiential environments are developed for education. It has recently created tools to support highly specialized learning in biochemistry and pediatric cardiology. Both projects required actual case studies, realistic models, and accurate realizations of processes. They use high end UNIX workstations, like the SGI, to create movies that are then delivered on more popular platforms like Windows and Macs. These lower end platforms are closing the gap with the higher end machines in terms of 3D capabilities. This means that it will be more common for people to become familiar with seeing, using, and creating 3D visualizations.

The goal of the pediatric cardiology project is to teach medical students, family physicians, pediatric residents, pediatricians, and fellows in pediatric cardiology about congenital heart disease. Figure 1.3 shows the heart and the transducer, a device that is placed on the patient's chest to probe the heart and take the echocardiogram of the patient. Students can then view what the echocardiogram shows, as the probe is placed in various locations around the heart.

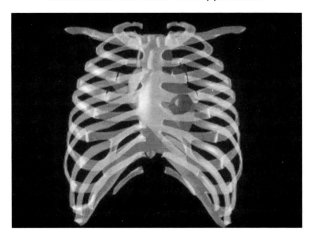

Figure 1.3 Heart and transducer within the chest wall, created by Sousan Karimi, Second Look Computing, University of Iowa. © Sousan Karimi.

1.6.2 Virtual reality

In recent years, virtual reality has emerged as a revolutionary human/computer interface, challenging everything to which we are accustomed. Research institutes around the world have demonstrated the potential of VR systems as a visualization tool and, as technology continues to improve, VR systems will become increasingly pervasive as tools for research and education.

The *CAVE* (Cave Automatic Virtual Environment), a multiperson, room-sized, high-resolution 3D video and audio environment, was developed as a prototype by the Electronic Visualization Laboratory (EVL) at the University of Illinois at Chicago in 1992. This projection-based system allows the movements of one viewer wearing a location sensor to control the perspective and stereo projections, while all the viewers, wearing stereo glasses, are equally immersed in the 3D image. There are now modules or interfaces linking most popular software, such as AVS, Data Explorer, and Sense8 World Toolkit, to the CAVE. Many scientific and educational applications have been developed for this environment, and EVL is actively engaged in transfer of the CAVE technology to businesses.

The CAVE is a theater $10 \times 10 \times 9$ feet, made up of two rear-projection screens for walls and a down-projection screen for the floor. Electrohome Marquis 8000 projectors throw full-color workstation fields (1024×768 stereo) at 96 Hz onto the screens, giving 2000×2000 linear pixel resolution to the surrounding composite image. Computer-controlled audio provides a sonification capability to multiple speakers. A user's head and hand are tracked with Ascension tethered electromagnetic sensors. Stereographics' LCD stereo shutter glasses are used to separate the alternate fields going to the eyes. An SGI Onyx with three Reality Engines is used to create the imagery that is projected onto the walls and floor.

The name CAVE is both a recursive acronym (Cave Automatic Virtual Environment) and a reference to 'The Simile of the Cave' found in Plato's *Republic*, in which the philosopher explores the ideas of perception, reality, and illusion. Plato used the analogy of a person facing the back of a cave alive with shadows that are his or her only basis for ideas of what real objects are. Figure 1.4 shows a sketch of the CAVE.

The *ImmersaDesk* offers a semi-immersive type of virtual reality. It features a 4 × 5 foot rear-projected screen at a 45 degree angle. This size and position allow a sufficiently wide angle view and the ability to look down as well as forward. The ImmersaDesk is a standalone system, as well as a development environment for the CAVE. This drafting table format virtual prototyping device uses stereo glasses and sonic head and hand tracking. The resolution is 1024 × 768 at 96 Hz. The ImmersaDesk is shown in Figure 1.5.

The *NII/Wall* is a large-screen, high-resolution, passive-stereo, projection display well suited for large audiences. The NII/Wall uses four Reality Engines spread across two Power Onyxes. Low-cost polarized passive glasses (like the cardboard glasses used for viewing 3D movies) can be used instead of the active stereo glasses used in the CAVE and ImmersaDesk systems.

The NII/Wall achieves its immersion by wide-screen projection, but unfortunately does not allow a way to look down, a problem with any normal audience seating arrangement. (Omnimax/Imax theater seating addresses this problem by steeply pitched seats). EVL is experimenting with large-area types of tracking, although it is only possible to track one person at a time. The NII/Wall is shown in Figure 1.6.

The CAVE™, ImmersaDesk™, and NII/Wall are EVL research projects. EVL collaborates with the National Center for Supercomputing Applications (NCSA) at the University of Illinois at Urbana-Champaign and the Mathematics and Computer Science Division of Argonne National Laboratory to further develop virtual reality as a scientific discovery and communications tool within the High Performance Computing and Communication community. EVL continues to advance visualization and virtual-reality research and development, and collaborates with NCSA and Argonne on virtual-reality application and toolkit development, with emphasis on supercomputing and networking research. EVL is developing the NII/Wall in collaboration with the University of Minnesota and NCSA.

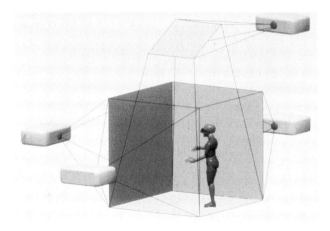

Figure 1.4 CAVE diagram by Lewis Siegel and Kathy O'Keefe, Electronic Visualization Laboratory, University of Illinois at Chicago, 1992. CAVE and ImmersaDesk are trademarks of the University of Illinois Board of Trustees.

Figure 1.5 The ImmersaDesk. © 1995 Jason Leigh, Electronic Visualization Laboratory, University of Illinois at Chicago.

Figure 1.6 The NII/Wall. © 1995 Jason Leigh, Electronic Visualization Laboratory, University of Illinois at Chicago.

References

[1] Judith R. Brown, Rae Earnshaw, Mikael Jern, John A. Vince, *Visualization: Using Computer Graphics to Explore Data and Present Information*, Wiley & Sons, 1995.

[2] Josef Albers, *Interaction of Color*, Yale University Press, Revised edition, 1975.

[3] Josef Albers, *Interaction of Color*, interactive CD-ROM edition for Macintosh computers, Yale University Press, 1994.

[4] L. G. Thorell, W. J. Smith, *Using Computer Color Effectively: An Illustrated Reference*, Prentice-Hall, 1990.

[5] M. Pauline Baker, Colleen Bushell, *After the Storm: Considerations for Information Visualization*, personal communication, 1994.

2
CSCV – Computer Supported Collaborative Visualization

Jason Wood, Helen Wright, and Ken Brodlie

2.1   Introduction

Visualization is a collaborative activity. Modern scientific research is rarely carried out by an individual. It needs the cooperative efforts of a group of scientists, with a range of complementary skills, to unravel the 'grand challenges.' These scientists – maybe at different sites, different institutions, even in different countries – need to collectively analyze data from simulations and experiments. Visualization is a key component of this analysis process; each member of the research team needs to look at the results from their special angle and with their special expertise, and share their interpretation with the rest of the team. Indeed, special expertise may need to be brought into the team at the visualization stage – the visualization expert to recommend the best technique, the artist to suggest the most effective style of presentation. Moreover, once the research is understood, the results need to be communicated to other workers, and indeed to students. This can be done in a passive way by presenting the results as a finished image or video, but much more effectively as a live, participative exercise – education is very much a collaborative experience.

Current visualization systems, however, see visualization more as a solo activity. Certainly scientists are well served by a range of powerful systems, such as IRIS Explorer [1], AVS [2] and IBM Data Explorer [3]. These are modular visualization environments (MVE) where, by means of a visual programming paradigm, the user selects a set of modules to fit together in a pipeline, transforming raw data to geometry and then to images. While these modules can be distributed across a network of processors, there is a single interaction point – a single user interface. Thus the research team mentioned above needs to cluster around a single workstation. The Renaissance team of scientists, artist, and visualization expert needs to physically come together; there is no hope of active collaboration in the dissemination of the results. We need to do better.

A helpful starting point is the time–place model often used by the Computer Supported Cooperative Working (CSCW) community to help position different activities [4] (see Figure 2.1). Existing systems clearly fit into the same time, same place quadrant of the model. Yet today's requirements extend well into the same time, different place quadrant – even to the different time, different place scenario.

In this chapter we look principally at extending current practice in visualization to allow different place, with some thoughts also on different time.

Visualization and Modeling
ISBN 0-12-227738-4

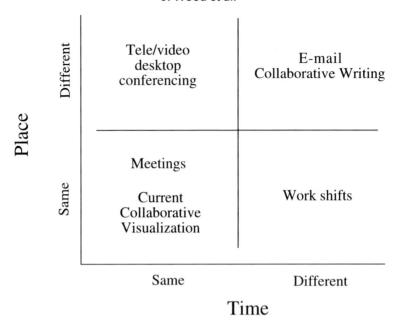

Figure 2.1   CSCW time–place model.

We begin by looking at other work in this new field, which we might call CSCV – computer supported cooperative visualization. It is helpful to place the different activities in the context of the elegant reference model of Haber and McNabb [5], which has acted as the foundation of the current set of systems. This leads us to the suggestion of a new model for CSCV. It is an extension of the Haber and McNabb model, powerful enough to encompass the requirements outlined at the start of this paper, and flexible enough to include as special cases the various earlier attempts at CSCV. This is described in section 2.2.

In section 2.3, we go on to show how our CSCV reference model can act as an implementation model for the extension of current MVEs to collaborative working. A specific illustration is given, where IRIS Explorer is extended from a solo to a collaborative environment. Finally in section 2.4 we look ahead to future work: tackling the different time issue; extending beyond visualization to wider problem-solving environments; and the potential of the World Wide Web for supporting collaborative visualization.

2.2   Reference Model for CSCV

Our reference model will draw on the Haber and McNabb model for visualization in a dataflow environment. They describe the visualization in terms of its component processes, which they categorize as filter, map, and render stages (Figure 2.2). Filtering involves taking some data from an input process and refining it, for example, to interpolate from an unstructured to a regular grid. Mapping the filtered data converts

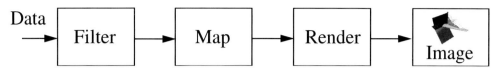

Figure 2.2   Haber and McNabb visualization pipeline.

it to a geometrical representation, such as a surface plot or isosurface, and finally the rendering stage generates a visible image from this geometrical information. Although it was developed to describe the style of dataflow visualization analysis as used by the family of MVEs such as IRIS Explorer, AVS, and IBM Data Explorer, the model can equally well describe turnkey systems. In these cases the individual process elements are hidden from the investigator, by contrast with an MVE where they appear explicitly as modules connected together in a pipeline.

The purpose of a reference model for CSCV will be to distinguish and describe different modes of working within a common framework. The following sections review current research in this area in the light of the existing Haber and McNabb model, subsequently proposing an extension to this which leads on naturally to the design of a toolkit for collaborative working within MVEs.

2.2.1   Sharing a complete application

We begin by examining examples of work which can generally be described as sharing a complete visualization application, whether turnkey or MVE. One way of doing this is via a product such as IBM Lakes [6] or Intel ProShare [7], where an application can be shared without alteration from its original, unshared form. The equivalent in the UNIX environment is to use a shared X mechanism [8]. Using these tools the entire user interface for the application is duplicated on a number of PCs or workstations, and a token passing system is used to determine whether a machine at any one time is acting as the master or as a slave. The master copy of the user interface is transmitted to the slaves each time a change is made so that all see the same output, thus the network load in this approach is substantial.

In terms of the dataflow pipeline model we view this as a single pipeline with many complete sets of control parameters, though the token passing mechanism ensures that only one set is active at a time (Figure 2.3).

A number of workers have achieved equivalent collaborative interaction by extending their existing software products or writing new ones. For example, one of the extensions which Pagendarm and Walter have made to their HIGHEND MVE system [9] allows two visualizers to work on the same data and produce identical images synchronously. Although the implementation is by means of separate pipelines operating on different machines, the synchronization ensures that, conceptually at least, the model is of a single pipeline with multiple controls. Furthermore, network traffic is reduced in their implementation because only status, layout, and remote cursor information is passed between machines. A similar capability is offered by COVISE (Collaborative Visual Simulation Environment [10]), a purpose-built, shared visualization system whose interface is based on the visual programming paradigm. Although all partners see identical screen representations at all times, the distribution

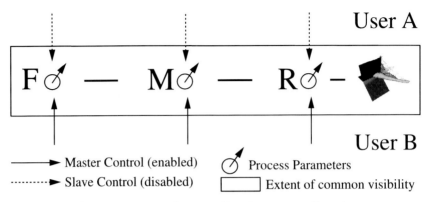

Figure 2.3   Sharing a complete application – user B acting as master.

of modules across different computers in the network is managed by the controller. The complete application can thus be optimized for different combinations of network and computer power.

2.2.2   Selective sharing of an application

A more complex model begins to emerge where the application is selectively shared, either in terms of the control being exerted over the processes, or in terms of the data which is flowing. One approach by Grave and coworkers within the PAGEIN project has been to extend two existing MVEs, IRIS Explorer and AVS [11]. Their approach has been to develop an interface panel containing those control parameters from within the network or map editor which are required to be shared. This panel is transmitted to all the partners, who make changes in turn using a token passing mechanism. These changes can be seen by all collaborators; however, remaining parameters in the map are private to the partner possessing the base application. Further sharing arises from the use of remote rendering facilities available in IRIS Explorer and AVS, whereby the base application can push the geometrical representation generated by the mapping stage to another workstation for local rendering. Viewing parameters can then be determined locally or synchronized between partners.

In terms of the pipeline model, an example situation is represented by Figure 2.4. Here, each partner has control of their own rendering process, whilst control of the mapping process is switchable between partners. The remaining processes, however, such as those in the filter stage, are only ever under the control of the owner of the base application, regardless of whether they are acting as master or slave at any particular time. Furthermore, the decision as to which control parameters to share is made at the implementation stage of the shared panel and is not changed during use. Gerald-Yamasaki [12] in his collaborative fluid flow visualizer also offers the possibility to distribute geometry data, and provides for shared and private contexts for rendering control.

We can also see from Figure 2.4 how a shared application can be implemented either as a single pipeline with multiple controls or as a replicated pipeline with duplicated control. This is evident if we look at the bifurcated render stage and suppose that R has

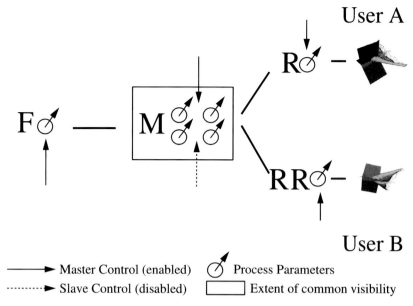

⟶ Master Control (enabled)	⊘ Process Parameters
┄┄┄⟶ Slave Control (disabled)	▭ Extent of common visibility

Figure 2.4   Selectively sharing an application – user A acting as master.

equivalent functionality to RR. Since both are operating on the same data, it follows that if control information is duplicated to each process, then the outcomes must be the same for user A and user B.

Yet another variant of the bifurcated pipeline can be seen in the CSpray system developed by Pang and colleagues [13]. This application is based on Spray [14], so called because the visualization metaphor is to use spray-cans of smart particles (sparts) to highlight interesting features in the data. Sparts leave abstract visualization objects (AVOs) in their path and the use of different spray cans is analogous to making different mappings of the data, which are then converted to images. A can is private to the creator of an AVO until he or she decides to make it public, whereupon other partners can see the AVO and request to use the can. This is the situation shown in Figure 2.5, where user B has assumed control of the mapping process initiated by user A.

2.2.3   Extended Haber and McNabb model

These different modes of CSCV can be drawn together into a single picture if we extend the traditional Haber and McNabb model to have intermediate import and export points for control information and data (Figure 2.6).

By focusing now at the data and control level, rather than at the user level, we arrive at a completely general paradigm for collaborative visualization. Each stage of a complete or partial pipeline can accept data and control information to enable it to operate collaboratively and export data in order to share the outcome. Control information from one pipeline can be exported to another in order to synchronize collaboration, as in the tight coupling mode described by Pagendarm and Walter. Each

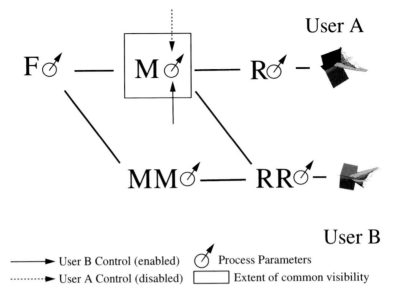

Figure 2.5   CSpray – User B controlling spray can initiated by user A.

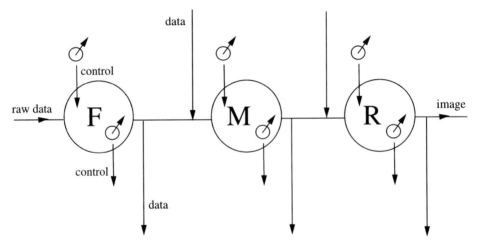

Figure 2.6   Extended Haber and McNabb model with intermediate in/outlet of control and data.

partner is modeled as having their own pipeline or partial pipeline, where in some cases this might consist of just a render stage with data imported from some other partner's mapping stage. Figure 2.7 shows user B's pipeline accepting geometry information from user A and viewing it independently. Figure 2.8 shows the same data being shared but now the two partners also synchronize their views by exchanging control information from their render processes.

   This model also allows easy resolution of the issue of public and private data. For example, if two users are collaborating on some mapping process, they can proceed in

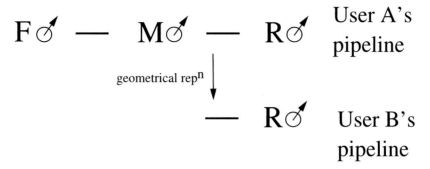

Figure 2.7   Users A and B view the same data in different ways.

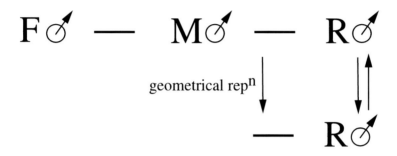

Figure 2.8   Users A and B synchronise their views.

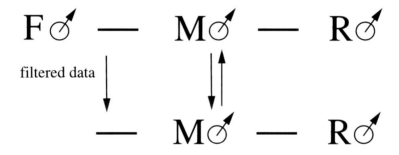

Figure 2.9   Users A and B collaborate on mapping stage (public data).

two ways. The first is to export the filtered data from A's pipeline into B's mapping stage and then to exchange control information (Figure 2.9). However, if the filtered data is to remain private to A, the alternative is to exchange control information at the mapping stage but then to export the geometrical representation (Figure 2.10). In this case, B's mapping stage consists just of a 'ghost' process which can generate appropriate control parameters for A's map process.

A further consequence of this model is that it suggests a paradigm for collaboration which is especially appropriate for extending existing MVEs, elaborated in the next section.

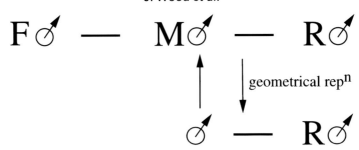

Figure 2.10   Users A and B collaborate on mapping stage but the filtered data remains private to A.

2.3   COVISA

We have implemented the extended reference model as part of the Co-Operative working in VIsualization and Scientific Analysis (COVISA) project at the University of Leeds. COVISA is a study aimed at understanding the requirements for group working in visualization and to this end we have built several demonstrators to test out different modes of working, basing our work on the visualization system IRIS Explorer.

2.3.1   Toolkit approach

The reference model presented in section 2.2 takes the approach of sharing both data and process control at all stages of the pipeline; in an MVE this equates to 'tapping off' the data at the point where it moves from one module to another and sharing it between collaborators. Sharing control of the pipeline can be implemented similarly, except that, rather than share the data flowing between modules, we share the parameters which control them.

   Our aim is to provide 'added value' to existing MVEs, to convert them from solo to collaborative tools. The open architecture of an MVE allows us to create new modules and add them to the system where they are used in the same way as standard modules. These new modules, when wired up in the same manner as the standard modules, can pass either data or parameters out of or into a pipeline. These extra modules then form a collaborative toolkit for the visualizer to build shared pipelines in any of the forms representable by the model. This approach is feasible in all of the MVEs, though the implementation details will be different.

2.3.2   Architecture for shared MVEs

MVEs build data flow applications by means of a visual editor (VE). Each of the stages F, M, and R of the visualization pipeline are realized by means of one or more modules within the VE, the flow of data being represented by connections, drawn as lines, between these modules. Thus the architecture for shared MVEs could be represented as in Figure 2.11A. This general architecture supports different instances

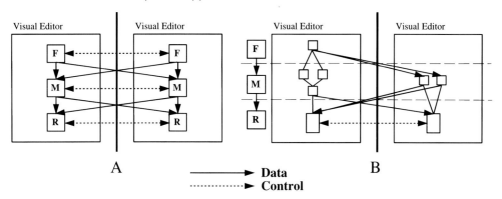

A

B

Data ————▶
Control ·············▶

Figure 2.11 Extended visualization pipeline.

of shared working. For example in Figure 2.11B, only the VE on the left has a filter stage, the output of which is shared by both VEs for mapping. The results of this mapping are recombined in both pipelines, with some control being shared at the rendering level.

The modules which comprise the collaborative toolkit must be able to form connections not only to modules in their own VE, but also to 'companion' modules in the second VE. Ideally this inter-VE connection must be done seamlessly: to facilitate this, we have developed the concept of 'collaboratively aware' (CA) modules. When launched, these modules cause their companion module to be launched automatically into the second VE and a connection to be formed between them. This connection allows bidirectional flow of data or parameters.

2.3.3 Implementation in IRIS Explorer

We have demonstrated the implementation of the above architecture in the MVE IRIS Explorer. The collaborative toolkit comprises a suite of modules that are collaboratively aware, one module for each of IRIS Explorer's internal datatypes, and a collaboratively aware server (CAS). When a CA module is launched into the VE, or Map Editor as the VE is known in IRIS Explorer, it connects to the server on its own machine, to register its existence and pass information about its type and the socket address on which it can be contacted. This information is passed to the server running on the collaborating machine, which effects the launch of the 'companion' module by generating a series of SKm (scheme) commands, SKm being IRIS Explorer's scripting language. Only simple items such as floats and strings can be passed into a module by means of SKm, so the address of the first module is retrieved from the server by making a temporary socket connection to it. Once this address is collected, the second module makes a direct, permanent socket connection to the first. This process is demonstrated in Figure 2.12, where user B has made the initial launch.

The server can be started at the initiation of a visualization session or, if part way through a session, it may be launched into the Map Editor as a module. The only information that is required is the machine name of the collaborator.

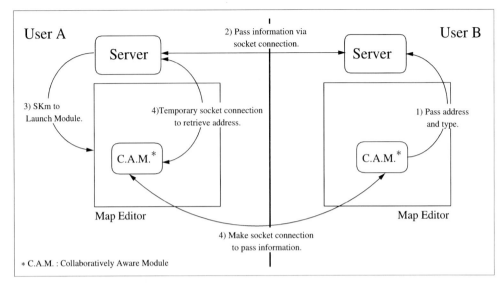

Figure 2.12   Launching a collaboratively aware module in IRIS Explorer.

2.4   Conclusions and Further Work

The tools described work well between two users, but in general we need to consider how to collaborate in larger teams. The extended reference model generalizes to more than two collaborators, hence we should be able to extend the architecture and implementation also. We envisage doing this by means of a central server through which all information passes, in addition to the local collaboratively aware servers (Figure 2.13). Although a central server presents a potential bottleneck when passing large quantities of data, its advantage lies in an ability to scale with increasing numbers of collaborators. A central server also allows partners to join and leave a collaborative session part way through. Clearly, as the number of collaborators increases, we need to make more formal provision for conference management in place of the present free-for-all mechanism.

The toolkit has been tested during development in a real-life situation involving a fuel engineer and a computation expert. Their experiences demonstrated the soundness of the basic concept but indicated improvements which could be made in the usage of the tools. Most notable was a need for both partners to see the pipeline topology in respect of those processes which were under dual control. This is in contrast to the current situation where the owner of the shared portion of pipeline is the only partner to see the process interconnections in full.

Our proposed solution to this difficulty is to provide a mechanism for shared construction of a pipeline, whilst retaining the ability to do private work at other times. The most fruitful avenue we have identified so far will be to use a journal record to distribute the actions of one partner to another's visualization session. A journal record should contain details of process launches, interprocess connections, and process control parameters; indeed, all of the user interactions with the VE which are needed to

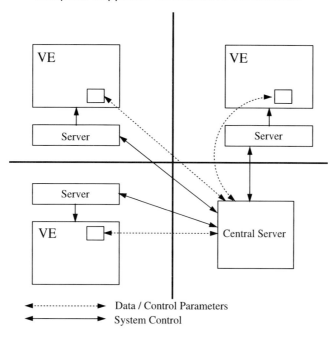

VE

VE

Server

Server

Server

VE

Central Server

◄·················► Data / Control Parameters
◄─────────► System Control

Figure 2.13   Collaborative visualization architecture for more than two users.

capture the construction of a portion of pipeline. To share this with another partner, the MVE must also be capable of receiving this information and carrying out the specified actions. Figure 2.14 shows a development of the architecture in Figure 2.13 which uses the journal in this way. We are about to commence a feasibility study of the MVEs referred to in section 2.1 to determine whether the existing facilities they offer make this approach viable.

We are also working on the transfer into COVISA of ideas from the recent GRASPARC project [15], which aimed to provide an integrated environment to support computation and visualization. A key feature of this support is a management process which stores computed results and simulation parameters at intermediate stages of the calculation, providing an audit of the progress of an experiment. Although originally developed for single-person working, we expect the GRASPARC ideas to move across quite naturally into COVISA since both projects are focused at the data and process parameter level. In addition to supporting work in the same time, different place scenario of collaborative working, the audit trail provides a convenient mechanism to support the different time, different place mode too. For example, one worker could develop a simulation to a certain point and store the computational record in the database, which could then be picked up and continued by another worker at some later time. Furthermore, utilizing a journal record as described above, the collaborating partner could also review the visualization steps which influenced the progress of the investigation. Combining this audit facility with the potential of the World Wide Web as a shared information repository opens up the possibility of truly global collaborative visualization and scientific analysis.

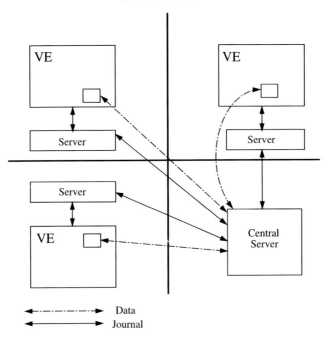

Figure 2.14   Collaborative visualization utilizing shared journal.

Acknowledgments

COVISA is a study funded by the Engineering and Physical Sciences Research Council of Great Britain. The project involves 30 staff-months effort expended over 2 years and is entering its second year.

Our thanks go to all who have contributed through discussion and technical assistance, notably Alison Tomlin and Justin Ware who used and commented upon the tools as they were developed. Special thanks, too, to Jeremy Walton of NAG Ltd for invaluable help with aspects of IRIS Explorer.

References

[1] IRIS Explorer 2.0, Technical Report, Silicon Graphics Computer Systems, Mountain View, 1992.
[2] Application Visualization System, Technical Overview, Advanced Visual Systems, Waltham, Mass, Oct. 1992.
[3] B. Lucas, G. D. Abram, N. S. Collins, D. A. Epstein, D. L. Gresh, K. P. McAucliffe, An architecture for a scientific visualization system, *Visualization '92*, pp. 107–114, IEEE Computer Society Press, 1992.
[4] L. M. Applegate, Technology support for cooperative work: A framework for studying introduction and assimilation in organizations, *J Organizational Computing*, 1: 11–39; 1991.

[5] Robert B. Haber, David A. McNabb, Visualization idioms: A conceptual model for scientific visualization systems, *Visualization in Scientific Computing*, pp. 74–93, IEEE, 1990.

[6] *IBM Lakes: An Architecture for Collaborative Networking*, R. Morgan Publishing, 1994 (ISBN 0-902979-13-2).

[7] ProShare Personal Conferencing, Intel Corporation, 1995. `http://www.intel.com/comm-net/proshare/index.htm`

[8] Wladimir Minenko, The application sharing technology, *The X Advisor*, 1: June 1995, Discovery Publishing Group. `http://landru.unx.com/DD/advisor/docs/jun95/jun95.minenko.shtml`

[9] H. G. Pagendarm, B. Walter, A prototype of a cooperative visualization workplace for the aerodynamicist, *Computer Graphics Forum*, 12(3): 485–496; 1993. EG 93 Conference Issue.

[10] COVISE: Collaborative Visualization and Simulation Environment. RUS: Regionales Rechenzentrum Universität Stuttgart, 1994. `http://www.uni-stuttgart.de/RUSuser/vis/Covise/covise.htm`

[11] CSCW in AVS and IRIS Explorer. ONERA: Office National d'Études et de Recherches Aérospatiales, 1995. `www.onera.fr/activites/en/informatique-projects-scientifiques.html`

[12] M. J. Gerald-Yamasaki, Cooperative visualization of computational fluid dynamics, *Computer Graphics Forum*, 12(3): 497–508; 1993. EG 93 Conference Issue.

[13] Alex Pang, Craig M. Wittenbrink, Tom Goodman, CSpray: A collaborative scientific visualization application, *Multimedia Computing and Networking*, San Jose. Calif., Feb. 1995.

[14] Alex Pang, Kyle Smith, Spray rendering: Visualization using smart particles, Proceedings of IEEE Visualization 1993 Conference, pp. 283–290, IEEE Computer Society Press, 1993.

[15] Ken Brodlie, Lesley Brankin, Greg Banecki, Alan Gray, Andrew Poon, Helen Wright, GRASPARC: A problem solving environment integrating computation and visualization, *Proceedings of IEEE Visualization 1993 Conference*, G. M. Nielson and D. Bergeron, eds, pp. 102–109, IEEE Computer Society Press, 1993.

3
An Integrated Visualization System for Modeling Pollutant Migration

M.D. Impey, K.J. Clark, J.P. Humm, S. Shah, M.J. Williams, and I. Curington

3.1   Introduction

There is a growing demand from consumers and legislators that the environmental impact of industrial processes be restricted to acceptable levels. To meet this demand often requires a detailed quantitative assessment of the fate of pollutants released into the environment. For processes such as the underground disposal of waste (radioactive; toxic; mixed waste) a key factor in a quantitative assessment is understanding the flow of groundwater through subsurface rocks and investigating how pollutants migrate through the groundwater and the effect of this on groundwater quality.

As a result, mathematical and computer codes for models of groundwater flow and pollutant migration have been extensively developed and are widely available. A major problem now is not computing a solution, but instead interpreting and communicating the significance of the computed solutions to non-specialists and decision makers. A key cause of this problem is that running models on realistic scenarios often requires a daunting range of specific mathematical, numerical and computational skills. Problem specification is often undertaken by editing a text input file, and viewing of results is done by porting results to a separate graphics viewer. This has resulted in many of the codes being used in batch mode, with a mathematical specialist running the code, a decision-maker reviewing the output results and returning requests for changes in problem specification, input data or output data format to the mathematical specialist. The inflexibility of this system precludes decision-makers from concluding a series of rapid what-if calculations and restricts the number of times the process can be applied iteratively to reach a solution.

What is required is a self-contained and interactive system enabling a non-mathematical expert to specify and solve a problem and have full access to the computed results. We argue that full interaction is best achieved by using visualization to collect information from a user, provide dynamic feedback, and display computed results. This poses a considerable challenge since the visualization aspects of the system should neither dominate the system to such an extent that basic functionality is compromised nor present the user with information in a potentially misleading manner.

Here we discuss the experience gained in developing a fully integrated, interactive

Visualization and Modeling
ISBN 0-12-227738-4

visualization system for subsurface pollutant migration. The focus is on the design of such a system, called MACRO-AFFINITY, that was developed by Quantisci using the visualization/development tools available in the software package AVS (Version 5.0) [1]. The chapter continues, in section 3.2, with a detailed description of the type of problems that are tackled in modeling subsurface pollutant migration and the key features that need to be specified in setting up a model solution. Section 3.3 sets out the principles used in designing an integrated, interactive visualization system to solve such problems. The implementation of the design principles is illustrated by a description of the MACRO-AFFINITY modeling system. Particular emphasis is placed on what information needs to be provided by a user at different stages in solving a problem, and what and how information is to be visualized. Section 3.4 describes the AVS software used in the development of MACRO-AFFINITY, focusing on the efficient implementation of design. Section 3.5 contains concluding remarks and comments.

3.2   Groundwater Pollutant Problems

The specification and solution of a groundwater pollutant problem can, typically, be split into the following stages:

1. Specification of the model region physical properties
2. Specification of the flow boundary conditions
3. Solution of the steady-state flow equations
4. Specification of the pollutant sources
5. Solution of the pollutant migration equations

In the following sections we consider each of these stages in more detail, with particular attention to the data required to undertake each step.

3.2.1   Specification of model region

In specifying the model region, basic geometric details are needed first. Although some calculations are done in three dimensions the current preference is for *two-dimensional* calculations in a region of a given *thickness*. The main reason for this is that often migration of a pollutant in a particular geological stratum is of interest. Therefore, specification of maximum and minimum (x, y) values and a thickness (in the direction perpendicular to the (x, y) plane) is sufficient.

The focus of many studies is to consider how details of the shape and size of a repository or its position relative to particular geological features (e.g., impermeable strata; fracture zones; faults) affects the migration of pollutants from the repository. It is thus important to be able to specify subregions in the model region, with each subregion representing a different natural or man-made material.

Within each subregion two specific flow properties have to be set: posority and permeability. The first provides a measure of how much of a material consists of open pores or fractures which can be accessed by water. The second indicates the ease with which water can pass through a material under a given forcing pressure gradient. A series of studies have shown that both the porosity and permeability of a rock are complex spatially varying functions, but that it is variations in the permeability that have most effect on pollutant migration. Thus the porosity is often regarded as a constant and attention is focused on characterizing and representing the *spatial variability* of the permeability. The main reason for this is that small length-scale variations in the permeability can affect pollutant migration behavior over much larger length-scales. Thus, obtaining a detailed high resolution map of the permeability is a key step in realistic modeling of pollutant migration.

Permeability measurements are often available at a number of points in the model region. A high-resolution *permeability map* can be obtained from this data using geostatistical methods first to quantify the spatial variability of field/experimental measurements of permeability, and second to generate a map (on a specified high-resolution grid) that interpolates the measurements and has the same mean, variance and spatial variability properties as the measurements.

3.2.2   Specification of flow boundary conditions

Having specified the geometry and physical parameters of the model region the next objective is to determine how groundwater flows through it. It is usually assumed that any migrating pollutants will be transported passively by the groundwater without affecting the groundwater flow and that density and thermal effects are negligible. Thus the solving for the groundwater flow can be conducted independently from and prior to solving for pollutant migration. Here we also restrict attention to migration through regions fully saturated with groundwater.

The groundwater is assumed to satisfy the following standard equations:

$$\boldsymbol{u} = -\frac{k}{\mu}\nabla P \tag{2.1}$$

$$\nabla.\boldsymbol{u} = 0 \tag{2.2}$$

where $\boldsymbol{u}$ is the groundwater velocity, k is the permeability, P is the water pressure, and μ is the water viscosity. Note that these equations are time-independent so that once the permeability is specified the only additional information required is that the *pressure* is set at two or more points in the model region. It is usual for the pressure to be set to a specified value along an external boundary of the model region. An additional constraint that is sometimes applied is that the flux across a given segment of the model region's external boundary be zero. Although these boundary conditions seem relatively simple, this is partly because the model region is often chosen with the specific intention that simple flow boundary conditions are applicable.

3.2.3   Solution of the groundwater flow equations

Provided valid pressure boundary conditions have been set, the solution of the groundwater flow equations is a relatively straightforward numerical exercise. The main action required is the specification of a *numerical grid* (finite difference or finite element) over which the governing partial differential equations (2.1), (2.2) are discretized. It is standard practice to use either the same grid as used in generating the permeability map, or a subdivision of it. Most numerical methods will also require the setting of a parameter against which the numerical convergence of the flow solution can be tested.

3.2.4   Specification of pollutant sources

The starting point for the specification and solution of the pollutant migration equations is to define where and how pollutant enters the model region. Since the *source of pollutant* being considered is usually a repository or other concentration of pollutant, a point source or subregion source is most often used. The temporal behavior of the source can be very complex but, most often, sufficient information can be obtained by considering either a pulse pollutant input or a constant decaying source.

3.2.5   Solution of the pollutant migration equations

A pollutant migrating through a water-saturated rock may be subject to a number of physical and chemical processes: molecular diffusion; adsorption to the rock; chemical reaction with other species in the groundwater; radioactive decay; and chemical degradation are most commonly considered. The numerical simulation of the migration of a chemically active pollutant is a very challenging task that is still the subject of much current research [2] so attention is usually confined to modeling the migration of chemically inert pollutants.

   Two numerical approaches to the numerical simulation of pollutant migration are currently in use. The first is a *continuum model*, based on a system of partial differential equations describing the spatial and temporal variation of pollutant concentration. The second is a *particle tracking* approach in which the movement of discrete packets of pollutant is tracked through the model region. Both approaches have been the subject of detailed research and quick, robust algorithms are available [3, 4]. The algorithms generally require three forms of input. First, *parameters* for each of the processes the pollutant will be subject to (for example, the diffusion coefficient, or the radioactive decay rate). Secondly, a *numerical grid* on which the continuum partial differential equations are discretized or which forms the spatial discretization of the model region for particle tracking algorithms. It is standard practice to use the same numerical grid for solving the pollutant migration equations as used in solving the groundwater flow equations (see section 3.2.3). The third input is a *time-step* for the algorithm, which is required because the position of the pollutant is time-dependent and so the numerical algorithms utilize a temporal discretization.

3.2.6   Analysis of results

The above subsections indicate the basic *input* required to specify and allow numerical solution of groundwater pollutant migration problems. Before considering the design of a visualization system for such problems, we need to consider what *output* (visual or otherwise) will be required at each stage of the specification and numerical solution process.

Output from specification of model region
Given the discussion in section 3.2.1, there are two main outputs from the specification of the model region. First, the division of the model region into *subregions* and secondly the *permeability map*. An additional derived output is the numerical grid on which the permeability map is defined.

Output from the groundwater flow equations
The two main outputs from the numerical solution of the groundwater flow equations are the computed *steady-state velocity* and *pressure* values at each numerical grid point in the model region. A third output is the numerical grid on which the velocity and pressure are computed.

Output from the pollutant migration equations
The pollutant migration equations are different from the groundwater flow equations in that their solution is time-dependent. Three outputs are of fundamental importance in interpreting pollutant migration. First, the temporal evolution of the *plume* as pollutants migrate from the source. Secondly, the temporal variation of the concentration at particular points. The results at these *monitor points* provide quantitative checks and are useful in cross-checking the numerical results with field or experimental measurements of pollutant concentrations. Thirdly, *breakthrough curves* which record the amount of pollutant crossing the external boundaries of the model region. These outputs indicate to an engineer/decision-maker the time and location at which pollutants are predicted to enter potentially sensitive areas (for example, underground drinking water supplies) and the amount of pollutant doing so.

3.3 An Integrated and Interactive Modeling System

3.3.1 Design principles

The input and output requirements listed above are both well known and widely accepted, and form the basis for a number of computer codes for solving groundwater pollutant migration problems. Given the discussion in section 3.1, we now consider how these basic requirements can be extended to form the design basis for a modeling system integrating problem specification, problem solution, and results analysis, allowing interactive modeling, rapid prototyping, and what-if calculations. The top-level design principle is to exploit graphical user interface (GUI) and visualization tools to allow the user to undertake steps in problem specification, solution, and diagnostics by direct graphical interaction with output results from previous steps.

A number of implementation-level design principles have been adopted by Quantisci in the development of integrated, interactive modeling systems:

- Divide problem into identifiable and manageable sections.
- Adopt a modular approach.
- Utilize third-party GUI and visualization software.
- Embed numerical solvers in modules, maintaining independence between numerical and visualization data structures.

- Allow multilevel input and output.
- Modules are responsible for checking whether they have sufficient and/or correct input data to run.
- Modules are responsible for local data structures.

The best way to describe the use of these principles is by illustration of their application. In the following subsections we describe the design of one modeling system, MACRO-AFFINITY, which used AVS (Version 5.0) as a development framework and provider of GUI and visualization tools.

3.3.2   Data flow and control

The sequential nature of the problem specification and solution process, described in section 3.2, means that the modeling system can be divided into four distinct sections each corresponding to a group of modules:

1. Specification of model region
2. Specification and solution of groundwater flow equations
3. Specification and solution of pollutant migration equations
4. Review of pollutant migration results

The GUI for MACRO-AFFINITY consists of four main *pages* (referred to as Pages 1, 2, 3, and 4 in the following discussion), corresponding to the four sections. An additional page, consisting of a 'Quit' button and four toggle (on/off) widgets, showing or hiding each of the four pages, provides top-level control.

Each of the four main pages consists of a graphics viewer and a module stack (Figure 3.1). Each module allows the user to carry out a specific task (for example: define (x, y) bounds for model region; draw subregions; etc.).

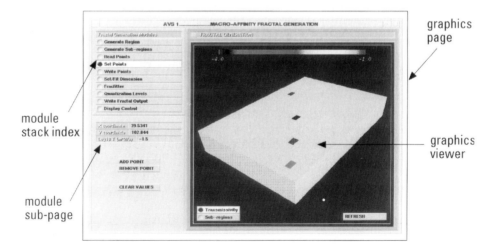

Figure 3.1   A MACRO-AFFINITY graphics page, including graphics viewer and module stack.

Module widgets (such as toggle buttons, dials, type-in boxes) which allow the user to control the execution of the module are placed on a module subpage. Rather than display all the module subpages at once, only one subpage is visible at a time. The module subpage is displayed immediately adjacent to a stack index, which consists of a column of toggle buttons each labeled with a module name. On clicking a stack index button, the corresponding module subpage appears. The stack index and the module subpages form the module stack.

In the group of modules associated with a page, one module is thought of as being the key output generator: the *generator module*. For example, when specifying the model region the key output is the permeability map. The additional *support modules* each provide independent input information to this output generator in a hierarchical manner (Figure 3.2).

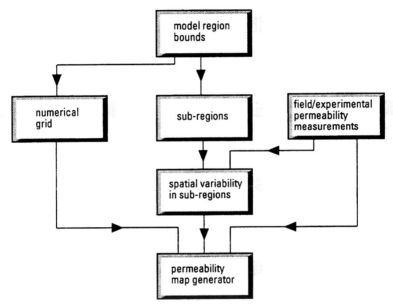

Figure 3.2   Schematic of the support module hierarchy for Page 1.

Individual support modules will only execute if data is available from other support modules prior to them in the hierarchy. Data from the support modules is used to update a graphical representation of the data to be input to the generator module. This graphical representation appears in the graphics viewer (or a supplementary graphics viewer) on the page on which the support modules are located. Data from the generator module is used as input to the support modules and graphics viewer on the next page (Figure 3.3).

An additional feature of this design is that the generator module can write data to an output file. Thus by including support modules on Pages 2, 3, and 4 that can read a file output by the generator module on the previous page and reconstruct its graphics output, MACRO-AFFINITY can be started at any page (Figure 3.4). Thus there is a multilevel input and output functionality.

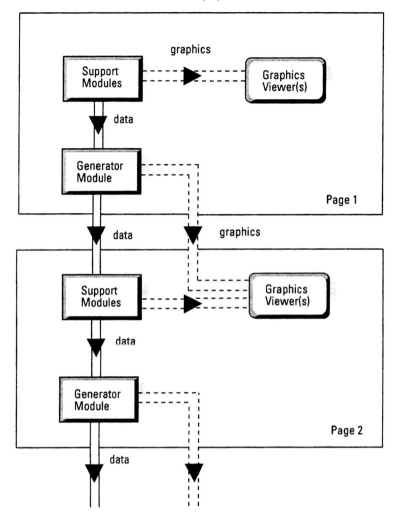

Figure 3.3 Schematic showing the support-generator design and the link between successive pages.

This design allows the user to apply GUI and visualization tools to specify part of the overall pollutant migration problem, with the visualization tools providing immediate information and feedback on actions taken. The following subsections provide more detail on the implementation of this design on each of the four pages. The support-generator approach and the implementation of the design principles are described in detail for Page 1. A summary is given for the other pages.

3.3.3   Page 1: Specification of model region

The output from the first generator module is a permeability map that is constructed using information on the model region bounds, subregions, the spatial variability in each subregion, and pointwise permeability measurements.

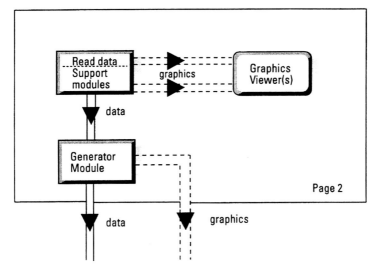

Figure 3.4 Schematic of the functionality of read data support module on Page 2.

The first module in the support module hierarchy allows the user to specify the Cartesian (x, y) coordinate bounds for a rectangular model region, and its thickness. This generates a three-dimensional block representation of the model region on the graphics viewer on Page 1 (Figure 3.5). The reason for using a three-dimensional

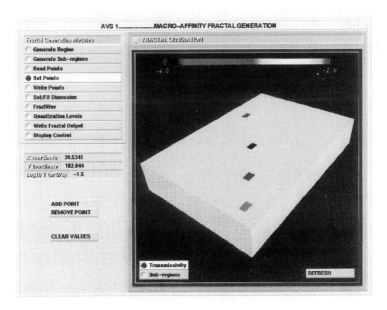

Figure 3.5 MACRO-AFFINITY Page 1, showing permeability data in the model region.

representation is to highlight that the thickness of the model region is important (since it affects the speed of pollutant migration) and, when the model region is a geological stratum, is of physical significance. The model region is initially uniformly colored gray.

The next support modules in the hierarchy allow the user to independently define the numerical grid on which the permeability map will be generated, define subregions, and import/manipulate pointwise permeability measurements.

The numerical grid generated is a simple rectilinear grid. The generator module requires only two parameters, namely the number of grid cells in the x-coordinate direction, and the number in the y-coordinate direction. The module has an option to overlay the grid mesh (formed by the grid cell boundaries) on the model representation. The subregion module allows the user to specify subregions of specified shape (rectangular, circular, . . .) and orientation in the model region. The module generates a wire-frame of the subregion boundaries which it places over the model region representation and the grid mesh. Since a circular subregion cannot be mapped exactly on a rectilinear grid, the user has an option to view how the subregions are mapped (discretized) onto the numerical grid, if it has been defined. Every grid cell is color-coded according to the subregion in which they are situated (determined by the position of the grid cell center).

A group of support modules allows the user to import text information on permeability measurements and interact with the permeability data set. The permeability data set is optionally displayed on the model region representation by color coding grid cells in which data is located (Figure 3.5). To avoid confusion the permeability data and subregion color-coding options are mutually exclusive. The data set can be examined by mouse point-and-clicks. Clicking on a color-coded grid cell, the location and value of the data point within the cell are displayed in type-in widgets on the module subpage. Existing data points can be modified or new ones added by clicking on a grid cell and entering the desired permeability value in the type-in widget. This facility is particularly important in what-if calculations, since it allows users to construct their own interpretation of data.

A final point of note here is that the visualization of the data is based on color-coding numerical grid cells, since the permeability map requires cell-based data. Each data point, however, has an exact (x, y) location, independent of the numerical grid. One of the support modules is thus responsible maintaining a list of the (x, y) locations and data values, and mapping these onto the grid. If the grid is changed, the module executes again to compute the new mapping. This is one example of the responsibility of modules for local data structures and the independence between numerical and visualization structures.

The final support module in the hierarchy allows the user to set parameters that, for the geostatistical method which is used to generate a permeability map, interpolate the permeability data set. The geostatistical method utilizes statistically *self-affine fractals* to generate realistic spatially variable permeability maps and requires at least three parameters (mean; variance; and fractal dimension) for each subregion [4]. Clicking the mouse in a subregion, the user is presented with a radio-button widget listing the options for the type of fractal used in generating the permeability map. When one option is selected, type-in widgets are displayed to indicate what parameter values need to be set for the chosen option. A diagnostics tool is also available, producing line-graphs constructed from the permeability data set to assist the user in choosing appropriate parameter values. The display of this line graph is controlled so that if the user selects a different subregion, the diagnostic line-graph from the original subregion is removed.

The use of the mouse to interact with the permeability data set and select subregions for the setting of geostatistical parameters could lead to possible conflicts. First, the user needs to be made aware of the functionality of the mouse, and secondly, different modules need to know how to process information coming from mouse clicks in a graphics viewer. The first conflict is resolved by use of the module stack. The user can only change the mouse functionality by selecting specific modules from the stack index. In addition, the functionality at a given time is clearly indicated by the one module subpage currently visible in the module stack. The conflict over how modules react to mouse-clicks is resolved by each module keeping a note of its position in the module stack. If it is not at the top of the stack it will not respond to mouse clicks. This is an example of the design principle that modules are responsible for checking when and how they execute.

As noted above, the generator module for Page 1 uses data from each of the support modules to generate a permeability map. The generator module is listed last in the module stack index and has only one user-accessible widget, an 'Execute' button, and a table (which cannot be overtyped) listing the data available. This is intended to highlight to the user that the module is the final destination for data from support modules and should be the last module to be executed on Page 1.

On execution, the permeability map generator checks that the input data is suitable. If it is not, execution is halted and a diagnostic message is displayed. Otherwise the input data is passed to a numerical subroutine in the module. The subroutine returns a numerical data structure to the module, which is then converted into a data structure suitable for display in the graphics viewer in Page 2 and/or output to a file. The use of different data structures for the numerical permeability map generator and the visualization of results may at first sight seem inefficient. In fact, the increase in efficiency gained from using the most suitable data structure within the numerical subroutine, both in terms of CPU and development time, more than offsets the conversion time. Additionally, if the visualization requirements are changed, only the conversion part of the module needs modification. This is the independence between numerical and visualization data structures referred to in the implementation-level design principles listed in section 3.3.1.

3.3.4   Page 2: Specification and solution of the groundwater flow equations

The generator module on Page 2 is a module containing the numerical subroutine solving the groundwater flow equations. Support modules enable the user to:

- subdivide the numerical grid used by the permeability map generator in order to provide a new numerical grid for the flow solver;
- specify pressure conditions at points in the model region or along the edges of the model region;
- examine and modify the permeability map;
- set the convergence criteria parameter.

The graphics viewer on Page 2 initially contains a three-dimensional block representation of the model region with numerical grid cells color-coded by permeability (Figure 3.6). A widget in the graphics viewer allows the user to change the color coding to show the set pressure conditions or the subregions. Again this visualization is cell-based, rather than node-based. A legend for the color coding is automatically updated depending on the data being displayed. Changes to the permeability map and set pressure conditions can be made in the same manner as changes to the permeability data set used by the permeability map generator on Page 1.

On execution of the generator module, a check is run on the data provided by the support modules. Provided these checks are satisfied, the generator module executes the numerical solver subroutine (which again uses data structures independent from the visualization data structures) and then converts data on the permeability map, the computed pressure, and the computed velocity magnitude in each numerical grid cell to a data structure suitable for cell-based visualization. The use of three scalar quantities $(k, p, |u|)$ rather than two scalars (k, p) and a vector (u) simplifies visualization since each of the scalars can be treated in exactly the same way, but currently some thought is being given to a vector representation of the velocity vector field.

3.3.5   Page 3: Specification and solution of the pollutant migration equations

The generator module on Page 3 is a module recording an animated series of results from the numerical solver of the pollutant migration equations. This generator module

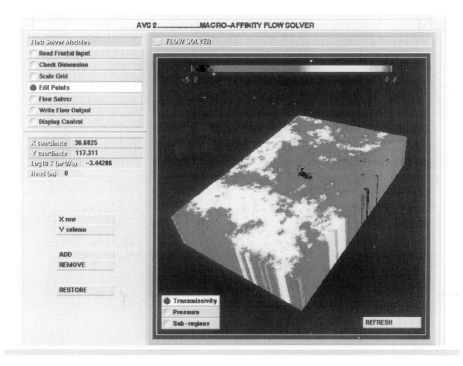

Figure 3.6   MACRO-AFFINITY Page 2, showing the permeability map.

is different from the previous two generator modules in that it does not directly provide visualization data structures to the graphics viewer on the following page. Instead it passes animation images to a file which can be read and visualized in the graphics viewer using a module on the following page. This allows the user to review and compare previously run calculations.

The support modules allow the user to:

- define pollutant source points by mouse point-and-click operations;
- define pollutant monitor points by mouse point-and-click operations;
- define the parameters for a particle tracking numerical subroutine which solves the pollutant migration equations;
- execute the particle tracking algorithm to generate an animated visualization of the temporal evolution of the pollutant plume;
- construct diagnostic line graphs.

From a visualization perspective, the particle tracking animation is of most interest. Initially the graphics viewer contains a three-dimensional block representation of the model region with the numerical grid cells color-coded by either permeability, pressure, or velocity vector magnitude (Figure 3.7). This cell-based visualization is constructed from the visualization data structures output by the generator module on Page 2. The particle tracking algorithm is based on a model for the movement of packets of

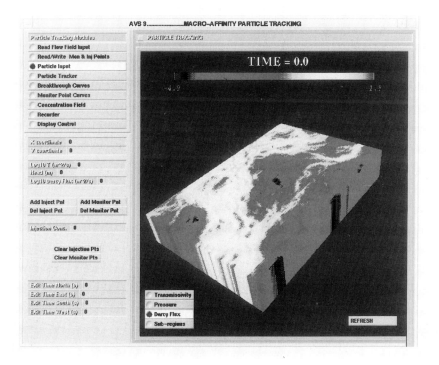

Figure 3.7 MACRO-AFFINITY Page 3, showing the groundwater velocity vector magnitude.

pollutant through the numerical grid cells. The results are thus cell-based and discrete, and this has to be reflected in the visualization. In addition there is a strong link between the groundwater flow solution and the pollutant migration (for example, fast flow channels are often the primary route for migration), so the user should be able to directly compare the pollutant migration paths with the flow velocity solution and possibly the permeability map or pressure solution. The visualization approach adopted is to construct a three-dimensional cell-based histogram overlaid on the model region representation, with the height of the histogram column in a numerical grid cell being proportional to the number of particles in the cell (Figure 3.8). This histogram is updated at a user-specified time interval as the particle tracking algorithm progresses. Features of the resulting animation are set by a number of parameters, such as the constant controlling the vertical scale of the histogram. The aim is to allow the user to quickly generate a series of animations until they find the viewing angle, time-step, vertical scale, etc. which provides the clearest images of the migration of the pollutant through the model region. These animation images can then be recorded to file by executing the generator module.

The three-dimensional histogram provides a very clear indication of the temporal evolution of the pollutant plume, but is somewhat qualitative. The use of monitor points allows the user to gather quantitative information in a manner which is directly analogous to taking field or experimental samples at selected points. An arbitrary number of monitor points can be set by clicking the mouse on the model region

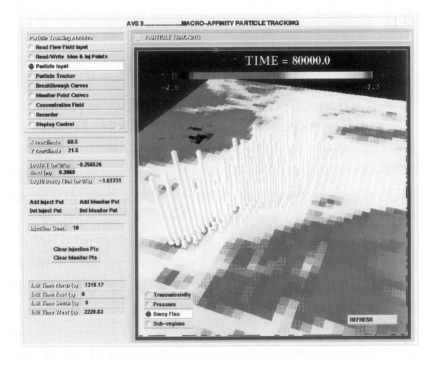

Figure 3.8   MACRO-AFFINITY Page 3, showing a detailed view of the pollutant plume overlaid on the groundwater velocity magnitude.

representation. Their set positions are denoted by colored markers. When the particle tracker is executed, the temporal variation of the concentration at each point is recorded. The result can either be written to a text file for future analysis or be displayed dynamically in a multiple line graph in an additional graphics viewer as the particle tracking algorithm executes. Additional useful quantitative information is obtained from breakthrough curves, which are constructed by computing the amount of pollutant that crosses given model region boundaries as a function of time. The breakthrough curve data is handled and can be viewed in a similar manner to the monitor point data.

3.3.6   Page 4: Review of pollutant migration results

The final page of MACRO-AFFINITY is the simplest (Figure 3.9). It consists of two modules. The support module allows the user to select a file containing animation images from a pollutant migration calculation. The generator module displays the images in a graphics viewer, with 'tape-recorder' style widgets allowing the user to play the animation sequence forwards or backwards or step through the sequence one frame at a time. This detailed, controllable view of the pollutant migration results together with the quantitative results provided by monitor point and breakthrough curve data is precisely the information that is required in assessing the impact of the pollutant on the environment.

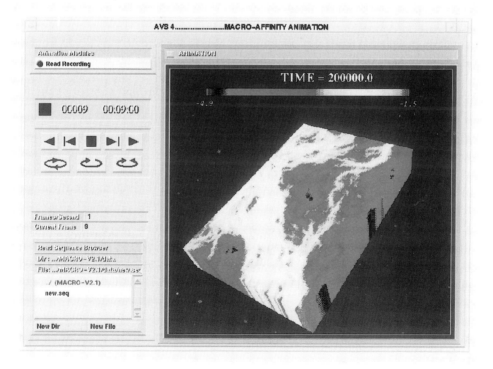

Figure 3.9   MACRO-AFFINITY Page 4, showing one frame in a recorded animation sequence.

3.4   Implementation of Design

3.4.1   Introduction

The requirements posed by a system such as MACRO-AFFINITY indicate the use of high-level reusable components, rather than a traditional, direct programming approach. The Application Visualization System (AVS) system provides a set of components and a development environment suited to the implementation and integration of analysis programs with visualization and interaction.

AVS is a 2D and 3D multiplatform data visualization environment, based on data flow and control interfaces between synchronous or asynchronous processes. It is used for data visualization and as a development system for visual applications. As such, it is a tool, where the appropriate parts may be used by an application, while irrelevant parts are left untouched in the base library. The AVS system serves as a foundation layer for interprocess communication, 3D graphics, user interface, and module development, while libraries of functional modules provide high-level application components for data manipulation. Visual application development attempts to solve two issues, first to shorten the time from prototype to completion, and second, to provide a rich suite of tools or application components to be used during application construction.

3.4.2   AVS development framework

The primary interface to AVS is through the network editor. The network editor is a visual programming interface, allowing graphical construction of applications by making mouse-directed connections between iconic program components. This visual representation is called a visualization network, or simulation network, and controls the data and execution flow in the application, through control of the flow executive.

User-developed or system-supplied modules are shown as small boxes in a scrollable library area, with colored ports on the top and bottom, representing input, output, and control parameter data structures. Modules are chosen for use by dragging the boxes from the library area to the network editor construction area. Modules are then connected together into functional networks by clicking and dragging on the colored ports. The network editor type-checks the allowable connections between modules based on data type.

The AVS system includes over 250 modules for input/output, data processing and display. The module libraries for scientific visualization are used for filtering and creating visual representations of data. Viewers, responsible for creating visible windows on data, receive representations from other modules in the network, and are responsible for handling mouse events, window system refreshes, or other display related events. In addition to the standard modules, a public domain library, maintained by the International AVS Center (http://iac.ncsc.org) has over 700 additional user-contributed modules.

The integration of numerical solver routines, multilevel input and output, and data structure conversion, is accomplished within AVS by creating new modules. The AVS system includes program-callable interfaces which enable externally supplied subroutines to be 'wrapped' as AVS modules. The principal task involved in such wrapping design is the use of standard AVS prescribed data structures for input and output. Also, control parameters and a default set of user interface widgets may be specified for user-supplied modules.

To assist with creation of new modules, AVS includes an interactive module generator, which, given choice selections on its user interface panels, will generate C source code and makefiles for new user-supplied modules. The automatically generated code is a template interface, where additional source lines are added by the programmer, such as subroutine calls to numerical processing libraries.

3.4.3 Data flow: modules and network

Flow executive

The purpose of constructing a network of modules is to provide a data processing pipeline in which, at each step, the output of one module becomes the input of another. In this way, data can enter AVS, flow through the modules of a network, and finally be rendered on a display or stored outside of AVS. This process requires that each module in the network be invoked at the appropriate time.

Overall network control in AVS is the responsibility of the AVS flow executive. As such, the flow executive manages the execution order of modules. The flow executive also supervises data flow between modules, keeping track of where data is to be sent, using a variety of transport methods. The flow executive is an implementation of a data flow architecture. This differs from standard monolithic applications in that data flow does not have a global memory space or program counter. An operation in data flow (i.e., a module) is enabled if and only if all the required input values have been computed. Enabled modules consume input values and produce output values. An application based on the data flow architecture does not introduce sequencing constraints other than those imposed by data dependencies.

AVS has extended the basic data flow architecture in a form called 'adaptive flow architecture'. Adaptive flow is optimized for a multiprocess computing environment, and includes direct module data communication pipes, upstream or feedback paths, shared memory configurations, in-place memory operators, and reentrant module execution.

Data flow control methods

Networks of modules are generally constructed interactively using the network editor. Fragments of networks can be saved as macros, or separate files, for merging into a larger application. Once a network is established, any change of data or parameter in that network is evaluated by the flow executive, which will direct the appropriate modules to respond to the change.

However, in managing complex applications, parts of the network can be created and deleted dynamically to optimize memory, or other resources. In this case the network is only partially constructed at the initial state of the application, and the remainder is constructed by the application itself.

Three independent methods are available to control the state of an AVS network:

• Mouse interaction with the network editor work area

- Typing commands at the interactive command prompt (command language interpreter, or CLI)
- Sending messages to the flow executive from within the program code of any running module

The MACRO-AFFINITY system uses dynamic control of this AVS mechanism to efficiently manage the flow of control and data to achieve:

- Dynamic menu user interface presentation to guide users through analysis
- Modification of the application network to accommodate user requests
- Signal control paths directly between processing functions as a global parameter space

The creation of feedback loops in the network topology is also possible, and extremely useful for direct data interaction. The output from downstream modules is fed back into optional secondary inputs of upstream modules, such that a loop is formed. By data-conditional behavior and parameter notifications, a series of processing steps may iterate over one data set, multiple data sets may be processed through a pipeline of operators, or data editing operations may be performed.

To create a data editing system, 3D mouse interaction with a graphics object is sent from the output of the 'Viewer' module to the input of a module responsible for the supply of the data. Under appropriate conditions, data may be selected, edited, added, deleted, or placed in the view under indirect control of an edit controller module, outside of the graphics display system. The MACRO-AFFINITY system uses this facility extensively to provide computational steering, model specification, and interrogation.

3.4.4   Panels and widgets

Every computational module in AVS allows for its parameters to be associated with interactive user interface elements. Floating point values may be controlled with dial, slider, or numeric text interfaces. Choice lists, radio-boxes, one-shot or toggle buttons are used for mode or choice selection parameters. User interface elements may be grouped and organized visually onto panels, scrolled areas, or stacks. These may be placed, framed, and titled using the AVS layout editor, or by procedural control through the CLI. Layouts may be constructed by hand using the interactive placement tools, then controlled dynamically through the application program. An example of this would be to control a special options panel to appear at a certain point during data processing. Message or other dialog boxes are generally used only through program interfaces, due to their transient nature.

Interfaces can be moved, re-sized, or re-parented during program execution to create specialized user interface arrangements. User interfaces in common use within an application may be stored as macros and reused in a number of distinct contexts to maintain a common look to the interface.

Specialized interfaces may also be created using external user interface design tools, or direct X/Motif programming. This allows for a number of strategies, including:

- Hiding the native AVS interface, replacing it with Motif

- Reparenting 2D and 3D display windows into Motif interface
- Direct X-window drawing or event handling on AVS interface
- Extending AVS interface with special Motif interaction widgets

3.5 Conclusions

We have discussed the growing demand for quantitative assessment of the impact of pollutants in the environment, and identified the communication of modeling results to nonspecialists and decision-makers as a key problem in meeting this demand. We have argued that integrated/interactive modeling systems provide a solution to this problem, particularly if visualization tools are used to provide users with direct access to input and output data. The commitment to such a modeling system has major implications for design, data management, and performance. We have focused on design issues, and outlined a number of design principles which have been adopted in the development of the application MACRO-AFFINITY.

The top-level design principle is to exploit GUI and visualization tools to allow a user to undertake the steps of problem specification, solution, and diagnostics by direct graphical interaction with results from previous steps. The lower-level design principles we have adopted are:

- Divide problem into identifiable and manageable sections.
- Adopt a molecular approach.
- Utilize third-party GUI software.
- Embed numerical solvers in modules, maintaining independence between numerical and visualization data structures.
- Allow multilevel input and output.
- Modules are responsible for checking if they have sufficient and/or correct input data to run.
- Modules are responsible for local data structures.

The use of third-party GUI and visualization software (such as AVS) by application developers (such as Quantisci) is a key point, and gives rise to many issues. Developers are seeking:

- Visualization tools that are or can be incorporated in a development framework
- Quantitative, scientific visualization tools with control over details such as axes, labels, contouring and colour scales
- Access to visualization data structures to enable direct graphical interaction by the user and feedback from the modeling system.

In turn, application developers have a responsibility to visualization specialists to ensure that:

- Visualization tools are used in a reasonable and appropriate manner
- Detailed consideration is given to the design of modeling systems incorporating visualization tools

- Reasonable provision is made for further development of visualization tools, for example by maintaining independence between numerical subroutines and visualization tools.

The success of MACRO-AFFINITY demonstrates that the design principles and requirements listed above provide a sound basis for cooperation between application developers and visualization specialists. Future developments will build on this to tackle the data management and performance issues that still remain if integrated modeling/visualization systems are to become more widely available.

References

[1] M.D. Impey, M.J. Williams, J.P. Humm, S. Shah, K.J. Clark, The MACRO-AFFINITY code (MACRO-AFFINITY Version 2.0): user guide and test case. Intera Report ID3618–2 Version 4, March 1995.
[2] S.P. Crompton, P. Grinrod, H. Takase, J. Woods, Multibarrier geochemical problems in two spatial dimensions, submitted to *Geochem. et Cosmichem. Acta*, 1995.
[3] P.C. Robinson, C.P. Jackson, A numerical study of various algorithms related to the preconditioned conjugate gradient method, *Int J. Mech. Eng.*, 21: 1315; 1985.
[4] P. Grinrod, M.D. Impey. Chanelling and Fickian dispersion in fractal simulated porous media. *Wat. Res. Research*, 29: 4077; 1993.

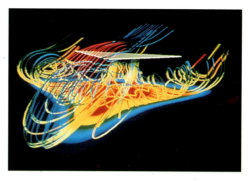

Plate 2. V/STOL 1989 20″x24″ PHSCologram. Dr Val Watson, Fergus Merritt, Chris Gong, and Vee Hirsch, Workstation Applications Office, NASA Ames Research Center/Sterling Software, Moffett Field, CA, in collaboration with (Art)[n] artists Stephan Meyers, and Ellen Sandor. Dan Sandin, Electronic Visualization Laboratory, University of Illinois at Chicago. Pressure and windflow around a vertical/ short take off and landing aircraft. The ground plate is colored according to pressure density, whereas the particle traces are colored by height above the ground: red is ground level, blue is the delta wing. ©Ellen Sandor.

Plate 1. Fourplay, 1990 20″x24″ PHSCologram. John Hart, Electronic Visualization Laboratory, University of Illinois at Chicago, in collaboration with (Art)[n] artists Stephan Meyers & Ellen Sandor. This is a juxtaposition of four related fractals, each of which has a certain 'four-ness' about it. The fractal in front is a 'quaternion Julia set' and in the back we see the 'Mandelbrot set' and the 'complex Julia set' A Julia set is a sort of strange attractor. A Mandelbrot set is an encyclopedia or map of all possible Julia sets. This map is a fractal, and it may be the most complex shape in mathematics. ©Ellen Sandor.

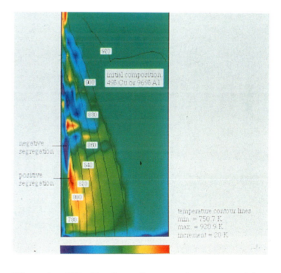

Plate 3. Lyapunov space. An image from an animated sequence, flying through the Lyapunov chaos space. Software and visualization are by John Knaack, Advanced Research Computing Services, Weeg Computing Center, University of Iowa. The visualization was done on a DECStation 5000 using AVS software. ©John Knaack.

Plate 4. Distribution of copper in a copper/aluminum mixture, with a contour plot showing the temperature range. The image illustrates computational fluid dynamics research by Dr Jun Ni and Dr Christoph Beckermann at the University of Iowa. Computation and visualization of data were performed at the Weeg Computing Center, Advanced Research Computing Services visualization laboratory. Visualization was done with Spyglass software. ©Jun Ni.

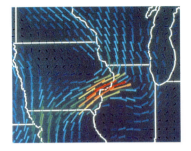

Plate 5 ROM wind vectors. This is a visualization from the Regional Oxidant Model (ROM), a computational air-quality model used for environmental studies at the US Environmental Protection Agency. Contact: Theresa Marie Rhyne, Martin Marietta Services Group, U.S. EPA Scientific Visualization Center.

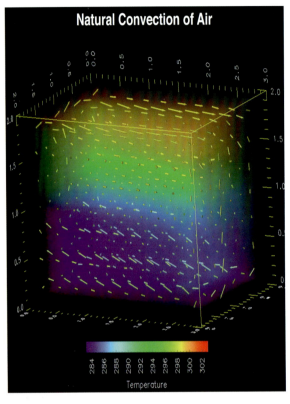

Plate 6 Air convection in a room, by Jun Ni and Tom Halverson. Data was generated by Ni on an IBM 3090 using PHOENICS software. Visualization was performed with Data Explorer software on an IBM RS6000 workstation. ©Jun Ni.

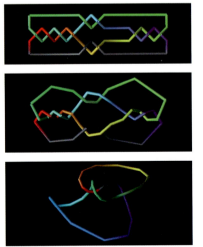

Plate 7 Frames from an animation of a knot in 3-space untangling. Visualization was done with Data Explorer on an IBM RS6000 workstation by Esmail Bonakdarian and Tom Halverson, Advanced Research Computing Services, Information Technology Services; Jonathan Simon, Mathematics; and Ying-Qing Wo, topology; University of Iowa. ©Jonathan Simon.

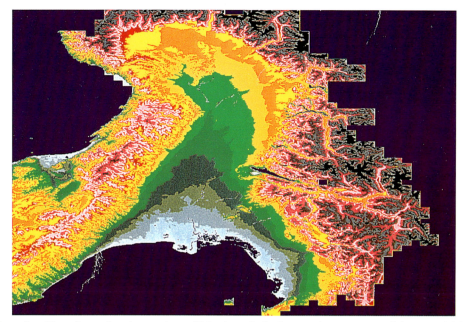

Plate 8. Two-dimensional overview of Northern Italy. Image shows extent of data available. Blue indicates seas and regions of on data. For legend see plate 10.

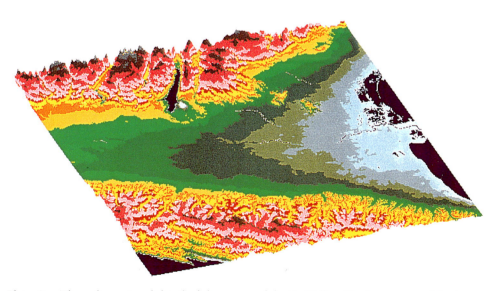

Plate 9. Three-dimensional detail of the centre of the Po Valley. The lower part of the image shows the Apennine mountains, with the Alps in the north. The Adriatic coast is clear in the east, and the Mediterranean in the lower left.

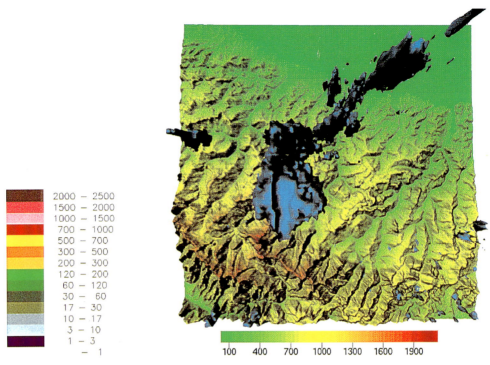

	2000 — 2500
	1500 — 2000
	1000 — 1500
	700 — 1000
	500 — 700
	300 — 500
	200 — 300
	120 — 200
	60 — 120
	30 — 60
	17 — 30
	10 — 17
	3 — 10
	1 — 3
	— 1

Plate 10. Left: Legend for plates 8 and 9. Right: See text. (Surface at 30 dBZ, 15:14.)

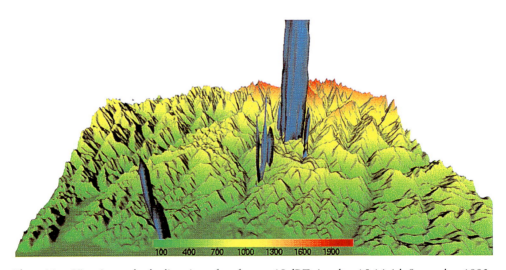

Plate 11. View in southerly direction of surface at 45 dBZ timed at 15:14 4th September 1993.

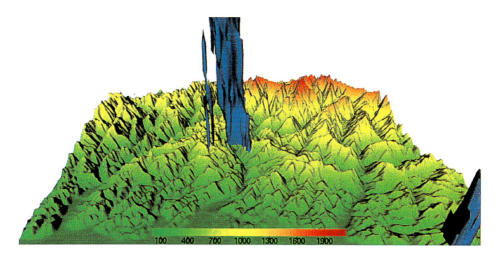

Plate 12. Display as plate 11 but time has progressed to 15:30. The isosurface value is unchanged and it can be seen how the storm has moved.

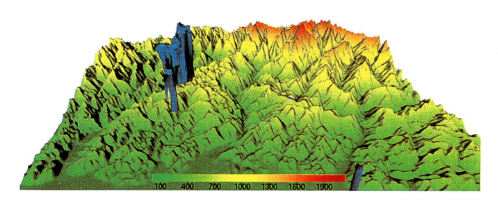

Plate 13. Final view, the time is now 15:45 and the surfaces are diminishing.

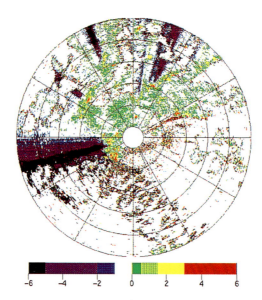

Plate 14. PPI of ZDR at 14:14 on 4 September 1993; range rings at 20 km intervals starting at 10 km.

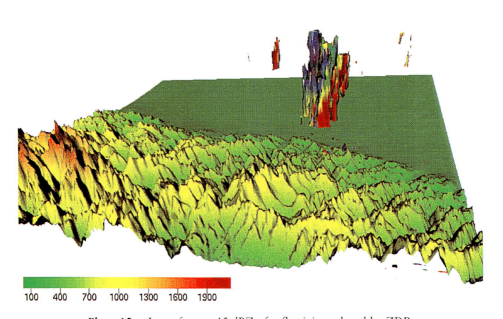

Plate 15. Isosurface at 45 dBZ of reflectivity colored by ZDR.

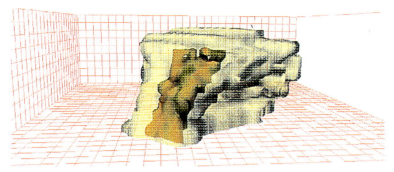

Plate 16. Data from Alberta Research Radar from 29 July 1991; isosurfaces of reflectivity at 35 and 60 dBZ at 16:40 MDT.

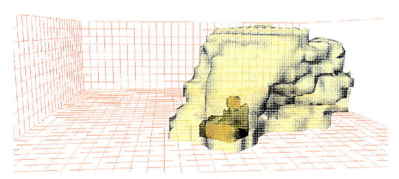

Plate 17. As plate 16 but at 16:46 MDT.

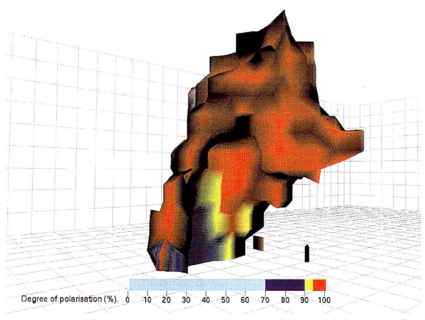

Degree of polarisation (%). 0 10 20 30 40 50 60 70 80 90 100

Plate 18. As plate 16 but isosurface of reflectivity at 57 dBZ colored by degree of polarization at 16:33 MDT.

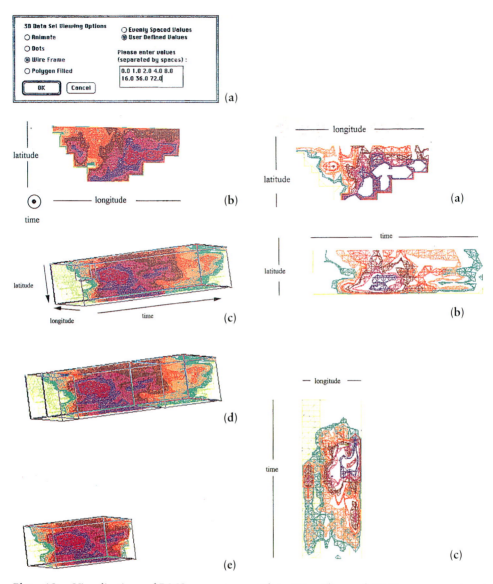

Plate 19. Visualisations of DMS concentration in the Southern North Sea. (a) Choice of thresholds in ascending order: greenish yellow, green, orange, dark orange, brown, pink, lilac, red. (b) End on view in ascending order of thresholds. Britain is located to the left and Continental Europe to the right. (c) Three-dimensional view of the whole data set using thresholds defined in (a). (d) Use of Volume Scan to select the time range. (e) Separate rendering of the range chosen in (d).

Plate 20. Slices of DMS concentration in the Southern North Sea. (a) Slice 10 in the time axis. (b) Slice 9 in longitude axis. (c) Slice 6 in latitude axis.

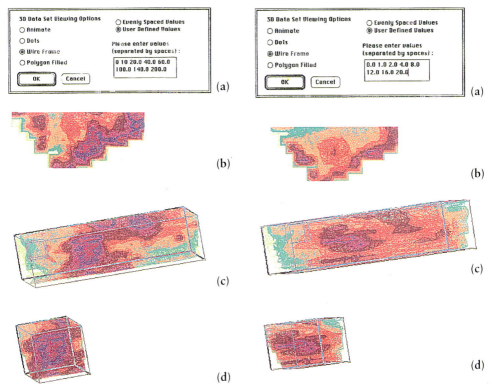

Plate 21. Visualisations of DMSPp concentration in the Southern North Sea. (a) Choice of thresholds in ascending order: greenish yellow, green, orange, dark orange, brown, pink, lilac, red. (b) End on view in ascending order of thresholds. Britain is located to the left and Continental Europe to the right. (c) Three-dimensional view of the whole data set. (d) Separate rendering of the ranges containing highest values.

Plate 22. Visualisations of Chlorophyll concentration in the Southern North Sea. (a) Choice of thresholds in ascending order: greenish yellow, green, orange, dark orange, brown, pink, lilac, red. (b) End on view in ascending order of thresholds. Britain is located to the left and Continental Europe to the right. (c) Three-dimensional view of the whole data set with thresholds defined in (a). (d) Separate rendering of the ranges chosen in (a).

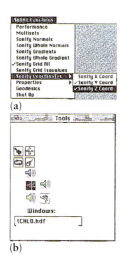

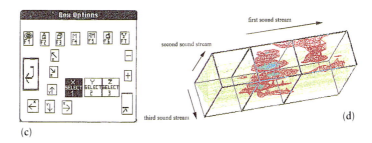

Plate 23. Sound Options for Visualisation Support (a) Sonification Function Option (Y and Z selected). (b) Sound Tools implemented in SSound as extensions of NCSA Image Toolbox. (c) Volume Scan Process Interface. (d) Organisation of Coordinate sonification in Sound Streams.

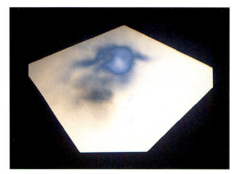

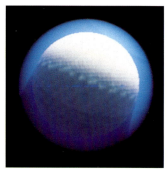

Plate 24. Shadows created by an object on a volume and on another object (what we call direct and indirect shadows). We can also see the shadow created by the volume on the largest object. The medium is not self-emitting. Its density varies from front to back and we can see the halo created by the primary light source inside this medium.

Plate 25. Simulation of a planet with a visible atmosphere. The planet is completely included in the volume. The medium emits blue light and has a small absorption coefficient. We can see the side of the planet which is illuminated by the primary light source (a large sun) as well as its dark side.

Plate 26. Representation of a self-emitting medium (here a surrealistic flame). This flame can be put in a realistic scene to represent fire. The boundaries are too sharp but this visual problem can be removed by adding perturbation functions to the volume modeling.

Plate 27. A more complex scene representing a room with foggy atmosphere. All the computations are made using the global illumination process. It takes four hours to compute on an IRIX 4 system which is relatively quick. We can represent either large media (like the atmosphere) or smaller media (like fog or fire) without any algorithm modification. Moreover, this representation is quick and easy to make.

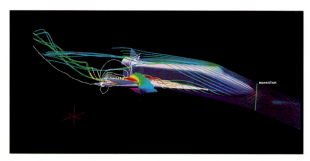

Plate 28. Virtual reality is used to manipulate streamlines and streaklines generated by numerical simulations of fluid flow.

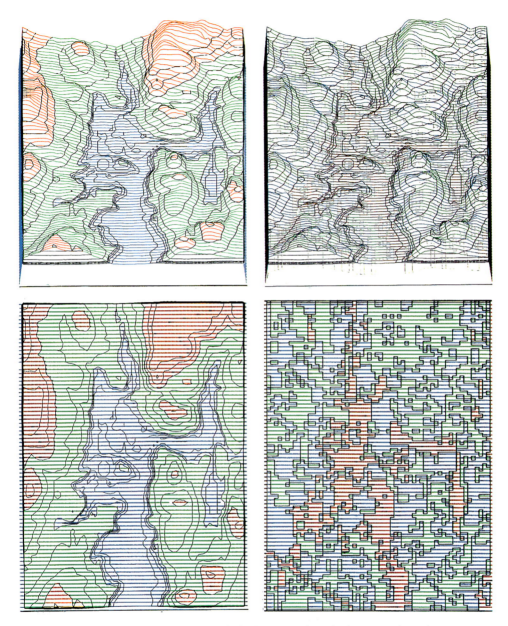

Plate 29 Surface contours, contour band shading, scan-line shading, zone boundaries, texture mapping. Experiments using OBLIX 1969-70. Honey Hill dam location studies showing the extent of the proposed lake (left in blue); and affected tree cover. (right, blue: coniferous, green: deciduous, brown: open space). [Laboratory for Computer Graphics and Spatial Analysis, Harvard University].

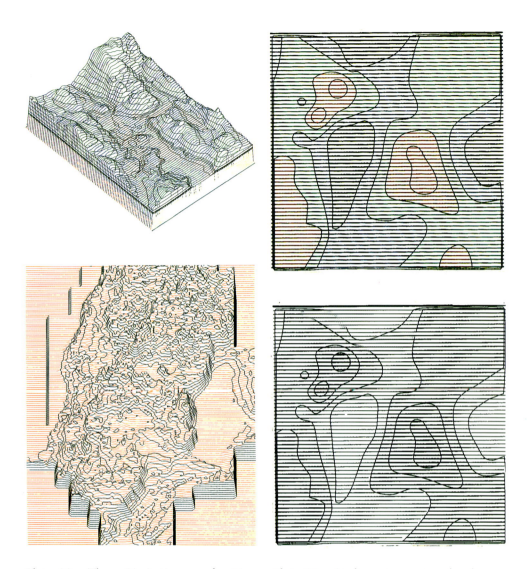

Plate 30. The Limitations of Line Symbolism. Studies showing the loss of intelligibility as the surface complexity is raised relative to grid resolution. An oblique view of the Honey Hill site compared with a terrain model of a more complex landscape. OBLIX 1969. [Laboratory for Computer Graphics and Spatial Analysis, Harvard University].

Plate 31. Studies using contour band scanline shading, OBLIX, 1969. Exploring the task of generating area shading and area symbolism, using different colours and continuously varying tone values over a region of an image. Changing line widths, as in the Moire patterns images, produce smooth changes in grey-scale. [Laboratory for Computer Graphics and Spatial Analysis, Harvard University].

4
Visualizing and Exploring Meteorological Data Using a Tool-Oriented Approach

Isabel Harb Manssour, Carla Maria Dal Sasso Freitas, Dalcidio Moraes Claudio, and Flávio Rech Wagner

4.1   Introduction

Despite the great interest in understanding meteorological phenomena, meteorology is a new science. Because of their economic and social importance, weather forecasts and the prediction of climatic and atmospheric phenomena are very important. These phenomena influence everybody and can seriously affect people and the economy, destroying lives, buildings, and plantations.

Since the middle of this century the technological progress of computers and equipment contributed to accurate observation of the properties of the atmosphere. Meteorologists began suddenly to work with large volumes of high-resolution data, and immediately computer graphics techniques came as the solution to a better representation of information.

Operational and research centers in weather forecasting usually work with a great volume of complex multivariate data, having to interpret them within a short time. A graphic system that helps the meteorologists conduct both daily forecasting and meteorological research is very important and perhaps essential.

This chapter presents the development of the VisualMet system for meteorological data visualization based on the tasks done by the meteorologists of the 8th Meteorological District, in the south of Brazil. This center collects meteorological data three times a day from 32 local stations and receives similar data from the National Institute of Meteorology, in Brasília. Such data result from observation of variables such as temperature, pressure, wind velocity, and type of cloud. These data are stored in a database and used for drawing (by hand) of pressure and temperature contour maps for presentation only.

As proposed in a methodology described in an earlier work [5], the tasks of meteorologists and the classes of application data were observed to define system requirements. System architecture and implementation follow a tool-oriented approach [6] and the object-oriented programming paradigm, respectively. The tool-oriented approach is based on the idea that scientific visualization systems must support the whole data analysis process, instead of being tools dedicated to producing pictures from data. A system following this approach must provide tools to support the visual exploration of datasets. An object-oriented implementation of the approach is based on classes that model both scientific data and visualization and exploration tools.

Visualization and Modeling
ISBN 0-12-227738-4

VisualMet presents an easy to use interface that improves meteorologists' daily tasks such as the drawing of contour maps. It also provides other tools like graphs and icon maps, to support different ways of visualizing and querying the same datasets.

When studying meteorological data visualization, we found that the systems described in the current literature do not work with data collected from local stations. They usually work with a regular grid of data, provided by some meteorological center, or with data resulting from simulation, radar, or remote-sensing instruments. A common aspect of this kind of system is that many of them require a previous knowledge of Computer Graphics techniques. In our case, however, the user needs a simple interface resembling the tools that they employ manually.

This chapter is organized as follows. As a case study we first describe the work done by the meteorologists at the 8th Meteorological District. Section 4.3 presents a review of the relevant work in this area. Section 4.4 contains a brief review of the tool-oriented approach as well as a presentation of the classes used to model the meteorological data and visualization tools. Implementation details of contour maps are presented with examples of images in section 4.5, while some conclusions are drawn in the last section.

4.2 Case Study

The 8th Meteorological District, located in Porto Alegre, collects data from 32 stations distributed in three states in the south of Brazil (Rio Grande do Sul, Santa Catarina, and Paraná). These data, called surface observation data (SYNOP data), are sent to the National Institute of Meteorology, in Brasilia. Satellite images, information received from the National Meteorological Center (NMC) and from the National Institute of Meteorology, and SYNOP data are used for local weather forecasting. Satellite images are used for visualization only and are not integrated with other variables, like wind velocity and temperature.

The work described uses only SYNOP data. A surface meteorological observation consists of measuring or determining the elements that, taken together, depict the meteorological conditions at a specific moment and in a specific place. In each station some data are collected by instruments and others by human observation. These observations and measurements are done in a systematic and uniform way, at fixed time intervals, to allow the capture of features and variations in atmospheric elements.

The observer does not make weather forecasts: he or she only reports the weather conditions at the moment of the observation. In meteorological centers these data support meteorologists' tasks: monitoring local conditions in each station; recording acquired data for meteorological and climatological statistical purpose; and distributing these data to local broadcast services and to other meteorological centers.

The stations are recognized by international identification numbers constituted by five digits. In these numbers, the leftmost two digits identify the block containing the region or country, while the other three digits represent the station number within the block. Each station also has a physical identification that encodes its geographical location expressed in latitude, longitude, and altitude.

SYNOP data are transmitted in encoded form to the 8th Meteorological District three times a day, at 09:00, 15:00, and 18:00, and stored in a local database. The decoding of these data produces values related to the cloud types, wind velocity, wind direction, temperature, dew point temperature, maximum and minimum temperature, pressure at station level, pressure at sea level, pressure tendency, past weather, present weather, and air humidity.

This information is used by meteorologists, three times a day, in the drawing (by hand) of a contour map, where some variables, such as temperature and pressure, are represented by contour lines, and others are represented numerically or by icons. The problems with this task are that (1) a new map must be drawn for each variable that one needs to represent, and (2) in every new map the meteorologist has to plot all the data concerning the stations and related information.

4.3 Related Work

4.3.1 Types and organization of meteorological data

Meteorological data consist of collected or calculated data that represent variables describing the behavior of the atmosphere in terms of temperature, pressure, wind, clouds, etc. Measures and observations are gathered in files that are further used in processing and/or visualization. Calculated data are those generated by numerical models of the Earth's atmosphere. These are stored as history files, containing arrays of variables indexed by time, representing physical variables as temperature, pressure, and wind velocity.

Data can be classified according to the type of value they represent. Scalar values represent variables that are obtained by sampling a function over some domain (in this case, the spatial–temporal domain). Some examples are temperature, pressure, and air humidity. Vector values are also sampled over some domain but instead of being represented by a single value, they have direction and magnitude. The most common example of this class of data in meteorology is wind velocity. Types of clouds are neither scalar nor vector values. We call data of this kind characteristic data, because they are not function values. Freitas and Wagner [5] show a complete classification of data for the development of a scientific visualization application.

Data is associated with spatial locations indexed by latitude, longitude and a vertical level. Considering time as another dimension, grids of meteorological data frequently contain billions of points. For example, the simulation of the dynamics of the atmosphere over a grid of 320 (longitude) × 160 (latitude) × 19 (vertical levels) per hour [15, 16] produces hundreds of megabytes of data per simulated day.

LAMPS (Limited Area and Mesoscale Prediction System) is an example of a mesoscale model system that works with a horizontal scale of 50 km and produces values associated with a four-dimensional array indexed by longitude, latitude, vertical level, and time [18]. The values associated with each space–time location may be, for example, the concentration of water in clouds. In the VIS-5D system [13] data are organized as a 2D array of 3D spatial grids. The 2D arrays are indexed by time and variable. Each cell of these arrays is a 3D rectangle of data.

Man–computer Interactive Data Access System (McIDAS), developed at the University of Wisconsin-Madison [12], supports different classes of data, such as satellite images, radar and laser–radar data, results of numerical models, and data gathered by remote-sensing instruments. These data are grouped in 2D and 3D grids of physical variables.

A system developed by the European Centre for Medium-Range Weather Forecast (ECMWF) and Brazil's Centro de Previsão do Tempo e Estudos Climáticos (CPTEC), METVIEW [25], uses the GRIB (two-dimensional fields and images) and BUFR (observation) formats, that were defined by the World Meteorological Organization (WMO). All data files are read, manipulated, and stored in a multilevel hierarchy. When a data request is issued, the system searches through a hierarchy of data repositories and creates a graphical representation.

4.3.2 Graphical representations

There are a lot of images that can be generated from meteorological data, depending on the variables that must be shown. In general, scalar values, such as pressure, temperature, and air humidity, are presented with false-color or contour maps, while vector values as wind direction and velocity are represented by depicting vector icons on maps that show the variable domain. These representations can be 2D or 3D maps, and frequently different variables are combined in a single image.

Bidimensional images consist, basically, of cartographic maps, where vector icons, related to wind information, and contour lines or false-colors, related to scalar data, can be depicted. Characteristic data can be shown by means of icons or glyphs. Satellite images are an example of bidimensional graphic representation.

Three-dimensional images enhance the realism of the representation of variables and phenomena. A typical example often used nowadays is the stereo pair. Papathomas [18] implemented this method for cloud visualization. Each representation consists of two images, one for the right eye, and the other for the left eye. The conjunction of these two images results in a three-dimensional scene. Alternative techniques used for the construction of three-dimensional images of meteorological data and phenomena are transparency and textures. These techniques are employed to associate features to the different layers of the atmosphere. Examples of this kind of image can be observed in the works developed by Max [15, 16] and Gelberg [11]. The display of contour lines, obtained through scalar variable interpolation, can also be done in a three-dimensional domain, as illustrated by Papathomas [19], who presents an image where the contour lines represent the dew point temperature, the pressure is represented by the shading of surfaces, and colors depict the temperature.

A variety of three-dimensional graphics are presented by Hibbard and Santek [12, 13]. A surface can be defined and exhibited in a wire-frame form or with texture and transparency to represent scalar data. Vector variables are exhibited as lines where orientation and thickness represent trajectory and magnitude, respectively.

4.3.3 Interaction facilities

The facility for interaction is of major importance in the acceptance of a meteorological visualization system, because of the complexity and large volume of data in this application. Meteorologists are scientific users, not computer scientists. They do not want to waste time creating or finding a new visualization program to execute with every new data set. Moreover, they would like to concentrate on the analysis of their data and not on the visualization process.

A scientific visualization system must provide interaction with data through their graphical representations. In general, rotation, viewing, and zoom control are present. Each different visualization technique requires parameters such as the interval between isolines, the positioning of a cut plane, or the threshold value for the depiction of an isosurface. These parameters are usually input by the user through buttons, dials, and menus [3]. This level of interaction is found with every visualization technique. However, the majority of scientific visualization systems offers as a high-level user interface a visual programming language based on the dataflow technique. AVS (Application Visualization System) [24], Silicon Graphics Iris Explorer, and IBM Data Explorer employ this technique, giving to the users the flexibility to design their own visualization pipelines as networks of basic modules. New basic modules can be programmed and put into the library for later use.

METVIEW [25] uses a distributed architecture based on the idea of service-oriented architectures, which allow for the combination of different services (such as data access, data manipulation, and visualization) in a single environment. Its main differences from the scientific visualization systems such as AVS and Data Explorer are integration with database management systems and a communication protocol. In this system the user creates objects and performs operations on them, without needing a computer graphics background.

In VIS-5D [13], however, the user interacts with a fixed rendering pipeline that supports atmosphere and ocean studies. To keep its interface simple, as described in a recent work [14], VIS-5D denies many rendering choices to its users. While VIS-5D is a post-processing system with such constraints, VIS-AD is an execution environment that enables scientists to define their data organization and the mappings to visual representations [14]. Users write algorithms in an interpreted language (with the flexibility of linking them to C or Fortran written functions). They can explicitly map variables declared in the algorithms to visual representations. On clicking a variable name in the text shown in a window, its icon appears in the display window. The displays are highly interactive, enabling, for example, rotation, zoom, animation, and adjustment of mapping colors.

4.4   System Design and Implementation

Taking into account the tasks performed by meteorologists in the 8th Meteorological District and the SYNOP data organization, we designed the system using the tool-oriented approach proposed by Freitas and Wagner [6]. This approach recognizes scientific visualization systems as collections of objects, where some objects are entities and others are tools [7]. Entities model data representing the phenomena under analysis; tools model the processes applied to data either for processing or visualization purposes. A brief description of this approach is given in the subsequent section.

VisualMet is being implemented on a Silicon Graphics workstation, because of its excellent performance in graphics applications. The source code is written using the programming language C++ and the graphical library GL [22]. The user interface was built using the Forms library [17], which is a powerful and simple package, with extensible facilities. This library has a great number of C routines and also uses the GL library.

4.4.1   The tool-oriented approach

The tool-oriented approach is based on the idea that scientific visualization systems must support the data analysis process, instead of being a collection of visualization tools. We have first identified the general goals of the data analysis process. Taxonomies for entities and attributes, goals and tasks were built from the analysis of representative case studies of simulation and scientific visualization problems [5]. These goals are to study the structure of an entity (or object), to understand static and dynamic properties of an entity, to compare properties of different entities, to compare properties of the same entity at different points in some spatial/temporal dimension, and to store and communicate acquired knowledge. The tasks executed by scientists in pursuing these goals are then stated as navigating the dataset, querying the dataset, selecting a data subset, computing (calculation, simulation), producing and storing data representations, and storing computed data.

These tasks are usually executed while observing visual representations. The analysis of the information conveyed by several existing graphical representations with the goals of visual interactive simulation and visual exploratory analysis led to a classification of visual representations and a methodology for selecting an adequate representation given an entity (or the entity's attribute) and a goal (an analysis task). The selection of visual representations is based on a classification of entity attributes (Table 4.1) [5].

The type of an attribute indicates the nature of values that it can assume. Attributes of type *characteristic* represent isolated features: there are no associated functions. This is the case of the height of individuals of some population or the predominant flora of some region. An attribute of type *scalar* denotes data that is sampled from a function over the domain of the attribute; examples are material density in medical data, temperature, or pressure in a flow of some gas. An attribute of type *vector* enables the representation of vectorial quantities such as the velocity of winds or other flows. So, while a *scalar* is a single integer or real value, a *vector* is a *n*-uple of integer or real values. Attributes of type *tensor* arise in application areas such as computational fluid dynamics and finite element stress analysis; a second-order tensor in 3D, for example, is represented by a matrix of nine components. The type *aggregation* is used to classify attributes that are collections or organizations of data of any type.

The nature or type of values corresponds to the classical data type concept. An attribute may assume alphanumerical, integer, real, or symbolic values. Symbolic values enable the representation of hierarchies.

The nature of the domain indicates whether an attribute can assume values from an enumerated set or from a continuous domain. For continuous domains, the values may be distributed either discretely or continuously. Considering a geographical area, an attribute that designates the height of the terrain is defined over a continuous domain, while another indicating the density of population in subareas is defined for regions in the continuous domain. Considering the fauna inhabiting this area, the number of individuals of each species is defined over an enumerated set; in contrast, the total fauna density is defined continuously over all the region.

Table 4.1 Classification of object attributes

Criteria	Classes	Meaning
Nature or type of characteristics	Characteristic	Isolated characteristic
	Scalar	Scalar variable, sampled from a function
	Vector	Vector variable, sampled from a function
	Tensor	Tensor variable
	Aggregation	Collection of attributes
Nature or type of values	Alphanumeric	Identification values
	Numeric	Ordinal values, discrete or continuous
	Symbol	Subattribute
Nature or domain	Discrete	Enumeration, finite or infinite set
	Continuous	All the points in 1D, 2D, 3D, nD space
	Cont-discrete	Regions in 1D, 2D, 3D, nD space
Domain dimension	1D	Defined data in 1D space
	2D	Value associated to point in 2D space
	3D	Value associated to point in 3D space
	nD	Value in n-dimensional space

The dimension of an attribute indicates whether the value is defined over a 1D, 2D, 3D, or higher dimensional space. Examples of the 1D domain are distances measured from a point or some characteristic observed for an entity over a period of time. Classical 2D and 3D data are values observed for geographical (planar) and spatial areas, respectively. Examples of higher dimensional data may be taken from applications that generate multivariate data: remote sensing applications and statistical data about populations. The dimension of an attribute enables the representation of spatial, temporal, spectral, and higher dimensional data.

Visualization techniques, in our approach, are indeed mapping tools from data to visual representations. Exploration tools are: navigation (synthetic camera, scroll bars), selection (2D and 3D cursors, cut planes, windows, line segments, volumes, constraints over attributes), query (simple reading, measuring), computation (deriving data), simulation (preparation of experiments, control of experiments), and storage (storage of data and images).

As can be seen from the above discussion, in our approach, tools assist the researcher in his or her tasks like any other instrument. For example, when observing a researcher studying the morphology of some animal species, we find the use of manual (concrete) tools like digital paquimeters, computational ones like statistical procedures applied in any order, and manual tasks like the drawing of parts of the animals' skeletons. We then realize that all the tools must be offered to the scientists without a specific order in their use. In exploratory research one cannot impose an order on the scientific thinking because this order is part of the researcher's methodology. He or she must freely select tools and apply them to the data in order to reach the final insight into the phenomena from which the data have been gathered. As artificial intelligence techniques are not (yet) applied in our approach to incorporate this knowledge, the reasoning that leads to the application of a particular tool is left to the researcher.

The tool-oriented approach proposes class hierarchies of entities and tools for developing scientific and simulation applications, following an object-oriented design methodology [20]. In this chapter we take this work and apply it to the problem of visualizing and exploring meteorological data, as will be described in the next section.

4.4.2 Modeling entities and tools

As stated above, the design of the system is based on the identification of two kinds of objects in the real world: entities, representing the phenomena described by the data gathered by the 8th Meteorological District, and tools, representing the processes applied to the data. In the system these two classes of objects are seen by the user as two independent collections, named 'Entities Base' and 'Tools Base'.

The Entities Base is a collection of data that is to be visualized or processed, and the Tools Base is a collection of tools used to process the data in order to derive new data, generate images, or return data values as a result of queries. Each base is presented to the user in a specific window. A main window contains only the help and quit buttons (Figure 4.1). The modeling of the entities is based on the methodology proposed by Freitas and Wagner [5], where the data are classified according to the four criteria presented in Table 4.1. SYNOP data represent the entities in our case study. They are samples of data, organized as ASCII files, that we call SYNOP files. SYNOP files are represented by icons in the Entities Base and identified by names that encode the date and hour when the sample was collected. Each sample is a collection of measures of the attributes presented in Table 4.2, for each station. The location of each station is stored in a separate file. The attributes of the data in the SYNOP files are classified according to the criteria shown in Table 4.1 (see Table 4.2).

Figure 4.1   System interface.

Table 4.2   Classification of SYNOP data

Surface information	Kind of attribute	Kind of values	Domain nature	Domain dimension
Clouds	Aggregation	Alphanum.	Cont-discrete	3D
Wind direction	Vector	Numerical	Continuous	2D
Wind velocity	Vector	Numerical	Continuous	2D
Temperature	Scalar	Numerical	Continuous	2D
Dew point temperature	Scalar	Numerical	Continuous	2D
Station pressure	Scalar	Numerical	Continuous	2D
Ocean pressure	Scalar	Numerical	Continuous	2D
Pressure tendency	Aggregation	Symbol	Continuous	2D
Past weather	Characteristic	Alphanum.	Cont-discrete	2D
Present weather	Characteristic	Alphanum.	Cont-discrete	2D
Max. to min. temperature	Scalar	Numerical	Continuous	2D
Air humidity	Scalar	Numerical	Continuous	2D

For modeling purposes we use the OMT (Object Modeling Technique), described by Rumbaugh et al. [20]. OMT uses three types of models to describe a system: the object model (to describe the objects in the system and their relationships), the dynamic model (to describe the interaction among the system objects), and the functional model (to describe the transformations to which data are submitted). This chapter presents only the object model, where the classes are represented by rectangles, showing the name of the class, the attributes' names, and the operations supported by the class. The subclasses are shown as a tree of rectangles with a special bifurcation that represents generalization, or with a lozenge that represents an aggregation. In designing the system, 'entities' and 'tools' appear as natural class types. In the implementation, there is another important class, the Interface class, that implements interaction with the user.

Figure 4.2 shows the modeling of the Interface class and its subclasses, following the OMT methodology. In fact, the subclasses are the three main windows existing in the VisualMet interface (Figure 4.1). The SYNOP entity is a class that models the samples (Figure 4.3). Each SYNOP entity is an aggregation of a class Sample, which in turn is an aggregation of a class Station.

Tools are represented by classes that model the processes that must be applied to the data. As we have already mentioned in the introduction of this section, the development of this system is based on a methodology [5] which also encompasses the classification of visual representations. To generate a visual representation of an entity, one must declare a mapping between a data object and a visual representation tool. The two classes we have already defined are the Map and the Graph classes. The Map class implements the exhibition of contour maps and icon maps (Figure 4.4). The Graph class is responsible for the generation of 2D and 3D graphics showing variables of interest (Figure 4.5). Another tool is the Record tool for saving and opening image files generated by VisualMet.

4.4.3   Functional description of tools

The user activates a tool by first selecting (using the 'point-and-click' technique) one or more entities in the Entities Base, and then selecting the desired tool in the same way.

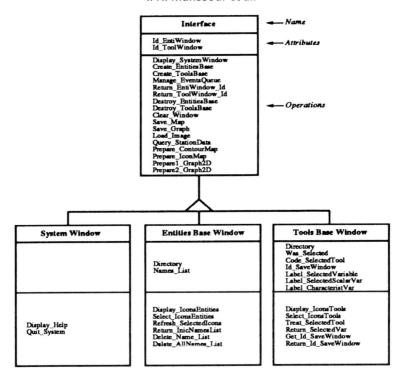

Figure 4.2   Modeling of the Interface class.

Tools already available allow the visualization of contour and icon maps, and 2D graphs. It is also possible to query attributes of stations that are displayed on maps. Selection and 3D Graph tools are under implementation.

An icon map is an image of the geographical distribution of the 32 stations with icons that represent values of variables at each station. Referring to the classification presented in Table 4.2, only the attributes that are of classes aggregation, characteristic, and vector can be displayed in an icon map.

When the user selects the Icon Map tool, the user is prompted (via a window) to specify the variable that must be shown. The icons employed in the image belong to a set commonly used by meteorologists of the 8th Meteorological District. Figure 4.6 shows an example of an icon map with the attribute concerning clouds plotted. In the upper left corner of this window the user can see the values of latitude and longitude of the cursor position in the icon map window.

The Contour Map is a tool employed to display scalar variables. This tool is selected in the same way as the icon map. By a parameter window the user can specify the name of the variables and the interval between lines. Since we have centered our work on methods for constructing isocontour lines from meteorological variables, the next section describes this tool in more detail. Figure 4.7 shows an example of a contour map. As in the icon map, the upper left corner of the window shows the latitude and longitude values, according to the cursor position in the window; the lower left corner shows the

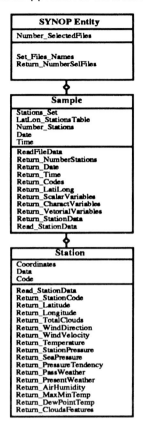

SYNOP Entity

Number_SelectedFiles

Set_Files_Names
Return_NumberSelFiles

Sample

Stations_Set
LatLon_StationsTable
Number_Stations
Date
Time

ReadFileData
Return_NumberStations
Return_Date
Return_Time
Return_Codes
Return_LatiLong
Return_ScalarVariables
Return_CharactVariables
Return_VetorialVariables
Return_StationData
Read_StationData

Station

Coordinates
Data
Code

Read_StationData
Return_StationCode
Return_Latitude
Return_Longitude
Return_TotalClouds
Return_WindDirection
Return_WindVelocity
Return_Temperature
Return_StationPressure
Return_SeaPressure
Return_PressureTendency
Return_PassWeather
Return_PresentWeather
Return_AirHumidity
Return_MaxMinTemp
Return_DewPointTemp
Return_CloudsFeatures

Figure 4.3   Modeling of the SYNOP data class.

value of the displayed variable for each contour line, which are presented in distinct colors.

The 2D Graph tool provides three different types of graph for scalar and vector variables. In the first one the user can select an entity and a variable, and then a simple bar graph is exhibited showing the value of this variable in the corresponding station. The second type is similar to the first one, but it allows the user to select three entities, related to data from one day's data (three samples). Finally, the third one allows the user to select a group of entities, one station, and one variable to generate a line graph with the variation of the selected variable in time.

The Query tool does not have an icon in the Tools Base because it is activated when the user positions the mouse over one icon on an icon map, or over one station identification on a contour map, and presses the left button. A window with the attributes of the selected station is then opened.

As mentioned earlier, the Record tool can be used to store images generated by the system, using an internal format. The user has to select the window that shows the desired image and then the icon of the Save tool in the Tools Base. The parameters for this tool are the name of the directory and the name of the file. The retrieval of a stored image is done by selecting the Open tool and entering the appropriate parameters.

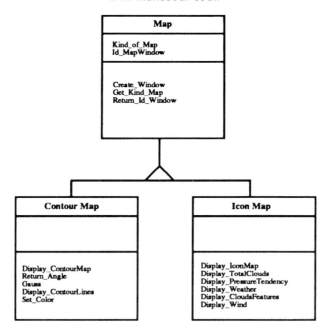

Figure 4.4   Modeling of the Map class.

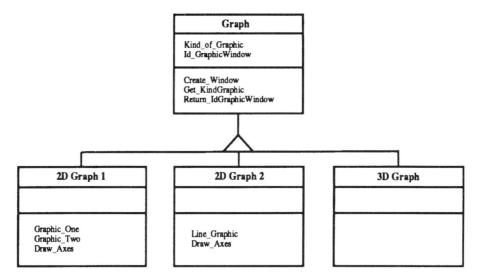

Figure 4.5   Modeling of the Graph class.

4.5   Contour Map Tool

In terms of the classification of acquired spatial scientific data, SYNOP data can be treated as scattered multivariate data, sampled over a bidimensional domain. Several researchers present algorithms to process these data in order to obtain the scalar field

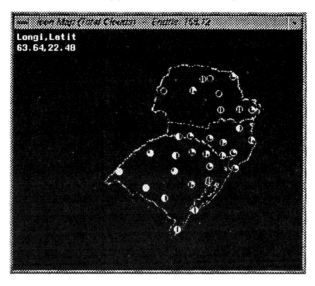

Figure 4.6   Icon map showing clouds.

that they represent [8–10] and produce the desired contour lines [21]. The study of several methods has led us to choose the multiquadric method described by Foley [8, 9].

The multiquadric method produces an approximation of an interpolant for scattered data, as shown below:

$$M(x, y) = \sum_{i=1}^{N} a_i \sqrt{(x - x_i)^2 + (y - y_i)^2 + R^2},$$

where $R^2 > 0$ and a_i satisfies the $N \times N$ linear system of equations $M(x_k, y_k)$, for $k=1,...,N$. This linear system is solved using the Gauss method [2].

After obtaining the interpolant, a second algorithm is used to generate the contour lines. This algorithm, based on that developed by Dayhoff [4], consists of a scan over a regular grid defined in the domain of the interpolant. For every row of the grid, a search is done looking for a point that belongs to the desired contour line. When this point is found, between two grid points (e.g. 1 and C1), the neighboring grid point of larger value is used as the center (C1), and plot points are found at successive angles of 45° along the lines extending to the eight points immediately adjacent, as shown in Figure 4.8. Linear interpolation is used to find the points of the contour line in each direction. If the contour line does not pass between the points (e.g. in the case of C1 and 4), the center of reference is transferred to the second point (4) around which contour points at 45° angles are searched for a new iteration.

A curve is terminated if the starting point is reached again (closed contour line) or if the edge of the grid is encountered. The latter happens in one direction, so it is necessary to come back to the first point and generate the other piece of the contour line that extends in the other direction.

The results obtained using these two algorithms are satisfactory, as can be observed in Figure 4.7. The only problem is the definition of the R value in the multiquadric method. This constant strongly influences the final result. The optimal choice for R^2 is

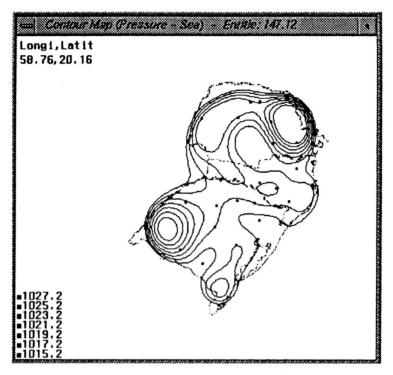

Figure 4.7   Contour map of pressure.

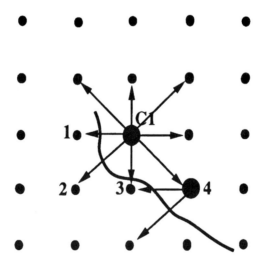

Figure 4.8   Angles of 45° along the lines extending to points adjacent to some center point.

an open research question. Experiments done by the author of this method [1, 23] indicate that it depends on the number of data points, the distribution of the (x_k, y_k) and the function values f_k.

4.6   Final Comments

The design goal of the system described in this work is to provide powerful tools for visualization and exploration of meteorological data in order to support the daily work of meteorologists in the 8th Meteorological District in south Brazil. Because of their lack of computer expertise, VisualMet must be very easy to use. This has been achieved by employing the tool-oriented approach that is strongly based on the analysis of the tasks accomplished by users.

The architecture of VisualMet is based on two collections of objects (data entities and tools), giving us the flexibility for extending it with new tools and also new data entities. The choice of an object-oriented methodology and language for design and implementation, respectively, enables the easy modification and extension of the system.

Currently, there are two tools under development, the 3D Graph tool and the Selection tool. Tridimensional graphs represent selected variables by longitude and latitude, either as line graphs or as surface graphs. The stations will also be plotted. The Selection tool will allow the user to select a group of stations to work with. As soon as the user selects a group of stations, a new entity with only these stations will appear in the Entities Base.

Acknowledgments

The authors express their gratitude to the 8th Meteorological District, which has provided all the information that supported this work. Thanks are also due to the partial support of CNPq and CESUP-UFRGS. We gratefully acknowledge Marcelo Gomes de Oliveira for the implementation of the class Graph tools.

References

[1] R.E. Carlson, Multi-stage algorithms for solving scattered data interpolation problems, Unpublished presentation at *4th Texas Symp. on Approximation Theory*, Texas A&M University, College Station, Tex, 1983.

[2] D.M. Claudio, J.M. Martins, *Numerical Calculation Computation – Theory and Practice*, Atlas Publishing House, São Paulo, Brazil, 1989.

[3] Cray Research, *Multipurpose Graphic System User Manual*, Eagan, 1991.

[4] M.O. Dayhoff, A contour-map program for X-ray crystallography, *Commun. ACM*, 6(10): 620–622; 1963.

[5] C.M.D.S. Freitas, F.R. Wagner, A methodology for selecting visual representations in scientific and simulation applications, *European Simulation Symposium*. Delft, The Netherlands, Oct. 1993, pp. 722–727.

[6] C.M.D.S. Freitas, F.R. Wagner, The tool-oriented approach for visual exploratory analysis, *VII Brazilian Symposium on Computer Graphics and Image Processing*, Curitiba, Brazil, Oct. 1994, pp. 197–203.

[7] I.H. Manssour, C.M.D.S. Freitas, D.M. Claudio, Tools for Metereological Data Visualization, *IX Brazilian Symposium on Computer Graphics and Image Processing*, Caxambu, Brazil, Oct. 1996, pp. 63–70.

[8] T.A. Foley, Interpolation and approximation of 3-D and 4-D scattered data, *Comput. Math. Appl.*, 13(8): pp. 711–740; 1987.

[9] T.A. Foley, D.A. Lane, Visualization of irregular multivariate data, *Visualization '90*, San-Francisco, Oct. 1990, pp. 247–254.

[10] R. Franke, Scattered data interpolation: Tests of some methods. *Math. Comp.* 38(157): 181–200; 1982.

[11] L.M. Gelberg, T.P. Stephenson, Supercomputing and graphics in the earth and planetary sciences, *IEEE Computer Graphics Appl.*, 7(7): 26–33; 1987.

[12] W.L. Hibbard, D. Santek, Visualizing large data sets in the earth sciences, *IEEE Computer*, 22(8): 53–57; 1990.

[13] W.L. Hibbard, D. Santek, The VIS-5D system for easy interactive visualization, *Visualization '90*, San Francisco, Oct. 1990, pp. 28–35.

[14] W.L. Hibbard, B.E. Paul, D.E. Santek, C.R. Dyer, A.L. Battaiola, M. Voidrot-Martinez, Interactive visualization of earth and space science computations, *IEEE Computer*, 27(7): 65–72; 1994.

[15] N. Max, R. Crawfis, D. Williams, Visualizing wind velocities by advecting cloud textures, *Visualization '92*, Boston, Mass., Oct. 1992, pp. 179–184.

[16] N. Max, R. Crawfis, D. Williams, Visualization for Climate Modeling, *IEEE Computer Graphics Appl.*, 13(4): 34–40; 1993.

[17] M.H. Overmars, Forms Library – A graphical user interface toolkit for Silicon Graphics workstations, Utrecht University, 1992.

[18] T.V. Papathomas, J.A. Schiavone, B. Julesz, Stereo animation for very large data bases: Case study – meteorology, *IEEE Computer Graphics Appl.*, 7(9): 18–27; 1987.

[19] T.V. Papathomas, J.A. Schiavone, B. Julesz, Applications of computer graphics to the visualization of meteorological data, *Computer Graphics*, 22(4): 327–334; 1988.

[20] J. Rumbaugh, M. Blaha, W. Premerlani, F. Eddy, W. Lorensen, *Object-Oriented Modeling and Design*, Prentice Hall, 1991.

[21] M.A. Sabin, A survey of contouring methods, *Computer Graphics Forum 5*, pp. 325–340. North-Holland, 1986.

[22] Silicon Graphics, *Graphics Library Programming Guide*. Silicon Graphics, Mountain View, Calif., 1991.

[23] A.E. Tarwater, A parameter study of Hardy's multiquadric method for scattered data interpolation, *Technical Report UCLR-53670*, Lawrence Livermore National Laboratory, Livermore, Calif., 1985.

[24] C. Upson, T. Faulhaber Jr., D. Kamins, D. Laidlaw, D. Schlegerl, J. Vroom, R. Gurwitz, A. Van Dam, The application visualization system: A computational environment for scientific visualization, *IEEE Computer Graphics Appl.*, 9(4): 30–42; 1989.

[25] B. Raoult, B. Norris, J. Daabeck, R. Cartaxo, G. Câmara, Distributed architectures for environmental visualization systems, *VIII Brazilian Symposium on Computer Graphics and Image Processing*, São Carlos, Brazil, Oct. 1995, pp. 249–256.

5

The Use of Visualization in the Examination of Work and Life Histories

Mark Fuller and Brian Francis

5.1 Scientific Visualization Systems

The term 'data visualization' is often used by statisticians as a modern term for a graphical representation of a set of data. In this chapter, we wish to draw a distinction between static graphical displays on the one hand, and scientific visualization on the other, which is carried out using highly interactive software, usually (but not always) producing three-dimensional (3D) representations, and with the availability of a wide set of tools providing interaction with the data, including zooming, panning, rotation, the manipulation of colors, shading, light sources, and the ability to 'fly' around objects in real time. The former displays are designed to be viewed on paper; the latter are designed to be viewed on a high-resolution computer screen driven by a high-performance workstation. Sending the output to videotape to provide a record of an interactive session is also possible.

Scientific data visualization [1], often referred to as ViSC (visualization in scientific computing) exploits modern developments in computer graphics to gain insight into scientific data. Traditional areas of scientific visualization are in engineering (e.g., computational fluid dynamics), in medicine (e.g., computed tomography), in meteorology, and in geology. Scientific visualization is typically used in these areas to add further information and interactivity to a graphical display of a real-life object or phenomenon. More recently, visualization has been used for geographical applications [2] and in other application areas such as number theory and simulation studies of computer systems [3] where the graphical representation has no a priori underlying physical model.

A modern visualization system is characterized not only by the provision of a set of highly interactive graphical tools, but also by the programming environment itself. Small, well-defined computational modules are assembled on the screen using a graphical editor, with links being added to define data flows between modules. In this way, new applications can be assembled and various displays created without the need for extensive code-writing.

The visualization literature emphasizes the distinction between exploratory visualization, analysis, and presentation [3]. This echoes the statistical literature. Although visualization can be used to great effect for the presentation of statistical analysis, the next sections concentrate exclusively on exploratory visualization to provide an exploratory statistical analysis of event histories as a precursor to more

Visualization and Modeling
ISBN 0-12-227738-4

formal statistical models. Our philosophy therefore follows Chatfield, who emphasized that initial data analysis can be used for model formulation and should be seen as complementary to more formal statistical modeling procedures [4].

We use the AVS system [5], although the general points made would apply to any modern visualization system [6].

5.2 Graphical Displays of Event Histories

Event history data is characterized for an individual by a set of multiple durations in each of a number of states, with additional complex covariate information varying over time. A typical work history for an individual will consist of records of that individual's employment state; typically containing the start and end date of each period of employment or unemployment, social class and industrial classification, the number of hours worked, and so on. Life history data may additionally contain records of other life events such as the individual's marital history, residential history, educational history, criminal history, medical history, and other demographic information such as the dates of birth of children and the size and composition of the individual's household over time. Life histories are special cases of event histories, which additionally would include shorter term studies such as the medical history of an individual since the first onset of an illness such as AIDS.

Although in many short-term studies event history data can be collected prospectively, it is common when assembling life histories for information to be collected retrospectively through questionnaire or interview, leading to problems of recall both for dates of state changes and associated covariate information. Such data is therefore characterized for an individual by a set of multiple durations in each of a number of states, with additional complex covariate information varying over time. Some durations in some states may be censored, and there may be missing data, both on the covariates, and on the durations and times for changes in state. The challenge in constructing any graphical display of such data is to allow the representation of both durations and state transitions in all variables relevant to an analysis. Such displays should allow for both the examination of a single event history and the comparison of multiple event histories.

An early graphical representation of work histories was suggested by Dex [7]. These are essentially line plots of individual career trajectories with time represented along the horizontal axis. Continuous, broken, and blank lines are used to illustrate full-time, part-time, and no work, respectively, and labels attached to the line represent other information, such as marriage and childbirth, the meaning of which is ascertained from an external key. This makes these diagrams rather difficult to interpret and limits their use as a tool for exploring large data sets.

Other authors have suggested alternative displays. Post and colleagues suggested a complex graphical display for the representation of an individual's psychiatric history [8]. The display contains information on drug treatments, periods of hospitalization, transitions between and levels of manic and depressive states, and external events affecting the patient's mental health. The representation is suggested as a graphical summary of an individual. Blossfeld and colleagues discuss various state diagrams, where movement from state to state in a single variable is plotted against time, but suggest that the clarity of these graphs decreases as the number of states and individuals increase, and that it is often difficult to track individual histories [9].

In constructing suitable new displays for event history data, we have been guided by Tufte [10], who stated that graphical excellence 'is that which gives the viewer the greatest number of ideas, in the shortest time, with the least ink, in the smallest space, and which tells the truth about the data.' He suggested that 'small multiples,' or *glyphs* in computer graphics terminology, are often useful when dealing with multivariate data. We take up Tufte's challenge and suggest suitable graphical objects for the exploratory display of individual event histories.

5.3   Event Histories as Objects

When analyzing event history data we are interested both in durations within states and also in transitions between states, together with associations with other time-dependent variables. It is clearly important that a graphical display be capable of representing all types of event history variables. We assume that the variables fall into one of seven possible types:

1. *Time variables*: age, calendar year, years in study
2. *Time-varying continuous variables*: number of hours worked, income
3. *Time-varying ordinal variables*: highest academic qualification
4. *Time-varying categorical variables*: occupational category, marital status
5. *Time-constant variables*: sex, ethnicity, place of birth
6. *Internal events*: parental death, date gained driving licence
7. *External events*: change of government, closure of major factory in locality

Time variables are those which measure the progress of an individual in time. Time-varying variables may vary within individuals as well as between individuals. Constant variables may vary between individuals, but not within a history. Internal events are events directly related to the individual, and will vary from individual to individual. External events, in contrast, affect the whole sample under study. It is clear that many variables can belong to more than one type. For example, age could be represented as a constant variable if treated as 'age at entry to study,' and number of children could be represented as time-varying continuous, ordinal, or categorical.

Earlier work by one of us used a similar categorization and suggested the construction of 'tulip plots,' consisting of circular glyphs, one for each individual [11]. Time runs clockwise around the tulip, which is subdivided into 'petals' of different color and variable thickness to represent different categorical and time-varying variables, respectively. The strength of this circular design is that it is a compact 'data-rich' summary of important variables of interest, showing durations and transitions. It can therefore be used as a plotting symbol in tabulations and scatterplots. However, its complexity cannot be increased greatly, and it is also less useful when state durations rather than transitions are the major aspect of interest. An alternative approach is to consider an event history as a linear object.

We therefore propose the formation of a 3D pencil-like object for each event history. The length of the pencil represents a time variable such as calendar time or age.

Different faces of the pencil represent different time-varying variables. Continuous or ordinal time-varying variables can be represented either by continuous changes in color, or alternatively by protuberances from faces of the object, with the height of the protuberances representing the values of the variable. Categorical time-varying variables are represented by changes in color or texture. Events can be marked by solid rings around the object, with different types or color of rings for each event type. Time-constant variables can be represented by different colors or glyphs at the end of each pencil, or by additional faces to the object.

Further refinements to this graphical representation can be proposed. A subset of event histories in a study may be censored; for these histories this information may be included in a display by superimposing (for example) an arrowhead on the top of the pencil. Missing time-dependent data may be represented using a neutral color such as gray. If some of the times of state changes are unknown within a history, abrupt color changes between different states may be replaced by a gradual blending of color between the states.

5.4   Multiple Event Histories and the Lexis Diagram

The Lexis diagram is used extensively as a graphical method of displaying demographic data. The original idea of this diagram is usually credited to Lexis [12], although Vanderschrick [13] gives an account of the development of such diagrams and suggests that other authors also deserve credit (Becker [14], Verwey [15]). The modern, modified form of the diagram [16] is shown in Figure 5.1. The x-axis represents calendar time t, and the y-axis represents age a. Deaths are represented by points in the age–time space. Each individual is represented in the diagram by a 45° line joining the time and age at birth to the time and age at death. Principal sets, of which Lexis defined three types, are parallelograms in the Lexis diagram. For example, those individuals born between T and $T + 1$, and dying between ages A and $A + 1$ will lie in the parallelogram identified by KLMN in Figure 5.1; this is a principal set of the first type.

Recently, Keiding [17] has investigated the utility of the Lexis diagram for statistical inference, and Goldman [18], working in the area of survival analysis, describes 'Eventgraphs' to represent the progress of individuals through a study. These are essentially Lexis diagrams with the axes reversed and with calendar time replaced by time of entry into the study.

This suggests that a development of the Lexis diagram could be used for complex event history data. Each Lexis line, representing the progress of an individual through time, would be replaced by a pencil representing the changing states of that individual over time on selected variables of interest. For a single variable this approach is attractive, but in general the resulting graph would be overcrowded and difficult to interpret. Can these ideas be extended into three dimensions?

Lexis also suggested an extension of his diagram to illustrate other irreversible changes of state such as termination of marriage during the lifetime of an individual [12]. He noted that such data from studies usually have an extra time dimension, with individuals entering this new state at varying ages. This led him to suggest a 3D extension to his diagram, where the x–z base plane had two dimensions, namely, year of birth and age upon entering the new state. The vertical y-axis would then represent

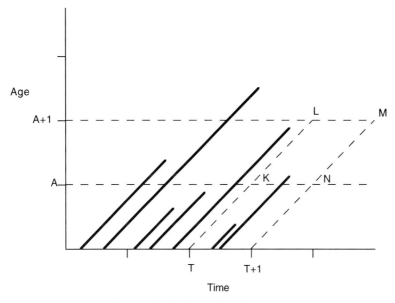

Figure 5.1   A Lexis diagram.

time spent in the study. In effect this approach would generate 3D age–period–cohorts displays of the raw data, and it provides us with a suitable spatial framework for visualization.

The choice of variables representing age and time in the x–z base plane now requires consideration. Both age (on the x-axis) and year (on the z-axis) can be represented either as constants for each individual (e.g., age on entering the study) or as continuously changing variables over the individual's lifetime. There are thus four possible displays which can be constructed, with suitable orientations of the pencils for each display. When both age and year are continuously varying, the resulting display will consist of angled pencils, at 45° to both the age and year axes. In contrast, if age is considered to be constant, the pencils will be vertical in the time–age plane, and angled at 45° in the time–year plane. With both age and year as constants, we have an underlying 3D Lexis diagram, with vertical pencils. The choice of an appropriate orientation will be guided by the analyst's proposed statistical model and the representation of time and age in that model.

If there is no suitable secondary time axis, then a variable indexing the individuals may be used as a substitute. This will space the histories equally along the z-axis. Variations on this display would sort the individuals into date, age, or other order before construction of the index variable.

Once the display has been constructed, suitable visualization tools can be used to explore the data. These include the following.

1. *Rotation, panning and zooming.* These tools are standard in modern visualization environments, enabling the analyst to view the data from different viewpoints and to fly around and through it. Zooming facilitates the inspection of subsets of individual histories in more detail.

2. *Clipping.* A clipping plane can be defined, with the effect that only portions of histories above, below, or intersecting the plane are displayed.
3. *Cropping.* Cropping is a more complex form of clipping. A 3D cropping box is specified, and only those histories within the box are displayed.
4. *Colour redefinition and lighting.* Color redefinition ensures that desired aspects of the histories are highlighted, and the manipulation of spotlights and background lights will improve the appearance of the 3D display.

An ideal set of tools would also include those available in dynamic graphics systems [19]. These would include the following.

5. *Identification.* The ability to identify case number or the values of other displayed variables on screen.
6. *Selection and brushing.* The ability to select a set of cases for subsequent highlighting or temporary deletion.
7. *Linked displays.* The linking of two or more displays, with highlighted objects in one display also highlighted in the remaining displays.

5.5   An Example

Davies and colleagues [20] used a binary logistic regression (controlling for heterogeneity) to examine the relationship between a husband's unemployment and his wife's participation in the labor force, as revealed by data from the Social Change and Economic Life Initiative (SCELI). Work and life histories were collected retrospectively for 1171 partnerships existing in 1987 in six UK localities, each history starting at the month of last marriage and continuing until the date of the survey. The investigation focused on the 'employment shortfall' effect noted in cross-sectional studies, where the wives of unemployed men are less likely to be working than the wives of employed men. The analysis revealed that there is little effect of husband's unemployment on his wife's employment status for the first 12 months, then a highly significant effect thereafter. The effect of the age of the youngest child is significantly negative and is particularly strong for couples with a child under 12 months old. Quadratic and linear terms representing age and calendar time were also found to be important.

We now use visualization techniques to re-explore this data set. In Figure 5.2, we display individual Lexis pencils, concentrating on three of the variables used in the above analysis – in anti-clockwise order, husband's employment state, wife's employment state, and a composite variable representing the age of the youngest child in the family. With a large number of histories to display, we adopt a simple color representation of state changes. For employment state, green is used for employed and red for unemployed for both the male and female in the partnership. Similarly, color is again used for the age of the youngest child, with brown representing no children in the household, blue representing under 1, magenta under 5, yellow under 11, and white under 16.

The angle between faces of the pencil is set to 45°. The anchor-point of each pencil on the base plane is offset along the x-axis according to female age at marriage (where $x=0$ represents females aged 16) and along the z-axis according to date of marriage

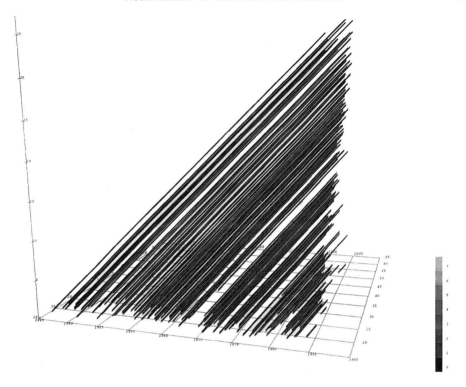

Figure 5.2   Visualization of 188 event histories using Lexis pencils.

(where $z=0$ represents 1947, the earliest marriage year in this study). The pencils are rotated by 45° about the age and year axes to indicate that time is continuously varying along both dimensions. The yellow base plane features blue bands to denote age 20, 30, 40, etc. and magenta bands to denote 1950, 1960, 1970, etc. These aid the viewer's orientation during interactive analysis.

Figure 5.2 shows the rendered display of all 188 histories. At this viewpoint, little of the detail can be seen of the individual histories, but the nature of the sampling scheme is now clear. Women contributing histories in the 1950s all married in the 1950s and were over 50 at the time of the survey. Conversely, women from all marriage cohorts contribute partial histories to the 1980s. It is possible to use this plot to search for histories which might have an influential effect on the regression parameter estimates of the calendar time and age variables. In this data set, there is no obviously influential history, and we proceed to examination of the display in greater detail.

If the display is rotated through a further 45° about the *y*-axis, it is possible to confirm graphically that all of the histories end in 1987, the survey date. Other rotations are possible: a conventional two-dimensional Lexis diagram can be produced by rotation so that the *x*- or *z*-axis is horizontal and the *y*-axis vertical.

We now zoom into the histories to view them in more detail. Figure 5.3 illustrates some typical histories for women aged around 25 marrying between 1966 and 1971. Immediately evident is the variation on female return to work patterns following childbirth, confirming the need to allow for heterogeneity in the model. Another feature

Figure 5.3 Zoomed detail of Figure 5.2, showing event histories starting around 1970.

of the data becomes immediately apparent; examination of the histories on the left side of the figure show that changes of state from green (shown as black) to red (dark gray) bars on the center face representing female employment history occur before changes of state from brown (black) to blue (medium gray) bars on the child history. In other words, the female partner stops work before the birth of a child. Although the data does not distinguish between adopted children and children born to the mother, we can realistically take this to be a pregnancy effect. This effect is unsurprising but was omitted from the original analysis.

Further examination of the histories (not shown here) also reveals evidence of differences between women marrying in early cohorts (pre-1960) and those marrying late (post-1970). The early group appear to have fewer state changes in female employment, and are less likely to reenter work than those in later marriage cohorts.

The above figures give snapshots of the visualization process. In any real application, the data would be explored in detail, using rotation, panning, zooming, and other visualization tools to gain insight into the data. Statisticians who have used 3D dynamic graphics software will be familiar with this process.

We can investigate these features of the display by reanalyzing the Kirkcaldy dataset. A new three-level factor representing pregnancy was introduced into the model: not pregnant or in first trimester, in second trimester, and in third trimester. There is a dramatic decrease in minus twice the log-likelihood of 859.5 on 2 df. The effects of pregnancy are dramatic, with the strongest effect, unsurprisingly, in the third trimester. If, in addition, the data set is divided into two cohorts, there is a further decrease in minus twice the log-likelihood of 465.8 on 18 df, with substantial differences in parameter estimates between the two cohorts.

5.6 Discussion

The above example illustrates that visualization software can aid the statistician in the analysis of event history and other longitudinal data. The software used is similar to other scientific visualization systems, which offer numerous benefits, including a powerful interaction capability, modularity and extendibility, and a graphics toolkit providing useful features such as slicing, texturing, rendering, and animation. However, there are also costs, which include a steep learning curve, plus the often complicated pre-processing of the data necessary to provide the visualization environment with data in the appropriate format, and the inability of the software to deal easily with abrupt color changes. There are also various tools which appear not to be currently available. First among these is an identification tool, to allow the user to examine values of variables and coordinates of a particular pixel point. The release of Explorer used for this study also appears to be lacking in its provision of suitable annotation tools for adding axes, labels, and titles to the rendered images.

The pencil objects proposed here, which are displayed in a 3D extension of the Lexis diagram, offer an appropriate compromise between complexity and understanding in their role of representing complex time-series data. The module to read the histories allows a subset of variables to be displayed, and the thickness and inter-face angle can also be specified by the user. Moreover, the plot can be adapted in various ways. For example, it is worth noting that the 3D Lexis diagram uses only one octant of the eight available in the full x–y–z space. The other octants with negative x, y or z values could be used to display mirror images of the Lexis diagrams, with different subsets of the data in other octants. One general application of this would be to split an event history sample by sex, and to display the males with positive y-values and the females with negative y-values.

Acknowledgments

We thank Professor Fred Smith and Dr Regina Dittrich for useful discussions on the Lexis diagram. This work was funded under the ESRC's Analysis of Large and Complex Datasets initiative (H519255029).

References

[1] B.H. McCormick, T.A. DeFanti, M.D. Brown (eds.), Visualization in scientific computing (special issue ACM SIGGRAPH), *Computer Graphics*, 21; 1987.
[2] H.M. Hearnshaw, D.J. Unwin (eds.), *Visualization in Geographical Information Systems*, Wiley, New York, 1994.

[3] P.R. Keller, M.M. Keller, *Visual Cues,* IEEE Computer Society Press, Los Alamitos, Calif., 1992.

[4] C. Chatfield, The initial examination of data, *J. R. Statist. Soc. A*, 148: 214–253; 1985.

[5] *AVS Developer's Guide* (1992) Advanced Visual Systems Inc., Waltham, Mass.

[6] K.W. Brodlie, J.R. Gallop, A.J. Grant, J. Haswell, W.T. Hewett, S. Larkin, C.C. Lilley, H. Morphet, A. Townend, J. Wood, H. Wright, *Review of Visualization Systems,* Advisory Group on Computer Graphics, Technical Report No. 9, 2nd Edition, 1995.

[7] S. Dex, *Women's Work Histories: An Analysis of the Women and Employment Survey,* Research Report No. 46, Department of Employment, HMSO, London, 1984.

[8] R.M. Post, P.P. Roy-Byrne, T.W. Uhde, Graphic representation of the life course of illness in patients with affective disorder, *Am J. Psychiatry*, 145(7): 844–848; 1988.

[9] H.-P. Blossfeld, A. Hamerle, K.U. Mayer, *Event History Analysis,* Lawrence Erlbaum Associates, Hillsdale, N.J., 1989.

[10] E.R. Tufte, *The Visual Display of Quantitative Information,* Graphics Press, Cheshire, Conn., 1983.

[11] J.T. Barry, S. Walby, B. Francis, Graphical exploration of work history data, *Quaderni di Statistica e Matematica Applicata alle Scienze Economico-Sociali*, 12: 65–74; 1990.

[12] W. Lexis, *Einleitung in die Theorie der Bevölkerungsstatistik,* Trübner, Strassburg, 1875.

[13] C. Vanderschrick, Le diagramme de Lexis revisité, *Population*, 5: 1241–1262; 1992.

[14] K. Becker, *Zur Berechnung vor Sterbetafeln an die Bevölkerungsstatistik zu Stellende Anforderungen,* Berlin, 1874.

[15] A.J. Verwey, Principles of vital statistics. *J. Statist. Soc. Lond.*, 38: 487–513; 1875.

[16] R. Pressat, *L'Analyse Demographique,* Presses Universitaires de France, Paris, 1961.

[17] N. Keiding, Statistical inference in the Lexis diagram, *Phil. Trans. R. Soc. Lond. A*, 332: 487–509; 1990.

[18] A.I. Goldman, Eventcharts: Visualising survival and other timed-events data. *Am. Statist.*, 46(1): 13–18; 1992.

[19] W.S. Cleveland, M.E. McGill (eds.), *Dynamic Graphics for Data Analysis,* Wadsworth, Belmont, Calif., 1988.

[20] R.B. Davies, P. Elias, R.D. Penn, The relationship between a husband's unemployment and his wife's participation in the labour force, *Oxford Bull. Statist.*, 54(2): 145–171; 1992.

6

The Full Volume, Simultaneous Visualization of Weather Radar Echoes with Digital Terrain Map Data

Justin J. Doick and Anthony R. Holt

6.1 Introduction

In this chapter we describe progress made towards a three-dimensional product for the interpretation of weather radar data. The radar as a remote sensor produces vast quantities of data in relatively short periods, with the quantity of data produced being dependent upon the number of polarization modes in operation. This makes the result of the radar an ideal application for visualization where further processing by computer merely generates an additional dataset. In the history of the radar, a number of two-dimensional displays have been established such as the PPI and CAPPI[1]. Other similar displays such as the HARPI [10] have been created and used in various studies. Here we aim to produce a full volume display which as yet has no firm foundation of use[2]. It is the anticipation that such a display might show facets of a storm that are not otherwise apparent to the operational forecaster. Current operational meteorologists use two-dimensional plots showing many variables, including wind direction and magnitude, pressure, and temperature. It may be useful to have a three-dimensional picture, and this may only be generated mentally. Thus there is some scope in such a display, but it should be informative and carry a clear meaning. It is often the case that three-dimensional imagery produced from modern packages such as IRIS Explorer [4] and AVS [5] are very complex to interpret. We require a well-defined output that may result in superior storm analysis and thus more accurate weather forecasts. A principal interpretation requirement is *location*. That is, a three-dimensional display of radar reflectivity is of little use if it is not possible to geographically locate the echoes. Further, it should be noted that the frequencies operationally used do not *see* clouds and as such a combined display could not be expected to precisely resemble what a viewer may have seen at the time of the storm. Rather, the radar sees the precipitation, be it rain, snow, or melting particles. Nonetheless, a display containing terrain should provide extra information about storm development, and should thus be the ideal solution.

---

[1] These terms are defined in Table 6.1 and are explained in the next section in a general discussion of the radar.
[2] NCAR are also looking into the possibilities of such a system, especially TDWR [6].

Visualization and Modeling
ISBN 0-12-227738-4

6.2   The Radar as a Meteorological Tool

The radar has been used in the study and forecast of weather situations since around 1947 [9]. It finds its source in World War II in the tracking of enemy aircraft, where weather echoes on the display were seen as distractions and unwanted artifacts. Since that time, the radar has been fully developed as an operational tool with a large skill basis called upon to study the collated data. In this section, we consider the radar as a data source, what data it collects, and what this data may mean. To consider the radar as an instrument is beyond the scope of this work.

Radar may be ground based, airborne, or spaceborne, but in this work we consider only the ground based radar. Each of these radar formats has a different set of specifics. The ground based radar is designed under various paradigms; most operate using a set of constant-elevation scans, but some operate helical scan techniques (see later) and so on. The radars producing data under the PADRE [19] agreement all operate under the following (simple) description. The radar collects *beams* (or *rays*) of data, each associated with angles ϕ and θ of *azimuth* and *elevation*, respectively. These are collected at constant θ whilst ϕ varies through 360°. As the full rotation is completed, θ is incremented to the next elevation angle that is to be sampled. Actually, the elevation angle is modified in the final few rays of the current elevation, and settled in the first few azimuth angles at the next. How far the elevation angle is altered will vary. Some radars operate a geometric scan scheme whereby many scans are performed at lower elevations, and few at increasing separations where the elevation is greater. The aim is to sample as great a volume as space in as short a time period as possible, concentrating on low altitudes where the majority of the scatterers are to be found. The MWRO in Montreal, Canada operates such a scheme.

Table 6.1   Acronyms used in this paper.

Acronym	Meaning
AVS	Application visualization system
C-Band	Radar wavelength ~ 5 cm
CAPPI	Constant altitude PPI
CSIM	Centro Sperimentale l'Idrologia e Meteorologia
DEM	Digital elevation model
DLR	Deutsche Forschungsanstalt für Luft-und Raumfahrt
DTM	Digital terrain model
ERA	Essex Radar Archive
MWRO	McGill Weather Radar Observatory
NAG	Numerical Algorithms Group
NCAR	National Centre for Atmospheric Research
PADRE	Polarization And Doppler Radar Experiment
PPI	Plan-Position Indicator
RADAR	Radio detection and ranging
RHI	Range–height indicator
SGI	Silicon Graphics Inc.
SMR	Servizio Meteorologico Regionale
TDWR	Terminal Doppler Weather Radar
UQAM	Université du Québec à Montréal

For a beam width of around 0.9°, the radar will collect around 400 beams at each elevation; each of these is an average of several consecutive rays where the azimuth angle is constantly varying at continuous intervals.

The radar collects data in two important modes, but data is displayed in many more. The first is the Plan Position Indicator or PPI. These are each associated with an elevation angle and are generally plotted in polar format. Each beam comprises a number of *bins*. The length of these bins is variable (radar hardware determined), but most radars will have a long and short range scan, and in the case of the CSIM radar there are 110 one-kilometer bins. The distance from the radar to the middle of each bin introduces the third principal radar parameter, *range*. This is associated with azimuth and elevation to individually identify radar bins. In contrast, where the radar is seen to increase the elevation constantly with azimuth, it scans in *helical* mode. This is the case with the Alberta radar [15].

The PPI is not suitable for direct iso-surface construction due to the three-dimensional surface that the data resides in. Thus we transform the data to a pseudo form, the Constant Altitude PPI or CAPPI. In this form, each slice represents a constant horizontal slice. Given a set of these, iso-surfacing may take place. The problems in generating a set of CAPPIs from a set of PPIs or a helical scan are clear! However, where data is to be advantageously displayed in Cartesian form the interpolation process may take place at the same time as the construction of the CAPPI set [11].

The second important data collection scheme is the Range Height Indicator or RHI. This is not presented in this paper but has been considered. In this mode, the radar is fixed at some azimuth, the elevation angle is then increased slowly to collect data at closer angular intervals than is the case with a PPI scan. At the preset maximum elevation, the azimuth angle is adjusted, and the elevation is now decreased in steps to around 0° elevation. The process is then repeated, until typically a sector scan has been completed. The sector may be around 20° in azimuth. Work has also been carried out on the construction of iso-surfaces from such a set of data. The initial task was to represent the *wedge* shaped set of data in a three-dimensional array.

6.3 Project Aim

In this section, we discuss why a combined display should be of any use. This gives the project motivation and a clear target. The display is justified through various important points which are discussed and substantiated. *This section considers aspects of three-dimensional visualization but uses the radar for data source as a discussion aid.*

Having produced a full volume display, the first thing that may be noticed is that an isolated three-dimensional surface is very hard to interpret. The meteorologist may be used to seeing planar views of radar data as in PPIs and other displays which may carry intuitive meanings and easily recognized patterns of weather behavior in the display. These skills need transferring to the interpretation of the new display which may or may not show the same facets. It may be that the new display will find application in identifying new and different storm development behavior. Essentially, the user must know how to interpret the display, and thus the user needs some interpretation clues.

The first challenge in interpreting a three-dimensional image is in gaining some notion of the directions of the axes. The user must determine what the eye vector is before appraisal can take place. Then magnitudes may be considered. The vertical scale needs to be such that the vertical variations in the data can be interpreted, but it should ideally be to scale with the horizontal plane scale. If not, then the scale factor should be apparent. The scale needs some user verification, and this may be achieved through some horizontal and vertical rule or else a grid box may be drawn around the dataset defining the extent of the data. The rulers can be just as difficult to place in three dimensions as the data itself, however, and thus may not lead to any additional clarity.

A solution to the problem may be to add terrain imagery. This, if possible, allows the user to mentally determine the position of the echo to at least some extent. Producing terrain imagery is an additional problem, where solutions may include aerial or satellite photographs or computer-modeled terrain based upon Digital Terrain Map (or DTM) data. There are further reasons for including terrain imagery in the display. It may prove possible to determine interaction between the terrain and storm development (and progression); this process is termed *orography* [1]. This, however, is under the provision that time-series data is provided at suitable temporal resolution. Not all sites are able to provide this, in particular research sites; the Alberta radar is one radar which did, at intervals of no more than 3 minutes. Either way, the task now includes the incorporation of two datasets which exist in different coordinate systems in different formats. Not the least of such concerns is the different data dimensionality that may be present in these data. There are further constraints in incorporating terrain into such an image. We should require that the vertical scale in the terrain match that in the vertical display of the radar echo. If this condition is not met, then the display does not portray the true situation and can only lead to misinterpretation of data with foreseeable connotations. Further, the space between the ground height and the echoes should be proportional to the scale used. There will always be such a gap, since the radar does not monitor across the surface of the Earth. The first reason is occlusion due to clutter (hills and buildings, etc.) and the second is beam elevation where, at increasing ranges, the beam is at progressively higher points above the Earth. Finally, we wish to manipulate both terrain and radar echo simultaneously. That is, should we wish to rotate the surface by some measure in the x and z axes, then the terrain should be updated accordingly. The point should also be made that we should consider whether the terrain should be visible through the echo when using a plan view. Alternatively, should merely the regions of terrain where there are no echoes located directly above be sufficient to gain the location information that is sought?

A further concern in three-dimensional visualization results from the fact that images are projected into two dimensions for display on VDUs and also for printing purposes. It is this which causes the occlusion of objects that are farther away, and difficulties in interpreting where each part of the display is geographically. The notion of introducing a terrain display was designed to help solve or alleviate this. When we then ask for multiple surface displays, such as is the case with more than one surface value or time step, there is a new problem introduced in that the display requires reduced opacity of the outer surface. This is not technically difficult within IRIS Explorer, where RGBA values allow opacity to be stored. However, in interpreting the display, we can now see both the front and rear of the surface (and all the other surfaces), which makes interpretation all the more difficult. The simplest way to interpret what is displayed is to rotate the image interactively until a user determines a view that shows the data correctly. It is possible to rotate through the x, y, and z axes simultaneously. The real shortfall is in producing hard copies, for example when documenting weather cases. Here (unless many images are to be produced, which may prove prohibitively expensive) the documenter must select a view that is all-encompassing, passing on a single interpretation which is correct. In many cases, the default projection angle leads to an incorrect understanding of the image. It may be that the image looks interesting and significant, but in reality may not be quite so. This may be demonstrated simply, through the use of a pair of sample result images.

6.4   A Realization

The task of visualization has been carried out under PV-Wave [23] on a Sun Station LX and IRIS Explorer [4] on an Silicon Graphics Indy workstation. However, the predominant task was carried out under the latter, which has been configured with 144 MB of RAM and the R4400 CPU daughter card upgrade. Thus the total system cost is now approximately[3] £10 000, and not an unrealistic proposal for an operations budget today. The decision was made to use such packages, rather than to develop a product from scratch, since initial progress would be faster and the end result would be as portable as the given package. The task is split into three: the first is to visualize the terrain from a DTM; then the radar data is to be visualized; and ultimately the two must be combined.

6.4.1   Terrain

General
This section briefly discusses the types, construction, and various uses of the DTM. Any two DTMs are more than likely to be provided in differing formats, and hence we discuss the visualization of a general, two-dimensional regularly gridded DTM which most other formats may be used to produce. Typically, the data will be tiled or cut to sheets due to its great volume. We consider also the construction of a suitable color map, which has relevance in the color map production for any given visualization. A DTM digitally represents heights above the Earth surface in some form of grid. Rather than a smooth contour line on a map, we now have a series of heights from which contours may be constructed. For further reading, consult reference [2].

   Under the PADRE agreement, DTMs were provided to complement the Italian radar data from CSIM and SMR. These radars are particularly useful since they they collect data fast enough to provide volume scan information. They are fairly close together (80 km apart) and permit the analysis of dual data. This has been considered in two dimensions in the reconstruction of full vector wind fields [13], and under further work there may be some interest in dual three-dimensional visualization. The second region to supply terrain data is DLR. We do not currently have access to DTM data for the other radar sources, McGill and Alberta.

Specifics
The Italian database was supplied by SMR (Bologna) [22]. The data is almost regularly gridded in that it is actually on a latitude/longitude grid. The lines of latitude are in fact

---

[3] At UK academic discounted prices.

parallel, but those of longitude tend together in the Northerly direction. However, for reasons of scale we wish to consider regions no larger than around 70 km × 70 km and thus make the assumption that the data exists on a regular grid. The error involved is less than 0.5%. The data is spaced at approximately every 220 m by 230 m. There were a number of problems with the raw dataset, not unexpected in a task of visualization. These included undefined values, negative heights, depth sampling, missing data, effects of tiling, and limits of digitization and accuracy (due to rounding, for example). Each of these were solved, and a resultant array of DTM data was produced.

The German DTM displayed none of the above problems and exhibited just a single feature. The data was very, very fine, being sampled at just 31 m by 21 m. The data had to be thinned. This level of resolution provides more detail than is used in a typical display. The DTM was supplied by DLR and it is hoped that combined displays constructed from the finely detailed RHI sector scans may benefit from this.

Color usage

Color models have been designed to portray altitude and gradient. Color is used for the feel of height, through the flat plains of Po Valley and Bavaria and into the valleys of the mountainous regions of the Alps and Appennines to the mountain peaks.

The use of color in scientific visualization is a process involving the use of perception [16]. Our needs are relatively straightforward, in that we wish to render terrain. Although we are not specifically interested in the terrain cover (some DTMs also store this information and additional factors, tree types, building heights, and so on), it is seen to be an important interpretation cue that seas and lakes are shown in blue. The color assignment may then proceed through the rainbow chart, or alternatively be tailored to the application. In addition, we wish the scale to 'suggest' increases in height. This may be achieved through increasing hues and a look and feel/adjust process. Each color band should be sufficiently different from every other, and be sharply defined from adjacent colors in the map. This is important so that image color to color scheme correlation may occur with ease.

In the specific case of our terrain modeling, we are discretizing an otherwise continuous dataset. That is, although terrain heights are rounded to the nearest meter, all heights are available from around −40 m and up to 4 km or more. In general this can be seen tobe nonbeneficial since some form of 'data hiding' occurs, and the true nature of the data may be misrepresented. The design of the color scheme will bin these values into a dozen or so height ranges. The bins may be completely manually defined, or alternatively histogrammatically determined or else based upon a logarithmic scale. The log scale has the advantage that it can be automatically generated, and applied to further DTM data sets.

Color maps can be and are defined to draw particular attention to particular details. Unless they are well designed, interest may be drawn to an incorrect region of the display. This is the expected behavior of a novice appraising a scientific visualization but might be ignored on just this basis. A lot of medical imaging, MRI and CAT scans for example are displayed merely gray-scaled on the basis of intensity. This is seen to be of greatest benefit to the radiographer. Clearly orange on a purple background stands out more than does purple on a black background and this effect may be used where it is important to highlight a feature in a display. For example, we only wish to draw attention to areas of missing data when appraising data quality and certainly not in the presentation of final results. In addition, these effects tend to make areas appear larger or smaller. Bright regions on black backgrounds stand out and lead to the incorrect interpretation of an image by a viewer.

An important example of the use of color is highlighted where two data sets possess something in common. For example, in time-series data, the values recorded may be expected to be different but the locations of the observations ought to be the same in each sampling. An example would be the height of the ground around a volcano measured 6 months apart. Or different parameters may be recorded, for example the height and temperature of the ground surrounding the volcano. Where the variables recorded differ, different color maps will be required to display the content of the data. Color plane switching may then occur to display the same data in different color schemes according to which data mode is being represented [21]. The latter is not feasible in IRIS Explorer, where a new color map must be read in or generated. Each object in the display pipeline is then rendered anew and redisplayed.

The visualization

To produce a three-dimensional surface, the DTM (subsection) is rotated around the x- and z-axes to produce the desired viewpoint, that is the eye vector. The result is projected into two dimensions (the plane $z = 0$) for display and printing purposes. Having projected the points, adjacent points are connected and hidden-line removal is performed. The surface may be displayed as a wire grid, or rendered using a lighting model such as Gouraud, or as above with color bands [4, 12, 23]. The given display may be manipulated through scaling, area selection, and viewpoint.

6.4.2   Radar

The radar data sources that have become available for this work include data collected by DLR (Germany), CSIM (Italy), and SMR (Italy) under the PADRE project. This data was archived under the same project into the Essex Radar Archive, or ERA. Other radar sources include ARC (Alberta) and McGill (Montreal, Quebec).

Intrinsically, each radar collects the same data. Radars sample data similarly and, whilst built by a multitude of different firms, they all work under the same principle. The major difference between data collected by radars today is the result of equipment fitted, for example whether the radar is Dopplerized or has polarization diversity facilities. Other system variables are the operational frequency, beam width, antenna size, pulse repetition frequency and rotation speed, but in each case the same data has to be stored. This can be a problem since each of these radars stores the data in radically different formats. The Essex Radar Archive in which all PADRE data has been converted to a common format, has the advantage that data can be visualized using the same routines for each data source, but this is associated with slower data access times. We aim toward a real-time operational tool where the data is provided immediately, and not from an archive; thus operational times will be faster than times previously reported [11].

The first, most crucial task in visualizing data is in importing it into the package; in this case, IRIS Explorer. As mentioned before, IRIS Explorer has a data type termed the curvilinear lattice. This may appear to be the ideal solution, to remove file headers (or allow the Data Scribe to perform this task using *patterns*) and to associate each data value (or radar resolution volume) with its coordinate (range, azimuth, and elevation). This (so far) has proved to be an elusive process. Additionally, it can be seen to be a disadvantageous solution, since all data stored within IRIS Explorer is of floating-point format, regardless of the format of the stored data. To use a curvilinear lattice to describe this data involves 4 bytes for the datum, and a further 12 for the coordinates. Clearly, a factor of 4 difference in memory requirements is quite detrimental to processing times. The most obvious alternative to these curvilinear surfaces is to interpolate the data to a Cartesian grid which may then be easily read into IRIS Explorer. This is a process that is used for visualization (and processing generally) by a number of institutions including the British Meteorological Office and the MWRO, although for differing reasons. Intrinsically, radar data is collected in three-dimensional polar coordinates and it can be seen that at greater ranges bin volumes are greater than at shorter ranges. This leads to data loss and nonperfect displays. Thus there are advantages and disadvantages in utilizing a Cartesian grid. However this is the solution implemented here for reasons of efficiency and practicality.

Having made the implementation decision to go with a Cartesian system, there are two immediate methods of gaining Cartesian data. The first is to consider a square grid of cells and to calculate which resolution volumes are incident with each. The second method is to process each volume, calculating the intersecting set of cells. In either method there will be cells which gain no value and cells which gain more than one value. This problem may be termed co-location and solutions include averaging all the values at a cell that are incident. However, for a more accurate display, we might weight these values on an area of overlap basis or on the distance to the center of the cell. Each of these improvements will add considerably to the processing time, clearly inappropriate in a real-time system. The solution most closely approximating the true solution, that is, one in which the user can detect no differences, should be considered suitable as an end result.

The first display considered is the creation of PPIs. These represent the simple format in which the data is collected and displayed planar. This is an important step since it provides a reference against which to check other systems displaying the same data. PPIs are not ideal for the construction of full volume data sets since they may be described as the surfaces of a set of cones with a common vertex. Little time is lost in creating such displays since the data will require extraction in any case. A different conversion routine is needed to produce the series of CAPPIs which are constructed from the PPIs and represent as closely as possible, a set of horizontal slices of data. The first slice is at some fixed height from the surface at the Earth (assumed flat) and successive slices are at constant increments in height. The true solution to this problem should include allowance for earth curvature and beam bending due to atmospheric effects. However, since we have confined our interest to limited regions, these effects will be small and have been neglected.

A usual requirement in radar displays (PPIs and CAPPIs), is the overlay of range rings and radials. These add geographical interpretation clues for the radar observer. Traditionally, radials are placed at 30° intervals in azimuth, with the first at 0°. The range ring placements will depend to some extent upon the radar's current operational range. Many radars normally operate in 110 or 120 km mode) and to around double this during intermittent long-range scans. Clearly, having range rings at short range increments for both displays would dominate one, and be a sparse facet in the other.

Hence at short ranges, a 20 km interval is not inappropriate. Producing these in an IRIS Explorer display (ultimately, the *Render* module) is far from an easy task. At the top level of usage, lines may be drawn using the module *Annotation* when correctly configured and having established a complex *Pick* connection. However, it is extremely complex to move the line and impossible to accurately place the line under this paradigm. Further, it is implausible to expect a user to place the lines each time the system is initiated. Finally, it is not possible to draw circles, and hence the rings are out of the question. Going to a lower level, at an advanced level of usage, it is possible to access line- and circle-drawing primitives under the *Geometry* data type through developing a new module. An alternative solution is to implement such an algorithm as the incremental line- and circle-drawing algorithms proposed by Bresenham [12, 17] and to include these as a bitmap into the Cartesian data prepared for radar display. If the bits are set at a suitable value out of the range of the radar parameter, then the color map may be used to *draw* the rings and radials as an overlay.

6.4.3 Combined product

In this section, we discuss the procedure to produce a combined display, and consider the difficulties that had to be solved in order to produce the end result. Many of the problems that have to be dealt with are IRIS Explorer-specific, that is, that package has to be configured to produce the desired product where it is not initially ideally suited to the task.

The first consideration is whether the relevant terrain section should match exactly the horizontal plane of the region of the echo. For example, it may be of interest to show a greater region of terrain so that during an animation it could be seen where the storm has come from and where it is going. If the terrain region is updated with each display, then a user may suffer some disorientation. This has not as yet proved possible, and a constraint of the current system is that the regions of each dataset must match.

The next problem to consider is data dimensionality. If two datasets are to represent the same region in IRIS Explorer, then they must have the same dimensionality. This is undesirable since, in producing terrain imagery, a dense two-dimensional grid is required. For a reasonable display, a dataset of 200 by 200 nodes might be considered. However, this causes easily anticipated problems with iso-surfacing where this data set of 80 000 bytes is only one of around 20 horizontal slices. Clearly iso-surfacing will be slow and this sort of resolution really is not required. A much-thinned dataset will produce images of acceptable quality. An aim of this work is that any resultant product should respond within real time where weather forecasting may prevent flooding [14] or even save lives. A Doppler radar can only be used to identify (as opposed to forecast) tornado signatures within 20 minutes of touchdown [18]. Here then, it can be seen that different dataset sizes would be both advantageous and superior.

The simple data type that IRIS Explorer uses for data communication is termed the *lattice*. Simply, this is a variable-dimension array (but does carry additional information). The more complex data type is the *pyramid*, which essentially manages a series of lattices; these find no application here. The remaining data types comprise *pick*, *parameter*, and *generic*. Data coordinates may be treated in three ways. They may be ignored, which implies that the data lies on a regular uniform grid. This grid may, ultimately, be scaled to represent any region with proportional inter-node spacing.

Alternatively, arrays may be provided of coordinate positions in the x and y directions when these are valid throughout the dataset. Here, irregular grids are catered for. The final alternative is the curvilinear lattice where each data point is associated with a point location. The location may be specified in one, two, three, or even more dimensions. In the case of radar data, the coordinates are spherical polar coordinates in three-dimensional space. Thus for each datum in, say, a reflectivity field, there are an additional three floating-point values to be stored. However, where several variables are available, as with polarization diversity and Doppler radars, the data location information need only be stored once. This is only valid so long as each data set was sampled similarly. Here an important compromise may be made. The data may be interpolated to a regular Cartesian grid at the cost of pre-processing and data co-location. The latter arrives from the radar data being collected in what may be modeled as a set of conical frustrums. These may not simply nor rapidly be represented on a Cartesian grid and many assumptions must be made. However, this can be accepted as a suitable solution which may very well be more efficient than the full curvilinear solution which must carry around a set of data coordinates. Additional constraints are apparent from the beam widening which takes place at greater ranges. Here, the radar resolution volumes become greater and correspond with a different number of Cartesian cells than do those volumes at closer ranges. This further leads to the possibility of some Cartesian cells not overlapping with any radar resolution volumes at all, and remaining void. This may cause problems in display, especially in the construction of full volume displays. This interpolation may be implemented in two directions. Firstly we may consider each resolution volume and determine which set of Cartesian cells are incident. There may then be cells which are incident with more than one volume, and some selection criterion must take place. This may be based on area weighting, absolute distance from cell to volume center, or any other suitable solution. Clearly, the closer the solution desired, the greater the required computation time. The alternative is to select each Cartesian cell in turn and calculate which radar resolution volume coincides. Each of these methods has connotations when reconsidering each dataset at a different resolution.

The cost of supporting data coordinates may be consolidated. Data and coordinates may be multiplied by some suitable factor of 10 and stored as a short rather than an integer or floating-point value. This results in a nett space saving of 50%. This (in IRIS Explorer) can lead to visual confusion since a user must select a value of 5000 when a surface of 50 dBZ is required. There are ways around this, but they are not immediately apparent to the casual or amateur user. This is also apparent in legends and automatically generated lines of annotation and file names. Further, it is of essence to store data in binary format rather than ASCII which is again smaller, but additionally more rapidly read and written by UNIX.

It is possible to solve the problem of different data dimensionality being used to represent the same terrain region as outlined above. This, however, requires utilizing the Module Builder [3]. It is true that a data set can be forced to represent a different region, but this is a manual process and only apparent through significant usage of IRIS Explorer. This would not be achieved, for example, by the end user. The basic problem evolves from lattices of dimension of n by m nodes being interpreted by IRIS Explorer as representing a region of n by m units, where the unit is irrelevant until a second dataset is to be incorporated, which must clearly be in the same units. The solution currently chosen manipulates the additional information supported by the lattice as suggested above. This is achieved through a module developed under this work.

Finally, we consider the question of scale. There are two aspects to this. Firstly, we need to maintain well-proportioned vertical scales in each of the display components. This is achieved through a simple linear mapping. The range of heights may be easily determined, in the case of the examples in the succeeding section this is a figure of around 2100 m. When displayed, the vertical range is determined by a mapping within IRIS Explorer, and may be around 0.03 to 30. These are not defined to take any units, merely maintaining correct ratio. There is, inevitably, some overlap in the vertical range of the two datasets. Radar echoes in our case exist between 500 m and say 10 000 m. It can be seen then that the vertical ratio is biased toward the echoes, and these are thus likely to dominate the display. We map these values into the internal scale given above, and gain a range of 7 to 105. These two values are entered into the module introduced in the previous paragraph. The lower end of this range determines the correct interaction between the mountain peaks and echo bottom, and the range (105–7) ensures proportional scaling. Secondly, the ratio of the vertical to the horizontal scale has to be considered. Since the terrain has a maximum height of around 2 km, and the storm echoes a maximum of around 10 km, the vertical height must be magnified compared to the horizontal extent in order for vertical variations to be visible. However, in order for this magnification to be reasonable, it is essential to limit the horizontal extent of the image. We have therefore restricted the horizontal extent to that of a square of side 74 km.

6.5 Results

In combined display output, the terrain and radar echo must clearly be displayed by the same package; this has been stated to be IRIS Explorer. However, the first results presented are those of terrain imagery produced using PV-Wave. When producing a dedicated visualization of a large area of terrain, PV-Wave produces what might be regarded as the superior output. However, when considering just confined regions for combining displays, IRIS Explorer seems superior. The iso-surfaces of reflectivity shown later are in blue in order to draw maximum contrast against the hues of the terrain imagery.

Plate 8 presents a two-dimensional overview of the extent of data provided for the north of Italy. Further data is provided for the southern areas. The image is (top–down) aligned in the west–east direction. It can be seen how the plain of the Po Valley is extremely flat, only rising by a few meters in its entirety. The Apennines can be seen in the left running down the length of Italy, and the Alps in the right towards Bavaria, Germany. Plate 9 shows a three-dimensional representation of the region containing the radars involved in the project. The origin of the display is at 44° latitude and 9° 27′ longitude, covering an area of 2° by 3° (or 334 km by 220 km). A combined legend for the terrain height in the two of these images is shown in Plate 10 (left). Heights are given in meters above sea level.

Plates 10 to 15 give various viewpoints and aspects of a storm that was tracked by the SMR radar in the early afternoon of 4 September 1993. The times considered here are 14:14 through to 15:45. For Plates 10–13 the terrain region represented takes its origin 93 km west of the radar, 73 km south, and is 74 km square. Each image contains a legend recording meters above sea level for the terrain shown. Plate 10 (right) shows a vertical view of reflectivity echo shape against terrain. This view gives little notion of vertical scale, but allows horizontal placement to be determined with ease. The display is timed at 15:14 and is a representation at 30 dBZ. The radar location may be very closely located at the top right corner of this display (in actuality, it is just a little further east).

The next three images use a new view vector which is generally south. This viewpoint gives more notion of the magnitude of the weather echo, and this can be seen against the height of the mountains (rising to 2140 m in these images). The first of this series, Plate 11, is timed as per the preceding image, but the surface is taken at 45 dBZ. The tall shaft in the middle of the image clears 7.5 km and at this value (from this radar) must represent a hail shaft. The next image, Plate 12, represents the same surface value but 15 minutes later. This gives an idea of how the storm may move and what might be achieved through animation of such data should it be available at finer temporal resolution. Finally, Plate 13 shows how the storm is dissipating. The next dataset available shows only very small surfaces remaining. The surface value is maintained to show how the storm has dissipated and gradually traveled east.

In Plate 14 we show a PPI of differential reflectivity, ZDR, at 14:14, showing the range rings and radials inserted as described above. The value of visualization can be seen immediately in the way that rays of negative ZDR are immediately apparent. Such rays are caused by differential attenuation between vertically and horizontally polarized waves when passing through regions of heavy rain. A number of regions of heavy rain can therefore immediately be identified. In Plate 15 we show an iso-surface of reflectivity at this time, colored by ZDR. This shows where the core of the storm is to be found, whilst at the same time the positive ZDR on the side close to the radar, accompanied by negative ZDR on the opposite side, again indicate the heavy rain. However, the latter is not as evident, since the effect of taking an iso-surface is to reduce the regions of weak reflectivity in the shadow of the core of the storm.

As a final example, we show in Plates 16 to 18 data from Alberta, Canada, from the Alberta Research Council radar showing a convective storm described by Holt and colleagues [20]. In Plates 16 and 17 we show two iso-surfaces of reflectivity, at 35 dBZ and 60 dBZ, at 16:40 and 16:46 local time. The core of the storm is shown by the 60 dBZ iso-surface, and it can be seen that there has been a rapid descent of the core at this time. Rapid descents of cores of precipitation can give rise to severe hazards, particularly for aircraft taking off or landing. Nevertheless, in devising displays for real-time use, it is important to ensure that effects are not sensitive to the precise iso-surface level being chosen. In Plate 18 we show the same storm at 16:33 with an iso-surface of reflectivity at 57 dBZ colored by a second parameter, 'degree of polarization.' It was shown by Holt and colleagues [20] that this parameter appears to reveal regions of strong updraught. In this figure, the lower degree of polarization values, indicative of the updraught, are seen close to the ground, with an overhang of strong reflectivity above. The latter is also a sign that an updraught region is to be expected, but it is only clearly seen through the three-dimensional visualization. These visualizations thus show that such displays enable the storm dynamics to be immediately appreciated by the user.

6.6   Conclusions

To achieve a good three-dimensional visualization system, low temporal spacing is required. It is established in specifying radar for operational use that fast scan times are required. Scarchilli [8] reports operational scan times achieved from a C-band radar with rotational speeds of 6° per second. However, for optimal use of polarization diversity, dwell times of 0.2 seconds are suggested and for collecting 360 beams at each of 20 elevation angles will require 20 minutes for a full volume scan. This period may be sufficiently long for a storm to move out of the area visible to the radar, but for this work is certainly long enough for a storm core to develop so that no useful animation may be produced. Thus, for useful response times, it is suggested here that, where possible, the radar need not elevate beyond 8°, which even then reaches 10 km altitude at a range of 70 km. Perhaps the major concern should be which products are most required from future radars. Or maybe, can the radar be requested (simply) to produce the vast number of scans for the optimal work suggested above on one day, and then on the next produce data more attuned to the needs of three-dimensional visualization? Clearly, the latter has to show its worth.

We have described the simultaneous three-dimensional visualization of radar echoes of reflectivity and the underlying terrain. This has been achieved with the purpose of creating a tool that can be used by the meteorologist in a real-time environment. The geographical region that can be considered is limited by the need to scale the vertical dimension relative to that of the horizontal.

Modern radar techniques allow the collection of more than one item of data from each resolution volume. Therefore, the problem now is to further develop simultaneous displays which contain information from more than one variable in addition to the combined terrain display. Such displays may potentially be able to distinguish regions containing heavy rain from those containing hail. This will permit the quality of storm warnings to be improved. Airport safety may also be increased with the identification of microbursts.

Acknowledgments

The authors acknowledge the European Union for funding the PADRE project under contract number EV5V–CT92–0181 which enabled this work to be completed. Our thanks are due to our partners in the project for kindly providing data. In particular, to Dr M. Chandra from DLR, Germany, and to Drs P.P. Alberoni and S. Nanni from SMR, Bologna, Italy. We also thank the Alberta Research Council for the use of their data, and Professor E. Torlaschi from UQAM, Montreal for helpful conversations. Many thanks are due to Mr Robert Watson for help with revising the figures.

Postscript

Prior to the publication of this chapter, Justin Doick was tragically killed in a road traffic accident. This chapter, based on his MSc thesis [7], now includes his research up until the time of his death. He is sadly missed by his family and colleagues alike.

References

[1] K.A. Browning, Organisation and internal structure of synoptic and mesoscale precipitation systems in midlatitudes, *Radar in Meteorology*, chapter 26a. American Meteorological Society, 1990.

[2] P.A. Burrough, *Principles of Geographic Information Systems for Land Resources Assessment*. Oxford Science Publications, reprinted edition (with corrections), 1987. Monographs on Soil and Resources Survey No. 12.

[3] M.A. Halse, *IRIS Explorer Module Writer's Guide*. Silicon Graphics, Inc., Mountain View, Calif, 1992–93.

[4] M.A. Halse, *IRIS Explorer User's Guide*, Silicon Graphics, Inc., Mountain View, Calif. 1st edition, 1992–93.

[5] Advanced Visual Systems Inc., *AVS User's Guide*, 1992 edition.

[6] National Weather Service Modernisation Committee. Toward a new national weather service, *Weather For Those Who Fly*, National Academy Press, 1994.

[7] J.J. Doick, *The visualisation of weather radar echoes*, Master's thesis, Mathematical and Computer Sciences, University of Essex, Colchester, UK, July 1995.

[8] G. Scarchilli, E. Gorgucci, Rain rate estimates by multi-parameter radar measurements, *COST 75 Workshop – Improved Rainfall Estimates Using Polarisation Diversity Radar*, Reading, UK, July 1995.

[9] J.I. Metcalf, K.M. Glover, A history of weather radar research in the U.S. Air Force, *Radar in Meteorology*, chapter 5. American Meteorological Society, 1990.

[10] L.J. Battan, *Radar Observation of the Atmosphere*, The University of Chicago Press, revised edition, 1973.

[11] J.J. Doick, A.R. Holt, Enhanced displays for advanced weather radars, *COST 75 International Seminar on Advanced Weather Radar Systems*, pp. 410–418, European Commission, Brussels, 1995.

[12] J. Foley, A. van Dam, S. Feiner, J. Hughes, *Computer Graphics Principles and Practice*. Addison Wesley, 2nd edn, 1990. The Systems Programming Series.

[13] R.J. Watson, D.H.O. Bebbington, A.R. Holt, A methodology for comparing meteorological radar from two overlapping sites, *COST 75 International Seminar on Advanced Weather Radar Systems*, pp. 167–177, European Commission, Brussels, 1995.

[14] D.K. Smith, *Natural Disaster Reduction: How Meteorological and Hydrological Services Can Help*, World Meteorological Organization, 1989.

[15] V.N. Bringi, A. Hendry, Technology of polarisation diversity radars for meteorology, *Radar in Meteorology*, chapter 19, American Meteorological Society, 1990.

[16] N. Gershon, From perception to visualisation, In Rosenblum *et al.* (eds) *Scientific Visualisation – Advances and Challenges*, pp. 129–139, Academic Press, London, 1994.

[17] Y.P. Kuzmin, An efficient circle-drawing algorithm, *Computer Graphics J.*, 9(4): 333–336; Dec. 1990.

[18] R. Davies-Jones, Tornadoes. *Scientific American*, pp. 34–41; Aug. 1995.

[19] A.R. Holt, The PADRE project, *COST 75 International Seminar on Advanced Weather Radar Systems*, pp. 492–497, European Commission, Brussels, 1995.

[20] A.R. Holt, P.I. Joe, R. McGuinness, E. Torlaschi, T. Nichols, F. Bergwall, D.A. Holland, Simultaneous polarization and Doppler observations of severe convective storms in central Alberta, *Atmospheric Res.*, 33: 37–56; 1994.

[21] R. McGuinness, A knowledge based colour graphics display system for multi-parameter weather radar data, *Int. J. Remote Sensing*, 9(3): 515–525, 1988.

[22] M.T. Carrozzo, A. Chirenti, D. Luzio, C. Margiotta, T. Quarta, Creation of a mean altitudes file.

[23] Visual Numerics, *PV-WAVE Command Language User's Guide*, June 1993, 4.2 edition.

7
Visualization and Sonification of Marine Survey Data

A.M. Day, R. Minghim, S.M. Turner and D.B. Arnold

7.1   Introduction

The process of extraction of information from measured data involves a number of different steps. Translating a set of numbers into a suitable representation to enable correct analysis is not a simple task. This is more significant in situations where models of temporal behavior of the phenomenon under observation are insufficiently defined and tested, as in the case treated here. This chapter is concerned with finding suitable representations of information collected in marine surveys so that the behavior of substances, their interrelationships, and variations in time of the concentrations of substances can be observed. The measurement, treatment, and visualization of DMS (dimethyl sulphide) is presented here and the procedure is generalized for other related substances. This section introduces the data handling and visualization processes. Sections 7.2 and 7.3 present the techniques developed and the geometric computations for manipulation of the original raw data. Section 7.4 presents some of the resulting images of the analysis process and the information they convey. Section 7.5 presents the sound functions utilized in the analysis process and the aspects of the data they can help identify. Section 7.6 presents the conclusions of the present work.

7.1.1   The data

Data collection in the natural environment is often compromised by environmental and logistical factors that can lead to damaged data sets. This is particularly the case for marine and atmospheric surveys where weather and equipment failure can generate discontinuities in data series and where the opportunity of study cannot be repeated.

   In earlier papers [4, 5] we described the application of 2D and 3D geometry to improve the results of a series of marine surveys, designed, inter alia, to determine the seasonal and spatial variation of the trace gas dimethyl sulphide (DMS). DMS, 'the smell of the sea,' is produced in surface seawater via a complex microbiological network, which is as yet poorly understood [16, 17]. DMS is emitted into the air, where its oxidation products (e.g., sulphur dioxide) play important roles in atmospheric chemistry, such as contributing to the acidity of precipitation and formation of cloud condensation nuclei [14].

   During 1989, measurements of the parameters associated with the evaluation of the sea-to-air flux of DMS were made as part of the UK NERC North Sea Community Research Project (May 88 to Oct. 89). For two weeks each month, RRS Challenger followed a 3300 km cruise track (Figure 7.1) between 120 stations at which physical, chemical, and biological measurements were made [23]. Data for DMS production and fluxes were collected on nine of these cruises (Feb. to Oct. 89) and details of sampling, analysis, and flux determination can be found in [24].

Although this project was reasonably fortunate with both weather and equipment reliability, the data sets for all the parameters are incomplete. The percentage of survey positions, within each cruise, at which a complete set of parameters were successfully measured, varies from about 35% to almost 100% data. Given the significant time taken to complete one cruise, the data need to be considered as being located in a 3D space, with axes corresponding to longitude, latitude, and time. Depth in the water is not considered since it is the concentration at the air–sea interface that controls the flux. Thus, the cruise track for any month can be represented, generally, as a spiral in space and time (Figure 7.2).

In the initial study [24], time was not considered and the data from each cruise were taken to represent the average value for the whole month. In addition, relatively simple methods were used for summation of the behavior of the system over the area of sea that was studied. Day employed a similar method, using algorithms based on the Delaunay triangulation and Voronoi tessellation of the survey points to estimate the variation in parameters over the area [4] (Figure 7.3). Although temporal information was not included in this work, the study showed that data interpretation through computational geometry could generate differences in the level of DMS emissions (Figure 7.4). In reference [5] these methods were extended by including consideration of the time dimension and by making use of the 3D Delaunay tetrahedralization. Here we have taken three data sets (DMS, DMSPp, and Chlorophyll) produced from the 'grid with scaled time' interpolation technique described in reference [5] and used them for experiments with visualization and sonification as described in the following sections 7.4 and 7.5.

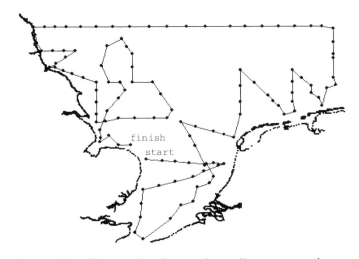

Figure 7.1   Planned cruise track to all survey stations.

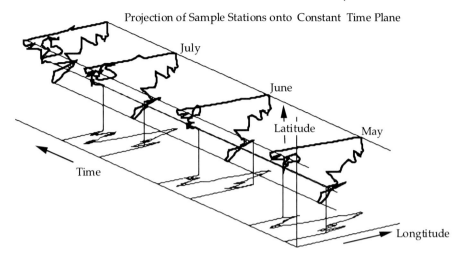

Figure 7.2   Spiral pattern of cruise position in space and time.

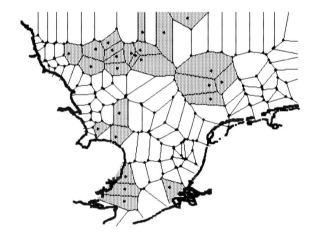

Figure 7.3   May Voronoi tessellation with missing samples shaded.

7.1.2   Multiple insights by multiple visualization techniques

The tasks of visualizing a data set and identifying patterns and behavior of the underlying processes pose a number of difficulties and the consequence is that interpretation is difficult. Data analysis can be enhanced by employing a number of different techniques on the same data set, allowing for different insights into the same information, redundancy and reinforcement of information, as well as speedup of interpretation. Nowadays a great number of different visualization methods are available and can be used and adapted for particular applications. In addition to visual methods of data mappings, the easy and inexpensive access to technology provides a greater number of devices and resources to support the process of data interaction and

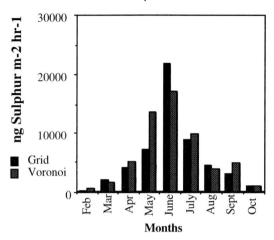

Figure 7.4   Grid and Voronoi spatially averaged flux.

understanding. In particular, sound has been successfully used as a tool for data mappings and interpretation, exploiting the capacity of human hearing to detect and analyze information.

Although not as powerful a sense as vision, hearing can help visualization tasks in a number of different ways, either by reinforcing visual information (supplementary) or by representing information that is not easy to convey graphically. In either case, sound helps to relieve the visual workload in graphical applications and improves sense of engagement. There are two basic ways humans can perceive sonic information in the environment. Those are *musical hearing* [13], whereby we interpret sounds by identifying their properties (pitch, duration, rhythm, intensity), and *everyday hearing* [8], which is the capability of identifying sound sources and dynamic events by listening to them (steps, car engines, door noises, key noises, and so on). Both types of hearing can be useful in computer interfaces.

Recently great progress has been made in understanding sound processing and in developing sound tools for data interpretation. Results have shown the adequacy of sound for a number of tasks, the adaptability of human hearing to new aural tasks, and the increase in performance when sound was employed with graphical presentations [12]. It was also possible to identify utility and frameworks for sound use in scientific and engineering applications [1, 18, 19]. Although usually requiring training, sound functions can support visual tasks and provide information on their own, provided correct sonic designs are made and appropriate integration into the graphic processes occurs. Based on these findings and, in a developed structure for sound representation of graphical and interaction entities, a system (SSound) was developed [20] to include data sonifications and sound perception aspects in a visualization system, and its utility for analysis of marine data or similar information is presented here.

The analysis of marine data included the creation, slicing and interaction of isosurfaces. The 'tetrahedralized' data were adjusted to a regularly spaced grid and isosurfaces were generated for particular values of concentration. Colour coding was manipulated until a satisfactory palette was defined that highlighted the particular information sought. The data were visualized by using a rather modified version of

NCSA's Image Software. Some of the modifications included: Volume Scan Function, Sound Functions, Isosurface Selection, and Volume Slicing. The system generates sound by use of a synthesizer module controlled by computer *via* MIDI, using pitch and timbre as independent channels for representation of data, in conjunction with stereo for orientation.

7.2   Geometric Computation

The problems of linear interpolation along a time axis, used with a bivariate method in 2D space, and the combination of different units (time and 2D space) are discussed in reference [22]. We have used a Delaunay triangulation to divide the 3D space into regions before interpolation and visualization are carried out. A detailed account of the triangulation method is given in reference [5], but for the purposes of this chapter a summary is given in the following.

In 3D, the triangulation (or tetrahedralization) has the property that the circumsphere of a Delaunay tetrahedron does not contain any point of the given set in its interior. One advantage of this type of triangulation is that it maximizes the minimum angle in the triangulation. This is useful for applications that use finite element methods and/or interpolations where long, narrow triangles are generally undesirable. The following method has been implemented.

The Delaunay tetrahedralization of the data points was computed for all 9 cruises for each parameter under investigation. We applied a scaling factor to the time axis before computing the tetrahedralization. A scaling of 500 was selected to bring the values for the range of interest on the time axis to approximately the same scale as the ranges of latitude and longitude in the data set. The effects of different ways of scaling of the time abscissa are discussed in reference [5]. To obtain an estimate of the parameter's values on any (scaled) date, the constant time plane (a 'slice') representing that date was intersected with the tetrahedralization. A regular grid of 19 by 9 positions (the grid points) was superimposed on every slice. The tetrahedron containing each grid point was identified and a data value was calculated using linear interpolation within the tetrahedron. It was necessary to use several slices (we have chosen 30) so that a fairly even spread of new data values was obtained across the volume of interest. This regular grid of data values can then be passed to the viewing package.

7.3   Computing the 3D Delaunay Triangulation

The 3D Delaunay triangulation (tetrahedralization) connects a set of 3D points using line segments such that the convex hull of the set of points is filled with nonintersecting tetrahedra. Furthermore, the sphere criterion must be satisfied, i.e., the circumsphere of the four vertices of any tetrahedron contains none of the other data points in its interior. Examples of the application of 3D Delaunay triangulations in the field of interpolation and contouring can be found in references [3] and [22], and algorithms for constructing 3D Delaunay triangulations can be found in references [2] and [9]. Edellsbrunner and Mücke [7] give an algorithm for constructing the 3D Delaunay from the 4D convex hull, using geometric transformations.

7.3.1   Local transformation algorithm

The program used in our work to create the 3D Delaunay triangulation for the North Sea data was implemented by Mücke [21] and is referred to as the 'Incremental/ Triangle Edge-Flip' algorithm by Joe [9]. Its operation is summarized in the following text. The triangulation is constructed in worst case $O(n^2)$ time and storage and is an extension of the 2D Edge-Flip algorithm of Lawson [11]. The 3D algorithm differs fundamentally from the 2D version, however, since the arbitrary scheduling of the sequence of flips will not necessarily produce a Delaunay triangulation. Joe [9] showed that, by adding the points one by one, and making the triangulation satisfy the Delaunay conditions each time, the method will always correctly build a Delaunay triangulation.

The local transformation procedure is based on the possible configurations of 5 distinct, noncoplanar points. The transformations consist of either Edge-to-Triangle flips or a Triangle-to-Edge flips. The code supplied by Mücke also uses the Simulation of Simplicity perturbation technique [7] so all degeneracies are effectively eliminated and special cases involving, for example coplanarity, are avoided during computation of the triangulation. Joe uses the term 'locally optimal' to describe two tetrahedra, with vertices $abcd$ and $abce$, sharing a common face abc and with d and e on opposite sides of abc. Additionally, the sphere criterion is satisfied so that the tetrahedron $abcd$ does not contain e in its interior. Joe proved that by starting with a special triangulation (4 vertices that are not coplanar and form a valid tetrahedron) it is possible to obtain a Delaunay triangulation by applying a finite series of local transformation procedures to nonlocally optimal transformable interior faces in an appropriate order. An outline of the basic algorithm is as follows:

```
ALG JOE.DELAUNAY
sort v₁, v₂,...vₙ lexicographically wrt x axis
create first tetrahedron using v₁,v₂,v₃,v₄
compute its centroid w
for i = 5 to n do
    let Tᵢ₋₁ be triangulation of first i−1 vertices
    for each boundary face vₐvᵦv𝒸 of Tᵢ₋₁ do
        if vᵢ is on opposite side of vₐvᵦv𝒸 from w then
            add tetrahedron vₐvᵦv𝒸vᵢ to triangulation
            put vₐvᵦv𝒸 on stack

    while stack not empty do
        get interior face vₐvᵦv𝒸 from stack
        if vₐvᵦv𝒸 is still in triangulation then
            find the two tetrahedra vₐvᵦv𝒸v𝒹 and vₐvᵦv𝒸vₑ sharing face vₐvᵦv𝒸
            if the circumsphere of vₐvᵦv𝒸v𝒹 contains vₑ then
                if vₐvᵦv𝒸 is transformable then
                    apply suitable local transforms (flips) to tetrahedra faces
        put each face on boundary of union of transformed tetrahedra onto stack
```

The algorithm described above can be improved in several ways which are described by Joe [9].

Inspection of the data interpolated for each grid slice from the tetrahedralization revealed several duplicate data points (i.e., with identical coordinates of longitude and latitude). A grid point would, therefore, have tested as being inside more than one tetrahedra. This effect was caused by overlapping colinear tetrahedron edges which are mostly likely to be created on the surface of the 3D convex hull of the tetrahedralization. The overlapping edges arise from the 'Simulation of Simplicity' (SOS) perturbation scheme of reference [7], which, in certain cases of degeneracy in the input data, such as colinear and coplanar points, will create 'perturbed' tetrahedra that in reality have zero volume. Our program therefore incorporates tests to identify 'zero-volume' tetrahedra in the grid slice stage and the interpolation adjusts according to the particular degeneracy found. For example, in the case of colinear overlapping edges we have used the shortest concurrent edge for interpolation at that point.

7.4   Visualization

Once the data were processed by the above algorithms, they were visualized in a number of different ways using Modified NCSA Image and SSound. Isosurfaces were generated from the information using thresholds that suited the investigation of the marine data and colors that were satisfactory for the end user. The grid organization was selected so that X-axis represented longitude, Y-axis represented latitude, and Z-axis represented time. The dimensions were $19 \times 9 \times 30$, as described in section 7.2.

It is clear from the experience of studying the collected information that it is not easy to extract all the necessary information contained in the data without using 'trial and error' visualization. For example, the palette was chosen after consultation with the end user, with colors selected after taking into account the appearance when rendered. This is important so that the user feels comfortable with the colors and can interpret the visualization easily. However, it is difficult to implement an automatic palette generation algorithm which takes into account perceptual variations between viewers.

Plate 19 shows some views of the set of data, for DMS. In the first view (b) all the chosen thresholds (a) are presented together, perpendicular to the view axis. This picture demonstrates what values are present and (to a limited extent) in what map coordinates they appear. Because the thresholds are rendered in ascending order, the span of higher values appears closer to the viewer than that of the lower values. It is possible to locate where the highest values occur, but no time information is identifiable. In (c), however, a 3D view of the same isosurfaces gives an idea of the occurrence of values in time. It is possible to identify the presence of values in time (when they appear or disappear), but it is not possible to localize the values in space (i.e., where they occur). Parts (d) and (e) show the use of Volume Scan, where a 'probe' can be moved and re-sized around the volume to localize specific portions of interest. This process is supported by sound functions as described in the next section.

Plate 20 presents samples of pictures that have been used to investigate the temporal behavior of DMS in the North Sea. Slices of minimum size in all three directions were obtained in order to try to identify patterns in the changes of the concentrations. Pictures like this offer insight into the variation with (a) time, (b) longitude, and (c) latitude. For example, (a), shows a time when high values were close to the continental coast, as well as in the middle, but the extreme high values were not present. In (b) it is possible to interpret changes at a particular longitude as showing that, as time progresses, some values change from one latitude to another while others seem to stay within certain latitudes. Similar observations can be made for longitude from (c). It is, however, difficult to visualize how DMS changes within the survey (with time, latitude, or longitude) and even this is only one aspect of an extremely complex system. Plates 21 and 22 show some visualizations generated for two other parameters related to the production of DMS (DMSPp and Chlorophyll).

In addition to static images of data and surface slices, the process of isosurface creation itself can offer some insight into the behavior of the object it represents. The generation of the surfaces promotes an 'incidental animation' that helps understanding of how the particular values are 'moving' from one slice to the other. The information is not precise, but may add to the conclusions on the subject.

Visual information may be the most powerful medium for data mappings, but if the data are complex and the visual channel is overloaded, alternative means of representation may offer valuable insights, especially if used in combination and as supportive tools. Sonic representation of information is one such case.

7.5   Sonification

Sonification functions were developed to use the volume data to assist in interpretation of isosurfaces. The basic processes were Coordinate Sonification (Plate 23(a) and (b)) and supportive sound cues for the Volume Scan process mentioned above (c).

Coordinate Sonification maps each coordinate to the frequency of a sound stream. Each axis (x, y or z) is mapped to a different timbre, so that different streams can be more easily distinguished when played individually or in combinations. The choice of frequency mapping can be used to convey additional information. For example, for the time axis (z) increasing pitch can be used to indicate movement forward in time. Similar mappings can be used for latitude and longitude. In Coordinate Sonification, variation in the rate of change of pitch means changes in the distribution of that particular value and 'jumps' in pitches represents absence of values in that particular region.

Coordinate Sonification can be used to indicate 'depth' whilst flat views are being plotted. For example, the flat views of isosurfaces in Plate 19(b) are generated by plotting each isosurface in order from low values to high values. As each surface is plotted, position indicates the values of two coordinates, pitch shows the 'depth' (time) and color the isosurface value. A step change in pitch will indicate a gap where the isosurface value is not found. This occurs where the isosurface is discontinuous (i.e., in two distinct parts).

During the display of consecutive isosurfaces the persistence of auditory memory allows the sound to be used to identify the dates at which particular values occur. For example, in displaying the two top values of Plate 19(b) (lilac and red) the display of lilac ends at a higher pitch than the display of red. This indicates that the highest value (red) stopped being found earlier in the year than the next highest value (lilac) as shown in Plate 19(c). The difference in final pitches indicates just how much earlier the red value ceases to be found.

Moreover, because the predefined timbre scales were normalized automatically to the ranges of the measured parameters, the aural presentations of their isosurfaces sound similar. However, the presentations are not mistaken for one another because they are complementary to the graphics, which direct their perception, but 'listening' to the different presentations offers an initial insight on coarse-grained similarities in behavior of the different substances. This is a by-product of the 'perception by contour' capability of human hearing.

The sonifications associated with the Volume Scan process (functions F1, F6, and F7 in Plate 23(c)) correspond to mappings of information from the contents of the volume probe to pitch, stereo field, and timbre, and the association between the volume probe and the whole of the volume. Here, 'contents' is represented by the measure 'occupation' which means how full or how empty a volume, subvolume, voxel, or probe may be, and its calculation is based on Marching Cubes strategy [15]. The ratio of the number of triangles inside the probe to the maximum possible number of triangles in a surface gives its 'occupation.' The 'occupation' of the volume probe is mapped to a tone followed by another tone that represents the part of the whole picture included in the probe (function F1). The Volume Scan sonifications are designed to help the search for aspects of interest inside the object under analysis. For example, with surfaces a high frequency means low occupation of the probe while a low frequency means high occupation. Using timbre, a full probe produces a heavy timbre while an empty probe gives a light timbre. Timbre is scaled by complexity of partials (overtones), where a flute is a light timbre and a buzzer is heavy. Two tones are presented in sequence. The first indicates the occupation inside the probe (full, empty, or in between) and the second tone indicates the relationship between what is in and out of the probe. Thus, with surfaces, the latter indicates what part of the whole object is inside the probe. Again, high frequencies mean that little of the whole object is inside while low frequencies mean the opposite.

The orientation of the probe is also mapped into a two-tone sonification. The first tone represents the occupation of the lower half of the volume probe in the selected direction (highlighted square in Plate 23(c)) and the second tone represents the occupation of the upper half of the volume probe in the selected direction. For example, if the frequencies are increasing, then most of the surface is toward the lower part; and if it is decreasing, then most of the surface is placed toward the higher part of the probe. Thus, the user is 'orientated' toward the 'more populated' part of the surface. Those two tones are also mapped to stereo distribution so that the left ear receives the tone for the lower part and the right ear the tone for the higher part. In this way the impression of the tone sequence is reinforced.

A further sonification, the Grid Sonification, maps values in the grid to pitches and the grid itself onto the screen. This is useful for finding values and comparing sharing of particular portions of the volume by different values [18]. In this case, the values themselves are mapped to pitch, high values to high pitches and low values to low pitches. The xy plane of the grid is mapped onto xy of the screen, with subdivisions corresponding to grid subdvisions. The Z axis is mapped left to right inside each rectangle of the grid. As the cursor is moved around the window, the user 'listens to the values.' Additionally, the Z position in the grid is mapped to quadraphonic (or stereo) speakers sited in front of and behind the user. Thus as the z index increases the sound 'moves' from back to front, giving the 'feeling' of depth to the volume. Additionally, if the user wishes to 'listen' only to the selected values (that is, the values of the isosurfaces), the timbre changes with isovalue, thus identifying the particular isosurface by timbre as well as pitch.

7.6 Conclusions

The techniques described here have shown the application of relatively simple geometric constructions in handling multivariate data sets involving nonhomogenous parameter types. We have based all our interpolation calculations on the Delaunay tetrahedralization. Previous applications of this technique have almost invariably been undertaken where the axes represent similar quantities, which is not the case for the data being analyzed here.

The analysis of the data highlighted the necessity to concentrate on studying the resulting pictures (or sounds) in order to be able to extract more information. This is to be expected in similar situations where there is no previous or little knowledge of the behavior of the phenomena under study. The use of isosurface generation is expected to be useful in understanding the processes involved, but is insufficient on its own. It has been possible to use sound to provide additional information which may prove useful as a supplement to the graphical display, as well as providing orientation. We expect this to be a positive contribution toward an integrated visualization model that involves more than one human sense through nonimmersive virtual reality. Interpreting sonic information requires training, but relatively simple mappings (like Coordinate Sonification) may offer a number of advantages to the user. Sound is a good tool for comparison. Pitch is very useful for sequences and timbre for identifying separate entities.

The choice of nonlinear mapping of values to the color palette was critical to improving the information gained from the plots of the data due to a small number of samples with very high values (i.e., the nonnormal distribution of data samples). By choosing different mappings of values to colors, further aspects of the data may be highlighted. This suggests that powerful interactive tools for palette definition are an important feature for visualizing data of this nature and that guidance based on perceptual 'rules' and the application should be formulated.

The end product of the application is intended to be a validated model of the processes involved in the production of DMS, DMSPp, and chlorophyll to evaluate their contribution to atmospheric sulfur. There is still some way to go to understanding the behavior of this complex system and improving the usefulness of the approach taken here will require integration of more understanding of the natural processes with the geometric modeling. Additionally, it will be necessary to take other physical, chemical, and biological data into account. Validation is envisaged as involving comparison of the results of running a theoretically based model with the empirical results. Additional visualization and/or sonification techniques will be needed to assist this comparison.

References

[1] P. Ashtheimer, Sonification Tools to Supplement Dataflow Visualization, *Scientific Visualization: Advanced Software Techniques*, P. Palamidese, ed., pp. 15–36, Prentice-Hall, 1992.

[2] D. Avis, B.K. Bhattacharya, Algorithms for computing *d*-dimensional voronoi diagrams and their duals, *Advances in Computing Research*, F.P. Preparata, ed., pp. 159–180, JAI Press, 1983.

[3] J.C. Cavendish, D.A. Field, W.H. Frey, An approach to automatic three-dimensional finite element mesh generation, *Int. J. Num. Meth. Eng.*, **21**: 329–347; 1985.

[4] A.M. Day, S.M. Turner, D.B. Arnold, Improved visualisation of marine data: Algae and acid rain, *Computer Graphics Forum*, **13**: 361–370; 1994.

[5] A.M. Day, S.M. Turner, D.B. Arnold, Incorporating temporal information in interpolating marine surveys, submitted for publication January 1995.

[6] N. Dyn, D. Levin, S. Rippa, Data dependent triangulations for piecewise linear interpolation, *IMA J. Num. Analysis*, **10**: 137–154; 1990.

[7] H. Edelsbrunner, E.P. Mücke, Simulation of simplicity: A technique to cope with degenerate cases in geometric algorithms, *ACM Trans. Graphics*, **9**(1): 66–104; 1990.

[8] W.W. Gaver, What in the world do we hear? *Ecological Psychology*, part 5, pp. 1–29. Lawrence Erlbaum Associated Inc., 1993.

[9] B. Joe, Construction of three-dimensional Delaunay triangulations using local transformations, *Computer Aided Geometric Design*, **8**(2): 123–142; 1991.

[10] F.P. Preparata, M.I. Shamos, *Introduction to Computational Geometry*, Springer Verlag, 1985.

[11] C.L. Lawson, Properties of *n*-dimensional triangulations, *Computer Aided Geometric Design*, **2**(3): 231–246; 1986.

[12] G. Kramer, *Auditory display: Sonification, audification and auditory interfaces*, Proc. ICAD'92, the First International Conference on Auditory Display, Addison-Wesley, 1994.

[13] G. Kramer, Some organizing principles for representing data with sound, *Auditory Display: Sonification, Audification and Auditory Interfaces*, The Proceedings of ICAD'92, the First International Conference on Auditory Display, Addison-Wesley , pp. 185–222, 1994.

[14] P.S. Liss, The sulphur cycle, *Climate and Global Change*, J.C. Duplessy, A. Pons and R. Fantechi, eds., CEC, Brussels, pp. 75–89, 1991.

[15] W.E. Lorensen, H.E. Cline, Marching Cubes: A high resolution 3D surface construction algorithm, *ACM SIGGRAPH, Computer Graphics*, **21**: 163–169; 1987.

[16] G. Malin, S.M. Turner, P.S. Liss, Sulfur: The plankton/climate connection, *J. Phycol.*, **28**: 590–597; 1992.

[17] G. Malin, S.M. Turner, P.S. Liss, Dimethyl sulphide: production and atmospheric consequences, *The Haptophyte Algae*, J.C. Green and B.S.C. Leadbetter, eds., Systematics Association, Vol. **51**, Clarendon Press, Oxford, pp. 303–320, 1992.

[18] R. Minghim, A.R. Forrest, Sound mappings for surface visualisation, *Proceedings of WSCG '95*, The Third International Conference in Central Europe on Computer Graphics and Visualisation 95, vol. II, pp. 410–420, 1995.

[19] R. Minghim, *On sound support for visualisation*, PhD thesis, School of Information Systems, University of East Anglia, UK, 1995.

[20] R. Minghim, A.R. Forrest, An illustrated analysis of sonification for scientific visualisation, *Proc. of the IEEE Visualization '95*, Atlanta, USA, Nov., 1995.

[21] E.P. Mücke, *Shapes and implementations in three-dimensional geometry*, PhD thesis, Dept. of Computer Science, University of Illinois at Urbana-Champaign. 1993.

[22] M.A. Sabin, Contouring – the state of the art, *Fundamental Algorithms for Computer Graphics*, R.A. Earnshaw, ed., NATO ASI series, vol. **F17**, Springer Verlag, 1985.

[23] J.H. Simpson, Introduction to the North Sea Project, *Understanding the North Sea System*, H. Charnock et al., eds., The Royal Society, Chapman and Hall, 1994.

[24] S.M. Turner, G. Malin, P.D. Nightingale, P.S. Liss, Seasonal variation of dimethyl sulphide in the North Sea and an assessment of fluxes to the atmosphere, *Cont. Shelf Res.*, submitted for publication April 1995.

8
Contouring Algorithms for Visualization and Shape Modeling Systems

A.L. Thomas

8.1 Background

The first studies in this collection were carried out in the Laboratory for Computer Graphics and Spatial Analysis, in the Graduate School of Design in Harvard University. The objectives of this work were to learn to program and use computers in applications in the environmental design and planning fields of architecture, landscape, urban planning, and in regional and geographical analysis work. Initially, this consisted of studies in how to automate existing graphical methods of analysis and presentation, but has led on to extensions to these methods which have become practical using the new technology.

Howard T. Fisher set up this laboratory in the mid-1960s to build and study computer application systems for design and planning work. An early success was the development of the computer cartography system called SYMAP [7]. At a time when computer drawing and display equipment, as we now know it, was still mostly at a laboratory development stage, this system harnessed a way of using the line printer as a cheap and ubiquitous graphic output device. This made SYMAP an accessible product for the growing number of computer centers serving universities, and city planning and government departments, where there was a need to produce 'working' maps and similar documents from the growing volume of digitally encoded data.

Algorithmically, line printer graphics can be classified as an early form of raster graphics. The image was produced by evaluating a property value at each node-point of a regular grid, and then representing the value by the appropriate symbol, color, or textured picture element. The graphical effects in the initial work were obtained by overprinting lines of text characters; in later studies special character chains were used on printers to get better quality images. This included experiments with picture elements made up from half-tone screen patterns – precursors of some of the current laser printing techniques.

SYMAP was set up to produce a series of different map types. One of these was the contour map. The basic mechanism was simple: where grid point values were known they could be classified into bands, depending on the contour intervals being used, then rendered using the corresponding symbolism for the contour band. However, the data rarely came set up in a grid in this way. Grid data usually had to be interpolated from a smaller set of data values distributed over the map area in the ways illustrated in

Figure 8.1. This interpolation defined a 'surface' from which the contour image could be generated.

A variety of mathematical ways existed for creating surfaces of this kind. Broadly speaking, the two extremes consisted of statistically fitting surfaces to approximate the given data point values, or interpolating a smooth continuous surface through the given data points. The interpolation process could use all the data points at once (Figure 8.1a to 8.1b), or be carried out in a piecewise manner, breaking the surface up into patches (shown in Figure 8.1c), only using points within each patch as it is interpolated: the choice depended on the characteristics of the interpolation which were required.

The early versions of SYMAP adopted the piece wise interpolation scheme but depended on a patch framework being defined manually. Data points were linked up to give quadrilateral patches which were then filled in on grid points using bilinear interpolation. This approach was time consuming and only viable where a particular arrangement of data points was going to be used many times. Later systems were greatly increased in flexibility and usefulness when Donald Shepard [12] developed a fully automated interpolation algorithm. Inverse-distance weighting factors were used to combine given data values to interpolate new ones onto undefined grid points. This approach removed the need to manually define a patch framework and made the contouring process much simpler to carry out.

The map generating subsystem developed for SYMAP was stripped down to its basic minimum configuration and linked to a multiple-subject, geographic database system called GRID [15]. This provided a tool for landscape architecture, urban and regional

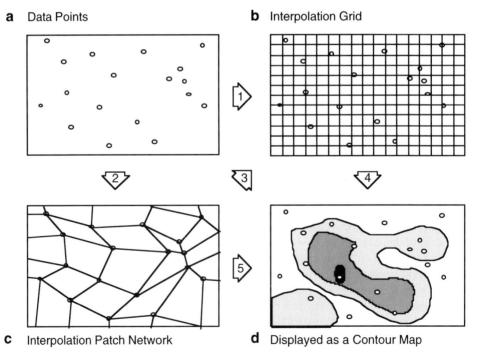

Figure 8.1   Contour generation from data point sets.

planning, and for geographic scale resource management studies. This system supported a variety of computer-based modeling forms of analysis, some providing simulation schemes for educational projects, some providing forecast data in economic and physical planning studies. The first study in this chapter exploring the use of contour drawings was developed using data collected and stored in the GRID system for one of these studies: a planning impact study for a proposed new dam in the Honey Hill region of New Hampshire [14].

8.2   OBLIX, an experimental cartography system

If contours are defined to be the set of lines which are created when a set of parallel planes intersect a surface in three dimensions, then it is clear that grid data lends itself to presentation in the form of contour drawings. If all the values along each row or column are projected upwards in the third dimension and linked together, the result is a 'contour' or 'profile' drawing for the surface. It is true that profile lines are not in the conventional orientation used for cartographic contour lines; a plan view of these profile lines cannot be used to show the shape of the surface. However, geometrically they are the same thing, and if these profile lines are viewed from an oblique angle the result is a 'block model' presentation of the surface, which as a graphic device works well in portraying the shape of the surface. This is partly because the grid provides a regular frame of reference, and partly because the lines of the profiles create a shading effect which, conforming to Lambert's illumination law, allows the viewer to perceive a surface representing the shape of the data distribution.

Frank Rens developed the SYMVU program to create block model drawings of this kind using the Calcomp plotter [11]. Using the array of data-values output from both SYMAP and GRID, this program generated profile block model drawings. Each profile was considered as a three-dimensional polygon, transformed as required by the viewing position. Profiles nearest to the observer were drawn first, but were only drawn where they were not masked by previously drawn profile sections as shown in Figure 8.2. To carry out this process it was necessary to implement a masking operation to clip any new section-lines which passed behind already drawn profiles. This mask was defined as the union of all previously drawn profile polygons. Each time that a profile line was completed this mask had to be updated to include any new outstanding areas.

In SYMVU Frank Rens implemented this operation as part of the line interpolation procedure which generated Calcomp plotting instructions. The mechanism is shown diagrammatically in Figure 8.3. The maximum y values for all profile line points so far drawn, are stored in an array, one for each x position of the plotting grid. Only new line points which have y coordinates greater than these stored values are plotted, and when they are they replace the existing values. A 20 inch plotter with 200 steps per inch only requires a Mask array of 4000 y values to support the program code:

```
IF y > Mask[x] THEN Mask[x] := y; Plot(x,y) END;
```

Including this statement in the plotting loop of Bresenham's line drawing algorithm [4] gave a very fast hidden-line removal procedure: an early example of the depth buffer principle. The only problem with this approach was that it was difficult to accurately retain or reconstruct the geometry of the hidden areas from these line clipping

102 A. L. Thomas

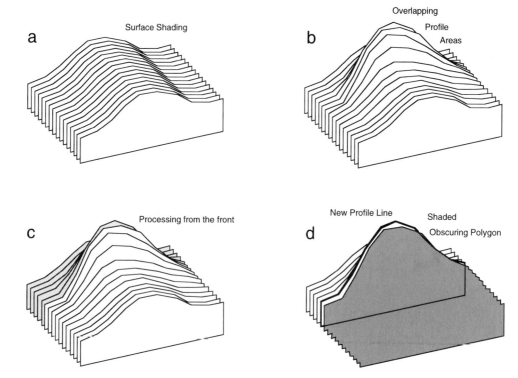

Figure 8.2 Profile block model drawing.

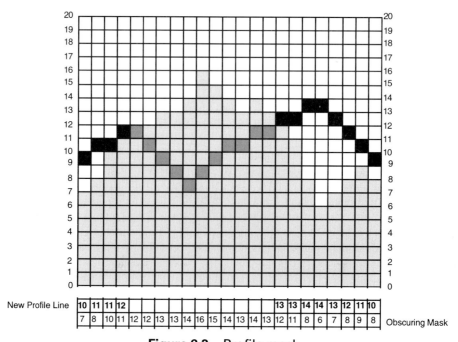

Figure 8.3 Profile mask.

operations which were carried out 'implicitly' in the innermost display loop, but were quantized to the plotter drawing grid.

Various desirable objectives, for example redrawing the block model to different scales with a minimum of calculation, needed this geometry to be defined in a more accurate form, and this led to an alternative approach being pioneered in the OBLIX program [18]. The initial target of this work was placing surface lines onto block model drawings, and then to simplify the hidden-line removal process, required to display surface features such as road networks, field boundaries, and surface contours, which a user might wish to overlay on an existing block model.

There were two strategies available. The first was the point sampling method of the profile mask, the precursor of the pixel-based depth buffer and ray tracing schemes that have been developed for rasterized images. The second was to define the boundary of visible regions. In this application there was the desire to present many different surface distributions overlaid on the same block model; consequently, if the visible regions of a particular block model could be determined once, the efficiency of the hidden-line, hidden-area removal process could be greatly improved for subsequent drawings.

One implementation of this idea was to create visibility areas as grid maps in a cartographic database [13]. These maps could then be used to 'sieve' other map data so that they could be projected directly onto the block model, with hidden elements already removed. The problem was that visibility areas did not appear to relate to any easily calculated property of an object's surface or its viewing point. The simplest accessible property which commonly used surface and object models provided was the result of classifying surface facets or points as facing the observer or facing away from the observer. For simple convex objects this might be enough to base a display algorithm on. However, curved concave objects presented problems.

The relationship between the visible area and the front- and back-facing regions of the surface of an 'L' shaped object with two concave facets is shown in Figure 8.4. On

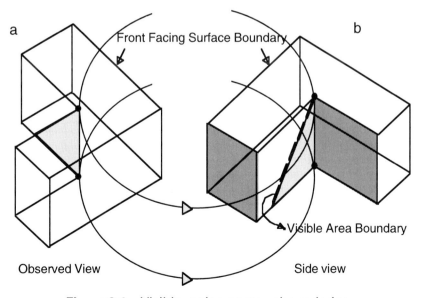

Figure 8.4   Visible region contour boundaries.

the left, Figure 8.4a, the boundary of the front-facing, in other words potentially visible, surface facets as the viewer would see them, are shown as a thicker line. On the right, Figure 8.4b, this line is shown as well as the boundary of the visible region, but viewed from a different position to show their true spatial relationship. If we distinguish the boundaries of these two areas as the *front-facing* boundary contour and the *visible area* (or *shadow*) boundary contour, then the first can be defined using local surface properties, and the second can be derived from the first by projecting it onto more distant front-facing surfaces. This gives a reasonably straightforward scheme for working with convex objects.

Hidden-line removal is illustrated in Figure 8.5 for convex objects. Intersection points between front-facing contour lines as they are projected onto the display screen are located and the depth priority of each line is found for related pairs of intersection points. The two alternative outcomes are shown for the two possible depth orderings in this case. The question was whether the self-overlapping front-facing contour shown in Figure 8.4 resulting from concave surfaces could be processed in a similar way.

In Figure 8.6a the front-facing boundary contour of a torus is shown projected on to the picture plane with the contour line segments *highlighted* which are separating a *nearer* back-facing surface section from a *further* front-facing surface section. In Figure 8.6b these pieces of the contour line have been removed since they can, by definition, never be seen. This allows the intersection between the two remaining line arcs to be determined using the simple priority test used for convex front-facing contours. Notice

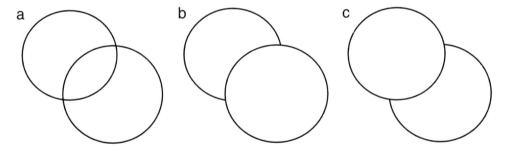

Figure 8.5   Simple convex curved surface silhouette contours.

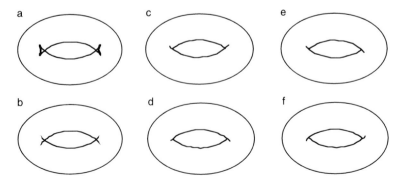

Figure 8.6   Concave curved surface silhouette contours.

in this case the intersections need not be taken in pairs, consequently, there are four possible alternative outcomes for these tests. These are given in Figures 8.6c–f.

The reason for adopting this approach is to establish a general way of tackling the problem of displaying objects with curved surfaces. There currently seem to be three general approaches. The first is defining these visibility contours, in terms compatible with the method being used to represent the curved surfaces of objects. The second is finding ways to convert the curved surface models into plane-faceted approximations. The third is using a sampling method, structured with respect to the viewing framework, such as the display of profiles, the use of depth buffers, or pixel-based ray tracing.

Exploring the first alternative: If curved-surfaced patches are being used to construct object models, then it is necessary to be able to define the boundary of front-facing areas in a reasonably direct way. It must then be possible to project these boundary lines centered on the viewing position as a ruled surface in the way shown in Figure 8.7, and finally it must be possible to define the line where this ruled surface intersects the rest of the patch (or other patches) to define the boundary edge lines for the visible areas of the object.

For curved surfaces, visibility can be given a quantitative measure by defining its value for a convex object as the angle between the surface normal at a point on the object's surface and the viewing ray from the viewing position to that point. This can be measured by calculating the dot product of the normal and the viewing ray vector, giving the cosine of this angle. The front-facing boundary contour can then be defined as the zero isoline of the distribution of this property over the surface of the object. This quantitative approach to visibility can be extended by subtracting from the front-facing measure 1.0 for each back-facing surface a viewing ray passes through before it reaches the surface point in question. This idea of a 'quantitative-invisibility' value [1] allows the visible surface contour to be defined as the zero isoline for this composite function.

If plane surfaces are used as patches, clearly the whole patch will be either front-facing or back-facing. This means that these visibility contours can only occur at the boundaries of plane patches. This approach simplifies the problem considerably: allowing the OBLIX strategy to work for line drawings and allowing the painter's algorithm to work as a fast rendering method for the raster display of complex faceted objects [10]. Notice that the visibility areas are the same as the areas illuminated by

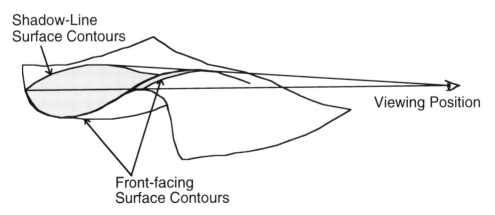

Figure 8.7 Piecewise construction of silhouette contours.

placing a light at the viewing position, hence the alternative name for this boundary, the *shadow-line* contour.

However, this discussion has assumed static scenes. If interactive editing creates moving objects in a scene, then the 'interference' problem must be considered as part of the display process. The possibility that object models may accidentally be made to overlap, and the catastrophic effect this can have on simple hidden-line removal algorithms, is one reason why the point sampling display methods based on ray tracing or the frame buffer have tended to predominate in interactive work because they are simpler to implement in a robust way.

In the case of visibility area calculations, it is necessary to check for interference each time objects are moved. This is because new boundaries may be needed to define the edges where surfaces intersect if objects have been made to overlap. These edges are often components of visibility area contours. When they are, it is essential to set them up correctly if the hidden-line process is to function correctly. Figure 8.8 illustrates the way that indiscernible movements perpendicular to the screen can substantially modify these contour lines, and how this can affect the final line drawing. In the first row the two objects do not overlap; in the second row two alternatives are shown where they do.

This example illustrates why this approach in its general form tends to be avoided: plane facet approximation or ray tracing methods are preferred ways of visualizing objects and scenes defined as mathematical models. However, having said this, these contours are valuable graphic elements. The artist is able to draw a curved-surfaced object as a quick sketch using only these lines. The efficient use of graphic space to present information can often profit from the use of these lines. In the OBLIX system they were found useful where it became desirable to suppress profile lines in order to present other surface distributions.

8.3   Generating Surface Symbolism for Block Models

In the OBLIX system it was found possible to generate a grid map of a study area classifying cells into three classes: totally visible, totally invisible, and partially visible.

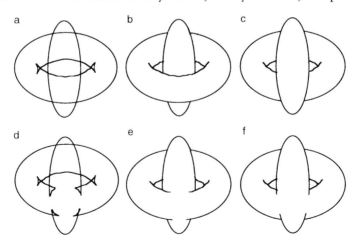

Figure 8.8   Interference effects on silhouette contours.

This grid data could then be used to reduce the hidden-line testing work for large areas of most block model drawings. From a cartographic system point of view this facility had several applications. The same operation was able to provide both hill-shading and inter visibility maps. Where this grid mapping information was being stored to process other map subjects, for display in block model form, the visible area contour lines associated with 'partially visible' cells could also be stored and linked to them. This simplified hidden-line removal makes it a two-dimensional clipping operation within the region of these 'partially visible' cells.

Where data was originally defined in other maps, for example road networks, it was simpler to clip this information in the base plane and then project the visible data onto the block model surface than to project and then check for visibility. Where surface lines were generated from surface properties, it was usually simpler to calculate these in the display space and carry out a more conventional hidden-line removal operation as part of the display processing.

During the time that OBLIX was being developed, other research workers in the Laboratory for Computer Graphics and Spatial Analysis were also exploring the potential of line plotter symbolism for generating cartographic images. Frank Rens had already completed the SYMVU program, and it was being used as a tool for further experiments, such as using moiré interference patterns to give contour band shading in the way illustrated in Example 8.1. Robert Cartwright developed the Calform system in experiments for Howard Fisher. A.L. Thomas and T.C. Waugh developed the first version of GIMMS [20]. A variety of ideas and possibilities were discussed and explored. It was the idea to develop variable-geometry symbols, *parametrized symbolism,* for grid data cells which was the breakthrough which allowed OBLIX to provide facilities not supported by SYMVU. The first application of this process to be exploited was drawing horizontal contour lines on to block model surfaces.

8.4   Horizontal Contours

Consider the values in the array of data from a grid map to be represented by vertical lines at the nodes of the grid in the way shown in Figure 8.9. The true surface that lies

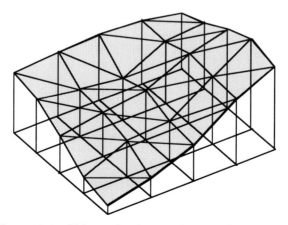

Figure 8.9   Triangular interpolation of grid data.

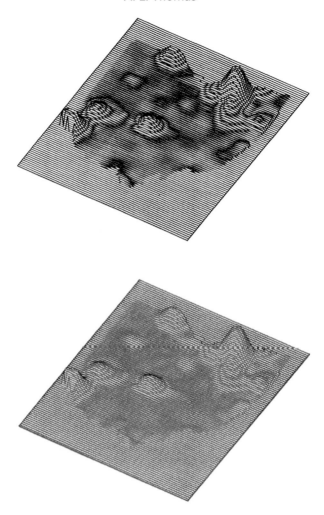

Example 8.1 Surface contours generated from moiré interference patterns. Experiments using SYMVU, 1969. Overlaying an undeformed grid on the profile grid of a parallel projection block model of the 'Population Density in Ohio.' (Laboratory for Computer Graphics and Spatial Analysis, Harvard University.)

between these sample points is not known and can therefore be filled in any way that is convenient and which is permitted by the nature of the application problem and the data. In the first versions of OBLIX a rectangular patch generated using bilinear interpolation was employed. However, though this was good enough to generate the 'Honey Hill' displays given in Examples 8.2 and 8.3, it became clear that the simplest, self-consistent approach was to triangulate the data-array cells, in the way shown in Figure 8.9, even though this gave an arbitrary orientation to symmetrically arranged data values.

Each triangle could then be filled in using a plane-surface facet. This simplified the

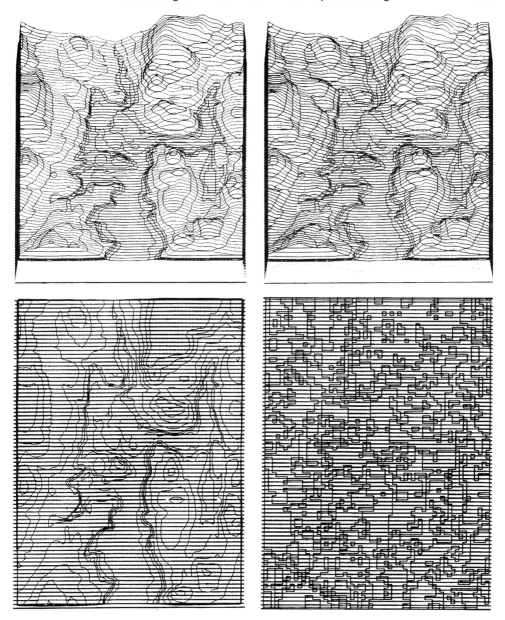

Example 8.2   (see also **Plate 29**) Surface contours, contour band shading, scan line shading, zone boundaries, texture mapping. Experiments using OBLIX 1969–70. Honey Hill dam location studies showing the extent of the proposed lake (left in blue); and affected tree cover (right: blue, coniferous; green, deciduous; brown, open space). (Laboratory for Computer Graphics and Spatial Analysis, Harvard University.)

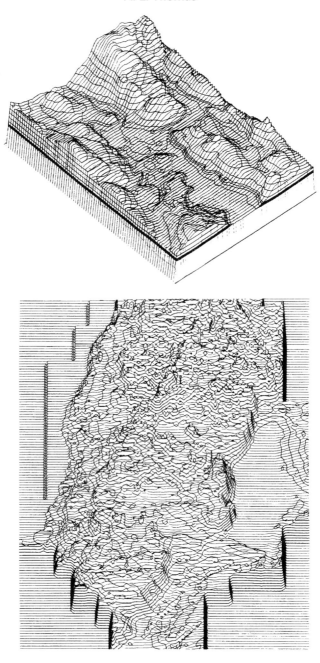

Example 8.3   (see also **Plate 30**) The limitations of line symbolism. Studies showing the loss of intelligibility as the surface complexity is raised relative to grid resolution. An oblique view of the Honey Hill site compared with a terrain model of a more complex landscape. OBLIX, 1969. (Laboratory for Computer Graphics and Spatial Analysis, Harvard University.)

next step, which was to produce the contour lines. Where interpolation using plane triangular patches is employed, contour lines will be made up from the straight line segments generated by intersecting these triangular surface patches with a set of parallel contour planes. All that is necessary to produce a drawing is to define the end points of these straight line segments, and this consists of finding the intersection points where the edges of the triangular patches cut each contour plane.

If the contour plane is taken to be horizontal then it can be represented by a single value giving its height, or value on a vertical axis, perpendicular to the base plane. This reduces the problem of finding the intersection of each triangle edge line with the contour plane to the geometric calculation shown in Figure 8.10.

The advantage of using a regular grid of data points and an array of corresponding values is that the structure of the interpolation triangles can be generated in a very simple way using the indexes of the array and the values stored in the array. The coordinates of the end points of the edge lines of the triangles will be an appropriately scaled function of the array's indexes, taken with the value referenced in the array by these indexes.

Similarly, the vertices of each triangle can be selected by using a pattern of index values defined relative to a base index position as shown in Figures 8.11 and 8.12. The programming task is to recast the calculation shown in Figure 8.10, to apply to the

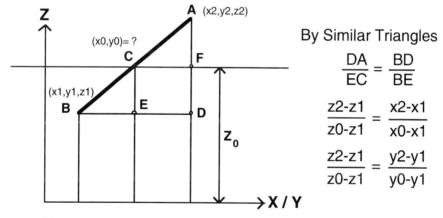

Figure 8.10   Intersecting an edge line with a contour plane.

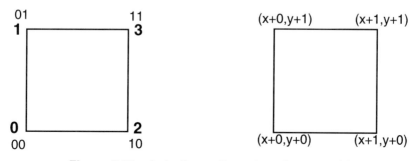

Figure 8.11   Labeling cell vertices from a grid.

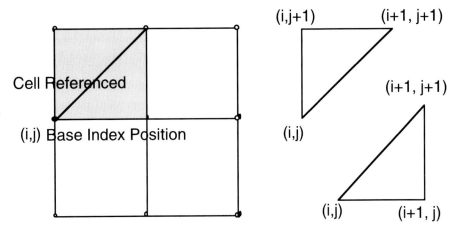

Figure 8.12   Defining triangles using array indexes.

appropriate lines generated by the selection procedure outlined in Figure 8.13. This can be done by designing a general solution to the contouring problem for one triangle as a procedure operating on generalized coordinates, for example (xa, ya, za), (xb, yb, zb), (xc, yc, zc), but calling this procedure from a selection procedure which passes real coordinates obtained from the current working position in the grid of data values. This approach allows the working position to be defined by the base index position in the array of grid values, and this allows the base position to be moved systematically through the array by using the appropriately formulated FOR loops. The example shown in Figure 8.12 illustrates how each base index position is used to reference two triangles.

```
PROCEDURE ContourSegment(VAR P1,P2,P3,Pa,Pb: PointVector; Z0:
REAL);
BEGIN
  Pa[0]  := 1.0;
  Pa[1]  := P1[1] + (Z0-P1[3]) * (P2[1]-P1[1]) / (P2[3]-P1[3]) ;
  Pa[2]  := P1[2] + (Z0-P1[3]) * (P2[2]-P1[2]) / (P2[3]-P1[3]) ;
  Pa[3]  := Z0 ;
  Pb[0]  := 1.0 ;
  Pb[1]  := P2[1] + (Z0-P2[3]) * (P3[1]-P2[1]) / (P3[3]-P2[3]) ;
  Pb[2]  := P2[2] + (Z0-P2[3]) * (P3[2]-P2[2]) / (P3[3]-P2[3]) ;
  Pb[3]  := Z0 ;
END ContourSegment;

PROCEDURE ContourTriangle ( VAR P1, P2, P3: PointVector; Z0: REAL;
              VAR Pa, Pb: PointVector; VAR J: INTEGER ): BOOLEAN ;

BEGIN
  J:= 0;
  IF P1[3] > Z0 THEN J:=J+1 END;
  IF P2[3] > Z0 THEN J:=J+2 END;
```

```
IF P3[3] > Z0 THEN J:=J+4 END;
CASE J OF
  1: ContourSegment(P2,P1,P3,Pa,Pb,Z0) |
  2: ContourSegment(P3,P2,P1,Pa,Pb,Z0) |
  3: ContourSegment(P2,P3,P1,Pa,Pb,Z0) |
  4: ContourSegment(P1,P3,P2,Pa,Pb,Z0) |
  5: ContourSegment(P1,P2,P3,Pa,Pb,Z0) |
  6: ContourSegment(P3,P1,P2,Pa,Pb,Z0) |
  ELSE RETURN FALSE END;
  RETURN TRUE;
END ContourTriangle ;
```

The parametric symbol approach to this problem is illustrated in Figure 8.13. There are two stages to this process. The first is defining a finite set of symbols, each with a different topology; the second is associating a geometry to the symbol depending on the local data values. The first stage for triangle-based contour generation is shown in Figure 8.13. Each vertex is classified as above or below a given contour level. This defines eight different patterns in the way shown. Using a label variable J defined by this selection sequence provides an elegant way of programming this task using a CASE statement. In this version of the triangle contouring function, written in Modula-2, the contour segments are passed back to the calling routine, (Pa,Pb). If the function returns the value *true* there is a segment to draw, if *false* then there is no contour segment to draw.

Once the contour line segments have been generated they can be transformed to correspond with the current viewing parameters. Where a cell is totally visible these lines can then be drawn out directly. Where they are only partially visible they need to be tested against the current obscuring polygon, to determine how much of each line can be seen. While developing this procedure it became clear that there were several ways in which the processing stages could be ordered. In the earliest system developed on the IBM 7090/94 there was only a limited amount of fast core memory. It was

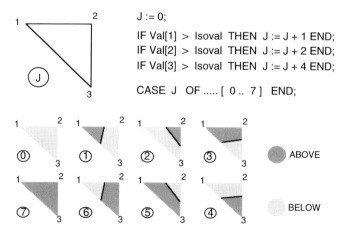

Figure 8.13 Contour line segments within a triangle.

therefore necessary to develop a processing strategy which limited the amount of memory necessary to complete the task. What evolved was a concept of 'local area' processing, sweeping data into and out of memory in a well-ordered way to avoid running out of space. This pragmatic approach led to an evolution of the ordered processing of profiles into the more general method called 'plane sweep' geometric processing.

Where a set of contour line segments is generated from a grid data cell, along with other line segments belonging to that cell, they can be treated as a list of line segments or they can be considered as a polyline with alternating visible and invisible elements. The latter approach allows a very simple use of ordering to be employed in carrying out the hidden-line clipping for this line segment set.

Since line segment (P1,P2) is oriented in a left to right direction, then the startup position will compare this line with the Obscuring Polygon line segment (Pa,Pb) (Figure 8.14). When this is complete because Pb < P2 in left to right order, the Obscuring Polygon is incremented to give line segment (Pb,Pc) which is also compared with line (P1,P2). Pc is now ahead of P2. This triggers the increment of the contour polyline to give (P2,P3). This line segment is oriented in the right to left direction. This is in the reverse direction, so it is compared with line segment (Pc,Pb). When this is complete, the leading point in this direction Pb is behind P3, so it is incremented in this direction to give (Pb,Pa). When this is complete, again Pa leads P3, so the contour polyline is incremented to give (P3,P4). The direction has reversed, so this is compared with (Pa,Pb) again. This process continues until the complete surface symbolism polyline has been clipped.

This mechanism worked very effectively for the small number of elements in a grid cell. To cope with a larger number of elements randomly ordered in space, this method had to be extended to give the plane sweep algorithm. The strategy was the same: to localize testing within a series of vertical bands. For randomly distributed line segments this was achieved by threading a sequence of ordering pointers through the list of point coordinate records making up the interacting polylines. The dashed line linking the Obscuring Polygon polyline and the Surface Symbolism polyline in Figure 8.14 illustrates the way this was done. In this case a first line (Pa,Pb) is taken from this ordered list. A second line is then selected from the sublist formed by the links between the two

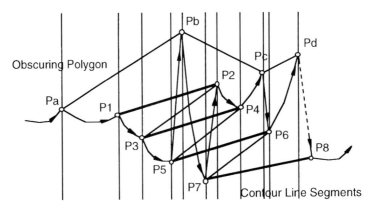

Figure 8.14   Plane sweep hidden-line clipping.

end points of the first line Pa to Pb. All the line segments encountered following this subsequence are compared with the first line. When complete, the first line is incremented to the next line in the ordered list, and so on. With a little refinement to avoid double testing of the same line segment pairs, this process sweeps across the diagram shown in Figure 8.14 testing each vertical band step by step. (Pa,Pb) is tested against (P1,P2), (P2,P3), (P3,P4), (P4,P5) and (P5,P6); (Pb,Pc) is tested against (P1,P2); and so on.

The first contouring algorithm was based on the cell classification shown in Figure 8.15. This employed a single rectangular patch obtained by bi-linear interpolation between the straight line edges of the cell, to give a hyperbolic parabaloid surface. However, inexactness in defining the visibility area boundaries using this approach led to the simpler scheme based on plane triangle patches being adopted. This did not prevent other surface symbolism being set up for the whole data cell. In Figure 8.16 the 'parametric symbol' set used for defining the boundaries of grid map zones is given, of the type illustrated in Example 8.2 for the Honey Hill project.

In these examples a map of the tree distribution of the area is 'painted' or 'texture mapped' onto the topographic surface, which is shown both as a color-shaded contour map and as a color-shaded contoured block model. The brown represents predominantly open space; the green represents predominantly deciduous trees; and the blue represents predominantly coniferous trees. The lines making up these boundary lines are made up from segments which can be mapped onto the interpolation surface being used. This means interpolating a point at the center of each edge line as well as at the center of each cell, for both the bilinear and the triangulated schemes.

In Example 8.2 it can be seen that not only are boundary lines drawn onto the surface but the profile lines are color-coded to shade the areas concerned. The grid map showing the tree distribution was shaded using a test sequence of the form:

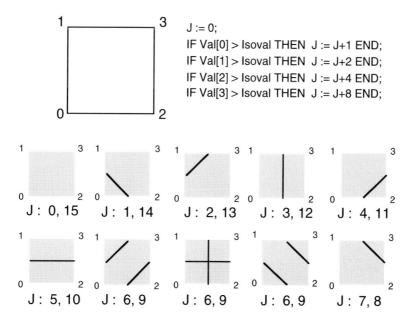

```
J := 0;
IF Val[0] > Isoval THEN  J := J+1 END;
IF Val[1] > Isoval THEN  J := J+2 END;
IF Val[2] > Isoval THEN  J := J+4 END;
IF Val[3] > Isoval THEN  J := J+8 END;
```

J: 0, 15   J: 1, 14   J: 2, 13   J: 3, 12   J: 4, 11

J: 5, 10   J: 6, 9   J: 6, 9   J: 6, 9   J: 7, 8

Figure 8.15   Bilinear interpolation contour tiles.

A. L. Thomas

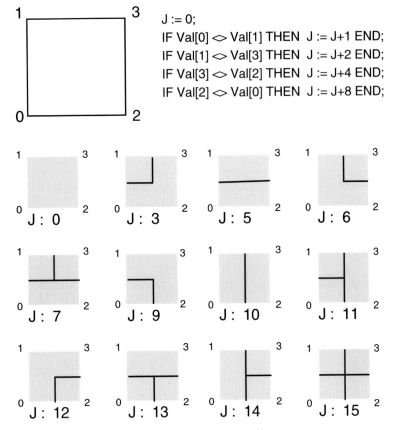

```
J := 0;
IF Val[0] <> Val[1] THEN  J := J+1 END;
IF Val[1] <> Val[3] THEN  J := J+2 END;
IF Val[3] <> Val[2] THEN  J := J+4 END;
IF Val[2] <> Val[0] THEN  J := J+8 END;
```

Figure 8.16   Grid cell boundary line segments.

```
IF Val[1] <> Val[3] THEN
   (*Draw two line segments of the appropriate colors *);
ELSE
   (*Draw one line segments of the appropriate color *);
END;
```

The color shading for the contour map and contour block model required a procedure to create the sequence of colored, profile-shading, line segments. Since a profile line segment of one cell, could traverse all the contour intervals, the simplest approach was to process the contours in the innermost loop of the display algorithm.

```
PROCEDURE ProfileShade( VAR P1,P2: PointVector; VAR Color:ColorArray;
          VAR Isoval: ContourArray; ContourNumber:CARDINAL);
VAR Pa, Pb : PointVector; J, i : CARDINAL;
BEGIN
   IF P1[3] < P2[3] THEN Pa := P1; ELSE Pa := P2; END;
   FOR i := 1 TO ContourNumber DO
      J := 0;
```

```
    IF P1[3] > Isoval [i] THEN J:= J+1 END;
    IF P2[3] > Isoval [i] THEN J:= J+2 END;
    CASE J OF
       |0 : IF P1[3] < P2[3] THEN Pb := P2; ELSE Pb := P1; END;
       |1,2: ContourPoint( P1, P2, Pb, Isoval [i] );    (* Figure 8.10 *)
    ELSE END;
    LinePlot ( Pa, Pb, Color [i] );
    Pa := Pb;
  END;
 END ProfileShade;
```

In developing these color-coded, shaded block models it became clear that the profile shading effect could only be maintained if the density of the different colored lines could be kept the same. The only alternative was to abandon the profile lines for this usage, and change to a system representing the shading effect directly by the appropriate choice of color and tone. This in turn required these areas to be evenly shaded with these colors if the modeling of the block model surface was to be rendered correctly. This change only became practical with the advent of the TV raster-based display systems. The important immediate development from these experiments was the realization that the complexity of the drawing with multisubject mapping reached an optimum point beyond which there was a very quick fall-off in clarity and readability, as shown in Example 8.3. The scan line area symbolism shown in Example 8.4, however, was a precursor of the raster shaded images to follow.

A separate sequence of studies was undertaken exporting contour and other cell-based symbolism to conventional mapping packages. This work was carried out as part of the development of the mapping facilities for GIMMS. This included algorithms for Delaunay triangulation, for Derichlet and Voronoi tessellations, for Point in Polygon classification, and for Polygon line shading, among others [19]. It was the line shading algorithm, developed for GIMMS, which provides the link with the next set of studies based on raster display systems.

8.5   Area Shading, Scan Conversion, Raster Displays

The first set of studies outlined above took the use of line symbolism to its practical limits for rendering three-dimensional objects. The starting point for the next set of studies was a polygon shading algorithm. The initial idea was to apply the plane sweep idea developed in the OBLIX system, making shading a form of polygon overlay exercise. If a parallel grid of lines is placed on top of a polygon then the approach outlined in Figure 8.14 looks possible, if a little complicated. Looking for ways to reduce and structure the computation it was realized that regular grids intersected straight-line sections of polygon boundaries with constant Δx and Δy stepping intervals. Particularly where a fine shading mesh was employed, this made it possible to follow the polygon boundary linearly interpolating these shading line end points, very simply and very quickly.

The only difficulty was matching up the resulting edge points into line segment pairs! However, it was pointed out that horizontal (or vertical, i.e., parallel to an axis)

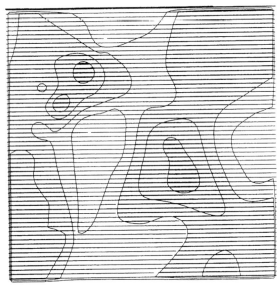

Example 8.4   (see also **Plate 31**) Studies using contour band scan line shading OBLIX, 1969. Exploring the task of generating area shading and area symbolism, using different colors and continuously varying tone values over a region of an image. Changing line widths, as in the moiré patterns images, produce smooth changes in grayscale. (Laboratory for Computer Graphics and Spatial Analysis, Harvard University.)

shading was easier to compute than oblique shading. At the cost of rotating the polygon boundary to the appropriate orientation, and rotating the shading lines back again, the problem became conceptually the simpler task of horizontal shading for which the linking problem was more easily solved. If the set of end point coordinates, in the rotated space, are co-ordinate sorted in (y,x) order, then shading line segments are naturally paired up in the output ordered list. Since the original shading data is created in ordered sequences, a natural merge sort algorithm gives a very efficient way to implement this process.

When this work was transferred to TV-based display systems, scan line shading was horizontal, so no rotation was needed. The approach seemed ideal. A polygon fill algorithm was evolved employing a scheme similar to the profile processing scheme outlined in Figure 8.3. Using the bucket sorting principle inherent in the use of depth-buffer memory, it was found that by using two 'profile buffers,' one for the left boundary of a polygon and one for the right boundary of a polygon, point data could be entered directly into these buffers from an edge line interpolation algorithm such as Bresenham's algorithm to give the scan line end points for a fast polygon fill procedure. The only limit was that the polygons could not be reentrant along their top or bottom boundaries.

Using a polygon fill algorithm of this kind to shade the triangles generated in OBLIX allowed the tone of the shading lines to be set to represent the illumination value of a surface, to give the shading effect previously approximated by the mesh of profile lines.

This half-tone illumination-based display process, pioneered by Brian Sprunt for block models in geographic work [16], gives the kind of result shown in Figure 8.17. One advantage which results from calculating the illumination and brightness levels of surfaces as a function of the light source position and the surface orientation is that it is possible to render images generated from non-grid-based data. In Figure 8.18 a site map of the University of Sussex is shown as a triangulated surface network. This network was produced by applying a Delaunay triangulation algorithm to a large data

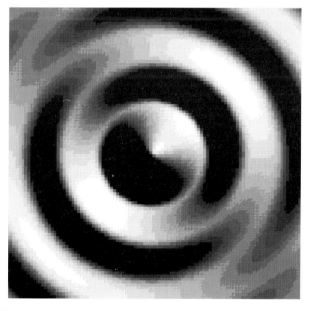

Figure 8.17   Halftone shading from a grid data set.

A. L. Thomas

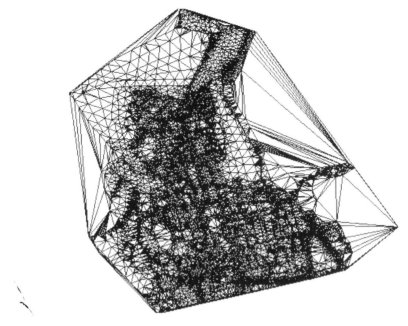

Figure 8.18   Delaunay triangulation, University of Sussex campus.

set of point-height values obtained from a site survey. Once the triangulated network had been defined, the same algorithm used to generate Figure 8.17 was used to create the site plan given in Figure 8.19. If this approach is to be used to generate block models, then grid data still has advantages, the primary one being that the regularly ordered structure provides a natural space-ordering which considerably simplifies the task of hidden-area removal.

The infill of triangles allows a different approach to be taken to hidden-line, and hidden-area removal. For a single surface the painters algorithm [10] will produce the image shown in Figure 8.20. The surface facets are transformed to correspond to the viewing direction and then rendered in an order taking the farthest away first. Nearer facets overwrite farther facets in the raster display buffer so avoiding complex visibility area calculations.

Although these images are at first sight better than their corresponding line-drawn counterparts, they are not strictly speaking comparable. The problem with an illustrative display, of which this is one, is that it is generally difficult to get detailed measured information from it. Given a technical drawing, and following the appropriate conventions, detailed information can be derived from it. A picture or visualization, in contrast, usually only gives a holistic effect from which it is difficult to get accurate geometrical information.

The traditional limits of the graphic form – the diagram and technical drawing at one extreme and the illustration or picture at the other – can be extended in the new developing computer environments. The static image still has the same limitations that it has always had, set by the visual perception system of the viewer. However, where the technical constraints in terms of time or cost prevented different graphic modes

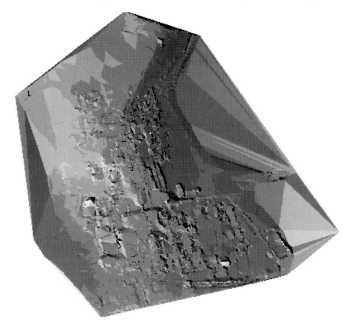

Figure 8.19   Shaded site plan, University of Sussex campus.

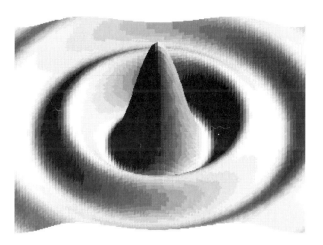

Figure 8.20   Half-tone shaded block model.

being merged, the computing environment is opening up new practical possibilities. In the case of block models it is now relatively easy to mix line symbolism used technically and area shading used pictorially. More than this is available from the new developing interactive graphics environments: not only synthetic photographic realism mixed with video-based 'real' realism, but also synthetic animation can be merged with standard video.

Different modes of display can be switched from one to another as different aspects of what is being shown need to be explored. Multiple coupled images can be placed in different windows. A text window can be set up as a digital meter to give a quantitative measure of properties selected in a visualization window display: for example, the distance between any two positions on a map following a given road network. The graphics display problem has become the system design problem of finding the most flexible and versatile way of implementing collections of interdependent geometric and rendering algorithms.

The site plan of the university campus becomes more useful for many applications if the contour lines shown in Figure 8.21 can be drawn on top of the shaded image. Similarly, a framework of grid lines is often useful to give a correct sense of distance within the space of the image. The image in Figure 8.21 was generated in two passes. This is reasonable in the case of a plan view but is not acceptable if a block model is to be rendered using the painters algorithm for hidden-area removal. In such a case each triangular facet needs to be rendered and then have its contour line segments drawn in before progressing to the next. The alternative is to use a different hidden-area removal strategy.

At first sight there would seem to be no difficulty completing each tile in turn. However, adopting this approach for the Sync function in Figure 8.22 produced the incomplete set of contour lines shown. The reason was simple in retrospect! The edge points of neighboring triangular facets are duplicated. When a properly implemented line interpolation algorithm is used, the edge line point set is totally replicated. Where line symbolism is created in a tile on this edge line, and the same symbolism is not duplicated in a neighboring tile which is drawn in later, then the line is overwritten and a gap is generated in the line symbolism in the way shown. There appeared to be two

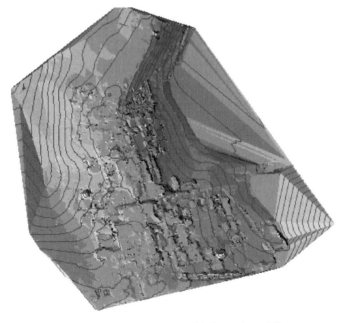

Figure 8.21   Shaded contour map, University of Sussex campus.

solutions to this problem. Either always duplicate overlain edge symbolism, or develop a more sophisticated tile fill procedure which does not overlap edges. The next study was an exploration of the latter approach.

8.6   Mutually Exclusive Tile Shading

Contouring triangular tiles generates an interesting problem when carried out in conjunction with shading operations. The problem arises because of the shading algorithm employed. In this algorithm the shading is defined by taking the outer points of the boundary lines for each scan line spanning the area. Where we have a surface

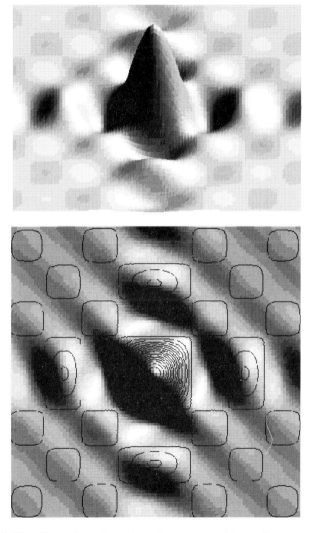

Figure 8.22   Sync function showing overwriting of contour lines.

covered by a set of abutting triangles, then it is clear that this shading algorithm will define areas which overlap for the sets of points which make up the common boundary line lying between them. For many applications this duplication is unimportant. In the painter's algorithm the overlap of one area by another is used to execute the simplest form of hidden-area removal. However, in the case of contour lines we could have the situation shown in Figure 8.23.

In Figure 8.23a two neighboring triangular tiles are shown. The four vertices labeled 1 to 4 are of height $h0$, $h1$, $h1$, and $h2$ respectively. Three contour lines will cut these two facets: $c1$ lies between $h0$ and $h1$, $c2$ exactly equals $h1$ and $c3$ lies between $h1$ and $h2$. The problem occurs in processing contour $c2$. In Figure 23b the classification of these two triangles is shown for the $c2$ contour. Only the top triangle will generate a contour line segment. Figures 8.23c and 8.23d show the way in which processing the top triangle first and the lower triangle second loses the $c2$ line segment.

This creates a problem which can only be solved by not overwriting existing patches where they include elements which will not be redefined in subsequent patches. In other words, where line symbolism is being drawn in on both the shared boundary lines of abutting triangles the line which is overwritten will be replaced, causing no problem; but given a line like the contour line which lies on the boundary but will only be generated for one patch, then the overwriting of boundaries must be avoided. There appears to be a basic principle here which can be applied in various ways depending on the context.

Each new patch must be shaded in so as not to cover any previously drawn patch area, but must provide the full extent of the new patch with its boundary lines so that any patch-related line segments for the new patch can be safely drawn in without fear of subsequent overwriting.

The detailed application of this principle depends on the order in which patches are processed. If adjacency information is part of the area boundary coding, as it would be in DIME and GIMMS files [6, 20], or in three dimensions in Volume-Matrix [19] or Winged Edge [2] data structures then a table of facets can be kept to flag areas which have already been rendered. This permits the appropriate edge points to be omitted so that the overlap of existing line symbolism is avoided.

There are many cases where this form of explicit information about neighbors is not provided, for example, if we are tessellating a surface using a regular rectangular grid

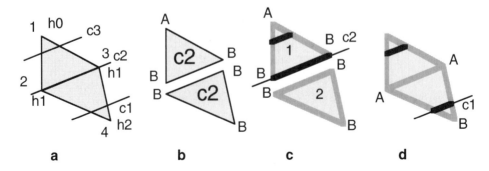

Figure 8.23   Contour line segments on tile boundaries.

in the way shown in Figure 8.24. In such a case the processing has to be ordered in some predefined way so that adjacency information can be deduced from the context.

If we are processing simple convex elements working down and across in the way shown in Figure 8.24 then each tile must be clipped in the way shown. Given this order of processing, the edge points to the upper left of a tile can be assumed to have already been painted in. A consistent treatment of boundary order will be necessary in order to classify the orientation of the edges of a tile. A counterclockwise convention to represent the interior of a polygon will give the scheme shown in Figure 8.25. If the order of processing is used to determine edge clipping, then concave boundary sequences need to be treated differently from convex sequences. The critical point,

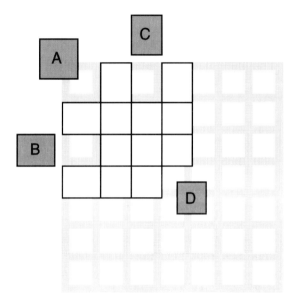

Figure 8.24   Nonoverlapping tiles on a grid framework.

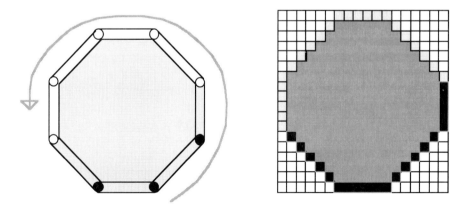

Figure 8.25   Convex tile boundary orientation used to clip edge points.

literally!, is shown in Figure 8.26. In convex tiles, vertex points shared by clipped edges and by nonclipped edges must be removed. In other words, the clipping operation dominates. However, the same vertex point for a concave sequence must be retained if complete nonoverlapping cover is to be provided for the overall study area. It can be seen that this makes it impossible to satisfy the 'complete cover' principle given above, if anything other than convex tiles are used for fill operations based on order and orientation in a local processing scheme.

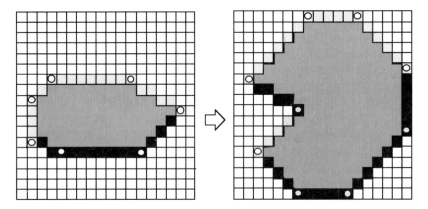

Figure 8.26   Concave vertex and edge clipping.

8.7   Contour Band Shading

In Example 8.2 the Honey Hill terrain model is shown band-shaded. The interval between contour lines is shaded with a uniform color code. In this example only one line from each grid cell row, is used for shading. Contour line segments were output as a file for use in GIMMS maps. In this case band shading was carried out by a general-purpose polygon shading routine. When further versatility was required, to provide band shading on block models, the option of using 'parametric symbols' was re-examined. The advantage that this offered was that a contour band inside a triangular patch was a convex shape and this could be shaded using the scan line shading algorithm based on line interpolation discussed above. The 'parametric symbol' approach is possible because contour lines on a plane triangular surface must be parallel. This limits the number of contour band patterns to three types. These are polygons with three, four, and five sides, respectively. However, although the number of patterns is limited, each band is generated by two adjacent contour levels. This means that a procedure has to be designed to run through the full contour sequence for each triangular facet. As Figure 8.27 shows, for n contour levels there are $n+1$ possible contour bands to define, and they could all occur within the same patch.

Basing the classification of a contour band symbol on the current contour line classification J, and the previous contour line classification K, the sequence of J–K pairs determines the number, and pattern of vertices needed to define the contour band polygons in each triangle. If an array of five point-vectors is used to store the contour band polygons (declared as type Hull), then it is possible to use the classification of the

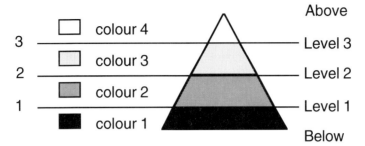

Figure 8.27   Contour lines and contour bands.

contour lines returned by the **ContourTriangle** procedure and their end points to specify the geometry and shape of each contour band in sequence.

The main cases which the contour banding procedure must cope with are shown in Figure 8.28. The process is controlled by a state variable S which can have three values. When $S = 1$ the process is in its start state. When $S = 2$ the process is stepping through intermediate level contours outputting contour bands. When $S = 3$ the final state is reached, when either all the contour levels have been processed or the current contour

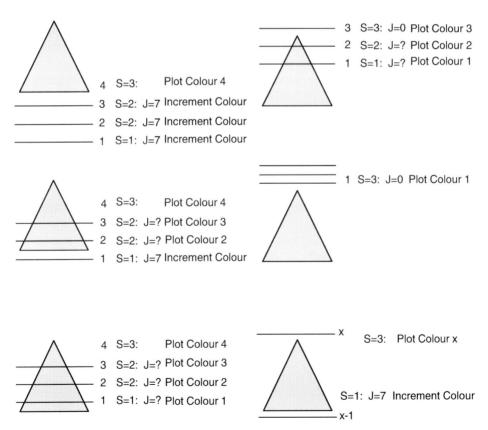

Figure 8.28   Different triangle to contour set sequence relationships.

is above all the vertices of the triangle. If after generating a contour $S = 1$, the system has to generate an 'opening' band. If $S = 3$ the system must create a 'closing' band. Otherwise, while $S = 2$ intermediate contour bands must be created from two neighboring contour line segments. In the latter case there are two possibilities: a simple four-vertex polygon, or a five-vertex polygon containing one of the triangle vertices as an extra boundary point.

In Figure 8.29 the way in which opening and closing contour bands are generated is shown. In each case part of the boundary is made up from two points from a contour line segment. The rest of the boundary is made up from either one or two points taken from the original triangle boundary, depending on the particular geometry of the case. The diagrams are set up to show how values passed to the contour band procedure are rearranged to maintain the boundary orientation of the polygon so that edge clipping can be carried out correctly. In the implementation shown no attempt is made to control the order in which the sequence of bands inside each patch is rendered. The assumption is made that a whole patch is filled in before any patch based line symbolism is applied to it. However, it is still necessary for the triangular patches to be processed in a correct order if line symbolism is not to be overwritten in the final completed image.

Because each triangular patch is planar, its contour line segments will be parallel.

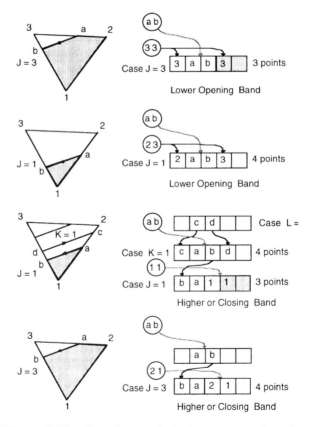

Figure 8.29 Opening and closing contour bands.

This limits the classification of consecutive contour segments to related pairs. In Figure 8.30, for example, the current line is classified as $J = 1$. The previous line segment could either also have been $J = 1$ or it could have been $J = 3$ or $J = 5$ depending on the orientation of the contour lines relative to the triangle framework.

This approach allows a reasonably simple mechanism to be set up which will generate these polygon patches and shade them in. The classification process using J and K determines which points will be required in each patch boundary. The key problem is how to set these points up in the order which corresponds with the oriented-boundary convention being used.

Figures 8.29 and 8.30 show how, by letting the selection procedure determine whether the resulting polygon will have three or four vertices, the simple order-swapping mechanism shown can be applied to all cases: *Take the previous middle two vertices in the polygon boundary array and, placing them into the outer two positions, then replace the middle two with the new contour segment end points.*

There are in fact two ordering mechanisms shown in Figure 8.30. The first of these is used in all cases and works with three- and four-point boundaries. The second is applied to modify the four-point boundary to a five-point boundary where an intermediate contour band is so placed that it spans one of the original triangle vertices.

Figure 8.31 shows how the various cases occur where five vertices are needed. These cases can again be identified using the J–K classification sequences. The first step is to create the standard four-point intermediate contour band; the second is to decide at which end of this polygon the extra point needs to be added, and then use the simplest swapping sequence to achieve this while maintaining the correct boundary order.

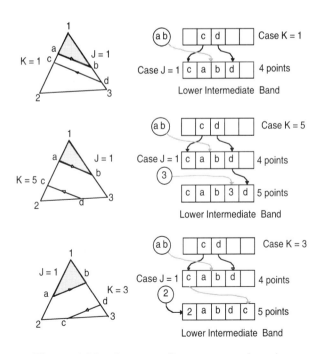

Figure 8.30   Intermediate contour bands.

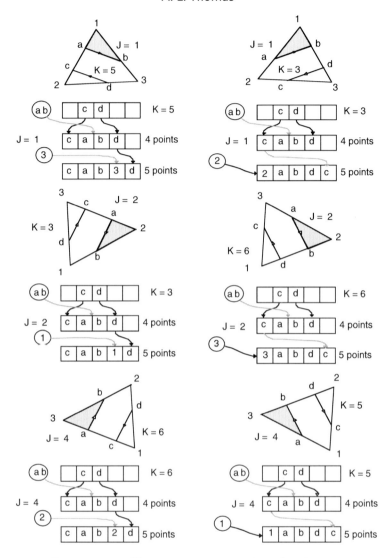

Figure 8.31   Five-vertex contour band polygons.

The result of this analysis is the code given in procedures **ContourBand** and **Band**. These procedures call the **ContourTriangle** procedure already described. The way in which the color shading is specified in these routines is simplified to the contour band indexes 0 . . . 15 which give the 16 grayscale levels shown in the figures.

```
PROCEDURE Band ( VAR Pa, Pb, Pc, Pd, Pe, Pf : PointVector;
               VAR P : Hull; VAR J, K, S, m : INTEGER; n : INTEGER );
BEGIN
     m := n+2;
     CASE S OF
```

```
|1: P[1] := Pa; P[4] := Pb; S :=2;
|2: P[1] := P[2]; P[4]: = P[3]; m := 4;
     CASE (K-J) OF
     | 1, 2, 4: CASE (K+J) OF
                | 5, 6, 10 : P[5] := P[4]; P[4] := Pb;
                | 4, 8, 9 : P[5] := P[1]; P[1] := Pa;
                ELSE END;
                m := 5;
     ELSE END;
  ELSE END;
  IF S = 3 THEN P[1] := Pe; P[4] := Pf; m := 5-n;
  ELSE P[2] := Pc; P[3] := Pd; END;
END Band;

PROCEDURE ContourBand ( VAR P1, P2, P3 : PointVector;
                        VAR Z0 : RPoints; n : CARDINAL);
VAR P : Hull; Pa , Pb : PointVector;
    L, K, J, S, k : INTEGER;
    m, i, Color : CARDINAL;
    Segment : BOOLEAN;
BEGIN
    K := 7; L := 7; S := 1; i := 1; m := 1; J := 7; Color := 1;
    P[1] := P1; P[2] := P2; P[3] := P3; P[4] := P1; k := 3;
    REPEAT
        IF i > n THEN S := 3;
        ELSE Segment := ContourTriangle(P1,P2,P3, Z0[i], Pa, Pb, J) END;
        IF J = 0 THEN S := 3; J := K; K := L; END;
        CASE J OF
        |1:    Band(P2, P3, Pa, Pb, P1, P1, P, J, K, S, k, 2);
        |2:    Band(P3, P1, Pa, Pb, P2, P2, P, J, K, S, k, 2);
        |3:    Band(P3, P3, Pa, Pb, P2, P1, P, J, K, S, k, 1);
        |4:    Band(P1, P2, Pa, Pb, P3, P3, P, J, K, S, k, 2);
        |5:    Band(P2, P2, Pa, Pb, P1, P3, P, J, K, S, k, 1);
        |6:    Band(P1, P1, Pa, Pb, P3, P2, P, J, K, S, k, 1);
        ELSE END;
        Color := i; L := K; K:= J;
        IF S > 1 THEN PolygonFill(P, k, Color); END;
        INC(i);
    UNTIL S = 3;
END ContourBand;
```

Applying these procedures to the University of Sussex Campus site data produced the image in Figure 8.32. Replacing the contour levels and introducing a function to determine the contour band color allowed the more complex image in Figure 8.33 to be produced, where the general shading reflects the orientation of the surface but narrow contour bands are defined where this shading is darkened sufficiently to see a superimposed pattern of contour bands. These, like the moiré pattern contour bands shown in Example 8.1, give a visual indication of both height and steepness of slope.

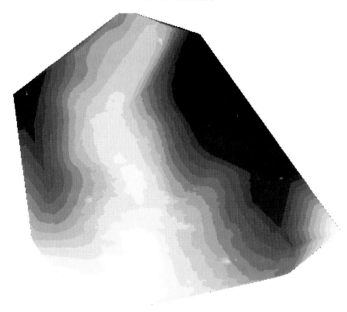

Figure 8.32   University of Sussex campus site contour band-shaded.

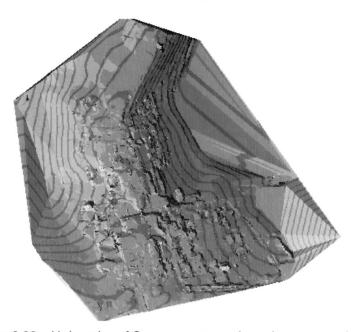

Figure 8.33   University of Sussex campus site using contour bands.

All seemed well with this analysis until a chance experiment was conducted on the band shaded image given in Figure 8.34 of an oblique view of a previously rendered block model. A series of pinholes appeared in the image, several pixels in size. A similar

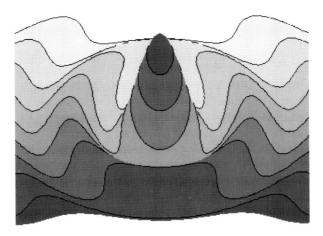

Figure 8.34 Viewing distance contoured onto a block model.

symptom had been encountered at an earlier stage of work, when a system line-interpolation algorithm was found to be incorrectly implemented. It gave a different set of points interpolating a line forward from that generated when interpolating the line backward; the result was a mismatch between abutting polygons when nominally they had identical edge lines. In order to avoid this kind of difficulty, all procedures above pixel level operations had subsequently been home written. This had up to this point successfully avoided further problems of this kind.

8.8   Polygon-Fill, Edge Clipping, and Quantization Errors

Since the errors were repeatable, and not a random printer artifact, a bug had crept into proceedings. It turned out to be a relatively difficult bug to pin down. Its tracking and capture are presented as the final study in this sequence on rendering block models. An example showing how these pinhole errors were generated can be set up in the way shown in Figures 8.35 and 8.36. The starting point is a triangulated grid with a contour line running across it defining a sequence of contour band polygons. Figure 8.35a shows the true geometry. In Figure 8.35b the grid of the display system is shown overlaid on this scheme.

Figures 8.36a and 8.36b show the result of rounding the real coordinates on to this display grid as integer coordinates. In (a) the contour band polygons are shown alternately shaded and unshaded to make them clearly identifiable. The result of this spatial quantization, shown in (b) is that several of the small polygons vanish.

Some of the difficult consequences of this quantization process can be removed by fairly simple actions; for example, null areas can be ignored or pruned out. In Figure 8.37 two modified patches A and D, and two other possible shapes which can be generated by quantization are shown as abstract graphs. Case D and these unlabeled cases are the graphs of triangular and rectangular patches where adjacent vertices have mapped onto identical points to give null areas which can be ignored. A, on the other hand, creates difficulties caused by the concave edge sequence generated when its

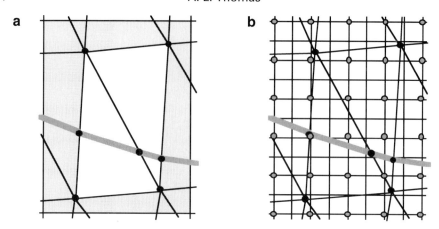

Figure 8.35   Contour band polygons on a display grid.

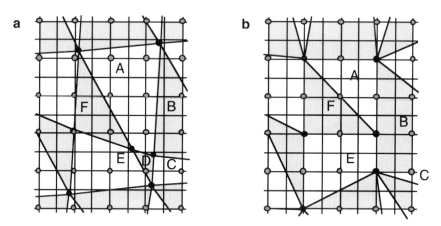

Figure 8.36   Quantizing polygon vertices to a display grid.

vertices are rounded to the display grid. The polygon fill algorithms illustrated in Figure 8.38 will successfully fill monotonic, nonconvex polygons as long as the concave edge sequences do not occur along the top or bottom boundaries of the polygon. However, the edge clipping of concave polygons cannot be achieved based on a spatial ordering strategy alone in a way that is compatible with the principle of 'complete cover' after each polygon-fill step. The only working strategy without explicit edge-adjacency information is to work with convex pieces. Unquantized contour band polygons are convex. Could this fact be used to avoid the problems?

There appeared to be two approaches to this task: Use integers in the display grid space or retain the original more exact floating-point representation. The latter would be self-consistent and would reduce the incidence of the difficulties considerably. However, there was the *possibility* that they could still emerge, occasionally, because the floating-point representation was also of a finite accuracy. Consequently, the first study was to see whether the problem could be resolved in the display-grid space, where it was more likely to occur and would be easier to locate and analyze.

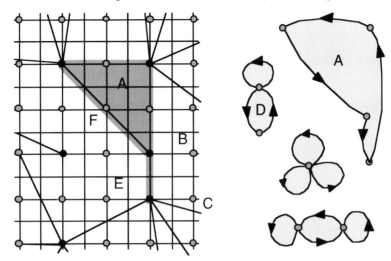

Figure 8.37   Lost areas and concave boundaries.

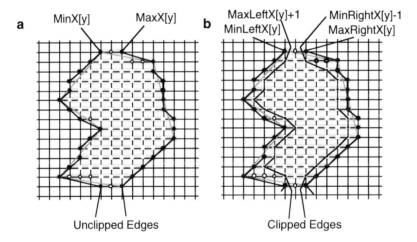

Figure 8.38   Polygon fill: clipped and unclipped edges.

In Figure 8.38a the simple area-fill algorithm is illustrated. As the boundary line of the polygon is interpolated, each point (x,y) is compared with an array of minimum and maximum x values – indexed on the appropriate y position in each array. This operation removes the edge line points, shown as heavy black circles in Figure 8.38, which would be internal to polygon-fill scan lines. It is these points which make the more complex approach illustrated in Figure 8.38b necessary for calculating the scan lines for an edge-clipped polygon. In this case the edge lines of the polygon have to be classified as belonging to the left edge or right edge of a figure, before being compared with MinLeftX and MaxRightX values to define the outer boundary of the polygon, and MaxLeftX and MinRightX to provide the clipped inner boundary of the polygon area. MaxLeftX+1 and MinRightX−1 give the left and right inner scan-line end points for a particular y value.

The procedures necessary to initialize and define these sequences of x values are **Box**, **InitScan** and **PolyScan**. Once all the scan line boundary values: $v[i]$, $v[i+1]$, $v[i+2]$, $v[i+3]$ are set up, the fill operation is completed by the **ScanFill** procedure.

```
PROCEDURE Box ( VAR x, y : Points; n : INTEGER;
                          VAR xmin, xmax, ymin, ymax : INTEGER);
VAR i : INTEGER;
BEGIN
    xmin := MAX (INTEGER);   xmax := MIN (INTEGER);
    ymin := MAX (INTEGER);   ymax := MIN (INTEGER);
    FOR i := 1 TO n DO
        IF x[i] < xmin THEN xmin := x[i] END;
        IF x[i] > xmax THEN xmax := x[i] END;
        IF y[i] < ymin THEN ymin := y[i] END;
        IF y[i] > ymax THEN ymax := y[i] END;
    END;
END Box;


PROCEDURE InitScan (VAR v : ARRAY OF INTEGER;
                         xmin, xmax, ymin, ymax : INTEGER);
VAR i, j, k : INTEGER;
BEGIN
    j := ymin*4; k := ymax*4;
    FOR i := j TO k BY 4 DO
        v[i] := xmin; v[i+1] := xmax; v[i+2] := xmax; v[i+3] := xmin;
    END;
END InitScan;


PROCEDURE PolyScan (x, y: INTEGER; VAR c, v: ARRAY OF INTEGER);
VAR i : INTEGER;
BEGIN
    i := y*4;
    IF c[0] <= 0 THEN
        IF c[2] = 1 THEN v[i] := c[3]; c[2] := 0; RETURN END;
        IF c[1] < 0 THEN IF v[i] < x+1 THEN v[i] := x+1 END; END;
        IF v[i+1] > x THEN v[i+1] := x END;
    END;
    IF c[0] >= 0 THEN
        IF c[2] = 1 THEN v[i+2] := c[4]; c[2] := 0; END;
        IF c[1] < 0 THEN IF v[i+2] > x-1 THEN v[i+2] := x-1 END; END;
        IF v[i+3] < x THEN v[i+3] := x END;
    END;
END PolyScan;
```

The mechanism employed in these routines is to initialize the $v[i]$ . . . to extreme values: MIN(INTEGER) and MAX(INTEGER) ready to run standard maximum or minimum selection algorithms respectively. If no clipped edge is encountered along a particular scan line then the inner point extreme values will remain unchanged, i.e., MaxLeftX will be left as MIN(INTEGER). This allows the test used in **ScanFill** to select the outer points to link up as a scan line because MaxLeftX will be less than MinLeftX.

If the inner point extreme values had been modified this test would have preferentially selected the inner points as scan line end points in the way shown in Procedure **ScanFill**.

```
PROCEDURE ScanFill (VAR v : ARRAY OF INTEGER;
                        Xmin, Xmax, Ymin, Ymax, color : INTEGER);
VAR i, j, k, m, left, right : INTEGER;
BEGIN
    j := Ymin*4; k := Ymax*4; m := Ymin;
    FOR i := j TO k BY 4 DO
        left := v[i+1]; right := v[i+3];
        IF v[i] > left THEN left := v[i]; END;
        IF v[i+2] < right THEN right := v[i+2] END;
        WHILE left <= right DO Pixel(left, m, color); INC(left); END;
        INC(m);
    END;
END ScanFill;
```

It is this primitive selection mechanism which caused the pinhole gaps in the image when the concave boundary sequence was encountered. Consider a polygon tile similar to *A* in Figure 8.37, shown in pixel level detail in Figure 8.39.

The various grid points which these procedures will select are shown as shaded circles in Figure 8.39. The problem is that the short vertical line segment at the bottom of *A* is oriented in a direction which, using the conventions of Figure 8.25, defines a clipped edge. The two scan lines traversed by this line will have clipped edge points

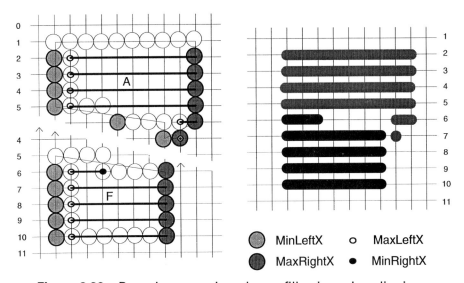

Figure 8.39 Boundary gaps in polygon fill using edge clipping.

defined. This means that the diagonal edge line which should be classified as an
unclipped line still gets clipped on its lowest scan line element. This means that when
the neighboring polygon is shaded, in the way shown, there is a resulting hole in the
image of four pixels. In order to locate conditions which would create this kind of error
it was necessary to set up a test for concave sequences in the polygon boundaries. If we
classify each line by the testing sequence:

```
j := 0;
  IF (x[i] < x[i+1]) THEN j := j+1 END;
  IF (x[i] = x[i+1]) THEN j := j+2 END;
  IF (y[i] < y[i+1]) THEN j := j+3 END;
  IF (y[i] = y[i+1]) THEN j := j+6 END;
```

then we get a value of j in the range 0 . . . 8 inclusive. The value 8 can be ignored as the
line consisting of a single point. This classification of edges can then be used to classify
vertices in the following way shown in Figure 8.40.

If we combine the classification of the two edges meeting at a vertex using the
0 . . . 7 classification, the result is the table of 64 cases shown in Figure 8.40. There
are only four conditions which are critical for handling the convex polygons created
by contour band shading. These are shown ringed in the table, and correspond to
the different junctions between clipped and unclipped edges which might occur in
the boundary of quantized convex polygons. In these four cases a vertex is classified
as 'concave' and this must be used to suppress clipping, by resetting the inner
boundary values to 'extreme values' for the scan line containing the 'concave'
vertex.

Procedure **PolygonFill** rounds a series of tile boundary coordinates to the integer
display grid and prunes out null areas. Procedure **PolyFill**, called by this routine, takes
this sequence of integer coordinates and classifies each edge, then taking this
classification in adjacent pairs ($c[i]$, $c[i+1]$) classifies each vertex. The concave cases are
flagged for treatment by the procedure **Lines**, which interpolates the edge points of the
tile boundary, and generates the arrays of scan line end points needed to fill each
polygon. These flags allow the interference of clipped and unclipped edges at concave
junctions to be suppressed. However, this is a 'fix' which allows tiles to be filled
without overlapping each other, but, it does not ensure that all edge lines are filled after
each tile fill operation has been completed. Occassionally with this approach, when tile-
based line symbolism falls on these unclipped edges, shown in Figure 8.41, they will be
overwritten by subsequent tiles.

It was initially hoped that since there were only four cases to handle in a special way,
and the patches were known a priori to be convex, a way would exist to avoid this need
to use a concave classification. This was based on the observation that these concave
sequences contain one edge which is only one grid step long. This can be considered
equivalent to the situation where a sloping straight line is interpolated onto a grid, and
the unit steps in the interpolation process required to give the line its slope are
separated out as distinct line segments. In other words, if the two lines making up the
concave sequence were taken together they could be considered as a single straight line
defined by grid point interpolation.

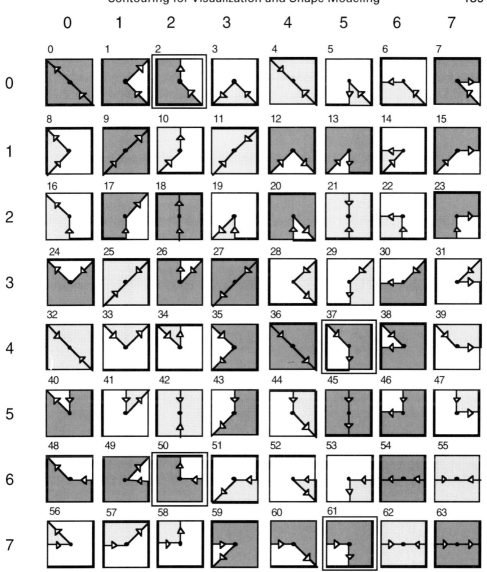

Figure 8.40   Edge to edge classification.

```
PROCEDURE PolyFill ( VAR x, y : Points; n, color : INTEGER);
VAR xmin, xmax, ymin, ymax, i, j, k, lastj : INTEGER; c : Points;
    v : ARRAY [0..2047] OF INTEGER;
    Color: ARRAY [0..4] OF INTEGER;
BEGIN
    Box (x, y, n, xmin, xmax, ymin, ymax);
    InitScan ( v, xmin, xmax, ymin, ymax);
    Color[3] := xmin; Color[4] := xmax;
    FOR i := 1 TO n-1 DO
```

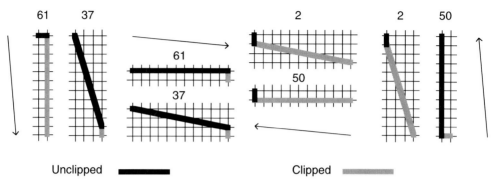

Figure 8.41   Edge lines subject to overwriting.

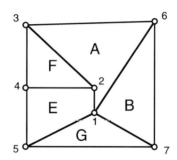

Figure 8.42   Concave and convex line sequences.

```
        j := 0;
        IF (x[i] < x[i+1]) THEN j := j+1 END;
        IF (x[i] = x[i+1]) THEN j := j+2 END;
        IF (y[i] < y[i+1]) THEN j := j+3 END;
        IF (y[i] = y[i+1]) THEN j := j+6 END;
        c[i]:= j;
END;
lastj := c[n-1];
FOR i := 1 TO n-1 DO
        j := c[i];
        CASE (8*lastj+j) OF 2, 37, 50, 61 : Color[2] := 1;
        ELSE Color[2] := 0; END;                        (*Concave Vertices*)
        lastj := j;
        CASE j OF
            |0, 1, 2 : Color[0] := 1 ;                  (*Right Edges*)
            |3, 4, 5, 6 : Color[0] := -1 ;              (*Left Edges*)
        ELSE Color[0] := 0 END;
        CASE j OF 0, 3, 5, 6 : Color[1] := -1 ;         (*Clipped Edges*)
        ELSE Color[1] := 1 END;
        CASE j OF 8, 7, 6 : ;                           (*Horizontal and Null Edges*)
        ELSE Lines ( x[i], y[i], x[i+1], y[i+1], Color, v, PolyScan); END;
```

```
    END;
    ScanFill ( v, xmin, xmax, ymin+1, ymax, color);
END PolyFill;


PROCEDURE PolygonFill ( VAR R : Hull; n, Color : INTEGER);
VAR x, y : Points; rx, ry, rz : RPoints;
    i, j : CARDINAL;
BEGIN
    FOR i := 1 TO n DO rx[i] := R[i,1]; ry[i] := R[i,2]; rz[i] := R[i,3]; END;
    rx[n+1] := rx[1]; ry[n+1] : = ry[1]; rz[n+1] := rz[1]; (*convert data structure*)
    FOR i := 1 TO n DO Scale ( rx[i], ry[i], x[i], y[i]); END;
    i := 1; j := 2;
    WHILE j <= n DO                              (*remove identical vertices*)
        IF (x[i] = x[j]) AND (y[i] = y[j]) THEN INC(j);
        ELSE INC(i); x[i] := x[j]; y[i] := y[j]; INC(j); END;
    END;
    n := i;
    IF n > 3 THEN PolyFill ( x, y, n, Color); END;      (*prune null areas*)
END PolygonFill;
```

The reason why any hoped for simplifications from this approach foundered is shown in Figure 8.42. For tile A in Figure 8.42 the edge sequence 12–23 could be classified as a single sloping line from 1 to 3. However all the neighboring tiles are simple convex areas. This means that if the sequence 12–23 is treated as an unclipped edge, which it would if it were considered to be a sloping line, then the standard treatment of tile E would cause the line segment 12 to be overwritten. There is no local test at this level of representation which can be used to signal a different treatment being required for the edge 12 in E, to match the treatment of line pair 12–23 as a single sloping straight line.

If these lines had not been quantized onto a grid, they would have the appropriately classified, matching slopes, for the edge clipping to work correctly in a self-consistent way, using only local tests. In the light of the given analysis, this would appear to offer the better solution. The only worry is that, when very small polygon zones are generated, as they can be by procedures like **ContourBand**, the same difficulties will occur in spite of using floating-point coordinates. The same 'concave' relationships will be generated, though much less often, because the floating-point representation also has a limited accuracy, and in the extreme is working on a grid. Two examples are shown in Figure 8.43 for different placements of the contour band polygon A, relative to the floating-point grid.

In both cases the small triangle D vanishes, and the floating-point coordinates for the area A give identical slope sequences, including a concave step, as before. The problem occurs with the placement of the vertical edge in this concave sequence. If it lies across the 'rounding' boundary between two display grid coordinates in the way shown, the result will be that given in Figure 8.44. In (a) the concave sequence has been removed, in (b) it has been magnified. In these diagrams the scale difference between the floating-point grid and the display grid has been considerably reduced to help illustrate the difficulty and then show its remedy.

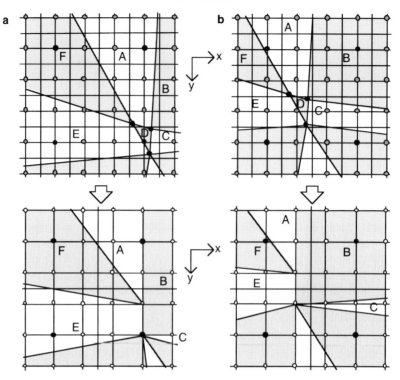

Figure **8.43**   Small triangles rounded onto the floating-point grid.

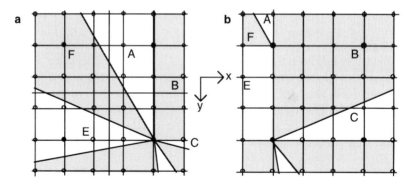

Figure 8.44   Rounding to the display grid.

A possible solution to this case is to process all the vertices in the network of tile boundaries and, where two vertices are within a certain distance of each other, larger than the finer grid but smaller than the larger grid, prune out one of the vertices. After this, classify the orientation of the remaining edges using real-valued coordinates. This operation must conform to a selection convention such as taking the coordinates in *coordinate order* for deletion, to avoid inconsistencies being introduced into the system.

In Figure 8.45 this distance test is shown being applied to the vertices of the vertical line segment which has been causing the problem. The result of pruning out the large coordinate is shown in Figure 8.46. This step is then followed by quantization to the display grid as before, using a rounding operation. All concave sequences at the floating-point scale will have been removed; however, rounding these adjusted floating-point coordinates to the display grid may still, for larger polygonal areas, introduce concave sequences all over again. However, transferring the classification of these edges from the floating-point level means the original '*convex-concave*' classification will be retained, and will be consistent for adjacent polygons.

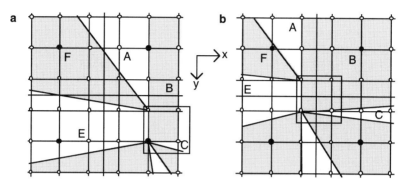

Figure 8.45   Removing points which are close to each other.

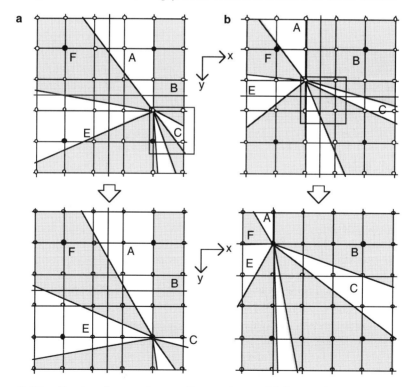

Figure 8.46   Coalescing and rounding points which are close to each other.

In Figure 8.46 the arbitrary but consistent selection of the smaller coordinate of a pair near enough to each other to be coalesced, caused the upper point of the vertical segment to be selected in Figure 8.46b. This could just as easily have been the neighboring lower point if the larger coordinate had been chosen. It can be seen that if a selection convention had not been adhered to, then the eight adjacent polygons could have been linked to either of the two closely placed points in an arbitrary way.

In fact if these polygons are processed independently this is exactly what would happen. The problem with this scheme is, though it works in this presentation, it is impossible to implement locally, in other words, based on a process which takes each polygon tile, independently, in turn. Without information about adjacent polygons there is no reason, for example, to change the top vertex of tile C. However it has to be changed to match the corresponding point in the neighboring area A which has been replaced by an adjacent vertex that it was too close to. To implement this scheme requires the edge adjacency coding methods developed in GIMMS, so the consequences of coalescing points can be worked through their neighborhood in a consistent way.

Other data structures than the adjacency links used in GIMMS can be used to achieve the same results. A traditional hierarchical arrangement which separates volumes, surfaces, edges, and vertices into separate sets, interrelated by pointers, so there is a unique definition of each entity, will also support this operation. If all the point coordinates in a vertex set are checked for 'nearness' to each other, and points which are within a certain distance of each other are given the same value, then elements composed from these vertices such as abutting polygon facets can be processed in a self consistent way, employing the method outlined above by rounding them to an appropriate display grid. A simple 'nearness' test can be carried out for the *Manhatten metric* shown illustrated in Figures 8.45 and 8.46 using a double application of the coordinate sort procedure in $O(n \log(n))$ time.

Where this or a related approach can be used the resulting quantized geometry with the floating point based classification of slope, will support a band shading process where contour line symbolism can safely be written onto shaded tiles as they are drawn in. This permits the use of the painter's algorithm to create images of the form shown in Figure 8.47, where mixed symbolism is employed. The image shows a shaded block model with standard profile lines drawn on top of a band shaded contour image giving the distance of each point on the block model surface from the display plane. This illustrates the *before* and *after* images generated *without corrected edge clipping*, and *with corrected edge clipping*.

It has to be observed that without further refinements, where a triangular tile is broken up into sub patches as is done in the case of contour band shading, the resulting edge points of the composite tile need not exactly match the edge line points defined by simple grid based interpolation between the triangles original vertices. This does not affect contour lines but other lines such as the profile lines shown in Figure 8.47 which fall on a triangle's edges could still end up being partially over-written unless they are duplicated on any adjacent triangle, filled in later. At first sight it appeared to be possible to duplicate contour lines which fall on triangle facet edges to avoid the overwriting problem shown in Figure 8.23. In order to do this, however, the contouring procedure had to be extended to distinguish triangle vertex points that are equal to contour levels from those which lie above or below the contour level, in the way shown in the procedure **ContourTriangle2** given below.

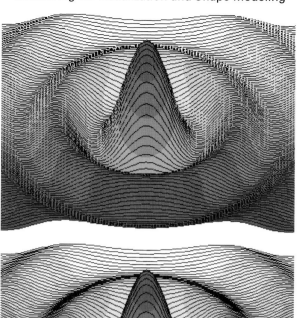

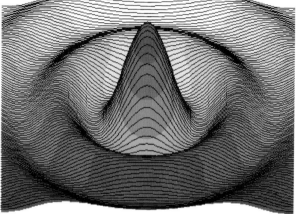

Figure 8.47 Mixed symbolism with and without corrected edge clipping.

In procedure **ContourTriangle2** when all the vertices are found to be below the current contour level: $Z0$ so that $J = 0$, then a further classification is carried out to test the vertices for equality with the contour level. When a single point is found to equal the contour level, the condition is ignored, when two vertices are found to equal it, they are used to define a contour line segment. If **A** denotes a vertex which is *above* the contour level, **B** a vertex which is *below* the level and **E** a vertex which is *equal* to the contour level, then a facet which is **AEE** and which before would have been classified as **ABB** would generate a contour line segment either way; whereas a triangle which is **EEB** and which would have been classified as **BBB** would not. Introducing the **E** classification allows edge line contours to be duplicated. When three vertex points are found to equal the contour level, either the whole triangle has to be ignored or filled with the color used to draw in the contour lines.

Duplicating contour lines on edge lines however does not solve all the difficulties. Figure 8.48 shows a condition where one vertex being equal to a contour level can produce a contour line segment which is so close to the triangle edge that its interpolation

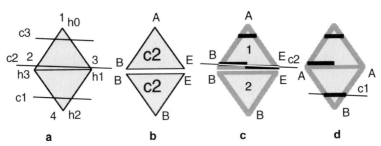

Figure 8.48 Contour lines partly overwritten by neighboring patches.

onto the pixel grid results in part or all of its constituent pixel points ending up on the
edge of the triangle. It can be seen that in this case the neighboring triangle cannot
generate the corresponding contour line points so they will again be overwritten when
the next tile is shaded in, unless some form of edge clipping is implemented.

```
PROCEDURE ContourTriangle2 ( VAR P1, P2, P3, Pa, Pb: PointVector;
          Z0: REAL; VAR J, H, K: INTEGER ): BOOLEAN;
BEGIN
    J:= 0;
    IF P1[3] > Z0 THEN J := J+1 END;
    IF P2[3] > Z0 THEN J := J+2 END;
    IF P3[3] > Z0 THEN J := J+4 END;
    CASE J OF
      0: IF K<0 THEN RETURN FALSE END;
         H:= 0;
         IF P1[3] = Z0 THEN H:=H+1 END;
         IF P2[3] = Z0 THEN H:=H+2 END;
         IF P3[3] = Z0 THEN H:=H+4 END;
         CASE H OF
             1: Pa:=P1; Pb:=P1;      |
             2: Pa:=P2; Pb:=P2;      |
             3: Pa:=P1; Pb:=P2;      |
             4: Pa:=P3; Pb:=P3;      |
             5: Pa:=P3; Pb:=P1;      |
             6: Pa:=P2; Pb:=P3;      |
             7: (*ignore or fill whole triangle with contour line color*)|
         ELSE RETURN FALSE END;                |
      1: ContSeg(P2,P1,P3,Pa,Pb,Z0)   |
      2: ContSeg(P3,P2,P1,Pa,Pb,Z0)   |
      3: ContSeg(P2,P3,P1,Pa,Pb,Z0)   |
      4: ContSeg(P1,P3,P2,Pa,Pb,Z0)   |
      5: ContSeg(P1,P2,P3,Pa,Pb,Z0)   |
      6: ContSeg(P3,P1,P2,Pa,Pb,Z0)   |
    ELSE RETURN FALSE; END;
    RETURN TRUE;
END ContourTriangle2;
```

A simpler way of solving this overwriting problem exists if a depth buffer can be used. Clearly, it is then possible to test a pixel position to see if it has already been filled in, so avoiding the overwriting of line symbolism by later patch shading. If the depth value of the existing entry is the same as the new depth value then it can be assumed that an adjacent tile has already been shaded in, and only new surface symbolism needs to be added if it is required. If the new depth value is greater than the existing depth value then clearly the existing surface is nearer than the current one so neither shading nor surface symbolism values should be entered. If the new depth value is less, then the new tile will be totally obscuring the old tile and both new shading and surface symbolism values can be entered into the display.

A related approach can be adopted for single, fully connected surfaces, by ordering the facets from the back working forwards, as in the painter's algorithm, but at the same time maintaining an array of pixel values for the leading edge of the section of the surface which has so far been rendered. This array will operate rather like the profile mask in Figure 8.3, but in reverse. Depth, z-values and y-values indexed on each x position for these edge points will allow the same test employed in the case of a depth buffer, to determine whether an edge has already been rendered and therefore needs to be clipped from neighbouring tiles or not. Most of the decisions can still be made using the edge classification shown in Figure 8.25, but the awkward cases in Figure 8.41 can be resolved point by point, by using a 'leading-edge' buffer of this kind.

This series of studies is one in a collection being carried out to provide a library of flexible graphic procedures to support an object oriented language environment, where depending on the operation being carried out the system must be capable of selecting and reordering operations automatically in the most efficient way. The procedures presented above have also been extended and modified in a series of experiments designed to find the best way of integrating image clipping and windowing with the contouring and rendering process.

In Figure 8.49 several polygons are defined on the display surface and the boundaries of these polygons are used to prime the polygon-fill boundary arrays. This gives an automatic texture-fill facility for these polygons, where the texture is defined functionally by the procedure needed to generate the images. Once the scan line boundary arrays have been primed, for each convex clipping polygon, there is no extra work involved. This therefore provides a flexible and useful general-purpose system facility. The combination of this polygon image clipping and the corrected contour band edge-clipping algorithms generates the pair of study images given in Figure 8.50.

The computational cost of this facility employing a naive approach will be $O(n.m)$ where n is the number of convex polygons making up the clipping area and m is the cost of rendering the infill image. This facility is being extended in another set of studies to fit within an image partitioning process designed to improve efficiency. As the lower example in Figure 8.50 shows, it is possible to partition the display area into mutually exclusive regions. This approach allows the two processes to be integrated within the framework provided by a third, which systematically subdivides the display space so the separate display tasks for each region are reduced in complexity and the overall performance for the total image moves toward $O(m)$.

A full analysis of this development falls outside the main theme of this chapter because further exploration of this topic requires the detailed study of a range of overlap and selection procedures. In two dimensions these include point-in-polygon,

Figure 8.49   Polygon-clipped oblique and plan views.

polygon overlay, polygon line clipping, and a series of windowing algorithms, while in three dimensions they also include Boolean-expression or constructive solid geometry modeling algorithms. The subject of three-dimensional modeling, however, leads on to the next set of studies which do come under the heading of this chapter. These are concerned with the production of three-dimensional contours, or isosurfaces.

8.9   Isosurfaces and Implicit Surface Rendering

Three-dimensional contours or isosurfaces can be constructed using virtually the identical algorithm to that employed in two dimensions. If data is provided on a grid

Figure 8.50   Polygon-clipped band shaded block models.

then contour segments, or surface facets in three dimensions, can be created for data cells set up by eight neighboring grid points in the way shown in Figure 8.51. Again these cells can be accessed sequentially by a nested set of repeat loops giving a base index position in the data array, from which the positions and data values of the remaining cell vertices can be calculated. This is done using the cell vertex numbering given in Figure 8.51, and the procedure **PointValue,** where a is the vertex number and $[i, j, k]$ gives the base index position of the cell in the overall data array.

```
PROCEDURE PointValue(a,i,j,k: CARDINAL; VAR V: ValueArrayType):REAL;
BEGIN
      RETURN V[ (a MOD 8) DIV 4+i, (a MOD 4) DIV 2+j, (a MOD 2)+k ];
END PointValue;
```

As in the two-dimensional case these cells need to be triangulated. In three dimensions there are more degrees of freedom with which to carry out this task. In Figure 8.52 three possibilities are shown: (A) and (C) giving a cell subdivided into six tetrahedra, and (B)

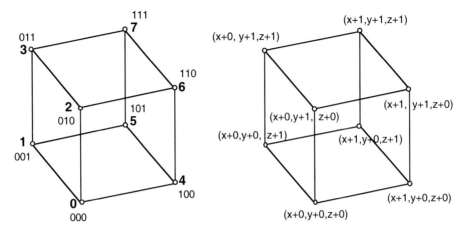

Figure 8.51   Three-dimensional grid cell labeling.

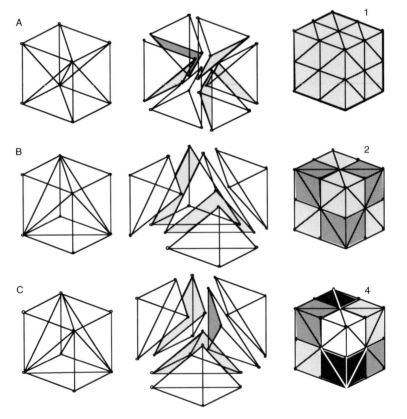

Figure 8.52   Triangulating schemes for three-dimensional cells.

subdivided into five. The initial choice of triangulation appears to be arbitrary. However, once a cell has been allocated a particular pattern then the patterns adopted for neighboring cells are constrained by the need to have adjacent faces between cells triangulated in the same way. In Figure 8.52, the correct correspondence between cells was achieved by reflecting the basic patterns in their joining faces.

```
PROCEDURE DisplayContourSurface (VAR Value : ValueArrayType;
                        I, J, K : CARDINAL; IsoValue : REAL);
VAR  i, j, k, t : CARDINAL;
BEGIN
    FOR k := K-1 TO 0 BY -1 DO
        FOR i := 0 TO I-1 DO
            FOR j := 0 TO J-1 DO
                t := (i MOD 2)*4 + (j MOD 2)*2 + (k MOD 2);
                CASE t OF
                1,2,4,7:
                Tetrahedron (Value,0,1,5,3,i,j,k,IsoValue);
                Tetrahedron (Value,0,5,6,3,i,j,k,IsoValue);
                Tetrahedron (Value,0,5,4,6,i,j,k,IsoValue);
                Tetrahedron (Value,2,3,0,6,i,j,k,IsoValue);
                Tetrahedron (Value,5,7,6,3,i,j,k,IsoValue); |
                0,3,5,6:
                Tetrahedron (Value,0,1,4,2,i,j,k,IsoValue);
                Tetrahedron (Value,1,3,7,2,i,j,k,IsoValue);
                Tetrahedron (Value,1,5,4,7,i,j,k,IsoValue);
                Tetrahedron (Value,4,6,2,7,i,j,k,IsoValue);
                Tetrahedron (Value,1,4,2,7,i,j,k,IsoValue); |
                ELSE END;
        END; END; END;
    END DisplayContourSurface;
```

In case (A) only one pattern was needed, in the case of (B) two patterns, and in the case of (C) four patterns, to achieve this matching. This switch in patterns between neighboring cells can be implemented using a classification function employing the cell's base index and a case statement in the way shown in procedure **DisplayContourSurface**. In this example, code is given for case (B) in Figure 8.52.

Each tetrahedron can then be processed in the same way that the triangular patches were in two dimensions, using the classification scheme shown in Figures 8.53 and

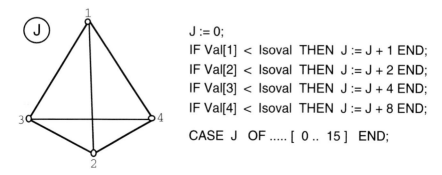

```
J := 0;
IF Val[1] < Isoval THEN J := J + 1 END;
IF Val[2] < Isoval THEN J := J + 2 END;
IF Val[3] < Isoval THEN J := J + 4 END;
IF Val[4] < Isoval THEN J := J + 8 END;

CASE J OF ..... [ 0 .. 15 ] END;
```

Figure 8.53   Classifying contour patterns for a tetrahedron.

8.54. A tetrahedron has four vertices, whereas a triangle has three. There are therefore four classifying statements generating 16 possible cases rather than the 8 shown in Figure 8.13. Each of these is illustrated in Figure 8.54.

In Figure 8.54 each of the possible Above–Below classifications of the tetrahedron is shown, along with the isosurface patch required in each case. The shaded region is the section of the tetrahedron above the given contour level. Again it can be seen that these patterns occur in pairs reflecting the two orientations of each surface patch which are possible. Each pair corresponds to a labeling pair n and $15 - n$. There are two patch types, a triangular and a quadrilateral patch. In the simple case the vertices of these isosurface patches are generated by linear interpolation along the appropriate tetrahedral edges. In both cases, patches are planar and can be rendered using polygon fill, or the quadrilateral patch can be divided into triangles, as shown in Figure 8.55.

```
PROCEDURE Tetrahedron(VAR Value: ValueArrayType;
                           a,b,c,d,i,j,k: CARDINAL; V0: REAL);

VAR s: CARDINAL;
```

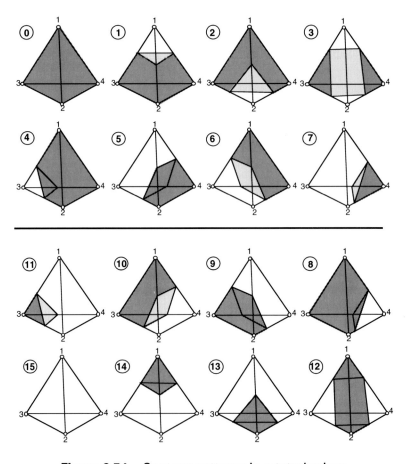

Figure 8.54   Contour patterns in a tetrahedron.

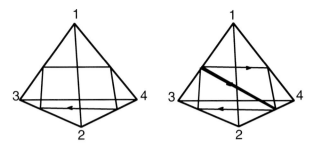

Figure 8.55   Triangulating quadrilateral contour facets.

```
BEGIN
    s := 0;
    IF PointValue(a,i,j,k,Value) > V0 THEN s := s+1; END;
    IF PointValue(b,i,j,k,Value) > V0 THEN s := s+2; END;
    IF PointValue(c,i,j,k,Value) > V0 THEN s := s+4; END;
    IF PointValue(d,i,j,k,Value) > V0 THEN s := s+8; END;
    CASE s OF
        |1: Triangle (a,b,a,d,a,c,i,j,k,V0);
        |2: Triangle (b,a,b,c,b,d,i,j,k,V0);
        |3: Quadrilateral(a,d,a,c,b,c,b,d,i,j,k,V0);
        |4: Triangle (c,a,c,d,c,b,i,j,k,V0);
        |5: Quadrilateral(a,b,a,d,c,d,c,b,i,j,k,V0);
        |6: Quadrilateral(b,d,b,a,c,a,c,d,i,j,k,V0);
        |7: Triangle (d,c,d,b,d,a,i,j,k,V0);
        |8: Triangle (d,a,d,b,d,c,i,j,k,V0);
        |9: Quadrilateral(a,c,a,b,d,b,d,c,i,j,k,V0);
        |10:Quadrilateral(d,c,d,a,b,a,b,c,i,j,k,V0);
        |11:Triangle (c,b,c,d,c,a,i,j,k,V0);
        |12:Quadrilateral(a,c,a,d,b,d,b,c,i,j,k,V0);
        |13:Triangle (b,a,b,d,b,c,i,j,k,V0);
        |14:Triangle (a,b,a,c,a,d,i,j,k,V0);
    ELSE RETURN END;
END Tetrahedron;
```

Source data in a three-dimensional grid format comes from body scanning systems such as MRI and CAT scanners. Without further information the isosurface generated by linear interpolation gives a resulting model and image which is probably as good as can be expected. The problem with this basic method is the coarse way in which smooth surfaces may get arbitrarily faceted depending on the positioning of the sampling grid. Figures 8.56 and 8.57 show the way that surface faceting varies over a well-known smooth surface giving a result which contrasts fairly strongly with what we expect to see. In this case, however, the use of linear interpolation not only introduces an error where plane facets do not match the true surface but also in many cases places the vertices of these facets, through linear interpolation, off the true surface position.

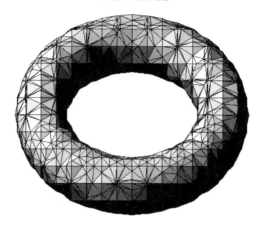

Figure 8.56   Linear interpolation: a torus as an isosurface.

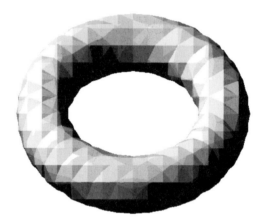

Figure 8.57   Linear interpolation: a torus as an isosurface.

8.10   Implicit Surface Modeling

Where the surface like this torus can be expressed as an algebraic equation, then it is possible to dramatically improve the approximated faceted model and the image of it produced by this isosurface modeling technique. Consider a sphere. A sphere can be represented by the equation

$$r^2 = x^2 + y^2 + z^2$$

This can be expressed in the functional form

$$f(x,y,z) = x^2 + y^2 + z^2 - r^2$$

where the surface required satisfies the equation $f(x,y,z) = 0$. This representation permits a series of nested surfaces to be defined where $f(x,y,z) = k$. These can be displayed by evaluating $f(x,y,z)$ on the node-points of a regular grid and then generating the contour surface for the required values of k. Using linear interpolation these will correspond to the results given in Figures 8.56 and 8.57 for the quartic polynomial representing a torus taking $k=0$. In the procedure **Tetrahedron** it can be seen that the faceting of the surface is based on point-values obtained at grid points. In the example given these are obtained from an array using an accessing function. This function **PointValue** could in the case of the torus or sphere equally well be set up to calculate the value of the function at each grid point when it is needed. The important observation is that the values at these nodes are calculated accurately: It is the linearly interpolated positions of the contour level values between these positions which are not. All that is necessary to improve this is to slide the positions of the isosurface facet vertices along the edges on which they were interpolated, tightening up the interpolated surface, moving all its facet vertices accurately onto the true surface. This can be done because all the interpolated points are located on edges where one end point is above the contour level and the other is below the contour level. This allows an approximation scheme based on binary subdivision to give a far more accurate placement of contour facet vertices in the way shown in Figure 8.58.

```
PROCEDURE Subdivide(X1,Y1,Z1,V1,X2,Y2,Z2,V2,V0:REAL;
                     Level: CARDINAL; VAR x,y,z: REAL);
VAR J: CARDINAL; V3: REAL;
BEGIN
    Level := Level + 1;
    x := (X1+X2) / 2.0; y := (Y1+Y2) / 2.0; z := (Z1+Z2) / 2.0;
    V3 := PointValue(x,y,z);
    IF Level < 10 THEN
        J := 0;
        IF V1 > V0 THEN J := J+1 END;
        IF V3 > V0 THEN J := J+2 END;
        IF V2 > V0 THEN J := J+4 END;
        CASE J OF
            | 3,4 : Subdivide(x,y,z,V3,X2,Y2,Z2,V2,V0,Level,x,y,z);
            | 1,2,6 : Subdivide(X1,Y1,Z1,V1,x,y,z,V3,V0,Level,x,y,z);
        ELSE END;
```

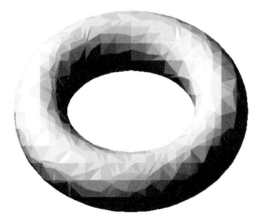

Figure 8.58   Torus as an implicit surface model.

```
      END; RETURN;
END Subdivide;


PROCEDURE PointInterpolate(a, b, i, j, k: CARDINAL;
                                          V0: REAL; VAR x, y, z: REAL);
VAR X1, Y1, Z1, V1, X2, Y2, Z2, V2: REAL;
BEGIN
    IF a < b THEN Swap(a,b); END;
    TransformPoint( a, i, j, k, X1,Y1,Z1);
    TransformPoint( b, i, j, k, X2,Y2,Z2);
    V1 := PointValue( X1,Y1,Z1 );
    V2 := PointValue( X2,Y2,Z2 );
    Subdivide( X1,Y1,Z1,V1, X2,Y2,Z2,V2, V0, 0, x,y,z);
END PointInterpolate;


PROCEDURE FrontFacing ( VAR P: Hull): BOOLEAN;
VAR r: REAL;
BEGIN
    r := P[1,1]*P[2,2] - P[1,1]*P[3,2] - P[1,2]*P[2,1];
    r := P[2,1]*P[3,2] - P[2,2]*P[3,1] + P[1,2]*P[3,1] + r;
    IF r < 0.0 THEN RETURN TRUE ELSE RETURN FALSE END;
END FrontFacing;


PROCEDURE Triangle ( a,b, c,d, e,f, i,j,k : CARDINAL; V0 : REAL);
VAR V1, V2 : REAL; P:Hull;
BEGIN
    PointInterpolate ( a,b,i,j,k,V0,P[1,1],P[1,2],P[1,3]);
    PointInterpolate ( c,d,i,j,k,V0,P[2,1],P[2,2],P[2,3]);
    PointInterpolate ( e,f,i,j,k,V0,P[3,1],P[3,2],P[3,3]);
    P[4] := P[1];
    IF FrontFacing (P) THEN TriangleShade(P); END;
END Triangle;


PROCEDURE Quadrilateral ( a,b, c,d, e,f, g,h, i,j,k : CARDINAL; V0 : REAL);
BEGIN
    Triangle ( a,b, c,d, e,f, i,j,k, V0);
    Triangle ( a,b, e,f, g,h, i,j,k, V0);
END Quadrilateral;
```

Where the interpolation is nonlinear it is simpler to subdivide the quadrilateral into two triangles in the way shown in Figure 8.55. Two further improvements to this process can be obtained. The first is to use smooth shading to get rid of the facet edges in the image. The second is to subdivide the surface facet triangulation further where the mid-point of a triangular facet is beyond a certain tolerance from the true surface. Where there is a sharply curving surface it may be necessary to also further partition edges. This is more complicated because neighboring triangles have to be subdivided to match such changes.

8.11   Smooth Shading and Contour Band Shading

Another advantage offered by implicit surfaces is that it allows us to calculate the normal to these surfaces at grid point nodes. This makes it possible to calculate the illumination values at triangle vertices and then interpolate them across each triangular facet to give Gouraud smooth shading, as illustrated in Figure 8.59.

Initially a separate routine was designed for this smooth shading task. However, when ways of improving its efficiency were being analyzed, it was realized that the contour band shading algorithm which had already been implemented could be set up to perform the same task.

```
PROCEDURE Normal ( x,y,z: REAL; VAR a,b,c,d: REAL);
BEGIN
    a := PointValue(x+delta,y,z) - PointValue(x-delta,y,z);
    b := PointValue(x,y+delta,z) - PointValue(x,y-delta,z);
    c := PointValue(x,y,z+delta) - PointValue(x,y,z-delta);
    d := sqrt(a*a + b*b + c*c); a := a/d; b := b/d; c:= c/d;
END Normal;

PROCEDURE TriangleShade ( VAR R: Hull );
VAR a,b,c,d, Z0: RPoints; P:Hull; i: CARDINAL;
BEGIN
    FOR i := 1 TO 3 DO
        Normal(R[i,1],R[i,2],R[i,3],a[i],b[i],c[i],d[i]);
        d[i] := IlluminationFunction( a[i],b[i],c[i],LightVector);
    END;
    FOR i := 1 TO 3 DO
        P[i,1] := R[i,1]; P[i,2] := R[i,2]; P[i,3] := d[i];
    END;
    Z0[1] := 0.0625;
    FOR i := 2 TO 16 DO Z0[i] := Z0[i-1] + Z0[1]; END;
    ContourBand( P[1], P[2], P[3], Z0, 15);
END TriangleShade;
```

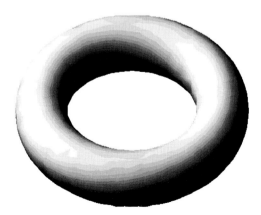

Figure 8.59   Smooth shaded torus using contour band shading.

These procedures can also be implemented in a way which allows them to be used efficiently in collaboration with window and polygon clipping procedures as illustrated in Figure 8.60.

If we start with an inappropriately complicated function for the given mesh resolution, it is clear that interactions with the sampling grid will produce unpredictable aliasing effects. The two studies cited above avoid this difficulty by restricting curved elements to smooth surfaces relative to the sampling framework. However, in these cases, it is still desirable to be able to change the accuracy with which the surfaces are approximated, particularly along silhouette edges, where the errors associated with linear approximation are usually most obvious, 'smooth shading' being able to remove most of the obvious visual discrepancies elsewhere.

The isosurface classification given in procedure **Tetrahedron** generates two surface patch types, shown in Figure 8.61, from which linear interpolation along edges

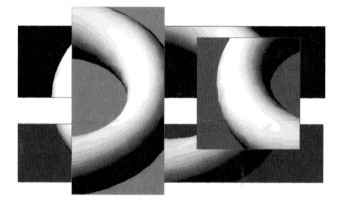

Figure 8.60   Smooth shaded images within a window clipping system.

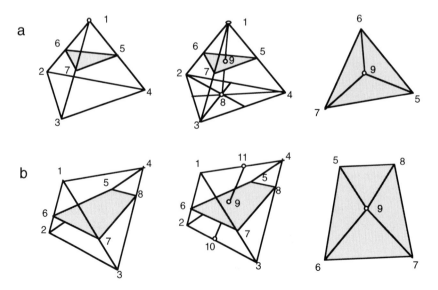

Figure 8.61   Subdividing isosurface patches within a tetrahedron.

produces a planar triangle and a planar quadrilateral. When nonlinear interpolation along edges is employed to give a more accurate definition of patch vertices, then the quadrilateral either has to be considered as a curved patch or has to be subdivided into planar triangles. If a planar patch is relatively large it is possible for its center point to be too far away from the true surface for the approximation scheme to be acceptable.

Figure 8.61 illustrates one way in which the quadrilateral and the triangular patches can be subdivided in a consistent way which will then support further subdivision if necessary. In case (a) the center of the base of the tetrahedron is linked to the apex of the tetrahedron in the way shown and the true location of the isosurface is calculated by binary subdivision along this line. The triangular patch is then subdivided by linking its vertices to this new center point. The decision whether this change should be made can be based on the difference between the position of this point along the center line and the linearly interpolated position along the same line, being greater or less than some predefined tolerance. A similar approach can be taken to case (b) except that in this case the interpolation line has to be set up between the center points of the two tetrahedron-edges which lie clear on either side of the quadrilateral patch in the way shown.

Joining the new patch center points to the vertices of the tetrahedron not only partitions the patches in the required way, it also generates new tetrahedra, each of which can be subdivided recursively until the mid-point positions of all the new planar patches fall within some tolerance of the true surface. To complete this scheme it is necessary to include a way of testing whether the mid-point of the edges of patches should also be moved to lie on the true surface. To do this, a local testing procedure is necessary if adjacency data-structures are not available.

Once the internal point of each patch has been tested, then the center points of each edge can also be tested. This can be done in a consistent way, using only local tests because of the matching subdivisions between neighboring tetrahedra, illustrated in Figure 8.62. The apex of each adjacent triangular facet can be linked to the mid-point of its base in an identical way. These lines can then be used to locate an accurate contour point, by applying binary subdivision recursively, as before, and the patch edge lines can then be linked to it in the ways shown in Figure 8.63.

Figure 8.63 illustrates the way that triangular and quadrilateral patches are subdivided so that edge splitting will not interfere with neighboring patches. An edge which does not meet the tolerance measure will trigger the subdivision of both neighboring subpatches, but the effect is contained within its local neighborhood, as shown. Although this scheme is self-consistent and works, it generates a series of null volumes in the recursive subdivision process. To avoid this, the classification in procedure **Tetrahedron** has to be extended to distinguish the nine cases shown in Figure 8.64 using the equality test sequence:

```
t := 0;
IF PointValue(a,i,j,k,Value) = V0 THEN t := t+1; END;
IF PointValue(b,i,j,k,Value) = V0 THEN t := t+2; END;
IF PointValue(c,i,j,k,Value) = V0 THEN t := t+4; END;
IF PointValue(d,i,j,k,Value) = V0 THEN t := t+8; END;
CASE t OF ....
```

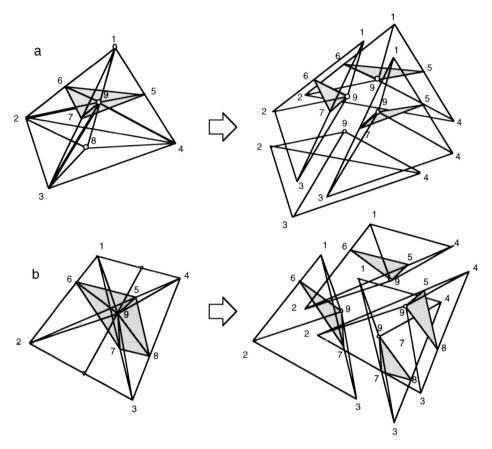

Figure 8.62   Subdivision of tetrahedral patches.

The use of the inequality test alone is unable to distinguish b3 from b1, or delete a5 and b2. In Figure 8.64 the equality test is required so that those cases where the isosurface patches pass through tetrahedral vertices can be properly identified. Cases a1, a2 and b1 all correspond to $t = 0$. Case b2 corresponds to when t is in {3,5,6,9,10,12} and a5 to when t is in {1,2,4,8}. a5 and b2 can be ignored as null patches. a3 corresponds to t is in {3,5,6,9,10,12}, a4 to t is in {7,11,13,14}, and a6 to t is in {1,2,4,8}. b3 corresponds to t is in {1,2,4,8}. All the remaining 'a' cases can be processed as triangular patches, as can b3. This leaves only b1 as a true quadrilateral patch. This more complex classification once the quadrilateral case has been subdivided in the way shown in Figure 8.62b results in all the subsequent subdivisions being of triangular patches.

This scheme works for a limited range of relatively smooth curved patches. Where the patch surface intersects the tetrahedral edges in the way shown in Figure 8.65, or when the surface does not intersect any edges at all, then this method is incomplete, and a way of subdividing the tetrahedron into sub-tetrahedra in a more appropriate way needs to be set up, as illustrated in Example 8.6.

a

b

c

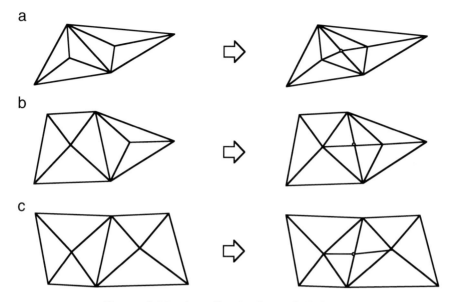

Figure 8.63   Localized edge subdivision.

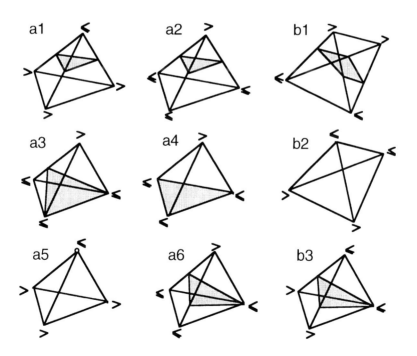

Figure 8.64   Classification of patches in a tetrahedron.

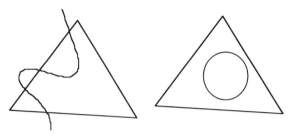

Figure 8.65 Patch intersections requiring full tetrahedral triangulation.

8.12 Blended and Parametric Surfaces

The use of isosurfaces to render implicit functions can be extended in a variety of ways. The surface is the locus of a particular value of an implicit function in space. If two functional distributions are calculated over the same space, they can be combined to give a composite distribution from which new isosurfaces can be generated. The functional values of two spheres, for example, placed at different centers, can be added together at grid point nodes and the resulting distribution contoured to give dumbell-shaped isosurfaces: an approach which was pioneered by J. Blinn in his 'Blobby' models [3]. Again there are a variety of ways in which separate distributions can be combined into one. The simplest is the Boolean combination which underlies the CSG, or constructive solid geometry, modeling technique. In Example 8.5, a model of a yellow rubber bath duck is shown generated using 'meta-balls.' This was produced by H. Sue in a series of studies exploring ways of modeling soft objects and texture mapping onto their surfaces [17].

Another series of studies is being carried out by S. Zhang [22] using a similar approximation approach for rendering parametric and blended surface patches for computer-aided design environments. Starting from a CSG or other polyhedral framework, this work sets up a triangulated polyhedral control structure made up from an ingon and an outgon polyhedron coupled together in a lattice of tetrahedra. A curved patch is then defined within each tetrahedron. These studies have been exploring the way different curved patches can be set up to satisfy continuity and smoothness criteria for an overall object surface. By expressing these patches in an implicit representation it is possible to approximate them using a similar display system to that outlined above.

In Example 8.6 the way a curved surface patch is defined by recursive subdivision of the control tetrahedron is shown. Following this the way that neighboring curved patches can be extended and blended together to give a smooth continuous join between the two original patches is illustrated. A smooth rendering of the final result is given as well as a color-coded sequence showing the two original patches and the blended area between them.

In Example 8.7 the blending of a sequence of point-based spherical functions is shown where the centers of the spheres are moved towards each other. In contrast, to the right, a study exploring the relationship between parametric patch modeling and algebraic surface patch modeling is given. In the latter case both three- and four-sided patches were used [22].

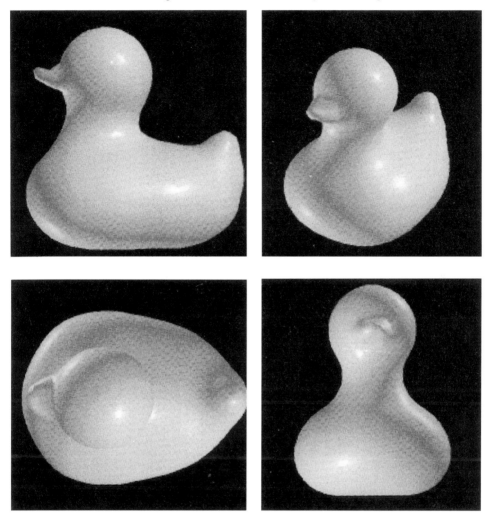

Example 8.5   Isosurfaces used to model soft objects. PhD studies, Hoylen Sue, 1995. A rubber duck modeled using 'meta-balls.' The first stage in a series of experiments on texture mapping surface information onto models of this kind. The objective was to create convincing animation sequences of soft objects being deformed, or changing shape. (Model Based Animation and Machine Vision Research Group, School of Engineering, University of Sussex.)

The reason for exploring this subdivision process in this detail is to provide a reasonably simple procedure which can be applied recursively to provide whatever level of accuracy the local situation requires. A particular case of interest is how to improve the polygonal silhouette of many smooth shaded objects. Where the normals used to calculate the illumination values at a patch's vertices indicate that the patch is virtually parallel to its viewing rays, the patch can be subdivided more finely to ensure that

A. L. Thomas

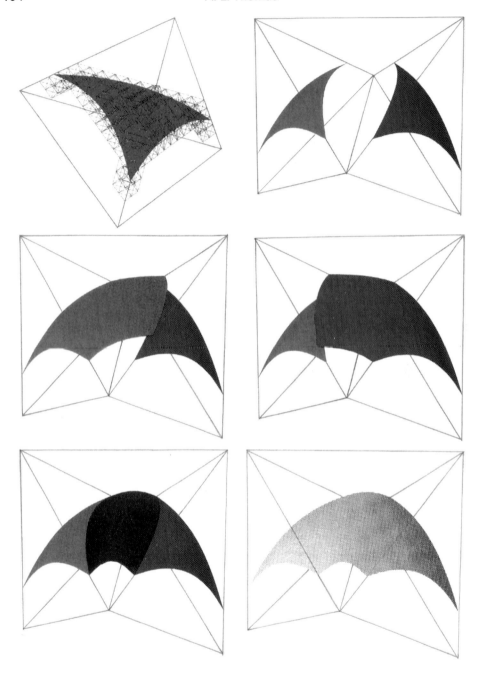

Example 8.6 Blending curved patches in a tetrahedral framework: C1 continuity (S. Zhang). (Model Based Animation and Machine Vision Research Group, School of Engineering, University of Sussex).

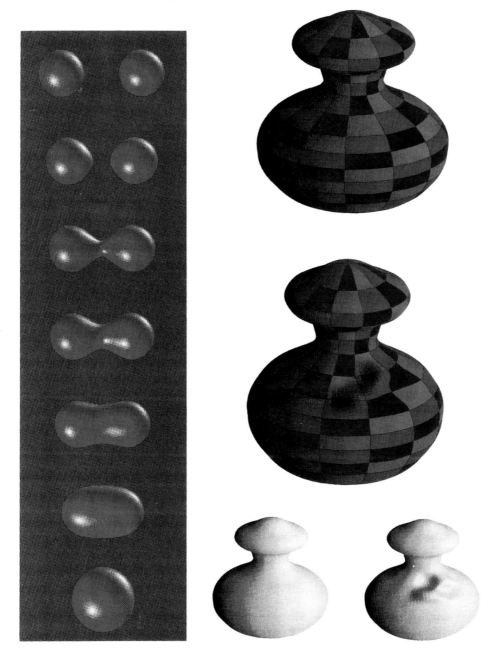

Example 8.7   Left: Metaball model of spheres joining (H. Sue). Right: Parametric patch model showing object deformation (S. Zhang). (Model Based Animation and Machine Vision Research Group, School of Engineering, University of Sussex.)

silhouette boundaries are accurately defined. Silhouette contours are important visual clues for understanding the shape of a smoothly curving surface. In the next series of studies, they were used to capture shape models directly from TV camera images.

8.13   Shape from silhouette contours

If we take a simple object against a highly contrasting background, we can extract the edge points of the object from any chosen point of view (using edge filtering). These edge points when linked up with the viewing position give a pyramid volume in which the target object must lie. If this process is carried out for the same object from points of view taken all the way round it, then the intersection of these pyramid volumes will give an approximate model of the object.

An experimental project was set up in which an object was placed in front of a TV camera and rotated to give such a systematic set of views. These were then processed to produce the required pyramids, which were then transformed into the correct overlapping spatial relationship with each other, and the Boolean intersection of the pyramids used as a CSG model to give the displays shown in Example 8.8.

In order to carry out this simple procedure it was necessary to generate the silhouette edges of the object images as a Boolean expression model. This was done in steps in the way illustrated in Figure 8.66. The silhouette of an object from a particular point of view is given in Figure 8.66a. The first step is to extract edge points using a standard image processing edge detection algorithm. The second step is to process

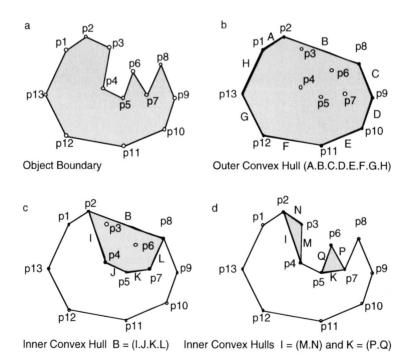

Figure 8.66   Object boundary: silhouette contour.

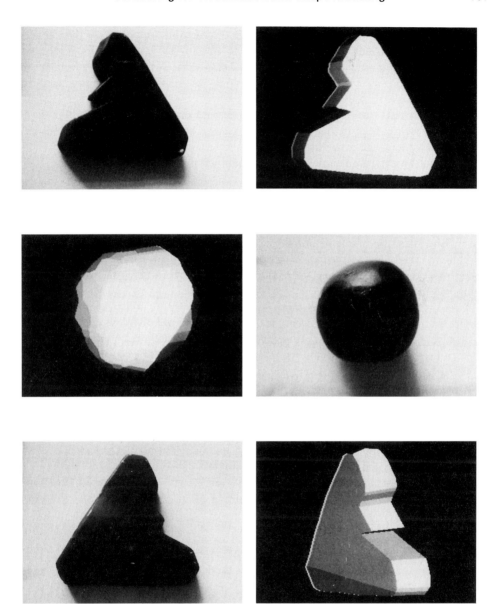

Example 8.8   Object models reconstructed from multiple silhouette contour pyramid projections being combined together and displayed as a Boolean expression model. Third-year undergraduate project, 1986, M.J. Lavington. (Model Based Animation and Machine Vision Research Group, School of Engineering, University of Sussex.)

these edge points and create their convex hull in the way shown in Figure 8.66b. All sequences of contiguous edge points not lying on this hull boundary are then collected together into sets which are then processed to obtain new convex hulls, as shown in (c). This is repeated recursively either until the size of the subset of edge points is small enough to ignore (a form of spatial filtering), or all the edge points have been accounted for.

Once the spatial decomposition has been carried out, each convex hull at its own level can be represented by the Boolean intersection or product of the edge lines of the polygon considered as plane half-spaces. These convex elements can then in turn be combined to give the Boolean expression model for this boundary in the form

$$\left(\text{A.C.D.E.F.G.H.} \left(\bar{J} + \bar{L} + (\text{M.N}) + (\text{Q.P}) \right) \right)$$

Each of these symbols corresponds to a straight line segment of this polygonal boundary. These lines can be converted into three-dimensional plane half-spaces by combining them with the viewing position in an appropriate way, giving a silhouette boundary pyramid with its apex at the eye, and tangent to the object being viewed.

These pyramid volumes taken from different viewing positions around the object illustrated in plan in Figure 8.67, can be combined by simple Boolean intersection. The advantage of using the CSG, Boolean expression modeling approach is that this operation is little more than list concatenation. The test objects and the geometric models generated from them using this approach are illustrated in Example 8.8. This process works but is limited. It can be improved. It is necessary, for example, to find some way of characterizing shape within concave areas of an object's surface which can never form part of a silhouette boundary. One possibility is to use the grayscale gradient of the interior region of a particular projection to reconstruct this shape information. In order to do this we need to examine the way in which the shading values relate to the shape of the object. The simplest of these is based on Lambert's law for the reflection from matt surfaces.

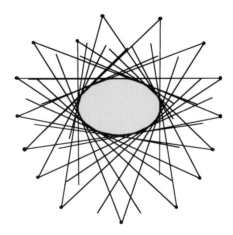

Figure 8.67   Multiple projections intersect to approximate the object.

8.14 Shape from Shading

If a surface of brightness B is viewed from different angles and if the surface is a matt surface then it will appear to be of the same brightness whatever the viewing angle. For this to be the case it can be seen by inspecting the diagrams in Figure 8.68 that a viewing tube of the same projected area A obtains its light energy from a smaller area of the surface for perpendicular directions compared to viewing the same surface from oblique directions. This means that the amount of light coming from each unit area of the surface that is being reflected in the oblique direction must be less than that in the perpendicular direction, because the area providing the reflected light in the oblique case is larger than the projected area, but the total reflected light energy is required to be the same. The same illuminating light energy is spread over more receiving area for oblique angle illumination than for perpendicular illumination, so the brightness of the surface will be greater for the perpendicular illumination than the oblique illumination.

To appear of equal brightness irrespective of the viewing direction a surface must obey Lambert's Law of reflection: $R = k.I.\cos\theta$, where R is the reflected light energy *per unit area of the surface*, and I is the incident light energy *per unit area of the surface*. θ is the angle between the normal to the surface and the viewing direction, and k is a constant related to the surface properties. The area of surface required *to give a unit projected area* will be $1/\cos\theta$, so multiplying this by R ensures that the *same projected area* of the surface will emit the same total light energy whatever the viewing angle is taken of the surface.

If a parallel beam of light is considered, illuminating a cone then, if the axis of the cone is parallel to the light direction, the illumination of the surface of the cone will be constant. If a cone with a shallower slope is taken, again with its axis parallel to the lighting direction, then a new surface of equal but different brightness will be obtained. If these two cones are intersected then it is clear that their relative positions can be

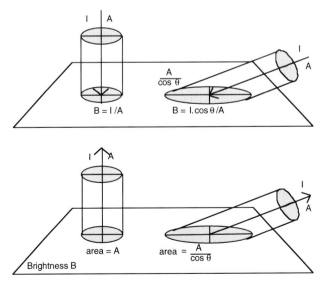

Figure 8.68 Light energy incident on and reflected from a surface.

varied in space, generating different boundaries between the two zones of brightness. This is illustrated in Figure 8.69. If it is assumed that a surface is smooth and matt, it has been shown theoretically that its shape can be derived from the illumination distribution on its surface [8]. However, the diagram in Figure 8.69 gives a more accessible portrayal of the problem. Real source data is quantized, both spatially on a grid in the case of a TV camera, and in the numerical values used in the grayscale representation. This means that though it may be possible to construct a surface cone of the kind shown, or a more sophisticated variant of it for a particular illumination value, if the light source direction is known, there is a cumulative error from the piece wise approximation of the surface using cones which results from the discrete steps in the received data.

In this visualization of the problem this is shown by the different positions in which the cones can be placed relative to each other which could still give the same grayscale distribution in a two-dimensional image. In Figure 8.70 the cross sections through a series of illumination cones are shown where the shading bands are reconstructed using

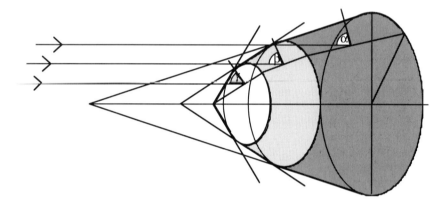

Figure 8.69   Shape reconstruction from illumination contour bands.

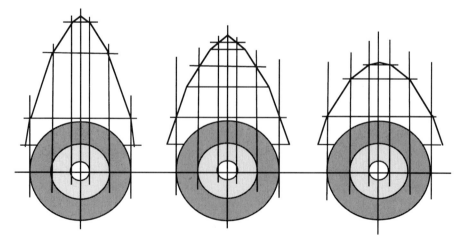

Figure 8.70   Reconstructed cross sections using equal illumination cones.

cones placed at the extreme positions which the contour boundaries make possible, and also a mid-range reconstruction. These diagrams suggest that the more contour levels there are the more tightly the reconstruction will be constrained.

8.15 Shape from Stereo Contours

Accurate reconstruction of three-dimensional objects is going to need more information than is provided by single grayscale images. It would also be useful to find a method which would work even where there were many light sources in a scene, giving complex illumination patterns on objects in the image being used to reconstruct the three-dimensional model of the scene.

The important consequences of Lambert's law are firstly that the brightness of a matt surface will depend on the strength and direction of the illuminating light falling on that surface. Secondly, the brightness distribution of an illuminated object will not be changed by changing the position it is being viewed from. This means that in stereo views of the same object the same points will appear to be of the same brightness. If Lambert's law were not being obeyed, this could not be assumed.

This property opens up one method of reconstructing an object's shape from stereo pair images. If each array of grayscale values making up each image is contoured, then it is possible to project these contours into three dimensions in the way shown in Figure 8.71. The potential advantage that this has over a similar approach applied to features in a scene is that firstly features have to be recognized, and secondly they have to be correlated with each other in the two separate stereo images; whereas the contours come from a continuous distribution, and even if the values are quantized on to a grid it is still possible to interpolate new values between the given data values.

If both eyes are centered on the same object point in space, then the centers of vision for the images seen by the two eyes should correlate automatically. If we process the contour distribution systematically out from this center, we are carrying out an ordered spatial search which automatically includes a form of cross correlation. If we explore this idea a little further we can start with the idealized geometrical layout shown in

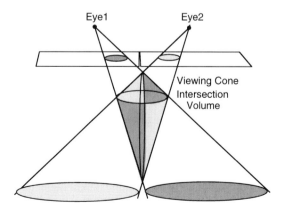

Figure 8.71 Viewing cone intersection volume for a contour ring.

Figure 8.72, where the intersection volume created by intersecting the two cones obtained from matching stereo image contours is shown.

If we could get the smooth surfaces shown in Figure 8.71 then, from a geometrical point of view, the problem would be reasonably easy to solve. However, even though we can contour the grayscales in the two stereo images as finely as we like, we have the quantization effects introduced by the pixel grid to contend with. The simplest interpolation is linear interpolation on grid lines joining the data point positions. If we assume that the location of a contour point on these grid lines can be found accurately enough for our purposes, we still have the problems generated by the straight line segments used to link these points together to give the complete contour line loops. The simplification obtained by using straight line segments is necessary to have a process which we can compute at a reasonable speed. By linking these edges to the viewing position we can generate a three-dimensional plane surface. The contour cones can then be made up, like the silhouette pyramids discussed above, by a sequence of plane half-spaces. The task then becomes one of intersecting these to obtain the intersection volume shown, and then extracting from it its equator line which will be the required three-dimensional projection of the contour we want.

In Figure 8.73 the way that this planar approximation creates inaccuracies that can create serious difficulties is illustrated. The two cones shown are convex; however, the intersection line generated by their intersection can be a saw-tooth or coronet structure of the form shown. The finer the angle between these intersecting cone surfaces the greater will be the vertical error displacement from the true line. It is necessary to find a method of smoothing this resulting intersection line to give an acceptable result.

The final study presents an exploration of a system which projects two stereo images onto a common plane in the way shown in Figure 8.74. This is set up so that the two images, obtained from aligned TV cameras or from an accurately placed beam splitter on one camera, have their raster lines parallel to the stereo axis joining the centers of the two images. This means that the images are lined up in the way shown in Figure 8.74a rather than in the unaligned way shown in (b) (which the arrangement in Figure 8.72 will produce). This means that local image comparisons can be carried out along corresponding raster lines. Figures 8.75 and 8.76 show a simulation of such a scheme

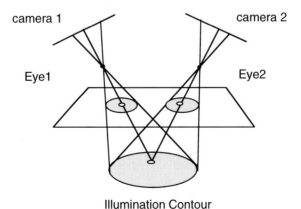

Illumination Contour

Figure 8.72   Point centered viewing.

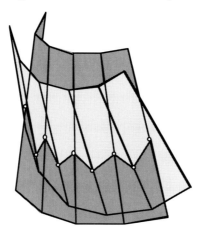

Figure 8.73   Intersecting contour cones giving a 'coronet' intersection line.

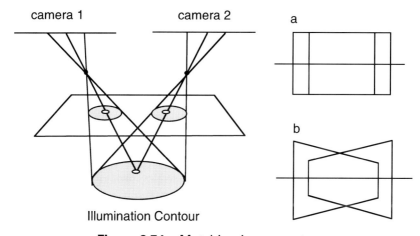

Figure 8.74   Matching image rasters.

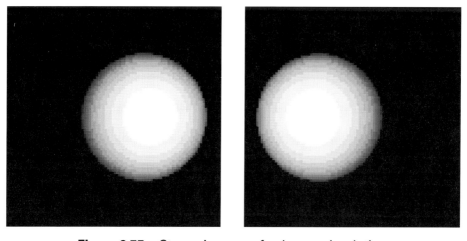

Figure 8.75   Stereo images of spheres: simulation.

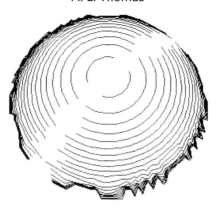

Figure 8.76   Geometric model reconstructed from stereo images.

giving the reconstructed contour lines in three dimensions. The reconstruction is shown rotated to a different viewing position from the one given in the two original images, to show the relative self-consistency of the result.

The advantage of this relatively simple approach is that contour point interpolation along raster lines avoids the worst of the errors shown in Figure 8.73. It also allows contour lines from one image to be correlated easily with contour lines from the second image. This can be done because the highest and lowest points of each contour loop theoretically fall on matching raster lines. When this is associated with the natural way that contour lines are nested in groups, it provides a highly structured framework within which to carry out feature correlation and object matching operations. Another possibility being investigated is the use of these theoretical properties to match up discrepancies between the two physical stereo channels being used to capture images. Finally, the assumption of Lambert's law as the basis of these experiments may mean that special surface treatment is necessary to allow object models to be captured in this way. However, one relatively exciting aspect of the current exploration is the observation that images in a mirror are further away than the mirror surface, so grouping and correlating contours based on Lambert's law may produce more interesting results than was originally expected when specular reflection was ignored.

Acknowledgments

Ideas, discussion, criticism and help from members of the Model Based Animation and Machine Vision research group, School of Engineering, University of Sussex: A. Cavusoglu, H. Sarnel, H. Sue, G. Jones, U. Cevik, N. Papadopoulos, D. Joyce, C. Saunders, A. Lim, S. Zhang, and B. Rey. Site data for the University of Sussex Campus was prepared by Christopher Saunders. Shape from stereo and shape from shading studies were carried out by Alan Lim. Use of Honey Hill datasets was provided by Steinitz and Rogers in the Laboratory for Computer Graphics and Spatial Analysis, in the Graduate School of Design, Harvard University.

References

[1] A. Appel, The notion of quantitative invisibility and the machine rendering of solids, *Proc. ACM 22nd National Conference*, 1967.

[2] B.G. Baumgart, *Winged Edge Polyhedral Representation*, Technical Report STAN-CS-320, Stanford University, Computer Science Dept, Palo Alto, Calif., 1972.

[3] J.F. Blinn, A generalisation of algebraic surface drawing. *ACM Trans. Graphics*, 1(3): 235–256, 1982.

[4] J.E. Bresenham, Algorithm for computer control of a digital plotter, *IBM Systems J.*, 25–30; Jan. 1965.

[5] P.G. Comba, A language for three dimensional geometry. *IBM Systems J.*, 7(3, 4); 1968.

[6] B.G. Cook, A computer representation of plane region boundaries, *Aust. Computer J.* 1; 1967.

[7] H.T. Fisher, SYMAP (1963–). Abstracts, Laboratory for Computer Graphics and Spatial Analysis, Graduate School of Design, Harvard University, I.1, 1966.

[8] B.K.P. Horn, Obtaining shape from shading information, in P.H. Winston, ed., *The Psychology of Computer Vision*, pp. 115–155, McGraw-Hill, New York, 1975.

[9] M.J. Lavington, *Automatic data entry for simple volume models*. BSc Final Year Project dissertation, School of Engineering and Applied Sciences, University of Sussex, Brighton, UK, 1986.

[10] M.E. Newell, R.G. Newell, T.L. Sancha, A new approach to the shaded picture problem, *Proc. ACM National Conference*, 1972, pp. 443–450.

[11] F. Rens. SYMVU (1967–). Abstracts, Laboratory for Computer Graphics and Spatial Analysis, Graduate School of Design, Harvard University, 1967.

[12] D. Shepard, *A Two Dimensional Interpolation Function for Computer Mapping of Irregularly Spaced Data*, Harvard Papers on Theoretical Geography, Laboratory for Computer Graphics and Spatial Analysis, Harvard University, March 1968.

[13] D. Sinton, *Views*, Abstracts, Laboratory for Computer Graphics and Spatial Analysis, Graduate School of Design, Harvard University, V45, 1969.

[14] C. Steinitz, P. Rogers et al., *Honey Hill: A Systems Analysis for Planning the Multiple Use of Controlled Water Areas*, Abstracts, Laboratory for Computer Graphics and Spatial Analysis, Graduate School of Design, Harvard University, V29, 1969.

[15] C. Steinitz, D. Sinton, *GRID: A Users Reference Manual*, Laboratory for Computer Graphics and Spatial Analysis, Graduate School of Design, Harvard University, 1968.

[16] B.F. Sprunt, *Computer generated half-tone images from digital terrain models*, MSc dissertation, Department of Mathematics, University of Southampton, UK, 1969.

[17] H. Sue, *Implicit models for computer animation*, PhD thesis, Model Based Animation and Machine Vision Group, School of Engineering, University of Sussex, Brighton, UK, 1994.

[18] A.L. Thomas, *OBLIX: A Two and Three Dimensional Mapping Program for Use with Line Plotters*, Abstracts, Laboratory for Computer Graphics and Spatial Analysis, Graduate School of Design, Harvard University, V50, 1969.

[19] A.L. Thomas, *Spatial models in computer based information sytems*, PhD thesis, University of Edinburgh, 1976.

[20] A.L. Thomas, T.C. Waugh, *GIMMS: Geographic Information Management and Mapping System*, Manual, Leyland Systems, Boston, Mass., 1970.

[21] T.C. Waugh, *GIMMS: Geographic Information Management and Mapping System*, Reference Manual, Program Library Unit, Edinburgh University, 1975.

[22] S. Zhang, A.L. Thomas, Free-form surface construction using Gregory patches, *Proc. Third International Conference in Central Europe on Computer Graphics and Visualisation*, 1995, pp. 338–346.

9
Fast Rendering of Participating Media in a Global Illumination Application

Laurent Da Dalto and Jean-Pierre Jessel

9.1 Introduction

During recent years, rendering methods have become increasingly close to reality. However, the memory and computation cost of these methods also increased strongly and required more powerful architectures. With the ability to make more calculations in less time and the development of large storage units, new methods of rendering appeared, taking physical and optical properties of the scenes into account. In spite of this evolution, equations representing these properties are not easy to solve and their storage costs are very significant.

The study of materials and light properties has been developed (in our research group also) but the application of participating media theory seems to be more difficult. This theory is very complex to apply in a rendering application because of the number and the complexity of equations required to represent such a medium. There are two kinds of existing methods. The first are analytic methods, in which the authors tried to simplify the mathematical model so they could solve the equations. It is necessary to find a way to solve the radiative transfer equation of the medium, which is a very complex integro-differential equation. Therefore, several restrictions are necessary to make this equation analytically soluable. Blinn [2] was the first to represent a gaseous phenomenon (Saturn's rings) but he made many simplifications to succeed in his simulation (low albedo medium, only simple scattering taken into account). Max [5] also used the model presented by Blinn but added shading volumes to take light sources into account. Finally, Nishita [7] also used an analytic method to represent participating media, with the restriction that the medium must have a uniform density. The volumes are represented by curved patches and he also used shading volumes.

Analytic methods are not very accurate for representing gaseous phenomena because they involve some restrictions on the medium properties (densities, scattering, isotropic medium, etc.). Therefore, other methods which do not modify the media properties have been presented. First there are statistic methods. One of the most famous of this family is the Monte Carlo method. Typically, this method allows the simulation of radiative transfers into the medium and the scene using the 'random walk.' This means that a probability distribution is associated with each property. This method requires considerable time to come close to reality and the errors generated are not easily controlled. Pattanaik [8] and Blasi [1] have developed this method.

Rushmeier [11] used the zonal method, which is close to the radiosity method, to compute the interaction between volumes and objects in the scene. Thus, she computed three kinds of form factors: volume–volume, volume–object, and object–object (classical form factor). However, the medium must be isotropic and this method takes only simple scattering into account. It is possible to apply this method to anisotropic media or media with high albedo, but the computation times are very considerable and it is very hard to implement.

The flows methods are more accurate than the zonal method. The aim of these methods is not to resolve an integro-differential equation (the radiative transfer equation for the medium) but to transform this equation in an equation system with partial derivatives. In order to this, it is necessary to separate the spatial dependence and the angular dependence of the luminance. Two important flow methods have been presented: spherical harmonics and discrete ordinates. The first is very suitable for isotropic media but requires a lot of computation time and memory for anisotropic media. It has been used by Kajiya [3]. The second one samples the volume into 'voxels' and the angular space in solid angles where the luminance is supposed uniform. Each voxel has a constant density. The method computes the propagation of the light energy through the voxels of the medium for each direction representing a solid angle. With this algorithm, it is possible to represent media with various albedos and to take multiple scattering into account. This method has been used by Patmore [9] and Languénou [4].

The aim of our work is to represent participating media as accurately as possible. This chapter describes a new method allowing the representation of media without constraint of size or number and with all their optical and physical properties. First, we introduce our representation model of the participating media. Then we will show how it was included in our global illumination application. Finally, we discuss the interest of such a model and present some results.

9.2   The Volume Representation

9.2.1   Shapes

In our application, any kind of analytical shape is accepted. The most basic shape is the sphere but this can be extended to ellipsoids, and more complex shapes created by the association of two or more basic shapes. Thus, we can use parallelepipeds created by the association of slabs. The shape can be extended to metaballs or to basic shapes distorted by noise in the form of any kind of perturbation functions (such as wavelets).

Any modelization based on analytic computation is possible and offers a wide range of possible volume shapes. However, as we will see below, the shape is not the most important parameter for representing realistic participating media. It is only used to determine the frontier of the medium. The realism is based more on the variation of the optical parameters than on the shape.

9.2.2   Properties

If we consider a point in the volume, it can be associated with a particle in the medium (or a molecule, depending on its size). The light energy entering the point is partly absorbed, partly scattered, partly reemitted. The point itself can emit light energy in a direction under consideration. These properties can be applied to all the points in the medium, giving it the same properties. These phenomena are represented in Figure 9.1.

In a real medium, these properties are very hard to evaluate because they can vary from one point to another in the same volume. Most of the latest proposed models require that at least one parameter be constant or uniform within the medium [4]. Therefore, a large number of small basic volumes is needed to approach a realistic medium. This is memory-expensive and requires more computation time to render. We therefore propose a new way of representing parameter variations without making any restrictive assumptions about the physical and optical phenomena.

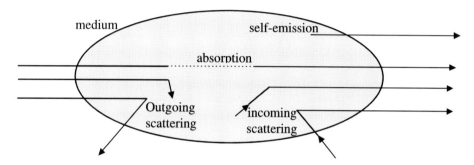

Figure 9.1 Optical phenomena associated with a participating medium.

Absorption and self-emission

The optical and physical properties of the volume are computed and stored only for the center point. Any other point of the medium is computed by taking distance and direction to the center point into account. Thus the self-emission and the absorption coefficients are defined a priori by the user for the center point. If we define only the coefficient value, we cannot have varying properties in the medium. Therefore, we associate with each property a propagation direction and function. This determines how the parameter representing the property will vary in the medium.

With this structure defined, we can compute the property of any other point of the volume using the equation

$$V_P = V_C \times Fx(Dist \times Direction.CP) \tag{1}$$

where V_C and V_P are the values of the current property for the center point and for the considered point, Fx is the propagation function, and C, P, CP, $Dist$ and $Direction$ are as defined in Figure 9.2.

If we define neither $Direction$ nor Fx then the property is considered uniform over the medium. If we define only Fx, then we consider that there is a circular variation of the parameter from the center to the volume borders. If we use a basic linear variation of the property then the distribution function Fx is replaced by a variation coefficient along the direction defined. Finally, in the most general case, we can use a nonlinear function (using exponent, cosines, powers, etc.) which will be applied as defined in (1).

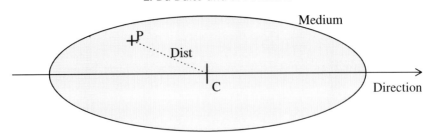

Figure 9.2   Definition of medium parameters.

With this model, we can have a wide range of variation for both absorption and self-emission. These properties are independent and therefore will be represented by two independent models. Moreover, the computation of the parameter value for one point of the medium does not require a great amount of time (depending on the propagation function complexity).

The self-emission and the absorption are the parameters of the volume that are easiest to compute because they are neither incoming nor outgoing direction dependent. The last parameter, the multiple scattering, needs a more complex definition, we will discuss now.

Multiple scattering
To model the multiple scattering, we must define the *phase function*. This function $\varphi(D_1, D_2)$ expresses the ratio of energy outgoing in the direction D_1 compared to the energy incoming from direction D_2. It incorporates two important properties that result directly from physics of light. D_1 and D_2 are defined as three dimensions vectors from V.

First, due to *Helmholtz reciprocity rule*, φ is symmetric relative to D_1 and D_2:

$$\forall\, D_1 \in V \qquad \forall\, D_2 \in V \qquad \varphi(D_1, D_2) = \varphi(D_2, D_1) \tag{2}$$

Second, due to the *energy conservation law*, φ has to fulfil the normalization condition

$$\forall\, D_1 \in V \qquad \frac{1}{4\pi} \int_{D_2 \in V} \varphi(D_1, D_2)\, dD_2 = 1 \tag{3}$$

Furthermore, φ is usually symmetric around the incident direction of the light and therefore $\varphi(D_1, D_2)$ depends only on the angle θ between D_1 and D_2. Therefore we can use θ as the only parameter of the phase function φ.

Let us briefly propose several phase functions detailed in [2].

Isotropic phase function
The simplest expression for φ is to suppose isotropic scattering:

$$\varphi(t) = 1 \qquad \text{where } t = \cos\theta \tag{4}$$

This is a good way to approximate the phase function without slowing down the application. Moreover, in a realistic medium (such as a cloud under natural sky lighting), this approximation can be very close to reality.

Rayleigh phase function
When particles are small compared to the wavelength, j is given by Rayleigh equation:

$$\varphi(t) = \frac{3}{4}(1 + t^2) \tag{5}$$

Mie phase function
When the particles are large compared to the wavelength, φ is given by Mie equation. Two useful approximations for foggy atmospheres are proposed [7]. The first one for hazy atmospheres is

$$\varphi(t) = \frac{1}{2} + \frac{9}{2}\left(\frac{1+t}{2}\right)^8 \tag{6}$$

And the second one for murky atmospheres is

$$\varphi(t) = \frac{1}{2} + \frac{33}{2}\left(\frac{1+t}{2}\right)^{32} \tag{7}$$

Henyey–Bernstein phase function
Henyey and Bernstein proposed a family of phase functions that has shown a good match to experimental data and permits to representation of a wide range of phase functions. The base equation for this family is

$$\varphi_k(t) = \frac{1 - k^2}{(1 - 2kt + k^2)^{1.5}} \quad \text{where } k \in \;]-1, 1[\tag{8}$$

The main advantage of Henyey–Bernstein phase functions is that they provide a continuum between forward scattering $(k>0)$, isotropic scattering $(k=0)$, and backward scattering $(k<0)$ (Figure 9.3).

Moreover, by taking a normalized sum of several $\varphi_k(t)$ with different values for k, many different phase functions can be obtained:

$$\varphi_k(t) = \sum_{i=1}^{n} r_i \varphi_{k_i}(t) \quad \text{where } \sum_{i=1}^{n} r_i = 1 \tag{9}$$

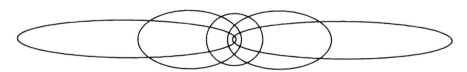

Figure 9.3   Henyey–Bernstein phase function for $k = -0.9, -0.6, 0, 0.6, 0.9$.

We implement this family of functions. Even if its expression is more complex than others, it permits the representation of numerous phase functions by making k vary and adding one to another. For example, isotropic and Rayleigh functions are very easy to represent using this model.

In our case, we assume the phase function is the same for all the particles (or the molecules) inside a volume. In fact, realistic media are composed of many different phase functions, but it is possible to approximate this by combining two or more media with different phase functions. In this case, the other parameters (absorption and self-emission) would be counted many times and therefore it is necessary to adapt them.

Multiple scattering implementation

As for the other parameters, the multiple scattering is stored only for the center point of the volume. From the phase function and depending on the direction of incoming energy, we can create a distribution function of this energy over the sphere. We therefore made a new structure containing the light energy reemitted in each direction. This is represented by the function $\phi(\theta, \gamma)$, where θ is the azimuth angle and γ the elevation angle. In order to implement this function, it must be sampled. Therefore the sphere, scanned by (θ, γ), is sampled into discrete values. We decided to sample the sphere in 26 points with a regular distribution.

We also need to store the lighting direction, which is the direction defined by the light source and the center point. Thus, we can determine the energy loss and compute the exact multiple scattering value for each point in the volume.

An error arises if we consider the multiple scattering function to be the same for all points of the medium (taking only the loss coefficient into account). In this case, we assume that the light rays entering the volume are all parallel. This can be true for a sufficiently distant light source, but it leads to a significant error if the source is near the medium. Therefore, in order to consider this parameter, we apply a rotation to the scattering function depending on the position of the point in the volume (see Figure 9.4). This computation is necessary if we want to take into account the real position of the light source.

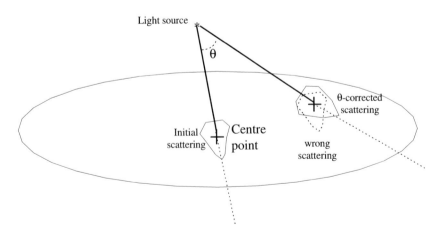

Figure 9.4   Multiple scattering correction.

Finally, when we need to know the scattering value, it is only for a considered direction. Therefore, we need to apply an interpolation computation between the sampled directions in order to compute the true value (linear approximation) of the selected direction.

While rendering, we need to know the energy contribution of each lighting source, so we store a multiple scattering function for each source illuminating the volume. For the light sources emitting energy below a minimum luminance value determined *a priori* by the user, we use a single function representing the participation of all these sources. The reason this individual storage will be detailed in the illumination process (section 4.3).

9.3   Volume Traversal

The model presented above has been implemented in a global illumination method. We use a grid of voxels to speed up the ray shooting [6]. Moreover, the illumination phase generates adaptive subdivision of objects depending on the shadows created [10]. This application can be executed using a parallel architecture of heterogeneous machines (controlled by PVM).

During the illumination and the rendering phases, many rays will be shot. We must take the existence of participating media into account. Therefore, each time a ray is shot, a new algorithm is applied. For each ray shot, we compute the intersection between the ray and each volume in the scene. If a medium is encountered before reaching a solid object then the medium participating updates the energy carried by the ray.

The principle is always the same for a particular ray:

```
FOR each volume in the scene DO
     IF there is an intersection between volume and ray THEN
          PtIn = Entering point of the ray into the volume
          PtOut = Outgoing point of the ray
          Pt = First intersection with a solid object
          IF Pt encountered before PtIn THEN
               The medium is behind the object => no need to take its participation
                                             into account
          ELSE
               IF Pt encountered before PtOut THEN
                    Update EnergyRay from PtIn to Pt (the object is in the volume).
               ELSE
                    Update EnergyRay from PtIn to PtOut.
               ENDIF
          ENDIF
     ENDIF
ENDFOR
```

This algorithm shows that we can consider volume-crossing objects or volume-containing objects, which is very useful (for example, we can model a planetary atmosphere by including the planet in a spherical volume representing the atmosphere). For the moment, we use only convex shapes for representing a medium, so we have only one entering and leaving point for a selected volume.

If a ray crosses a medium, we must compute its energy variation due to the volume. For this, we sample the ray into the volume by taking regular spaced points along its path (see Figure 9.5). Only the latest sample is not regular because it depends on the position of the leaving point along the ray path.

We compute the value of each property of the medium for each point sampled (self-emission, scattering, and absorption). The first two properties can be considered as point values. The absorption must be computed along the distance between two sampled points. This is done using Bouguer's law expressing the attenuation A between two points P and P':

$$A(P, P') = e^{-\tau(P, P')} \tag{10}$$

where t is the optical depth between P and P'. The optical depth can be defined by an absorption coefficient α and a scattering coefficient σ:

$$\tau(P, P') = \int_P^{P'} \alpha(P'')\, dP'' + \int_P^{P'} \sigma(P'')\, dP'' \tag{11}$$

In our case, we define β as the absorption coefficient stored for the center point and corresponding to the ratio of energy absorbed along a unit path. This coefficient takes the simple scattering into account. Thus, equation (11) could be rewritten:

$$\tau(P, P') = \int_P^{P'} \beta(P'')\, dP'' \tag{12}$$

It is important to emphasize that self-emission and absorption will not vary during the illumination, whereas the multiple scattering function will be updated at each phase. Therefore, when we consider the scattering, we only take a part of the total light energy scattered into account. However, it is impossible to consider the total energy scattered until we reach the radiosity convergence, that is when all the energy has been distributed into the scene (mathematical convergence).

9.4　Illumination Process

During the illumination process, media are considered like objects in the scene but are selected and illuminated using a different algorithm. In fact, for one selected source, we

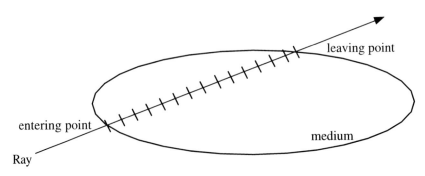

Figure 9.5　Sampling of a ray crossing a medium.

first compute the medium illumination and then illuminate the solid objects. This sequence is not an arbitrary selection. It is important because the illumination of a medium creates a new multiple scattering function linked to the current light source. When we illuminate the other objects, there may be media between light and selected objects. This sequence permits one to consider the multiple scattering factor due to the light source under consideration when the visibility ray crosses participating media.

9.4.1   Volume illumination

In a classical global illumination application, we compute the form factor between the selected light emitter and all the objects in the scene. We use the extended progressive radiosity process to compute these illuminations.

First, a light source is selected as the most emissive patch in the scene. Now we have to compute the form factor between this patch (represented by a triangular face) and the volumes. However, we cannot compute a classical form factor because the volume is not represented by a patch. It is necessary to create a new algorithm for this step.

We shoot a ray (or several rays) from the light source to the center point of the volume. We compute the energy attenuation due to the distance between the light source and the entering point. Then, we apply the traversal sampling algorithm described before from the entering point of the ray in the volume to the center point. This give us the true amount of energy entering into the center point. Using the phase function, we distribute this energy in all the sampled directions as described before. Thus, we create the multiple scattering function associated with the current light source. In the work so far, objects or media existing between the light source and the medium under consideration are not taken into account so, for the moment, shadows created by others objects upon the volume are not computed (see Figure 9.6).

The shadows problem is not resolvable during the illumination process. Considering that we have represented a medium by its center point, it is impossible to compute the shape of the shadows cast onto the volume without considering each point (or at least each point at its border). We will show how this phenomenon can be taken into account during the rendering process.

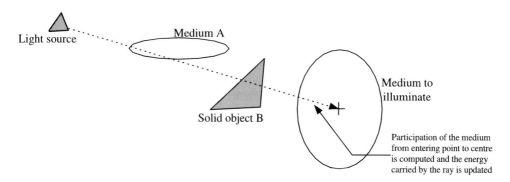

Figure 9.6   Medium illuminated by a selected patch source. Neither medium participation of *A* nor occlusion of *B* is taken into account: the ray always reaches the center of the medium to be illuminated.

9.4.2   Solid object illumination

The illumination process for solid objects is not essentially different from the classical global illumination process. As before, we compute the form factor between the light source patch and the selected object patch to be illuminated, but now we consider also the media existing between the two patches. These volumes may and will update the light energy carried by the ray shot. The medium may contain the light emitter or the patch to be illuminated or may just be in the path of the ray between the two objects (see Figure 9.7). This step creates the shadows of the media upon the solid objects. They may be real shadows or (if the media have important scattering and self-emission values) highlighted spots corresponding to the shadows.

9.4.3   Computing shadows on volumes

At present, shadows on volumes are not considered. Under real illumination, this phenomenon may be very important. Shadows contribute to the illumination in two ways. The first may be called *direct shadow* and is represented by the shadows made by objects or other media on a volume under consideration. The second is *indirect shadow*, which is the shadows created on the objects behind the volume. For example, if there is a patch between the light source and an object, there is a shadow on this object. Now if a medium is created between the object and the occluder then there is a direct shadow of the occluder on the volume and an indirect shadow of the occluder on the object. These two phenomena must be considered using different algorithms.

Direct shadows
If an object occludes a volume partly or totally, the light contribution of the occluded source is not considered. This is why we store each light contribution in a different multiple scattering function. The absorption and the self-emission values will not be modified.

When we compute the real multiple scattering SC, we sum each scattering function SC_i where i varies from 1 to the number N of sources illuminating the volume:

$$SC = \sum_{i=1}^{N} SC_i \qquad (13)$$

Now we shoot a ray from the selected point in the volume to each stored light source. If the ray reaches another object before hitting the light source then this light source

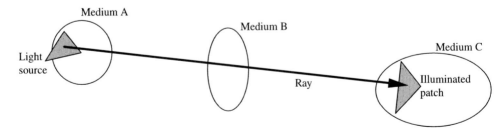

Figure 9.7   Solid object illumination. The ray traversals of the media *A, B,* and *C* are computed and update the energy carried by the ray.

does not illuminate a selected point in the volume. Thus, for this point the equation becomes

$$SC = \sum_{i=1}^{N} \delta_i SC_i \quad \text{where } \delta_i = 1 \text{ if the source illuminates the patch else } \delta_i = 0 \quad (14)$$

and so on for each light source that does not contribute to the point illumination. Thus, we compute the real scattering for each point sampled in the volume and we create shadows on the volume. Making this computation for each point sampled in the volume, we also take into account the effects of the shadows in the volume (see Figure 9.8).

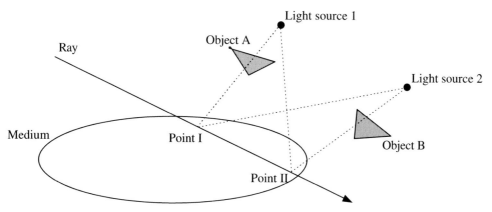

Figure 9.8   Direct shadows on the volumes. *A* creates a shadow on I by the occlusion of 1 (but I is illuminated by 2); similarly for *B* creating a shadow on II by the occlusion of 2 (but II is illuminated by 1).

Indirect shadows

The indirect shadow phenomenon is very easy to consider. In fact, it can be associated with the shadow created by one object on another modified by one or more media existing between the two objects.

In classical illumination, if the object to be illuminated is occluded by another then the form factor does not need to be computed. Now, even if the light source does not reach the selected object, we compute the energy that may be collected due to the media traversal (self-emissive and scattered energy). Thus, we consider the shadow as a direct shadow in a classical way and update the energy returned by the ray shot to create the real indirect shadow.

9.5   Rendering process

During this step, rays are shot from the observer into the scene. Now we must consider the contributions of the participating media and render them. We compute the ray intersection with all the media in the scene. In our classical application, we only need to know the first intersection with solid objects and, thus, compute the pixel color. We always compute the first object intersection, but before returning the pixel color we need to determine whether the ray intersects some media before reaching the object. Moreover, if the ray leaves the scene without hitting anything, it is also very important to determine whether or not it crosses any media before exiting.

We can rewrite the classical rendering process in the following algorithm:

```
FOR each pixel of the viewer screen DO
    PtObj = First intersection point of the ray with an object
    IF PtObj Exists THEN        // There is an intersection with a solid object
        Compute PixelColor using classical ray shooting
        FOR each volume DO
            IF the ray intersects the volume before reaching the object THEN
                Update PixelColor considering volume traversal
            ENDIF
        ENDFOR
    ELSE                        // There is no intersection with a solid object
        PixelColor = BackGround Color
        FOR each volume DO
            IF the ray intersects the volume THEN
                Update PixelColor considering volume traversal
            ENDIF
        ENDFOR
    ENDIF
ENDFOR
```

There are two cases. The first is when the ray intersects an object; then we must compute only the participation of the media along the path of the ray before reaching the object (or the media that contain the selected object). The second is when the ray leaves the scene; then we just compute all the volume participation existing.

9.6   Results

So far we have only worked on very basic scenes because the aim of our research was first to represent media with their real properties. In a basic scene with only one medium and one or two objects, we can easily study the effect of single parameter variations. Once parameter variations are well known, we will be able to produce more complex scenes.

Plate 24 shows the shadows created by an object on a volume and on another object (what we call direct and indirect shadows). We can also see the shadow created by the volume on the largest object. The medium is not self-emitting. Its density varies from front to back and we can see the halo created by the primary light source inside this medium.

Plate 25 is a simulation of a planet with a visible atmosphere. The planet is completely included in the volume. The medium emits blue light and has a small absorption coefficient. We can see the side of the planet which is illuminated by the primary light source (a large sun) as well as its dark side.

Plate 26 is a representation of a self-emitting medium (here a surrealistic flame). This flame can be put in a realistic scene to represent fire. The boundaries are too sharp but we can remove this visual problem by adding perturbation functions to the volume modeling.

Finally, Plate 27 is a more complex scene representing a room with foggy atmosphere. All the computations are made using the global illumination process. It takes four hours to compute on an IRIX 4 system which is relatively quick. As we see, with our model, we can represent either large media (like the atmosphere) or smaller media (like fog or fire) without any algorithm modification. Moreover, this representation is rather quick and easy to make.

9.7   Conclusion and Future Directions

With this new approach for modeling participating media, we have strongly reduced the time and the memory costs for representing media. All optical and physical properties are represented and can vary inside the medium. These variations can be nonlinear using any analytic function (even very complex ones). All shadows are computed, even those created by volumes or objects on a medium. This phenomenon, which can be very difficult to consider, is very easy to take into account using our method. We can use any kind of analytic volume to represent a medium. So far we have only used ellipsoid or parallelepiped models. Furthermore, it is possible to introduce objects into the media without modifying the algorithm. Objects may be partly or completely included in a volume; the algorithm is the same in both cases. Unfortunately, for the moment, we must make some assumptions for the scene geometry: the primary source may not be inserted into a medium.

We have also begun the implementation of realistic materials (with bidirectional reflectance) and realistic lights (with spectral and spatial distribution). This will allow us to create scenes based on realistic physical and optical properties.

This work is developed in association with CESR (Centre d'Etude Spatial des Rayonnements), which provides theoretical tools and realistic data. The aim of the association is to represent radiative transfers into a forest. We aim to be able to study the way a forest grows depending on the light energy it receives.

Finally, we plan to further develop this method. We would like to be able to create more complex media using more complex geometrical shapes. For example, we could use wavelets or implicit functions to disturb the shape of the volume. We will also use more complex variation functions for the medium parameters. These functions will create the perturbations needed to represent realistic media without using very complex shapes (in this case, the volume shape will represent the spatial space where the phenomenon must be considered). It seems that this solution is the easiest and the best way to create realistic media such as clouds. Some details need to be corrected, such as media illumination and relations between medium and solid objects. We will develop our model further to consider these phenomena.

Bibliography

[1] P. Blasi, B. Le Saëc, C. Schlick, A rendering algorithm for discrete volume density objects, *Proc. Eurographics 93*, 12(3), Barcelona, September 1993, pp. 201–210.

[2] J. Blinn, Light reflection functions for simulation of clouds and dusty surfaces (Proc. SIGGRAPH'82, Boston, Mass., 1982), *Computer Graphics* 16(3): 21–29; 1982.

[3] J.T. Kajiya, B.P. Von Herzen, Ray tracing volume densities (Proc. SIGGRAPH'84, Minneapolis, Minn., 1984), *Computer Graphics* 18(3): 165–174, 1984.

[4] E. Languénou, K. Bouatouch, M. Chelle, Global illumination in presence of participating media with general properties, *5th Eurographics Workshop on Rendering*, Darmstadt, 1994, pp. 69–85.

[5] N. Max, Light diffusion through clouds and haze, *Computer Vision, Graphics and Image Processing* 33: 280–292; 1986.

[6] C. Metge, R. Caubet, A discrete global illumination method, *Proc. 4th Discrete Geometry for Computer Imagery*, September 1994, pp. 100–120.

[7] T. Nishita, Y. Miyawaki, E. Nakamae, A shading model for atmospheric scattering considering luminous intensity distribution of light sources, Proc. SIGGRAPH'87, Anaheim, Calif., 1987), *Computer Graphics* 21(4): 303–310; 1987.

[8] S.N. Pattanaik, *Computational methods for global illumination and visualisation of complex 3D environments*, PhD thesis, Birla Institute of Technology and Science, India, February 1993.

[9] C. Patmore, Simulated multiple scattering for cloud rendering, *ICCG 93 Conference Proc. IFIP*, 1993, pp. 59–71.

[10] M. Paulin, J.P. Jessel, Adaptative mesh generation for progressive radiosity: a ray-tracing based algorithm, *Proc. Eurographics 94*, Oslo, 1994, pp. 421–432.

[11] H. Rushmeier, K. Torrance, The zonal method for calculating light intensities in the presence of a participating medium, Proc. SIGGRAPH'87, Anaheim, Calif., 1987, *Computer Graphics* 21(4): 293–302; 1987.

10
Comparison between Different Rasterization Methods for Implicit Surfaces

Nilo Stolte and René Caubet

10.1 Introduction

Implicit surfaces can be defined by functions of the kind:

$$F(x, y, z) = 0$$

An interesting property of this kind of function is its ability to determine whether a point is inside (when $F(x, y, z) < 0$), outside (when $F(x, y, z) > 0$), or on (when $F(x, y, z) = 0$) the surface. The sphere ($x^2 + y^2 + z^2 - r^2 = 0$, where r is the ray) and the plane ($ax + by + cz + d = 0$, where a, b, and c are the normal vector components and d is an arbitrary constant) equations are the simplest examples of implicit functions. All implicit functions that can be completely defined analytically are called *analytical implicit functions*. These are the functions that are considered in this article. There are still other kinds of implicit surfaces that cannot be expressed analytically, which are called *procedural implicit functions*, since they are defined procedurally [4]. The surfaces of this kind must rely on other representations to estimate the normal vector, since they do not allow derivative calculations [13]. Conversely, in analytic implicit functions the normal vector can be calculated by deriving the function equation in relationship to each axis, applying the point coordinates to the derivatives expressions, and normalizing the vector. In other words, each component of the normal vector first has the same components as the gradient in the point and is normalized afterwards.

The analytic implicit functions can be subdivided into two main groups: algebraic implicit functions and nonalgebraic implicit functions. The algebraic implicit functions [14] can be reduced to polynomials by algebraic manipulation, that is, they contain only arithmetic operations and integer powers.

Nonalgebraic surfaces cannot be reduced to polynomials. One particularly useful example is the 'blobby model' [1, 3, 12] where negative algebraic expressions are placed as exponents of exponential functions. These exponential functions are added (and/or subtracted) and made equal to a constant (C, below):

$$\sum_{i=0}^{n} b_i \cdot e^{-a_i f_i(x,y,z)} = C$$

When the objects are quite near one to the other, the resulting surface is a fusion between the several algebraic surfaces in the exponents. This fusion is controlled by the parameters a_i and b_i which change the exponential form. The exponential is used as a *blending function* (Figure 10.1) which gives the amount of mixing in relationship to the distance from the functions' ($f_i(x, y, z)$) origins. The main interest of this kind of surface is modeling and animation facilities. Other advantages are the exact simulation of certain physical phenomena: electron clouds, molecules, isopotential fields, etc.

Similar effects can be obtained with algebraic surfaces. Addition of two exponential functions in the 'blobby model' corresponds to multiplying the two algebraic functions that were in the exponents in the 'blobby model' [14]. The disadvantage of using this kind of algebraic surface is that the modeling and animation facilities are reduced. Nevertheless, polynomial blending functions [2, 5] (Figure 10.2) allowed even more flexibility in animation and modeling than exponential blending functions. If the functions to be blended are algebraic and polynomial blending functions are used, the implicit function obtained is algebraic. However, this kind of algebraic surface is very flexible and even simpler to manipulate than 'blobby models.' Blending nonalgebraic functions allows a wider variety of forms, but the resulting surface is nonalgebraic.

Algebraic surfaces are more easily rendered than nonalgebraic surfaces. Ray tracing algebraic surfaces of arbitrary order is straightforward using Collins's theorem [9]. Numerical techniques for ray tracing nonalgebraic surfaces are generally unstable. An elegant method for ray tracing this kind of surface was proposed by Kalra and Barr [10]. They calculate Lipschitz constants to subdivide the surface and to ray trace it. The method always converges and works for algebraic and nonalgebraic surfaces.

Duff [6] proposed another method for ray tracing CSG trees of algebraic surfaces, but the subdivision method works also for nonalgebraic implicit surfaces. The basic

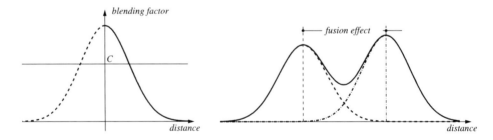

Figure 10.1 'Blobby model' blending function and its effects.

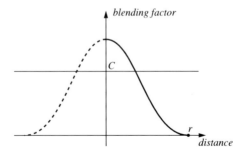

Figure 10.2 Polynomial blending function.

principle is the same as in Kalra and Barr [10]: subdivide the surface until a certain level and ray trace the surfaces contained in the subregions crossed by a ray. To subdivide the implicit functions he uses interval arithmetic. In fact, Kalra and Barr's method 'is a sort of interval arithmetic without intervals' [6].

Taubin [21, 22] presented a method for rasterizing implicit algebraic curves which can also rasterize implicit algebraic surfaces [22]. Although showing the surfaces directly in the 'voxel' format, he suggests converting the voxels into polygons using a technique known as 'marching cubes' [11] and afterwards using conventional methods to render the polygons. We propose the direct visualization of the voxel volume by keeping the normal vector in the middle of the voxels and using a high subdivision level. To avoid the high memory consumption we store the voxels in an octree. This approach allows us to render the surfaces using our fast discrete ray tracing [16–19], or a Z-buffer algorithm considering each voxel a point of the surface. This latter visualization method significantly enhances the interactivity with no loss in image quality, but with less realism than in ray tracing generated images. The image quality is generally better than using polygons. In the case when all projected polygons are smaller than a pixel, the quality obtained is equivalent. Nevertheless, we still have the advantage that it does not require polygonization.

Bloomenthal and Wyvill [4] have presented several techniques for modeling implicit surfaces. We do not claim interactive modeling in our method but an acceptable level of interactivity in the visualization process. Nevertheless, a good interactive modeling level can be obtained by limiting the voxel space resolution, which allows faster prototyping as proposed in Bloomenthal and Wyvill [4]. Bloomenthal and Wyvill [4] recommend octree display, as proposed here, for a coarse representation of the surface or for volume rendering hardware. The advances in graphics hardware and the memory lowering prices in these later years are drastically changing this situation. Even software advances have contributed to reversing this situation. An example is the adaptive subdivision method proposed by Duff [6]. Instead of calculating curvatures as observed in [2], this subdivision method uses simple interval arithmetic, which is computationally inexpensive on most of today's machines.

On the other hand, near real-time interactive modeling could be achieved using our method with special blending functions. 'Blobby' models use exponentials as blending functions (Figure 10.1) with negative exponents. An inconvenience of using these blending functions is that their values are never zero. This implies that a full function evaluation is needed to calculate its value. If a huge number of functions are considered, as in biological molecular models, the rasterization is very time-consuming. In these cases approximations usually have to be made [3, 7], which are often undesirable. To avoid these problems, other kinds of blending functions can be used [2, 5]. We can design blending functions that go to zero for a relatively short distance. We show in Figure 10.2 a polynomial blending function given by a Bezier curve. The curve's appearance is similar to exponentials but with the advantage of having local influence. Only distances between zero and r need to be considered. In this case rasterizations of huge biological molecular models are feasible in quite short time. Even interactive modeling can be envisaged using this approach, assuming that most changes are local and can be rasterized almost in real time. The octree display time can be significantly enhanced by storing the voxels in a linear octree. Since the implicit surface subdivision methods subdivide the space in the same order in which an octree is traversed, the voxels generated are already sorted into the linear octree. In the linear octree the coordinates of each voxel should be explicitly stored. To save space, memory can be allocated in eight voxels groups, each group representing one octant, as done in many linear octree implementations [8, 20]. The linear octree would be a chained list of octants. Each octant would contain a pointer to the next octant, the coordinates of the octant (the last voxel coordinate bits are given by voxels' positions in the octant as in standard octrees), and eight pointers, each one pointing to the corresponding voxel (or a null pointer if the corresponding voxel is empty). To display the octree the chained list would be linearly traversed and all the voxels would be obtained very efficiently. The voxel search in this octree can be done with the help of a hash table, as done in many linear octree implementations [8, 20].

The voxel-based visualization methods have been neglected until recently, but their importance is remarkable. Mathematicians could finally analyze implicit functions interactively. Implicit surfaces could easily be ported to medical imagery to simulate tumors, organs, prostheses, etc. The investigation of new forms using implicit surfaces could count on well-known mathematic expressions whose derivatives are easily calculated, and many other mathematic properties could easily be derived from their equations. Physical simulations using implicit surfaces could easily be obtained. All these applications are very difficult using procedural implicit surfaces: Since they have no equation they need to be converted into polygons [4] or voxels [13] in order to estimate the normal vectors, for example.

These applications are ready to profit from the benefits of voxel representation of implicit surfaces. Consequently the performance of implicit surface rasterization algorithms is very important to the increase of these benefits. The rasterization quality is also very important, since a better rasterization implies a better representation of the surface. We here make a comparison between different rasterization methods for the two most used implicit surfaces: algebraic implicit functions and exponential implicit functions.

10.2   Implicit Surface Rasterization Methods

10.2.1   Kalra and Barr's subdivision method

The subdivision method proposed by Kalra and Barr [10] can be used to rasterize implicit surfaces. It consists in a recursive subdivision where certain regions in space are divided into eight subspaces, called octants. This is the same construction logic used to build an octree. In fact we do use an octree in our discrete ray tracing system [16–19] and our interactive visualization software. However, direct memory allocation for the octree using this method is not recommended, since the method only guarantees discarding octants where the surface does not pass through but does not guarantee that there is really a piece of surface inside an octant. We subdivide the surface up to a maximum level and allocate the memory only when the subdivision arrives at this level. Using a linear octree, as remarked previously, would enhance the performance of this process, since no intermediate octree levels exist and several optimizations can be done.

The octant rejection condition applies when the norm of the maximization of the partial derivatives over the octant multiplied by the half of the octant diagonal is less than the absolute value of the function value at the middle of the octant. The significance of this test can be seen as a sphere centered in the middle of the octant with ray greater than octant's diagonal. Therefore it rejects the octants where the surface has no intersection with this sphere and when the surface is not totally inside it. Since this sphere is greater than the octant, the test can catch pieces of the surface that pass close to the octant, but does not necessarily pierce the octant. Hence the 'tightness' of the rasterization depends directly on the maximization of the partial derivatives. This means that if this maximization is overestimated the rasterization will take more time, since more subdivisions are necessary to correctly rasterize it, or if we limit the number of levels the quality of the rasterization will be poor. On the other side, underestimating the maximization can translate as errors in the rasterization. To accelerate the process, Kalra and Barr proposed to test in advance whether there is variation in sign in the function values at the eight octant vertexes. This would clearly indicate an intersection between the surface and the octant, since negative function values indicate that the vertex is inside the surface and positive function values indicate that the vertex is outside the surface.

10.2.2   Duff's subdivision method

Duff [6] has proposed another method for rasterizing algebraic and nonalgebraic implicit functions. He uses interval arithmetic for calculating function values. Snyder [15] has extended the idea to other computer graphics problems. Interval arithmetic generalizes traditional arithmetic, guaranteeing exactness of results inside an interval. A certain value in interval arithmetic is given by two values, the lower and the higher bounds of the interval that contains the real value. All arithmetic operations are then redefined to work in this interval, giving as a result another interval defined by the resulting lower and higher bounds. To use interval arithmetic in a computer, we should use floating-point arithmetic and modify the interval in such a way that the real value we want to represent is in a computer-representable floating-point interval. To guarantee exactness we must change the rounding mode to minus infinity in lower-bound calculation and to plus infinity in higher-bound calculation. Interval arithmetic can be generalized to other mathematical operations such as integer powers and transcendental functions.

   The rasterization is done by subdividing the space in an octree-like way as seen in the preceding method. Each subdivided octant is represented by three intervals, one for each variable (x, y, z), where the lower and higher bounds correspond to the octant bounding coordinates. The result of applying these intervals in the function (in interval arithmetic) is an interval. If the interval lower bound is greater than zero then the octant is totally outside the surface. If the interval higher bound is less than zero then the octant is totally inside the surface. In both cases the octant is rejected. Otherwise the octant might intersect the surface and merits being further subdivided. We note at this point that this method clearly has a much more efficient octant elimination heuristic. In the preceding method, if we calculate the value of the function in the eight vertexes, and if all the values are negative or positive, we cannot eliminate the octant. With the interval arithmetic we can. Hence we can expect that this method will be faster than the preceding one. Nevertheless, this must be verified experimentally.

Interval arithmetic

Duff and Snyder [6, 15] have simultaneously but independently introduced interval arithmetic to solve computer graphics problems. Duff concentrated on 3D implicit function subdivision and Snyder on more general problems like silhouette edge detection, surface polygonization, minimum distance determination, etc.

Interval arithmetic guarantees that the exact result of any arithmetic operation is between two values, called *interval bounds*. Any real number is represented by two interval bounds. For example, the coordinates, X, Y, and Z are represented in interval arithmetic as

$$X = [x, X]$$
$$Y = [y, Y]$$
$$Z = [z, Z]$$

These interval bounds in our case are the coordinates of the octant's boundaries. Substituting in the implicit function equation each regular variable by the correspondent interval and each regular operation by the respective interval operation produces an interval version of the function, which Snyder [15] calls an *inclusion function*. We can verify if the surface does not pass through the octant simply testing whether the resulting interval does not *include* zero, that is, when the inclusion function resulting interval does not *include* a solution for the regular function $F(x, y, z) = 0$. Then if the resulting interval does not include zero, the function certainly does not have a zero into the octant, therefore the surface does not pass through the octant.

The interval arithmetic operators are:

$$X + Y = [x + y, X + Y]$$
$$X - Y = [x - y, X - y]$$
$$X \cdot Y = [\min(xy, xY, Xy, XY), \max(xy, xY, Xy, XY)]$$
$$X / Y = [x / y, X / y] \text{ if } 0 \notin [y, Y]$$

These operators are not enough for the functions used in practice. To include any algebraic expression we need

$$X^n = \begin{cases} [x^n, X^n] \ n \text{ odd or } x \geqslant 0 \\ [X^n, x^n] \ n \text{ even or } X \leqslant 0 \\ [0, \max(-x, X)^n] \ n \text{ even and } 0 \in [x, X] \end{cases}$$

To include exponential functions with negative exponents, which are useful as blending functions in 'blobby' models, we have

$$e^{-X} = [e^{-X}, e^{-x}]$$

Any other function can be converted to interval arithmetic similarly by breaking the function into monotonic intervals [6].

10.2.3   Taubin's rasterizing method

Taubin [22] has proposed another rasterization method that works for algebraic implicit surfaces only. It also uses space subdivision in octree-like fashion like the preceding methods. The method first translates the origin to the middle point of the octant. Subsequently, the algebraic implicit function is simplified and converted to a single variable polynomial. If the evaluation of this new function for the half-octant size gives a positive value, then the octant does not intersect the surface. The simplification starts by grouping all the terms of the same degree together. Then for each one of these groups the coefficients' absolute values are added to form a new coefficient. The three variables are then substituted by just one variable, which is raised to the power corresponding to each group's degree. Finally, the coefficient which does not multiply any variable is subtracted from the rest of the polynomial. Notice that the entire polynomial evaluation is not necessary if a partial result is already negative or zero. We suggest then that for each polynomial term we test whether the result is negative or zero before the next term is considered. Even with this optimization, we are not sure whether this method is really more efficient than the preceding ones. This must be verified experimentally. Nevertheless, we have opted not to examine this algorithm based on the following observations:

- It rasterizes only algebraic functions.
- For each octant it recalculates the polynomial in Taylor series using Horner's algorithm, which requires the function in the polynomial forms.
- It does not rasterize well near singular points.

10.3 Comparative Results

Kalra and Barr's method is not very appropriate for rectangular regions since it rejects regions outside a sphere. This is equivalent to the spherical bounding volume problem. It is not very effective for long narrow objects. Duff's method is more suited to rectangular regions. Therefore it can be used to eliminate long, narrow regions more effectively than Kalra and Barr's method.

We used only cubic octants, which aids Kalra and Barr's method better than Duff's. In any case, Duff's method was always faster than Kalra and Barr's method. However, Duff's method always used more memory than Kalra and Barr's method. This indicates that Kalra and Barr's method is 'tighter' than Duff's, at least for cubic regions. On the other hand, Kalra and Barr's method is very sensitive to functions like the heart (see Figure 10.5). In this case Kalra and Barr's method took practically twice as much time to rasterize. We can also observe that algebraic functions take less time to be rasterized than an almost equivalent form given by exponential functions in both methods (Figures 10.3 and 10.4). This was expected, since algebraic expressions are faster to evaluate than exponential functions. We also note how Kalra and Barr's method is sensitive to singular points. This sensitivity was also noted in the normal vector calculation near singular points in both methods. The fact that Kalra and Barr's method uses partial derivatives explains its sensitivity near singular points, since the normal vector is also calculated using the partial derivatives. At singular points the partial derivatives are zero, which explains this behavior. Duff's method is insensitive to singular points.

All rasterizations were generated into a Crimson SGI workstation with 100 MHz R4000/R4010 processors. Memory occupation in Tables 10.1 and 10.2 are given in

N. Stolte and R. Caubet

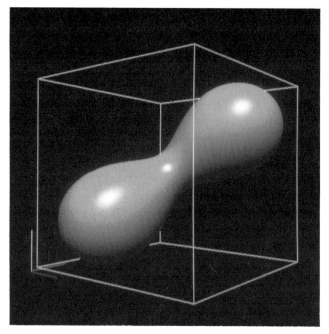

Figure 10.3   Image 1 → $f(x, y, z) \cdot g(x, y, z) - 0.058 = 0$, where
$$f(x, y, z) = (x - 0.78)^2 + (y - 0.78)^2 + (z - 0.78)^2 + 0.001$$
$$g(x, y, z) = (x - 0.23)^2 + (y - 0.23)^2 + (z - 0.23)^2 + 0.001$$

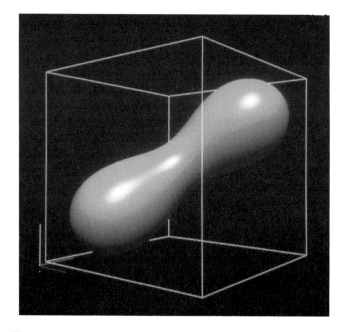

Figure 10.4   Image 2 → $e^{((x-0.78)^2+(y-0.78)^2+(z-0.78)^2)\cdot 3.25} + e^{((x-0.23)^2+(y-0.23)^2+(z-0.23)^2)\cdot 3.25} - 0.9 = 0.$

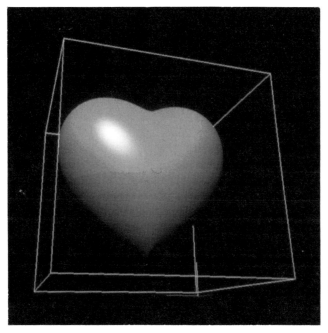

Figure 10.5   Image 3 → $(x^2 + y^2 + 2z^2 - 1)^3 - y^3(x^2 + 0.1 \cdot z^2) = 0$.

4 KB blocks. All images were generated into the same machine using our interactive voxel visualization software. This software uses an octree to store the voxels and GL primitives to display each voxel as a 3D point.

Table 10.1   Rasterization times for Kalra and Barr's method.

	Image 1		Image 2		Image 3	
3D resolution	Time	Memory	Time	Memory	Time	Memory
512^3	0′34″	6263	1′26″	5730	0′58″	6594
256^3	0′08″	2185	0′22″	2056	0′13″	2350
128^3	<0′01″	1171	0′05″	1103	0′06″	1252

Table 10.2   Rasterization times for Duff's method.

	Image 1		Image 2		Image 3	
3D resolution	Time	Memory	Time	Memory	Time	Memory
512^3	0′21″	8165	0′50″	7802	0′25″	7330
256^3	0′05″	2661	0′09″	2574	0′05″	2456
128^3	<0′01″	1289	<0′02″	1254	<0′01″	1234

10.4 Conclusion

The importance of implicit surface rasterizing methods has recently been emphasized. A number of applications can be devised. The use of implicit representation is a very convenient way to represent 3D objects, since it is very general. Planes, quadratic surfaces, parametric and more exotic surfaces can be expressed under the implicit form. Hence it is a very high level modeling tool. In addition, it is very compact, allowing the representation of very complex scenes with less memory consumption.

We have proposed two rasterizing methods based on existing implicit surface subdviding techniques. Unfortunately, as far as we know, no comparison between these methods in terms of quality or performance has been given. We have proposed experimental comparison between these two methods. These results will be very useful to those desiring to implement such rasterization methods.

All three methods overestimate the size of the octant in one way or another. The search for better methods, in which this size is exact or is better approximated, is a constant concern in this research area. Finding such methods will allow more precise and perhaps faster rasterizations.

We have proposed visualizing implicit functions directly in their voxel format with the help of an octree. This allows a near to real-time interaction at quite high resolutions.

References

[1] H.B. Bidasaria, Defining and rendering of textured objects through the use of exponential functions, *Graphical Models and Image Processing*, 54(2): 97–102; 1992.
[2] Eric Bittar, Nicolas Tsingos, Marie-Paule Gascuel, Automatic reconstruction of unstructured 3D data: Combining a medial axis and implicit surfaces, *Eurographics 95*, pp. 457–468, Blackwell, 1995.
[3] James Blinn, A generalization of algebraic surface drawing, *ACM Trans. Graphics*, 1(3): 235–256; 1982.
[4] Jules Bloomenthal, Brian Wyvill, Interactive techniques for implicit modeling, *Computer Graphics*, 24(2): 109–116; 1990.
[5] Mathieu Desbrun, Marie-Paule Gascuel, Animating soft substances with implicit surfaces, *Siggraph 95*, pp. 287–290, ACM Press, 1995.
[6] Tom Duff, Interval arithmetic and recursive subdivision for implicit functions and constructive solid geometry, *Computer Graphics*, 26(2): 131–138; 1992.
[7] Akira Fujimoto, Takayaki Tanaka, Kansei Iwata, ARTS: Accelerated ray tracing system, *IEEE Computer Graphics Appl.*, 6(4): 16–26; 1986.
[8] Andrew S. Glassner, Space subdivision for fast ray tracing, *IEEE Computer Graphics Appl.*, 10(4): 15–22; 1984.
[9] Pat Hanrahan, Ray tracing algebraic surfaces, *Computer Graphics*, 17(3): 83–90; 1983
[10] Devendra Kalra, Alan Barr, Guaranteed ray intersections with implicit surfaces, *Computer Graphics*, 23(3): 297–306; 1989.
[11] W.E. Lorensen, H.E. Cline, Marching cubes: A high resolution 3D surface construction algorithm, *Computer Graphics*, 21(4): 163–169; 1987.
[12] Shigeru Muraki, Volumetric shape description of range data using 'blobby model,' *Computer Graphics*, 25(4): 227–235; 1991.

[13] Alan Norton, Generation and display of geometric fractals in 3-D, *Computer Graphics*, 16(3): 61–67; 1982.

[14] Thomas W. Sederberg, Techniques for cubic algebraic surfaces, *IEEE Computer Graphics Appl.*, 10(4): 14–25; 1990.

[15] John M. Snyder, Interval analysis for computer graphics, *Computer Graphics*, 26(2): 121–130; 1992.

[16] Nilo Stolte, René Caubet, Discrete ray-tracing high resolution 3D grids, *The Winter School of Computer Graphics and Visualization 95*, pp. 300–312, Vaclav Skala, 1995.

[17] Nilo Stolte, René Caubet, Discrete ray-tracing of huge voxel spaces, *Eurographics 95*, pp. 383–394, Blackwell, 1995.

[18] Nilo Stolte, René Caubet, Fast high definition ray tracing implicit surfaces, *5th DGCI – Discrete Geometry for Computer Imagery*, Clermont-Ferrand, 1995, pp. 61–70.

[19] Nilo Stolte, René Caubet, Lancer de rayons discret pour des grilles de hautes résolutions, *Montpellier'95 – L'interface des Mondes Réels et Virtuels*, pp. 335–344, EC2 & Cie, 1995.

[20] Kelvin Sung, A DDA traversal algorithm for ray tracing, *Eurographics'91*, pp. 73–85, North Holland, 1991.

[21] Gabriel Taubin, Distance aproximation for rasterizing implicit curves, *ACM Trans. Graphics*, 13(1): 3–42; 1994.

[22] Gabriel Taubin, Rasterizing algebraic curves and surfaces, *IEEE Computer Graphics Appl.*, 13(1): 14–23; 1994.

11
High-Speed and High-Fidelity Visualization of Complex CSG Models

Subodh Kumar, Shankar Krishnan, Dinesh Manocha, and
Atul Narkhede

11.1 Introduction

Rational spline surfaces are routinely used to represent solids in engineering design. Splines also find application in modeling body parts for medical imaging and molecules for drug design, among other things. In addition, solid models composed of polyhedra, spheres, cones, tori, prisms, solids of revolution, etc. are widely used in CAD/CAM, virtual reality, engineering simulation, and animation [12, 24]. All these solids can also easily be represented in terms of rational spline surfaces. These solids and their Boolean combinations, i.e., union, intersection, and difference, are used to generate large-scale models like those of airplanes, ships, automobiles, submarines, etc. (see Figure 11.1). These models are typically represented as thousands of CSG trees (for an example of a CSG tree see Figure 11.2) with up to a hundred Boolean operations on primitives corresponding to surfaces of high parametric degree. Many of the current solid modelers do not compute analytic and accurate B-reps for these models and represent

Figure 11.1 Pivot: Part of the submarine storage and handling system model.

Visualization and Modeling
ISBN 0-12-227738-4

CSG tree
Boolean operations on solids

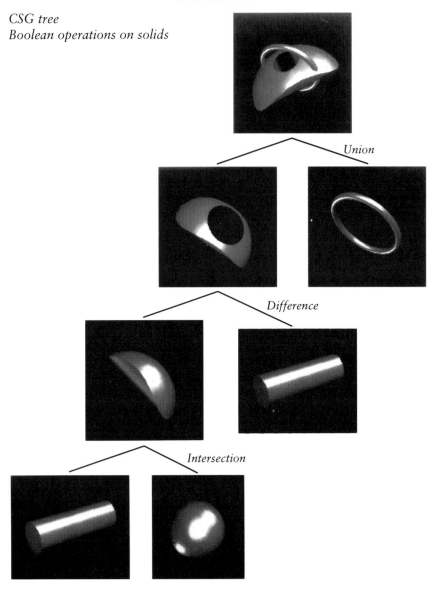

Figure 11.2　CSG tree.

them as millions of polygons. Current graphics systems are not able to render such complex polygonal models at interactive frame rates. Thus there is a wide body of applications that benefits from accurate CSG display based on a spline visualizer.

Main contribution
We present algorithms and systems to display CSG and spline models at interactive frame rates. The main components are

- *Model conversion*: Computation of accurate B-reps from the CSG models and their representation in terms of trimmed spline models.
- *Representation*: An accurate and efficient representation of the high-degree trimming curves.
- *Display*: Fast and accurate rendering of models composed of trimmed spline surfaces.

Our solid modeler can accurately compute Boolean combinations of solids composed of more than 30 high-degree curved primitives and their CSG combinations. Its application to parts of a submarine storage and handling system composed of about 2000 CSG trees resulted in a B-rep consisting of more than 30 000 trimmed surfaces, which can be rendered at interactive rates on Pixel-Planes 5 [6] by our display system.

11.1.1   Prior work

There is a large volume of work in the modeling and rendering literature related to model conversion, displaying large data sets, and multiresolution modeling. We categorize it into four types as follows.

Direct rendering of CSG models

Some graphics systems include capabilities to directly render CSG models [9, 15]. However, they either restrict the number of CSG operations or the degrees of the primitives or are not able to render complex models. Algorithms based on enhanced Z-buffer often require multiple rendering passes along with fast rasterizing systems for such primitives [25]. Other techniques and systems for direct rendering are based on ray casting [14, 23] and are currently not fast enough.

CSG to B-rep conversion

There is considerable literature on computing B-reps from CSG solids defined using polyhedral primitives, as surveyed in [12, 24]. A number of techniques to improve the robustness of such systems have been proposed as well [26]. However, no such robust algorithms and systems are known for solid models composed of curved or spline primitives [12, 24]. The main problem lies in accurate, robust, and efficient computation of the intersection of spline surfaces. Surface intersection is an active area of research and some of the recent papers have proposed algorithms to compute all components and piecewise linear or spline approximations to the intersection curves based on tracing methods [12, 13, 17, 29]. However, these representations are either inaccurate or inconsistent for Boolean operations on complex models. Therefore, some of the current solid modelers use polyhedral approximations of these primitives and compute the B-reps of the resulting solids in terms of polygons. This method can potentially lead to data proliferation and inaccurate representations.

Visualization of large data sets

Current high-end graphics systems are not able to render polygonal representation of complex models described using millions of polygons at interactive frame rates. Many algorithms based on visibility preprocessing and multiresolution modeling have been proposed for faster display of such models [4, 7, 8, 10, 21, 30, 31, 33]. However, visibility methods have been shown useful for densely occluded polyhedral environments only [31]. Most of the current simplification algorithms are restrictive and no efficient algorithms with guaranteed error bounds are known for general topologies [11].

Rendering spline surfaces

Many algorithms are known in the literature for tessellating spline surfaces and rendering the resulting polygons [1, 2, 19, 20, 22]. In particular, Rockwood et al. [22] presented the first real-time algorithm for rendering trimmed surfaces. Given a NURBS model, Rockwood et al. decompose it into a series of trimmed Bézier surfaces, split the trimmed surfaces into patches bounded by monotonic curve segments, and triangulate the resulting patches. However, it is not fast enough for complex models and its implementation as part of SGI's GL library can render surfaces composed of at most a few hundred trimmed Bézier surfaces at interactive rates on an SGI Onyx [19].

11.1.2   Overview

Given a CSG model, our solid modeler represents each primitive as a collection of Bézier surfaces, performs accurate Boolean operations, and represents the B-rep as a collection of trimmed Bézier surfaces. It represents the trimming curves as piecewise algebraic space curves along with bounding volumes. It makes use of algorithms for surface intersection, polygon triangulation, domain partitioning, and ray shooting to compute the B-reps. Given a collection of trimmed Bézier surfaces, our display system tessellates them into triangles and renders them on the graphics pipeline. It performs visibility culling and dynamically tessellates the surface as a function of viewing parameters. As opposed to decomposing the trimming curves into monotonic segments, our system uses an algorithm for triangulating nonconvex polygons. In particular, it makes use of frame to frame coherence computing *incremental triangulation*. On parallel graphics systems, the display system makes use of multiple processors for tessellation, minimizes communication between processors, and load balances the work between polygon generation and polygon rendering.

The ability to compute varying resolutions of the B-reps in terms of trimmed curves and surfaces is fundamental to the performance of the overall system. As compared to earlier systems for rendering such models, it has the following advantages.

- *Fidelity*: A high degree of fidelity of display is essential for any meaningful visualization and design validation. Our B-reps for CSG models are more accurate than those generated by modelers using polygonal representation for the curved primitives and the final solids. Besides rendering, it is also useful for other applications like collision detection.
- *Rendering*: Our algorithms based on visibility culling and dynamic tessellation generate fewer polygons for the spline models. Furthermore, we can easily generate on-line any *level-of-detail* with correct topology using incremental computations. This is in contrast with the difficulty of computing multiresolution models for large polygonal datasets of arbitrary topology with visible artifacts introduced due to few and discrete levels of detail. Our method results in *better images and faster display*.
- *Memory*: The memory requirements for our B-reps are about an order of magnitude

lower than for polygonal models and their multiresolution representations. On the other hand, our display system needs more processing power for on-line triangulation of the multiresolution representations.

The rest of the chapter is organized in the following manner. Section 11.2 presents the notation used in the rest of the chapter and the multiresolution representation for the trimming curves. Section 11.3 describes model generation, representation, and the underlying algorithms. We present the display system in Section 11.4 and discuss the overall implementation and performance on parts of the submarine storage and handling system model in Section 11.5.

11.2   Model Representation

We use boldface letters to represent vector quantities and surfaces. Lower-case letters are used for representing points and curves in a plane and upper case letters for points, curves, and surfaces in $\mathcal{R}^3$. A tensor product Bézier surface $F(s, t)$ is represented as

$$F(s, t) = \sum_{i=0}^{m} \sum_{j=0}^{n} V_{ij} B_i^m(s) B_j^n(t)$$

where $V_{ij} = \langle w_{ij}x_{ij}, w_{ij}y_{ij}, w_{ij}z_{ij}, w_{ij} \rangle$ are the control points of the patch in homogeneous coordinates and

$$B_i^m(s) = \binom{m}{i} s^i (1 - s)^{m-i}$$

is the Bernstein polynomial [5]. The domain of the surface is defined on the unit square $0 \leq s, t \leq 1$ in the (s, t) plane. Trimmed surfaces are defined on a subset of $[s, t] \in [0, 1] \times [0, 1]$ domain using trimming curves, $t_1, t_2, \ldots, t_p$. The trimming curves are represented as piecewise linear curves, Bézier curves, or piecewise algebraic space curves. Each of them is an oriented curve, i.e., it has a starting point, q_0 and an ending point, q_k (as shown in Figure 11.3). Each trimming curve *trims out* the part of the surface that lies on its right. It does not allow self-intersecting trimming curves. The region of the surface that is not trimmed out is also referred to as the trimmed region.

11.2.1   Representation of solids

Each solid S comprises planar faces and trimmed Bézier surfaces. The data structure for the solid includes the number of surfaces, representation of each surface, and an adjacency graph $\Gamma(S)$ representing the connectivity between all the surfaces (Figure 11.5). Each planar face is defined as an anticlockwise ordering of the vertices and for each Bézier surface $F(s, t)$; the cross-product $F_s \times F_t$ points to the outer normal. As a result, we can perform *local* in/out tests at any point on the boundary of the solid.

Each vertex v_i in the adjacency graph corresponds to a surface F_i of the solid. Two vertices v_j and v_k are connected by an edge, iff the two surfaces F_j and F_k share a common boundary. The common boundary may be along the edges of a planar face or a boundary curve or trimming curve for a Bézier surface.

11.2.2   Representation of trimming curves

The intersection curves of two surfaces correspond to the vector equation $F(s, t) = G(u, v)$. This results in the following three scalar equations:

$$F_1(s, t, u, v) = X(s, t)\overline{W}(u, v) - \overline{X}(u, v)W(s, t) = 0$$
$$F_2(s, t, u, v) = Y(s, t)\overline{W}(u, v) - \overline{Y}(u, v)W(s, t) = 0 \qquad (1)$$
$$F_3(s, t, u, v) = Z(s, t)\overline{W}(u, v) - \overline{Z}(u, v)W(s, t) = 0$$

where the domain of the variables is restricted to $0 \le s, t, u, v \le 1$. We use a recently developed algorithm for computing the intersection of rational parametric surfaces [17]. In this algorithm, we maintain an accurate analytic representation of the intersection curve in the domain of the two surfaces. This can be used to obtain accurate trimming curves during the CSG operation. The algorithm computes a start point on each component of the intersection curve and decomposes the domain such that each resulting region contains at most one component of the intersection curve. Along with the analytic representation, the algorithm also computes a series of points on each component. Its performance is output sensitive and can compute all the components of the intersection curve of 50 pairs of surfaces in about 20 seconds on an SGI Onyx. Its application to the representation of $F(s, t)$ in Figure 11.4 after a few intersections is shown in Figure 11.3. The trimming curves corresponding to the surface intersection are represented as a union of components (c_i) of the algebraic space curve. Each component consists of:

1. Start and end points q_0 and q_k.
2. Rectangular bounding box b_i ($[u_1, v_1] \times [u_2, v_2]$) in the domain of the surface bounding c_i.
3. An axis-aligned bounding box B_i in $\mathcal{R}^3$ bounding the image of that component (I_i).
4. The surface parametrizations $F(s, t)$ and $G(u, v)$ and the equations $F_1(\ ), \ . \ . \ . , F_3$ $(\ )$ in equation (1) describing the curve.

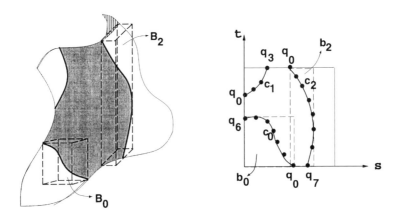

Figure 11.3   Representation of trimming curves.

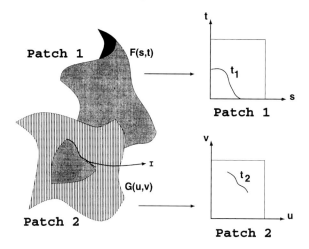

Figure 11.4 Intersection of two surfaces.

The incremental rendering algorithm in section 11.4 needs a piecewise linear representation of the trimming curve as a function of viewing parameters.

At the lowest level is the straight line joining q_0 and q_n. To generate more points on the curve, the algorithm simultaneously traces the trimming curve c_i in the domain and the intersection curve I_i on the surface.

This tracing algorithm is in fact quite slow and it is impractical to trace each trimming curve each frame. Fortunately, due to coherence between frames, this step is not required very often. In fact, for each curve of length l in $\mathcal{R}^3$ we compute, off-line, Kl points on the curve, where K is a user specified constant. At run time we evaluate more

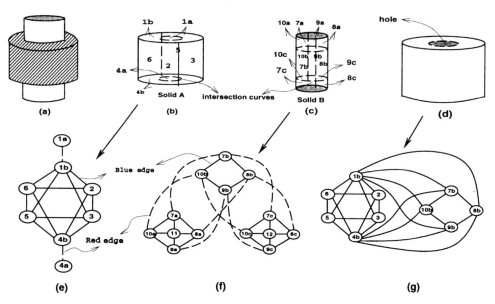

Figure 11.5 Adjacency graph computation for a difference operation.

points as we need them. Further, when the required tessellation of the curve goes down, we retain the extra points subject to availability of memory. For most frames we just choose points from the pretessellated curves. The point closest to the required tessellant is chosen. For large models this method becomes impractical. In such cases we approximate the curve with splines, ensuring that the number of splines does not increase too much. For details of the algorithm we refer the reader to Kumav et al. [16].

11.3   Model Generation

In this section, we describe the solid modeling system used for computing B-reps from CSG trees. Free-form surfaces have been used previously in modeling systems. The Alpha_1 [3] and Geomod [32] modeling systems use NURBS to describe the B-rep. The primitives may correspond to polyhedra or solids whose boundaries can be represented in terms of rational spline surfaces. This is a fairly rich class of objects and can be used to model almost all the solids used in CAD/CAM and simulation applications. Currently our system handles primitives composed of tensor-product surfaces only, but can be easily extended to include solids defined using triangular surfaces. It makes the following set of assumptions for each Boolean operation:

- All primitives are *regularized* solids [12] and all Boolean operations result in regularized solids. That is, the closure of the interior of the solid corresponds to the original model.
- The intersection between all pairs of overlapping surfaces is well-conditioned and there are no degeneracies.

The system does not explicitly check whether these assumptions are satisfied. In some cases, it can detect these cases while running the algorithm.

The algorithm for B-rep computation performs a depth-first traversal of the CSG tree and computes the B-rep of solids at each intermediate node of the tree. The algorithm for Boolean operation between a pair of solids involves trimmed surface intersection, ray-shooting, adjacency graph computation and surface normal orientation of the resulting solid. In this section we give a brief overview of the algorithm.

11.3.1   Surface intersection

A basic operation in the computation of B-reps from a CSG model is the intersection of two surfaces. Given two Bézier surfaces, $F(s, t) = (X(s, t), Y(s, t), Z(s, t), W(s, t))$ and $G(u, v) = (\overline{X}(u, v), \overline{Y}(u, v), \overline{Z}(u, v), \overline{W}(u, v))$, represented in homogeneous coordinates, the intersection curve is defined as the set of common points in $\mathcal{R}^3$. However, the degree of the intersection curve can be as high as $4m^2n^2$ for two $m \times n$ tensor-product surfaces and the curve cannot be exactly represented as a Bézier curve (for most cases) [12]. Typical values of m and n are 2 or 3 and can be as high as 10 or 15 in practice. In addition, the intersection curve may consist of multiple components, closed loops, singularities, etc., which add to its geometric complexity. A number of algorithms based on subdivision, lattice evaluation, and marching [12, 13, 17, 29] are known. These algorithms compute piecewise linear or spline approximations of the intersection curve. However, when it comes to computing the B-reps of CSG models defined using a series of Boolean operations, these representations may not guarantee the following.

1. *Robustness and accuracy*: The algorithm for Boolean operations repeatedly computes intersection of trimmed surfaces with rays in space and other trimmed surfaces. With approximate representations, the errors at each level of the tree propagate and it becomes difficult to compute B-reps accurately and robustly for models defined with more than seven or eight CSG operations.
2. *Consistent representation*: The rendering algorithm based on dynamic tessellation needs a multiresolution representation of the trimming curves. Furthermore, in order to prevent cracks, the trimming curves (e.g., curves t_1 and t_2 in Figure 11.3) corresponding to the intersection curve (curve I in Figure 11.3) should be consistently tessellated into piecewise linear segments in the domains of surfaces $F(s, t)$ and $G(u, v)$. An off-line piecewise linear approximation does not provide a multiresolution representation. Generating a densely tessellated linear approximation using a small step size can lead to data proliferation. It is nontrivial to compute consistent spline approximations to t_1 and t_2 such that their images correspond to the same curve and there are no cracks while rendering.

11.3.2   Intersection between trimmed surfaces

Given two solids, S_1 and S_2, with m and n surfaces, respectively, the algorithm for Boolean operations initially computes the intersection curve between their boundaries. This includes computation of intersection between all possible overlapping surfaces. In the worst case, all the mn pairs can intersect, but that is uncommon. To speed up the computation, the algorithm first checks bounding volumes and convex hulls for intersection. It encloses each surface by an axis-aligned bounding box, projects the bounding box along the X, Y, and Z axes, sorts the resulting intervals, and computes the overlapping bounding boxes. Each Bézier surface is contained in the convex hull of its control points [5]. For each pair of overlapping bounding boxes, the algorithm checks whether the convex hulls of their control points intersect. This is reduced to a linear programming problem in three dimensions and solved using Seidel's incremental linear time algorithm [27].

Let $F(s, t)$ be a trimmed surface and its trimmed subset in the domain $0 \le s, t \le 1$ be bounded by curve segments $t_1, t_2, \ldots, t_k$. To compute its intersection with another trimmed or nontrimmed surface $G(u, v)$, it initially treats each parametrization as a nontrimmed surface and computes all the components of the intersection curves in the domain $0 \le s, t, u, v \le 1$ [17]. Let these components be denoted as $c_1, c_2, \ldots, c_p$, as shown in Figure 11.6. Let the corresponding components in the domain of $G(u, v)$ be $\bar{c}_1, \bar{c}_2, \ldots, \bar{c}_p$. Given these components, it computes a partition of the domain of $F(s, t)$. This partitioning [16] is first done on the polygonal approximation of the domain. The intersection points are then improved in a second step using a more exact curve intersection. The first step ensures that the more accurate second step converges quickly.

The new trimming curves arising from intersection with various surfaces are merged together and eventually the domain of intersecting surfaces is partitioned into two or more regions. The boundaries of each component are composed of portions of t_i and c_i.

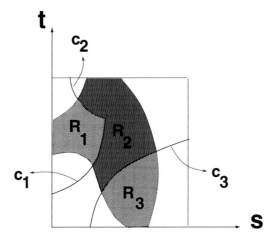

Figure 11.6   Partitioning the domain based on intersection.

11.3.3   Computation of the new solid

The location of a point with respect to a solid (in/out) is a fundamental operation in the computation of the new solid. Given a point P, we shoot a ray from the point in any direction and compute all its intersections with the boundaries of the solid. If the number of intersections is odd, the point is inside the solid, otherwise it is outside. The intersection of rays with trimmed Bézier surfaces is computed using eigenvalue methods [17]. Checking whether the resulting point lies inside the trimmed domain is based on planar triangulation [28].

The intersection curves between the boundaries of the two solids partition the surfaces into multiple regions. These regions have the property that all points in their interior are either inside or outside the other solid. Further, it is easy to show that two adjacent regions, separated by the intersection curve, cannot *both* lie inside or outside. Depending on the Boolean operation, the regions composing the B-rep of the solid are chosen as follows.

- *Union*: A region of S_1 is part of the new solid if it lies outside S_2 and vice versa for the regions of S_2.
- *Intersection*: A region of S_1 is part of the new solid if it lies inside S_2 and vice versa for the regions of S_2.
- *Difference*: A region of S_1 is part of the new solid if it lies outside S_2. A region of S_2 is part of the new solid if it lies inside S_1.

In practice, doing a containment classification test (inside/outside test) for each region of S_1 and S_2 is expensive. The number of surfaces and regions tends to grow rapidly with each Boolean operation. To speed up the process we make use of adjacency graphs of the two solids, $\Gamma(S_1)$ and $\Gamma(S_2)$. The partitioning of surfaces into multiple regions induced by the intersection curves changes the structure of the adjacency graphs. For example, in Figure 11.5e the vertex 1 corresponding to a surface in solid S_1 is split into regions corresponding to 1*a* and 1*b*. New adjacencies are introduced between the vertices due to intersection curves. We refer to the new edges as *red* edges and the original set of edges as *blue* edges. All the red edges in Figures 11.5e and f are shown using dashed lines. After computing the new vertices and edges, the algorithm computes all connected components of the graph considering only the blue edges. For example, the subgraph consisting of vertices *7a*, *8a*, *9a*, *10a*, *11* represents one connected component in Figure 11.5f. Each connected component of one solid lies completely inside or outside the other solid. We perform ray shooting tests on one of these components. Based on the result, we propagate it to the rest of the graph such that no two adjacent components have the same result. The adjacency graph of the solid resulting from the difference operation is shown in Figure 11.5g. The new edges between these solids correspond to pairs of intersecting surfaces between S_1 and S_2 (e.g., *1b* and *7b*). See Figure 11.7 for some example solids.

11.4 Display System

In this section, we describe the trimmed NURBS visualization system. This system subdivides NURBS into trimmed Bézier surfaces [5, 19], which allow more efficient display than general splines. Our algorithm tessellates the surfaces into triangles and renders these triangles using the standard graphics pipeline. Special attention is paid to the prevention of cracks between adjacent surfaces along the common boundaries and intersection curves. The system makes use of algorithms for back-patch culling (an extension of back-face culling for polygons to Bézier patches), bounds for triangulation, and coherence between successive frames for general NURBS models, presented in [19].

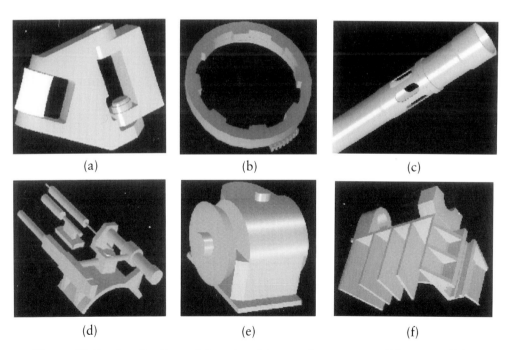

(a)   (b)   (c)

(d)   (e)   (f)

Figure 11.7 Application of the algorithm and system to different solids.

In this section, we extend and improve the algorithms presented in [18] to handle trimmed surfaces and B-reps of CSG models described in the previous section.

Given a Bézier surface and the viewing parameters, the algorithm tessellates the domain into rectangular cells based on a size criterion and an estimation of curvature of the surfaces. It ensures that the image of each cell is smaller than a user specified tolerance *TOL* in the screen space [19] and, as a result, generates a smooth image after Gouraud or Phong shading of the polygons corresponding to the cells. This way we can achieve the required degree of fidelity in the display. To speed up the display process, the algorithm incrementally adds or deletes triangles as a function of the viewing parameters. The algorithm for trimmed surfaces traces the trimming curve on the grid of isoparametric u and v lines in the parametric domain [18].

In brief, the rendering algorithm for trimmed patches is as follows.

1. Create rectangular cells from the uniform tessellation of the surface based on *TOL* for the surface.
2. For *each* trimming curve:
    (a) Compute the required tessellation for the curve: $n_t(TOL)$.
    (b) Tessellate the curve into $n_t(TOL)$ straight line segments.
    (c) March along the piecewise linear curve segments marking all the domain cells it crosses. Since the trimming curves are tessellated into piecewise linear segments, there is no need to calculate the exact intersections of the high-degree algebraic curves with the cell boundaries. We only need to do the following:
        (i)   Identify the cells whose bounding edges are intersected by the curve segments.
        (ii) For each bounding edge of the rectangular cell, maintain the order in which the segments cross that cell.
        (iii) If the trimming curve is contained in a cell, it intersects no cell edges. Mark such cells also.
3. Triangulate each unmarked cell that lies in the trimmed region of the surface by adding a diagonal.
4. The marked cells form a staircase-like polygonal chain[1] as shown in Figure 11.8.

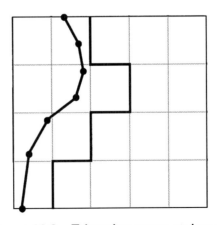

Figure 11.8   Trimming curve staircase.

[1] This chain can be degenerate, e.g., it is null if a trimming curve is contained in a cell.

The trimming curve forms another polygonal chain offset from the staircase. Partition this region across cell edges.

5. What results is a set of planar straight line graphs (PSLGs). Triangulate each PSLG. (We use Siedel's algorithm [28].) To prevent cracks in the display, no additional points on the curve are introduced in the region partitioning step or the triangulation step.

11.4.1 Tessellation of surfaces

Since we are targeting engineering applications, we assume that models are regular solids: there are no self-intersecting patches. Still, some patches can be highly curved and polygonizing such patches can cause an incorrect topology. This is demonstrated by an example in Figure 11.9. Such behavior occurs when a tessellant for some part of the patch intersects some other part of the patch, i.e., a part of the patch is too close to another. (This *distance* is not measured along the patch but normal to it.) Since this case rarely occurs in practice, we adopt a simple solution – for such patches we ensure that the tessellation step is smaller than the smallest such offending distance of the patch. The drawback, of course, is that such patches get tessellated too densely. Another solution that works well in practice is to subdivide such patches that have offending distance smaller than a user specified tolerance.

11.4.2 Tessellation of trimming curves

The trimming curves corresponding to surface intersections are represented as piecewise algebraic space curves, as described in section 11.2.2. Our algorithm computes projected area of the bounding box B_i for each trimming curve on the screen space. Based on the area it computes $n_t(TOL)$, the number of points needed for the piecewise representation of the trimming curve. The algorithm computes these points using the tracing algorithm presented in section 11.2.2. The step size Δ for the tracing algorithm is set equal to $L/n_t(TOL)$, where L is the length of the main diagonal of B_i.

Analogously to patches, trimming curves with high curvature can cause the violation of the regularity constraint on the topology – the piecewise tessellation of the curves can be nonsimple. Unfortunately, this happens rather often in practice. As a result,

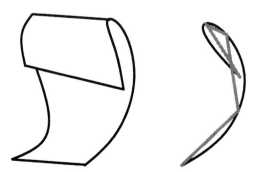

Figure 11.9 Topology violated by the tessellation. The picture on the left is a patch. The picture on the right shows a self-intersecting tessellation of a boundary curve.

increasing the tessellation of such curves causes an explosion of tessellants, and hence a more efficient solution is warranted.

For each trimming curve the algorithm finds a *nonsimple skeleton*. This is a gross piecewise representation of the curve such that the part of the curve between any two points on the skeleton is *split-monotonic* with respect to the segment joining those points. *Definition*: A curve c is split-monotonic with respect to a line l if the following property holds for any line l' perpendicular to l:

> If c intersects l' at points p_1 and p_2 such that there does not lie any other intersection of c and l' between p_1 and p_2 along l', then the points p_1 and p_2 split the curve in two parts neither of which intersects l'.

We find the skeleton by starting with the polygon connecting all the points of inflection and do a naive[2] diagonal-based subdivision to eliminate nonessential points from this polygon. If we pick the points on the skeleton, no nonsimple polygons are generated. Notice this is not much unlike Rockwood's [22] monotone decomposition of trimming curves, except that we avoid the overhead of actually doing the decomposition and dividing the patches. Example images generated by our system are shown in Figures 11.10 and 11.11.

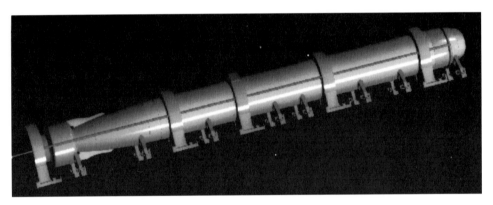

Figure 11.10   Parts of submarine storage and handling system: shipping model.

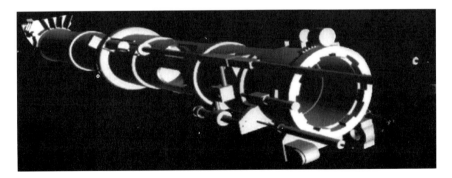

Figure 11.11   Parts of submarine storage and handling system: tube model.

[2] This is an off-line process.

11.4.3   Crack prevention

A trimming curve of a patch is a sequence of curves of intersection with neighboring patches. Each of these component curves is shared by two patches. To avoid cracks we need to make sure that the curve gets tessellated into the same segments in $\mathcal{R}^3$ for both the patches. Since we are looking for a parallel tessellation algorithm with no inter-process communication, and we would like the freedom to assign adjacent patches to different processors, we need to tessellate each patch independently.

Each preimage of the intersection curve (the trimming curves in the domain of two patches) uses the same bounding box (in $\mathcal{R}^3$) B_i in its data structure. Therefore the same values of $n_t(TOL)$, L, and Δ are used for the trimming curves in different domains. The tracing algorithm evaluates points on the intersection curve as a function of Δ and uses their preimages to obtain points in the domain ((s, t) or (u, v) coordinates). Therefore, the images of piecewise linear representation of each trimming curve match identically in $\mathcal{R}^3$ and the resulting image has no cracks. This evaluation of points is an expensive operation, but due to coherence only a few points need to be computed for any frame.

The standard patch boundaries are not treated as curves of intersection. We do not need to evaluate bounds in $\mathcal{R}^3$ for these curves.

11.4.4   Load balancing

Our tessellation algorithm takes special care to eliminate any communication between processors. Currently, most graphics systems do not offer sufficient communication bandwidth between processors to sustain large volumes of information transfer. Most available bandwidth is typically used up by the triangle rasterization. Thus we have to be especially careful to distribute patches between processors so as to reduce load imbalance. The problem is that in any visualization application, the tendency to zoom in on parts of the model is high, causing the tessellation and triangulation time of such patches to increase. Hence there is a need for patches in the zoomed-in region to be distributed across processors. This is handled by doing a round-robin distribution of primitives based on the adjacency information, so that adjacent patches do not lie on the same processor. But such distribution reduces the effectiveness of our visibility algorithm based on view frustum culling. We group patches into clusters and cull all patches of a cluster if the bounding box of the cluster is off-screen. If adjacent patches are grouped in a cluster, the bounding box fits them tightly and is more effective. Finding an optimal balance of this trade-off remains an open problem.

11.4.5   Incremental computations

In an interactive application there is typically a small change in the viewing parameters between successive frames. As a result, the bounds for tessellation of a surface and its trimming curves do not change much. Our algorithm exploits this property by making use of the triangulation at the previous frame and computing a small number of extra triangles for the current frame. The incremental algorithm for decomposing the domain into cells divides some of them into rectangular subcells or merges adjacent cells into supercells [19]. These subcells or supercells are used as normal cells for successive frames. For trimmed surfaces this results in small changes in cell intersections and triangulation and we do not need to retrace each trimming curve or triangulate each region.

As the value of $n_t(TOL)$ for a trimming curve increases or decreases between frames, the algorithm computes additional points or takes a subset of the original set of points. The algorithm makes use of the piecewise linear approximation of the trimming curve and computes additional points corresponding to the line segments of maximum length. It uses the start point of the maximal line segment as (s_0, t_0, u_0, v_0) and new value of $\Delta = L/n_t(TOL)$ for the tracing algorithm. For deletion the algorithm removes points corresponding to line segments of minimal length. It keeps track of the maximal and minimal lengths for subsequent frames.

Depending on the change in cell decomposition and piecewise approximation of the trimming curve, the algorithm only retraces the portion of the trimming curves belonging to the subcells or supercells and computes intersection with their boundaries. The new set of crossings is used to either decompose the original triangulation of a region or merge the triangulations of two or more adjacent regions. This is quite like the algorithm in [18], except that we avoid the per-cell cost. The cost of our algorithm is dependent on the actual intersections of the cells with the curve segments. If a grid line is added between two grid lines, we potentially need to retriangulate all parts of the staircase it intersects. (Additionally it may intersect full grid cells which are trivially subdivided.) For each staircase intersection we need to insert a point, a sequence of points, or a sequence of points, or a sequence of rectangles into the current triangulation. The basic idea is to first delete the features intersected by the feature being added or deleted. This creates a polygonal hole in the triangulation. When deleting the feature we retriangulate the hole polygon. When adding a new feature, we insert the feature into the hole polygon and then triangulate it. Further details are presented in [16].

11.5   Implementation and Performance

The algorithms presented above have been implemented and applied to a number of solids comprising the model of a submarine storage and handling system, made available to us by Electric Boat, a division of General Dynamics. The model consists of about 2000 solids. Many of the primitives are composed of polyhedra and conicoids like spheres or cylinders. Additional primitives include prisms and surfaces of revolution of degrees 6 and more. A few of the primitives are composed of Bézier surfaces of degree as high as 12. Most of the CSG trees have heights ranging between 6 and 12 and some of them are as high as 30. The B-reps of many of the solids consist of more than 40–45 trimmed Bézier surfaces and some of them have up to 148 surfaces.

11.5.1   Model generation

The running time of the system varies on different solids. In particular, it depends on the number of Boolean operations, the number of intersecting pairs of surfaces, and the number of connected components generated. In most cases, it spends about half the time in computing intersections between pairs of surfaces and the other half in ray shooting and computing the components of new solids. Its performance on a small subset of solids from the model has been highlighted in Table 11.1. The solids are shown in Figure 11.7.

Table 11.1 Performance of the solid modeling system

Model	Number of primitives	Number of CSG operations	Running time (min)	Number of patches (in B-Rep)
Figure 11.7a	23	20	2.6	137
Figure 11.7b	6	5	0.8	89
Figure 11.7c	6	5	0.7	116
Figure 11.7d	28	27	3.4	169
Figure 11.7e	11	10	1.1	69
Figure 11.7f	22	21	3.1	146

A major problem in the application of our system to different models is numerical accuracy of computations and its impact on the robustness of the entire system. The problem of building robust solid modeling systems based on floating-point computation is fairly open and no good solutions are known [12]. In our case, the algorithm uses tolerances at different parts of the overall algorithm. Depending on the values of the tolerances, the robustness of the algorithm can vary considerably.

As an input, the user specifies a set of four tolerance values and they are used as part of the surface intersection algorithm, for ray shooting, merging intersection curves, and detecting planar overlaps. The surface intersection algorithm normalizes the input surface parametrizations and ensures that the output of the intersection algorithm has certain digits of accuracy. The intersection algorithm is based on iterative numerical algorithms and we set the termination criterion accordingly. Similar criteria are used in computing the intersection of trimming curves represented as piecewise algebraic curves. At the end of every CSG operation, the system makes sure that the topology of the resulting solid is consistent (i.e., the solid boundary partitions $\mathcal{R}^3$ into two or more regions).

11.5.2 Display

The display system has been implemented on an SGI Onyx and Pixel-Planes 5 graphics system. On Pixel-Planes 5 it uses multiple graphics processors (GPs) for visibility computations, evaluating Bézier functions, and triangulating polygons. The trimmed Bézier surfaces are evenly distributed over different GPs and the system associates each surface with the parent solid for visibility computations. Each GP has about 2.5MB of memory for storing the surface representations and caching the triangle vertices and their normals. The system uses a dynamic memory allocation scheme for caching triangles.

The rendering algorithm produces topologically correct triangulations. As we zoom in or out on a model, it produces varying levels of detail incrementally and *no visual artifacts* appear. The trimming algorithm also works for trimming curves represented as piecewise linear or spline curves. Compared to Rockwood et al.'s algorithm [22], our trimming algorithm is faster by a factor of 7 or 8 on models consisting of about 200 surfaces on an SGI Onyx. It also produces fewer triangles. We used SGI's GL library implementation based on the algorithm of [22] for comparison.

We evaluated the performance of our system on parts of a submarine storage and handling system. The model was designed using Catia CAD system. This version of

Catia does not support Boolean operations on curved geometries[3] and therefore generates a dense polygonal B-rep for each model. Different models, their polygonal representation (from Catia) and trimmed Bézier representation (from our solid modeling system) are listed in Table 11.2. Pixel-Planes 5 graphics system can barely render 3–10 frames per second on the polygonal representation on a combination of these models (389 721 polygons). Furthermore, the image quality is poor when we zoom onto a part of a model. On the other hand, our display system can render the multiresolution representation (20 928 trimmed Bézier surfaces) at 12–25 frames a second at good resolutions.

Table 11.2   Comparison of our solid modeling system with Catia

Model name	Figure no.	Catia's B-rep polygon count	Our B-rep trimmed Bézier count
Pivot	Figure 11.1	73 269	4 435
Shipping	Figure 11.10	52 107	3 346
Tube	Figure 11.11	31 846	1 452

11.6   Conclusion

We have presented a system for generating an accurate B-rep for CSG models composed of curved primitives and rendering the resulting primitives on current graphics systems. Its application to parts of a submarine storage and handling system model helped us improve the overall frame rate by 3 to 4 times, as compared to directly rendering the polygonal B-rep. The main benefits in image quality, memory requirements, and rendering performance come from the multiresolution representation of the B-reps. However, our display system needs more processing (CPU) power for incremental triangulation computation. We are currently working on efficient memory management, load balancing, and performance enhancement of the display system to achieve interactive visualization of the entire submarine storage and handling system model. We are also working on more efficient algorithms to perform split-monotonic subdivision.

Acknowledgments

We are grateful to Fred Brooks, Anselmo Lastra, and members of UNC Walkthrough group for productive discussions. The CSG model of the submarine storage and handling system was provided to us by Greg Angelini, Jim Boudreaux, and Ken Fast at Electric Boat; thanks go to them. Supported in part by Alfred P. Sloan Foundation Fellowship, ARO Contract P-34982-MA, NSF Grant CCR-9319957, ONR Contract N00014-94-1-0738, ARPA Contract DABT63-93-C-0048 and NSF/ARPA Center for Computer Graphics and Scientific Visualization.

---

[3]The latest version of Catia does support curved geometries.

References

[1] S.S. Abi-Ezzi, L.A. Shirman, Tessellation of curved surfaces under highly varying transformations, *Proc. Eurographics'91*, pp. 385–397, 1991.

[2] C.L. Bajaj, A. Royappa, Triangulation and display of rational parametric surfaces, *Proc. Visualization'94*, pp. 69–76, IEEE Computer Society, Los Alamitos, Calif., 1994.

[3] E. Cohen, Some mathematical tools for a modeler's workbench, *IEEE Computer Graphics Appl.*, 3(7): 63–66; 1983.

[4] T. Derose, M. Lounsbery, J. Warren, *Multiresolution Analysis for Surfaces of Arbitrary Topology Type*, Technical Report TR 93-10-05, Department of Computer Science, University of Washington, 1993.

[5] G. Farin, *Curves and Surfaces for Computer Aided Geometric Design: A Practical Guide*, Academic Press, 1993.

[6] H. Fuchs, J. Poulton et al., Pixel-Planes 5: A heterogeneous multiprocessor graphics system using processor-enhanced memories, *Proc. ACM Siggraph*, 1989, pp. 79–88.

[7] T. A. Funkhouser, *Database and display algorithms for interactive visualization of architecture models*, PhD thesis, CS Division, UC Berkeley, 1993.

[8] N. Greene, M. Kass, G. Miller, Hierarchical z-buffer visibility, in *Proceedings of ACM Siggraph*, 1993, pp. 231–238.

[9] J. Goldfeather, S. Molnar, G. Turk, H. Fuchs, Near real-time csg rendering using tree normalization and geometric pruning, *IEEE Computer Graphics Appl.*, 9(3): 20–28; 1989.

[10] H. Hoppe, T. DeRose, T. Duchamp, J. Mcdonald, W. Stuetzle, Mesh optimization, *Proc. ACM Siggraph*, 1993, pp. 19–26.

[11] P. Heckbert, M. Garland, Multiresolution modeling for fast rendering, *Proc. Graphics Interface*, 1994.

[12] C.M. Hoffmann, *Geometric and Solid Modeling*, Morgan Kaufmann, San Mateo, Calif., 1989.

[13] M.E. Hohmeyer, A surface intersection algorithm based on loop detection, *Int. J. Comput. Geometry Appl.*, 1(4): 473–490; 1991. Special issue on Solid Modeling.

[14] G. Kedem, J.L. Ellis, The ray-casting machine, *Parallel Processing for Computer Vision and Display*, pp. 378–401, Springer-Verlag, 1989.

[15] M. Kelley, K. Gould et al., Hardware accelerated rendering of csg and transparency. *Proc. ACM Siggraph*, 1994, pp. 177–184.

[16] S. Kumar, S. Krishnan, D. Manocha, A. Narkhede, *Representation and display of complex csg models*, Technical Report TR95-019, Department of Computer Science, University of North Carolina, 1995.

[17] S. Krishnan, D. Manocha, *An efficient surface intersection algorithm based on the lower dimensional formulation*, Technical Report TR94-062, Department of Computer Science, University of North Carolina, 1994.

[18] S. Kumar, D. Manocha, Efficient rendering of trimmed NURBS surfaces. *Computer-Aided Design*, 27(7): 509–521; 1995.

[19] S. Kumar, D. Manocha, A. Lastra, Interactive display of large scale NURBS models, *Symposium on Interactive 3D Graphics*, Monterey, Calif., 1995, pp. 51–58.

[20] W.L. Luken, Fuhua Cheng, *Rendering trimmed NURB surfaces*, Computer science research report 18669(81711), IBM Research Division, 1993.

[21] J.R. Rossignac, P. Borrel, *Multi-resolution 3d approximations for rendering complex scenes*, Technical Report RC 17697, IBM T.J. Watson Research Center, 1992.

[22] A. Rockwood, K. Heaton, T. Davis, Real-time rendering of trimmed surfaces, *Proc. of ACM Siggraph*, 1989, pp. 107–117.

[23] S. Roth, Ray casting for modeling solids, *Computer Graphics and Image Processing*, 18(2): 109–144; 1982.

[24] A.A.G. Requicha, J.R. Rossignac, Solid modeling and beyond, *IEEE Computer Graphics Appl.*, 31–44; Sept. 1992.

[25] J. Rossignac, J. Wu, Correct shading of regularized csg solids using a depth-interval buffer, *Eurographics Workshop on Graphics Hardware*, 1990.

[26] M. Segal, Using tolerances to guarantee valid polyhedral modeling results, *Proc. ACM Siggraph*, 1990, pp. 105–114.

[27] R. Seidel, Linear programming and convex hulls made easy, *Proc. 6th Ann. ACM Conf. on Computational Geometry*, Berkeley, Calif., 1990, pp. 211–215.

[28] R. Seidel, A simple and fast randomized algorithm for computing trapezoidal decompositions and for triangulating polygons, *Comput. Geometry Theor. Appl.*, 1(1): 51–64; 1991.

[29] T.W. Sederberg, T. Nishita, Geometric hermite approximation of surface patch intersection curves, *Computer Aided Geometric Design*, 8: 97–114; 1991.

[30] W.J. Schroeder, J.A. Zarge, W.E. Lorensen, Decimation of triangle meshes, *Proc. ACM Siggraph*, 1992, pp. 65–70.

[31] S.J. Teller, *Visibility computations in densely occluded polyhedral environments*, PhD thesis, CS Division, UC Berkeley, 1992.

[32] W. Tiller, Rational b–splines for curve and surface representation, *IEEE Computer Graphics Appl.*, 3(6): 61–69; 1983.

[33] G. Turk, Re-tiling polygonal surfaces, *Proc. ACM Siggraph*, 1992, pp. 55–64.

12
Texture Potential Mapping: A Way to Provide Anti-Aliased Texture without Blurring

R.J. Cant and P. Shrubsole

12.1 Introduction

Early real-time graphics systems, such as the Apollo landing simulator, gave us an insight into the practicality of interacting with 3D environments. Such systems used scenes built from flat, polygonal surfaces which could be rendered sufficiently quickly with the technology of the time. Early improvements in realism were achieved by incorporating lighting effects and Gouraud shading. Their main criticism, however, was their lack of realism due to the extreme smoothness of surfaces. Not only were the scenes visually uninteresting, but it was found that pilots training on flight simulators were unable to make use of visual motion cues when 'flying' at low altitude. However, as greater processing power became more readily available, methods were devised to try to give a better representation of surfaces, thereby adding richness to the scene and linking more closely to their 'real-life' counterparts. The most startling difference can be observed by overlaying a predetermined pattern to each surface (see Figures 12.1a and 12.1b). Thus, the demand for realism has meant that texture mapping has become a vital component in the graphics rendering pipeline for a wide range of applications. However, the process of accurately mapping texture values to the display requires a significant amount of computing power.

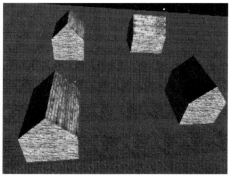

Figure 12.1 (a) A simple rendered scene using flat shading. (b) The same scene using texture mapping.

Visualization and Modeling
ISBN 0-12-227738-4

Normal real-time image rendering methods require that, instead of mapping the texture values on a polygon in 3D space to the screen, screen pixels are effectively mapped onto a region of the texture. This means that whilst image results will be fine when the transformed screen pixels are of the same order of size, shape and orientation as the stored pixels, when the size of the transformed pixels in texture space varies, aliasing can readily occur, resulting in a variety of false patterns and moiré fringing effects depending on the nature of the textures being mapped. Such effects can sometimes pass unnoticed in still images, but when the scene moves the texture will change and move in unexpected ways. Therefore, a method of finding the average texture value within the pixels needs to be adopted. A number of techniques have been proposed to do this; a good survey of them is given in [1]. To our knowledge, only a few methods have been proposed for real-time usage. All of these techniques suffer from one or other deficiency. The problems include the inability to cope with an arbitrary texture pattern, inadequate suppression of aliasing, a tendency to unnecessarily blur the texture pattern, and inefficiency or complexity, making a real-time implementation impractical.

A new technique is therefore desirable for improving the quality of texture mapping in high-performance real-time graphics architectures, provided that this can be achieved with a comparable computational cost to that of existing methods.

This chapter describes a new type of texture mapping algorithm called Texture Potential mapping that is optimized for the constraints of hardware systems and can easily be embedded into a single or multiprocessor graphics pipeline.

12.2   The Mapping Process

Since the basis of adding planar texture patterns to smooth surfaces is mapping, the texture problem reduces to the specification of a transformation from one coordinate system to another. The most commonly used method is to scan in screen space (x, y) and find the transformation that maps to texture space $u(x, y)$ and $v(x, y)$. Thus, the amount of work done during a point to point transformation for a polygon in object space is directly proportional to the number of pixels the polygon covers in screen space.

This can be summarized as

```
for y
    for x
        compute u(x, y) and v(x, y)
        copy TEXTURE[u, v] to SCREEN[x, y]
```

The mapping from screen space to texture space can be deduced by applying a perspective matrix transformation expressed in homogeneous form:

$$[xw \ yw \ w] = [u \ v \ 1] \begin{bmatrix} A & D & G \\ B & E & H \\ C & F & I \end{bmatrix}$$

Hence the values of u and v are evaluated by finding the inverse of this matrix:

$$[uq \ vq \ q] = [x \ y \ 1] \begin{bmatrix} EI-FH & FG-DI & DH-EG \\ CH-BI & AI-CG & BG-AH \\ BF-CE & CD-AF & AE-BD \end{bmatrix} = \begin{bmatrix} a & d & g \\ b & e & h \\ c & f & i \end{bmatrix}$$

Resulting in

$$u = \frac{ax + by + c}{gh + hy + i} \quad \text{and} \quad v = \frac{dx + ey + f}{gh + hy + i}$$

Since the formulas for u and v are quotients of linear expressions, they can be computed incrementally when using scan line methods for rasterization. This further reduces the computational cost to 3 additions and 2 divisions per screen pixel.

12.3   Aliasing

If the method described above is used on a point to point basis, the centers of each of the screen pixels are mapped to single texture values, then large chunks of the original texture might well be ignored, whilst the points that are being considered depend on the interaction between the grid of the texture store and that of the screen. This is analogous to the classic 'jaggies' aliasing effect, where edges within a pixel are not sufficiently sampled (i.e., sampling takes place below the Nyquist rate). Texture aliasing arising from low sampling rates, however, can often deteriorate picture quality more seriously than 'jaggies' do, since every pixel within a face will be affected, rather than just those along the edges. Furthermore, in a real-time system, the effect is still worse because textures will map at different orientations for each frame at a rate of 30 to 60 frames per second. The apparent movement of the patterns will not correlate with that of the actual scene and the resulting texture will appear to swim and scintillate [2].

Such a problem can be dealt with effectively by making use of a procedural texture [3]. With a procedural texture it may be possible to evaluate the average texture within a pixel analytically – but there are few choices of 'texture function' which allow this, the major option being patterns built from superpositions of sinusoids. With such a system, exact sampling of texture is possible, resulting in high quality anti-aliased images. Some early flight simulator texture mapping systems utilized this approach. The drawback of this method is that the range of possible patterns is severely limited and hence it is not possible to reproduce the majority of textures found in the real world.

A static example of the problem is illustrated by Figures 12.2a and 12.2b. The texture being mapped consists of a combination of two sinusoidal patterns at right angles. We have chosen this pattern because it shows up aliasing problems very clearly, whilst it can also be correctly sampled analytically. In both figures, the pattern is being mapped onto an infinite plane at a shallow angle to the viewing direction. In (a) the pattern has been correctly sampled analytically, using a Gaussian filter. The two sinusoids fade out progressively at long range when their wavelength becomes shorter than the size of the screen pixel. The result is that in the distance the pattern degenerates into moiré fringing. One might think that this problem could be overcome by simply taking significantly more samples within a pixel. Unfortunately this does not work very well if the samples are taken on a regular pattern, as Figure 12.2c, which has

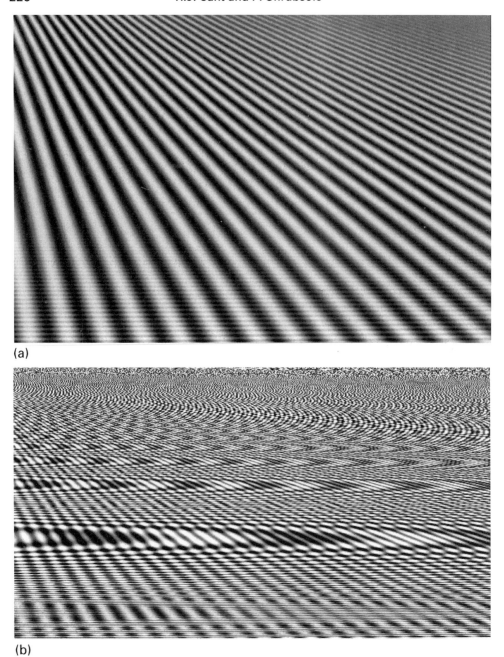

(a)

(b)

Figure 12.2 (a) The procedural texture is mapped analytically, producing excellent anti-aliased results. (b) The same texture is mapped on a point to point basis. Extreme aliasing effects and fringing are exhibited as the texture becomes compressed with distance. (c) Aliasing effects are reduced by taking 16 samples at the same points within each pixel. (d) Effects of aliasing reduce further if the samples are taken randomly within each pixel.

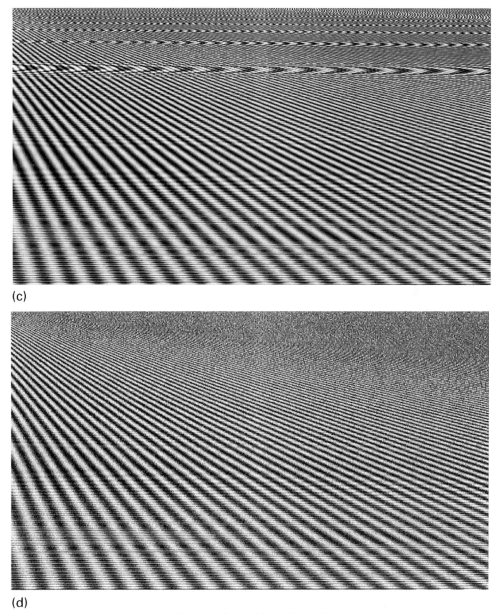

(c)

(d)

Figure 12.2   (Continued)

16 samples per pixel, shows. This is because the grid of samples still 'beats' with the texture. If the samples are taken at random points then the fringing can be replaced by noise, but the cost of this is that the sample points can no longer be determined incrementally. This will substantially increase the processing time required to render each surface in a 3D scene. This is illustrated in Figure 12.2d.

More subtle techniques are therefore required that retain as much of the original texture as possible whilst keeping the sampling rate low.

12.4   Established Methods of Anti-Aliasing Texture in Real Time

12.4.1   MIP mapping

Williams [4] deals with the problem of texture aliasing by making use of several images of the texture at various resolutions, each of which is derived from the original by averaging down to lower resolutions. When a transformed screen pixel is covered by a collection of texture pixels, the MIP map pixels corresponding to this collection most closely are used to give a filtered value. Since only a limited number of the tables may be stored, values from two adjacent tables must be blended in order to deal with the transition of one resolution to another across a surface.

MIP mapping has the advantage of speed since only two bilinear interpolations are required to get a value from each adjacent table plus an additional interpolation between the two values. However, this is generally at the expense of accuracy. For example, a perspective projection may well require that the texture be compressed in only one direction. This will result in blurring of the original texture in both directions as the MIP map goes down to lower resolutions at greater viewing distances. Figure 12.3 illustrates the effect of blurring using a MIP map. The pattern used is as in the previous figures and, once again, the pattern is mapped onto an infinite plane at a shallow angle.

The choice of scale for the MIP map must be governed by the highest frequency that occurs within each pixel, in this case the horizontal lines, otherwise aliasing will occur. The side effect of this is that the other component of the texture is suppressed while it is still large enough to be clearly seen. The only way in which this problem could be overcome would be to greatly increase the number of MIP maps to include ones which

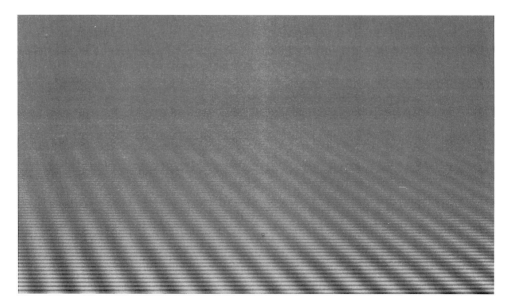

Figure 12.3   Effects of aliasing are not easily observable here, but the texture becomes blurred sooner than necessary.

resample the texture asymmetrically. The number of maps required to cover all possibilities makes this approach impractical.

12.4.2   Summed area table

Crow [5] devised a scheme in which a single table of entries calculated from the original texture is used from which a sum of texture values lying within a given rectangle can easily be determined. Thus, if we place a bounding rectangle around a transformed pixel in texture space, an average texture value can be determined by evaluating the sum of texture values within it, using the summed area table, and then dividing this value by its area. The idea of making use of such a table is neat in that it does not require us to actually look at each of the texture values within the rectangle at render time.

This method has the advantage over MIP mapping that a virtually continuous range of texture densities can be obtained in two directions independently. This improvement is well illustrated in Figure 12.5a, which has the same texture pattern and viewpoint as Figure 12.3, but uses the summed area technique in place of MIP mapping. The extra processing required to perform the Summed Area Table method comes from the fact that now four bilinear interpolations are required to map each of the corners of the screen pixel to texture space in order to obtain a bounding rectangle.

To see where the summed area method becomes significantly less accurate, consider a screen pixel that has undergone a perspective bilinear transformation to texture space (see Figure 12.4). It can be seen that a bounding rectangle may not suffice when the surface is viewed at rotations about more than one axis. Such pixels will also occur at the edge of the screen when the field of view is wide. These cases therefore need to be taken into consideration, since excessive blurring will be observed when they occur. This effect is illustrated in Figure 12.5b. The same texture pattern has been used as before, but this time, it has been rotated by 45° before being stored. This rotation has been reversed by the viewing transformation creating a long, thin pixel footprint at 45° as shown in Figure 12.4. As with the MIP map, the outcome is that the vertical stripes are suppressed sooner than is necessary.

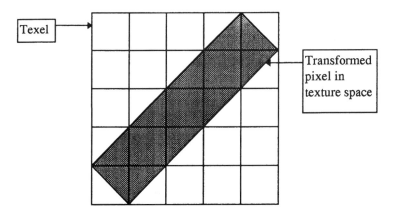

Figure 12.4   Illustration of how the summed area table ignores substantial areas of the texture at certain orientations.

R.J. Cant and P. Shrubsole

(a)

(b)

Figure 12.5   (a) Effects of blurring are removed with the summed area table, but this is a favourable orientation. (b) Effects of blurring and fringing are evident here with the summed area method. This is due to the orientation of the texture and the type of texture used.

To illustrate the fact that such a problem can occur with realistic texture patterns we have included Figure 12.10a which shows a pattern that could be used to represent a tiled surface. When this pattern is rotated to a similar angle to that of Figure 12.5b, a similar blurring effect is observed.

12.4.3 Adaptive precision method

In an attempt to solve this problem, Glassner [6] extended the summed area method by iteratively trimming away the excess areas of the bounding rectangle. This requires the geometry of the transformed screen pixel, relative to its bounding box, to be detected. The excess areas are then subdivided into rectangles which can then be deducted from the original sum (see Figure 12.6).

Although the technique minimizes the error produced by the summed area method, it is found that an estimate on the number of subdivisions that need to be made for good results is difficult to produce accurately, leading to unpredictable results. Furthermore, the classification of general quadrilaterals tends to make the overall process algorithmically burdensome. Such an algorithm would be difficult to optimize or implement in hardware. A particular problem arises from the larger number of accesses which may need to be made to the table for each pixel. In a highly optimized system these accesses will be the dominant factor in determining system performance.

12.4.4 Other methods of anti-aliasing texture

Other well-established methods have less application in real-time systems since they tend to work in texture space (such as Feibush-Levoy-Cook [7]). This means that a

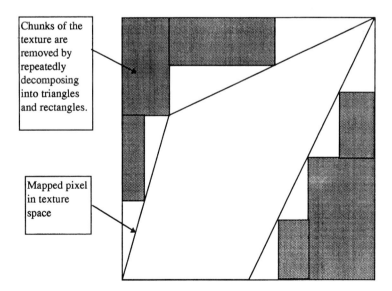

Chunks of the texture are removed by repeatedly decomposing into triangles and rectangles.

Mapped pixel in texture space

Figure 12.6 Illustration shows how the adaptive precision method is used to reduce the texture to within the boundaries of the warped pixel.

great number of transformations from texture space to screen space may well occur for a single pixel.

12.5   New Method: Potential Mapping

Having examined the range of texture anti-aliasing methods, it becomes evident that there is a bias, whether in favor of efficiency, leading to spurious areas of the resulting texture, or in favor of texture integrity, where computation is greatly increased and hardware implementation becomes impractical. It would therefore seem appropriate to balance the scales of efficiency and integrity by developing a new method that takes all of the following factors into account:

- A simple algorithm
- Ability to cope with general texture patterns at any orientation
- Speed
- Ability to implement in hardware
- Minimal aliasing
- Minimal blurring

Our method is based on the idea of finding a quick way of performing the integral of the texture pattern over the area of the transformed pixel which avoids the problems of the summed area table without introducing too much algorithmic complexity.

If we assume a screen pixel to be square, then its resultant image after rotation and a perspective transformation of its corner points will be a general quadrilateral. Ideally we would like a method that deals with the quadrilateral directly without approximating it to any simpler shape. Furthermore, as with Crow, we would like to avoid having to look at each and every texture pixel that lies within the transformed pixel when determining the average texture value (i.e., when finding the texture sum and the area of the quadrilateral).

Consider Gauss' theorem in physics, in which the charge contained within a volume can be found by traversing only the surface of that volume. If this is reduced by one dimension then, by analogy, the texture contained within a transformed pixel can be found by traversing only the boundary. This is essentially the principle behind potential mapping.

Potential mapping for a given screen pixel is done by tracing around the boundary of its transformed pixel in texture space. For each texture coordinate, we calculate a corresponding 'potential' value which is based on the actual texture intensities down a column in texture space (see Figure 12.7). The total texture intensity bounded by a transformed pixel within that column is then found from the corresponding upper and lower 'potential' values on the boundary of the pixel. If we integrate this over all the columns within the transformed pixel, an average intensity value can be deduced. Since the 'potential' values only need to be calculated once for each texture map, they can be pre-computed and stored, leaving only one operation per texture column and only one division per transformed pixel in order to average over the area.

The method can be summarized algorithmically:

for u (left of transformed pixel to right)
  find v_{lower} and v_{upper}
  find 'potential' across texture column, $P(v_{lower}, v_{upper})$
  Texture Sum = Texture Sum + $P(v_{lower}, v_{upper})$
  Area = Area+ $(v_{upper} - v_{lower})$
 Average Intensity = Texture Sum / Area

The algorithm clearly shows that the problem of finding the summed area has now been reduced to one dimension (i.e., the u direction) such that the number of iterations required becomes solely dependent on the width of the transformed pixel. Note that we could alternatively make use of horizontal texture strips and sum in the v direction just as easily.

The task of implementing potential mapping optimally can be divided into two: the construction of a table of 'potential' values such that $P(v_{lower}, v_{upper})$ is computationally inexpensive, and finding v_{lower} and v_{upper} as we trace around the pixel.

12.5.1 Evaluating potential values

As the boundary of the transformed pixel is being traced in texture space, the summed texture values lying within each vertical strip need to be evaluated. This can be achieved

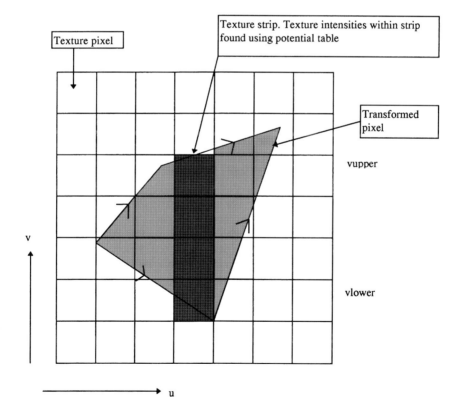

Figure 12.7 Illustration showing how texture strips are found whilst the texture pixel is traced (note arrowheads around pixel boundary).

optimally by first building up a table of 'potential' values. These values are derived from the texture by storing a cumulative sum of texture values down each column of the original texture. Figure 12.8 illustrates this.

Now we can find the 'potential difference' (or summed texture), P, across the upper and lower texture values in a vertical strip by simply subtracting the upper and lower potential values corresponding to v_{upper} and v_{lower}, i.e.,

$P(v_{lower}, v_{upper}) = p[u, v_{lower}] - p[u, v_{upper}]$
where $p[u, v] = \Sigma_{i=0; l<=v+1} T[u, i]$, is prestored in a potential table,
and $T[u, v]$ is the texture value obtained from the texture table at (u, v).

12.5.2   Tracing around transformed pixels

As with Crow's method, the four corners of the screen pixel need to be bilinearly mapped into texture space (note that only one corner need be mapped for pixels lying within a screen polygon, see later). One way of performing the tracing operation is to start with the extreme top left corner of the transformed pixel in texture space. We then find the gradients to its nearest lower and upper corners, and next the gradients from those corners to its farthest right corner. Since we are ultimately dealing with discrete texture pixels, the values of v_{lower} and v_{upper} can be evaluated trivially using unit increments in u.

This method, known as the DDA algorithm, has drawbacks, however, since four divides must take place to find each gradient and the process of rounding v to an integer takes time [8]. The need for divide operations can be removed by using Bresenham's line drawing algorithm. This also has the advantage of guaranteeing accuracy, which helps to prevent double counting of contributions.

When the slope of a line is greater than 1, the usual procedure is to exchange the x and y (in this case u and v) coordinates and plot the line 'on its side.' In the present case we do not want to do this because it would result in more than one entry per column.

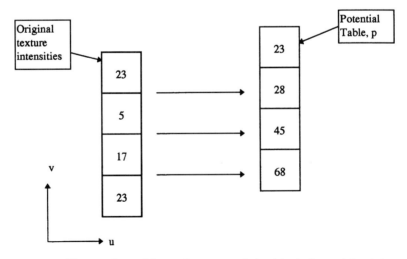

Figure 12.8   Illustration of how the potential table is found for later use.

To compensate for this, a complicated calculation of the integration measure would be needed. Instead we just continue to use the algorithm in its original form, allowing near vertical lines to be sparsely populated.

The consolidation of subpixel displacements into whole pixels nominally requires a division for each step along the line. In the normal Bresenham algorithm [9] this is reduced to a simple subtraction because we know that, for a line at less than 45°, the only possible answers are 0 and 1. In the present case we do not have this restriction but we can still know the answer in advance to an accuracy of one unit if we calculate the integer part of the slope first. This might seem to cancel the original advantage, but because the gradients are the same for all pixels in a scan line in screen space, this can be done just once per line. Similarly, left and right gradients for pixels in a column are the same and can be shared (see Figure 12.9).

We can make further efficiency savings by noting that adjacent pixel corners are shared between screen pixels, so that only one bilinear mapping need be made for each

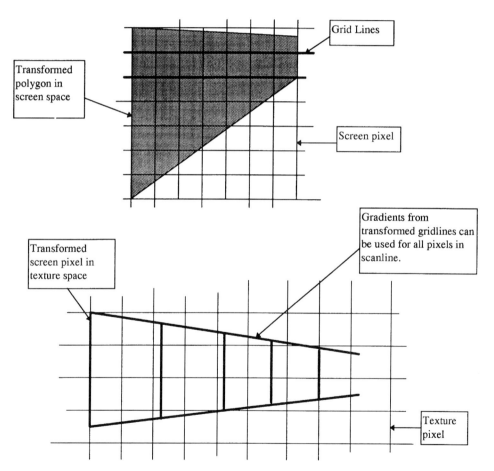

Figure 12.9 Illustration showing how the cost of finding the gradients around each transformed pixel in texture space can be reduced by mapping gridlines in screen space prior to texture mapping.

pixel except at the edges of the polygon. This commonality also applies to the pixel edges, allowing a possible saving of a factor of 2 in the time taken to trace around each pixel.

There is one particular case when the calculation leads to a summed texture of 0! This occurs when the fractional values for v_{upper} and v_{lower} lie within the same texture pixel. In order to avoid extending the algorithm to overcome this problem (since we would like to keep it as simple as possible for hardware implementation purposes), we can use the fact that the fractional v_{upper} and v_{lower} values are always distinct if texture mapping is to take place. If we double the resolution of the potential table in the v direction, so that the new table values are the average of consecutive pairs of the old table values, then we can simply force upper values of v in a strip, to access the upper values in the table, and the lower values of v to access the lower values in the table. Thus we ensure that the summed texture is always greater than zero without incurring any modifications to the algorithm. To continue to exploit the commonality of edges between neighboring pixels we must arrange for the two sets of values to be retrieved using the same memory access.

Note that when tracing around pixels which lie on the edge of a polygon, it is possible to use the polygon edge rather than the pixel edge. The result of this is to provide improved anti-aliasing of the edges of textured polygons. This is a further advantage of potential mapping compared to the MIP map, which prefilters the texture and cannot 'know' where the polygon boundary will lie.

Results of the potential mapping algorithm show that the effects of blurring and aliasing are significantly reduced when compared with MIP mapping (Figures 12.3 and 12.10a respectively) and when compared with the summed area method (Figures 12.5 and 12.10b respectively). The residual moiré fringing which can be seen is caused by the top-hat style filter which has been used. To eliminate this fringing, it would be necessary to use a filter such as a Gaussian which has a more gradual fall-off at the edges. Unfortunately, this is difficult to achieve without resorting to a brute force integration technique involving all the texels which lie within and around the projected pixel edges.

Since the texture patterns used in these images represent a severe test of a texture anti-aliasing system, it is likely that the kind of patterns used more commonly in practical applications will not display the effect so strongly. If the residual fringing is a problem it can easily be eliminated at a cost of slight blurring by passing the final image through a filter before display. (In practice, a final adjustment of the monitor focus can achieve the required effect at zero cost.)

12.6   Implementation and Performance Considerations

Unlike methods such as the MIP map or summed area table, the time taken per pixel by our algorithm will vary according to the scale and orientation of the texture. Consequently we cannot specify a fixed performance level for this algorithm.

We have included in our text programs extra instructions to count the amount of time being taken by each stage in the process. For a full screen image of texture at a shallow angle, as shown in the illustrations above, the results show that the inverse perspective transformation takes 12% of the time, set-up operations take 40%, and the

(a)

(b)

Figure 12.10 (a) Using the potential mapping technique the excessive blurring noticed in Figure 12.3 is removed without introducing significant aliasing. (b) The effects of blur, aliasing, and fringing are greatly reduced when using potential mapping even with the unfavorable texture orientation, as used in Figure 12.5.

remaining 48% is spent tracing around the edge of the pixels. At a less favorable orientation of the texture map (when the projected pixel is very long in the nonintegrated direction) the time spent tracing around pixels increases by 50%. Since the time taken to perform the inverse perspective transformation will be the same as for the other algorithms and the set-up operations that need to be done for each pixel are likely to be comparable to those required by the summed area table method, these proportions give an approximate guide to relative performance.

This suggests a degradation by roughly a factor of 2 in speed compared to the summed area table and between 2 and 4 compared to MIP mapping, depending on how many samples and scales the MIP map uses. When the texture system is being optimally used, most of the time the texels will be of similar scale to the screen pixels. In these circumstances, the number of entries which need to be summed for each pixel edge will normally be only one or two. In consequence, the time taken to trace around the pixels will disappear (the time taken for the first point on each edge has been included in the set-up time) and our algorithm will be only marginally slower than the summed area table or MIP map.

The variation in performance with texture scale and orientation may not matter for real applications because only a small proportion of textured polygons will be presented at time-consuming angles. However, it is possible to combine our algorithm with a one-dimensional MIP map which operates in the nonsummed direction. Using this approach, the number of texture potential values which need to be accessed to create each pixel can be limited to 16 in the worst case without degrading the image significantly. Using two different techniques in the two directions thus produces a better result than either of them individually.

On a single processor using current technology, none of the algorithms are capable of real-time performance, so interactive systems will require multiple processors or special hardware. Our algorithm is well suited to parallel processing using a pipeline architecture because it easily decomposes into the stages of transformation, pixel edge set up, pixel edge tracing and the summation of the final results. A subdivision work based on giving each processor a separate area of the screen can also be done quite easily because the only data which needs to be communicated between processors is the sums over pixel edges and they only need to be passed between nearest neighbors. Multiple copies of the potential map would be needed to avoid conflicts between the processors.

All these estimates assume that all the instructions other than the divide and the reciprocal take a single cycle and no allowance can be made for cache misses. Such assumptions correlate well with the use of a modern DSP style processor such as the TMS320C40 with all external memory being single cycle SRAM. In many systems the external memory is much slower than the cache and instructions which do not access it run very much faster than those that do. In such a system the number of external memory accesses provides an alternative performance measure. It is likely that the only external accesses in any of the algorithms will be the reads from the texture map or potential.

On this measure our experiments have shown that potential mapping requires a minimum of 2 and an average of 7–10 accesses per pixel, as against 4 for the summed area table and 2–8 for MIP mapping (depending on the version used). Simply averaging all the texels within a pixel would have required between 20 and 30 accesses on average in the cases we tested.

In a hardware implementation, these memory access requirements are the only critical factors because almost all the other operations are simple logical or arithmetic ones which can be pipelined and parallelized into a single-cycle architecture without using excessive numbers of gates. We can deduce that our method is 2–4 times slower than the summed area table or MIP map techniques, both of which have some deficiency in anti-aliasing performance. It is about 2 or 3 times faster than the brute force approach which produces similar quality output. Compared with multiple random samples it produces better output at a slightly lower cost.

12.7 Conclusions

As remarked above, the justification for the potential mapping method is that it should be faster than existing high-quality methods and produce better quality results than existing fast methods. In the preceding section, we have shown that the theoretical performance of our technique is a useful improvement over the simple approach of averaging all texels within a pixel. The illustrations demonstrate that it also avoids the problem areas which affect faster techniques.

Whilst the new method is somewhat slower than those in current use, it is interesting to note that this speed differential is outweighed by the technological advances of recent years. Consequently, a potential mapping system, implemented with current technology will have a better price/performance ratio than would have been possible using MIP mapping or the summed area table at the time at which they were first proposed.

Potential mapping is therefore worthy of serious consideration as a texture anti-aliasing system for future image generation systems (Figure 12.11).

(a)

Figure 12.11   (a) A more realistic texture pattern is used with the summed area method.

(b)

Figure 12.11   (b) The same texture is used with the potential mapping method.

References

[1] P. Heckbert, Survey of texture mapping. In K.I. Joy (ed.) *Computer Graphics: Image Synthesis*, Computer Society Press, 1988, pp. 321–322.
[2] J. Dudgeon, Algorithms for texture mapping. In *Proceedings of the 23rd South Eastern Symposium on Systems Theory*, 10–12 March 1991, Columbia SC. Sponsored by the IEEE, pp. 613–617.
[3] B. Schachter, Long crested wave models, *Computer Graphics and Image Processing*, 12: 187–201; 1980.
[4] L. Williams, Pyramidal parametrics, *Computer Graphics*, 17(3): July 1983.
[5] F. Crow, Summed area tables for texture mapping, *Computer Graphics*, 18(3); July 1984.
[6] A. Glassner, Adaptive precision in texture mapping, *Computer Graphics*, 20(4): Nov. 1986.
[7] A. Feibish, M. Levoy, L. Cook, Synthetic texturing using digital filters, *Computer Graphics*, 14(3): July 1980.
[8] Foley, van Dam, Feiner, Hughes, *Computer Graphics, Principles and Practice*, Addison-Wesley, 1990, pp. 72–81.
[9] J.E. Bresenham, Algorithm for computer control of a digital plotter, *IBM Systems J.*, 4(1): 25–30; 1965.

13
Extended Algebraic Surface Generation for Volume Modeling: An Approach through Genetic Algorithms

Herve Luga, Rodolphe Pelle, Alain Berro and Yves Duthen

13.1 Introduction

Volumes can be defined by implicit surfaces using mathematical equations such as $f(x, y, z) = 0$ where f is a 'potential' function. Such a definition is interesting because it allows compact representation of complex objects which usually require a large set of primitives such as meshes. For example, a sphere of radius r could be described by the equation $x^2 + y^2 + z^2 - r^2 = 0$ instead of a mesh of hundred faces. Moreover, this simplifies their transformation and animation [3]. Deforming soft objects like balls or 'jello' could be achieved by direct modification of their mathematical equation.

Extended algebraic surfaces known as 'blobby models' [2] offer great advantages because of the continuous aspect of fields that derive from them. A surface is defined by an isovalue of a scalar field produced by generating primitives.

These algebraic surfaces provide smooth and soft shapes which are very difficult to achieve with other modeling methods. Consequently, they are well suited for representation of natural objects like human faces [8] or physical objects (clouds, for example). Rendering such surfaces can now be achieved efficiently [9]. Several optimization methods can be applied to accelerate rendering or manipulation of such

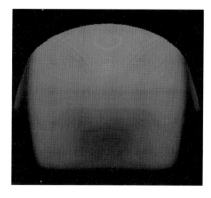

Figure 13.1 Example of a field produced by two primitives.

Visualization and Modeling
ISBN 0-12-227738-4

surfaces. The Kalra and Barr method uses field gradient and Cauchy–Lipschitz conditions to verify whether the fields is secant to a particular cube.

Blinn [2] defined a subset of implicit surfaces. These surfaces are defined as a weighted sum of primitives:

$$V(x, y, z) = \sum_{i=1}^{N} f_i(x, y, z)$$

A primitive is defined by the function $f_i(x, y, z) = b_i \cdot e^{-(a_i g_i(x,y,z))}$, where $g_i(x, y, z)$ is an algebraic expression and b_i the weight of the primitive. This approach permits the representation of a large set of surfaces. Moreover, these surfaces are easily derivable and are consequently well suited for mathematical transformations.

13.2   Modeling Implicit Surfaces

The main problem that has to be solved in order to determine the distribution of primitives which shape a particular field is in deep correlation with the parameters defining them. The slight modification of any one of them will affect the whole field and then the whole surface. Several modeling methods have been proposed to produce implicit surfaces; we show here two of them with their advantages and drawbacks.

13.2.1   The Muraki method

Muraki [8] proposed a deterministic approach based on the Blinn's model. This method proceeds by the segmentation of primitives, which permits the minimization of an energy function. This function computes the differences between range data points and current surface. Each primitive, defined by five parameters, is of the form

$$f_i(x, y, z) = b_i \cdot \exp\left\{-a_i\left[((x - x_i)^{2/\nu_i} + (y - y_i)^{2/\nu_i})^{\nu_i/\mu_i} + (z - z_i)^{2/\mu_i}\right]\right\}$$

Therefore, this method does not cover the whole range of primitives defined in the Blinn model. In the case of objects defined by many points, this systematic and linear exploration of space is not efficient and depends on the range data distribution. Consequently, this approach cannot ensure the optimal solution.

13.2.2   The Tsingos modeler

Tsingos [10] provides a real-time modeler which allows interactive use of such surfaces for object generation. This modeler operate on skeletons which define the center of the primitives. The association of such skeletons defines complex objects which are real-time rendered by the use of discrete techniques. This modeler does not deal with other surface definition models.

These two approaches do not provide an easy and adaptive method to convert objects defined by 3D meshes or NURBS to implicit surfaces. Moreover, they use a restrictive subset of the implicit surfaces, limiting the interest of the Blinn model.

13.3   Fitting 3D Model to Implicit Surfaces

Our goal is to provide a model that can automatically generate implicit surfaces as a replacement of another volume modelization. We expose here an application of our approach to the translation of 3D meshes into extended algebraic surface definitions.

We consider a subset of Blinn's functions which allows a large class of surface definitions. These functions are defined by the equation

$$f(x,\, y,\, z) = \sum_{i=1}^{N} b_i \cdot e^{-(a_i \cdot f_i(x,y,z))}$$

where

$$f_i(x,\, y,\, z) = \frac{(x - xc)^{px}}{dx} + \frac{(y - yc)^{py}}{dy} + \frac{(z - zc)^{pz}}{dz}$$

Such an expression allows the creation of a wide variety of potentials including elliptics, superquadrics, and cubics.

Each primitive of the surface is defined with 11 parameters. Therefore, our surfaces are defined by $N \times 11$ parameters where N is the number of primitives in the surface. We have to tune these parameters to make the surface match those of the specified original object. This matching must take into account the spatial distribution of the original model. Then, we need an optimization algorithm for generating these surfaces.

13.4   Optimization Algorithms

Considering the chosen state space, one could attribute to each value a hundred (in fact this is very small) possible states. So we have $N \times 100^{11} = N \times 10^{22}$ points in our state space. Several optimization schemes could be considered to solve our problem. We now look at some of these, discussing of their advantages and drawbacks.

- *Deterministic approaches*: These approaches are based on a deterministic exploration of the state space. They provide robust algorithms such as branch and bound. These methods are very efficient in the case of *low dimension* state space. Therefore, they are not well fitted to our problem.
- *Systematic approaches*: These approaches perform systematic exploration of the state space. Because of the large size of our state space, if we suppose that computing the volume described by an equation took 10^{-3} seconds, we need $N \times 1.9 \times 10^{19}$ years to compute the solutions which cover the whole state space. Thus, this method cannot be applied.
- *Stochastic approaches*: These approaches are based on a stochastic exploration of the state space. They are characterized by a random generation of points in the state space. According to the optimization process, these points are gradually bearing to a point which represents one solution of the given problem.

Simulated annealing [7]

This optimization model mimics the physical process used in the annealing of materials. This process takes place in two stages: (1) The solid is heated to its melting point; (2) The heat is reduced in a particular way to give to the solid a minimal energy state. Applied to mathematical optimization, the solid states represent possible points in the state space. The function to optimize is the energy of the solid.

At a given step i of energy E_i, a new step j of energy E_j is generated by local modifications of i. If $(E_j - E_i) \leq 0$ then j is chosen as the new state. If $(E_j - E_i) > 0$, j has the probability P_j to become the new state where

$$ P_j = \exp\left(\frac{E_i - E_j}{k_b \cdot T} \right) $$

K_b is the Boltzmann constant and T represents the current temperature of the system. At the beginning of the process, T is high and is progressively decreased. When T is near 0, the process has reached a stable state which is assumed to be near the optimal solution.

This optimization process could not be applied to our problem because the size of the state space is unknown a priori. Furthermore, this process is not efficient when several solutions are equivalent.

Genetic algorithms

These search and optimization algorithms have been introduced by Holland [5]. They use as a model the natural evolution process to provide a robust search technique in complex environments.

This method mimics the environmental pressure on a population of data structures that represent the genetic codes of the solutions to the problem. Each individual of the population, called a chromosome, is evaluated against the environment and receives a payoff. This measure, provided by a 'fitness' function, has to estimate the ability of an individual to solve the problem. For example, finding the global maximum of a simple unidimensional mathematical function could use the function value f_i of an individual C_i as a fitness (Figure 13.2).

The best fitted chromosomes can spread their characteristics to form a new population or a new generation. Spreading characteristics is achieved by crossing the individual in a similar way to the natural DNA crossing-over (Figure 13.3). This

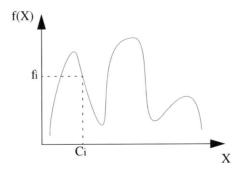

Figure 13.2   Example of a simple fitness.

Parents   Childs

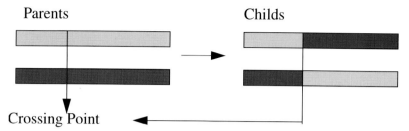

Crossing Point

Figure 13.3   Genetic cross-over.

process is iterated until convergence of the population to the optimal solution (Figure 13.4).

The original population is generated through a stochastic process which can be limited to a subset of possible individuals to cover well-fitted positions in the state space.

Coding a problem consists in the choice of a pertinent data structure (the chromosomes), which has to 'encapsulate the abstraction' of a problem and the definition of a fitness function that defines the pressure of the environment for a particular problem.

Because of the nonlinearity of the problem and the wide size of the state space, we choose genetic algorithms which provide an efficient and robust optimization method in nonlinear environments [4]. Furthermore, the operations provided by genetic search such as crossing (cross-over operation) and creating (mutation operation) match the progressive aspect of solving such a problem. They can act with a high abstraction level for both the space of solutions and the way to explore it.

13.5   Adaptation of Genetic Algorithms to Our Problem

This section describes the chromosome representation, the fitness function, and some additional operators needed to apply genetic algorithms to our problem.

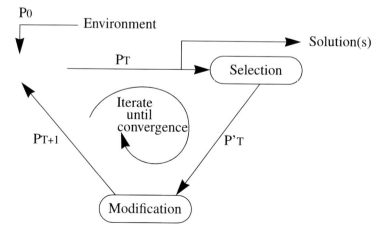

Figure 13.4   The cycle of a genetic algorithm.

13.5.1 Chromosome representation

As stated before, our chromosome must describe the mathematic equation of the field, which is:

$$f(x, y, z) = \sum_{i=1}^{N} b_i \cdot \exp\left[-a_i\left(\frac{(x - xc)^{px}}{dx} + \frac{(y - yc)^{py}}{dy} + \frac{(z - zc)^{pz}}{dz}\right)\right]$$

According to the fact that the original object could be normalized, we choose to limit the parameters values in the ranges

$b_i \in [-1, 1]$
$px, py, pz \in [0, 20]$
$xc, yc, zc \in [-1, 1]$
$dx, dy, dz > 0$

Here, b_i is a 'blending factor' which represents the relative importance of a particular primitive within the global field; px, py, pz are used to describe the shape of a particular primitive, a value near 1 describes a sphere. Bigger values tend to modelize cubes.

Let V be the isovalue of our field. If $\sum_{i=1}^{N} b_i < V$ the equation $f(x, y, z) = V$ has no solution, so there is no need to compute the fitness of individuals which match this condition. The genetic code used defines N primitives containing 11 parameters in a linear way. Thus each chromosome is an array of $N \times 11$ real numbers (Figure 13.5).

According to our surface definition, each chromosome contains $N \times 11$ parameters. As we do not know a priori the number of primitives needed to describe the surface, N could change according to the selection process. On the other hand, this definition ignores the differences between the parameters and their deep correlation. Therefore, genetic operations such as cross-over and mutation must be adjusted to take into account the specificity of each primitive of the weighted sum. Several crossing schemes have been tested, including the following.

- *Standard crossover*: a random cross point is chosen along the two chromosomes without taking into account the primitives distribution. The left parts of the two parents are exchanged, producing two new chromosomes.
- *Block preservative crossover*: same as above but the cross point is chosen between two primitives.
- *Statistical crossover*: crossing two chromosomes acts by randomly choosing a cross point which represents two primitives A_i and B_j and a real number $\lambda \in [0, 1]$. These primitives are weighted to produce two offspring A'_j and B'_j according to the scheme:

$$A'_j = \lambda \cdot A_i + (1 - \lambda) \cdot B_j$$
$$B'_j = (1 - \lambda) \cdot A_i + \lambda \cdot B_j$$

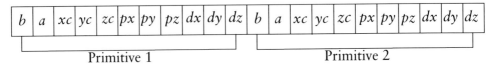

b	a	xc	yc	zc	px	py	pz	dx	dy	dz	b	a	xc	yc	zc	px	py	pz	dx	dy	dz

Primitive 1   Primitive 2

Figure 13.5 Example of a simple chromosome composed of two primitives.

This last crossing method seems to be more efficient in our problem because it takes into account the mathematical specificity of each primitive.

13.5.2   The fitness function

We now have to define a fitness function in order to compare our generated implicit surface with an existing object. This function must take into account the spatial volume occupation differences between the two objects. Moreover, this function must be generic for trading with several volume models.

Comparing range values
The simplest fitness function we can imagine consists in comparing, for a set of points, the field values on these points with the isovalue V. Let P be the set of points, fitness is then described as:

$$\text{Fitness} = \sum_{x,y,z \in P} |f(x, y, z) - V|$$

This definition is interesting because it provides a simple method for evaluating an individual performance. However, this fitness function does not ensure the behavior of the equation between two points (Figure 13.6).

A method for obtaining better results is to compute normal differences at these range points. The new fitness becomes:

$$\text{Fitness} = \sum_{x,y,z \in P} |f(x, y, z) - V| + \sum_{x,y,z \in P} \left\| \overrightarrow{f(x, y, z)} - \overrightarrow{N(x, y, z)} \right\|$$

$N(x, y, z)$ represents the value of the normal at the point (x, y, z). This solution gives better results but, if we want to get a realistic conversion of the base object, we need to compute this formula for a large set of points (Figure 13.7).

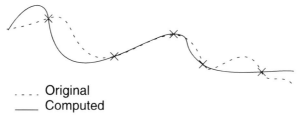

  · · · · Original
  _____ Computed

Figure 13.6   Differences between an original and a computed curve.

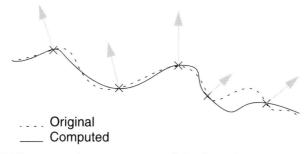

  · · · · Original
  _____ Computed

Figure 13.7   Differences between an original and a computed curve with comparison of normals.

The octree comparison as a 'fitness' function

Nonlinear octrees [6] have been used for a long time in fast rendering techniques. They define a spatial subdivision of a volume that contains an object by recursively dividing space into 8 equal cubes.

Our evolution process begins with the construction of the octree of the original object. The fitness function is then defined by comparison of the spatial and volumic occupation between this octree and those of the implicit surface generated by the current chromosome. This function gives a percentage which represents the volumic and spatial matching between both octrees at a given level of decomposition. This level of decomposition is adaptive. In fact, it is used to modify the environment pressure according to the mean fitness of the global population. When a large part of the population has reached an acceptable matching level, the decomposition level is upgraded to make the environment more aggressive toward the population.

This fitness function (Figure 13.8) completes the genericity constraints inherent to this kind of problem because it does not take into account the modelization method of the original object. Moreover, octree acceleration methods for implicit surface visualization [1] could be applied to accelerate the evaluation of chromosomes.

In that section we have defined the adaptation of genetic algorithms to our optimization problem. We can then apply this optimization process to the conversion of an original meshed object to an implicit defined one.

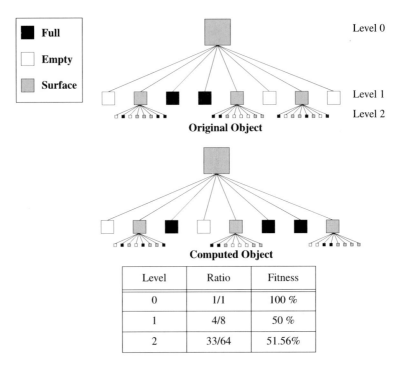

Level	Ratio	Fitness
0	1/1	100 %
1	4/8	50 %
2	33/64	51.56%

Figure 13.8   The octree fitness function.

13.6   Results

Our optimization process begins with a random population of 200 individuals and a decomposition level of 3 on which we apply the genetic algorithm. After 27 generations, the primitives of the best individual are located in the volume defined by the original object and the decomposition level is then upgraded to 5. At generation 50, the best chromosome has a fitness of 80%. The worst individual of generation 90 then scores 83%. There is now only a slight difference between the best individual of the current generation and the original object. We then increase the decomposition level to 7.

Finally, generation 112 provide an individual that matches 99.53% of the original object, so that the visual aspects of both objects do not differ. This experiment corresponds to the object #1 in Figure 13.9.

The second experiment is more difficult because of the aspect of the original object #2. The optimization process begins with placing primitives. Then mutations introduce new primitives which slowly converge to the shape of the object. The convergence process is achieved at generation 200 (Figure 13.10).

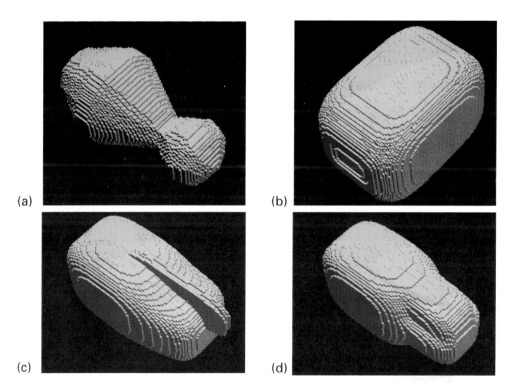

(a)

(b)

(c)

(d)

Figure 13.9   (a) Visualization of the octree generated by the original object #1. (b) Best individual from the initial (random generated) population. (c) Visualization of the best surface at generation 27 which scores 76% (level of decomposition (LOD) = 4). (d) Visualization of the best surface at generation 90 which scores 83% (LOD = 6).

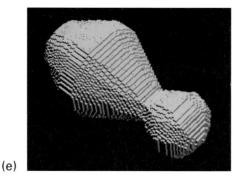

(e)

Figure 13.9   (contd) (e) Final object from generation 112.

13.7   Conclusion

Volume representation is limited in traditional approaches by the requirement for a lot of numerical data. Extended algebraic surfaces solve this problem by generating a wide variety of volumes with a mathematical equation.

We have presented a new approach for converting objects into implicit surfaces using genetic algorithms. This method provides a robust, automatic but adaptive model independent of the original object representation. This conversion is computed using an

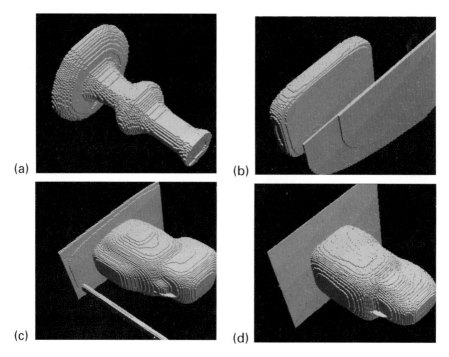

(a)   (b)   (c)   (d)

Figure 13.10   (a) Original object #2. (b) Best individual from initial generation. (c) Best individual of generation 30 which scores 68.66% (LOD = 5). (d) Best individual of generation 32. Artifacts present at generation 30 were eliminated.

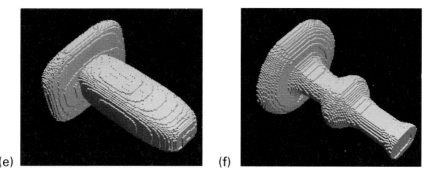

(e) (f)

Figure 13.10 (contd) (e) Intermediate object from generation 100. (f) Final object from generation 200.

octree as a 'fitness' function which compares the volumic and spatial differences between both objects. We have applied this method for converting a meshed object. The experiments show the effectiveness of our conversion process.

Furthermore, the original octree can represent volumic constraints. It would then be possible to build algebraic surfaces responding to such spatial restrictions. We are now working on an extension of the Blinn model to generate surfaces represented by more general mathematical expressions.

References

[1] D. Kalra, A. Barr, Guaranteed ray intersections with implicit surfaces, *Computer Graphics*, 1(3): 297–306; July 1989.

[2] J. F. Blinn, A generalization of algebraic surface drawing, *ACM Trans. Graphics*, 1(3): 235–256; 1982.

[3] M.P. Gascuel, An implicit formulation for precise contact modeling between flexible solids, *Proc. Siggraph'93*, Anaheim, Calif., *Computer Graphics*, 313–320; Aug. 1993.

[4] D.E. Golberg, *Genetic Algorithm in Search, Optimisation and Machine Learning*, Addison-Wesley, 1989.

[5] J. Holland, *Adaptation in Natural and Artificial Systems*, The University of Michigan Press, Ann Arbor, 1975.

[6] C.L. Jackins, Tanimoto Octrees and their use in representing 3D objects, *Computer Graphics and Image Processing*, 14: 249–270; 1980.

[7] S. Kirkpatrick, C.D. Gelatt, M.P. Vecchi, Optimization by simulated annealing. *Science*, 220: 671; 1983.

[8] S. Muraki, Volumetric shape description of range data using blobby model, *Computer Graphics*, 25(4): 227–235; 1991.

[9] N.J. Stolte, First high definition discrete ray tracing implicit surfaces, submitted to *Discrete Geometry*, 1995.

[10] N. Tsingos, M.P. Gascuel, Un modeleur interactif d'objets definis par des surfaces implicites, *Proc. AFIG'94*, Toulouse, Dec. 1994.

14
Acceleration Techniques for Volume Rendering

Mark W. Jones

14.1 Introduction

Volume rendering offers an alternative method for the investigation of three-dimensional data to that of surface tiling as described by Jones [1], Lorensen and Cline [2], Wilhelms and Van Gelder [3], Wyvill et al. [4], and Payne and Toga [5]. Surface tiling can be regarded as giving one particular view of the data set, one which just presents all instances of one value – the threshold value. All other values within the data are ignored and do not contribute to the final image. This is acceptable when the data being visualized contains a surface that is readily understandable, as is the case when viewing objects contained within the data produced by CT scans. In certain circumstances this view alone is not enough to reveal the subtle variations in the data, and for such data sets volume rendering was developed [6–9]. The underlying technique employed by volume rendering is given in section 14.2 presented with the aid of a volume rendering model introduced by Levoy [6]. Section 14.3 examines various other volume rendering models and the differing representations they give of the same data. A more efficient method for sampling volume data is presented in section 14.4 and acceleration techniques are covered in section 14.5. In section 14.6 a thorough comparison is made of many of the more popular acceleration techniques with the more efficient method of section 14.4. It is shown that the new method offers a 30–50% improvement in speed over current techniques, with very little image degradation and in some cases no visible degradation. A review of existing methods, systems and techniques is given in section 14.7.

14.2 Volume Rendering

Many of the three-dimensional data sets that need to be visualized contain an interesting range of values throughout the volume. By interesting, it is meant those parts of the volume to which the viewer's attention must be drawn in order for the viewer to gain insight to the physical phenomena the data represents. If the range of values is small, as for example the visualization of the human skull from CT scans, then a surface tiling method will suffice. Most data sets do not fall into this category, but rather have a larger range of values or several different values which need to be represented in the visualization. Such data sets need a method which can display the volume as a whole and visualize correctly those data values in which the viewer is interested.

Visualization and Modeling
ISBN 0-12-227738-4

The method known as *volume rendering* or *direct volume rendering* allows just that by rendering (visualizing) the whole of the volume according to some definable criteria which describe those data values that are interesting, and how they should be dealt with.

14.2.1   Classification of data

In a typical data set every voxel contains some material property such as object density, probability, pressure, or temperature. These data values have been measured or calculated in the *volume generation* stage. Visualization of the data set will be based upon an interpretation of these values, which is defined by those values that are of interest, and how they will influence the overall visualization. The data is converted from the values originally contained within the sampled volume into data in which each value indicates the importance of the corresponding voxel in the volume. These values are usually scaled linearly between the maximum and minimum representable by the number of bits available for each voxel. For example, for an 8-bit representation, points with a value of zero are uninteresting, and points with a value of 255 are most interesting, with all other values scaled linearly between these. These values are used to compute opacity for each voxel by normalizing them to lie between 0 and 1. An opacity of zero indicates that the point is transparent, and therefore will not be seen, and a value of 1 is opaque and will not only be seen but will *obscure* points behind it. All other values are semitransparent and will be seen with varying degrees of clarity. Each voxel is also given a color, again based upon its value and/or position, which is combined according to opacity with all voxels behind it during the visualization.

This process of converting the original data values into values of opacity is known as the *classification* process. It can be carried out with the use of a lookup table (LUT) using the very simple algorithm below.

```
for k = 1 to z
   for j = 1 to y
      for i = 1 to x
         voxel'[i, j, k] = LUT[voxel[i, j, k]]
```

The LUT will either have been defined by some expert who can decide between those values that are interesting and those that are not, or defined as the result of interaction. The user will adjust the values in the lookup table according to the images produced in order to direct the visualization of the data based upon what information needs to be gathered from the data and what view is desired of the volume.

Usually a more advanced classification process has to be carried out. In the case of data which has been generated by a medical imaging device, several stages of preprocessing may be carried out before the final gray level volume is created. This preprocessing consists of some or all of the following steps:

- *Filtering of original images*: The original images can be spatially filtered to remove noise using techniques such as median, modal and k-closest averaging filters. Other filters could be used to detect and enhance edges [10–12].
- *Interpolation of images to create the 3D volume of gray level values*: Often the data

is of a much higher resolution in the x and y image axes compared to the number of images (z axis). In some cases the resolution can differ by a factor of 20 [13]. If a regular volume is required which has equal dimensions in each axis, new slices must be interpolated between those already known [14, 15].

- *Segmentation of volume*: In medical applications it is desirable to display the different objects contained within the data separately, or to attach a different attribute, such as color, to each object. In order to display, for example, the spinal column, from a set of CT scans, the object in question has to be located and separated (segmented) from the surrounding objects. There is no automatic segmentation algorithm that works in all cases [16, 17] although interactive segmentation has proved to be successful [18–21].

  A typical segmentation process involves the user locating within a slice a seed point in the object they are interested in, from which a region is grown using thresholds. The thresholds define a range of values which encompass the object. The result of the region growing can be viewed in 3D, and parameters can be adjusted to correct the region interactively. Commonly regions that are incorrectly connected can have the *bridges* eroded, and regions that should be connected can be merged together using dilation. Currently segmentation is being used successfully to identify all parts of the human body (section 14.7.8).

- *Opacity classification*: Often the straightforward mapping of value to opacity does not result in an accurate display of surfaces contained within the volume. In medical imaging, visualization often has to display the interface between surfaces such as air/skin, skin/muscle, and muscle/bone. These surfaces can be best visualized by setting the opacity according to a function of the gradient of the data [6]. Using this method the gradient is calculated using equation (3) (see later) and the opacity is assigned accordingly, such that voxels in the vicinity of the object interfaces (high gradients) will have high opacity.

The next step is to determine the representation of the volume. The image comprises a regular grid of points, each of which can be assigned a certain color. The image is calculated as a representation of what would be seen from a certain viewpoint, looking in a particular direction, under certain conditions. With the viewpoint and direction known, a ray originating from each pixel in the image can be traced through the object domain.

The light and shade of each pixel is calculated as a function of the intensity along the ray originating from that pixel. The value of each pixel is governed by how the volume rendering model interprets the intensity profile, and thus visualization of the data is determined by the model.

The continuous intensity signal along the ray is reconstructed by taking samples at evenly distributed points on the ray and it is these samples that are evaluated by the model.

14.2.2 Levoy's rendering model

The rendering model popularized by Levoy [6] is that of assuming the volume to be back-lit by a uniform white light. The light passes through the volume and is attenuated by the opacity it encounters on the path it tracks through the volume. The resulting light that reaches the image is the light that exits the volume. Each pixel is also given a color which is determined by the *color* of each sample along the ray. The colors are chosen in a color classification process which is similar to the opacity classification process, except the color is a triple of red, green, and blue. The color at each sample can also depend upon the lighting model chosen, as will be described later.

Each voxel value in the volume is given by the function

$$f: \mathbb{R}^3 \Rightarrow \mathbb{R} \tag{1}$$

where $f(x)$ = measured value at x if $x \in \mathbb{N}^3$ otherwise $f(x)$ = value trilinearly interpolated from the 8 closest neighbors of x.

The quadruple $\langle r, g, b, \alpha \rangle$ at each data point is calculated from the lookup table for the value at those points.

$$\langle r, g, b, \alpha \rangle = \mathrm{LUT}(f(x))$$

where r, g, b, and α are the red, green, blue, and opacity components respectively. A function

$$g: \langle r, g, b, \alpha \rangle \times \mathbb{R}^3 \Rightarrow \mathbb{R} \tag{2}$$

is defined such that $g(\alpha, x)$ = the opacity at the point x trilinearly interpolated from its 8 closest neighbors; $g(r, x)$ = the red at that point; and so on.

For each pixel p in the image, where $p = \langle i, j \rangle$, $i = 1, \ldots, I_x$, $j = 1, \ldots, I_y$, where I_x and I_y are the dimensions of the image in the x and y axes, a ray R_p is traced into the object domain. If the ray intersects the volume of data, the length of the ray passing through the volume will be $l = |R_p|$. If the ray is sampled at intervals of τ, there will be $K = l/\tau$ samples, each given by $R_p(n)$ where $n = 1, \ldots, K$. $R_p(1)$ is the ray entry point and $R_p(K)$ is the last sample before the ray exits the volume. The color and opacity at each sample is given by the function g, and for the nth red sample would be $g(r, R_p(n))$. If attenuation of a back light with color Background = $\langle B_r, B_g, B_b \rangle$ is assumed as the rendering model, the resulting pixel color triple $\langle p_r, p_g, p_b \rangle$ is given by $\langle C_r, C_g, C_b \rangle$ where for each pixel p

$C = Background$
for $n := k$ **downto** 1 **do**
   $opacity = g(\alpha, R_p(n))$
   $C_r = (1 - opacity) \times C_r + opacity \times g(r, R_p(n))$
   $C_g = (1 - opacity) \times C_g + opacity \times g(g, R_p(n))$
   $C_b = (1 - opacity) \times C_b + opacity \times g(b, R_p(n))$
endfor
$p = \langle C_r, C_g, C_b \rangle$

This algorithm contains no view-dependent visual cues which may aid the understanding of the visualization. These can be added in the color accumulation stage by calculating the spatial point of each sample and applying a shading operator to it before compositing that color. The simplest shading operator is to depth-cue the data.

The process of depth cueing involves calculating the distance z, from the ray origin (pixel) to the sample point. The color at the sample point is then attenuated according to some function based upon that distance. The simplest function is to multiply the colour intensities by $(1 - z/Z)$ where Z is the maximum distance in the scene.

It is also possible to apply a shading technique such as Phong's by determining a normal to the data at the sample point which can be used in a similar way to a surface normal. The normal can be calculated by trilinear interpolation from the normals of its 8 closest voxel neighbors, whose normals are calculated using difference operators.

For voxel x, y, z in a data set where each voxel is a unit cube, its normal G is calculated using

$$G = (g_x, g_y, g_z)$$
$$g_x = f(x + 1, y, z) - f(x - 1, y, z)$$
$$g_y = f(x, y + 1, z) - f(x, y - 1, z) \quad\quad (3)$$
$$g_z = f(x, y, z + 1) - f(x, y, z - 1)$$

The result of shading is a value between 0 and 1 which can be used to multiply the color for a sample before being composited.

14.2.3   Results

Using this algorithm and suitably defined classification functions, images such as that of Figures 14.1 and 14.2 are created.

But what is the intended interpretation of these images? Firstly the classification functions must be examined. In the case of Figure 14.1, values below 50 have been set to be transparent (that is $\alpha = 0$). Values between 50 and 100 have been set to $\alpha = 0.15$ and the colors set to $\langle r = 1.0, g = 1.0, b = 1.0 \rangle$, values between 100 and 200 set to $\alpha = 0.15$ and the colors set to $\langle r = 1.0, g = 0.0, b = 0.0 \rangle$, and above 200, $\alpha = 0.8$, $\langle r = 0.0,$

Figure 14.1   Volume rendering of AVS Hydrogen data set.

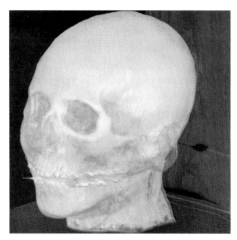

Figure 14.2   Volume rendering of CT head data set.

$g = 0.0$, $b = 1.0\rangle$. The image indicates that values above 200 (up to 255) occur in two distinct ellipsoidal sections, and values between 50 and 200 occur in two larger ellipsoids and a torus around the center. In this case the interpretation is correct. The lighting model has given the eye the required cues to determine the *shape* of the volumes contained within the data, and the coloration and opacity have allowed the three separate ranges to be distinguished.

   In the case of the CT image (the data having values −1117 to +2248), values below −300 have been set to be transparent and values between −300 and 50 set to $\langle r = 1.0$, $g = 0.79$, $b = 0.6\rangle$, $\alpha = 0.12$. These values contain the range for the skin in the CT images. The other range we are interested in are those values that produce the skull, 300–2248, and therefore these are set to $\alpha = 0.8$ and $\langle r = 1.0, g = 1.0, b = 1.0\rangle$. The interpretation is also correct in this case, the skin is mostly transparent, thus revealing the skull contained within. The lighting functions provide enough information to understand the surfaces, both exterior (skin) and interior (skull).

14.3   Volume Rendering Models

14.3.1   Maximum value images

For many applications, specific viewing models other than the one mentioned in section 14.2.2 are employed to present visualizations. The simplest is the widely used maximum value visualization[1] [22]. For this approach the maximum sampled value along a pixel's ray is the value used for that pixel's color. This method avoids the need for expensive shading calculations and composition operations, and therefore requires less computation than using a model such as Levoy's. The method is generally used to produce visualizations in which the data is rotated, so that the visualizer can identify

---

[1]Personal communication with K. S. Sampathkumaran of Washington, USA in which he stated that for medical applications maximum value projection gave a valuable insight to the hotspots within the data.

areas of high value (hot spots). This type of visualization results in images not unlike x-rays, and therefore is particularly useful in the medical profession where the users of such methods are familiar with radiographs.

The main problem with this method is the fact that images 180° apart are identical. For animations of rotating objects this produces the effect of the object seeming to turn back and forth rather than rotate. Depth cueing can be employed to avoid this problem by attenuating the image according to the depth at which the maximum value occurs, and indeed, animations produced using depth cueing provide far more depth information than those without.

14.3.2   X-ray images

The maximum value images of section 14.3.1 produce images that look like radiographs. X-ray images of the data can be produced by simulating how the rays pass through the volume, calculating the absorption due to the density of the volume. If the density, p, along each ray from 0 to l is

$$\rho = f(t), \quad 0 \leq t \leq l \tag{4}$$

the density of material along the path of the ray is

$$\int_0^l f(t)\, dt \tag{5}$$

This can be calculated quite simply using either Simpson's rule (with three ordinates):

$$\int_0^l f(t)\, dt \approx \frac{1}{3} d(y_0 + 4y_1 + y_2) \tag{6}$$

or the trapezium rule:

$$\int_0^l f(t)\, dt \approx \frac{1}{2} d(y_0 + 2y_1 + \cdots + 2y_{n-2} + y_{n-1}) \tag{7}$$

where d is the distance between each sample. As $d \to 0$ the approximation becomes more accurate.

The image displayed is a function of the material density – for example, the inverse of the material density – and normalized to use the full range of brightness of the display. The result is an image which looks similar to a radiograph.

14.3.3   Standard model without normal shading

The main computational expense with the standard model is the shading calculation done at each sample position within the volume. If this could be removed, the amount of computation required could be dramatically reduced. One way would be to completely disregard shading operations and display the color and opacities directly. This results in an image generated rapidly that contains no shading cues but does contain enough information to identify interesting areas within the data set.

Alternatively, the expensive calculation of data normals can be disregarded, with the data being shaded using depth cueing. This gives the same look upon the data as the method without any shading at all, and in addition provides some feeling of the distance of the objects within the data. The drawback to both methods is the fact that valuable curvature information is not present in the images they produce.

14.3.4   Sabella's method

A major contribution to the subject of producing alternative images from 3D data sets is that of Sabella [7]. The volume data is treated as a varying-density emitter, where the density is a function of the data itself. Sabella regards this to be an equivalent model to a particle system where the particles are sufficiently small. Rays originating from each pixel are traced into the volume data set as described in section 14.2 and the volume is sampled as before. Sabella's viewing model calculates four parameters – the peak value occurring along the ray, the distance where it occurs, the attenuated intensity, and the center of gravity of the field along the ray. A combination of three of these four parameters is then mapped to the Hue, Saturation, and Value (HSV) model.

The peak value and distance are self-explanatory, whereas the attenuated intensity needs more explanation. It is taken to be the brightness, B, along the ray, where

$$B = \int_{t_1}^{t_2} \exp\left(-\int_{t_1}^{t_2} \tau p^\gamma(\lambda)\, d\lambda\right) p^\gamma(t)\, dt \tag{8}$$

The variables and expressions of this equation are described in [7].

The $\int_{t_1}^{t} p^\gamma(\lambda)\, d\lambda$ represents the number of particles in the volume along the ray that spans between t_1 and t, where t_1 and t_2 are the ray entry and exit points of the value data, t is the ray parameter, $t_1 \le t \le t_2$, and p is the density.

The term $\exp\left(-\int_{t_1}^{t_2} \tau p^\gamma(\lambda)\, d\lambda\right)$ could be regarded as the transparency for simplicity, and is in fact proportional to transparency. The integral therefore calculates the contribution to the final intensity of particles along the whole ray, and the attenuation of the light due to the density of the particles.

It is shown that equation (8) is the continuous form of the discrete equation

$$\sum_{i=1}^{n} b_i \prod_{j=1}^{i-1} \theta_j \tag{9}$$

where b_i can be considered as the brightness at sample i, and θ_j is the transmittance (that is transparency) of sample j, $0 \le \theta_j \le 1$. The term $\prod_{j=1}^{i-1} \theta_j$ calculates the attenuation due to all the samples *in front* of sample i, and therefore the product $b_i \prod_{j=1}^{i-1} \theta_j$ is the contribution of sample i to the intensity. The sum of all contributions gives the brightness, B.

A practical method of computation can be derived from this equation:

```
B = 0.0;
o = 1.0;
for i = 0 to length do
    B = B + b_i × o
    o = o × θ_i
endfor
```

The peak value parameter is mapped to Hue, and the attenuated intensity is mapped to Value. Either the centroid or distance is mapped to the saturation parameter. This has the effect of allowing color to represent the maximum values and the distance parameters to give depth information in the form of saturation, leading to what can most easily be described as fog. The attenuated intensity parameter gives an impression of the distribution of the data.

14.4 Efficiency Aspects of Volume Rendering

The volume rendering method as described in section 14.2 is a costly process to compute due to the number of samples that have to be determined. In this section a new method which reduces this computation is presented. The method has been developed as a result of analyzing where work is done in the volume rendering process. This section introduces the idea of choosing the distance at which samples are made along the ray such that computation can be reduced. The method requires a bare minimum of precalculation (a few tens of mathematical operations), and works without constraints for arbitrary viewpoints. In section 14.4.1 the calculations required by the volume rendering process are examined. In section 14.4.2 the process of choosing the sampling distance to reduce the number of calculations is introduced, and in section 14.4.3 the effect this has on computational time and the images produced is investigated. Section 14.4.4 outlines some view artifacts that this method introduces during animation loops, and suggests how these may be overcome. Section 14.4.5 offers conclusions for this method.

14.4.1 Computation involved during volume rendering

The algorithm has been described elsewhere [6] sufficiently for implementation, but in each case, although the spacing for the sampling is described, the value is left up to the reader. In the majority of cases a value of 1 unit will be chosen for simplicity, where each voxel in the data set has length 1 unit in each dimension. Figure 14.3 indicates the situation.

The spatial position of the ith sample along the jth ray is given by $p_j(i)$. The value which is sampled at that point is given by $S_{p_j(i)}$ where the sample is calculated by trilinear interpolation from the 8 neighboring voxels that make up the cube that contains the point $p_j(i)$. The sampled value is usually the interpolation of the value and normal from each of the 8 neighboring voxels [23], or the interpolation of the opacity and color components and normal from each of the 8 neighboring voxels [6].

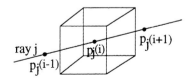

Figure 14.3 Ray passing through cube sampled at even intervals.

In order to calculate the normal of the sample $S_{p_j(i)}$ in Figure 14.3, the normals at each voxel $v_0, \ldots, v_7$ must be determined using an appropriate method, such as central differences. This involves the calculation of 8 central differences, each of which involves 3 subtractions, 6 voxel lookups (equation 10) and one normalization step.

$$
\begin{aligned}
G &= (g_x, g_y, g_z), \\
g_x &= f(x + 1, y, z) - f(x - 1, y, z), \\
g_y &= f(x, y + 1, z) - f(x, y - 1, z), \\
g_z &= f(x, y, z + 1) - f(x, y, z - 1).
\end{aligned} \tag{10}
$$

The normalization step (equation 11) involves 3 subtractions, 2 additions, 3 multiplications, 1 square root, and 3 divisions.

$$
n' \leftarrow \frac{n}{|n|} \tag{11}
$$

To calculate the normals at each of the 8 cube vertices requires a total of 16 additions, 48 subtractions, 24 multiplications, 24 divisions, 8 square roots, and 48 voxel lookups.

If the offsets in the cube for each axis are r_x, r_y, and r_z (Figure 14.4), the values at $p_j(i)$ are calculated using trilinear interpolation as follows:

$$
\begin{aligned}
t_0 &= (v_1 - v_0)r_x + v_0 \\
t_1 &= (v_3 - v_2)r_x + v_2 \\
t_2 &= (t_1 - t_0)r_y + t_0 \\
t_3 &= (v_5 - v_4)r_x + v_4 \\
t_4 &= (v_7 - v_6)r_x + v_6 \\
t_5 &= (t_4 - t_3)r_y + t_3 \\
v_{p_j(i)} &= (t_5 - t_2)r_z + t_2
\end{aligned}
$$

which involves 7 subtractions, 7 additions, and 7 multiplications for each value that must be interpolated and a total of 8 voxel lookups. Furthermore, if a value such as opacity is required, a further classification table lookup is necessary. If the value being interpolated is the normal, each v_i is now a triple and the calculations are therefore trebled. Also, each step must be normalized, so a further 7 normalization calculations are required. A summary of the total required computational operations is given in Table 14.1.

As can be seen from the table, normal interpolation is the most expensive operation, particularly with its 15 roots and 45 division operations. When this is put into context

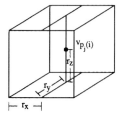

Figure 14.4 Trilinear interpolation within cube.

Table 14.1 Calculations required for trilinear sampling process

Operation	Normal	rgbα	Value
+	51	28	7
−	90	28	7
÷	45		
×	66	28	7
$\sqrt{}$	15		
Voxel l.u.	48	8	8
Table l.u.		32	

with the operation of the algorithm, it is realized that for a large image (500×500) and a large data set ($256 \times 256 \times 256$) this normal interpolation can be done up to a maximum of 100 million times (number of rays × the maximum ray length). It is this figure that led to the investigation of ways to reduce the calculation.

One immediate solution is to precompute the normals at each of the voxels in a preprocessing step. The problem with this is the extra storage required – for a data set of $256 \times 256 \times 256$ an additional 200 MB of storage is needed (12 bytes for a normal per voxel). As a result of the usual problems of memory size, disk size, and swapping it is far better for them to be calculated on the fly. In reality far fewer normals are computed during image computation since not all voxels contribute to the final image when adaptive termination is used. In an experiment with the CT head data of 7 million voxels, only 2 million voxel normals were computed.

14.4.2 Choosing the stepping distance

By choosing the stepping distance to be 1 unit, the samples may occur anywhere within the data set, that is to say, there are no means by which the computational cost can be reduced by taking advantage of where sample positions occur. It can be seen that since these samples can occur anywhere within the cube, trilinear interpolation for the values must be used. If the samples were to occur within the face of each cube, then only bilinear interpolation would be required. This reduces the need to know the normals at all 8 neighboring voxels to only needing to know them at the 4 face neighboring voxels. The stepping distance can be chosen so this situation occurs by calculating how far along the ray must be traveled to cross between successive cube faces parallel to a particular axis. By starting the ray on that face boundary, it is ensured that by using the correct step distance each sample will be in a face, and therefore only bilinear interpolation is required.

The stepping distance is calculated by determining which axis the ray travels fastest in – that is, for a given length of ray which axis it will travel farthest in. The rays are then adjusted to start in the closest face perpendicular to that axis, and then each sample will occur in a face perpendicular to the axis. Face interpolation functions are used depending upon in which face interpolation has to take place (perpendicular to the x, y, or z axis). The ray is adjusted simply by scaling the stepping distance of the *fast voxel traversal* algorithm of Amanatides and Woo [24] so that the quickest axis has a stepping distance of 1 (2 division operations), and the fractional part of the sample point position is altered so that it is zero in the fastest axis and contains the fractional placement in the other two axis (2 divisions, 2 multiplications, 2 subtractions, and 2 additions). The fast voxel traversal algorithm then continues as normal.

The effect this has is twofold. Firstly it is no longer necessary to calculate the normal from 8 neighbors, but rather from 4, halving the number of central difference calculations. Secondly, bilinear interpolation is used:

$$t_0 = (v_1 - v_0)r_i + v_0$$
$$t_1 = (v_3 - v_2)r_i + v_2$$
$$v_{pj(i)} = (t_1 - t_0)r_j + t_0$$

where r_i and r_j are the offsets along the two axes (Figure 14.5). This involves 3 subtractions, 3 additions, and 3 multiplication operations for each value that must be interpolated, and a total of 4 voxel lookups. The total computational operations required are summarized in Table 14.2, with the old values in brackets. It can be observed that about 50% of calculation can be saved using this method.

14.4.3 Testing

The effect this has on computational time was tested by implementing the standard volume rendering algorithm using trilinear interpolation and then modifying it to

Table 14.2 Calculations required for bilinear sampling process

Operation	Normal	rgbα	Value
+	23 (51)	12 (28)	3 (7)
−	42 (90)	12 (28)	3 (7)
÷	21 (45)		
×	30 (66)	12 (28)	3 (7)
√	7 (15)		
Voxel l.u.	24 (48)	4 (8)	8
Table l.u.		16 (32)	

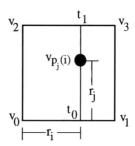

Figure 14.5 Bilinear interpolation within cube face.

calculate the required interval size, therefore allowing bilinear interpolation to be used. The algorithm was implemented on a DEC 3000 model 400 Alpha workstation and tested on the UNC Chapel Hill CT head and superoxide dismutase electron density map (SOD) data sets, and the AVS Hydrogen data set. Since the new method increases the interval size, a certain amount of time will be saved due to the fact fewer samples will be taken along the ray. In order to eliminate this effect, the standard algorithm was modified so that it calculated the interval size, and used trilinear interpolation rather than bilinear interpolation (called Jump in tables). Taking this time into account allows the true saving to be revealed. One final point is that the interval size can vary between 1 when the viewing angle is axis aligned and $\sqrt{3}$ when the viewing angle is at 45° to each axis. Therefore, testing is carried out at various angles to give differing interval sizes. The results appear in Tables 14.3 and 14.4.

Table 14.3   Computation times for hydrogen data set

Angle	Standard ray termination				Adaptive termination			
	Standard	Jump	Bilinear	Gain	Standard	Jump	Bilinear	Gain
45,45,45	113.16	69.18	39.10	26.6%	73.18	54.30	40.10	19.4%
0,90,0	111.53	113.78	65.73	41.1%	64.20	65.53	50.50	23.4%
45,0,45	114.46	84.21	47.11	32.4%	73.73	61.93	35.77	35.5%

Table 14.4   Computation times for CT head data set

Angle	Standard ray termination				Adaptive termination			
	Standard	Jump	Bilinear	Gain	Standard	Jump	Bilinear	Gain
45,45,45	365.85	276.57	141.71	36.9%	96.88	84.40	54.61	35.3%
0,90,0	401.67	448.60	244.36	39.2%	103.23	112.50	74.18	28.1%
45,0,45	344.49	351.67	183.01	46.9%	98.68	100.98	64.68	34.5%

The normal calculations dominate the volume rendering process, and by reducing the number required and simplifying the interpolation process, substantial savings can be obtained as indicated by the tables. In fact the computation time has been reduced by about 30–40%. This reduction is to be expected since the amount of computation done during normal calculation is reduced by 50% and also the fact that normal calculation requires a large proportion of the running time when compared to the constant calculations that are made, such as calculating ray entry and exit points to the volume.

It is interesting to note (from the Jump column) that, on increasing the step size, computational time also increases in some cases. This is because the step size is not significantly greater than 1, and some extra calculations involved when determining the number of samples outweigh any saving.

The method gives a better gain for the normal ray terminating method because a higher percentage of the computation time is spent calculating normals, for which the method offers a 50% speedup.

Examination of the image produced shows very little degradation in quality. This is to be expected since the samples are still being taken at evenly spaced intervals and are taken in such a way that all values along a ray are used in the sampling process. There is no difference between images 14.6b and c, since both have the same interval size. There is a difference between images 14.6a and b which have been produced with an interval size of 1 and 1.732 units, respectively. This difference is caused by samples being taken with larger intervals using the same compositing formula:

$$o_i^{out} = (1 - o_i)o_i^{in} + o_i \quad \text{for } i = 1, \dots, n$$

where n is the number of samples, o_i is the opacity at sample i, and o_i^{out} and o_i^{in} are the opacities coming into and going out of i. The interval length does not come into this formula, and therefore in a volume of constant value, n samples with an interval length of m will give the same opacity for n samples with an interval length of 1.

If $m > 1$ the volume sampled with the larger interval size will seem more transparent than the volume traversed with an interval size of 1. This is quite acceptable since the opacity values are a subjective scheme to allow the presentation of the data. For static images there is no problem.

Figure 14.7 shows the resulting images for the CT head test data set.

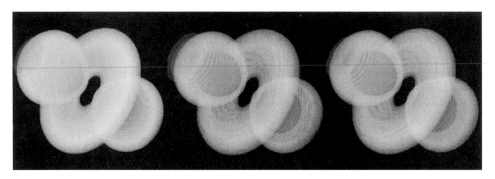

Figure 14.6 (a) Trilinear interpolation. (b) Increased interval size. (c) Bilinear interpolation.

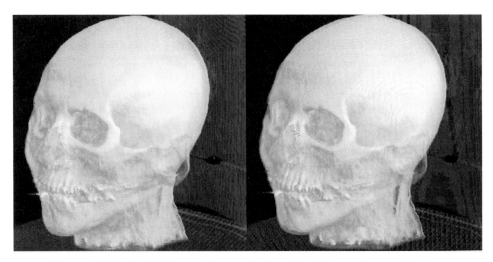

Figure 14.7 (a) Trilinear interpolation. (b) Bilinear interpolation.

14.4.4 Animation

As mentioned in the previous section, increasing the interval size increases the transparency of the volume. This does not cause problems for static images, but for animation, where the viewpoint from which the data is seen from varies, the interval size is variable and during a rotation the transparency may be perceived to rise and fall. A practical solution is to raise each value in the opacity classification table to some power proportional to the step size. Figure 14.8 gives two images, with differing interval lengths, produced using the modified classification table. As can be seen, the transparency of the images corresponds quite closely.

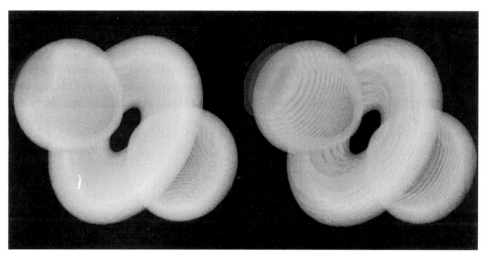

Figure 14.8   (a) Trilinear interpolation. (b) Bilinear interpolation.

14.4.5 Discussion

By analyzing exactly how many operations are carried out during volume rendering, it has been possible to concentrate on a method that reduces these operations by about 50%. This substantial reduction has been achieved through the use of a variable interval size which is dependent upon viewpoint and is calculated in order to make each sample fall within a cube face. This allows bilinear, rather than trilinear, interpolation to be used, with the associated reduction in computational complexity. This saving has been analyzed both qualitively and also through the effect it has on the execution times of the volume rendering process. Since normal calculation is the main burden of volume rendering, a reduction by 50% of the operations required should result in a large reduction in computation time. This reduction is observed to be around 30% and reasons for this were given in section 14.4.3. The images produced by the method are shown to be good representations of the volume, and problems that arise during animation where the viewpoint changes have been investigated. A practical solution to avoid these artifacts has been given, and testing shows it to be acceptable. This method compares well with other acceleration techniques (section 14.5) since it gives a similar reduction in time without the large trade-off in image quality that other methods suffer.

This method involves very little computation to determine the stepping distance, and suffers from no constraints on the viewing direction and viewpoint.

14.5 Acceleration Techniques

The volume rendering process has been identified as being very costly in terms of computation, and many methods exist that accelerate the computation time. This section reviews several acceleration techniques.

14.5.1 Adaptive rendering

Most of the expense involved in volume rendering is due to the fact that so many samples are taken along each ray during the compositing process. Since the number of rays is dependent upon image size, the larger the image the more expensive it becomes to render the data set. Adaptive rendering attempts to reduce the workload by concentrating computation in areas where it is most needed. This technique can be applied quite simply to volume rendering by assuming that the resultant image will contain large areas of coherency (color and intensity). The principle is to ray trace the volume at a low image resolution, and by treating four neighboring pixels which have been ray traced as corners of a square the remaining pixels can be colored using bilinear interpolation. This coarse image can be regarded as the first image in a sequence of images that progressively become more and more refined. The refinement process takes place by adaptively concentrating on areas with greatest change. If the pixels at the corners of the square vary by more than a given tolerance ε, the square is divided into four smaller squares and the new unknown corner points are computed. The process of computing the interior pixels using bilinear interpolation is repeated, and a new image can be displayed. This process is carried out until the corners of the square vary by less than ε or the size of the square is one pixel. At this point the image is correct to a tolerance of ε. The effect of this method is that computation is concentrated in areas where features change sharply, for example, along the edge of an object. By relaxing the tolerance, fewer pixels are truly sampled but more image defects become apparent, and so there is a trade-off between image quality and speed. This method was also presented in [20, 25]. The image in the middle of Figure 14.9 is a volume rendering of the hydrogen

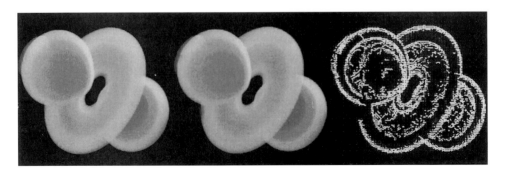

Figure 14.9   The adaptive rendering process.

data using the adaptive rendering method with squares of an initial size of 16 and a tolerance of $\varepsilon = 0.0275$ (or a difference of 7 intensity values out of 256). The image on the right shows the pixels that were actually ray traced, the rest being interpolated from these. The number of rays traced is 34 335 as opposed to 160 000 for the image produced by the standard method on the left. Whereas the standard method took 129.4 s, the method using adaptive rendering took 53.0 s. All images are 400×400.

14.5.2   Template-based volume viewing

In section 14.4 it was shown that the process of trilinearly interpolating sample positions and function gradients along the ray is the most computationally intensive component of the volume rendering process; thus any method that avoids this will reduce the computation required. The template based method of Yagel and Kaufman [23] calculates a ray template which is a path of voxels through the volume. This template can be moved over the image construction plane in such a way that the volume is sampled uniformly without gaps (Figure 14.10). The ray template indicates which voxels are to be sampled, and these voxels are sampled without trilinear interpolation, with their gradients calculated using central differences. This is valid if it is assumed that the value in the volume does not vary over the cube represented by one voxel, which is not generally the case. The template is constructed so that it is either 6-way or 26-way connected. In this case 26-way connection is chosen because it results in fewer samples and allows the volume to be sampled uniformly without repetition. The image is formed by projecting and resampling the image construction plane to the desired dimensions.

14.5.3   Adaptive termination

The original volume rendering algorithm composites color and opacities in a back to front manner. If at any time a fully opaque sample is encountered, the samples

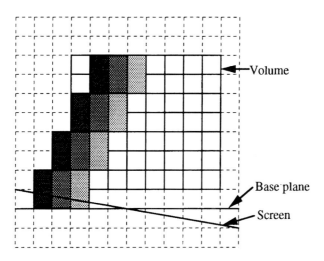

Figure 14.10   Using template to sample the volume.

composited up to that point have no bearing on the final pixel color since they are obscured. This is an undesirable situation since expensive interpolation and gradient operations are effectively ignored and do not make any contribution. In order to prevent this, the ray should be traced in a front to back manner so that in the event of an opaque sample, the ray can be terminated, and so no further samples need to be taken along the ray [26].

Using the definitions from section 14.2.2, the front to back algorithm for each pixel *p* is

$$C = Background$$
$$o = 1.0$$
$$n = 1$$
while $(n < K \text{ and } o \neq 0.0)$ **do**
$$C_r = C_r + o \times g(\alpha, R_p(n)) \times g(r, R_p(n))$$
$$C_g = C_g + o \times g(\alpha, R_p(n)) \times g(g, R_p(n))$$
$$C_b = C_b + o \times g(\alpha, R_p(n)) \times g(b, R_p(n))$$
$$o = o \times (1 - g(\alpha, R_p(n)))$$
$$n = n + 1$$
endwhile

The front to back compositing function is slightly more complicated, but also allows the use of adaptive termination to stop the rendering process when a useful image has been calculated. In the compositing function it is observed that as the accumulated transparency o approaches 0, the sample taken does not contribute significantly to the final pixel color [26]. In fact the contribution is less than o, so for $o < \varepsilon$ where ε is some small tolerance level, we can *adaptively terminate* the ray no matter how far it has traveled through the volume. Since the opacity along the ray reaches high values very quickly, when passing through slightly opaque solid matter, the ray is terminated long before it has passed through all of the volume, and thus large amounts of unnecessary computational effort can be saved. If the tolerance ε is relaxed, rendering time is reduced although the image contains more artifacts.

14.6   Comparison of Methods

For the comparison of all the different methods, three test data sets were used – AVS Hydrogen, University of North Carolina (UNC) CT head, and UNC superoxide dismutase electron density map (SOD). Each test program was written in C on a DEC Alpha 3000/400 workstation using as much common code as possible to make timing comparisons fair. Each data set was rendered from a particular viewpoint under certain conditions for an image size of 400 × 400 to give the time. Such a large image was chosen in order to allow the differences between the methods to be more marked. The images were compared qualitatively (how they looked). The results for the CT head data are given in Table 14.5, results for the AVS Hydrogen data are given in Table 14.6, and for the SOD data in Table 14.7.

For the CT head (Figures 14.11–14.13) there is no qualitative difference between any of the images using the standard viewing model. From these comparisons it would seem

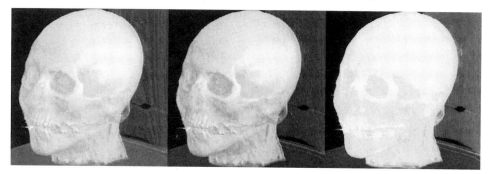

Figure 14.11   (a) Standard method. (b) Adaptive termination. (c) No shading.

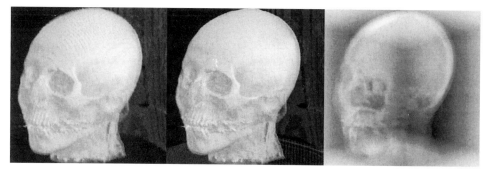

Figure 14.12   (a) Template method. (b) Bilinear method. (c) X-ray method.

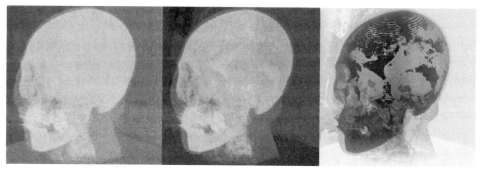

Figure 14.13   (a) Maximum method. (b) Maximum with depth cue. (c) Sabella's method.

that the bilinear method with adaptive termination is the one that produces the best results quickly for this data set, being over 7 times faster than the method without any optimizations. An animation loop was created for the CT head using the adaptive termination technique, with and without the adjustment of the step size to enable bilinear interpolation. Using the normal method, the animation took 2 h 6 min 12 s to produce, as opposed to 1 h 16 min 6 s with bilinear interpolation. There is no visual difference between the two, which would suggest that the bilinear method can be used where high-quality accurate images are required using the least computational time.

Table 14.5 Results of different methods using CT head data

Method	Adaptive termination	Figure	Time (s)
Standard	No	11a	731.37
Standard	Yes ($\varepsilon = 0.1$)	11b	190.01
No shading	Yes ($\varepsilon = 0.1$)	11c	81.09
Template	Yes ($\varepsilon = 0.1$)	12a	10.10
Bilinear	Yes ($\varepsilon = 0.1$)	12b	98.25
Jumps	Yes ($\varepsilon = 0.1$)		140.93
Bilinear	No		292.64
Jumps	No		503.63
X-ray	N/A	12c	97.66
Maximum	N/A	13a	99.71
Depthmax	N/A	13b	106.23
Sabella	N/A	13c	133.61

The template method is by far and away the fastest method – taking only 10 seconds for the test data – but produces a very coarse image. The image is adequate to gain a rough idea of the data and is ideal for quick visualizations, since it shows the main features. The problem with this method is that the time is not scalable, that is, it is constant for all image sizes, unlike the other methods, which are scalable. It was found that a 100×100 image created using the bilinear method, and scaled up, took half the time of the template method to compute and produced a comparable image, the only difference being the fact that the bilinear image was slightly smoother than the template image and contained less sharp delineations of features which had provided good indicators in the case of the template method.

The x-ray, maximum, and maximum with depth cue methods produce alternative views of the data in reasonably quick times. The maximum and x-ray methods produce similar images in much the same time. When using the maximum method to produce animations, the head looks as if it is swinging from side to side, rather than rotating, due to the fact that images 180° apart are identical. This situation was somewhat improved by using the depth cueing method, and produces a better animation.

Finally, the Sabella image of the skull is interesting, but it can only be used to show how the image differs from the standard methods. The image it produces in the case of the CT head serves no real purpose since the method was not intended for use on such data sets.

For the AVS Hydrogen data set (Figures 14.14–14.16) the image produced by the Sabella method shows the data distribution originally using color. Fogginess shows depth, and together they convey a lot of information, showing the structure of the data. The image looks good, but it needs effort to interpret the information.

The x-ray, maximum, and maximum depth images all look very similar, and show the two *hot spots* and a general fuzziness around the toroidal section.

The only difference between the adaptive method and the standard method is that the adaptive image looks duller because brighter areas to the back of the volume are not contributing, due to the ray terminating. It was found that by making the error bound ε tighter, this effect is reduced, and the time to produce the image increases. It was

Figure 14.14 (a) Standard method. (b) Adaptive termination. (c) No shading.

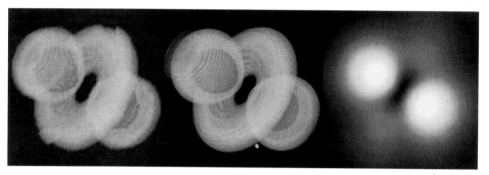

Figure 14.15 (a) Template method. (b) Bilinear method. (c) X-ray method.

Figure 14.16 (a) Maximum method. (b) Maximum with depth cue. (c) Sabella's method.

found that for $\varepsilon = 0.05$ the image produced by the adaptive method looks identical to the image produced by the standard method and took 146.28 s, a saving of 25%. The template method produces a coarse image which looks very fuzzy. It gives a rough idea of the data spread, but the image is weak and dull. This is due to the fact that fewer samples are taken along the ray, and therefore less light is contributed to the final intensity. The method without shading also produces the image quickly and gives a good impression of the data, although the lack of shape information from the shading detracts from the image. The bilinear method produces good clean images, but they are

Table 14.6 Results of different methods using AVS Hydrogen data

Method	Adaptive termination	Figure	Time (s)
Standard	No	14a	202.32
Standard	Yes ($\varepsilon = 0.1$)	14b	130.94
No shading	Yes ($\varepsilon = 0.1$)	14c	30.67
Template	Yes ($\varepsilon = 0.1$)	15a	1.95
Bilinear	Yes ($\varepsilon = 0.1$)	15b	55.00
Jumps	Yes ($\varepsilon = 0.1$)		104.45
Bilinear	No		69.88
Jumps	No		131.88
X-ray	N/A	15c	26.76
Maximum	N/A	16a	25.98
Depthmax	N/A	16b	29.87
Sabella	N/A	16c	36.62

slightly more transparent, and therefore dull, because fewer samples are taken along the ray. Nevertheless, the images are still very useful.

This problem also occurs with the SOD data (Figures 14.17–14.19), but the bilinear method results in an image that is even more weak and dull. Any impressions of curvature are lost as shading is not enforced over large coherent areas. In this case the

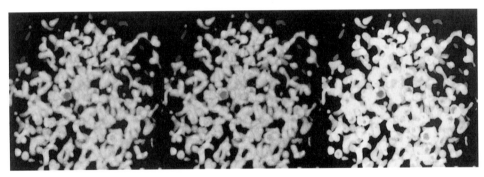

Figure 14.17   (a) Standard method. (b) Adaptive termination. (c) No shading.

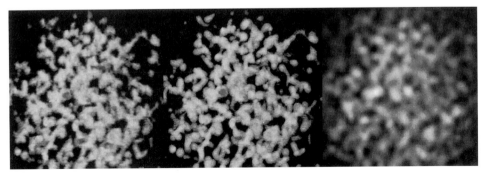

Figure 14.18   (a) Template method. (b) Bilinear method. (c) X-ray method.

Figure 14.19   (a) Maximum method. (b) Maximum with depth cue. (c) Sabella's method.

Table 14.7   Results of different methods using SOD data.

Method	Adaptive termination	Figure	Time (s)
Standard	No	17(a)	108.80
Standard	Yes ($\varepsilon = 0.1$)	17(b)	99.95
No shading	Yes ($\varepsilon = 0.1$)	17(c)	56.01
Template	Yes ($\varepsilon = 0.1$)	18(a)	3.37
Bilinear	Yes ($\varepsilon = 0.1$)	18(b)	51.68
Jumps	Yes ($\varepsilon = 0.1$)		73.55
Bilinear	No		49.81
Jumps	No		72.98
X-ray	N/A	18(c)	43.79
Maximum	N/A	19(a)	42.44
Depthmax	N/A	19(b)	47.83
Sabella	N/A	19(c)	59.66

method produces useful images, but they do not contain as much information as some of the other models and methods.

The image produced by the template method suffers even more from dullness and is very fuzzy. The method is still useful though, because it is so fast, and could be used to produce animations quickly to gain an overall impression of the data.

The image produced by the standard method with adaptive termination is duller than images produced without, and in this case the saving in time is not so significant, and in conclusion not worth the slight degradation in image quality. A good impression of the hot spots contained within the data can be gained through images produced without shading, and also through images produced using the x-ray, maximum, and maximum with depth cueing methods, which also bring out the blobby structure of the data quite well.

Finally, the image produced using the Sabella model produces what is arguably the best image, with a clear indication of hot spots, with a good feel for the lumpy structure of the data, conveying the depth of the data well.

14.7   A Review of Other Volume Rendering Techniques

The main viewing models available for the rendering of 3D data sets have been
described and compared in sections 14.2 and 14.3. The more important acceleration
techniques have been reviewed in sections 14.4 and 14.5, with comparative tests
made about their speed and image quality in section 14.6. This section is a review of
the other techniques and systems that are available for the visualization of volume
data.

14.7.1   Splatting

One large area that has been focused on is that of projecting the volume data set onto
the image plane to produce the image. This differs from previously described
techniques in that rather than a pixel by pixel traversal of the image, and a mapping
from image space to object space, the volume is traversed in a cell by cell order with a
mapping from object space to image space.

In footprint evaluation [27], Westover suggested projecting each sample within
the data set onto the image plane, and *spreading* the energy of the sample according
to its *footprint*. The footprint is obtained by applying the view transformation to a
generic footprint which can be calculated by assuming that the reconstruction kernel
is a sphere. The kernel's footprint is determined, and the energy spread is calculated
according to some function, such as a Gaussian. The relative merits of footprints of
various sizes (5×5 to 101×101) are described in the paper. The advantage of this
method is the fact that each sample is projected onto the image and rays no longer
have to be traced into the volume to integrate samples to find their contribution.
This allows the application of parallel processing techniques since each processor
can operate on a subset of the data rather than requiring access to the data as a
whole.

This work was extended by Crawfis and Max [28], where the authors present an
ideal reconstruction formula. Their goal was to produce a formula which produced
splats with smooth densities, so that the structure of the individual splats was not
visible. Their example is that of a cube of $n \times n \times n$ voxels, each emitting an intensity of
1, and having no opacity. The projection of such a cube should be as constant as
possible. The function they calculate produces a variation of at most 1 part in 256.
They also describe how to map textures onto the splats with the use of hardware
texture mapping (Silicon Graphics Rendering Machines and Iris Explorer) to produce
animations, and motion blurred images of 3D vector fields.

The work is also extended by Laur and Hanrahan [29], this time by approximating
splats with Gouraud shaded polygons. The work they present is concerned with the
production of real-time rendering for interactive applications. Real-time rendering is
achieved by encoding the data as an octree, and projecting nodes of the octree using the
splatting technique. Each node in the tree is associated with an error, the idea being that
the node with greatest error is the node to be divided next in the refinement process.
Using this method the user would be able to move a low-resolution representation of
the object in real time, which would be progressively refined whenever the user paused
to consider the image.

14.7.2   Curvilinear grids

One aspect of volume rendering that does not receive so much attention is that of the display of curvilinear grids. The grids usually arise as the result of computational space being warped around an object of interest. A typical example is a computational fluid dynamics simulation of an aircraft wing, where the mesh has a much lower resolution away from the wing than in the vicinity of it. Distances between neighboring points can vary by a factor of 10 000 over the whole data set. Conventional ray casting methods run into difficulty since rays can enter and exit through any cell face, and also reenter cells (Figure 14.20). Max and colleagues [30] went some way to addressing this problem by dividing nonconvex cells up into convex cells and nonconvex cells which are guaranteed to have only one ray span intersection for a given viewpoint.

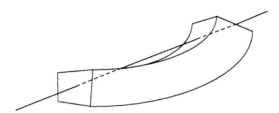

Figure 14.20   Ray can exit and reenter curvilinear cells.

Alternatively, the large curvilinear grids could be resampled by a regular grid, and then ray casted. This method is problematical, since resampling would have to be carried out with a small step size to retain accuracy. This would result in a large increase in the volume of data. A larger step size would not result in such an increase in the amount of data, but has the problem that fine details in the data would be lost.

These problems can be avoided by using projection methods [8, 31–33]. Wilhelms and Gelder [31] show how accurate integration and composition can be performed on cells in order to project the cells correctly onto the image plane. Wilhelms [33] also compares the projection and ray casting methods and shows that a speed-up of 50–150 times is quite reasonable. A comparison of the different methods for projection was made by Williams [32], in which various methods are described for the projection of tetrahedral meshes. The order of traversal presents a problem, but once solved [34, 35], cells can be projected easily, usually in the form of hardware Gouraud shaded polygons.

It is also worth mentioning the work presented by Frühauf [36], which essentially solves many of the problems associated with the ray casting of curvilinear grids. In this paper the author shows how computational space can be unfolded into a regular grid. The same transformation can be performed on the light rays so that, instead of sampling along straight rays in curvilinear space, samples are taken along curved rays in a regular computational space. This solves the problems of finding neighbors, and the ray/cell intersections. The ray direction is stored at each node as a vector, and some *particle tracking* technique, such as Runge–Kutta, is used to determine where the next sample occurs along the ray. Results show that very little error creeps into the ray paths, which therefore allows the production of accurate images.

14.7.3   Data compression

The data sets requiring visualization are often very large. In fact they are usually larger by an order of magnitude than data sets that can be handled easily. A typical data set can be around 16 MB. Techniques which reduce the volume of data can often have the advantage that images are also quicker to produce [37, 38].

Udupa and Odhner [37] extend their data model [39] to cater for volume rendering. In their method they assume (for a large reduction in data and image rendering times) that the opacity functions (of section 14.2.1) have been defined using gradient operators such that voxels away from object boundaries contribute very little, if at all, to the image. This allows them to define a data structure which encodes the data as a *shell* around an object boundary. The shell is then projected using a back-to-front or front-to-back method, and since only voxels within the shell rather than all the voxels in the scene domain are projected, large reductions in rendering time are achieved. They report that shell rendering is nearly 1000 times faster than a straightforward implementation of a standard ray casting method.

Volume compression was the focus of the work of Ning and Hesselink [38], where data is replaced by indexes to a codebook. Using vector quantization, the authors use nearest-neighbor mapping of every k-dimensional input vector X to some vector X_i selected from a finite codebook of candidate vectors. The original data can be replaced by the index i, which allows the data to be compressed. They chose the voxel value, normal, and gradient magnitude for a block of b^3 voxels as the vector to be compressed, and found that a compression ratio of 5:1 could be achieved for practical data sets. The rendering times of the data set increased by 5% due to the overhead of checking a table entry to uncompress the data. They also show how faster rendering can be achieved by rendering the codebook entries from the viewpoint and compositing the result along each ray. Since the codebook has only a few entries, rendering of the codebook entries takes negligible time. The rendering of the data is now reduced to a composition of the codebook renderings that occur along the ray, which avoids the need to perform costly trilinear interpolation and shading calculations at each sample along the ray. A speed up of about 10:1 was achieved using this method of volume rendering, although there is loss of image accuracy since the codebook is only representative of the data and not all possible ray entry and exit points for a given view can be catered for.

14.7.4   Spatial techniques

Spatial techniques seek to explore coherency within the data to accelerate rendering. An additional data structure is constructed using the data, which can then be used to accelerate the rendering, usually by allowing rays to skip over portions of the volume that are uninteresting. The most popular spatial subdivision technique is that of the octree [40, 41], which was applied to volume rendering by Levoy [26]. In a preprocessing step an octree is constructed where each node is divided if it contains a voxel which has nonzero opacity. Each divided node branches into eight subtrees, one for each of the subvolumes constructed when the volume is divided in half in the x, y, and z directions. The ray is traced through the octree, using information within the nodes to jump over large areas of noncontributing (zero opacity) voxels. Most of the computation during volume rendering is the trilinear interpolation of sample values along the ray from surrounding voxels. By knowing in advance that all values within a subvolume are going to produce an opacity of zero, which would result in no contribution to the image, the ray can safely skip over that subvolume to the next sample point. This would avoid the costly sampling process for all samples along the ray within that subvolume, resulting in a reduction of computational cost and therefore time. Although a speed-up was reported by Levoy [26], it was shown that this was not the case [1]. In addition to this problem, any change of opacity function would require the octree to be recomputed.

The fact that the octree does not speed up ray casting is also mentioned by Yagel and Shi [42]. The authors suggest that the additional cost of tracing the ray through the octree can be avoided by storing the octree information at the empty voxels as uniformity information. Using this process, empty voxels are assigned a value which represents which level of the octree they are in, which can then be used to cause the ray to leap forward to bring it to the first voxel beyond the uniform region.

Other methods are discussed by Yagel and Shi [42] in which either an additional volume or the data volume itself is used to store proximity flags or values. The idea behind this is to place a shell of flags, or shells of values representing distance, around the object which will enable an efficient ray tracking algorithm to switch from an efficient space jumping rapid traversal algorithm to an accurate ray traversal algorithm. The proximity flags would indicate that a surface was near, or, more efficiently, the shells of distance values would indicate how far a ray can jump without encountering an object. These methods suffer from the fact that 3D preprocessing is required that must be repeated for any change in the data.

Yagel and Shi [42] also show how a method retaining starting depths for rays can accelerate ray casting of successive images in a rotation by avoiding the need to calculate a traversal of empty voxels in front of the object. They show how to avoid some of the problems associated with rotated objects covering objects previously visible and report a speed-up of 2 to 6 times. It should be noted that this speed-up applies to ray traversal and, since in many applications it is the ray compositing step that is the most time consuming (see section 14.4.1), a significant speed-up in the volume rendering process may not be observed.

Spatial techniques are also used by Subramani and Fussell [43], in order to store interesting voxels in a k–d tree. This tree is obtained by using a median cut space partitioning algorithm to efficiently divide space up so that either branch, at any one time, removes a similar number of voxels. Bounding volumes are also used at nodes to efficiently encapsulate the voxels within each subtree. This leads to an efficient subdivision of space – the k–d tree, which can be efficiently ray traced. The authors report a reduction of over 90% in the amount of data that needs to be considered in order to produce the image, although they do not discuss rendering acceleration times.

One other acceleration method is the polygon assisted ray casting (PARC) technique of Avila and colleagues [44]. The object is simply approximated by polygons which can be projected onto two depth buffers – a front projection and a back projection. These two depth buffers will contain the start and end points for each ray of the image, and in this way the ray does not traverse parts of the volume that do not contribute to the final image. The problem with this method is that of how to choose the polygonal representation of the object. This can be achieved by using the faces of subvolumes of the data which contain a surface, and merely requires the decision of how fine the subvolumes should be. The method has the advantage that costly unnecessary ray sampling is avoided, and therefore produces images with less computation.

14.7.5   Shading techniques

The problem of interactive shading on less powerful graphics workstations was addressed by Fletcher and Robertson [45]. Interactive shading is desirable since it allows researchers to move light sources around their data in real time, thus giving a better understanding as to the three-dimensional nature of their data. Another benefit is the experimentation of light source positions during the production of animation sequences without the need of rerendering each frame. Interactive shading is achievable by computing a restricted table of n normals (where usually $n = 256$). The normal calculated for each pixel in the rendered image is then mapped to the normal in the table that has the closest matching direction to it. In recalculating the image with different shading parameters, only the intensities resulting from shading the normals within the table need to be computed. These values can then be mapped back onto the image to produce the new image. This results in a substantial reduction of computation – to a level most graphics workstations can handle. The main problem is the fact that only a restricted subset of normals can be reproduced accurately. One example image [45] is that of a hemisphere which has been shaded with this technique, and has resulted in a hexagonal faceted image, each hexagon centered about a known normal. Their solution is to dither the normals using a process similar to the Floyd–Steinberg algorithm for dithering. They report images can be shaded at rates of 47 to 139 fps on a DEC 5000/200.

14.7.6   Volume seeds

Ma and colleagues [46] present a method in which the user is given interactive control of the final volume rendered image. The user can alter variables such as the opacity table and voxel colors in real time through the use of a *cache*. The idea is that the volume is ray traced from the given viewing direction, and the value of each sample along the ray is stored in a three-dimensional array. This array is simply traversed, and voxel values are looked up in the classification table in order to perform the compositing step. Since costly trilinear interpolation of the sample values is no longer required, real-time compositing of the image is achievable.

The user is also given control of the *volume seeds* technique. The user can place a seed anywhere in the volume with the effect that voxels close to the seed are enhanced, and those farther away are made more transparent. The example given [46] is that of placing a seed in the throat to make the spine in the neck area easier to see. The effect is achieved by increasing the opacity of close voxels and reducing the opacity of farther away voxels using a simple function. Real-time control is achieved by combining the seed placement with the volume caching to give users full investigative control over their data.

14.7.7   Systems and environments

Techniques can be regarded as the precursors to fully fledged systems that provide environments for data visualization. Commercial examples would be those of AVS,

Data Explorer, and the public domain Khorus packages. These all work on the data-driven flow model and are based on the linking of modules to form networks (Figure 14.21). The commercial packages tend to be well known, and widely used, but very often it is the *homegrown* software that incorporates innovative features.

A simple but effective system is reported by Corrie and Mackerras [47]; the authors point out that one of the major benefits of their system is its flexibility in producing images over systems, such as AVS, which limit the user to a number of fixed rendering techniques. This flexibility is achieved by using a shading language, rather than a user interface. It is therefore flexible and extensible. The example visualizations and code shown in the paper [47] are for the standard shading model for volume rendering [6, 8], Sabella's model [7], and a proprietary shader for the Dominion Radio Astrophysical observatory. The authors report that allowing a higher level shading language does result in a loss of efficiency when it comes to computing the images, with the example that their implementation of standard volume rendering takes about 1.7 times as long to render an image.

Montine [48] takes a low-level approach to the task of providing a visualization language and provides just the basic functions for visualization. These functions are classified as to which object they operate on (volume – the original data; environments – lighting conditions and viewing parameters; and images). To visualize a set of data the user must provide the appropriate calls to all the functions. This requires low-level knowledge from the user as to what the available functions are, but in this way provides the user with a powerful environment.

Smart particles are introduced by Pang and Smith [49] as a way of providing a framework for visualization. Using existing techniques usually associated with 3D data sets, such as isosurfacing, particle tracking, and volume rendering, the authors

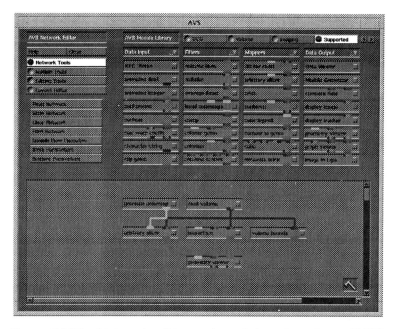

Figure 14.21   Network editor and module palette from AVS™.

endeavor to show how an effective but easy to use system can be made using the *sparts* (smart particles). The sparts are sprayed into the data set in much the same way as paint is sprayed from spray cans. Sparts can be of several forms such as surface seeking, volume penetrating, or flow tracking. Sparts can also operate on the data, and leave messages for other following sparts. The authors indicate that their system allows the user the flexibility of exploring their data using a simple and intuitive tool – the spray can. It is an effective tool since complex visualizations can be built up by using different combinations of sparts.

An example of a visualization environment actually being used would be that of Yoshida and colleagues [20] in which the authors demonstrate the effectiveness of their system in support of neurosurgical planning (CliPSS – Clinical Planning Support System). They show the simple step by step process a user follows to produce data which can be used for surgical planning. Each slice is edited interactively to remove unnecessary data, such as the bed. The surgeon can use an extraction function to extract the volume of interest (VOI) by defining two threshold parameters and a seed. CliPSS then uses region growing to extract the VOI by grouping voxels together until a boundary is found. Boundaries are distinguished by moving a $7 \times 7 \times 7$ filter across the volume, calculating statistics locally from the voxels. The surgeon is given the option of rendering the VOI as a surface (isosurfacing) or as a volume (volume rendering). Surgical planning is supported by using a stereotactic frame which fits over the head of the patient. Using this frame a correlation between the computer model and patient can be made. The surgeon can plan entry points, direction, and depth to probe for a target lesion on the computer. The surgical instruments can be attached to the stereotactic frame and positioned accurately over the lesion. The surgeon then knows the direction and depth to which he must probe. Using this tool operations are made much safer for the patient.

14.7.8 Anatomical atlas

Karl Heinz Höhne and his colleagues at the University Hospital Ependorf, Hamburg, are working on a project to segment and label the whole of the human anatomy [16–18, 50, 51]. Their main aim is to provide a hypermedia system for anatomical study, enabling students to control their exploration of the body. They used their generalized voxel model [50] to store the available information about each voxel – its gray level value as obtained from CT or MRI, and its membership to parts of the body, or functional areas or a lesion. In addition to this model, and the graphical capability of the system, is a knowledge base which encodes the relationship between all the different regions (for example, of the brain). The method by which the model is constructed and the functionality of the system is described in [18] with additional information about producing the images of blood vessels in [51]. In order to isolate each entity within the brain, they first perform a semiautomatic segmentation to extract voxels belonging to the skull, brain, or ventricular system. From this model an anatomist can examine the data slice by slice and identify and label regions. Each region is extracted by selecting it using region filling, thresholding, and pixel selection. Basically the anatomist would point to an object, and define data thresholds which would identify the voxels that belong to the object as those that can be reached by a path of voxels with values between the threshold values. For troublesome regions pixels can be included or removed in a way similar to using a paint package. Once an object has been selected it is given an entry in the knowledge base indicating its name and functionality – for example [50], '*gyrus calcarinus is part of the lobus occipitalis.*'

With this model the user can explore the human head with ease. A typical enquiry could be to start with the whole head, and indicate a cut and depth. This cut would be performed and the user can point to the revealed anatomy and query the database to find out its nature. The database will provide a label to each object and show the user where the object occurs in the knowledge tree. Cut planes can be taken, but could ignore specified objects such as eyes. X-ray images can be simulated with the addition of being able to enquire what has contributed to the resulting intensity along the ray. The knowledge tree itself can be queried – for example, the user could select an object from the tree and ask for it to be displayed.

The resulting system is a powerful exploration tool, giving users a very natural feeling of dissection as they explore the brain. Höhne estimated that about one person-year was spent on the segmentation of the brain during the construction of the brain atlas. The group is now extending its work to the whole of the human anatomy [17].

14.7.9 Image segmentation

It has already been mentioned in the previous sections that image segmentation is a necessary tool in order to extract the various parts of the voxel model, so that each object can be examined in isolation. The problem is that there is no one method that can automatically segment complex objects from voxel data. Most methods rely on interaction, in the form of the user selecting voxels within a slice that are within the volume of interest and filling the volume in 3D within a certain range. The range is defined using thresholds and the region is defined simply as all those voxels that can be reached from the start voxel by a path of voxels that have values that lie between the thresholds. The thresholds can be defined by allowing the user to probe the data, displaying the values of voxels pointed to by the user within a slice. Examples of this method can be found in [18–21].

Algorithms which perform automatic segmentation on images (for example, [11]) are used to perform semiautomatic segmentation of voxel data. The regions produced using an automatic method will often have false connections (or bridges) to other regions, or will be split from regions that they should be joined to. One simple method to solve the first case is to shrink the voxel model by n voxels (where n is small, typically $n = 1$), and then grow it by n voxels. This will have the effect of removing links of n voxels wide [50, 52]. Other methods use the image processing techniques of erode and dilate to erode away the bridges or dilate the region to join it to others [53, 50].

Yoo and colleagues [54] show the difference between syntactic and semantic classification. In syntactic classification, geometric clipping is used to cut away parts of the volume not required, and intensity values are mapped to opacity using mappings such as gradient value. They point out that these operate on the whole volume and cannot distinguish between features such as the different bones in a leg. Semantic classification isolates the different parts of the volume interactively. First the regions are segmented automatically, and connected in the form of a branching tree. This tree is traversed interactively by the user in order to select the object of interest. They remark on the effectiveness of their system by giving the example that the extraction of the brain, which previously took 40 minutes, now takes about 10 mouse button clicks in a few seconds.

14.8 Conclusion

This chapter has been concerned with the production of images from volume data using the method of volume rendering. A thorough comparison of the more popular viewing models was given in sections 14.2 and 14.3. The new work presented in section 14.4 was concerned with the acceleration of image production, and was compared to the existing acceleration methods of section 14.5. Section 14.6 presented a thorough comparison of these methods, in terms of computational requirements and image quality. A thorough review of many recent developments of volume rendering was given in section 14.7.

References

[1] M.W. Jones, The visualisation of regular three dimensional data, University of Wales Swansea, UK, July 1995.

[2] W.E. Lorensen, H.E. Cline, Marching Cubes: A high resolution 3D surface construction algorithm, *Proc. SIGGRAPH '87*, 21(4), pp. 163–169, ACM SIGGRAPH, New York, July 1987.

[3] J. Wilhelms, A. Van Gelder, Octrees for faster isosurface generation, *ACM Trans. Graphics* 11(3): 201–227; 1992.

[4] G. Wyvill, C. McPheeters, B. Wyvill, Data structures for soft objects, *The Visual Computer* 2: 227–234; 1986.

[5] B.A. Payne, A.W. Toga, Surface mapping brain function on 3D models, *IEEE Computer Graphics Appl.*, 10(5): 33–41; 1990.

[6] M. Levoy, Display of surfaces from volume data, *IEEE Computer Graphics Appl.*, 8(3): 29–37; May 1988.

[7] P. Sabella, A rendering algorithm for visualizing 3D scalar fields. In *Proc. SIGGRAPH '88*, 22(4), pp. 51–57, ACM SIGGRAPH, New York, August 1988.

[8] C. Upson, M. Keeler, V-Buffer: Visible volume rendering, *Proc. SIGGRAPH '88*, 22(4), pp. 59–64, ACM SIGGRAPH, New York, August 1988.

[9] L. Carpenter, R.A. Drebin, P. Hanrahan, Volume rendering, *Proc. SIGGRAPH '88*, 22(4), pp. 65–74. ACM SIGGRAPH, New York, August 1988.

[10] J.D. Foley, A. Dam, S.K. Feiner, J.F. Hughes, *Computer Graphics, Principles and Practice*, 2nd edn. Addison-Wesley, 1990.

[11] A. Low, *Introductory Computer Vision and Image Processing*, McGraw-Hill, Maidenhead, Berkshire, UK, 1991.

[12] P. Burger, D. Gillies, *Interactive Computer Graphics*, Addison-Wesley, 1989.

[13] M.W. Jones, M. Chen. A new approach to the construction of surfaces from contour data, *Computer Graphics Forum, Proc. Eurographics '94*, 13(3), pp. C-75–C-84, Cambridge University Press, Cambridge, UK, 1994.

[14] G.T. Herman, J. Zheng, C.A. Bucholtz, Shape-based interpolation, *IEEE Computer Graphics Appl.*, 12(3): 69–79; 1992.

[15] M.W. Vannier, J.L. Marsh, J.O. Warren, Three dimensional computer graphics for craniofacial surgical planning and evaluation, *Proc. SIGGRAPH '83*, 17(3), pp. 263–273, ACM SIGGRAPH, New York, July 1983.

[16] A. Kaufman, K.H. Höhne, W. Krüger, L. Rosenblum, P. Schröder, Research issues in volume visualization, *IEEE Computer Graphics Appl.*, 14(2): 63–67; 1994.

[17] A. Pommert, B. Pflesser, M. Riemer, T. Schiemann, R. Schubert, U. Tiede, K.H. Höhne, *Advances in medical volume visualization*, Technical Report, Eurographics, 1994 (ISSN 1017–4656).

[18] K.H. Höhne, M. Bomans, M. Riemer, R. Schubert, U. Tiede, W. Lierse, A volume-based anatomical atlas, *IEEE Computer Graphics Appl.* 12(4): 72–78, July 1992.

[19] T.R. Nelson, T.T. Elvins, Visualization of ultrasound data, *IEEE Computer Graphics Appl.*, 13(6): 50–57; 1993.

[20] R. Yoshida, A. Doi, T. Miyazawa, T. Otsuki, Clinical planning support system – CliPSS. *IEEE Computer Graphics Appl.*, 13(6): 76–84; 1993.

[21] D.R. Ney, E.K. Fishman, Editing tools for 3D medical imaging, *IEEE Computer Graphics Appl.*, 11(6): 63–70; 1991.

[22] R.S. Avila, L.M. Sobierajski, A. Kaufman, Visualizing nerve cells, *IEEE Computer Graphics Appl.*, 14(5):11–13; 1994.

[23] R. Yagel, A. Kaufman, Template-based volume viewing, *Computer Graphics Forum, Proc. Europgraphics '92*, 11(3), pp. C-153–C-167. Cambridge University Press, Cambridge, UK, 1992.

[24] J. Amanatides, A. Woo, A fast voxel traversal algorithm for ray tracing, *Proc. Eurographics '87*, Amsterdam, The Netherlands, August 1987, pp. 3–9.

[25] M. Levoy, Volume rendering by adaptive refinement, *The Visual Computer*, 6: 2–7; 1990.

[26] M. Levoy, Efficient ray tracing of volume data, *ACM Trans. Graphics*, 9(3): 245–261; 1990.

[27] L. Westover, Footprint evaluation for volume rendering, *Proc. SIGGRAPH '90* 24(4), pp. 367–376, ACM SIGGRAPH, New York, August 1990.

[28] R.A. Crawfis, N. Max, Texture splats for 3D scalar and vector field visualization, *Proc. Visualization 93*, pp. 261–266, IEEE CS Press, Los Alamitos, Calif., 1993.

[29] D. Laur, P. Hanrahan, Hierarchical splatting: A progressive refinement algorithm for volume rendering, *Proc. SIGGRAPH '91* 25(4), pp. 285–288, ACM SIGGRAPH, New York, July 1991.

[30] N. Max, R. Crawfis, D. Williams, Visualization for climate modeling. *IEEE Computer Graphics and Applications*, 13(4): 34–40; 1993.

[31] J. Wilhelms, A.V. Gelder, A coherent projection approach for direct volume rendering, *Proc. SIGGRAPH '91*, 25(4), pp. 275–284, ACM SIGGRAPH, New York, July 1991.

[32] P.L. Williams, Interactive splatting of nonrectilinear volumes, *Proc. Visualization '92*, pp. 37–44, IEEE CS Press, Los Alamitos, Calif., 1992.

[33] J. Wilhelms, Pursuing interactive visualization of irregular grids, *The Visual Computer*, 9: 450–458, 1993.

[34] P.L. Williams, Visibility ordering meshed polyhedra, *ACM Trans. Graphics*, 11(2): 103–126; 1992.

[35] A. Van Gelder, J. Wilhelms, Rapid exploration of curvilinear grids using direct volume rendering (extended abstract), *Proc. Visualization '93*, pp. 70–77, IEEE CS Press, Los Alamitos, Calif., 1993.

[36] T. Frühauf, Raycasting of nonregularly structured volume data. In *Computer Graphics Forum, Proc. Eurographics '94*, 13(3), pp. C-293–C-303, Cambridge University Press, Cambridge, UK, 1994.

[37] J.K. Udupa, D. Odhner, Shell rendering, *IEEE Computer Graphics Appl.*, 13(6): 58–67; 1993.

[38] P. Ning, L. Hesselink, Fast volume rendering of compressed data, *Proc. Visualization 93*, pp. 11–18, IEEE CS Press, Los Alamitos, Calif., 1993.

[39] J.K. Udupa, D. Odhner, Fast visualization, manipulation, and analysis of binary volumetric objects, *IEEE Computer Graphics Appl.*, 11(6): 53–62; 1991.

[40] H. Samet, R.E. Webber, Hierarchical data structures and algorithms for computer graphics. *IEEE Computer Graphics Appl.* 8(3): 48–68; 1988.

[41] A.S. Glassner, Space subdivision for fast ray tracing, *IEEE Computer Graphics Appl.*, 4(10): 15–22; 1984.

[42] R. Yagel, Z. Shi, Accelerating volume animation by space-leaping, *Proc. Visualization 93*, pp. 62–69, IEEE CS Press, Los Alamitos, Calif., 1993.

[43] K.R. Subramani, D.S. Fussell, Applying space subdivision techniques to volume rendering, *Proc. Visualization 90*, pp. 150–159, IEEE CS Press, Los Alamitos, Calif., 1990.

[44] R.S. Avila, L.M. Sobierajski, A.E. Kaufman, Towards a comprehensive volume visualisation system, *Proc. Visualization 92*, pp. 13–20, IEEE CS Press, Los Alamitos, Calif., 1992.

[45] P.A. Fletcher, P.K. Robertson, Interactive shading for surface and volume visualization on graphics workstations, *Proc. Visualization 93*, pp. 291–298, IEEE CS Press, Los Alamitos, Calif., 1993.

[46] K.L. Ma, M.F. Cohen, J.S. Painter, Volume seeds: A volume exploration technique, *The Journal of Visualization and Computer Animation*, 2: 135–140; 1991.

[47] B. Corrie, P. Mackerras, Data shaders, *Proc. Visualization 93*, pp. 275–282, IEEE CS Press, Los Alamitos, Calif., 1993.

[48] J.L. Montine, A procedural interface for volume rendering, *Proc. Visualization 90*, pp. 36–44, IEEE CS Press, Los Alamitos, Calif., 1990.

[49] A. Pang, K. Smith, Spray rendering: Visualization using smart particles, *Proc. Visualization 93*, pp. 283–290, IEEE CS Press, Los Alamitos, Calif., 1993.

[50] K.H. Höhne, M. Bomans, A. Pommert, M. Reimer, C. Schiers, U. Tiede, G. Wiebecke, 3D visualization of tomographic volume data using the generalized voxel model, *The Visual Computer*, 6: 28–36; 1990.

[51] A. Pommert, M. Bomans, K.H. Höhne, Volume visualization in magnetic resonance angiography, *IEEE Computer Graphics and Applications*, 12(5): 12–13; 1992.

[52] K.D. Toennies, J. Udupa, G.T. Herman, I.L. Wornom III, S.R. Buchman, Registration of 3D objects and surfaces, *IEEE Computer Graphics Appl.* 10(3): 52–62; 1990.

[53] L. Caponetti, A.M. Fanelli, Computer-aided simulation for bone surgery, *IEEE Computer Graphics Appl.*, 13(6): 86–92; 1993.

[54] T.S. Yoo, U. Neumann, H. Fuchs, S.M. Pizer, J. Rhoades, T. Cullip, R. Whitaker, Direct visualization of volume data, *IEEE Computer Graphics Appl.*, 12(4): 63–71; 1992.

15
Physically Based Rendering of Metallic Paints and Coated Pigments

Patrick Callet

15.1 Introduction

A new approach for modeling colored phenomena appeared at the end of the 1980s with the works of Gary Meyer on colorimetry [13]. This physically based modeling of color, often called the 'spectral approach,' was quickly adopted and a quest for spectral data began. The present work does not directly consist in presenting a colorimetric or lighting process model for computer graphics. It rather concerns the modeling of the physical interaction of light with coated materials, and the elaboration of more accurate visualization models, since it refers systematically to the concept of the electromagnetic field and not only to light energy. The calculation of interference colors is possible when use is made of this notion; the perceived radiance is then computed with optical constants (dielectric functions or, equivalently, refractive indices) only. However, the physical laws governing the interaction of light with materials require not only spectra (e.g., reflection or transmission spectra) but also some more pertinent data to provide access to a more realistic behavior of this interaction between light and materials. The lighting process constitutes a significant field of investigation for simulating realistic environments in computer generated imagery; unfortunately, colored phenomena depend not only on light properties but also on material properties as we have already mentioned. The present work is an attempt to unify some notions about color production, using (but not exclusively) real parameters of materials in relation to the visible light; these pertinent data allow the simulation of *physical* or *chemical colors*. After a short historical survey, the complete electromagnetic-based model of interference colors is presented using *complex refractive indices* for *all the materials* involved. Some sections are devoted to pigments properties, such as the geometrical effects due to their size or shape. Computer synthesized pictures illustrating the model presented were computed with a distributed ray tracing algorithm operating in the AC1C2 colorimetric space, using a method developed by Meyer [13]. Employed under certain conditions this method drastically reduces the number of samples to be used in the spectral representation of colored phenomena.

15.2   Short Historical Survey

The historical starting point of our model can be found in the works of Lippmann.[1] In 1985 Bridgeman proposed a model of reflectance for metallic paints using a radiative transfer formulation [3] unable to account for angular variations of the reflected light. In computer graphics applications, angular variations of all colored phenomena are very important when a realistic appearance is required. During the same international event, Mondial Couleur'85, Franz [8] described the optical properties of pearlescent mica pigments and their use in automotive coatings. This formulation was a completely electromagnetic one, since it used only optical constants in formulating color. A second article in Mondial Couleur'85 exposed some colorimetric aspects of the difficult problem of measuring the reflectance spectrum and the chromaticity of interference pigments as a function of the optical layer thickness; this description is due to Hofmeister [12]. More recently a model of surface and subsurface scattering effects has been developed by Hanrahan and Krueger [11] in the interesting case of radiative transfer applied to a microscopic level in stratified media. Neglecting particle absorption but including scattering, this model cannot predict the production of physical colors combined with chemical color effects. Within classical rendering techniques the first occurrence of an interference colors model was by Smits and Meyer [16], while in ray tracing Dias [6] presented a dielectric formulation of the interference phenomenon. The model developed here accounts for absorption inside the coating and constitutes an enhanced version of a former one [4]. The first approach to the optical model described below can be found in optics textbooks [2] while the description of painting materials can be found in more specialized literature [9, 10].

15.3   Thin Films and Interference Colors

The model presented below is a generalization of an interference model for dielectric materials. The classical description of interference colors involves refractive indices only. In this model the main idea governing its elaboration lies in the systematic use of *complex refractive indices*. This model is restricted to materials in optical contact and having smooth surfaces.[2] These materials assumed sufficiently homogeneous so that internal scattering (Mie scattering by individual particulates and Raman scattering by molecules) can be neglected. The optical characteristics of the materials are, in this case, reduced to their effective optical constants, i.e., complex refractive indices. Our main determination will consist in modeling the specular component of the reflected light by a dielectric–metal system. Thus, for simplicity our description will start with a dielectric–dielectric tandem for which preceding works have already been presented in the computer graphics field [6, 16]. A further development presenting no mathematical difficulties, but somewhat tedious, will include the complex refractive index characterizing each material. These indices are generally extracted from tables of constants for very high-purity materials.

---

[1] Gabriel Lippmann received the Nobel Prize for Physics in 1908; he first formulated an interference process of color photography.
[2] No fractal profiles will be studied here.

15.3.1   Optical path calculations

When an incident ray strikes the external boundary of a coated material with a smooth surface, it is partly reflected in the specular direction and partly transmitted inside the coating, where a similar process takes place. This refracted ray is then subjected to an infinite number of internal reflections and refractions. The coating looks like a wave-guide for visible light. The electric field of the plane wave associated with the emergent ray outside of the layered material is phase-shifted from the previous emergent ray. This shift, written φ, is given by equation (1) where δ means the minimal optical path difference between two successive rays of wavelength λ (in vacuum). According to the notation indicated in Figure 15.1 this path difference is evaluated for two successive rays whose relative phases are, e.g., φ_0 and φ_1. Thus, the phase of the second ray is shifted from that of the first, following the optical path difference

$$\delta = n_2(AD + DC) - n_1AB, \quad \delta = 2en_2\cos\theta_2$$

Using the Snell–Descartes law $n_1\sin\theta_1 = n_2\sin\theta_2$ applied to the phase boundary between the surrounding medium whose refractive index is n_1 and the coating whose refractive index is n_2 leads to

$$\varphi = \frac{2\pi}{\lambda}\delta = 4\pi\frac{e}{\lambda}\sqrt{n_2^2 - n_1^2\sin^2\theta_1} \tag{1}$$

This expression is quite similar to the expression given by Beckmann and Spizzichino [1] when they define a roughness criterion, known as Rayleigh criterion, which also refers to interference. In the whole text of this article the refractive indices and all other quantities will be written with subscripts relating to the medium they characterize. The

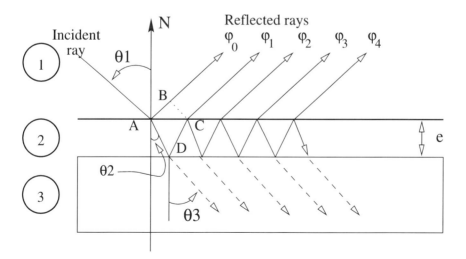

Figure 15.1   Interference system for a uniformly coated material.

typical geometry of an interference system is indicated in Figure 15.1. The three media involved are numbered as follows: 1 for the surrounding medium (often the air); 2 for the coating itself; and 3 for the substrate.

15.3.2   Reflectance of a uniformly coated material

The dielectric formulation of the interference phenomenon leads to a classical function that is described in many optics textbooks and was previously used in a computer graphics context by Dias [6]. Thus, the global amplitude of the electromagnetic field reflected by a homogeneous dielectric film uniformly deposited on another dielectric film is given by

$$r_{123} = \frac{r_{12} + r_{23} \exp{(i\varphi)}}{1 + r_{12}r_{23} \exp{(i\varphi)}} \tag{2}$$

This equation is valid for either polarization of the incident radiation and is also valid for either reflected amplitude. The generalization of formula (2) is made by replacing r_{12} and r_{23} by complex amplitudes according to the notation $\hat{r}_{12}$ and $\hat{r}_{23}$. With complex amplitudes and complex refractive indices appear the complex cosine function and therefore complex angles of refraction. These terms involve some more complicated relations since we account for absorption. However, these complications can be dealt with by using complete Fresnel formalism. In the following we will describe all the terms necessary for fast computation in the rendering phase. Thus, the classical dielectric reflectance of thin films is recalled:

$$|\hat{r}_{123}|^2 = \frac{r_{12}^2 + r_{23}^2 + 2r_{12}r_{23}\cos{(\varphi + \beta_{23})}}{1 + r_{12}^2 r_{23}^2 + 2r_{12}r_{23}\cos{(\varphi + \beta_{23})}} \tag{3}$$

to permit comparison with the next formula (4) obtained when replacing all the reflected amplitudes by relations of the form: $\hat{r}_{ij} = \rho_{ij}\exp{(i\beta_{ij})}$ in which $i, j = 1, 2$ or $i, j = 2, 3$.

$$|\hat{r}_{123}|^2 = \frac{\rho_{12}^2 + \rho_{23}^2 \exp{(-2\varphi_1)} + 2\rho_{12}\rho_{23}\exp{(-\varphi_1)}\cos{(\varphi_0 + \beta_{23} - \beta_{12})}}{1 + \rho_{12}^2 \rho_{23}^2 \exp{(-2\varphi_1)} + 2\rho_{12}\rho_{23}\exp{(-\varphi_1)}\cos{(\varphi_0 + \beta_{23} + \beta_{12})}} \tag{4}$$

where φ_0 and φ_1 are linked to the angle of incidence θ_1 as exhibited in equation (1), with a complex refractive index $\hat{n}_2$ for the coating leading to

$$\varphi = 4\pi\frac{e}{\lambda}n_2(1 + i\kappa_2)\cos{\theta_2} = \varphi_0 + i\varphi_1 \tag{5}$$

As this important theoretical result in equation (4) is valid for either polarization of the incident light, we will evaluate their contributions separately. For natural light or unpolarized light sources the resulting reflectivity will simply be

$$|\hat{r}_{123}|^2 = \frac{1}{2}\left(\left|\hat{r}_{123}^{\parallel}\right|^2 + \left|\hat{r}_{123}^{\perp}\right|^2\right)$$

The most apparent differences between equation (3) and equation (4) lie in the presence of exponential damping factors and of an additional term in the cosine functions. Notice that the arguments of these cosine functions differ slightly in numerator and denominator. When the coating is highly absorbing, i.e., when φ_1 is important, this coating completely hides the substrate; then, equation (4) reduces to $|\hat{r}_{123}|^2 = |\hat{r}_{12}|^2$. Inversely, when this coating is removed, equation (4) reduces to $|\hat{r}_{123}|^2 = |\hat{r}_{23}|^2$. Between these two asymptotic situations, all colorations are possible, depending on the thickness of the coating. All the preceding terms in equation (4) will be evaluated in the next subsection.

Reflection coefficients of each layer
The characterization of each material being dependent on its own refractive index, i.e., absolute refractive index, we need to use relative indices for the determination of the Fresnel factors associated with each phase boundary. Thus, for the phase boundary between the surrounding medium and the coating, we have a relative refractive index $\hat{n}_{12}$ such as

$$\hat{n}_{12} = \frac{\hat{n}_2}{n_1} = n_{12}(1 + i\kappa_{12}) \tag{6}$$

and for simplicity we will used n_{12} and κ_{12}

$$n_{12} = \frac{n_2}{n_1} \quad \text{and} \quad \kappa_{12} = \kappa_2 \tag{7}$$

The amplitudes of the reflected fields for parallel and perpendicular components of the incident light are given by the Fresnel formulas depending on the relative refractive index and on the angle of incidence. These formulas are

$$r_{12}^{\perp} = \rho_{12}^{\perp} \exp\left(i\beta_{12}^{\perp}\right) = \frac{\cos\theta_1 - \hat{n}_{12}\cos\theta_2}{\cos\theta_1 + \hat{n}_{12}\cos\theta_2} = \frac{\cos\theta_1 - \hat{n}_{12}q_{12}\exp i\gamma_{12}}{\cos\theta_1 + \hat{n}_{12}q_{12}\exp i\gamma_{12}}$$

$$r_{12}^{\parallel} = \rho_{12}^{\parallel} \exp\left(i\beta_{12}^{\parallel}\right) = \frac{\hat{n}_{12}\cos\theta_1 - \cos\theta_2}{\hat{n}_{12}\cos\theta_1 + \cos\theta_2} = \frac{\hat{n}_{12}\cos\theta_1 - q_{12}\exp i\gamma_{12}}{\hat{n}_{12}\cos\theta_1 + q_{12}\exp i\gamma_{12}} \tag{8}$$

where $\cos\theta_2 = q_{12}\exp(i\gamma_{12})$, i.e., explicitly

$$\cos\theta_2 = \sqrt{1 - \frac{1 - \kappa_{12}^2}{n_{12}^2(1 + \kappa_{12}^2)^2}\sin^2\theta_1 + i\frac{2\kappa_{12}\sin^2\theta_1}{n_{12}^2(1 + \kappa_{12}^2)^2}} \tag{9}$$

from which are easily extracted the modulus and the phase of this complex number:

$$q_{12} = \left(1 + \left[\sin^2\theta_1 - 2n_{12}^2\left(1 - \kappa_{12}^2\right)\right]\frac{\sin^2\theta_1}{|\hat{n}_{12}|^4}\right)^{\frac{1}{4}}$$

$$\gamma_{12} = \frac{1}{2}\arctan\frac{2\kappa_{12}n_{12}^2\sin^2\theta_1}{|\hat{n}_{12}|^4 - n_{12}^2(1 - \kappa_{12}^2)\sin^2\theta_1} \tag{10}$$

The expressions for q_{12}, γ_{12} involve the squaring of the relative refractive index because it appears squared in equation (1)

$$\frac{1}{(\hat{n}_{12})^2} = \frac{1 - \kappa_{12}^2 - 2i\kappa_{12}}{n_{12}^2(1 + \kappa_{12}^2)^2}$$

Now we can evaluate the damping factor j1 and the phase factor j0 as defined in equation (5)

$$\varphi_0 = 4\pi \frac{e}{\lambda} n_2 q_{12}(\cos\gamma_{12} - \kappa_2 \sin\gamma_{12})$$

$$\varphi_1 = 4\pi \frac{e}{\lambda} n_2 q_{12}(\kappa_2 \cos\gamma_{12} + \sin\gamma_{12}) \tag{11}$$

Thus all the terms relative to the interface between the surrounding medium and the coating have been obtained. The complete Fresnel factors for this interface are

$$\rho_{12}^{\perp} = \frac{\sqrt{\left(\cos^2\theta_1 - q_{12}^2|\hat{n}_{12}|^2\right)^2 + 4n_{12}^2 q_{12}^2(\sin\gamma_{12} + \kappa_{12}\cos\gamma_{12})^2\cos^2\theta_1}}{\cos^2\theta_1 + q_{12}^2|\hat{n}_{12}|^2 + 2n_{12}q_{12}(\cos\gamma_{12} - \kappa_{12}\sin\gamma_{12})\cos\theta_1}$$

$$\beta_{12}^{\perp} = \arctan \frac{2n_{12}q_{12}(\sin\gamma_{12} + \kappa_{12}\cos\gamma_{12})\cos\theta_1}{q_{12}^2|\hat{n}_{12}|^2 - \cos^2\theta_1} \tag{12}$$

$$\rho_{12}^{\|} = \frac{\sqrt{\left(|\hat{n}_{12}|^2\cos^2\theta_1 - q_{12}^2\right)^2 + 4n_{12}^2 q_{12}^2(\kappa_{12}\cos\gamma_{12} - \sin\gamma_{12})^2\cos^2\theta_1}}{|\hat{n}_{12}|^2\cos^2\theta_1 + q_{12}^2 + 2n_{12}q_{12}(\cos\gamma_{12} + \kappa_{12}\sin\gamma_{12})\cos\theta_1}$$

$$\beta_{12}^{\|} = \arctan \frac{2n_{12}q_{12}(\kappa_{12}\cos\gamma_{12} - \sin\gamma_{12})\cos\theta_1}{|\hat{n}_{12}|^2\cos^2\theta_1 - q_{12}^2} \tag{13}$$

The same procedure will be applied to the calculation of the Fresnel terms characterizing the phase boundary separating the coating and the substrate, resulting in the parallel and perpendicular components:

$$r_{12}^{\perp} = \rho_{23}^{\perp}\exp\left(i\beta_{23}^{\perp}\right) = \frac{\cos\theta_2 - \hat{n}_{23}\cos\theta_3}{\cos\theta_2 + \hat{n}_{23}\cos\theta_3} = \frac{q_{12}\exp(i\gamma_{12}) - \hat{n}_{23}q_{13}\exp(i\gamma_{13})}{q_{12}\exp(i\gamma_{12}) + \hat{n}_{23}q_{13}\exp(i\gamma_{13})}$$

$$r_{23}^{\|} = \rho_{23}^{\|}\exp\left(i\beta_{23}^{\|}\right) = \frac{\hat{n}_{23}\cos\theta_2 - \cos\theta_3}{\hat{n}_{23}\cos\theta_2 + \cos\theta_3} = \frac{\hat{n}_{23}q_{12}\exp(i\gamma_{12}) - q_{13}\exp(i\gamma_{13})}{\hat{n}_{23}q_{12}\exp(i\gamma_{12}) + q_{13}\exp(i\gamma_{13})} \tag{14}$$

Since the two materials in optical contact are supposed to be absorbing substances, the expression of the relative refractive index is a little more complicated:

$$\frac{\hat{n}_3}{\hat{n}_2} = \hat{n}_{23} = n_{23}(1 + i\kappa_{23})$$

$$n_{23} = \frac{n_3}{n_2}\left(\frac{1 + \kappa_2\kappa_3}{1 + \kappa_2^2}\right) \quad \text{and} \quad \kappa_{23} = \frac{\kappa_3 - \kappa_2}{(1 + \kappa_2\kappa_3)} \tag{15}$$

The Snell–Descartes law applied to each interface where the materials are in optical contact can be written as

$$\hat{n}_1 \sin \theta_1 = \hat{n}_2 \sin \theta_2 = \hat{n}_3 \sin \theta_3 \qquad (16)$$

The chain of equalities in relation (16) above, links the optical constants of the external medium to those of the most internal one, whatever the number of deposited films. In multilayered systems this behavior of light propagation is maintained. For example, the technology of multiple thin films involves a very high number of coatings for the specification of the required optical transparency in very high-quality optical instrumentation. These films are generally composed of completely transparent dielectric substances whose characteristic thickness (optical depth), varying according to a peculiar wavelength, depends on the desired result, i.e., the magnification of the reflectivity or transmittivity function. In this way, the absolute optical constants of the substrate are directly used.

$$\hat{n}_{13} = n_{13}(1 + i\kappa_{13}) \qquad (17)$$

In a very similar way, for $\cos \theta_3 = q_{13}\exp(i\gamma_{13})$, with θ_3 the angle of refraction inside the substrate,

$$q_{13} = \left(1 + \left[\sin^2\theta_1 - 2n_{13}^2\left(1 - \kappa_{13}^2\right)\right]\frac{\sin^2\theta_1}{|\hat{n}_{13}|^4}\right)^{\frac{1}{4}}$$

$$\gamma_{13} = \frac{1}{2}\arctan\frac{2\kappa_{13}n_{13}^2\sin^2\theta_1}{|\hat{n}_{13}|^4 - n_{13}^2(1 - \kappa_{13}^2)\sin^2\theta_1} \qquad (18)$$

If $Q = q_{12}/q_{13}$ and $\Gamma = \gamma_{13} - \gamma_{12}$, using equation (14) then

$$\rho_{23}^{\perp} = \frac{\sqrt{\left(Q^2 - |\hat{n}_{23}|^2\right)^2 + 4n_{23}^2Q^2(\kappa_{23}\cos\Gamma + \sin\Gamma)^2}}{Q^2 + |\hat{n}_{23}|^2 + 2n_{23}Q(\cos\Gamma - \kappa_{23}\sin\Gamma)}$$

$$\beta_{23}^{\perp} = \arctan\frac{2n_{23}Q(\kappa_{23}\cos\Gamma + \sin\Gamma)}{|\hat{n}_{23}|^2 - Q^2} \qquad (19)$$

$$\rho_{23}^{\parallel} = \frac{\sqrt{\left(Q^2|\hat{n}_{23}|^2 - 1\right)^2 + 4n_{23}^2Q^2(\kappa_{23}\cos\Gamma + \sin\Gamma)^2}}{1 + Q^2|\hat{n}_{23}|^2 + 2n_{23}Q(\cos\Gamma - \kappa_{23}\sin\Gamma)}$$

$$\beta_{23}^{\parallel} = \arctan\frac{2n_{23}Q(\kappa_{23}\cos\Gamma + \sin\Gamma)}{|\hat{n}_{23}|^2Q^2 - 1} \qquad (20)$$

which are the last calculated terms for the application of the expression (4) to yield the reflectivity. To speed up all computations in the rendering phase with ray tracing we decided to tabulate equation (4). This storage requires 10 double-precision floating-point numbers, i.e., all the following terms: $\rho_{12}^{\parallel}$, $\rho_{12}^{\perp}$, $\rho_{23}^{\parallel}$, $\rho_{23}^{\perp}$, $\beta_{12}^{\parallel}$, $\beta_{12}^{\perp}$, $\beta_{23}^{\parallel}$, $^3{}_{23}^{\perp}$, φ_0, φ_1 for each wavelength in AC1C2 and for each degree of incidence.

Relation between K and κ

It is not yet very common to deal with complex refractive indices. The notion of absorption that lies within this concept can be linked to a more macroscopic parameter defined as the *absorption constant K* generally given for a unit thickness of material. In an absorbing but nonscattering medium, the Beer–Lambert law expresses the decrease of an incoming flux of light energy after the crossing of this medium of thickness d. Let Φ be this emergent flux and Φ_0 the incident one. The Beer–Lambert law states

$$\frac{\Phi}{\Phi_0} = \exp(-Kd)$$

If a model of plane waves is used for the description of the electromagnetic field associated with the incident light of wavelength λ propagating in the direction defined by the unit vector u, then the electric field of this wave is of the form

$$E = E_0 \exp i(k.r - \omega t) = E_0 \exp i\omega\left[\frac{\hat{n}}{c}(r.u) - 1\right]$$

where E_0 is the amplitude of this incident electric field. The radiance perceived by a human observer, proportional to the square of the reflected field, is expressed

$$\frac{\Phi}{\Phi_0} = \exp\left(-2n\kappa\omega\frac{d}{c}\right)$$

which leads to the relation between the macroscopic absorption constant K and the imaginary part of the refractive index κ characterizing the absorbing medium:

$$K = 4\pi\frac{\kappa}{\lambda} \tag{21}$$

In the next subsection and following sections it will be seen how this model for interference in homogeneous and absorbing media is immediately applicable to several cases of industrial interest.

15.3.3 Generalization to thick films

Upon increasing the thickness of the coating, the interference fringes disappear and a new uniform coloration takes place. Predicting the color of such materials is difficult, if not practically impossible. A thick, uniform coating magnifies the reflectivity of the coated surface: a process which has been applied in the coating of mirrors by opticians. Today, a great number of materials are concerned with coating. Several kinds of coatings are already possible and of interest for industry, e.g., synthetic diamond deposited on polystyrene. Some other current applications concern compact disk manufacturing and, more generally, optical surface coating to prevent grooving.

15.4   Metallic paints and coated pigments

To obtain a metallic paint aspect, it is possible to use several kinds of pigments, for example, metallic coated flakes (often aluminum or bronze) with titanium dioxide or coated mica[3] pigments [8]. This coating being a major compound in many industries fields (e.g., paints, soaps, plastics, cosmetics) it is used in our computations. Several other coatings (e.g., iron or chromium oxides) are also used to adjust the desired finish, possibly in a multilayered system. The colors produced by these techniques depend mainly on the coating thickness and the number of these coatings. This very important effect is illustrated in Figure 15.3. A general description of almost all the possible optical interactions within a coated material, including coated pigments, is presented in Figure 15.2. In the reflectance model presented here the backscattering due to individual flakes has been neglected and a uniformly sedimented flake distribution is considered, i.e., with the flakes lying approximately in the same plane parallel, to the phase boundaries. An extension of the interference model for thin layers has produced some pleasing results for metallic paints. A typical metallic paint formulation consists of: a transparent colored coating with highly reflecting lamellar aluminum pigments placed at about constant depth and with parallel orientations to the boundaries of the painted surface. When this manufacturing principle is followed it becomes impossible to obtain either a completely white or completely black metallic paint, white being produced by maximum scattering and minimum absorption while it is exactly the contrary with black.

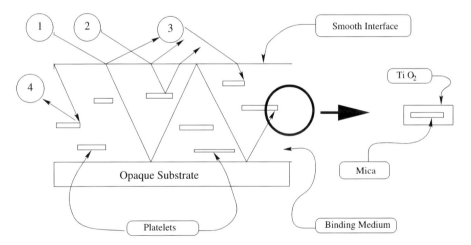

Figure 15.2 Typical geometry for metallic paints. 1, Multiple reflected/refracted ray. 2, Single reflection on a platelet. 3, Direct scattering. 4, Backscattering. The binding medium is generally a nitrocellulose-acrylate lacquer.

[3] The most common sources of mica are:
1. *Muscovite* K_2Al_4 $[Si_6Al_2O_{20}]$ $(OH, F)_4$
with refractive indices for the sodium D line given by $\alpha = 1.552 - 1.578$, $\beta = 1.582 - 1.615$, $\gamma = 1.587 - 1.617$.
2. *Paragonite* Na_2Al_4 $[Si_6Al_2O_{20}]$ $(OH)_4$
with refractive indices for the sodium D line given by $\alpha = 1.564 - 1.580$, $\beta = 1.594 - 1.609$, $\gamma = 1.600 - 1.609$.
These two biaxial crystalline substances are colorless in thin sections.

15.4.1 Brief characterization of coated pigments

Some pigments are themselves composite materials, i.e., having a coating so that their 'own color' cannot be predicted with a single refractive index but with two or even more refractive indices combined with the thicknesses of the coatings. Some coated pigments[4] are composed of a spherical (even elliptical) silica kernel on which the classical pigment is deposited, usually employed alone. As it increases the reflectivity of the coated surface, the coloring power of this kind of pigment is about 30% or 40% greater [7]. From spectral data given by Dotsenko et al. [7] we have found some reasonable refractive indices for pigments such as cadmium yellow, cobalt blue, and iron oxide red[5]. Some of them are used to compute the radiance in the 3D scenes presented. According to the notation $\hat{n}_e = n_e(1 + \kappa_e)$, refractive indices are indicated in Table 15.1. These values are computed for four wavelengths defined in the AC1C2 colorimetric space, according to Meyer's specifications [13].

Metallic coated pigments are very often employed for automotive coatings.

When there is some special requirement, e.g., nonelectrically conductive paints, mica-based pearlescent pigments are used. These pigments are sometimes produced in combination with absorptive pigments. They are obtained by depositing thin layers of high refractive index metal oxides around flat platelets of mica as a substrate, as presented in Figure 15.3. Pearlescent effects are easily produced by depositing thin layers of titanium dioxide on each face of a mica flake. The platelets that are used as a substrate have a mean thickness of 0.4 μm and a diameter ranging from 2–150 μm. These platelets are manufactured in several size distributions. Lead carbonate or bismuth oxychloride are also used as coated substances. We will shortly describe some characteristics of mica coated pigments because they are also employed in the cosmetics industry. Mica coated pigments present many advantages, among which is the fact that they are mechanically and chemically extremely stable, nonconductive, and dispersible in organic or aqueous solvents. Thus the combination of two or more transparent materials in a layered system produces brilliant colors, and these colors are interference

Table 15.1 Some complex refractive indices for common pigments. The optical constants of iron oxide red pigment are used in the computed images.

λ	Cobalt blue		Cadmium yellow		Iron oxide red	
(nm)	n	κ	n	κ	n	κ
631.4	1.804 100	0.455 380	2.350 000	0.000 081	2.708 600	0.012 660
557.7	1.500 000	0.050 160	2.446 900	0.002 148	2.739 050	0.110 655
490.9	1.500 000	0.002 618	1.584 580	0.027 082	2.281 820	0.052 590
456.4	1.500 000	0.001 928	1.715 680	0.035 871	2.288 720	0.052 431

[4] Pliny indicates that, in antiquity, a complicated mixture of *cæruleum* and *lutea* was used as an artificial chrysocolla ($CuCO_3$, $Cu(OH)_2$), probably a mixture of Egyptian blue with a white pigment. Coated pigments are historically very ancient materials employed in paintings.
[5] Red pigments obtained by direct grinding of hematite (Fe_2O_3) contain trace amounts of Ca, Ti, Cr, Mn, Cu, Zn, Sr, Ba, Hg, Pb. One can find [15] some slightly different values for the refractive index of hematite or other minerals. The refractive index for this negative uniaxial crystal is given, as for almost all materials, for the sodium D line (at 689.3 nm) only.

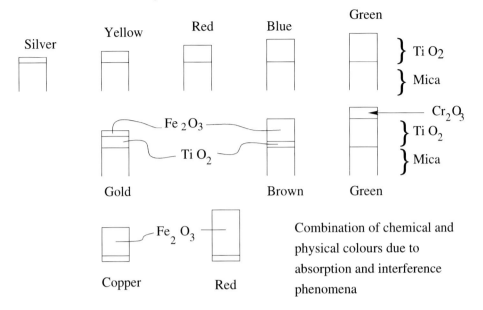

Figure 15.3   Color of some mica coated pigments of several thicknesses.

colors, obtained without any coloring agent – 'colors without colorants'. Several factors are necessary to characterize interference colors: the kind of metal oxides used, the layer thickness on mica, and the particle size distribution of the flat platelets. The elaboration of the coated pigment requires the control of certain parameters, such as the time of deposition for the coating. Brillant and lustrous color effects can be generated by

- Controlled deposition of a transparent TiO_2 layer on mica, where interference colors depend on the layer thickness.
- Combination of an interference layer with an additional coating of an absorbing metal oxide (Fe_2O_3 or Cr_2O_3).
- Controlled deposition of an absorbing, high refractive index metal oxide (Fe_2O_3) on mica, simultaneously showing interference and absorption colors, i.e. metallic colored luster with a nonmetallic pigment.

In the natural world, as opposed to the synthetic world, interference colors due to a similar but more complicated process are encountered in the beautiful luster of mother-of-pearl and generally in all the nacreous product of animals. Mother-of-pearl is formed by concentric layers of an alternating system of thick layers of calcium carbonate (aragonite) and thin layers of conchialin (an organic substance). The appearance of a painted surface depends on the size of the pigments used in the paint formulation. For mica pigments, this influence is shown in Table 15.2. We have neglected the influence of the size of pigments on the scattering diagram and have dealt only with specular reflectance. Specular reflectance is computed with a classical function for roughness applied to the pigment surface. The Beckmann and Spizzichino

Table 15.2 Influence of the size range on the appearance of mica pigments after incorporation

Size range	Appearance
3–15 µm	Mat luster
5–20 µm	Silky luster
10–50 µm	Pearly luster
30–130 µm	Glistening
50–150 µm	Spangly

model [1] for optical roughness is used throughout the computations and modifies the orthotropic diffuse diagram deduced from the Lambert law. The size of pigments nevertheless influences the final aspect of a painted surface because it influences the covering capacity of that paint.

15.5   Results

A set of six pictures is included and should be read from left to right and from top to bottom. This presentation follows an increase in the thickness of the coatings. The interference fringes become less visible when the thickness of the coating increases. Figure 15.4a shows interference patterns produced by a thin absorbing film of iron oxide (uniformly deposited crystalline hematite on pure iron) for various thicknesses. Figure 15.4b shows the influence of the external roughness on the shininess for a constant thickness greater than in the preceding image. Figure 15.4c exhibits the transition between thin and thick coatings. Figure 15.4d presents the influence of the thickness on the color production caused by the same absorbing coating of iron oxide red deposited on aluminum platelets. Figure 15.4e shows the effect of a 10 µm coating of crystalline iron oxide (central sphere) compared to pure iron (lateral spheres). Figure 14.4f is equivalent to 15.4e with copper oxide on copper.

15.6   Conclusion

The model presented here offers many capabilities in the rendering of some colored phenomena. It can be applied to coated or uncoated materials and needs only optical constants and thickness as natural parameters. As it is always difficult to obtain spectral data for a single coating, we have chosen this alternative approach, using an 'effective medium' description of heterogeneous media. One can notice that the spectral reflectance curves for various materials depend on a special preparation of the surface sample used in data acquisition. Here refractive indices extracted from tables of optical constants were used, along with previous work on the rendering of paints and opaque plastic materials [5]. The optical constants found in the tables concern materials with a very high purity level. For more usual materials, the relation between the real and the ideal optical properties has not yet been studied very well. Nevertheless, a more electromagnetic-based model of stratified media that includes internal scattering, connecting fundamental optical properties of materials to their macroscopic

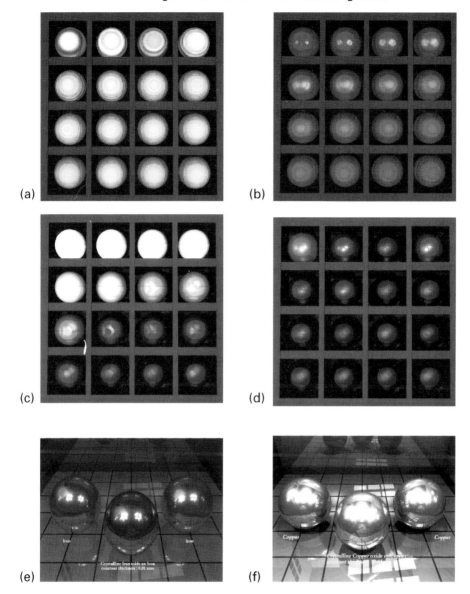

(a)

(b)

(c)

(d)

(e)

(f)

Figure 15.4 (a) Interference patterns produced in thin absorbing films. (b) Influence of roughness on shininess (constant thickness). (c) Pearlescent effects obtained with smooth variations of the coating thickness. (d) Metallic paint rendered with coated pigments. The successive coatings are growing in the 400–750 nm range in steps of 50 nm. (e) Thick coating of iron oxide red uniformly deposited on pure iron (center). (f) Thick coating of copper oxide uniformly deposited on pure copper (center).

parameters, has yet to be explored. A generalization could be implemented on the basis of these two analyses of color simulation (theories of *effective media* and theory of *stratified media*). Whatever the model of color simulation, the problem of its validation is encountered. In a spectral approach to the rendering of color the 'real' is usually conceived as being embodied in the notion of the (energetic) reflection or transmission spectrum. This assumption does not concern only the validity or accuracy of the data that must be introduced in the models of rendering. Unfortunately, color is not equivalent to energy.

Color synthesis needs to draw upon the great experience and knowledge of color manipulation and formulation accumulated by artists over the centuries. A possible way to build a highly realistic rendering program is illustrated by the famous art historian Erwin Panofsky [14] when describing the very subtle effects obtained by 'The Master of Flémalle' (cf., chapter 6, pp. 152–153). He writes:

> The whole picture was built up from bottom to top by superimposing 'rich' and therefore translucent paint (viz., pigments tempered with a fat medium, mostly, though not exclusively, oil) upon 'lean' and therefore more or less opaque paint (viz., pigments tempered with other, aqueous media or, possibly, an emulsion). Lighter and darker tones were produced by applying the translucent colors over an opaque underpainting – significantly called dood-verw, 'dead color,' in Dutch and Flemish – which preestablished the light values and, to some extent, the general color; and finer gradation – in certain cases even an optical mixture of two colors – was achieved by applying further films of pigment. As a result, the light is not entirely reflected from the top surface of the picture, where opaque pigments appear only in the shape of highlights. Part of the light penetrates the coat or coats of translucent paint to be reflected from the nearest layer of opaque pigment, and this is what endows the pictures of the old masters with their peculiar 'depth.' Even the darkest tones could never turn opaque, and ultimately the whole multiple coat of paint would coalesce into a hard, enamellike, slightly uneven but uniformly luminous substance, irradiated from below as well as from above, excepting only those sporadic whites or light yellows which, by their very contrast to the transparent depth of the surrounding pigments, assume the character of 'high lights.'

Panofsky indicates the way to define a very complete reflectance model for composite materials. The complexity of such a rendering program thus remains in the mathematical and physical formulation of the associated model.

References

[1] Piotr Beckmann, André Spizzicchino, *The Scattering of Electromagnetic Waves from Rough Surfaces*. Pergamon Press, London, 1963.
[2] Max Born, Emile Wolf, *Principles of Optics–Electromagnetic Theory of Propagation, Interference and Diffraction of Light*, Pergamon Press, Oxford, 1975.
[3] Tony Bridgeman, The reflectance of metallic paints, *Mondial Couleur 85*, F. Parra, ed., AIC, 1985.
[4] P. Callet, Interferences, couches minces et peintures métallisées. *Int. J. CADCAM and Computer Graphics*, 9(1–2): 251–264; 1994.
[5] Patrick Callet, Simulation de la couleur des milieux diffusants opaques, *Actes de MICAD 93*, Yvon Gardan, ed., pp. 81–97, Hermès, Paris, 1993.
[6] Maria Lurdes Dias, Ray tracing interference color, *IEEE Computer Graphics Appl.*, 272(17): 54–59; 1991.

[7] A.V. Dotsenko, A.M. Efremov, V.G. Sofronov, Ligh attenuation by spherical two-layer particles having a coating of coloured pigments, *Opt. Mekh. Promst.*, 55, 1988. [Translated into English in *Sov. J. Opt. Technol.* 55(9): 556–557; 1988.]

[8] Klaus-Dieter Franz, High luster mica pigments for automotive coatings, *Modial Couleur 85*, F. Parra, ed., AIC, 1985.

[9] R.J. Gettens, G.L. Stout, *Painting Materials*. Dover, New York, 1966.

[10] Pierre Grandou, Paul Pastour, *Peintures et vernis*. Hermann, Paris, 1988.

[11] Pat Hanrahan, Wolfgang Krueger, Reflection from layered surfaces due to subsurface scattering. In *Computer Graphics Proceedings*, Paris, 1993, pp. 81–97, Siggraph Annual Conference Series.

[12] Franz Hofmeister, Colourimetric evaluation of perlescent pigments, *Mondial Couleur 85*, F. Parra, ed., AIC, 1985.

[13] G.W. Meyer, Wavelength selection for synthetic image generation, *Computer Vision, Graphics and Image Processing*, 41: 57–69; 1988.

[14] Erwin Panofsky, *Les primitifs flamands*, collection 35–37. Hazan, Paris, 1992. [Original version: *Early Netherlandish Painting*, Harvard University Press, 1971.]

[15] David Shelly, *Optical Mineralogy*, Elsevier, 1990.

[16] B.R. Smits, G.W. Meyer, Newton's colors: Simulating interference phenomena in realistic image synthesis. In *Conference Proceedings of Eurographics Workshop on Photo-simulation, Realism and Physics in Computer Graphics*, K. Bouatouch, ed., INRIA/IRISA, 1990.

16
Modeling of Growing Biological Processes Using Parametric L-Systems

Huw Jones, Andrew Tunbridge, and Paul Briggs

16.1   Introduction

The realistic modeling of growing plants is a major research issue in computer graphics. Probably the most extensively used method is that of L-systems, first introduced by Aristid Lindenmayer [6] to describe biological structures and later developed as a visualization method [10]. Alvy Ray Smith III developed a similar technique which he called 'graftals' [12]. The method is effective in the way that complex structures can be described by relatively simple rule sets. This, the method adopted and adapted for this study, is described in more detail below.

Visually convincing effects are created by direct simulations of the appearance of particular tree types which allow stochastic variation in the depiction. The maple model shown by Bloomenthal [2] and maple, birch, and hornbeam forms created by Thum [13] (Figure 16.1) are examples which include textured tree bark and individual leaf detail (Figure 16.2). DeReffye and colleagues [11] used botanical laws based on 'knowledge' of the plant (such as age, growing conditions or the physics of branches)

Figure 16.1   Synthetic maple, birch, and hornbeam models by Jon Thum.

Visualization and Modeling
ISBN 0-12-227738-4

Figure 16.2 Details of Jon Thum's maple tree models.

to influence the form generated. The method allows stochastic variation and produces images of a range of plant species and varieties. Holton [5] models a tree structure as a sequence of strands, each running unbroken from the tree base (or root) to a terminating leaf or branch. The thickness of a structural element such as a branch or trunk depends on the number of internal strands passing through it, and effects of gravity, length, and nutrition are simulated.

The methods presented below are developments of the standard L-systems approach. The 'growth' of a branching structure is affected by simulated 'nutrient' flow. Parameters represent levels of nutrients and internally created energy in each element of the plant structure; these 'flow' through the structure during its development. The parameters model, in a simplistic sense, the biological influences on plant growth and enable varying environmental features to affect the structure.

16.2   L-Systems in General

An L-system [10] is specified by three elements: an 'alphabet,' a defined 'axiom,' and a set of 'productions.' The system is essentially a set of rules for generation of a string of alphabetic characters. The depiction of an L-system is through interpretation of the string characters as geometric elements which can be related to structural parts of an object to be simulated.

String development begins with an axiom, which is a 'word' (a collection of characters or a single character from the permitted alphabet). Structures are generated by recursive application of the productions or replacement rules to the axiom. Productions are rules for replacing a character by a word (which may itself be a single character). These rules, applied simultaneously to all characters, generate relatively complicated words or text strings after a few iterations. Interpretation of string characters as geometric entities is usually related to turtle graphic commands used in the language LOGO [1]. Typical alphabet characters and their turtle interpretations are 'F,' representing a forward drawing step of given length d, '+' for a left turn of given angle δ and '−' for a right turn of the same angle. These are implemented by performing the relevant activity and updating the current state of the drawing 'turtle,' which is maintained as a Cartesian location (x, y) and a turtle direction θ. Thus, when the symbol 'F' is encountered, the turtle state is updated to

$$\{(x', y'), \theta)\} = \{(x + d \cos(\theta), y + d \sin(\theta)), \theta\}$$

with the line from (x, y) to (x', y') being drawn. The symbol '[' denotes the start of a branch, implemented by pushing the current turtle state onto a stack data structure. When the branch is complete, the end of the branch is indicated by the symbol ']', when the turtle is reset to the state popped off the stack. The symbol 'f' is sometimes used to represent a forward step equivalent to F, but without any line being drawn.

When the branching angle δ is set to 45°, the effect of applying the production

$$F \rightarrow F\,[-F + F\,]\,F\,F$$

four times to the axiom F is shown in Figure 16.3. The symbol F is replaced by the string to the right of the arrow at each stage. By convention, any symbol which does not have a production is unchanged. The effect of the first two stages of string generation is shown in Table 16.1 – inclusion of further stages would soon fill the page. When the sequence of strings is interpreted as a drawing, the overall size of the image is kept the same in this example by reducing the length of each F drawing step by one third at each stage. The figure shows how recursive application of the production generates an object with an almost organic nature, resembling a stylized plant structure. The regular nature of the structure makes it unconvincing as a 'plant,' although an object of reasonable complexity is created in relatively few stages. Rules which reflect the uncertainty of natural plant forms must be implemented to give more realistic plant interpretations.

Less regular shapes are generated by allowing random variation in the drawing rules, varying the branching angles and/or lengths of F forward drawing steps according to given stochastic distributions. One of the beauties of L-systems is in the limited use of storage needed to generate relatively complicated images. If depiction of a growing plant is required, this feature must be compromised by holding the random number associated with each feature as a parameter of that feature. For example, the turn angle of the main lower right branch of Figure 16.3 is represented by the third string symbol ('−') at stage 1 (Table 16.1), but by the 11th symbol at stage 2. It is practically impossible to track a particular feature with regard to its location within the string. A practical way of maintaining the value of this particular angle is to store the random

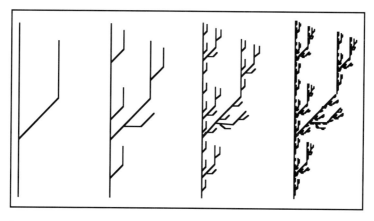

Figure 16.3   An L-system with production F → F [−F + F] F F.

Table 16.1   Two-stage recursive application of F [–F + F] F F to the axiom F.

Stage	String generated
0	F
1	F [–F + F] F F
2	F [–F + F] F F [–F [–F + F] F F + F [–F + F] F F F [–F + F] F F F [–F + F] F F

value designated to it as a parameter pointed at by the string symbol when it is first generated. This is where the concept of parametric L-systems begins.

   This method would produce plants with different geometric forms but with identical topological structures. Similar, but not identical, plant-like forms can be generated by stochastic variation of production rules. This can create images representing different instances of plants from the same 'genus,' as shown in Figure 16.4. This uses the production

$$F \begin{cases} \overset{0.95}{\longrightarrow} & F [+ F] [< F] F [- F] F \\ \overset{0.05}{\longrightarrow} & \varnothing \end{cases}$$

indicating that the upper replacement rule is to be used with probability 0.95, the lower, indicating a 'null' result or deletion of the character (like allowing a branch to be snapped off), with probability 0.05. The symbol '<' indicates a right turn of 30°. Stochastic variation at the drawing (or string interpretation stage) is introduced by deviating the angle of each F forward drawing step by −2°, 0°, or 2° with equal probability. The first of the seven growths in Figure 16.4 has suffered an L-systems 'late frost,' being obliterated by chance at its first stage.

   Context-sensitive L-systems, another method for producing some structural irregularity, use productions which are dependent on neighboring string symbols. The result of applying a production may depend on the character appearing to the left (the left context) of a character or its right along its branch level (the right context) or both. L-systems interpretation can be extended to three-dimensional domains by introducing roll, pitch, and yaw angle symbols. These features, and others, are fully described by Prusinkiewicz and Lindenmayer [10], and readers are encouraged to refer to this excellent text for full development of the ideas hinted at here.

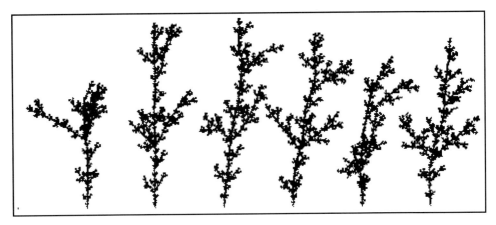

Figure 16.4   Seven stochastic L-systems growths from the same 'genus.'

These methods still suffer from separate development of the string, representing the topological structure of the object produced, and its geometric interpretation. In nature, these are not independent. The location of a branch within a plant influences its development. For example, its growth rate may be affected by its being frequently shaded by other features or its orientation to prevailing wind. Recent work in 'environmentally sensitive' L-systems overcomes this problem. Prusinkiewicz and colleagues [9] show appealing images of synthetic topiary, achieved by introduction of a 'query module.' The L-systems string is interpreted as a geometric structure as it is developed (or 'grown'), location parameters (typically Cartesian coordinates) being held as parameters of each relevant string character. 'Query modules,' inserted as string characters, test these coordinate values against location constraints and affect the production rules according to the result. For example, if a query module falls outside some predefined region of space, the branch growing from it is terminated, equivalent to pruning a plant growth against a spatial shape. Tying of location information to the string means that the L-systems structures become less compact. However, in an age of relatively cheap computer memory, the modeling opportunities offered by this technique make it attractive. This method is used later in the creation of a simplistic model of tree growth by passing 'nutrient' and 'energy' parameters. The relatively simpler concept of a fungal growth simulation is introduced first, as an intermediate stage.

16.3   Simulation of a Fungal Growth Using Parametric L-Systems

Prosser and Trinci [8] present a comprehensive mathematical model of fungal growth based on underlying biological processes. This mechanistic model is the basis of a simulation of the growth of a particular type of fungus, *Aspergillus nidulans* [15].

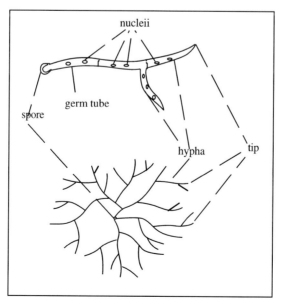

Figure 16.5   Typical structure of a mycelium.

Figure 16.5 shows the basic structure of the fungus, with typical features of molds grown in Petri dishes. A whole network is called a *mycelium*, with individual threads called *hyphae*. These can be considered as tubes filled with a liquid (the cytoplasm), comprising chemicals and tiny structures (such as the nuclei which control some growth processes) needed to sustain and develop the fungus. Hyphae extend by growing at their tips; branch hyphae are usually formed behind the tip. Hyphal tubes are divided, in some fungi, by walls called septa. A septum may form a complete or partial barrier to flow of cytoplasm. A new mycelium typically starts with spore germination to form a single hypha or germ-tube. A colony, generally lying roughly within a circle, is formed by elongation and branching. Radial extension is approximately constant, whilst the total length of the mycelium increases exponentially.

The cytoplasm contains vesicles, cytoplasmic structures containing nutrients necessary for extension of the hyphal tip. Vesicles are produced throughout the hypha and flow toward the hyphal tip [8]. It is believed that vesicles fuse with the hyphal tip when they reach it, their contents being used to fuel the extension of the tip.

New septa (cross walls) are generated according to the following model, observed by Trinci [14]. The apical compartment, that portion of hypha that lies between the tip and the next septum, contains four nuclei. As the tip extends, the volume of cytoplasm contained in this compartment increases. When the volume of cytoplasm per nucleus in an apical compartment reaches a critical value, the four nuclei divide to form eight nuclei. When this division is complete, a new septum is formed across the middle of the apical compartment, separating the nuclei into two clusters of four. The septum gradually grows to its maximum size, giving greater resistance to flow of vesicles as it grows.

When the number of vesicles in part of a hypha between two septa reaches a critical concentration, the vesicles fuse with part of a side-wall of the hypha, causing the wall to swell and eventually branch at that point. Because septa have a constraining effect on the flow of vesicles, this usually occurs in the part of a hypha just behind a septum. Flow of vesicles through the hypha just before the branch is divided so that some flow into the branch, the remainder flowing toward the original flow direction.

An alphabet of seven characters plus the usual branch start and end symbols is used to model this growing structure, each character representing a segment of the structure. Figure 16.6 shows part of a mycelium modeled in this way. The character T represents a growing tip, A is an apical segment (lying just behind a tip), segment M contains a septum, B is a branch initiator, S is a normal segment, and P and G (not shown in Figure 16.6) represent an ungerminated and germinated spore, respectively. A parameter associated with each character represents its vesicle content. A fraction of the vesicle content of each element is passed to its right context in the string, with this proportion being divided between main and branch sections at character B, representing the base of a branch. The section depicted in Figure 16.6 would be represented in an L-system string as

$$... S S B [S S B [A A A T] M A T] M A A T$$

Sixteen productions are used to control growth of the string from its axiom P, representing an ungerminated spore. They serve two purposes. The generation of vesicles within segments and their distribution along the mycelium is modeled by adjusting parameter values at each 'clock tick,' indicating flow from left to right of the string; this is usually achieved without amending the characters themselves. When parameter values achieve certain thresholds indicating that vesicle level within a segment has achieved a significantly high value, or when signals are passed from the right context indicating a change of state, the nature of the characters in the string may change. The following list indicates the permitted character changes; reference to Figure 16.6 should help in understanding the entries.

P → GT   an ungerminated spore germinates and grows a tip when its vesicle content achieves a threshold;

T → AT   a tip grows forward leaving an apical segment behind it when it achieves a certain size;

A → M   an apical segment becomes a septum on a signal that its right context has achieved a certain size;

A → S   an apical segment becomes a normal segment when its right context has changed to a septum;

S → B[T]   a normal segment becomes a branch segment with a growing tip when its parameter value achieves a threshold.

Full details of these productions and of threshold levels that directly model *Aspergillus nidulans* are given by Tunbridge and Jones [15]. It should be noted that the parameter passing is deterministic, always generating the same string, but the model could be made more realistically variable by allowing stochastic parameter passing and generation rules. The number of growing tips and the total hyphal length generated (found from the number of segments, which are considered to have standard lengths), are remarkably close to the values reported by Prosser and Trinci [8], indicating the aptness of the model.

Once a string representing the mycelium's topological structure has been generated, this must be interpreted geometrically to generate an image of the fungus. This

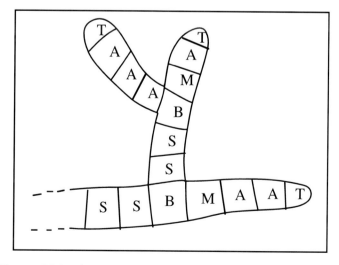

Figure 16.6   L-system characters modeling a mycelium.

separation of topological creation from geometric interpretation means this implementation shares the limitation of simple L-systems in that the growth is independent of the geometrical location of the string elements. This is an unreal feature, as the mycelium growth may be inhibited locally by exhaustion of the external nutrient stock, possibly explaining why mycelia tend to grow circular colonies in an outward 'search' for nutrients. At the drawing stage, this is simulated by deviating the drawing direction of a segment randomly towards a radially outward direction from the colony's origin at a spore. Branch angles and growing directions are also randomly perturbed to give a more realistic appearance. Part of a typical simulation of *Aspergillus nidulans* is shown in Figure 16.7. The 2D drawing gives a good interpretation of the mycelium, whose hypha cross over each other in a very narrow slice of the third dimension.

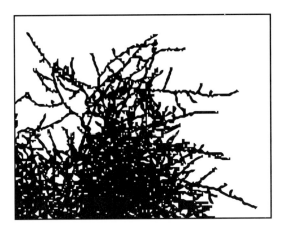

Figure 16.7 Part of a simulation of *Aspergillus nidulans.*

16.4 Simulation of Tree Growth: A Simple Parametric L-System Model

The above simulation of a fungus shows how a parameter can be used to model the way in which nutrients, vesicles in this case, pass along and enable growth of a branching structure. This idea has been extended to model an interpretation of the biological processes underlying general plant growth, in particular the growth of general tree structures. We are aware that this is a complex activity (see, for example, Evans [4]), but have found that the modeling of two simple processes can create reasonable simulation of the general effect of tree growth.

   The organs of a plant can be categorized as roots, stems, leaves, and reproductive organs. This study considers the activities of roots, stems, apical (growing) buds, and leaves. The root of a plant absorbs nutrients (water and minerals) from the soil and passes them to the stem. It would be possible, in an extended study, to model the roots as a branching L-system, using this development to affect the amount of nutrient absorbed. This process has been assumed to have occurred in this case study; a controlled amount of 'nutrient' dependent on stem breadth is simply passed into the growing stem by a parametric process starting at the left of the L-system string.

Leaves are the principal photosynthetic organs, although some photosynthetic tissue is also found in stems. Photosynthesis is the biological process which uses radiated energy from the sun to turn water and organic compounds into 'food' for growth. This process takes place in algae and some bacteria as well as green plants. The overall effect of this complex activity is to produce organic compounds, starches and sugars, from carbon dioxide extracted from the air and water and minerals extracted from the soil. These compounds are removed from photosynthetic sites by the process of translocation.

The translocation system of a plant is simplified as a bidirectional parameter passing system in an L-system interpretation, with nutrients from the soil passing 'up' the tree to the apical buds and leaves, and 'energy' (sugars and starches) created in the leaves through photosynthesis being redistributed about other plant features. At each time step of the L-system development, nutrients taken up at the root level will be passed 'up' the plant structure (from left to right of the string), with each stem section absorbing a percentage of the nutrient as it passes along. Some of the remaining nutrients will be 'used' to extend growing apical buds, with most being used to drive the photosynthetic process in leaves. Energy so created is then redistributed by a similar reverse parameter passing process. Nutrient and energy levels affect the thickness of stem elements. Each stem section is considered to contain a number s of 'strands,' after the method described by Holton [5]. A stem element is eventually depicted as a generalized cylindrical section with radius equal to $K\sqrt{s}$, where K is a rendering configuration parameter. The way that s and hence stem thickness is affected by nutrient and energy distribution is indicated below.

Some of this energy will eventually find its way to the root. This could be used to drive development of the root structure in a future implementation, but in this study the effect of its growth is related to the thickness of its base stem element. The functions of the major modeled features in the L-system string are indicated below.

Root R (nutrient, energy). The solitary root character exports nutrients to its right context, which must be a stem segment. The amount of nutrient passed is proportional to the number of strands in this stem section. The energy content is not used in this implementation, but is included in the data structure as it would be useful if an L-systems root structure were to be grown.

Stem S (strand, nutrient, export nutrient, export energy). A stem segment imports nutrient from its left context (when this is a root or stem), imports energy from its right context (leaf or stem), exports nutrients to its right context (apical bud, leaf, or stem), and exports energy to its left context (stem or root). This is defined by the following basic production, which is specifically implemented as a number of separate context-sensitive productions to take account of all possible left and right contexts.

$$S(s, n, x, e) \rightarrow S(s + n, \text{importNutr} *N + \text{importEnergy}*E,$$
$$(1 - N)*\text{importNutr} + D*\text{importEnergy},$$
$$(1 - D - E)*\text{importEnergy})$$

Proportion N of the nutrient imported and E of energy imported are absorbed to enable thickening. Control of parameters E, D (energy used for development), and N affects the general tree structure, as shown in examples below.

Apical bud A (nutrient). An apical bud accumulates imported nutrients from the left context until its content achieves a given threshold. The effect at this stage will depend on the type of tree being modeled. In the example implemented below, A converts into a string of type

$$[S[L]A]S[L]A$$

adding one forward stem segment and a leaf, with a similar initial branch structure created (Figure 16.8). Parameters and directional indicators of roll, pitch, and yaw changes have not been shown to simplify the description. New stem segments are created with one initial strand. Construction of this section is important in the modeling of particular plant species. This is the 'engine' that drives the tree's topological growth.

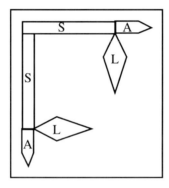

Figure 16.8   Conversion of an apical bud.

Leaf L (scale, age, nutrient). The leaf is the important photosynthetic element, importing nutrient from and exporting energy to its left context. Exported energy is calculated as the product of a universal sun factor H, which could be dependent on time, and imported nutrient. In practice, the amount of energy produced diminishes with age of a leaf. This feature has not been implemented, but the structure allows for this development in future implementations. The leaf is also aged by a set amount each 'clock tick.' When the age of the leaf reaches 70% of its maximum, it 'falls to the ground.' This is implemented by replacing string element L by GL, where G is a 'ground' feature, reducing the y-coordinate of the turtle location to zero for drawing of the next leaf element. Again, parameters have not been indicated here to simplify the description. On depiction, leaf colors are affected by the age parameter and the leaf element is eliminated from the L-system after its age reaches a maximum threshold. The scale parameter is used to generate an image of the leaf from a canonical standard description in the form of a simple polygon. Leaf size grows to a maximum value dependent on age. It could also be made to depend on environmental factors.

The rules indicated above give a simple description of the effects implemented. Full descriptions of all productions used, data structures, rendering parameters, and color settings (using Open GL as a rendering engine [7]) are given by Briggs [3]. No attempt has been made at this stage to model a particular genus of tree. The intention of this study is to indicate the aptness of the method. Examples illustrated below show that naturalistic tree like structures can be 'grown' by the method, and that the shape of structures can be affected by amending parameters for nutrient absorbed from the soil, radiated energy from sunlight, and absorption of nutrients and energy within structure elements. Future implementations could include other features such as fruit and flowers as intrinsic parts of the L-systems alphabet.

16.5 Simulation of Tree Growth: Implementation of the Model

The axiom for the illustrations shown is set to

$$RSS[L]A$$

representing a double stem segment growing from a root, with a growing apical tip and a leaf. Figures 16.9a and b shows how trunk and branch thickening is satisfactorily simulated for an L-system generation of 100 stages. Preset parameters for this simulation are

Nutrient absorbed	$N = 0.02$
Energy absorbed	$E = 0.01$
Energy for development	$D = 0.1$
Solar energy	$H = 1$
Maximum leaf age	60

Branching angles are subject to stochastic variation when allocated to give a more natural irregular appearance. No clash detection has been implemented, so branches may sometimes be seen to pass through each other on close scrutiny of Figure 16.9b.

By changing the parameters given above, markedly different growth effects are produced. For example, by changing the nutrient flow parameter N to 0.05, more nutrient is absorbed within stem segments, allowing them to grow more thickly. The consequence of this is that less nutrient is available for the development of leaves and hence the photosynthetic effect is diminished, producing a structure with thicker trunk and less foliage (Figure 16.10). Parameters here are as for Figure 16.9 except for the change of N from 0.02 to 0.05.

The parameter E, representing energy absorption within stem sections, is increased from its previous setting of 0.01 to 0.04 in Figure 16.11. This means that 96% of energy received from the right context by a stem section is exported to its left context, with 4% absorbed to contribute to stem growth. This leads to increased thickening of stems compared to Figure 16.9. In Figure 16.11, all parameters other than E are set as in Figure 16.9. This includes drawing parameters, such as lengths of cylinder sections and random angle variations, so it is clear from Figures 16.9, 16.10, and 16.11 that factors N and E have considerable influence on the tree shape.

By associating a query module, as explained by Prusinkiewicz and colleagues [9],

314   H. Jones et al.

(a)

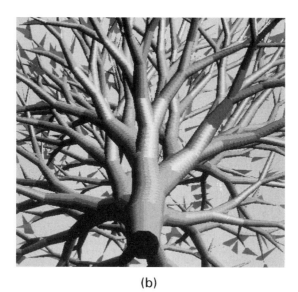

(b)

Figure 16.9 A generated tree (a) from the side, (b) from below.

with each leaf, the effect of having part of the structure in shade can be simulated. In Figure 16.12, the location of each leaf is queried before the amount of energy created by the photosynthetic effect is calculated. The supplied sun energy H is set to a lower value for leaves to the left of the structure (where $x < 0$) than to the right. The effect on the tree structure is clearly visible, with the region to the left being less well developed and having thinner branches. This effect has been more clearly demonstrated in other examples using greater differences in the values of H. Two other effects are shown in Figure 16.12. Leaf colors are changed with age and those older than 70% of the maximum set age are detached from the tree using the G 'ground' symbol (all leaves are depicted as simple shaded plane quadrilaterals for simplicity). Real plants reseed when seeds fall from the plant and germinate to create new growths. Although the concept of flower to fruit to seed development is not implemented in this study, its feasibility is

Figure 16.10   Tree with higher nutrient absorption.

Figure 16.11   Tree with higher energy absorption.

demonstrated by allowing a small proportion of the fallen leaves to behave as seed would in the real situation. Several leaves close to the trunk in Figure 16.12 have reseeded, one is clearly visible to the left of the trunk.

16.6 Summary

The two major case studies illustrated in this chapter demonstrate the usefulness of parametric L-systems for modeling nutrient and energy flows in plant growth. One

Figure 16.12　Shade affecting growth, fallen leaves and reseeding.

models a limited form of plant structure directly, the other takes a more simplistic interpretation of a more general model. Both these studies were undertaken as the project phase of a MSc program, so were subject to time constraints. Although the studies are complete in themselves, this explains why some potential improvements have not yet been implemented, and the models have potential for further development. For example, in the simulation of fungus growth, the passage of nutrients is deterministic. It would be relatively simple to re-run the system with stochastic vesicle generation laws. In the tree simulation, no attempt has yet been made directly to model existing trees. The illustrations are of a generic tree-like structure. There is no clash detection between branches, and no attempt is made to create realistic impressions of tree bark and leaf structure. Although the effect of shading has been shown clearly, the models have no self-shading. In spite of these accepted limitations, the result is a convincing demonstration of the validity of the method; a simplistic interpretation of the mechanisms of nutrient and energy flow through the structure produces life-like features. The effects of leaf aging and detachment and the potential for seed generation within a more complex model have been shown. This could be a take-off point for a wide range of potential applications.

References

[1] H. Abelson, A.A. diSessa, *Turtle Geometry*, MIT Press, Cambridge, Mass., 1982.
[2] J. Bloomenthal, Modeling the mighty maple, *Computer Graphics*, 19(3): 305–311; 1985.
[3] P. Briggs, *Plant growth simulation using L-systems*, MSc Computer Graphics project dissertation, Middlesex University, London, UK, 1995.
[4] G.C. Evans, *The Quantitative Analysis of Plant Growth*, Blackwell, London, UK, 1972.

[5] M. Holton, Strands, gravity and botanical tree imagery, *Computer Graphics Forum*, 13(1): 57–67; 1994.

[6] A. Lindenmayer, Mathematical models for cellular interaction in development, parts I and II, *J. Theor. Biol.*, 18: 280–315; 1968.

[7] J. Neider, T. Davis, M. Woo, *OpenGL Programming Guide*, Addison Wesley, Reading, Mass., 1993.

[8] J.I. Prosser, A.P.J. Trinci, A model for hyphal growth and branching, *J. Gen. Microsc.*, 111: 153–164; 1979.

[9] P. Prusinkiewicz, M. James, R. Měch, Synthetic topiary, *ACM SIGGRAPH '94*, 351–358, 1994.

[10] P. Prusinkiewicz, A. Lindenmayer, *The Algorithmic Beauty of Plants*, Springer-Verlag, New York, NY, 1990.

[11] P. deReffye, C. Edelin, J. Françon, M. Jaeger and C. Puech, Plant models faithful to botanical structure and development, *ACM SIGGRAPH'88*, 22(4): 151–158; 1988.

[12] A.R. Smith, Plants, fractals and formal languages, *ACM Computer Graphics*, 18(3): 1–10; 1984.

[13] J. Thum, *Jon's Trees*, MSc Applied Computing Technology project dissertation, Middlesex University, London, UK, 1993.

[14] A.P. Trinci, Wall and hyphal growth, *Science Progress*, 65: 75–99; 1978.

[15] A. Tunbridge, H. Jones, An L-Systems approach to the modeling of fungal growth, *J. Visualization and Computer Animation*, 6(2): 91–107; 1995.

17
Additive Technologies for Direct 3D Rapid Prototyping

Jack Bresenham

17.1 Subtractive and Additive RP Processes

Graphics and manufacturing have always gone well together. Drafting was one of the early computer graphics application successes. Physical design of parts benefited greatly from introduction of computer graphics design systems. An early graphics design system was the Alpine project undertaken jointly by IBM and General Motors in 1964. In those days a computer terminal was so expensive relative to the cost of an engineer that a design department might be split into shift work to share one workstation among three or more engineers. Now, of course, computing costs are so affordable it is not uncommon to provide a graphics workstation on each engineer's desk for sporadic use.

As computer-aided design systems emerged from the research era to ordinary everyday use in engineering, it still was not uncommon to have the system's end product be a set of drawings. Drawings were a familiar communication medium for manufacturing. Even with the advent of numerically controlled (NC) tools, drawings continued to be the primary description for parts. NC part programmers would read the drawings to prepare NC tapes in a computer language such as APT. The tape would be carried (sneaker net?) to manufacturing where the NC milling, lathing, and drilling operations would be completed and then quality control would use drawings to verify in-spec production of a prototype or finished part. NC tool operations removed material, wood or metal typically, from a block. To distinguish newly emerging technologies in the general area of automated fabrication (autofab), the descriptor *subtractive rapid prototyping* now is applied to such NC processes.

As a brief aside, I can remember being involved in an early NC process at IBM in late 1964. In Gene Lindstrom's development computation laboratory to which I had recently returned after finishing my degree, Chuck Corley left on vacation and I was to sit in for him to help prepare the paper tape NC input for the strip housing part in IBM's 2321 data cell drive mass storage unit. The part had the shape of a six or eight inch long, two or three inch wide fish hook. Its actual shape had been calculated from the standing wave pattern of the tape strip moving at high speed. Engineers sampled the differential equation solution at many points and prepared a table of measurements for the engineering drawing formally released to manufacturing. My task was to write a 7094 Fortran program and produce the APT tape for manufacturing. No one could find the descriptive equations, so points from the drawing were used to fit a polynomial to control the tool path. Computer modeling was tolerated but hand-drawn discrete drawings ruled the roost.

Today's computer numerically controlled (CNC) machines certainly make the whole process much more accurate and efficient. I would hazard a guess that computer graphics support of the new additive RP technologies, like early part programming support for subtractive RP, has ample opportunity to be substantially enhanced. Here I discuss some of these new technologies for quick-turnaround manufacturing. I believe they offer a significant growth application area in which computer graphics must play an important part.

In contrast to the NC approach of removing material from a block of plastic, metal or wood, the additive technologies for RP build up a part, layer by layer, much like the inverse of the separated slices seen in CAT, MRI, or PET images. A very thin cross-sectional layer or slice is created repetitively. Each successive horizontal slice rests upon and bonds to the top surface of its predecessor horizontal cross-section layer to build up the complete part from seamlessly joined, individually formed, thin laminations.

Typically, the part being built rests on an elevator platform that is either dropped or raised a small distance, say 0.0254 to 0.254 mm, to allow the part to be deposited or grown in stacked, thin, cross-sectional slices. The technique permits rather complex parts to be built up. Difficult interior patterns that would be a problem for a subtractive NC process or would take a long preparation time to be done by mixed casting and assembly operations can often be straightforwardly accommodated by additive RP processes. Fabrication of honeycombed chambers, toothed gears, and nested objects can be accomplished using the cross-sectional layer build-up technique of the various additive RP processes.

Why should RP be of interest? Terry T. Wohlers' article in [1] estimates that about 950 RP systems are installed and operating around the world. Wohlers' examples provide an insightful, business based answer:

> Rapid prototyping can save organizations both time and money. For example, Mack Industries(Troy, Michigan) has cut in half the time it takes to build wood patterns using Helisys' Laminated Object Manufacturing (LOM) system. AMP's Automotive/Consumer Business Group (Harrisburg, Pennsylvania) saved four months and $80,000 on one project using 3D Systems' StereoLithography Apparatus (SLA). Biomet (Warsaw, Indiana) builds custom patella implants in 2 hours using Stratasys' Fused Deposition Modeling (FDM) system when conventional (non-RP) techniques would take 8 to 12 hours. Using Cubital's Solid Ground Curing (SGC) system, Stature Machining (Warren, Michigan) saved Whirlpool $22,000 and 3 weeks of time on a blower-housing project. Hewlett-Packard (San Diego, California) estimates they have saved $20,000 and weeks on one project using DTM's Selective Laser Sintering (SLS) system.

17.2   StereoLithography

StereoLithography is typically touted as the 'oldest' commercially available additive RP technology. It is based upon Charles Hull's patent filing of 8 August 1984. 3D Systems corporation was spun off from UVP, Inc. of San Gabriel, California, in March 1986 when the patent for UVP's 'StereoLithography Apparatus' (SLA) patent was issued. 3D

Systems, now headquartered in Valencia, California, introduced its original device, SLA–1, at the Autofact exposition in Detroit in November 1987. In less than a decade, the additive RP industry has grown remarkably. Competitive technology alternatives to StereoLithography, too, are less than a decade old. Additive RP is a young, developing industry that needs good solid modelers and fully closed 3D surface modelers to realize its full potential; good graphics support is essential for additive RP growth.

3D Systems' StereoLithography [2] produces parts by exposing an actinic photopolymer resin using a laser beam. Tiny voxels of the liquid resin solidify as the path of the laser traces through the horizontal area of a full cross-sectional layer. An elevator on which the base layer of the growing part rests is lowered after a brief solidifying interval. Resin flows across the top layer and the next layer is traced out. After production, the part is removed from the fabrication vat of liquid resin, thoroughly cleaned, then cured by further exposure to UV light to properly harden it.

Surface finish can be enhanced with sand or bead blasting. A part can be painted if desired. Not unlike the early NC undertakings, successful part building takes skill in CAD design, knowledge of resin property alternatives, and effective control of numerous build parameters of the devices unique to each RP technology and vendor. Viscous resin properties obviate any horizontal instances, but sides off a true vertical can exhibit a very small propensity for a three-dimensional analog of 'the jaggies.' A graphics algorithmist could claim (tongue-in-cheek perhaps) that in objects built using any of the various additive RP technologies, anti-aliasing is achieved with sandpaper, rasp, or file. It remains to be seen whether 'stair steps' will become the 3D surface equivalent of 2D jaggies in rastered lines.

Early resins were brittle and shattered easily if dropped after hardening. Today there is a wide selection of resins that do not exhibit such properties. To counter the perception of brittle photopolymers, Formation Engineering, Gloucester, UK, has fabricated an SLA-made hammer, used the hammer to pound a nail into a block of wood, then extracted the nail using the hammer's claw. Use of possibly carcinogenic, highly toxic materials was an early concern that has also been allayed owing to development of new resins and cleaning substances. The first SLA-1 had a rather small vat that constrained the size of part that could be built. Photopolymer resin choices were limited. Today each of these challenges has been pretty well addressed. If you should consider StereoLithography or any of the additive technologies, it is a good idea to be certain you have current, up-to-date information as the materials, machines, software, and just about all aspects of the technology continue to evolve and change at a rapid pace.

17.3 Solid Ground Curing

An alternative fabrication technology employing photopolymers is the *solid ground curing* (SGC) system, Solider, developed by Cubital, Ltd, headquartered in Raanana, Israel. Their approach employs an intense flood of ultraviolet radiation to solidify a full horizontal layer at once. Rather than trace out a cross-section area with a narrow laser beam, SGC first charges a glass mask plate to form a pattern that is a negative image of the cross-section. Black electrostatic toner adheres to the ion-charged portions of the plate in an approach much like that used in the xerographic process to form images in a modern copier.

The resin is flashed so that transparent, clear areas of the glass mask plate permit exposure for solidification at each layer while toner-covered, black regions block UV exposure of cross-section areas that represent voids in the part being fabricated. Unhardened liquid is suctioned away; the residual thin voids then are filled with molten wax. After cooling, the composite layer of wax and solidified polymer is milled to produce a flat surface of precisely controlled thickness ready for the next layer. Upon completion of the full part, wax filler is removed.

Use of the wax filler precludes any need to build up temporary support structures to hold cantilevered or separated elements in a layer as must be done in some other systems. The Cubital process, like other RP technologies, has the ability to fabricate composite mechanical structures with integrated moving parts, such as a football referee's whistle, in a single pass without requiring post-processing assembly. Subtractive RP processes can not build such parts without assembly.

17.4 Selective Sintering

Selective sintering is the process promulgated by DTM corporation headquartered in Austin, Texas. Their Sinterstation system uses powder, rather than a liquid, to build up a part layer by layer. After a thin layer of powder is spread evenly with a roller, a CO_2 laser provides the energy beam to heat a small voxel of material to the temperature at which it melts and fuses or sinters. The part platform is dropped, new powder is added to form the basis for the next layer, and the sintering laser beam trace for each cross-section layer is repeated until the part is complete. A variety of powders including nylon, investment casting wax, polycarbonates, ceramics, and metals can be used. DTM corporation evolved from Carl Deckard's master's thesis at the University of Texas-Austin in 1986.

17.5 Droplet Deposition

Droplet deposition is the province of Soligen, an RP company headquartered in Northridge, California. The technology comes from research at MIT led by Emanuel Sachs and Michael Cima. Soligen's Direct Shell Production (DSP) system was introduced in 1993. The essence of the process is to lay down a controlled thickness of powdered material, not unlike the sintering approach, then, in a raster scan, selectively deposit drops of a liquid adhesive or binder to form each successive horizontal cross-section layer.

Standard ink-jet nozzles, like those used in ordinary 2D ink-jet printing, apply the liquid binding adhesive. Not surprisingly, the term three-dimensional printing is used by its originators to describe the process of droplet deposition. A variety of powder/adhesive combinations, including plastics, metals, ceramics, and glasses, offer potential. The concentration has been on building ceramic structures to fabricate molds subsequently used directly for investment casting.

17.6   Fused Deposition Modeling

Fused deposition modeling (FDM) is an alternative RP process offered by Stratasys, Inc., headquartered in Eden Prairie, Minnesota. Stratasys was founded in late 1990 to pursue an extrusion approach based upon a 1992 patent issued for the invention of S. Scott Crump. Their 3D Modeler product uses a robotically guided extrusion nozzle to form successive laminations of a part. A spool of 0.050 inch diameter filament provides the thermoplastic material that is melted and squeezed out for deposition across each layer. The material solidifies upon deposition and requires little cleanup. The system is small enough to truly qualify for use in 'desktop manufacturing.' It uses thermoplastic filaments of a machinable wax, an investment casting wax, polyolefin, and polyamide.

17.7   Laminated Object Manufacturing

Laminated object manufacturing (LOM) is yet another additive RP technology offered by Helisys, Inc. of Torrance, California. Their LOM machine uses sheet material, such as polyethylene-coated paper ('butcher paper'), to build up successive layers of a part. A thin sheet of paper, from 0.0038 to 0.0100 inches thick, is placed upon the previous layer. Heat and pressure laminate the new sheet to the top layer of the cumulative part. A CO_2 laser cuts the outer and inner outlines of the new layer cross-section. Portions not to be part of this layer's cross-section then are cross-hatched by the laser for later removal. The resulting part looks, feels, and acts like wood. As is the case with Cubital's Solider and DTM's Sinterstation, Helisys' LOM machine needs no temporary support structures that require later removal from the finished part itself; support material is, however, inherently present in each of these approaches and the finished part must be removed from the excess material. No post-curing is necessary; finished parts are typically sealed with a spray coating of polyurethane.

17.8   RP Representation Opportunities

All RP fabricators use a three-dimensional representation of the part to be built. The 3D digitized model may be the result of scanned images [3] or CAD images. Unique program support for a specific RP fabrication device will typically do the slicing of the 3D geometric model to provide cross-sectional layers. A commonly used de facto standard format for RP device input is the .STL format originally introduced by 3D Systems as input for its SLA machines. The .STL format is essentially a triangulated surface representation with associated outward-pointing normals accompanying the triangles. As merely a list of triangles with no associated topological connections, .STL files lose any geometric or topological robustness that the original data may once have had. Flaws such as cracks, self-intersecting surfaces, zero-thickness surfaces, and orphan surfaces [4] pose problems for RP fabrication.

There is room for considerable improvement in graphics tools for RP support. There's also room for considerable opportunity. It is always informative to hear a 'consumer' of one's 'product' voice an opinion, so I will close with Burns' [5] challenge to us in computer graphics:

Today's CAD programs are not easy to use, are not easy to learn how to use, and usually have substantial limitations as to what can and cannot be designed on them.

We need to focus not only upon better topologically robust technical interfacing but also upon improved ease of use and user friendly human interfaces.

References

[1] T.T. Wohlers, Solid modeling and rapid prototyping, *Handbook of Solid Modeling*, D.E. LaCourse, ed., ch. 19. McGraw-Hill, New York, 1995.

[2] P.F. Jacobs, *Rapid Prototyping and Manufacturing; Fundamentals of StereoLithography*, Society of Mechanical Engineers, Dearborn, Michigan, 1992.

[3] C. Zollikofer, M.S. Ponce de León, Tools for rapid prototyping in the biosciences, *IEEE Computer Graphics Appl.*, 15(6): 48–55; 1995.

[4] M.J. Bailey, Tele-manufacturing: rapid prototyping on the Internet, *IEEE Computer Graphics Appl.*, 15(6): 20–26; 1995.

[5] M. Burns, *Automated Fabrication*, Prentice-Hall, Englewood Cliffs, NJ, 1993.

Further Reading

J.H. Bøhn, Removing zero-volume parts from CAD models for layered manufacturing, *IEEE Computer Graphics Appl.*, 15(6): 27–34; 1995.

J. Bresenham, P. Jacobs, L. Sadler, P. Stucki, Real virtuality: StereoLithography–Rapid prototyping in 3-D, *Computer Graphics: (Proc. ACM SIGGRAPH'93)* Annual Conference Series, pp. 377–378, 1993.

V. Chandru, S. Manohar, C.E. Prakash, Voxel-based modeling for layered manufacturing, *IEEE Computer Graphics Appl.*, 15(6): 42–47; 1995.

X. Sheng, I.R. Meier, Generating topological structures for surface models, *IEEE Computer Graphics Appl.*, 15(6): 35–41; 1995.

P. Stucki, J. Bresenham, R. Earnshaw, Computer graphics in rapid prototyping technology, *IEEE Computer Graphics Appl.*, 15(6): 17–19; 1995.

18
The Challenge of Virtual Reality

Lawrence J. Rosenblum and Robert A. Cross

18.1 Introduction

Virtual reality (VR) is a demanding research area that requires inputs from numerous disciplines while attempting to meet stringent timing requirements [21]. The (as yet unrealized) goal of a VR system is the development of a virtual environment that is presented with such high precision that the user perceives it as real. This realism is more than graphical, for objects in the virtual environment must also act in physically appropriate ways. Objects must react appropriately to gravity, friction, collisions, etc. and the environment should contain nonvisual feedback that leads to a sense of realism (e.g., audio and haptic).

  VR has presented a compelling concept: a natural and effective interaction between user and computer. However, the concept has proved difficult to implement. Indeed, only recently due to increased computational power has the field begun to advance to where effective VRs are now beginning to appear. VR has stringent performance requirements. To maintain the illusion of 'immersion,' frame rates must be kept high and system latency in responding to user's actions must be minimal. Interface designs to VRs are still poorly understood and often are application specific. Many disparate technologies must be integrated within the environment. The technical difficulties, in turn, generate complex research issues that often require a multidisciplinary approach. This chapter examines some of the research and technology issues faced in constructing virtual environments today. In addition we examine selected applications that demonstrate current state of the art in VR.

18.2 Fundamental Requirements

Three primary requirements of a virtual reality system are *immersion, interaction,* and *visual realism* [4, 7]. A user should feel immersed in the scene, transparently interacting with a visually realistic simulated environment. The recent report of the US National Research Council on virtual reality [9] does not attempt to define VR but mentions the following characteristics: a man–machine interface between human and computer; immersion with a 3D object; objects have spatial presence independent of the user's position; and the user interacts with objects using a variety of motor output channels to manipulate them. The report notes that the extent to which a virtual environment is designed to simulate a real environment is application

Visualization and Modeling
ISBN 0-12-227738-4

specific (so we could, for example, have a VR representation of abstract mathematical spaces).

Systems to date have emphasized the visual and, to a lesser degree, the auditory channels. Haptics is an important additional feedback. Significant progress is being made in force feedback, while tactile feedback is less advanced. Olfactory and gustatory feedback also have potential value, but these are research topics not yet ready for inclusion in VR systems. The same is true for adding common external stimuli such as wind and heat to a virtual environment.

18.2.1 Immersion

Immersion requires physically involving the user, both by capturing exclusive visual attention and by transparently responding to three-dimensional input (e.g., through a head-tracker, 3D mouse, wand, data glove, or fully instrumented body suit). As virtual reality is a highly visual environment, the combination of these requirements – proper rendering from and smoothly tracking the movement of the viewpoint (i.e., the user's eye) – is the most important factor in producing an effective sense of immersion [20, 30].

Immersion does not necessarily require the use of the head-mounted displays that are the most common method for presenting the visual channel in a virtual environment. The CAVE developed at the University of Illinois-Chicago accomplishes immersion by projecting on two walls and a floor and allowing the user to interactively explore (using head tracking) a virtual environment [8]. The Responsive (or Virtual) Workbench, developed at the German National Research Center for Mathematics and Computer Graphics and introduced in the United States at the Naval Research Laboratory [15] is predicated on the idea that for some applications it is not desirable to immerse the user fully inside the scene. Rather, the immersion takes place as the user reaches over a table, above which the 3D image rises. For applications such as medicine, where a surgeon doing presurgical planning does not want to be inside the data but rather wishes to stand in front of an operating table with a virtual patient, this paradigm has proved powerful.

18.2.2 Interaction

The user interacts through the three-dimensional control devices to investigate and control the virtual environment. To maintain the user's sense of immersion in the scene, the displayed view of the environment must be updated quickly (through rapid rendering speed) while the input devices must be tracked smoothly (i.e., with low control lag time) [11, 20].

The minimal and optimal performance requirements for interaction with a virtual reality system are summarized in Table 18.1. Useful interaction requires a minimum of 10 frames per second and control lag of less than 0.1 seconds; however, such minimal performance does not generate a sense of high-quality immersive interaction. Optimal interaction requires a frame rate of at least 60 Hz, with control lag less than 50 milliseconds [29, 30].

Table 18.1   Measures of a user's interaction ability

Characteristic	Minimum for interaction	Maximum for interaction
Frame Rate	10 frames/s	60–70 frames/s
Control Lag (Latency)	0.1 s	0.03–0.05 s

18.2.3 Visual realism

Virtual reality also requires visual realism, accurate representation, and presentation of visual cues and information about the virtual environment. Just as they do in real environments, visual cues should provide intuitive conscious and unconscious information about the virtual environment [7, 12]. For example, a 'walk-through' simulation of an actual environment seeks a level of fidelity sufficient to 'fool the user' in order to maximize the information provided by the visualization. Table 18.2 summarizes many of the problems faced in architectural design or other visually realistic systems [6].

Table 18.2   Examples of issues for visual realism in VR

Topic	Issue
Lighting	Point vs. area sources, spectral response
Shadows	Hard (point source) vs. soft (area source)
Optics	Propagation of light and global illumination, surface materials, and complex (non-planar) reflectors
Perception	Depth-of-field, glare, dark adaptation, anti-aliasing

While movement toward realism in VR is important, the fundamental limitation in VR today is the inability to draw enough polygons to provide the required level of detail while still maintaining interactivity. This topic has produced several threads of research. In the ship walkthrough described in section 18.6.7, extensive use is made of texture mapping. The texture maps include transparency. By representing complex objects as a texture which is mapped onto a single polygon, detailed objects (e.g., grated walkways and link chains) are realistically represented without a large polygon count. This technique is both visually satisfying and allows for displaying a sizable area of the ship while letting the virtual environment respond to the user's movements. However, texture mapping is limited by the restrictions it places on physical fidelity as interaction with components of a single texture-mapped object is impossible (e.g., picking up one link of a texture-mapped link chain). One solution is to cache detailed geometries of the objects and replace the texture-mapped object with the geometrical model when a user is close enough to interact with the object. A second approach has been to develop algorithms for multiresolution modeling. This approach utilizes the fact that far-away objects need not be seen at high resolutions, so algorithms represent objects at different levels of detail to reduce rendering time. This approach works well in moderately simple environments, but does not necessarily scale well when the space becomes extremely large and complex. One method under investigation is to use curved surfaces to represent the objects and then tessellate these surfaces into triangles for final rendering [17]. The third approach to minimizing the number of polygons to be rendered is to determine which objects are visible from various viewpoints. By preprocessing this information, considerable speedups have been obtained in architectural walk-throughs.

18.3 Information Channels

The primary purpose of virtual reality is to provide information about the simulated environment. Contemporary technology provides the ability to convey information through widely varying information channels including visual, auditory, and haptic data.

18.3.1 The visual channel

Display technology is the most mature information channel and is the primary form of data in most virtual reality applications. Rendering the large numbers of pixels necessary for a proper sense of immersion at the rendering speed required for high-quality interaction consumes the largest portion of the computational resources used by a VR system. Stereo views may, in the worst case, double that overhead by requiring that two complete views be rendered (one for each eye) for each stereo frame. However, since stereopsis is less of a factor beyond a visual distance of 3 meters (outweighed by motion parallax at longer range) some rendering overhead can be avoided by re-use of image and occlusion data between individual eye views.

Visual complexity is necessary to create a sense of immersion in the virtual environment; in particular, the disparity between the two images of a stereo view drives the user's sense of stereopsis. Though photorealism may be too complex for interaction in the near term, contemporary graphics hardware does provide approximations to complex rendering methods [2]. In particular, texture mapping hardware can greatly increase the user's perception of surface complexity without added geometric data (e.g., an image of grass, texture mapped onto a ground plane, is perceived as a grassy field by a flight simulator pilot at high altitude).

18.3.2 The auditory channel

Auditory feedback can provide detailed three-dimensional static and movement information about the surrounding real or virtual environments [12]. In an interactive visualization system, auditory feedback can provide useful control information that, in visual form, would disrupt the immersion of the virtual environment [16, 21]. In applications such as combat simulation, quickly calculated realistic sound is a critical aspect of immersion [15, 19]. The issues of introducing the auditory channel to a virtual environment span the entire range of research in acoustic perception. Of particular interest is the need to fully understand 3D transfer functions. Commercial systems can do a good job today of defining a single user acoustic transfer function and providing 3D sound to someone inside a head-mounted display. However, providing 3D sound inside a room to VR users not in head-mounted displays (i.e., responding to a group leader whose head movements are being tracked) remains an unsolved problem. Sound tends to be a more discrete channel than the visual with, for example, angular resolutions greater than or equal to 1 degree. The ability to perceive sound source distances tends to be poor. A great deal of research has been conducted on extracting a given sound source from multiple sources at different spatial locations, but little is known about the ability to localize a given source in such a background of interference.

18.3.3   The haptic channel

Haptic or force feedback is the least mature of the three information channels discussed here. Its development is motivated by its potential to provide useful direct manipulation and control information on an intuitive level. For example, inter-object relationships and forces could be made clear through a sense of touch or a level of resistance in the manipulator (as in the University of North Carolina's Nanomanipulator [28]).

Haptics has received less research than the visual and auditory channels, with most research and development having been driven until recently by the requirements of telerobotics. Most current haptic interfaces can be categorized as either (1) body-based gloves or exoskeletons that track the position of the finger, hand, or arm and (2) devices such as 'joysticks' that both sense certain actions of the hand and provide force feedback [9]. While force feedback and exoskeletons have made significant progress on both sides of the Atlantic – see Encarnacao et al. [10] for recent European activity – there has been less effort and success to date on devices providing such nonforce haptic feedbacks as texture or temperature. With force feedback devices becoming available, some at 'moderate' cost, research efforts are taking place to evaluate the role of haptic feedback as part of multimodal interactions within virtual environments.

18.4   Control Methods

As interaction is a primary feature of virtual reality, a VR system must have accurate, smooth, and effective methods of control. Most important for an interactive application, visible control lag (time from control input to visual result) must be low. The three most common control methods in current VR systems are position tracking, speech, and physical devices, including manipulators and simple props.

18.4.1   Position tracking

The most intuitive control method for VR involves tracking the user's position in order to provide direct control over virtual objects' orientation and position. Often, this involves attaching an electromagnetic or ultrasonic tracker to the appropriate control (e.g., a glove) or body part.

This technology faces difficult problems. The requirements of immersion and effective control make the user intolerant of control lag and tracking noise [29, 30]. Unfortunately, many common systems fail in both categories beyond a limited envelope (e.g., electromagnetic trackers may be effective only within a 1-meter sphere and face severe degradations in a metallic environment). Current research concentrates on prediction and filter methods to eliminate these latency and error limitations.

While laser tracking [9] and other technologies show promise, these are not yet economically feasible for most research institutions. Such methods also have line-of-sight limitations.

18.4.2   Speech

The advantages of speech control are literally self-explanatory. Current commercial systems are capable of recognizing arbitrary same-dialect speakers using simple preprogrammed grammars without user-specific training. Such systems can allow VR to avoid difficult implementation issues and hardware limitations. For example, a human anatomy application might recognize 'grab gall bladder' as a synonym for the end result of dissection and careful selection of a relatively small organ. The gall bladder will then be removed from the body and appear before the user. Such interactions are difficult to achieve using hand movements (gesture recognition) due to the highly accurate tracking requirements that would be required as well as the current lack of appropriate haptic feedback.

There have been impressive strides made in recent years in expanding the number of words and accuracy of commercial speech recognition systems and they have been incorporated into several VR systems. For fixed, limited operations they work rather impressively. However, as VRs become increasingly complex, so will the operations to take place. It is not reasonable to expect a user, unless very strongly motivated, to memorize a large set of permissible vocabularies and grammars. The long-term solution to using speech in VR lies in research advances now being made in natural language recognition.

18.4.3   Devices or manipulators

Physical armatures can avoid some of the limitations of the other tracking and control methods; e.g., the sensors in a waldo can provide the same position and orientation information as an EM tracker without the transmission and interference problems. Likewise, a large device also has more internal volume to contain the large sensors and motors required to provide effective force feedback. Of course, these advantages are contrasted with new problems; multiple control arms may physically collide. Such physical interference is less common with EM trackers.

On a simpler scale, physical props can enhance immersion and interaction. For example, physical buttons placed correctly relative to a virtual control panel provide implicit touch feedback while a joystick is essential to control a flight simulator [13, 27]. As used by Hinckley and Stoakley, physical props are combination input/output devices.

18.5   Hardware Issues

Clearly, the computing and communication hardware foundation of a VR system determines its ability to interact with complex environments.

18.5.1   Computing hardware

Contemporary graphics hardware provides fast, polygon-based scan conversion rendering with approximations to more complex effects such as texture mapping, fog, lighting, etc. [2]. However, as this paradigm is fundamentally oriented towards rendering polygons as portions of scan lines, its maximum level of visual fidelity is limited in complex environments (e.g., nonplanar surfaces with realistic material types are difficult to simulate using graphics hardware alone) [6]. Even if such levels of fidelity are unnecessary, current designs do not scale well. Incremental performance improvements are expensive and eventually are restricted by the physical limitations of the chassis case.

In contrast, general-purpose computing hardware can both correctly model objects' physical interactions in the simulated environment (e.g., collision detection) and render the resulting scene with high fidelity. Of course, without dedicated graphics hardware support, such simulation systems tend to be orders of magnitude too slow for interaction.

18.5.2   Networking and communication

Systems involving human interaction require minimal latency for the arrival of network communication packets and the high-speed generation of video frames. However, virtual environments with large numbers of simultaneous participants (or 'players') would, using naive communications methods, require direct high-bandwidth connections between all simulation nodes. This is currently unreasonable in cases with 10 000 players at physically remote sites.

18.5.3   Parallel and distributed computing

Current network technology increases the feasibility of distributed computing for virtual reality. ATM networks provide low latency and high bandwidth, necessary for real-time simulations controlling the virtual environment. Pixel-based rendering methods, such as ray tracing, are more suited to distributed rendering than scan conversion while also providing higher accuracy, lower distortion, levels of detail and fidelity, etc. [6].

18.6   Contemporary Applications

The following applications illustrate the issues discussed above. Training has been the great success story for VR over the past 5 years. From the demonstration prototypes of a half-decade ago, VR has gone on to develop proven, useful training systems. Medicine and manufacturing/design are two other application domains that show great promise. Additional areas where researchers and technologists are experimenting with the value of VR include information visualization, telecommunications, and hazardous operations. While the virtual environments in the applications discussed below place the largest emphasis on the presentation of visual data, they also illustrate the emerging need for solutions to other problems such as haptic feedback and distributed computing. We focus here on a selection of US applications; European applications were recently examined by one of the authors [10, 23, 24].

One of the important recent trends in VR applications has been the way in which the field has begun moving from demonstrations of VR toward implementable applications. Noteworthy is the success of the applications of sections 18.6.2 and 18.6.6 in performing the necessary human studies to demonstrate that VR was indeed an effective tool for the application.

18.6.1   The Virtual Wind Tunnel

One of the most challenging and exciting areas in scientific visualization over the past decade has been the development of a variety of tools for visualizing vector and tensor fields [22, 25]. The problem is important because of the complex geometrical and topological considerations that arise when examining both collected and simulated fluid flow data. Fluid flow analysis impacts numerous scientific and technological problems ranging from aircraft and automobile manufacturing through the creation of new, useful materials and the understanding of the impact of ocean currents on the environment. The Virtual Wind Tunnel project at NASA/Ames [5] is a virtual environment designed for the exploration of 3D simulation-generated unsteady flow fields. A boom-mounted six degrees of freedom stereo CRT system is used for viewing. A hand position-sensitive glove controller is used for injecting traces into the virtual flow field. A multiprocessor graphics workstation is used for computation and rendering. Users insert and interact with rakes, streamlines, and other representations of fluid flow. Plate 28 illustrates the Virtual Wind Tunnel's capabilities.

18.6.2   Phobias

The Acrophobia project at the Georgia Institute of Technology used virtual reality to examine fear of heights [14], which is clinically defined as anxiety upon exposure to heights, avoidance of heights, and having the fear interfere with normal daily functions. In normal treatment, the psychologist will accompany the patient through a succession of tasks involving height with the task difficulty increasing. Thus, use of VR offers several advantages: lower cost (less time spent by the psychologist, who need not accompany the patient on tasks), a less intimidating environment, and safety. The virtual reality treatment comprises three stages: a virtual 'see-out' elevator inside a 49-story virtual hotel (Figure 18.1), balconies of several different heights, and bridges over a river and through a canyon. This research includes careful statistical studies that demonstrate the benefits of virtual reality. The work is now being extended into a project to assist those with fear of flying.

18.6.3   Scientific visualization

Researchers at the University of North Carolina (UNC), lead by Professor Frederick Brooks, have a long history of leading edge explorations of scientific data utilizing virtual reality and often including force feedback. UNC is known for its explorations of the role of virtual reality in viewing, assembling, docking, and manipulating molecules [3]. The UNC Nanomanipulator [28] is a virtual-reality interface to scanning probe microscopes. Surface rendering is performed by the Pixel-Planes 5 massively parallel graphics engine. Force-feedback devices allow the operator to 'feel' the surface under study.

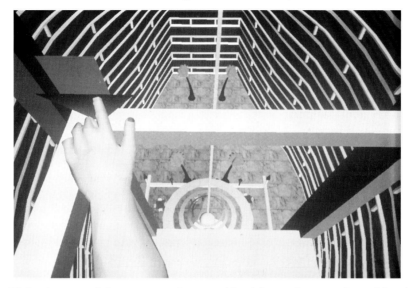

Figure 18.1   In one of three scenarios used in this study, a patient rides up and down in a glass enclosed elevator. (© Larry Hodges, GUU Center at the Georgia Institute of Technology; used with permission.)

18.6.4   Remote collaboration

An ongoing challenge for VR is to integrate VR with networking to facilitate remote collaboration in problems ranging from manufacturing through modeling and simulation. This issue can be subdivided into two classes. Some applications require complex interactions among a limited number of participants, while others, such as military simulations, require servicing thousands of players. Large, multiuser virtual environments must keep each entity aware of others' actions. This places considerable demands on the workstation I/O, network bandwidth, and the underlying architecture. One approach to this challenge, developed at the Naval Postgraduate School, is NPSNET [19]. NPSNET is a large-scale software package designed for networking that is capable of simulating articulated humans and ground and air vehicles in the DIS networked virtual environment of 250–300 players. NPSNET is the first 3D virtual environment to make effective use of the multicast backbone of Internet in order to avoid direct connections between all sites. It also makes extensive use of dead-reckoning to predict object position and reduce visual latency in low-bandwidth situations. The software architecture logically partitions a virtual environment by associating spatial, temporal, and functional classes with network multicast groups.

18.6.5   Medical training on the Responsive Workbench

The Responsive Workbench [16] integrates the simulated virtual environment directly into the user's real world. Objects are displayed on a table in 3D. The user interacts with this virtual scenario and manipulates it as if real Interaction with the computer can be performed using the keyboard, speech, lightpen-selected menus, or a variety of other interfaces. The Workbench is a nonimmersive virtual environment where the user stands in front of the 3D stereoscopic images. VR applications that have been successfully developed on the Workbench include medical training and surgical planning, architecture, and fluid flow at the German National Research Center for Mathematics and Computer Science (GMD) [15]. Based in part on research seen at GMD, the Naval Research Laboratory (NRL) in the United States fabricated its own design of the Workbench in 1994 and is using it for command and control, simulation-based design, and medicine. Three advantages of the Workbench are illustrated in Figure 18.2. Unlike HMDs, the Workbench supports multi-user collaboration in real, rather than virtual, space. Secondly, natural interactions are more readily available. For medical training, a user may pick up and examine a bone or internal organ using a data glove. However, gesture recognition has its limits: multiple organs may have to be removed to reach a small, nonvisible one, and it is difficult to put bones or organs back exactly in the proper place. Accordingly, voice recognition is also used as an interface. Finally, our initial experience indicates that looking down at an image rising above a horizontal tabletop appears, at least for these applications, to provide superior information perception for a user compared with wall-mounted horizontal or other angled displays. For medicine, in particular, the environment replicates the manner in which a doctor would examine a patient on an operating table.

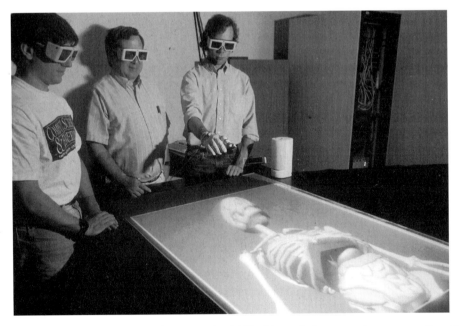

Figure 18.2 NRL's Virtual (Responsive) Workbench is seen demonstrating the human anatomy. The team leader has both a data glove for gesture recognition and a microphone for voice pickup and recognition.

18.6.6   Training for the Hubble Telescope repair

In 1990, following the launch of the Hubble Space Telescope, astronomers discovered flaws in its optical systems. Training for a repair mission became a major NASA focus for more than 3 years and this training included the use of VR [18]. The goal was to provide the repair team with knowledge of both the telescope hardware and repair procedures. Figure 18.3 illustrates a typical training scenario for this mission. The training enhanced both cognitive and psychomotor skills. As we know, the repair mission was successful. In addition to the training for the mission's success, a post-flight survey was taken. This was used to conduct an analysis demonstrating that members of the flight team judged, on average, that the VR training had had a positive effect on their performance during the mission. Moreover, audio and visual cues were judged to have helped the participants. Discomfort in the virtual environment had a negative but acceptable impact on team members. This project demonstrates the role that VR can play for situational training where on-site training is difficult or impossible.

18.6.7   VR for situational planning and training

As seen in section 18.6.6, VR is demonstrating success in training personnel for operations where classroom instructions are insufficient but in-situ training is dangerous or expensive. Figure 18.4 shows a scene from a VR project at NRL for

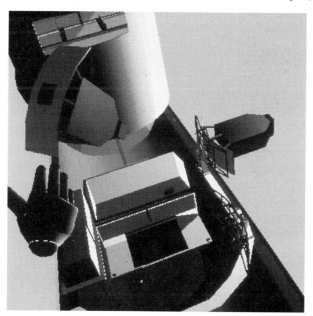

Figure 18.3   A scene from the virtual environment used to train the flight team for the change out of the Hubble Space Telescope's Wide-Field Planetary Camera. The new camera is still stowed in its parking fixture in the Space Shuttle's payload bay (right) while the old camera (left), already removed from the telescope, is being transferred to its parking fixture (lower right).

Figure 18.4 A scene showing a portion of the ex-USS Shadwell, a decommissioned ship used by NRL for virtual firefighting and damage control experimentation. Texture mapping is used to portray complex objects such as grated walkways, cylindrical pipes, and linked chains while minimizing polygon count.

shipboard firefighting and damage control. The ex-USS Shadwell, a decommissioned ship, is used by NRL for experimentation in damage control. Portions of the ship where fires are set were modeled and used to create a virtual environment that included fire (both visual and acoustic) and smoke. Noteworthy in this effort was the use of complex texture mapping to effectively portray complex objects, such as grated walkways and linked chains, while keeping the polygon count sufficiently low to maintain effective interactivity. Another important trend in situational training has been developing the ability to place 'avatars' (the graphical representation of human participants) and actors (virtual human figures with associated behavioral characteristics) within a scene [26]. Figure 18.5 shows the use of avatars in a situational training environment at Sandia National Laboratories. Behaviors are currently inserted into this virtual environment interactively, but there is movement toward autonomous actors with predefined behavioral characteristics that probabilistically determine their actions.

18.6.8   Understanding medical trauma

One of the more fascinating applications of VR has been its use to simulate perceptual anomalies. An example of this is the recent work of Rita Addison, an artist who had been involved in a serious car accident with a resulting brain injury. Working within the CAVE at the University of Illinois, Chicago (and with Marcus Thiebaux of UIC generating the code), Addison was able to portray changes in perception [1]. Among the effects generated were hemiahapia (the loss of peripheral vision), clouding (seeing as if through a viscous film), proprioceptive (equilibrium) damage, and agnosia (the

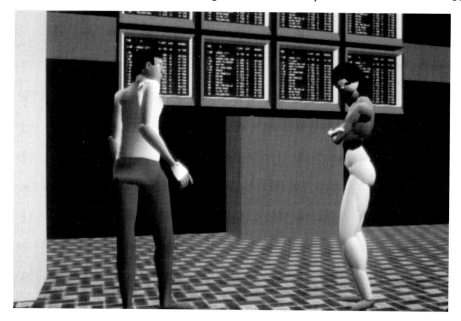

Figure 18.5 A human represented by an avatar and a computer-generated actor engage in a training exercise in a virtual airport.

inability of the higher cortical pathways to interpret signals from the optic nerve. Addison has called this effort 'a profound catharsis for me. It helped me accept and adapt to chronic impairments and fight my way through depression. It provided a safe yet powerful way for me to serve as witness to the trauma' [6].

18.7 Summary

The above discussion illustrates some of the important problems and issues facing current virtual reality research. As illustrated by the example applications, some of these problems are near solution; in particular, visual fidelity in high-end virtual reality systems is impressive. Other problems have yet to be solved in a commercially feasible way, leaving room for future virtual reality research to continue toward truly realistic virtual environments.

Acknowledgments

The authors thank the other members of the VR Laboratory in the Information Technology Division of the Naval Research Laboratory as well as our sponsors, the Defense Advanced Projects Research Agency (DARPA) and the Office of Naval Research (ONR). The NRL version of the Responsive Workbench was developed by Durbin, Obeysekare, Rosenblum, Templeman, and Cross along with summer interns Greg Newton (Georgia Institute of Technology) and Jim van Verth (University of

North Carolina). The 'Shadwell' walk-through was developed by Tate, Rosenblum, and Obeysekare along with summer interns Tom Myers and Drew Kessler (Georgia Institute of Technology) and Jyoti Agrawal (University of North Carolina), Dan Fasulo (University of Washington) and Amit Shalev (George Washington University). David Tate, Tony King, Jim Templeman, and Linda Sibert developed the version used for training last August, developed the test plan, and conducted the test aboard the Shadwell. Plate 28 and Figures 18.1, 18.3 and 18.5 were provided by Steve Bryson of NASA/Ames, Larry Hodges of the GVU Center at the Georgia Institute of Technology, R. Bowen Loftin of the NASA/Johnson Space Center, and Sharon Stansfield of Sandia National Laboratories, respectively. Special thanks goes to these contributors and their team members for making this work available.

References

[1] R. Addison, Detour: Brain deconstruction ahead, *IEEE Computer Graphics and Applications*, 15(2): 14–17; 1995.
[2] K. Akeley, RealityEngine graphics, *Computer Graphics (Proc. Siggraph '93)*, 27: 109–116; 1993.
[3] F.P. Brooks Jr., M. Ouh-Young, J.J. Batter, P.J. Kilpatrick, Project grope – haptic displays for scientific visualization, *Computer Graphics (Proc. Siggraph '90)*, 24: 177–185; 1990.
[4] S. Bryson, Real-time exploratory scientific visualization and virtual reality, *Scientific Visualization: Advances and Challenges*, L.J. Rosenblum et al., eds., Ch. 5, pp. 65–86, Academic Press, London, UK, 1994.
[5] S. Bryson, C. Levitt, The virtual wind tunnel, *IEEE Computer Graphics Appl.*, 12(2): 25–34; 1992.
[6] R.A. Cross, Interactive realism for visualization using ray tracing, *Proc. Visualization '95*, Nov. 1995, to appear.
[7] R.A. Cross, A.J. Hanson, Virtual reality performance for virtual geometry, *Proc. Visualization '94*, Washington, DC, Oct. 1994, pp. 156–163.
[8] C. Cruz-Neira, D. Sandin, T. DeFanti, Surround-screen, projection-based virtual reality: The design and implementation of the CAVE, *Computer Graphics (Proc. Siggraph 93)*, 27: 135–142; 1993.
[9] N.I. Durlach, A.S. Mavor (eds.), *Virtual Reality: Scientific and Technological Challenges*, National Academy Press, 1995.
[10] J. Encarnacao, M. Goebel, L. Rosenblum, European activities in virtual reality, *IEEE Computer Graphics Appl.*, 14(1): 66–74; 1994.
[11] T.A. Funkhouser, C.H. Squin, Adaptive display algorithm for interactive frame rates during visualization of complex virtual environments, *Computer Graphics (Proc. Siggraph '93)*, 27: 247–254; 1993.
[12] E.B. Goldstein, *Sensation and Perception*, Wadsworth Publishing Company, 1980.
[13] K. Hinckley, R. Pausch, J.C. Goble, N.F. Kassell, A survey of design issues in spatial input, *Proc. UIST '94*, Nov. 1994, pp. 213–222.
[14] L.F. Hodges, B.O. Rothbaum, R. Kooper, D. Opdyke, T. Meyer, T. North, J.J. deGraff, J. Williford, Virtual reality for exposure therapy, *Computer*, 28(7): 27–34; 1995.
[15] W. Krueger, C.A. Bohn, B. Froehlich, H. Schuth, W. Strauss, Wesche, G., The Responsive Workbench: A virtual work environment, *Computer*, 28(7): 42–48; 1995.
[16] W. Krueger, B. Froehlich, The responsive workbench, *IEEE Computer Graphics Appl.*, 14(3): 12–15; 1994.

[17] S. Kumar, D. Manocha, A. Lastra, Interactive display of large-scale NURBS Models, *Proc. Interactive 3D Conference*, 1995.

[18] R.B. Loftin, P.J. Kenney, Training the Hubble space telescope team, *IEEE Computer Graphics Appl.*, 15(5): 31–37; 1995.

[19] M.R. Macedonia, M.J. Zyda, D.R. Pratt, P.T. Barham, S. Zeswitz, NPSNET: A network software architecture for large scale virtual environments, *Presence*, 3(4); Fall 1994.

[20] M. Regan, R. Post, Priority rendering with a virtual reality address recalculation pipeline, *Computer Graphics (Proc. Siggraph '94)*, July 1994, pp. 155–162.

[21] L.J. Rosenblum, S. Bryson, S.K. Feiner, Virtual reality unbound, *IEEE Computer Graphics Appl.*, 15(5): 19–21; 1995.

[22] L.J. Rosenblum, R.A. Earnshaw, J. Encarnacao, H. Hagen, A. Kaufman, S. Klimenko, G. Nielson, F. Post, D. Thalmann (eds.), *Scientific Visualization: Advances and Challenges*, Academic Press, London, 1994.

[23] L.J. Rosenblum, European Research Activity Reports – II, *Computer Graphics*, Feb. 1994.

[24] L.J. Rosenblum, European Research Activity Report – III, *Computer Graphics*, 167–173; May, 1994.

[25] L.J. Rosenblum, F. Post, Visualizing fluid flow, *Computer*, 26(6): 98–100; 1993.

[26] S. Stansfield, A distributed virtual reality simulation system for situational training, *Presence*, 3(4); Fall 1994.

[27] R. Stoakley, M. Conway, R. Pausch, Virtual reality on a {WIM}: Interactive worlds in miniature, *Proc. CHI '95*, 1995.

[28] R.M. Taylor II, W. Robinett, V.L. Chi, F.P. Brooks, W.V. Wright, R.S. Williams, E.J. Snyder, The nanomanipulator: A virtual-reality interface for a scanning tunneling microscope, *Computer Graphics (Proc. Siggraph '93)*, 27: 109–116; 1993.

[29] C. Ware, R. Balakrishnan, Target acquisition in fish tank VR: The effects of lag and frame rate, *Proc. Graphics Interface '94*, May 1994, pp. 1–7.

[30] M.M. Wloka, Lag in multiprocessor VR, *Presence*, 4(1): 50–63; 1995.

19
A Simple System for Animation of Natural Phenomena

A. Gareau and D. Vandorpe

19.1   Introduction

Classical animation systems generally use polygons to describe the objects. This model is very simple to use and powerful interfaces can be developed. Object trajectories can be controlled using key-frames. Due to graphic card performance, such systems allow very realistic creations in short development times for low costs. However, the animator needs to control all the objects: If collisions occur, the response must be simulated by hand. Thus, if even not very complex objects are in collision, it is impossible to find a realistic response. This is the most important problem of descriptive systems.

With physical control of the interaction, the realism of the animation could be improved, but the algorithms are completely different. Physical and mechanical relations must be used. The generation process can be divided into two parts. First the geometric and mechanical properties of the objects are described, then the objects are allowed to evolve under the influence and control of physical laws. We make the assumption that, if good laws are used, the animation will look realistic. But such systems are not very easy to use, because it is difficult to find the constraints needed to achieve the intended goal (animators always try to work to a scenario). Interfacing is also a problem. Animators are not physicists: It is very difficult for them to describe trajectories with parameters like density, momentum, speed, force, etc. To produce a good result, tests with different parameters are necessary. For simple animations, the same results could be obtained faster with key-frame systems.

Previous systems have not been able to generate natural objects like clouds, rain, or water. Of course, it is possible to simulate water with a large textured polygon, but it is impossible to interact with it: If you touch it, you will not see waves. In fact, special effects are usually generated by external packages, and integrated into the final film by the animator. For very long sequences, this is very laborious, and interactions are impossible. Special effects are generated by graphical systems, but they can be described physically. They should be integrated like real objects into a physical system; then they can interact with the other objects.

Different systems have been developed to simulate evolving natural phenomena. Water can be simulated using parameters such as

- the depth of the sea;

- the height of the waves;
- the shape of the beach.

Fournier [2] and Peachey [11] create very realistic simulations taking such parameters into account.

Clouds are usually generated using textures, but doing animation by such a method is not realistic because there is no movement. A cloud should be able to collide with a mountain, and the wind can modify its shape. Kajiya [8] proposes the use of quadrics subject to constraints to describe the shape of clouds. The visualization of volume densities given by the quadric allows very realistic effects.

Sea waves and clouds seem to be very easily described using a physical system. In fact, many other graphical effects can be described using physical laws. Reeves [13] in the movie *Star Trek II* simulates the creation of the planet Genesis with large explosions generated by a particle system. His system has been extended to generate grass under the influence of wind, rain, etc.

Such systems are used as tools. We propose to integrate them into a large and general physical system, and consider them as objects of the animation. Clouds, the sea, trees, etc. could then interact with all the other objects: clouds could touch the mountain; a stone would create waves on the water.

All the interactions between the objects will be implemented using forces and geometric transformations. We assume that all the other interactions can be translated into forces or geometric transformations. Objects could then interact very simply.

First, we present the system architecture. Then we describe the different types of objects we test. Finally, we study some examples and present conclusions.

19.2   System Architecture

We choose to use agents and messages in our system for the following reasons.

- Each object of the animation can be considered as an autonomous agent living in a virtual world.
- The creation of new types of agents does not modify already existing agents.
- The behavior of an agent depends only on the list of messages it is able to respond to. It can respond to a message by performing an action that can produce messages for other agents.
- Messages allow abstraction. Orders are sent to objects: We do not need to know which internal functions will be used.

The agents communicate using messages. This can be done using two different methods:

- Calling public functions
- Sending requests to a communication task

We choose the second solution, because all the requests are sent to the same part of the application, called the *communication task*. The objects are then totally code-independent. This task is able to perform several functions such as requesting control (filter, broadcast, delay, destruction, etc.) and statistical evaluation followed by internal control by detection of abnormal activity. All these operations are easily performed without being excessively time-consuming in terms of simulation times.

Agents can be represented as shown in Figure 19.1. The body part of the agent has the form

```
while (1)
  {
    wait(message)
    switch(message.type)
      {
        case MOVE :  ...
                     function1()
                     send(amessage)
                     ...
        case DIE   :  ...
        ...
      }
  }
```

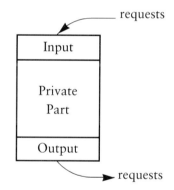

Figure 19.1   Agent representation.

Requests are sent between objects working on the same machine, but it is possible to send requests via the network to other machines. It is easy to realize a true distributed model. Only few lines of the communication task need to be modified; the rest of the code is unchanged. Of course, optimizations could be implemented to put on the same machine agents that communicate frequently. Various methods have been developed to get the best performance on a given configuration of machines. The more time-consuming the agents are, the more important is the acceleration.

Finally, we get a very simple architecture (Figure 19.2).

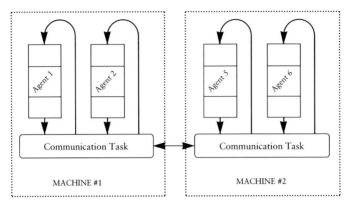

Figure 19.2   System representation.

19.3   Object Description

To test our system, we first developed current objects used for effects like water, clouds, trees, or mountains. Other objects (scenario, collision detector, generator) are necessary for animation control.

19.3.1   Scenario

We develop the simplest scenario possible. Its goal is to send requests for creation, management, and destruction of objects. The scenario is simply composed of a list of messages to be sent that is given by the user. A real language needs to be developed to provide real control of the objects. However, the control provided by the scenario could be sufficiently important that some investigation should be made for this part of the system. For example, the scenario could provide interactions with the user and high-level control functions of the objects. Gancarsky in [3] proposes such a system for high-level control of animation.

19.3.2   Generator

We use the simplest primitives possible to represent the objects. We use only points, particles, edges, or faces. The primitives are simple and can be exchanged with all other objects (in particular the collision detector). However, the user description cannot always be made with such simple primitives and it is necessary to use more descriptive models.

The list of models we propose below is not complete and can be extended easily.

- *Particle sources.* Rain, jets of water, or explosions can be simulated by particles but it is impossible and pointless to give all the positions by hand. We propose the use of generation shapes which are described by a geometric primitive (position, size, and color). The particles are ejected from the surface of the generation shape with various speeds. The number of particles generated per second is not constant. We use relations given by Reeves in [13] to modify the particle generation density. Thus, an explosion can easily be simulated by a sphere generating a very large number of particles in a very short time. Figure 19.3 presents an example with four different sources (sphere, disk, segment, rectangle).

- *Image.* This primitive was introduced simply in order to simulate the explosion of a photograph into small pieces of confetti. Interesting effects (such as turbulence or gravity) can be applied to the fragments.
- *Fractal height fields.* Mountains (Figure 19.4) are one of the most important objects we see in nature. A flat landscape does not look realistic; humans like to see something in the background. We use a very simple algorithm based on a recursive subdivision of an initial square into smaller squares perturbed by a Gaussian function. This is called the algorithm of the middle-point [6].
- *L-Systems.* Some natural objects have very particular geometrical structures, such as trees, flowers (Figure 19.5), or shells. These can be generated by algorithms. A very

Figure 19.3   Sources.

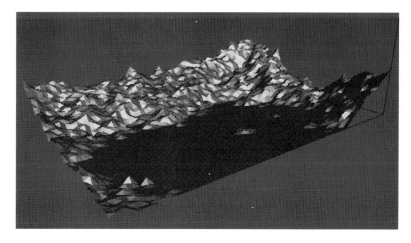

Figure 19.4   A mountain.

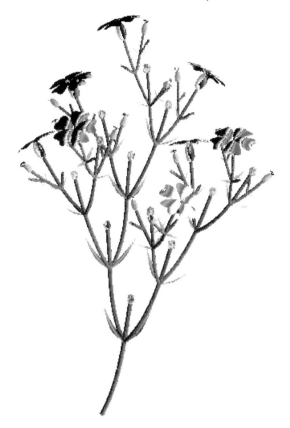

Figure 19.5   Flowers generated by an L-System.

simple method based on grammar is provided by L-Systems. An object is described by a list of derivation rules. Derivations are applied to an initial word and the resulting word can be used by a graphic turtle to generate the geometric description. But in nature objects do not look so perfect. We do not always want to generate identical objects, so the application of rules will be controlled by probabilistic relations and geometrical transformations are modified using a small random transformation. A good description of L-Systems can be found in [6] and [12].

- *List of polygons*. This is the classical method for description of solid objects (Figure 19.6). A large collection of software uses this model.
- *Constructive solid geometry*. CSG is a very powerful model for volume object representation. Complex objects with many curves are described using very few primitives. CSG allows exact representation of objects such as spheres, cones, or tori, whereas polygons provide only an approximation. The object (Figure 19.7) is described using our geometrical language [1] with only nine primitives. We are not able to use CSG for animation, so we transform this representation into particles using an algorithm described in [4].

Of course, this list of generators can be extended easily with other models.

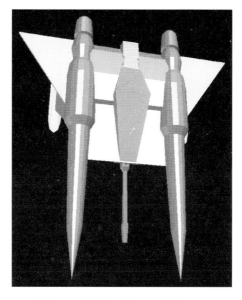

Figure 19.6 A star fighter.

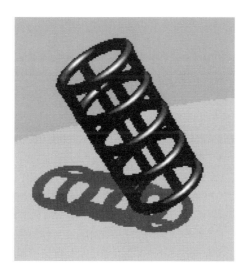

Figure 19.7 A strange spring.

19.3.3 Collision detector

Objects are independent and cannot access the descriptions of the other objects, which are private. Accordingly, we create a special object called the Collision Detector which receives messages from objects that want to detect collision with others.

First, objects send their bounding boxes if they move. If an intersection is detected using the bounding boxes, a message is sent to the two colliding objects in order to get the list of graphical primitives which are in the intersection zone. Then the exact collision can be computed and if necessary a message is sent to the two objects to compute the response to the collision.

In fact, only one instance of this object is created during a simulation. But if the objects evolve into two parallel worlds, it could be possible to create a detector for each virtual world.

19.3.4 Particle system

Different types of particle systems have been developed: the first was presented by Reeves [13]. A particle system is a large collection of small elements called particles. They have attributes of position and velocity; size, color, transparency, and shape; and lifetime.

During the simulation:

1. New particles are generated into the system.
2. They move and modify their attributes.
3. Old particles die and are deleted.

Reeves uses his system to generate fuzzy objects like explosions, clouds, fire, or grass. Such objects do not have real shape and we do not know exactly how they move, but we can find basic laws that produce the same effects. In this system, particles are only used as graphical elements.

In fact, physical laws can be used to control the particles' movements. Particles are also considered as small elements of material. Various systems have been developed using ad hoc control laws [5, 9, 16, 19, 25]:

- *Global attraction–repulsion.* All the particles are in repulsion and attraction with all the others. Lennard-Jones proposed a law for the force computation. For each pair of particles, a force F_{ij} is created:

$$F_{ij} = \frac{A}{r_{ij}^n} - \frac{B}{r_{ij}^{2n}} \tag{1}$$

where r_{ij} is the distance from p_i to p_j. For different values A and B, soft or hard objects can be generated. For example, Gascuel uses such a system in order to simulate complex soft objects like a blob splashing on the floor.
- *Coupled system.* The particles are in interaction with all the others only for collisions. The attraction forces needed for the cohesion of the objects are generated using links between adjoining particles. These links look like springs. Thus, elastic objects are created. Different types of spring can be used.

We propose to use a coupled particle system to control the object deformation. The different steps of our animation algorithm are as follows.

1. *Collision detection.*
   For all the particle pairs (i, j) if distance $(i, j) < r_i + r_j$ then

$$Fc_{ij} = k_0(r_i + r_j - d_{ij}) \tag{2}$$

2. *Links.*

   For all the links (i, j)

$$Fl_{ij} = k_1(l_{ij}^t - l_{ij}^0) \tag{3}$$

   where l_{ij}^0 is the length of the spring at rest.

3. *Couples.*

   For all the couples (i, j, k) compute

$$Fa_{ijk} = C_0(\theta_{ijk}^t - \theta_{ijk}^0) \tag{4}$$

   where θ_{ijk}^0 is the angle at rest.

4. *External forces.*

   We do not only want to see objects flying in space; we would like to act upon them. We introdce interactions using constraints such as gravity, wind, vortices, or obstacles. Other actions can easily be added to the system.

5. *Bringing positions up to date.*

   The relations we will use are similar to the ones used by Velho [18]. We use the Lagrange equation:

$$m_i \frac{d^2 x_i}{dt^2} + v \frac{dx_i}{dt} + \phi_i = 0 \tag{5}$$

   where m_i = node mass, x_i = position, v = damping coefficient, and ϕ_i = external and internal forces applied to the node.

   Previously we computed different forces applied to the particles. We deduce the final forces:

$$\phi_i = \sum_j Fc_{ij} + \sum_j Fl_{ij} + Fe_i + v\, v_i \tag{6}$$

   Then we can deduce the acceleration:

$$\gamma_i = \frac{\phi_i}{m_i} \tag{7}$$

   The new speed is

$$v_i^{t+\delta t} = v_i^t + \delta t\, \gamma_i \tag{8}$$

   and the new position is

$$x_i^{t+\delta t} = x_i^t + \delta t\, v_i^{t+\delta t} \tag{9}$$

   In fact, most of the time is spent on collision detection. This requires a lot of tests that are pointless. The complexity is $O(n^2)$. We should test collisions only for particles which are near to each other. Many partition algorithms have been developed [7, 14, 17]. We propose to subdivide the simulation space into smaller regions. Each particle is placed into a region and then we just have to test for collisions with particles which are in the same region.

If we subdivide the working space into n arrays, and fix the number of particles in each array to a, then the complexity is only $a^2 O(n)$.

19.3.5 Rigid objects

Rigid objects are not used in order to create special effects; we use them to interact with the objects used for special effects. They are described by a list of polygons and we can apply transformations (translation, rotation) to them. Two different trajectory modes can be used:

- *Path* – the object follows a path defined as in key-frame systems.
- *Force* – accelerations and forces can be applied. An integration using Euler's method is done to find the trajectory.

19.3.6 Water

Water could be simulated using particles, but a very large number of particles would be created and only a small proportion of them would be useful. We propose to physically modelize the surface of water. All the interactions with the water should be implemented using forces. We will use the model of water described by O'Brien and Hodgins [10]. The water is simulated by a list of columns of water. Waves will appear if columns do not have the same height. Each column is connected by pipes with its neighbors, so the sea can be regarded as a large graph of water columns (Figure 19.8).

Physical laws are used to determine flow in the pipes. The pressure of a column in the grid at position $[i, j]$, P_{ij} is

$$P_{ij} = h_{ij}\rho g + p_0 \tag{10}$$

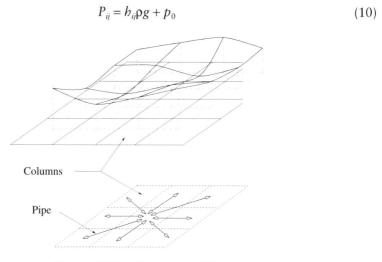

Columns

Pipe

Figure 19.8 Water model.

where h_{ij} is the height of the column at $[i, j]$, g is the acceleration due to gravity, and p_0 is the atmospheric pressure.

Then for each pipe from column $[i, j]$ to is neighbors $[k, l]$, the pressure differential is

$$\Delta P_{ij-kl} = P_{ij} - P_{kl} \tag{11}$$

so the acceleration of the fluid in the pipe is

$$a_{ij-kl} = \frac{c \, \Delta P_{ij-kl}}{m} \tag{12}$$

where c is the cross-sectional area of the pipe and m is the mass of fluid in the pipe.

We assume the acceleration to be constant during a small time period, Δt. The flow in the pipe is

$$\Phi_{ij-kl}^{t+\Delta t} = \Phi_{ij-kl}^{t} + \Delta t \, c \, a_{ij-kl} \tag{13}$$

so the volume change of a column is

$$\Delta V_{ij} = \Delta t \sum_{kl} \frac{\Phi_{ij-kl}^{t+\Delta t} + \Phi_{ij-kl}^{t}}{2} \tag{14}$$

Finally, the new heights of the columns can be computed. More details of this model can be found in [10].

19.4 Constraints

Constraints are necessary to make objects move. In nature, objects are under the influence of constraints, like wind or gravity acting on a tree, which make them evolve.

Constraints must be applied to the objects at each time step. Many very large messages need to be sent in order to get geometrical information and send the forces to be applied. For this reason we decide that constraints will not communicate using messages. Information is received and sent using functions.

Constraints are currently applied to a specified object and not to the others, so a constraint will be associated to a specified object (Figure 19.9).

Initially, only simple constraints have been used. These allow classical interactions. This list could easily be extended with more sophisticated constraints. The different types of constraints already used are as follows.

- *Set position.* This is useful to set the position of objects. For example, a sail moving because of the wind is fixed to the mast at three or more places. A chain hanging between two posts is constrained by the position of the two extremities.
- *Keep the distance between two points.* In order to maintain the cohesion of deformable objects, it can be useful to set the distance between two points. This constraint can be simulated by a strong spring, but, due to the time step integration, computational divergence could appear. It is more efficient to use a geometric constraint.

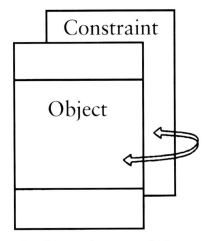

Figure 19.9   Constraints association to objects.

- *Set speed*. It can be useful to fix the speed of an object (for example, of a car on a highway).
- *Acceleration*. We create different types of acceleration (uniform, axial, punctual). We can then simulate the Earth's gravity, another planet's attraction, and so on.
- *Vortex*. A vortex is defined by a position, a direction, a rotation speed, and a vertical speed. This is a classic example of cloud deformation (Figure 19.10).

Other constraints could be created, but these are sufficient for classical animation.

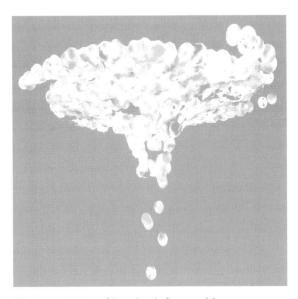

Figure 19.10   Clouds deformed by a vortex.

19.5   Results and Comments

19.5.1   Tree example (Figure 19.11)

The simulation of a tree is realized using a particle system. The particles are created by a generator using an L-System. We use only one derivation rule, applied four times:

```
T -> ^^(*(^^^)@(^^^)@(^^^)@(^^^))%T
```

Four constraints are applied to the tree:

- Gravity
- Wind (horizontal acceleration)
- Two fixed positions for the feet of the tree

19.5.2   Water example (Figure 19.12)

To simulate waves, the water is not created with a horizontal surface: Waves already exist at the beginning of the simulation. Then wave propagation will appear without any external interactions.

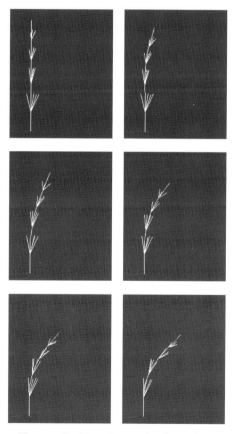

Figure 19.11   A tree in the wind.

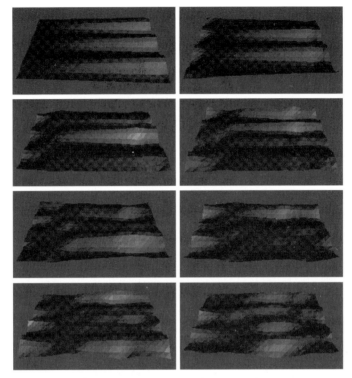

Figure 19.12   Waves.

19.5.3   CSG objects

CSG objects are used for geometric description; using a renderer, an image can be generated (Figure 19.13). For the physical animation, we use particles: The object can then be displayed using two different representations (particles or links between masses: Figure 19.14).

Our system is able to generate a CSG-tree description using a list of particles if they have previously been created by a CSG-tree [4].

It is possible to animate objects with good detail, described by a small number of primitives (Figure 19.15). For example, a ball usually defined by many polygons is defined by only one CSG-primitive.

19.5.4   Rendering problem

Some effects cannot be generated using only simple primitives like points, spheres, edges, and faces. For example, a tree is composed of thousands of leaves. It is possible to physically simulate a leaf by a particle and display a sphere. But it would be better to display small green textured polygons. A package needs to be developed to generate more complex output files mixing the physical description and complex geometric descriptions. It would then be possible to display trees with leaves looking like orange or cherry tree leaves without doing a new simulation.

Figure 19.13   A basic CSG primitive.

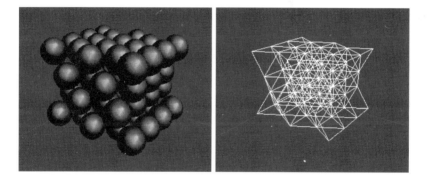

Figure 19.14   Two representations of a CSG object.

To simulate rain, for example, we need to visualize small segments whose length depends on the speed of the droplets. All the physical information (masses, age, etc.) could be used by the display processes in order to generate more complex images.

19.6   Conclusion

It is easy to generate animations of natural phenomena taking into account interactions between objects. To achieve this, we use:

- Autonomous agents communicating with messages. This model is not too time consuming and allows a distributed implementation of the agents.
- Translation functions from high to low level geometric descriptions.
- Simple geometric primitives for the agent geometry description which allow fast development of new objects.
- Physical parameters (force, mass, speed) for interaction and simulation computation.

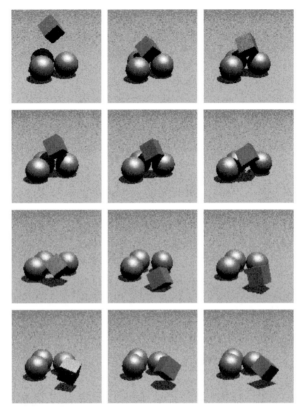

Figure 19.15   A cube falling on spheres with bouncing effects.

In testing our system, we do not try to get the best images possible. If necessary, more complex description files can be generated and used by a ray tracer.

All the simulations shown above have been computed in a few minutes or seconds. We do not need to use high-performance algorithms. In fact, natural phenomena can be simulated without high-performance machines. However, the rendering step can be very long if high image quality is needed. For example, the rendering of a cloud using ray tracing of volume densities can take hours, whereas the physical simulation can be done within a few minutes.

To produce something really usable by end-users, graphical capabilities must be added to the system.

References

[1] T. Excoffier, *Utilisation due langage 'G' pour coder les arbres CSG*. Rapport de recherche, LIGIA, université Claude Bernard, Lyon I, 1989.
[2] A. Fournier, W.T. Reeves, A simple model of ocean waves, *ACM SIGGRAPH 86*, 20(4): 75–84; 1986.

[3] P. Gancarsky, *Le controle de l'interactivité et du temps dans la production d'animations*, PhD thesis, Université Louis Pasteur, Strasbourg I, Dec. 1988.

[4] A. Gareau, T. Excoffier, E. Tosan, A particle system using csg for description and visualization, *Computer Animation*, 175–183; May 25–28, 1994.

[5] M.P. Gascuel, A. Verroust, C. Puech, Animation and collisions between complex deformables bodies, *Journées Graphiques Gros-Plan 1990*, 1–20; Nov. 1990.

[6] D. Saupe, H.-O. Peitgen, *The Science of Fractal Images*, Springer, 1988.

[7] D. House, Coupled particles: theory. *ACM Siggraph'92 Course Notes: Particle system modeling, animation and physically based techniques*, 16: 3.1–3.8; July 1992.

[8] J.T. Kajiya, B.P. Von Herzen, Ray tracing volume densities, *Computer Graphics*, 18(3): 165–174; 1984.

[9] A. Luciani, S. Jimenez, J.L. Florens, O. Raoult, C. Cadoz, Modeles comportementaux: vers une approche instrumentale de la synthèse d'images, *Bigre*, 67: 259–272; Jan. 1990.

[10] J. O'Brien, J.K. Hodgins, *Dynamic simulation of splashing fluids*, Technical report, Georgia Institute of Technology, 1994. Technical Report Number: GIT-GVU-94-32.

[11] D. Peachey, Modeling waves and surf, *ACM SIGGRAPH 86*, 20(4): 65–74; 1986.

[12] P. Prusinkiewicz, M. Hammel, E. Mjolsness, Animation of plant development, *Computer Graphics*, 351–360; 1993.

[13] W.T. Reeves, Particle systems: a technique for modeling a class of fuzzy objects, *ACM Siggraph'92 Course Notes: Particle system modeling, animation and physically based techniques*, 16: 1.2–1.19, July 1992.

[14] H. Samet, *The Design and Analysis of Spatial Data Structures*. Addison Wesley, Reading, Mass., 1989.

[15] D. Tonnesen, Modeling liquids and solids using thermal particles, *ACM Siggraph'92 Course Notes: Particle system modeling, animation and physically based techniques*, 16: 4.22–4.29; July 1992.

[16] D. Tonnesen, Spatially coupled particle systems. *ACM Siggraph'92 Course Notes: Particle system modeling, animation and physically based techniques*, 16: 4.2–4.21; July 1992.

[17] G. Turk, *Interactive collision detection for molecular graphics*, PhD thesis, University of North Carolina at Chapel Hill, 1989.

[18] L. Velho, J. Miranda Gomes, A dynamics simulation environment for implicit objects using discrete models, *Second Eurographics Workshop 91*, Sept. 1991, pp. 183–190.

[19] A. Witkin, Particle system dynamics. *ACM Siggraph '92 Course Notes, An Introduction to Physically Based Modeling*, B1–B12, July 1992.

20
Geometric Model and Visualization of Breaking Waves

Atsumi Imamiya and Dong Zhang

20.1 Introduction

Modeling of water waves is an important research subject in natural phenomena modeling [1–3]. In this chapter, we try to set up a model which can express breaking waves on a computer. Various kinds of ocean wave models have been presented to date. In the earliest, ripples were expressed as sine waves. Later, Gerstner presented the famous classical water wave model [4]. In 1981, Nelson Max proposed a three-dimensional wave model with simple wave theory [5]. Perlin gave more complex patterns of ripples or waves by summing band-limited noise to make texture maps [6]. Peachey [7] and Fournier and Reeves [8] constructed models that address waves that are refracting and breaking. Further, Masten used a well-known power spectrum of waves under steady wind and infinite fetch to Fourier synthesize the surface [9]. Pauline combined the wave composition principle and refraction, and presented a method based on wave tracing similar to ray tracing [10]. Because these models are based on linear small-amplitude wave theory, the algorithms are simple, the calculation burden is small, and the results of simulations of small-amplitude waves are often satisfactory. However, if the real conditions are widely different from the restricted conditions above, the theory will no longer be usable. Therefore, it is very difficult to express breaking waves like a plunging breaker with the models mentioned above. Furthermore, research on the modeling of breaking waves is very difficult because there is no complete theory of breaking waves yet.

20.2 Basic Model

According to the theory of fluid mechanics, if water is considered as a kind of incompressible and irrotational ideal fluid with constant density, then water waves can be defined by the following differential equation and boundary conditions.

Laplace's equation:

$$\Delta\phi = \nabla^2 = 0 \tag{1}$$

Visualization and Modeling
ISBN 0-12-227738-4

Dynamic boundary condition:

$$\frac{\partial \phi}{\partial t} + g\,\xi + \frac{\Delta \phi}{2} = 0 \tag{2}$$

Kinematic boundary condition:

$$\frac{\partial \xi}{\partial t} = \frac{\partial \phi}{\partial z} - \frac{\partial \phi}{\partial x}\frac{\partial \xi}{\partial x} - \frac{\partial \phi}{\partial y}\frac{\partial \xi}{\partial y} \tag{3}$$

Kinematic bottom boundary condition:

$$w = \frac{\partial \phi}{\partial z} = 0 \tag{4}$$

We can obtain two water wave models based on methods for solving the equation: one is based on the finite element method, or boundary element method, and another is based on linear small-amplitude wave theory. The former can be regarded as an incomplete model because the equations are nonlinear and the initial conditions even as turbulent water are unknown, which makes the calculation extremely large and also nearly impossible to solve. The latter one is got by simplifying above equations. We added the following conditions.

(a) The deformation of the water surface is very small.
(b) The wave movement is slow, so that the terms of equal to or higher than the second power of velocity can be discarded.
(c) The change of steepness of shade of the wave is very small.

Fluid mechanics can provide a set of linear equations that gives a first approximation to the behavior of water wave, so obviating the need for complex nonlinear calculation. Most water wave models are based on the linear small-amplitude wave theory [4–10].

We assume that each particle on the free surface describes a circle around its rest position (x', y', z'), the XY plane is the plane of the sea at rest, and the Z axis points upward; then the equation of motion of a particle in the XY plane is

$$x = x' + H\sin(kx' - \omega t)$$
$$z = z' - H\cos(kx' - \omega t) \tag{5}$$

This is the well-known Gerstner model. The model can be seen as the curve generated by a point P at a distance r from the center of a circle of radius $1/k$ rolling over a line at distance $1/k$ from the X axis (see Figure 20.1).

Fournier considered orbits of particles as ellipses in which the major axes orient toward the slope of the bottom, and proposed the following model:

$$x = x' - H\cos\beta\, S_x \sin(k\,x' - \omega t) + H\sin\beta\, S_z \cos(k\,x' - \omega t)$$
$$z = z' - H\cos\beta\, S_z \cos(k\,x' - \omega t) + H\sin\beta\, S_x \sin(k\,x' - \omega t) \tag{6}$$

Neither Gerstner's model nor Fournier's model can depict plunging waves. Here, we transform equation (7), guided by the finite amplitude wave theory, into equation (8).

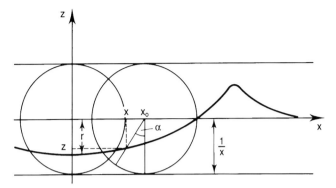

Figure 20.1   The trochoid wave.

$$\frac{\partial \phi}{\partial x} = -C + Ck\xi$$

$$= -C + Ck[p_0 + p_1\cos(kx - \omega t) + p_2\cos(2(kx - \omega t)) + p_3\cos(3(kx - \omega t)) + \cdots]$$

$$\frac{\partial \phi}{\partial x} = Ck[p_0 + p_1\sin(kx - \omega t) + p_2\sin(2(kx - \omega t)) + p_3\sin(3(kx - \omega t)) + \cdots] \qquad (7)$$

If $i \to \infty$, $a_i \to 0$;

$$x(t) = x' + a_0 t + a_1\sin(kx' - \omega t) + a_2\sin(2(kx' - \omega t)) + a_3\sin(3(kx' - \omega t)) + \cdots \quad (8a)$$

If $i \to \infty$, $b_i \to 0$;

$$z(t) = z' + b_0 t + b_1\cos(kx' - \omega t) + b_2\cos(2(kx' - \omega t)) + b_3\cos(3(kx' - \omega t)) + \cdots \quad (8b)$$

Both equation (5) and equation (6) may be considered as a special case of equation (8). Further, equation (8) can be simplified to our basic model.

$$x = x' + f_1(\xi) H\sin(kx' - \omega t + \alpha_1(\xi))$$
$$z = z' + f_2(\xi) H\cos(kx' - \omega t + \alpha_2(\xi)) + f_3(\xi) H\cos(2kx' - 2\omega t) \qquad (9)$$

Here, H = wave amplitude, k = radian wavenumber (2π/wavelength λ), ω = radian frequency, β = angle between sea bottom and surface, ξ = surf similarity parameter,

$$\xi = \frac{\tan\beta}{\sqrt{H/\lambda}} \qquad \text{(see Figure 20.2)} \quad (10)$$

(x', z') = central point of water particle movement, and f_i, α_i = unknown functions of the parameter ξ.

The shapes of waves generated by Gerstner's model, Fournier's model, and our model are shown in Figures 20.3a, b, and c, respectively. In Gerstner's model and Fournier's model, the orbits of water particles are ellipses and oblique ellipses, respectively. However, in our model, the orbits of water particles look like butterflies (see Figure 20.3d).

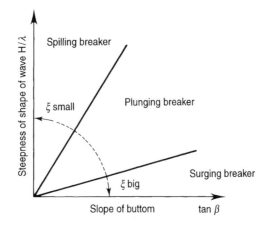

Figure 20.2 Surf similarity parameter ξ.

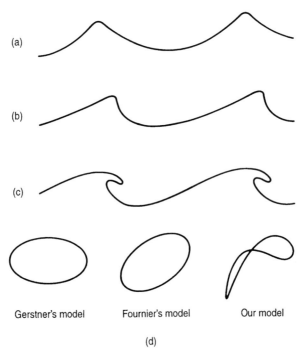

Figure 20.3 Examples of waves generated by (a) Gerstner's model; (b) Fournier's model; (c) Our model; (d) The orbits of water particles.

To determine the unknown functions, several wave patterns are needed. Here, the curve composed of sampling points of the famous Kanagawa-Oki Waves (see Figure 20.4) is used as an original wave pattern, and other patterns can be generated by applying equation (11) to the original wave pattern. Here, (x_i, z_i) are the coordinates of the ith sample point, j is the number of iterations at the ith point.

Figure 20.4   Kanagawa-Oki Waves.

$$x_i^{(j+1)} = \frac{x_{i-1}^{(j)} + 2x_i^{(j)} + x_{i+1}^{(j)}}{4}$$

$$z_i^{(j+1)} = \frac{z_{i-1}^{(j)} + 2z_i^{(j)} + z_{i+1}^{(j)}}{4} \tag{11}$$

Assuming that β and λ are constant, the wave height of wave pattern WP_i is H_i; then ξ_i corresponding to wave pattern WP_i can be calculated by

$$\xi_i = \frac{\tan \beta}{\sqrt{H_i/\lambda}} \tag{12}$$

It is possible to approach a certain wave pattern by adjusting the assumed values of the five unknown functions in equation (9). In other words, it is necessary to calculate the optimum values of f_i, α_i as the model approaches the wave pattern. This problem can be regarded as an unconstrained optimization problem in a space of five parameters. It is very difficult to search for the optimum values with the steepest descent method because the coincidence is very sensitive to the parameters and there are many peaks in the five-dimensional space. Here, we adapt a method based on the genetic algorithm.

20.3   Wave Pattern Approaching Method Based on the Genetic Algorithm

As a successful method for nonlinear optimum value searching the genetic algorithm (GA) [11] has been applied to graphic object layout, image pattern recognition, and so on. Here, the GA is applied to wave modeling.

20.3.1   Basic definition of GA

The structure of information fields in an individual is called the *genotype*. Here, we define each individual as corresponding to each point in the five-dimension search space, with the genotype G_k

$$G_k = (\alpha_1, \alpha_2, f_1, f_2, f_3)$$

The population is composed of individuals with G_k. The length of the population (number of individuals) is defined as 32. We can evaluate each individual in this population, and put selection, cross-over, or mutation into operation on an individual in the population (see Figure 20.5).

The phenotype of each individual is a wave form generated by putting the parameters of the individual into equation (13):

$$x = x' + f_1 H \sin(kx' + \alpha_1)$$
$$z = z' + f_2 H \cos(kx' + \alpha_2) + f_3 H \cos(2kx') \qquad (13)$$

Let m be the number of sample points of the wave pattern; the coordinate of each sample point is (X_{pti}, Z_{pti}), $i = 0, 1, \ldots, m - 1$; the square of the wave pattern is ΔS_{pti}; and the square of the wave generated by equation (13) is ΔS_{wsi}. Let $s = \min(\Delta S_{pti}, \Delta S_{wsi})$, $b = \max(\Delta S_{pti}, \Delta S_{wsi})$, $P_{si} = s/b$, then fitness G_s is defined as follows:

$$G_s = \frac{(\Sigma \Delta P_{si})}{m} \qquad (14)$$

	α_1	α_2	f_1	f_2	f_3
Individual 1	α_{11}	α_{12}	f_{11}	f_{12}	f_{13}
Individual 2	α_{21}	α_{22}	f_{21}	f_{22}	f_{23}
			... ...		
Individual n	α_{n1}	α_{n2}	f_{n1}	f_{n2}	f_{n3}

Figure 20.5   Genotype, individual and population.

20.3.2   Genetic operation

We use the fitness to evaluate each individual in the population, and remove the individuals with lower fitness values while keeping the individuals with higher fitness values. New individuals generated by cross-over or mutation operations will take the place of the selected individuals.

Assume each term of the genotype as a cross-over segment. Select two individuals out of the surviving individuals in a random way. New individuals can be generated by exchanging information between the selected segments of the two individuals.

Mutation on a term of an individual means changing the value of this term by a probability. Here, there are two kinds of mutation operation. One is similar to the

Hooke–Jeeres direct search method [12]. The purpose is to find a local optimum value as soon as possible. The other operation is to use a random value within a limited range instead of a corresponding term of the individual. The purpose is to get rid of a local solution of lower fitness value so as to find a better solution.

The above operation will loop until the final conditions are fulfilled. Since fitness above 0.8 is enough for our problem, we regard a solution above 0.8 as an optimum solution. An optimum solution as the model approaches a wave pattern can be obtained by the genetic algorithm mentioned above.

20.3.3   Determination of unknown functions

Assume that optimum solutions corresponding to each wave pattern are

$$
\begin{array}{llllll}
WP1: & \alpha_1(\xi_1), & \alpha_2(\xi_1), & f_1(\xi_1), & f_2(\xi_1), & f_3(\xi_1) \\
WP2: & \alpha_1(\xi_2), & \alpha_2(\xi_2), & f_1(\xi_2), & f_2(\xi_2), & f_3(\xi_2) \\
\vdots & \vdots & \vdots & \vdots & \vdots & \vdots \\
WPm: & \alpha_1(\xi_m), & \alpha_2(\xi_m), & f_1(\xi_m), & f_2(\xi_m), & f_3(\xi_m)
\end{array}
$$

We can determine the unknown functions from these solutions. For example, we have the points $(\xi_1, f_1(\xi_1)), (\xi_2, f_1(\xi_2)), \cdot \ \cdot \ \cdot, (\xi_m, f_1(\xi_m))$; the approximate equation along these points is

$$
F_1(\xi) = a_0 + a_1\xi + a_2\xi^2 + a_3\xi^3 + \cdots \tag{15}
$$

We calculate each value of a_i by the method of least squares, and assign them to equation (15), to get

$$
F_1(\xi) = 2.25176 + 2.40138\xi + 0.81728\xi^2 - 0.0881\xi^3 \tag{16}
$$

We can determine other unknown functions in the same way:

$$
F_2(\xi) = -1.459336 + 1.154276\xi - 0.32182\xi^2 - 0.030234\xi^3 \tag{17}
$$

$$
F_3(\xi) = -1.340143 + 1.5999\xi - 0.572427\xi^3 - 0.063266\xi^3 \tag{18}
$$

$$
\alpha_1(\xi) \approx -0.785 \tag{19}
$$

$$
\alpha_2(\xi) \approx 0.5233 \tag{20}
$$

The whole model will be completely determined by putting each function into equation (9).

20.4   Influence due to Circumstances

The shapes of waves are strongly affected by wind and the shape of the ocean floor. The relationship between wind speed V and the average of the highest one third of the waves $H_{\frac{1}{3}}$ is

$$H_{\frac{1}{3}} = 7.065 \times 10^{-3} \, V^{2.5} \tag{21}$$

Here, we assume wind speed V constant, and reflection of waves and friction of the sea bottom are ignored: only the influence of topography of ocean floor is considered.

20.4.1   The influence of the slope of the bottom

There are mainly two types of breaking waves. One is the spilling breaker, the other is the plunging breaker. Spilling breakers happen on shores of gentle bottom slope. Plunging breakers happen on shores of steep bottom slope. If the slope of the bottom and the steepness of the shape of waves changes as waves move forward, the surf similarity parameter ξ turns out to be a function of t. Assume that both slope of the bottom $\tan\beta$ and wavelength λ are constant, and the shoaling coefficient is K_s, then

$$H = k_s H_0 = \frac{H_0}{\sqrt{\tanh kd * \left(1 + \dfrac{2kd}{\sinh 2kd}\right)}} \approx \frac{H_0}{\sqrt{\tanh kd}} \approx \frac{H_0}{\sqrt{kd}} \tag{22}$$

Substitute equation (22) into equation (10):

$$\xi_i = \frac{\tan\beta}{\sqrt{H_i/\lambda}} = A\sqrt[4]{d(t)} = A\sqrt[4]{d_0 - ct} \tag{23}$$

Here, A is a constant, d is the depth of water, d_0 is the initial depth of water, and c is the speed of water. For waves progressing on a slope whose angle β is 30°, the changes of the wave shape as time t changes are shown in Figure 20.6.

20.4.2   Influence of refraction

Wave fronts will curve as the wave is moving from place to place in its own direction. Wave orthogonals will also curve in shallow sea. This is called refraction. The changes of refraction angle (see Figure 20.7) can be calculated by Snell's law of refraction:

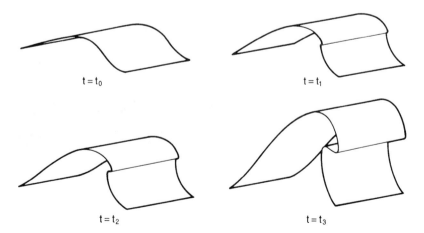

$t = t_0$ $t = t_1$

$t = t_2$ $t = t_3$

Figure 20.6   Changes of wave shapes.

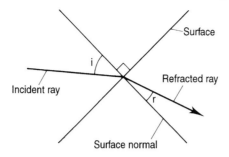

Figure 20.7   Refraction angle.

$$\frac{\sin i}{\sin r} = \frac{c_i}{c_r} \approx \frac{d_i}{d_r} \tag{24}$$

The changes of the wave ray direction depend on the incident angle and the depth of the water. For instance, two different topographies of the ocean floor are given in Figure 20.8. With the two topographies, which can be expressed with contour lines, for a difference between two neighboring contours Δd of 3 and d_0 is 120, the effects of refraction are different (see Figure 20.9a,b). If Δd or d_0 changes, then the effects of refraction change as well (see Figure 20.9c,d).

The relation between deep sea wave height and shallow sea wave height is

$$\frac{H}{H_0} = K_s K_r = K_s \sqrt{\frac{b_0}{b}} \tag{25}$$

Here, K_r is the refraction coefficient, and b_0 and b are intervals of wave orthogonals in deep sea and shallow sea (see Figure 20.10). According to equation (25), when wave rays are focused, the wave height will increase; when they diverge, it will decrease.

The examples of breaking waves generated by our model are shown in Figure 20.11. Figures 20.11a and b correspond to the topographies shown in Figures 20.8a and b, respectively. In Figure 20.11b, the effects of refraction from the topography shown in

Figure 20.8   Two topographies of the ocean floor.

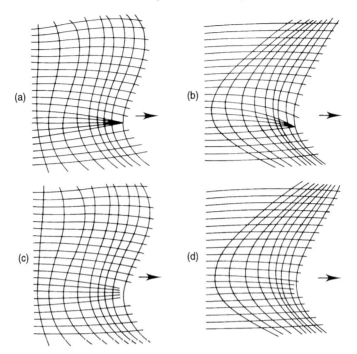

Figure 20.9   Effects of refraction.

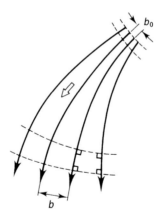

Figure 20.10   Interval of orthogonals.

Figure 20.8b are considered; the result is that the central part of the wave grows higher and both side parts get lower.

20.5   Expression for breaking spray

Visualization of breaking waves should be able to describe not only the shape of waves but also spray. Since spray is generated simultaneously with breaking waves, the limit

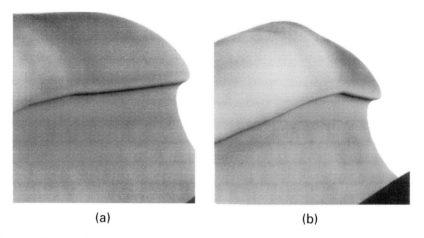

(a)   (b)

Figure 20.11   Examples of plunging breaker generated by our model.

condition for breaking wave generation can be regarded as a a threshold for spray generation.

Let the slope of wave form SW and limit slope of breaking waves LSW be

$$SW = \frac{H}{\lambda}, \qquad LSW = 0.142 \left(\tanh \frac{2\pi d}{\lambda} \right) \qquad (26)$$

then, the limit condition for spray generation is

$$SW \geq LSW \qquad (27)$$

The spray can be modeled by a particle system [13, 14]. The number of spray particles N is defined as follows. Let $MeanParts = (SW - LSW)\,C$, then

$$N = MeanParts + Rand(\ ) * VarParts \qquad (28)$$

Here, *Meanparts* is a main value, *Varparts* is a variable value, *Rand*( ) is a random function, and C is a constant value.

When spray is generated on top of breaking waves, the density of spray particles is not uniform. The density function of spray particles for the plunging breaker $p(x)$ may be defined as (see Figure 20.12)

$$P(x) = \frac{2N}{l^2} x \qquad (29)$$

We suppose that spray particles move in parabola. The attributes of spray particles would include initial location, speed vector, size, color, transparency, lifetime, and so on.

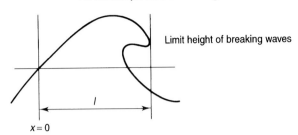

Figure 20.12   The definition of *l*.

20.6   Conclusion

This is the first application of GA to the modeling of breaking waves. The method based on GA given here is successful. With this method we have solved the problem of generating breaking waves, which has not been achieved before.

Since this model is obtained for certain specific wave patterns, the model would change if the patterns changed. The model will be a simulation corresponding to natural breaking waves if shapes of natural breaking waves are used as wave patterns. This may be significant because no perfect breaking wave theory exists yet.

We have considered the effects of depth of water, shape of ocean floor, and wave refraction, discussed the changes of wave shape as time changes, and given examples of breaking waves corresponding to different topographies.

Although this genetic method is useful for finding the optimum solution, the possibility still exists that only local solutions are found. Evaluation methods and the genetic rule should be improved, and the research on modeling breaking spray should be developed further.

Acknowledgments

The authors thank C. Shou and Q. Meng for polishing up the paper, and T. Sakamoto and Y. Funato for preparing figures.

References

[1] J.D. Foley, A. VanDam, S.K. Feiner, J.F. Hughes, *Computer Graphics,* Addison-Wesley, Reading, Mass., 1990.
[2] B. Kinsman, *Wind Waves,* Prentice-Hall, Englewood Cliffs, N.J., 1965.
[3] P. Haack, P. Glravert, V. Schlegel, The modeling of extreme gravity waves: an approach towards a numerical wave channel, *Proc. 1st. Int.Conf. Moving Boundaries,* 1991.
[4] F.J.V. Gerstner, Theorie der wellen, *Ann. der Physik,* 32: 412–440; 1809.
[5] N.L. Max, Vectorized procedural models for natural terrain: Waves and islands in the sun set, *SIGGRAPH'81 Conference Proceedings,* pp. 317–324, ACM, New York, 1981.
[6] K. Perlin, An image synthesizer, *SIGGRAPH'85 Conference Proceedings,* pp. 287–296, ACM, New York, 1985.

[7] D.R. Peachey, Modeling waves and surf, *SIGGRAPH'86 Conference Proceedings*, pp. 65–74, ACM, New York, 1986.

[8] A. Fournier, W.T. Reeves, A Simple Model of Ocean Waves, *SIGGRAPH86, Conference Proceedings*, pp. 75–84, ACM, New York, 1986.

[9] G.A. Masten, P.A. Watterberg, I.F. Mareda, Fourier synthesis of ocean scenes, *IEEE Computer Graphics Appl.* 7(3): 16–23; 1987.

[10] P.Y. Ts'o, B.A. Barsky, Modeling and rendering waves, *ACM Trans. Graphics*, 6(3): 191–214, 1987.

[11] D. Goldberg, *Genetic Algorithms in Search, Optimization, and Machine Learning*, Addison-Wesley, Reading, Mass., 1989.

[12] J. Kowalik, *Methods for Unconstrained Optimization Problems*, American Elsevier, New York, 1968.

[13] W.T. Reeves, Particle Systems – A technique for modeling a class of fuzzy objects, *Computer Graphics*, 17(3): 359–376; 1983.

[14] W.T. Reeves, Approximate and probabilistic algorithms for shading and rendering structured particle systems, *Computer Graphics*, 19(3): 313–322; 1985.

21
Visualizing Motion Characteristics

Bart MacCarthy and Mark Caulfield-Browne

21.1 Introduction

Engineering design has seen radical changes in the last 15 years. Changes have resulted from rapid technological advances in many engineering disciplines and fundamental developments in the way in which the design function is perceived in engineering businesses. Equally important have been the developments in design modeling, visualization and modification, and the handling and transmission of engineering design data.

Today, CADCAM technologies and systems are commonplace and taken for granted in most engineering environments. However, such systems are frequently rather limited, often providing only 2D drafting capability. Three-dimensional surface and solid modeling is still considered to be advanced in many sectors. A fundamental distinction can be made between systems which provide purely aesthetic design capability and those which are required to model physical laws, principles, and constraints. More limited progress has been made in the visualization and modeling of physical systems in areas of engineering design such as fluid dynamics, kinematic analysis, and deformation analysis. The development of graphical modeling and visualization tools for this category of application usually presents many difficulties and challenges.

In this chapter we discuss the application of visualization and modeling principles to the problem of planar motion specification. The specification of motion is crucial in many areas of engineering design, in particular in relation to high-speed mechanisms and mechanical systems. A range of problems in motion design arise in areas as diverse as automotive engineering, packaging, printing, food processing, and textile machinery.

We first present, in a descriptive manner, the nature of motion design problems and the limitations of traditional graphical and mathematical approaches. The application of polynomial spline functions for motion design problems is then discussed. An overview of the spline function method is presented. The potential of the spline function method for computer-aided motion design is highlighted. The development of a computer-aided engineering tool called MODUS (motion design using splines) is described. The functionality of MODUS in a range of applications is described. The advantages, benefits, and difficulties of the approach are discussed.

21.2 Motion Design

The central problem in planar motion design is the selection of a motion which satisfies imposed constraints in terms of displacements, velocities, and accelerations (and sometimes higher order characteristics) and also generates good dynamic performance. Constraints may be of different types. Thus a discrete constraint is a condition imposed at a specific point in a motion; e.g., a motion may be required to achieve a specific displacement and velocity at a particular instant in a motion interval. Constraints may also be continuous over a segment of a motion; e.g., a motion may be required which does not exceed a specified acceleration over a segment. Constraints may also be hard or soft. Thus a hard constraint could be a zero acceleration condition specified at the end of a motion interval. A soft, or desirable constraint, might be the requirement for a smooth transition from a constant velocity segment to a point of maximum deceleration.

The common objectives in motion design problems are to satisfy all hard constraints and balance the many soft constraints in an attempt to obtain acceptable overall dynamic performance characteristics in the system being designed. The effect of the motion characteristics is usually a limiting factor in high-speed performance. Maximum 'smoothness' or monotonicity is usually a desirable goal in almost all motion design problems.

Traditional design methods relied on graphical techniques. In automotive cam design, for instance, complex graphical methods were developed in the postwar period for this highly constrained motion design problem [4]. It has been clear for many decades that the motion selected in this application is critical for high-speed performance.

It may sometimes be possible to generate motions from dynamic models. However, the number and types of constraints usually result in intractable mathematical problems. Many mechanism designers have developed specific methods for specific problem areas, based on an intuitive feel for good dynamic performance characteristics. However, traditional design methods are very limited for handling complex motion design problems.

For planar motion specification, the mathematical problem reduces to a non-standard interpolation problem [6]. A smooth mathematical function must be found which satisfies all the hard constraints and as many of the soft constraints as possible. Viewed in this manner, the mathematical function defines the motion's displacement, and its derivatives define velocity, acceleration, and higher order characteristics.

Numerous mathematical function types have been proposed. Approaches based on trigonometric segments and polynomials have been the most popular. Such functions provide a range of possibilities for simple motions. However, they are very limited for complex motions and do not provide any flexibility to control the motion characteristics directly. Trignometric segments in particular are usually limited when anything other than boundary conditions are specified.

21.3 Motion Specification Using Splines

Polynomials are usually thought of as exhibiting sufficient flexibility for mathematical interpolation problems [3]. However, there are two major limitations with using polynomials for the more general nonstandard interpolation problems found in motion design:

1. The order of a polynomial solution for an interpolation problem is determined by the number of constraints. High-order polynomials may oscillate wildly. This detracts from the maximum smoothness requirement for motion design problems.
2. Polynomial interpolation gives a unique solution. Hence, there is no flexibility to control the characteristics of the motion. Thus, 'tuning' a motion to obtain satisfactory overall characteristics is not possible. For example, a designer may be satisfied with the overall characteristics of a motion but might wish to reduce the level of maximum acceleration.

Thus, polynomial interpolation is limited for motion design. MacCarthy and Burns [5] and MacCarthy [6] have investigated the potential of polynomial spline functions for planar motion design problems. A spline function is made up of a set of polynomial segments, joined in a manner such that the function has a prescribed degree of smoothness across the full interval. The join points between segments are called knots.

It has been shown that, under certain nonrestrictive conditions, a set of discrete motion constraints can be satisfied exactly by a whole families of spline functions. For a given set of constraints, once the order of the spline function is chosen, the number of knots can be determined. Each knot has an interval in which it can be placed with respect to the constraints. Once the position of each knot is specified in its interval, then the spline function is uniquely defined. A different choice of spline order and/or knot positions would give a different spline solution with different characteristics.

The spline function method has many advantages for motion design and specification:

- Very complex motion constraints can be specified.
- Infinite families of solutions are provided for most problems.
- Three approaches are possible for designers to interact with the motion:
    selection of spline order (e.g. cubic, quartic, quintic, etc.)
    selection of knot positions
    addition, deletion, or modification of constraints
- Spline functions can approximate any of the standard motions.
- When spline solution methods are implemented with a B-spline basis, the numerical computation is stable, accurate, and very fast, allowing the possibility of an interactive computer-aided engineering tool to be developed.

The foregoing is an overview of the theory of polynomial spline functions applied to motion design problems. A more formal mathematical outline is now presented.

21.4   The Mathematics of the Spline Function Method

Assume that we have a set of interpolation constraints where derivatives may be specified in addition to y-values. Thus at any x-value, in addition to a y-value we may specify first, second, and higher derivatives. The only stipulation we will make is that there are no gaps in the derivatives specified, e.g., if a second derivative value is specified at a point then the first derivative value must also be specified. The x-values for such a set of constraints may be specified as a set of nondecreasing real numbers $x_1,$

$x_2, \ldots, x_n$. Repeated x-values indicate that derivative values have been specified in addition to the y-value. The total number of constraints specified is n.

A spline of order k is a function which is made up of a set of polynomials of order k or less, joined in such a manner that the function is continuous and has $k-2$ continuous derivatives over its entire interval. Thus a cubic spline function (order $k = 4$) is continuous and has continuous first and second derivatives.

We will now consider spline functions of order k, defined on the interval $[x_1, x_n]$ which satisfy all the interpolation constraints noted above. Let us assume that the spline functions have m knots, $\lambda_1, \lambda_2, \ldots, \lambda_m$ which lie strictly inside the interval $[x_1, x_n]$. It can be shown [6] that a spline of order k with m interior knots can satisfy all the constraints if

$$m = n - k \tag{1}$$

and

$$\lambda_i \in (x_i, x_{i+k}) \qquad i = 1, 2, \ldots, m \tag{2}$$

Effectively, we require the ith knot to lie in the interval between the ith and $(i + k)$th constraint. A number of further technicalities should be noted:

- The most amenable representation of the spline function for solution of the interpolation problem is not the usual polynomial power series representation. A linear combination of β-splines ([2, 3, 8] gives rise to the most stable and fastest solution procedures. In addition, the computation of the spline and its derivatives is also very rapid using β-splines.
- The β-spline approach allows a more general situation to be developed where knots are allowed to coincide. At such a point, the continuity of the spline is reduced accordingly.
- The spline function method using β-splines requires additional external knots [2]. These may be handled quite easily in computation.

The computation of a spline requires constraints to be specified first. Then an appropriate spline order is selected. The maximum order is determined by the total number of constraints. The minimum is determined by the maximum number of derivatives specified at any point. A valid knot set can then be specified. A linear equation system can be developed and a linear equation solver can be applied to obtain the spline coefficients. Evaluation of the spline and its derivatives is then a straightforward matter.

21.5   An Interactive Graphical Approach for Motion Design

It was clear in the late 1980s that the spline function approach had the potential to be used as an interactive graphical tool in a computer-aided engineering environment, to allow designers to explore many potential design alternatives even for the most complex motion design problems. In particular, it was clear that the method provided some natural design interaction 'tools' with which to visualize, modify, and tune the motion characteristics. A research project at the University of Nottingham began to develop such a tool called MODUS – motion design using splines.

An initial decision was taken to develop a core motion generation module on which application modules could be built. The system requirements were identified as follows.

- Exploit the full functionality of the spline interpolation method to solve general motion specification problems.
- Provide an interactive, graphical, user-friendly interface.
- Provide 'tools' which could be used to alter the characteristics of designed motion.
- Utilize the full processing power of computer hardware.
- Guide the user towards better motion design solutions.
- Be usable by both experienced and occasional users.
- Allow links to motion design applications.
- Allow system developments and upgrading.

In order to develop these ideas it was decided to use a windows-based graphical user interface. The MODUS system was developed and implemented on a SUN 3/80 workstation in a UNIX environment. The SUN environment used SunView tools (SUN Visual/Integrated Environment for Workstations). The system uses canvasses, panels, text, and tty subwindows.

Three principal motion design 'handles' or 'tools' were identified – spline order, knot placement, constraint modification. It was envisaged that motion design cycles would usually be iterative and that skilled motion designers would move toward improved solutions by seeing the effect of changes to design parameters almost instantaneously. However, it was considered desirable from the outset to give designers helpful search tools to explore solution spaces for problems. Ultimately, it was hoped to provide interactive optimization techniques which could search automatically for better solutions.

An overview of the MODUS system is presented here. See Caulfield-Browne [1] for a more detailed discussion. Figure 21.1 shows a top level conceptual model of the system architecture. The system contains the following modules.

Data input and data file manipulation. Initial input data (i.e., a set of discrete constraints) is entered either directly by the user or is retrieved from a file. Data checks are made for consistency and validity. Allowable spline orders are displayed. Spline order is then specified. Initial knot placement may then be carried out. Allowable knot intervals may be displayed. Initial knot placement may be done interactively via the mouse and cursor (or keyboard) or an automatic choice may be made. The automatic choice always produces a valid set of knots.

Spline motion curve calculation and display. The system solves the necessary linear system of equations, via the computational spline routines provided, and obtains the coefficients of the unique spline defined by the data previously specified. The spline function and its derivatives, i.e., displacement, velocity, acceleration, and jerk, are then evaluated across the data interval. The system functionality is highly dependent on the quality of the display. Using the best available computational routines [2, 3], it has been

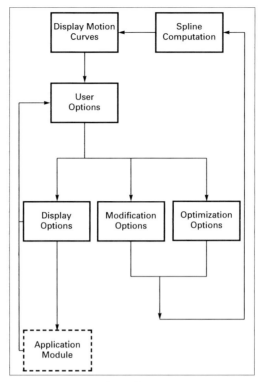

Figure 21.1   MODUS main design loop.

possible to generate high-quality displays of the motion and its characteristics, almost instantaneously. Figure 21.2 illustrates a screen schematically. In addition, it is possible to produce motion data to high precision for subsequent use in applications or application modules. The display of the motion and its characteristics uses a windows environment to allow simultaneous viewing. Four motion windows are provided and each window can accept graphical input via the mouse and cursor. A control panel in the display (top right hand in Figure 21.2) contains a host of user option buttons, some of which are described below.

User display options. There are a number of options which provide information on the current motion, e.g., current motion constraints, spline order, and current knot positions. There are also further application-specific options allowing such things as inertia torque, and radius of curvature to be computed. MODUS allows these facilities to be extended. These options are controlled through subwindows when they are requested. An option also exists to invite an application module to use the current motion or to transmit the motion to an application module.

User modification options. The main motion design tools available to the user may be described as interactive modification options. These options are a central feature of MODUS and their development in an interactive graphics environment represented a

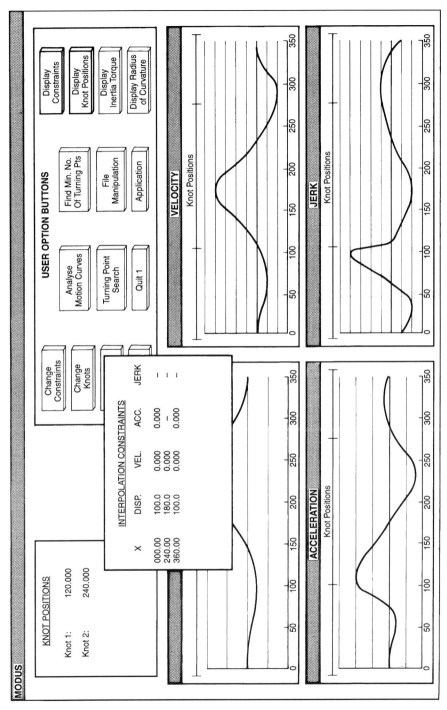

Figure 21.2 Display of defined motion parameters.

considerable achievement. The first interactive option is knot placement. The permissible interval for each knot may be highlighted in any of the motion windows. Knot movement is usually carried out by 'clicking' on the appropriate knot and 'dragging' the knot to the required position. A further 'click' indicates to the system that the desired position has been found. The system then recomputes the spline coefficients and evaluates the spline and its characteristics. Coincident knots are allowed and add to design flexibility [8]. Keyboard entry of knot positions may be selected for higher precision than the graphical display allows.

The second interactive option is spline order. Order change may be carried out graphically or via the keyboard. Order change results in a contingent change in the number of knots and hence knot positioning always follows an order change. The third interactive option is constraint modification, which again can be carried out graphically or via the keyboard. Constraint position does not affect the number of knots but may affect their positioning. The addition or deletion of a constraint results in a change in the number of knots required for a solution and hence repositioning and recomputation is necessary.

The development of these three user modification options represented a considerable achievement. When used together in an interactive and iterative design environment, they provide a very significant design aid.

User optimization options. In engineering design generally and in motion design in particular, the concept of a unique optimal solution is usually inappropriate. Most problems are highly constrained. Multiple, and sometimes conflicting, objectives occur frequently. In addition, there are usually a large number of variable parameters with nonlinear relationships. Analytical optimization is usually out of the question and numerical approaches are very difficult. The approach taken in MODUS is to provide helpful routines in searching for solutions with improved characteristics. Two analysis options are provided. One searches for the position and number of turning points in the currently defined displacement curve. A second option indicates the minimum number of turning points possible in the current displacement curve with the current constraints. This gives the user some indication of the potential 'smoothness' of the solution. A search option may be selected which searches the spline solution space for a solution which achieves the minimum number of turning points. The search is based on knot positions and is reasonably efficient for a small numbers of knots.

The application module for cam design. The first application module which has been developed is for radial plate cam design. The designer first uses the motion generation module to define a displacement/rotation diagram using actual follower lift values in the required units. A motion is then selected which satisfies the specified constraints and has desirable velocity, acceleration and higher order characteristics. Essentially, the cam application module computes the coordinates of a radial cam profile which will achieve the displacement function selected. On selection of the cam design option, the designer specifies follower type and inputs relevant cam specific data. A number of options are then possible.

The cam profile may be computed in radial or orthogonal coordinates. The cutter path coordinates, the pressure angle, and the cam curvature may also be generated.

These may be incremented to the required precision for manufacture. The data is held in a file window which may be scrolled for observation. A plot of the cam profile may be rotated on the screen for viewing. Follower type may be changed or cam follower data may be reentered. The user may utilize an option to return to the motion. The system uses best practice in the cam design area to build on the flexibility in the core module.

Figure 21.3 shows a screen from MODUS which has the four primary windows displaying the otion characteristics – displacement, velocity, acceleration, and jerk. The top left-hand subwindow shows the current data which has been specified. In the top right-hand subwindow, the option to modify a constraint has been chosen and the plate shows this being done graphically in the velocity subwindow.

Figure 21.4 shows a screen where all the options available to the user are displayed as 'buttons' in the top right-hand subwindow. The pop-up panels show the results of choosing the analysis option from the user option buttons. The position of turning points in the displacement curve and the minimum number of turning points possible with the current data set are given.

Figure 21.5 shows the beginning of a knot movement procedure where the allowable knot interval is displayed above each motion characteristic subwindow. If the knot is 'dragged' along the interval, its position is indicated numerically on the screen.

Figure 21.6 shows a screen following the selection of a cam application module. A cam type selection has been made and data relevant to that cam configuration has been supplied. The cam application module has then used the motion developed with the motion generation module to generate the cam profile displayed. The file below contains all the data needed for further analysis and manufacture. If any feature of these data is unacceptable, e.g., pressure angle or curvature, then the user may return to the underlying motion and make adjustments where appropriate.

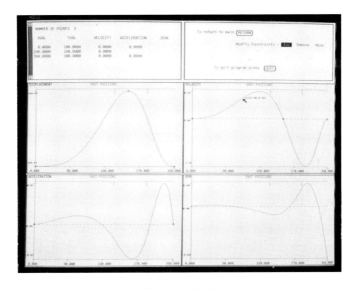

Figure 21.3

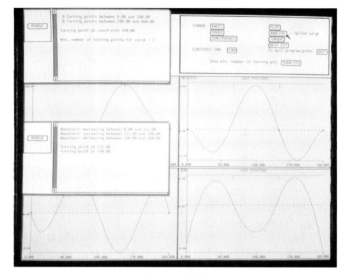

Figure 21.4

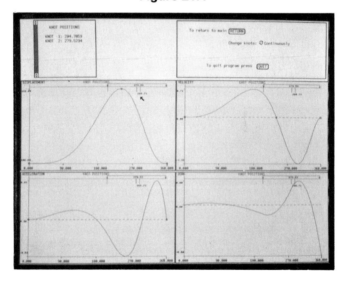

Figure 21.5

21.6   Applications of MODUS

The system has been applied successfully to a full range of theoretical, practical, experimental, and real-world problems (see Caulfield-Browne [1, Chapter 6]). An experimental investigation has evaluated the effect of the motion design handles provided in MODUS for cam design. Dynamic tests have been carried out on a set of experimental cams designed using MODUS. The cams were designed to highlight the effects of knot placement, spline order, and constraint modification. The observed

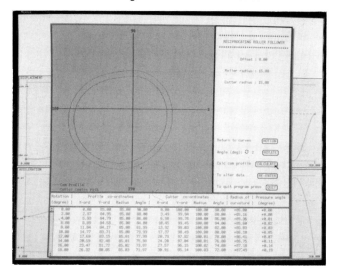

Figure 21.6

effects in experiments indicate clearly the power of the design flexibility inherent in MODUS.

MODUS makes light work of the traditional problem areas in cam design. In particular, problems with precision points, asymmetric motions, nonstandard end-conditions, and rise-and-return motions pose little difficulty. More complex problems such as incorporating periods of constant velocity are also easy to handle.

MODUS has been applied to problems in the design of high-speed textile cam mechanisms with many complex constraints. The system has been used in the design of cam-driven feeder mechanisms and spring-loaded plate cams. Improved results were obtained in comparison to traditional approaches. Recently, the system has been used to design the motion for an embroidery mechanism and a cylindrical cam-driven tool changing device on a CNC machine.

In all these cases, the benefits of using MODUS were clear:

- The ease with which complex constraints could be specified
- The speed with which design solutions could be generated
- The potential for evaluating a range of solution options for a given problem

These benefits could only be generated with a visual interactive system such as MODUS.

21.7 Conclusions, Research Issues, and Further Work

This paper has described the development of MODUS – a visual, interactive motion generation system, applicable in a range of engineering design areas. The system uses the spline function method and an overview of the theory has been presented here. The functionality of the system has been described and the applications and benefits have been highlighted. When used in an interactive and iterative manner, the system guides the user toward improved design solutions very rapidly.

The system is still a prototype. A number of problem areas still exist. It is not always possible to provide the user with a good initial solution quickly if the data is complex. Often it requires an experienced user to work with the data to move toward an acceptable solution space. It would be very beneficial to be able to achieve this automatically.

The system has highlighted a number of mathematical difficulties on the boundaries of kinematics and approximation theory [7]. These difficulties are particularly relevant to the development of optimization methods for searching solution spaces. This is the main area where future developments will lie.

Acknowledgment

This research was funded by the Electro-Mechanical Committee of EPSRC and the authors are grateful for their support.

References

[1] M. Caulfield-Browne, *The application of spline functions for kinematic design*, PhD thesis, University of Nottingham, UK, 1994.

[2] M.G. Cox, *Practical spline approximation*, NPL report DITC 1/82, 1982.

[3] C. de Boor, *A Practical Guide to Splines*, Springer, 1978

[4] P. Hollingworth, R.A. Hodges, The history and mathematical development of cam profile design in ROVER, *AutoTech 1991*, IMechE Publications C427/1, 1991.

[5] B.L. MacCarthy, N.D. Burns, An evaluation of spline functions for use in cam design, *J. Mech. Eng. Sci.*, 199(3): 239–248; 1985.

[6] B.L. MacCarthy, Quintic splines for kinematic design, *Computer-Aided Design*, 20(7): 759–765; 1988.

[7] B.L. MacCarthy, C.S. Syan, M. Caulfield-Browne, Splines in motion – an introduction to MODUS and some unresolved approximation problems, *Numerical Algorithms*, 5(1–4): 41–50; 1993.

[8] L.L. Schumacher, *Spline Functions: Basic Theory*, Wiley, 1981.

22
A Physically Based Approach to Visualizing Behavior of Flexible Mechanical Parts

Hiromasa Suzuki, Mikio Terasawa, Teruyoshi Fujiwara,
Kouji Yoshizaki, and Fumihiko Kimura

22.1   Introduction

Mechanical products often contain many parts made of flexible materials such as plastics and rubber. Their flexibility is used for realizing various functionalities of the product. The aim of this research is to develop a system to visualize kinematic motion and deformation of those flexible parts for assisting designers at an early design stage. What is particular to this early design stage is that the system must support designers in examining many design alternatives, rather than refining a single design. For this purpose, the system must be 'handy,' that is, it must have designer-friendly interface and quick response. At the same time, accuracy of the result of the analysis does not matter so much.

What will be discussed in the paper is an approach for developing such a system. The idea behind the system is that visualization is done by combination of three different models: an analysis model, a deformation mapping model, and a graphics model. The graphics model is a faceted geometric model representing the shape of a part, and is used mainly to render the part. The analysis model captures the overall physical properties of a part. One typical example of this analysis model is a beam model. When a part can be considered as a beam in static, dynamic senses, it is efficient to use the beam model by neglecting details of the part's shape. Another analysis model proposed in the paper is a simple FEM model. The motion and deformation calculated by these analysis models are applied to graphics models by deformation mapping models. The deformation mapping model is similar to FFD (free form deformation) [3].

Another concept is the scenario. If contacts between parts varies along their motion, the situation of the system of the parts changes dynamically. It is hard to deal with all the possible transitions between situations. The scenario is introduced to describe a desired sequence of motion states and events. This chapter will demonstrate some examples of the system, which include analyses of a plastic latch fastener and a locking mechanism of a ball point pen.

22.2   Modeling Scheme

In our approach, movement and deformation of an object are visualized in the scheme of a two-step mapping between the following three kinds of models as shown in Figure 22.1.

386   H. Suzuki et al.

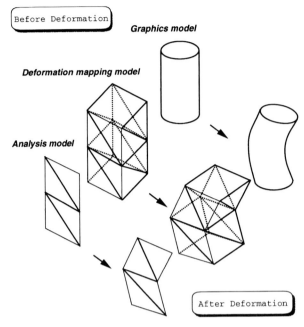

Figure 22.1   Modeling scheme.

1. Graphics model
2. Analysis model
3. Deformation mapping model

The graphics model represents the shape of an object and is used to render the object and to check collisions among objects. As is usual in computer graphics, the graphics model is a polyhedron of triangular faces. For mechanical products, a graphics model is easily generated by contemporary solid-based three-dimensional CAD systems through their capability to triangulate the faces of solid models.

An analysis model is used for computing the motion and deformation of objects. It can be an FEM (finite element method) model or a simple beam structure model. In this figure, a two-dimensional FEM model is shown.

The motion and deformation computed with the analysis model are mapped to the graphics model via the deformation mapping model. As shown in Figure 22.2, the deformation model 'surrounds' the graphics model. In other words, the shape of the graphics model, namely, the positions of the vertices, is determined by the deformation mapping model.

Advantages of this scheme are the following:

● *Motion and deformation features.* Fundamental properties of the motion and deformation of an object are determined by an analysis model. Thus, by selecting an analysis model properly, the characteristics of the motion and deformation can be obtained. For instance, if an object is a very complicated shape, but can be regarded as a beam structure as a whole, a cantilever model from the material strength theory can be used as a deformation mapping model.

• *Computational efficiency.* The independence between a graphics model and a deformation mapping model is also beneficial for the reduction of computational complexity, which is important for achieving an interactive system.

In the following sections we describe the details of deformation mapping model and two kinds of analysis models. We are particularly concerned with such mechanisms as shown in Figures 22.6 and 22.14.

22.3 Linear Deformation Mapping Model

In Figure 22.2, a kangaroo is represented as a graphics model. The wire frame that surrounds the graphic model is a deformation mapping model [4]. Displacements of the deformation mapping model are linearly mapped to those of graphics models. In Figure 22.3, let X_{j1}, X_{j2}, X_{j3} be the vertices of a face j in a deformation mapping model and x_i be the vertex i of a graphic model which is contained in a tetrahedron consisting of X_{j1}, X_{j2}, X_{j3} and the frame origin, then x_i can be expressed as

$$x_i = e_{ij1}X_{j1} + e_{ij2}X_{j2} + e_{ij3}X_{j3}$$

$$= \begin{pmatrix} x_{j1} & x_{j2} & x_{j3} \\ y_{j1} & y_{j2} & y_{j3} \\ z_{j1} & z_{j2} & z_{j3} \end{pmatrix} \begin{pmatrix} e_{ij1} \\ e_{ij2} \\ e_{ij3} \end{pmatrix}$$

$$\equiv X_j e_{ij} \tag{1}$$

where e_{ij1}, e_{ij2}, and e_{ij3} are the constants. If we calculate e_{ij} that satisfies equation (2) in advance,

Figure 22.2   Linear mapping of deformation.

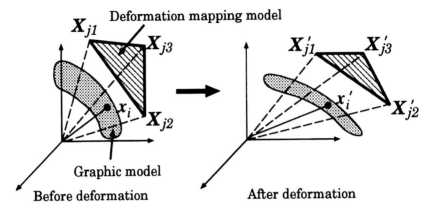

Figure 22.3   Deformation mapping scheme.

$$e_{ij} = X_j^{-1} x_i \tag{2}$$

the vertex x_i' of the graphic model corresponding to X_j' of the analysis model after deformation is given by

$$x_i' = X_j'' e_{ij} \tag{3}$$

By this linear mapping technique, the cost of dynamic analysis is reduced and the effect becomes global since the number of vertices of analysis models is less than that of graphic models. The range of deformation can be controlled by the shape of deformation mapping models.

22.4   FEM Model and Its Application

22.4.1   FEM model and deformation mapping model

The most powerful method for computing the deformation of a structure is the FEM (finite element method). It is straightforward to adopt the FEM model as an analysis model within the modeling scheme. In FEM an object to be analyzed is decomposed into a finite number of elements, each of which takes a simple shape of a triangle or a rectangle. The vertices of those elements are called *nodes*, of which displacements are computed.

In this system, FEM of two-dimensional triangular elements for the planar strain analysis is implemented, by which we can compute displacements of each of the nodes under external load and fixing constraints [2].

As shown in Figure 22.4, the deformation mapping model and this FEM model have a projective relationship. The nodes of the FEM mesh model corresponds to the vertices of the deformation mapping model in such a way that the projections of the vertices are the corresponding nodes of the FEM model. Thus the displacement of the nodes of the FEM model are directly mapped to those of the vertices of the deformation mapping model.

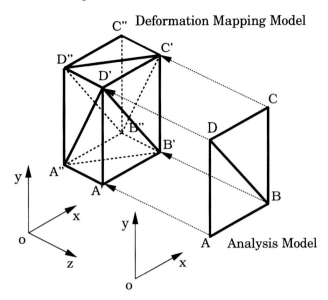

Figure 22.4 Relationship between deformation mapping model and analysis model.

The computation with FEM usually tends to be complex and time consuming, as the model becomes complex. In particular, the computation time is sensitive to the number of elements, which increases according to the complexity of the shape. However, as described above, our modeling scheme allows the use of simpler FEM models than needed in ordinary FEM analyses.

24.4.2   Computation of deformation

Let the displacement vector to be computed $u = (u_1, v_1, u_2, v_2, \ldots, u_N, v_N)^{\mathrm{T}}$ where u_i, v_i are displacements of ith node in x and y directions, respectively, and N denotes the number of nodes. In the same way, we can define an external load vector $f = (f_1, g_1, f_2, g_2, \ldots, f_N, g_N)^{\mathrm{T}}$ where f_i, g_i are external force applied to ith node in x and y directions, respectively.

Then u is given by computing the following system of linear equations:

$$K \cdot u = f \qquad (4)$$

where K is a stiffness matrix. K is constructed by summing the so-called elemental stiffness matrix k^j, $(j = 1, 2, \ldots, M)$ where M is the number of elements. The elemental stiffness matrix represents the local relationship between the forces applied to the nodes of an element and their displacements. k^j is determined with the shape and thickness of the element and also its material properties such as Young's modulus and Poisson's ratio. By adding up these small elementary stiffness matrices of all the elements, we obtain the total stiffness matrix K.

Some of the nodes are fixed to the ground. This constraint for the ith node is represented by equations of $u_i = 0$ and $v_i = 0$ and is incorporated into equation (4). A congruent gradient method is used to solve the equation.

24.4.3   Rigid element

In addition to the elastic elements, we introduce a rigid element. This rigid element is used for representing a portion of a mechanical part which is considered rigid. Such a portion can be represented by setting the material of elastic elements to be very hard; but incorporating such hard elements makes the computation unstable.

A fundamental property of the rigidity is that the distance between two arbitrary points of the material is constant. As far as the triangular element is concerned, the distances between their three nodes are kept constant during deformation.

Let us consider the rigidity constraint between nodes i and j in Figure 22.5. Let p_i, p_j be the positions of the nodes i and j, respectively. Vector r_{ij} denotes the vector from node i to node j. For two nodes before deformation, the following equation holds:

$$\|r_{ij}\|^2 = \|p_i - p_j\|^2 \tag{5}$$

where $\|\cdot\|$ is Euclidean norm.

After some deformation of the object, those nodes i and j are displaced by u_i and u_j, respectively. The distance of the vector between those two nodes r'_{ij} now becomes

$$\|r'_{ij}\|^2 = \|(p_i + u_i) - (p_j + u_j)\|^2 \tag{6}$$

From the condition of rigidity, this norm must be equal to $\|r_{ij}\|^2$ given in equation (5).

$$\|r'_{ij}\|^2 = \|r_{ij}\|^2 \tag{7}$$

By substituting the right-hand side with equation (5), we obtain

$$\|(p_i + u_i) - (p_j + u_j)\|^2 = \|r_{ij}\|^2 \tag{8}$$

$$\|p_i - p_j\|^2 + 2(p_i - p_j) \cdot (u_i - u_j) + \|u_i - u_j\|^2 = \|(p_i + u_i) - (p_j + u_j)\|^2 \tag{9}$$

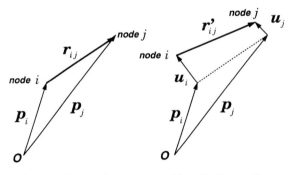

Before Deformation   **After Deformation**

Figure 22.5   Rigidity constraint.

Assuming the displacement is small enough, the second-order term of displacement can be neglected. Finally, we get a linear constraint equation of the rigidity constraint:

$$(\boldsymbol{p}_i - \boldsymbol{p}_j) \cdot (\boldsymbol{u}_i - \boldsymbol{u}_j) = \boldsymbol{r}_{ij} \cdot (\boldsymbol{u}_i - \boldsymbol{u}_j) = 0 \tag{10}$$

We can incorporate this constraint into the stiffness equation (4) and obtain the following equation. The details of this derivation are given in the Appendix.

$$R^{\mathrm{T}}KR\bar{u} = R^{\mathrm{T}}f \tag{11}$$

22.4.4   Application

The FEM analysis model described in the previous section is applied to the visualization of motion of the U-shaped snap fit shown in Figure 22.6. The snap fit consists of an elastic snap and hook. The snap moves downward, then contacts with the hook, and finally loses contact to be a resting position. They are modeled by using the FEM analysis model including both elastic and rigid elements as shown in Figure 22.7.

In Figure 22.6 some portions of the graphics model is outside the analysis model. However, the deformation mapping model automatically associates these portions to the nearest part of the analysis model.

The visualization of the motion and deformation is done by the following procedure.

1. Specify the initial and final positions of the snap. The snap is moved along the straight path between those points.
2. Calculate the movement direction and distance Δ which the snap travels in time frame Δt.
3. The snap is located at the initial position.

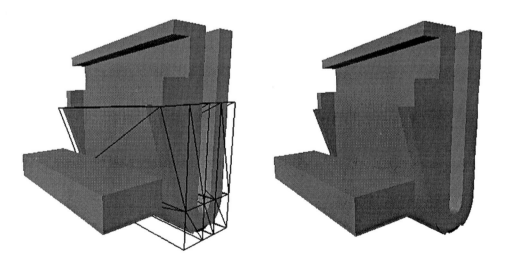

Figure 22.6   *Graphics model, deformation mapping model for U-shaped snap fit.*

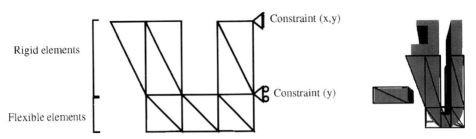

Figure 22.7 Analytic model for U-shaped snap fit.

4. Move the snap by Δ.
5. Check the intersection between the snap and hook.
6. If no intersection is detected, go to (4).
7. In case some intersections occur, the system tries to resolve them by applying contact forces to deform the parts. The problem is to find nodes to which the contact forces must be applied and their strength. This problem is discussed below.
8. Go to (4) keeping these contact forces.

The above problem is not actually solved in our current implementation. The information about elements where the intersection will occur and nodes to which the contact force must be applied is given to the system. This means that the system cannot handle unexpected intersections.

However, by assuming that the user of the system has a rough idea about how the snap moves and deforms, it could be validated that it is not terribly difficult to provide such information. We will discuss this point in terms of a scenario in the following section.

In addition to this intersection check, when the system detects the intersection it calculates the values of the contact forces to be applied. By letting Δ be a small value, the intersection is also expected to be small. Such small intersections between two triangles are classified into two cases of point–line intersection and point–point intersection as shown in Figures 22.8 and 22.9, respectively.

In case of point–line intersection, forces are applied to the nodes A, B and C in Figure 22.8. We apply f to A and $-f/2$ to B and C orthogonal to $\overline{BC}$. The amount of the force f is determined as follows. First a force f_0 large enough to separate those two parts is

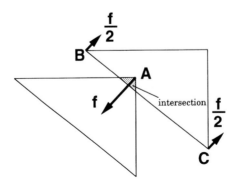

Figure 22.8 Point–line intersection.

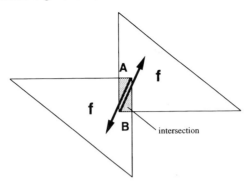

Figure 22.9   Point–point intersection.

applied. Then the contact force is searched by using a binary search method in the range [0, f_0]. In case of point–point intersection, contact forces f and $-f$ are applied to the nodes A and B in the direction of $\overline{AB}$. The magnitude of f is calculated in the same way as in the point–line case.

Figure 22.10 shows frame images selected from an animation generated by this method. At the 30th frame the contact occurs, and from the 60th to 90th frames the part deforms while keeping contact. It takes about 50 seconds to compute those 120 frames of animation with SGI IRIS/Indigo (CPU MIPS R4000).

22.5   Cantilever Model and Its Application

22.5.1   Part model

FEM models are generally used to model various kinds of deformations, while beam models are often used in design practices because of their simplicity. In this section, a cantilever model is introduced as an analysis model. Here the particular concern is a mechanical part such as shown in Figure 22.11. This mechanism has three elements 1, 2, and 3. Elements 1 and 3 are rigid, and element 2 is deformable. The deformable element 2 is represented as a cantilever beam.

The part has a coordinate frame to represent its location and position in the world coordinate frame. Each element is also associated with a local reference frame. These frames are related to each other to form a tree structure of which the root is the reference frame of the part. For instance, the motion and deformation of element 3 are described in its reference frame, and are relative to those of element 2. The deformation of the element 2 is described in its local reference frame.

22.5.2   Analysis model

The motion of a part is basically controlled by Newtonian dynamics [5]. The deformation of the element 2 is calculated as a cantilever as shown in Figure 22.12. The deformation y is given by

$$y = \frac{P}{6EI_z}(x^3 - 3l^2x + 2l^3) \tag{12}$$

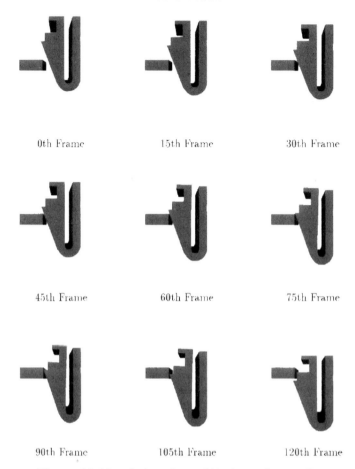

Figure 22.10   Animation of U-shaped snap fit.

where P is the load at the end, E is the Young's modulus, I_z is a momentum of inertia of area, and l is the length of the cantilever; x is a coordinate along the axis of the beam measuring from the fixed end.

The deformation mapping model is a simple prism-like structure that surrounds the cantilever. Figure 22.13 shows how the deformation mapping model in the middle is applied to bend the model in the left. The result is shown in the right figure.

The displacement value of each of the vertices of this deformation mapping model is calculated by

$$y = \frac{y_{max}}{2l^3}(x^3 - 3l^2x + 2l^3) \tag{13}$$

The vibration of the cantilever is also considered. The natural frequency of a beam with a lumped mass attached to its end is given. In case the attached mass m is of the same order of the mass m of the beam itself, the lowest natural frequency is given by

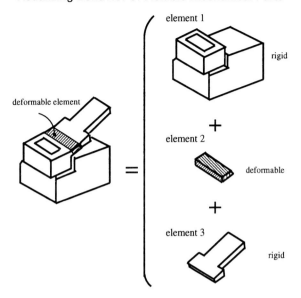

Figure 22.11   Parts and elements of modular jack.

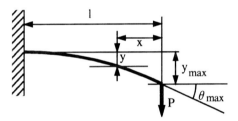

Figure 22.12   Beam model.

$$\omega = \sqrt{\frac{3EI}{(m + 0.236m_3)l^3}} \tag{14}$$

We assume that element 2 vibrates in this lowest frequency mode whenever it is excited to vibrate.

22.5.3   Motion scenario

It is not an easy task to calculate all the behavior of the mechanism from only the shapes of objects and other physical properties. In this approach, the concept of motion scenario is used [1]. Motion of a mechanism can be classified into several distinct motion states. A motion state represents a typical state of motion of objects. As shown in Figure 22.14, the latch first moves down, hits against the lock to begin deforming, then slides along the lock, and finally loses contact with the lock. Those steps are called the *motion state*, and their sequence the *motion scenario*. The

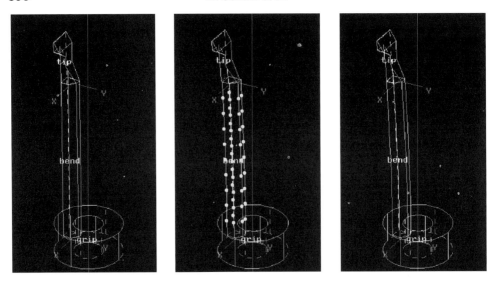

Figure 22.13 Deformation of cantilever model.

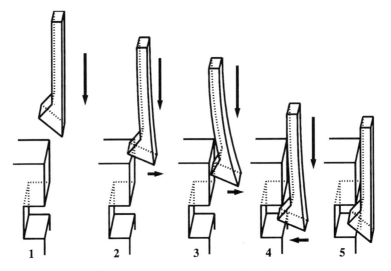

Figure 22.14 Latch mechanism.

mechanical system transfers from one state to another at the occurrence of *event*, such as collision and separation. More precisely, the motion scenario is a sequence of states and events.

Designers have an idea of how the mechanical system works and thus it is not terribly difficult to specify the motion scenario. Of course, they do not have to describe the details of the motion, such as positions and velocities, which are calculated by the analysis models. Using the motion scenario, the computation becomes much easier, since it is not necessary to consider all the possible behaviors.

A motion scenario can have a branch. For instance, if the latch moves fast and hits hard against the lock, it will jump. Then it may touch down on the lock's surface, otherwise it may jump over the lock as shown in Figure 22.15. In the event of collision, we choose succeeding motion states based on the physical conditions.

Free motion states

In this state no objects are in contact; instead they move freely, for instance, when a latch moves down as shown in Figure 22.14(1) or when it jumps as shown in Figure 22.15. The system computes its acceleration from all the external forces, such as a driving force, the gravity force, and friction forces. The deformable element 2 may vibrate.

Collision event

A collision event occurs when two separated objects intersect each other (Figure 22.14(2)). This intersection is checked with graphic models. In case of intersection, the system determines position of the contact (contact points and surface). Then it calculates impulsive momentum. The momentum is assumed to apply in the normal direction of the collision surface. This momentum may generate the velocity for the latch so that it moves apart from the lock. Following this event, the mechanism goes into a *jump* motion state.

Jump motion state and convergence event

This motion state after the collision event represents the situation in which two objects move apart with some relative velocity. This motion state lasts for an infinitesimal amount of time.

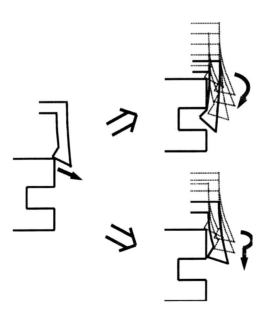

Figure 22.15   Branching of motion states.

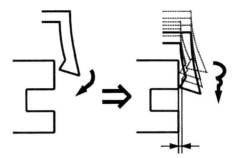

Figure 22.16   Convergence event.

As shown in Figure 22.16, if this velocity is small, and if an elastic restoration force generates the acceleration in the direction opposite to the velocity, the object may experience collision again after a small amount of time. In this manner, the mechanism may repeat jumping and colliding, and under some condition converges to the stable state. Then the convergence event occurs. After this event the mechanism goes into a contact motion state, or immediately into a stay state via a stop event.

Contact motion state and separation event

In the contact motion state the two parts slide while keeping their contact under the elastic force of the deformation element. The contact motion state lasts as far as the contact point lies on the contact surface. In this state, contact forces at the contact point and their friction forces are calculated. Elastic restoration forces from the cantilever are also taken into consideration.

The contact motion state ends when the contact point moves out of the contact surface. This is dealt with as a *separation* event. The mechanism transfers into the free motion state.

Stop event and stay motion state

If forces to the part are balanced and its velocity is zero, the stop event occurs. The system goes into a stay motion state.

22.5.4   Application

Figure 22.17 shows a mechanism which functions to lock the tip of a ball point pen. As the head of the pen is pushed, the tip projects out of the body. This mechanism locks the tip. By pushing the head again, the tip is unlocked and returns back to the original position. This tricky mechanism is realized by the elastic cantilever contacting with the groove as shown in the figure.

Based on the above concepts, a prototype system is developed to handle a cantilever model and motion scenario. A difference from the example in section 22.4 is that the cantilever model has the deformation in two different directions. A motion scenario is described and animations are generated as shown in Figures 22.18a, b, and c. Figure 22.18a shows a process to push out and lock the tip of the ball point pen, while Figure 22.18b shows the process to restore it into the body of the pen.

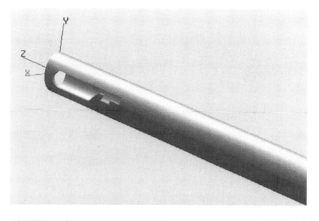

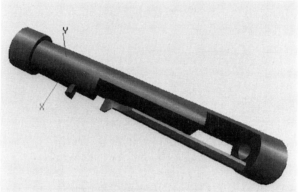

Figure 22.17 Graphics model.

Figure 22.18c shows a case where the pushing force is so large that the tip is not properly locked.

22.6 Conclusion

A method for visualizing the motion and deformation of flexible parts in a mechanism is proposed. The method is based on a mapping framework and the concept of *scenario*. Brief experience with this method persuades us that even a physically simple analysis is useful for designers to gain better understanding of their conceptual designs. It is considered that the system is a visualization system rather than a full simulation system, in the sense that it does not compute physical behavior that is completely accurate.

Future work includes development of more sound theories and algorithms for modeling motion and deformation of flexible objects in contact states. We are also developing a general scenario management system for handling motion states and events.

H. Suzuki et al.

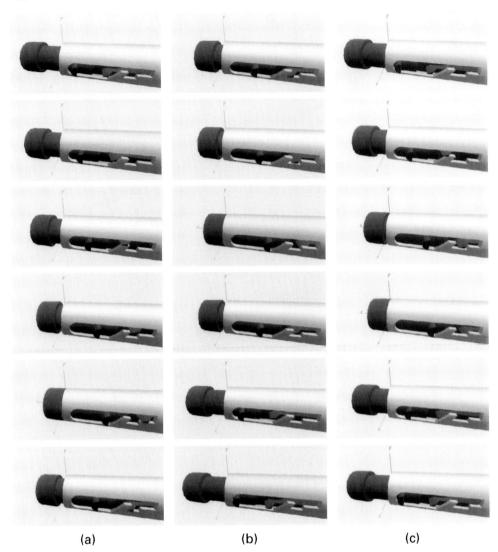

(a)   (b)   (c)

Figure 22.18 (a) Push out and lock the tip. (b) Restore the tip. (c) Failure to lock the tip.

Acknowledgment

The authors would like to thank Mr. Bryan Moser for his valuable comments.

References

[1] Devendra Kalra, Alan H. Barr, Modeling with time and events in computer animation, *EUROGRAPHICS '92*, 11: C45–C58; 1992.

[2] H. Mori (in Japanese), *FEM in C Language*, Morikita Publishers, 1989.
[3] Thomas W. Sederberg, Scott R. Perry, Free-form deformation of solid geometric models, *ACM Computer Graphics*, 20(4): 151–160; 1986.
[4] Mikio Terasawa, Fumihiko Kimura, Collision response for deformable models based on Hertz's contact theory, *J. Visualization and Computer Animation*, 5: 209–224; 1995.
[5] J. Wilhelms, Dynamics for everyone, *IEEE Computer Graphics Appl.*, 7(6); 1987.

Appendix

By defining the elements of r_{ij}, u_i, u_j as $\mathbf{r}_{ij} = (r_x, r_y)$, $\mathbf{u}_i = (u_{xi}, u_{iy})$, $\mathbf{u}_j = (u_{jx}, u_{jy})$, and substituting equation (10), the following equation is obtained:

$$r_x(u_{ix} - u_{jx}) + r_y(u_{iy} - u_{jy}) = 0 \tag{15}$$

A new parameter $\bar{u}_{ix}$ is now introduced to represent the left hand side of this equation:

$$\bar{u}_{ix} = r_x u_{ix} - r_x u_{jx} + r_y u_{iy} - r_y u_{jy} \quad (= 0) \tag{16}$$

Then solve this equation for u_{ix}:

$$u_{ix} = \frac{1}{r_x}\bar{u}_{ix} + u_{jx} - \frac{r_y}{r_x}u_{iy} + \frac{r_y}{r_x}u_{jy} \tag{17}$$

This equation can be represented as a matrix form:

$$
\begin{pmatrix}
u_{1x} \\ u_{1y} \\ \vdots \\ u_{ix} \\ \vdots \\ u_{Nx} \\ u_{Ny}
\end{pmatrix}
=
\begin{pmatrix}
1 & & & & & & \\
& \ddots & & & & 0 & \\
& & \ddots & & & & \\
\cdots & & \frac{1}{r_x} & 1 & 0 & -\frac{r_y}{r_x} & \frac{r_y}{r_x} & \cdots \\
& & & & \ddots & & \\
& 0 & & & & \ddots & \\
& & & & & & 1
\end{pmatrix}
\begin{pmatrix}
u_1 \\ u_2 \\ \vdots \\ \bar{u}_{ix} \\ \vdots \\ u_{Nx} \\ u_{Ny}
\end{pmatrix}
\tag{18}
$$

Using the same procedure for other u_{ix} and u_{iy} which are constrained by rigidity constraints, we obtain

$$u = R\bar{u} \tag{19}$$

where R is sum of matrices in the form of equation (18). This is a matrix which transforms displacement vector constrained by the rigidity constraint, $\bar{u}$, to u.

Substituting equation (19) into equation (4), we obtain

$$KR\bar{u} = f \qquad (20)$$

Multiplying by R^{T}, the coefficient matrix becomes symmetric. The result is equation (11):

$$R^{\mathrm{T}}KR\bar{u} = R^{\mathrm{T}}f \qquad (21)$$

By solving this equation under the condition $\bar{u}_{ix} = 0$ in equation (16), we obtain $\bar{u}$. Then we get u by equation (19).

23
Visualizing and Animating Implicit and Solid Models

Brian Wyvill and Kees van Overveld

23.1   Introduction

Interest has grown since the early 1980s in the idea of using an isosurface in a scalar field as a modeling technique. In the work described here *skeletal implicit surfaces* are used as a viable method for building models. A skeleton is composed of a number of geometrical skeletal elements such as points and lines. A scalar (or potential) field is manufactured by summing contributions from the fields defined around each skeletal element. Jim Blinn introduced the idea of modeling with isosurfaces as a side effect of a visualization of electron density fields [1]. Such models have various desirable properties including the ability to blend with their close neighbors. These models have been given a variety of names, in particular: *Blobby Molecules* (Blinn), *Soft Objects* (Wyvill) [23] and *MetaBalls* (Nishimura) [17]. Jules Bloomenthal pointed out that these models could be grouped under the more general heading of *implicit surfaces*, defined as the point set $F(P) = 0$ [2].

Figure 23.1   BCSO concert grand piano.

Visualization and Modeling
ISBN 0-12-227738-4

Implicit surface modeling techniques are now beginning to penetrate the animation industry. Several examples in commercial animation exist, including at least one commercial system (the MetaEditor – Meta Corporation), an interactive editor which uses metaballs.

Another technique for defining complex geometric objects composed from more elementary geometric primitives is constructive solid geometry (CSG; [12, 19]). The application fields of the two methods appears to be quite different. Implicit surface models (ISM) have been used mainly for the description of cartoon-like models, whereas CSG has been used by the engineering industry and often applied where an object has to be manufactured using numerically controlled machining.

Our own modeling and animation system (*GraphicsLand*) combines both of these modeling techniques in a manner that exploits their advantages. A system that combines CSG and implicit surface objects was also developed by Geoff Wyvill [26], using ray tracing to both traverse the CSG tree and render the objects. In this work our approach is quite different in that we do not use ray tracing; instead we have developed a polygonizing algorithm to facilitate prototyping and interactive editing and improve the design cycle of such objects.

Some CSG systems use algebraic functions to define blends between primitives (e.g. SvLis [4]) which also provides a polygonizer for visualizing of the models (see [21]). However, our system is rather different in the way that models are defined.

Combining ISM and CSG modeling results in a surface definition which we refer to as *Boolean compound soft object*, or BCSO for short) which consists of a Boolean expression with union, intersection, and set difference operators. The geometric primitives that form the operands are *soft objects* bounded by the isosurfaces resulting from suitable potential fields. These potential fields are parametrized by configurations of so-called *skeletal elements*. The resulting system, unlike most CSG systems, combines blended and unblended primitives. In this chapter attention is focused on some new animation methods developed for use with these BCSO objects. Following this introduction, the paper is organized as follows; section 23.2 provides an overview of implicit modeling techniques, section 23.3 with rendering and section 23.4 with animation.

23.2   Skeletal Implicit Surface Models (ISMs)

The basic idea is that a model can be built from a primitive skeleton by combining elements such as points, lines, polygons, circles, and splines. A surface representing a blended offset from the skeletal elements is calculated and visualized. The skeletal elements are linked hierarchically. In animation, at each frame an implicit surface encloses the skeleton calculated using the techniques described in [3], allowing the model to change shape over time. In general, any three-dimensional object can be a part of the skeleton, as long as it is possible to determine the distance from a given point in space to the object. Skeletons are useful for several reasons:

- Skeletons provide intuitive representation for many natural objects.
- Skeletons themselves are easily manipulated and displayed.
- Skeletons provide a more concise representation than parametric surfaces.

The skeleton is surrounded by a scalar field $F_{total}(P)$ (equation 1). The intensity of the field being the highest on the skeleton, and decreasing with distance from the skeleton. The function $F_{total}(P)$ relates the field value (intensity) to distance from the skeleton has an impact on the shape of the surface, and determines how separate surfaces blend together (see [9]). The surface is defined by the set of points in space for which the intensity of the field has some chosen constant value (or isovalue, thus the name *isosurface*). Fields from the individual elements of the skeleton are added to find the potential at some chosen point (values can be negative or positive). The value at some point in space is calculated as follows:

$$F_{total}(P) = \sum_{i=1}^{i=n} c_i F_i(r_i) \tag{1}$$

where P is a point in space
$F_{total}(P)$ is the value of the field at P
n is the number of skeletal elements
c_i is a scalar value (a weight which can be a positive or negative)
F_i is the blending function of the ith element
r_i is the distance from P to the nearest point Q_i on the ith element.

The evaluation of $F_{total}(P)$ has two steps. The first step involves finding the nearest point Q_i on the skeletal element to the given query point P and calculating the distance between them. This procedure depends on the geometry of the skeletal element and can be very simple (trivial in the case of a point skeleton), or quite complex in the case of spline curves and patches, when an iterative or numerical method is necessary. The second step involves evaluation of the blending function, which may be modified by noise or other perturbation functions as described in [9]. The shape of the surface is controlled by applying local or global transformations, such as scaling, translation, and rotation, to the elements of the skeleton, by changing the blending functions or any of the parameters decribed in equation (1).

23.3   Rendering

CSG and implicit surface systems are similar in that the underlying model description has to be visualized. There are two basic approaches for each type of representation:

- For CSG systems, find a boundary representation (b-rep) and render the model as boundary fragments (mostly converted to polygon meshes); alternatively, the object may be ray traced while the CSG expression evaluation takes place for each ray while being traced [8].
- An implicit isosurface, once polygonized, is just a polygon mesh that can be rendered as it stands. Alternatively, it may be rendered directly via ray tracing. Although this is often too computationally expensive for many applications, it has been demonstrated that CSG-type Boolean combinations of several isosurfaces can be obtained by evaluating the Boolean expressions along with the ray intersections in a manner similar to standard CSG [26].

Skeletal implicit surfaces are defined by *black box functions* which, given a point, provide a value and, in the case of points on the surface, a surface normal. These surfaces can be visualized by ray tracing, finding the ray surface intersection by one of a number of numerical techniques. A good survey of these techniques is given in [28]. A popular method of rendering implicit surfaces is to first convert the surface to a polygonal approximation. A survey of methods of doing this *polygonization* is detailed in [16]. In an interactive environment, the surface must be visualized as fast as possible, to keep up with changes to a model entered interactively by the user. An additional advantage of the polygonization approach is the availability of a full 3D approximation of the implicit surface which allows for fast viewing from arbitrary directions.

Most currently existing techniques for the polygonization of implicit surfaces are based on data structures that allow spatial indexing: either a voxel-based structure [2] or the hash-table structure of [23] may be used. Some inherent disadvantages of these data structures exist. Firstly, the data structure comprises a partitioning of the space rather than a tesselation of the surfaces to be polygonized. Especially in the case of animation (e.g., in the computer animation *The Great Train Rubbery* [24]), this is likely to cause geometric artifacts that are fixed with respect to space, thus moving in an incoherent way over every moving surface.

Second, there is an apparent mismatch between the number of triangles that is generated by these algorithms and the complexity of the surface that is approximated: even relatively smooth and flat segments of an implicit surface usually result in large numbers of facets. Bloomenthal [2] uses an adaptive version of the spatial indexing data structures, an octree, in order to reduce the number of polygons produced in tesselating an implicit surface. This indeed reduces the number of polygons generated, but full advantage of large cells can only be taken if the flat regions of the surface happen to fall entirely within the appropriate octants. The algorithm proves in practice to be considerably slower than the uniform voxel algorithm of [23], and is complicated to implement. There are many problems to solve, including avoiding the introduction of cracks in the surface where a subdivided region is adjacent to a less subdivided region.

A new, fast, adaptive algorithm called *ShrinkWrap*, was offered by Overveld [18]. Earlier algorithms approximate the surface by a discrete set of samples plus some connecting topology; the interpretation of the value of this curvature in the sampled points is not at all clear. For instance, the surface may be highly curved between two adjacent sample vertices, but if it happens to be flat in these vertices we will not know and the tesselation is likely to miss this curved feature. In the ShrinkWrap algorithm the tesselation consists of a mesh of triangles, but the error analysis takes place on the edges of the triangles (the chords) rather than on the triangles themselves. Chords are considered as approximations of segments of curves in the implicit surface. The algorithm is limited to single manifolds and intially approximates the surface with a tetrahedron. The chords forming the sides of the triangles are compared against a Lipschitz based set of criteria to decide whether or not to subdivide the triangle. The Lipschitz criterion bounds the variation of the derivative of a function between neighbor points in the domain of that function (see also [10]). If a chord is split, the new midpoint is then forced onto the surface by an iterative method. For further examples and details of the algorithm see Overveld [18].

23.4   BCSO Models

Boolean compound soft objects use black box primitives, or skeletal elements. The primitives available in our system along with the defining geometry in parentheses are listed below.

- Sphere (point)
- Cylinder with hemispherical ends (line segment and radius)
- Cone with hemispherical ends (line segment and two radii)
- Ellipsoid (three orthogonal vectors)
- Torus (point, two radii and normal vector)
- Polygon (point list and normal vector)
- Plane (point and normal vector)
- Bezier curve (control points and normal vector)

The last two of these primitives are infinite in extent and in our system only closed manifold surfaces can be polygonized, thus they can only be visualized after the appropriate CSG operation. The above primitives are found to be very useful; however, a virtually unlimited set of primitives could be defined.

These primitives are assembled firstly into blended groups or *gangs*. The skeletal elements within one ISM gang become a CSG primitive. There are no visible non-C^1 junctions within those elements. On the other hand, two ISM primitives are combined in the CSG sense, and hence a visible junction arises there. So both types of junctions are supported within one surface representation scheme. When ray tracing is employed for ISMs, CSG-type operations can be performed on-the-fly where the operands are individual ISMs [26], but ray tracing is computationally expensive. On the other hand, when all ISMs are polygonized first, then CSG-type operations can be performed afterward on the resulting polygon meshes [15], since they are closed manifolds, but this has a high complexity in terms of the number of triangles in the meshes involved: the fully triangulated meshes of all input ISMs have to be available, even if a given ISM only contributes for a small fraction of its surface. Also, this strategy cannot be used if one of the participating CSG-primitives (ISMs) is unbounded, as for instance when intersecting with a planar half-space in order to 'cut an object in half.' In our proposal of BCSOs we perform the CSG operations on-the-fly while polygonizing the *resulting* surface. This means that the complexity is linear in the number of triangles of the resulting surface only, even if some of the contributing ISMs would have given rise to much larger triangular meshes.

If the resulting BCSO is used for further manipulations that require a parametrized representation, the number of triangles can be reduced using resampling [20], and next the use of, e.g., *Loop patches* [11], so if need be, ISMs can serve in a CAGD context. BCSOs serve as an extension of the variety of shapes that may be modeled with plain ISMs, so they may be applied in the same areas.

An example of a BCSO object is shown in Figure 23.2. The spokes are ISM cones blended with each other and the outer torus. A second torus has been subtracted to make the wheel flange. Two planes intersect with the wheel to flatten the sides and a third torus is subtracted to make a circular groove. Finally two planes are intersected and subtracted from the wheel to show details of the blended and nonblended shapes.

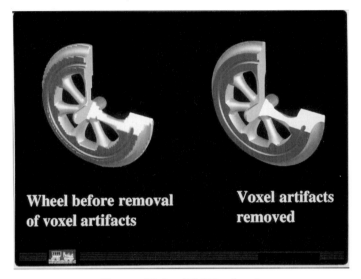

Figure 23.2   BSCO wheel.

23.4.1   Polygonizing a BCSO surface

Although it is possible to render BCSO surfaces with existing ray tracing techniques, it is essential to have a method for producing a polygonal surface approximation for prototyping and interaction when designing models.

Given a scalar field function $f = f(x, y, z)$, the Uniform voxel Subdivision Algorithm of [23] estimates intersections of the isosurface $\{(x, y, z) \,|\, f(x, y, z) = 0\}$, to be polygonized, with the 12 edges of a cubic voxel, on the basis of the $f(x_c, y_c, z_c)$ values, $c = 0, \ldots, 7$, in the 8 corner vertices (x_c, y_c, z_c) of that voxel (see Figure 23.3).

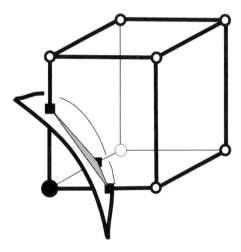

Figure 23.3   A cubic voxel intersected by an isosurface.

Here, the front lower left corner vertex (solid circle) has $f > 0$ whereas the other corner vertices (open circles) have $f < 0$. A vertex with $f > 0$ classifies 'in' with respect to the isosurface and a vertex with $f < 0$ classifies 'out'. In the case where an intersection of that edge with the isosurface exists, the extreme vertices of a voxel edge are classified differently. Cases where an edge contains one intersection are indistinguishable from cases where there are any odd number of intersections. Similarly, the occurrence of an even number of intersections goes unnoticed.

The intersection points (solid squares) are estimated by interpolation of the values of f in the corner vertices. In our implementation the user can choose between fast linear interpolation or a slower, more accurate numerical method such as *regula falsi*. The shaded triangle in Figure 23.3 is the mesh element that originates from this voxel. Any intersections found are connected by piecewise planar surface elements (triangles), and the collection of all these triangles forms the triangulated polygon mesh that approximates the isosurface.

In order to generalize towards CSG expressions in isosurfaces, we assume that instead of a scalar function $f(x, y, z)$, we have an n-component vector function $f_j(x, y, z)$, $j = 0, \ldots, n - 1$. Each of the components f_j constituting a *gang*, a group of blended ISM primitives, gives rise to its own isosurface; each isosurface can be seen as the boundary of one gang (CSG primitive).

To see how this works out, we study a 2D version first (see Figure 23.4). Here C_1 and C_2 are two isovalue contours that both intersect voxel edge A–B. They give rise to (estimated) intersections p_1 and p_2, respectively. Suppose C_1 is the boundary of ISM primitive 1 whereas C_2 bounds ISM primitive 2, and we want to polygonize the boundary of the object $DIFF(1, 2)$. It can be seen from Figure 23.4 that p_2 is the relevant intersection of the two. In the discussion that follows, the CSG operations are denoted as *DIFF*, *UNION*, and *INTSCT*, for difference, union, and intersection, respectively. The arguments of these operators will be either numbers of ISM primitives (the above j) or other CSG operations.

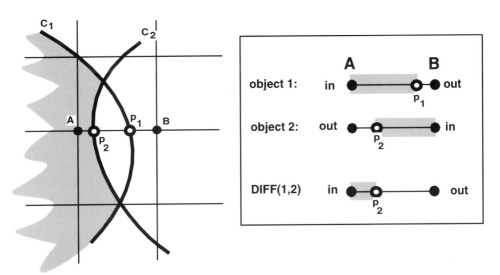

Figure 23.4 CSG operations on ISM gangs.

In general, we observe that depending on the in- or out-classifications of each of the components f_j in A and B we can determine, for each of the operators *DIFF*, *UNION*, *INTSCT*, which of the intersections is the relevant one. Note that there does not always have to be a relevant intersection: If the resulting BCSO isosurface does not pass through the edge AB, the 'relevant intersection' is not defined. We only consider intersections between two CSG primitives in a voxel, so the number of cases to be considered is limited and can be implemented via a table (see [29]). The table has 16 entries corresponding to the 16 possible combinations of edge vertices A and B being inside one of the two surfaces that intersect in this voxel. For example for Figure 23.4 A is inside the gang whose surface is given by C_1 and outside C_2. B is inside C_2 and outside C_1. Two intersections are possible and for the *DIFF* operator the correct intersection is P_2, which can be found from the table as the minimum of P_1 and P_2. In this case the table would give no intersection for either *UNION* or *INTSCT*.

The algorithm proceeds by first building the voxels with the appropriate vector of field values at each vertex. Each gang is identified in the vector by a unique number. The Boolean expression is parsed in the usual way and a CSG binary tree is built as indicated in the CSG tree diagram in Figure 23.9. The tree is traversed and the appropriate intersection is found and a triangular mesh is built.

23.4.2   CSG and ISM junctions

Junctions in the boundary between surface fragments of different CSG primitives are generally not C^1. It requires special primitives to obtain smooth blends [14, 22]. Alternatively, filleting and rounding operations may apply to the boundary representation of the CSG object [5]. The implicit functions used in ISM that give rise to the resultant isosurface are in general differentiable everywhere in 3-space, so the surface is smooth everywhere. Since there is no notion of explicitly represented junctions in ISM, it is not possible to get non-C^1 boundaries anywhere (see, however, [6]).

Although the algorithm described in section 23.4.1 gives an adequate and consistent polygonization for the smooth parts of the resulting BCSO surface, the non-C^1 junctions are reproduced poorly. This is due to the fact that the voxel structure that underlies our polygonization algorithm has a uniform distribution, which is adequate under the assumption that for smooth surfaces the curvature of the polygonized surface is distributed more or less uniformly over space. (In fact, it can be rather wasteful in areas of large curvature radii. Adaptive polygonization techniques (see, e.g., [2, 22]) should be used to make this more efficient, but we do not focus on adaptive techniques here.) The 'smoothness'-assumption does *not* hold, however, in the vicinity of the non-C^1 junctions, and therefore severe voxelization artifacts may show up in these areas.

Unlike implicit blends, CSG operations should result in sharp contours between primitives. Again we first study the problem in 2D. Consider Figure 23.5. Here we have again the configuration that two isovalue contours, C_1 and C_2 intersect. The intersection point is $x = (x, y, z)$, but this is of course a priori unknown and we should try to find an approximation to it. Suppose that the CSG expression is *DIFF*(2, 1) where the interior region associated with curve C_1 is on the left of C_1 and the interior region associated with C_2 is on the right of C_2. Then the two relevant intersections between the resulting contour and the voxel edges are found to be p_1 and p_2,

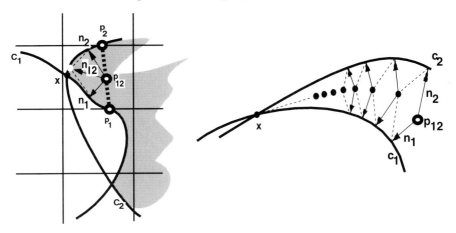

Figure 23.5 Approximating the intersection of two implicit contours. Left: p_{12} is a first guess. Right: iterating to get a more accurate approximation of x.

respectively. The contour is calculated from these intersection points, we would obtain the dashed line $p_1 p_2$ as a segment of the contour. Since this is quite far from the actual intersection point, the non-C^1 junction is not very well reproduced. Instead we observe that we should find an estimate for x such that $f_1(x) = f_2(x) = 0$ where f_1 and f_2 are the scalar field functions for the two ISM primitives with contours C_1 and C_2, respectively. Assuming we have a starting point which is not too far off, an iterative numeric technique has been implemented which produces a better intersection point combined with a splitting scheme to produce smaller triangles to describe such junctions. Details of this are given in [29].

23.4.3   Building the piano

An example of a more sophisticated BCSO object is shown in Figure 23.1. The piano is made from the primitives mentioned above except that the main body uses a curved half space defined by a parametric curve. A piecewise planar parametric cubic curve is defined along with an *up* direction and a normal in the plane of the curve which points toward the positive side of the primitive. The curve is extruded in the *up* direction, for example, to form the curved side of the piano case. To extend the extruded piecewise curve so that it forms a half-space, a planar extension is added at each end. Each plane has the same *up* as the curve and is defined by the last or first two control points along the curve. The piano was designed using the polygonizer to prototype the model; it is a scale model of a 9-foot Steinway concert grand. Figure 23.6 shows a diagrammatic representation of a 2D slice through the primitives that make up the piano body including the parametric curve. Two large cylinders form the basis for the piano and the curve is subtracted to form the body. A smaller version of the body was also built and subtracted from the outer body to give the side walls. The piano demonstrates blended primitives as in the piano legs and pedals, and nonblended as in the keyboard. The plant in Figure 23.1 is not a BCSO model but is defined by an L-System designed by Dr Przemek Prusinkiwicz and Mark Hammel at the University of Calgary.

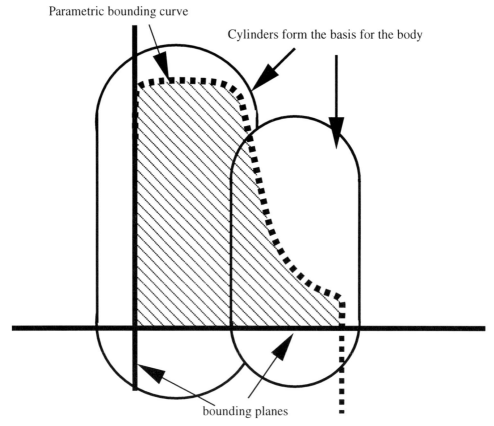

Figure 23.6   Diagrammatic representation of CSG objects for piano body.

23.5 Metamorphosis

Implicit surface models have proved to be very useful for animating characters whose shape changes over time. Various techniques have been described, for example:

- Path following
- Negative primitives
- Metamorphosis
- Collision detection
- Warping

The first three of these techniques are detailed in [28], the fourth in [6] and the fifth in [27]. Adding CSG operations to our system introduces a number of problems. In this work we have currently looked at one of the most interesting of these, that is, extending the metamorphosis algorithms described in [25]. The problem is that, given a source model and a destination model, an automatic way has to be found for manufacturing a series of inbetween models that best suggest a smooth transition from source to destination. This has previously been addressed using the following techniques:

- Hierarchical matching
- Surface inbetweening (SIN)
- Cellular inbetweening (CIS)
- Fourier volume morphing

Typically, each model will consist of a number of primitives and the problem will be to decide how each primitive of each of the source and destination models is to be interpolated. In our system models are stored as a hierarchy, in fact a graph structure that includes recursive cycles (see [13]).

The SIN technique makes no assumptions about matching; a weight is applied to each primitive, the value of c_i in equation (1). The weights on the source primitives are varied from 1 down to 0 over the time for the metamorphosis. This causes the isosurface representing the source object to shrink around each primitive. At the same time the weight for the destination primitive is increased, also as a function of time, from 0 to 1. Typically, the functions used are for the source $w_s = \sin(t)$ and for the destination $w_d = \cos(t)$.

Cellular matching is used in conjunction with the other techniques. Objects may occupy different volumes of space. The bounds of the source and destination objects are found and the space is subdivided into a number of cubic voxels. The number of these voxels in each dimension is the same for source and destination, but the size of a voxel depends on the bounds. The primitives from each object are sorted into the appropriate voxel. They are then interpolated either by changing the attributes of like primitives, or using the weighting functions of the surface inbetweening technique mentioned above.

Another technique which used surface inbetweening as its base was introduced by John Hughes [7], who observed that implicit objects are represented by a field of values which could be treated as a 3D signal and Fourier transformed into the frequency domain. The inbetween models are interpolated in this domain and the intermediate model is then inverse Fourier transformed back to the spatial domain.

23.6 BCSO Metamorphosis

The techniques in the previous section depend largely on the primitives contributing toward a global field. Thus the same techniques can in general be applied to BCSO objects. There are two major problems: Firstly, ISM primitives do not include infinite half-spaces such as a plane, whereas BCSO models do. If no infinite half-space primitives were included, matching primitives for source and destination models could be described, except that each object could potentialy use a different CSG expression, which is the second problem.

23.6.1 Using SIN

If BCSO objects do not contain infinite half-spaces, they can be dealt with quite adequately with existing techniques. Figure 23.7 shows some frames from a sample animation. The source object is a BCSO ellipsoid. The destination object consists of a similar ellipsoid and has a cylinder (the ISM version of a cylinder is not infinite but has

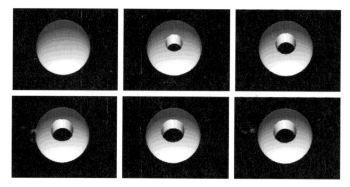

Figure 23.7   Cylinders of increasing weight subtracted from an ellipsoid.

hemispherical ends) removed from the ellipsoid. This can be achieved by introducing a zero-weighted cylinder as part of the source object and using the Boolean expression from the destination object. The weight of the second cylinder is increased over time; the difference operation does not affect the source object in the first frame as the cylinder is initially zero weighted.

23.6.2   Moving planes

Figure 23.8A shows a half space plane intersected with a sphere. The SIN heuristic would gradually increase the weight on the destination object from 0 to 1 while decreasing the weight on the source object. This method cannot be used in this case. The plane primitive is surrounded by a field which has the contour value on one side and zero on the other, essentially the plane is either present or not and cannot be weighted to bring it gradually into effect as can the other primitives. The plane can, however, be moved to a position where it has no effect i.e. outside the display contour of the source object and suitably matched to the destination object. The position of the plane can then be interpolated at each frame. In the example given the effect will be to gradually cut the sphere as in 23.8A. A gang (blended group of ISM primitives) has two iso-values (contours) associated with it, the inner contour which forms the surface of the model and the zero contour, beyond which the gang has no contribution to the field. The plane should be moved that its initial position is outside the inner contour for the entire gang.

In general the plane to be moved could be deeply nested in the CSG tree. The plane must be moved if it is part of an object consisting of other planes this group may at some point higher in the tree be intersected (or differenced) with some non-half-space primitives. To calculate where the plane must be moved to, it is necessary to list all the gangs which have this relationship with the subject plane. Consider the following example.

In Figure 23.9 there are two spheres in gang 0 which blend together. Planes of gangs 1,2,3 are defined to be parallel to each of the major axes, and are intersected to form a corner which is subtracted from gang 0. Plane 4 is subtracted from the resulting object as shown in the CSG tree diagram in Figure 23.9.

The algorithm used for finding a list of gangs which have to be considered before moving the plane is as follows:

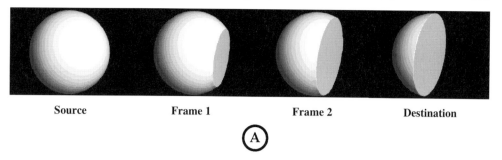

Source   Frame 1   Frame 2   Destination

(A)

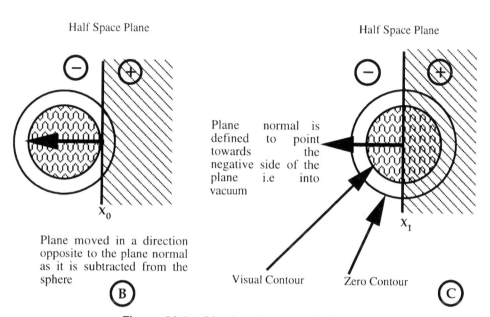

Half Space Plane   Half Space Plane

Plane normal is defined to point towards the negative side of the plane i.e into vacuum

X_0

Plane moved in a direction opposite to the plane normal as it is subtracted from the sphere

(B)

X_1

Visual Contour   Zero Contour

(C)

Figure 23.8   Moving planes technique.

```
1. Traverse the tree to find the plane we are looking.
   set current node to this node, set a flag to indicate
   that this node has been visited.
2. While the current node is not the root
   begin
     set current node = parent of current node
     if this node is 'u' continue to go up
     if the type is 'i' or 'd'
       begin
         visit right or left child that has not been visited.
         (i.e., the sibling of the node previously just visited)
         traverse the subtree adding all nonplane primitives to the list.
         if the list is not empty exit
       end
   end
end
```

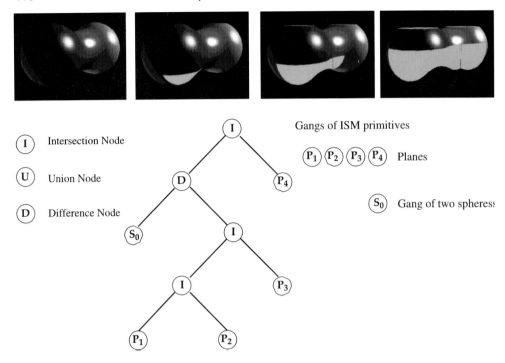

Figure 23.9   Moving planes nested in the CSG tree.

```
3. Return the list of gangs
   if the list is empty the plane can be ignored.
```

We get a list of all the soft primitives that are intersected or differenced with the plane in question. In our experience it has not been common to use union operations with infinite planes. At some point the object has to be bounded otherwise it cannot be rendered in our system; currently the system does not search for gang members that are unioned with the subject plane.

As a further example, the wheel of the train used in the 1986 animation *The Great Train Rubbery* [24], is shown in Figure 23.10 as the source object. The destination object is the wheel of Figure 23.2.

Conclusions

Some techniques for modeling, rendering, and animating implicit surfaces have been presented. Attention has been focused on combined ISM/CSG techniques to produce BCSO models. A new algorithm for metamorphosis has been presented which allows two BCSO models to be interpolated.

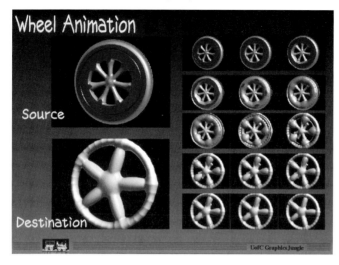

Figure 23.10   Sample frames from morph between ew and old wheel.

Acknowledgments

I thank the many students who have contributed so greatly to this research. I also thank Kees van Overveld, who is my coworker in developing the *ShrinkWrap* and *Breakfast* algorithms and the work on the BCSO polygonizer. Thanks also to Jules Bloomenthal for his encouragement and ideas over the years. I am particularly in debt to my brother, friend, and colleague, Geoff Wyvill, who started the whole thing off by solving a problem in scientific visualization, the solution to which turned out to be so useful for building models. Thanks also to the Banff Centre for Fine Arts for letting me take accurate measurements of *Camille*, a Hamburg Steinway concert grand piano.

This work is partially supported by the Natural Sciences and Engineering Research Council of Canada in the form of a research grant and equipment grants.

References

[1] James Blinn, A generalization of algebraic surface drawing, *ACM Trans. Graphics*, 1: 235; 1982.

[2] Jules Bloomenthal, Polygonisation of implicit surfaces, *Computer Aided Geometric Design*, 4(5): 341–355; 1988.

[3] Jules Bloomenthal, Brian Wyvill, Interactive techniques for implicit modeling. *Computer Graphics*, 24(2): 109–116; 1990.

[4] Adrian Bowyer, *Svlis Introduction and User Manual* 2nd edn, Information Geometers, 47 Stockers Ave., Winchester, UK, 1995.

[5] H. Chiokura, F. Kimura, Design of solids with free form surfaces, *Computer Graphics Proc. SIGGRAPH 83*, 17(3): 289–296; July 1983.

[6] Marie-Paule Gascuel. An Implicit Formulation for Precise Contact Modeling Between Flexible Solids. *Computer Graphics (Proc. SIGGRAPH 93)*, 313–320; Aug. 1993.

[7] J. Hughes, Scheduled Fourier volume morphing. *Computer Graphics (Proc. SIGGRAPH 92)*, 26(2): 43–46; July 1992.

[8] F.W. Jansen, *Solid Modeling with Faceted Primitives*, PhD thesis, Delft University of Technology, Netherlands, 1987.

[9] Z. Kacic-Alesic, B. Wyvill, *Controlled Blending of Procedural Implicit Surfaces*, Technical Report 90/415/39, University of Calgary, Dept. of Computer Science, 1990.

[10] D. Kalra, A. Barr, Guaranteed ray intersections with implicit functions, *Computer Graphics (Proc. SIGGRAPH 89)*, 23(3): 297–306; July 1989.

[11] Charles Loop, Smooth spline surfaces over irregular meshes, *Computer Graphics (Proc. SIGGRAPH 93)*, 303–310; Aug. 1993.

[12] Martti Mantyla, *An Introduction to Solid Modeling*, Computer Science Press, Rockville, Md. 1988.

[13] Charles Herr, Michael Chmilar, Brian Wyvill, A software architect for integrating modelling with kinematic and dynamic animation, *The Visual Computer*, 7(2/3): 122–137; Mar. 1991.

[14] A. Middleditch, K. Sears, Blend surfaces for set theoretic volume modelling systems. *Computer Graphics (Proc. SIGGRAPH 85)*, 19(3): 161–170; 1985.

[15] B. Naylor, J. Amantides, J. Thibault, Merging BSP trees yields polyhedral set operations. *Computer Graphics (Proc. SIGGRAPH 90)*, 224(4): 115–124; Aug. 1990.

[16] Paul Ning, Jules Bloomenthal, An evaluation of implicit surface tilers. *IEEE Computer Graphics and Applications*, 13(6): 33–41; Nov. 1993.

[17] H. Nishimura, A. Hirai, T. Kawai, T. Kawata, I. Shirakawa, K. Omura, Object modelling by distribution function and a method of image generation, *Journal of papers given at the Electronics Communication Conference '85*, J68-D(4), 1985. [In Japanese.]

[18] Kees van Overveld, Brian Wyvill, Potentials, polygons and penguins. An efficient adaptive algorithm for triangulating an equi-potential surface, 31–62; 1993.

[19] A.A.G. Requicha, Representations for rigid solids: theory, methods, and systems. *ACM Comput. Surv.*, 12(4): 437–464; Dec. 1980.

[20] W. Schroeder, J. Zarge, W. Lorensen, Decimation of triangle meshes. *Computer Graphics (Proc. SIGGRAPH 92)*, 26(2): 65–70; July 1992.

[21] J. Woodwark, K. Quinlan, The derivation of graphics from volume models by recursive division of the object space, *Proc. Computer Graphics 80 Conference, Brighton, UK, Online*, pp. 335–343; 1980.

[22] J. Woodwark, A. Bowyer, Better and faster pictures from solid models, *Computer Aided Eng. J.*, 3(1): 17–24; Feb. 1986.

[23] Geoff Wyvill, Craig McPheeters, Brian Wyvill, Data structure for soft objects. *The Visual Computer*, 2(4): 227–234; Feb. 1986.

[24] Brian Wyvill, The Great Train Rubbery. *SIGGRAPH 88 Electronic Theatre and Video Review*, (26); 1988.

[25] Brian Wyvill, Jules Bloomenthal, Geoff Wyvill, Jim Blinn, Alyn Rockwood, Thad Bier, Jim Cleck, *SIGGRAPH '90, Course Notes, Course #23, Modeling and Animating with Implicit Surfaces*, 1990.

[26] G. Wyvill, A. Trotman, Ray tracing soft objects, *Proc. CG International 90*, 1990.

[27] Brian Wyvill, Explicating implicit surfaces, *Proc. Graphics Interface 1991*, pp. 164–173.

[28] Brian Wyvill, Jules Bloomenthal, Geoff Wyvill, Jim Blinn, John Hart, Chandrajit Bajaj, Thad Bier, *SIGGRAPH '93, Course Notes, Course #25, Modeling and Animating with Implicit Surfaces*, 1993.

[29] Brian Wyvill, Kees van Overveld, *Constructive Soft Geometry: The unification of CSG and Implicit Surfaces*. Technical report, University of Calgary, Dept. of Computer Science, 1995.

24
Visual Simulation of the Chewing Process for Dentistry

Karol Myszkowski, Galina Okuneva, Jens Herder,
Tosiyasu L. Kunii, and Masumi Ibusuki

24.1   Introduction

Most tooth restoration work in dental clinics is done by dentists and accompanying technicians using traditional methods. In the case of high-quality and long-life restoration materials like porcelain or metal, the process of producing an inlay, onlay, or crown (all of which we shall call *restorations*) requires significant resources, in terms of both time and manpower. Usually a mold of the prepared tooth or die is taken. It is used by the technician to prepare a cast restoration, which in most cases must be adjusted by the dentist to have proper occlusal contacts with opposing teeth. At least two visits by the patient to the clinic are required to perform even simple restorations using this technology.

We describe research done as part of the ongoing Intelligent Dental Care System project. The goal of this project is to enhance the quality of dental treatment, accelerate restoration design and manufacturing (ideally a single visit to the clinic should be sufficient to complete treatment of a tooth), and reduce the human labor factor.

The general structure of the dental care system is shown in Figure 24.1. The process of creating a restoration starts with the measurement of the surface of the tooth under treatment, measurement of the surfaces of the jaws, and measurement of the positions of the jaws.

The next step is *initial design* of the shape of the restoration. The shape is partially constrained by the shape of the preparation/die, and these parts will be reconstructed from measurements. The free (remaining) surfaces are taken from a library of shapes and/or a database, with further adjustments to individual characteristics of the patient.

The resulting shape is checked for articulation problems by articulation simulation software. The articulation simulation detects basic articulation problems associated with the generated shape of the inlay/onlay or crown.

The information thus obtained is fed to shape generation software to change the shape so as to avoid the problems. We thus get an iterative process for designing/checking the occlusal surface. Basic geometric features of the occlusal surface of the tooth (such as cusps, ridges, and fossae) are preserved where the properties of the restoration material allow efficient reconstruction.

The final shape is thus based on measurement data, library/database information about basic tooth features, general gnathological rules, and the results of articulation

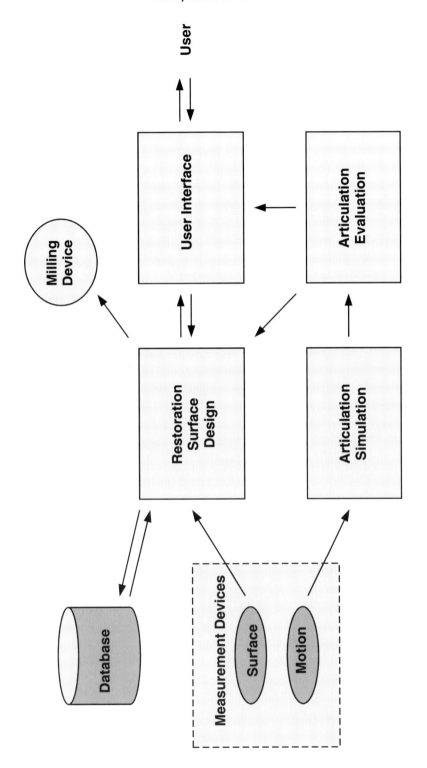

Figure 24.1   General structure of the IDCS.

optimization. The features unrelated to occlusion are therefore based on previously stored data and the individual features of the patient. The user interface allows the dentist to interrupt at any moment and to perform manual adjustment of a shape, using the database and articulation simulation software. The shape is given to a milling device, which manufactures the designed restoration.

We focus here on the evaluation of articulation and its visual representation.

24.2   Articulation Model

As seen from the general structure of the system, an outstanding feature of the system is the use of automatic articulation simulation for diagnosis of occlusal disorders and prevention of new disorders that can appear after performing the restoration. The simulation is based on measurements of real motion data of the lower jaw and of the surface of the teeth in the jaws. We are currently working on two approaches to the reconstruction of motion between the measured points, *geometric modeling* and *direct reconstruction* via interpolation. The first approach is more computationally expensive, but requires less measured data.

1. *Modeling of the jaw joints.* The modeling requires an appropriate geometric model usable for deriving characteristics of the system of the chewing process; we make the following basic assumptions:

- The upper and lower jaws are rigid bodies.
- The position of the lower jaw with respect to the upper jaw defines completely the state of the whole system.
- The set of all possible positions of the system is three-dimensional and is determined completely by a position of a single point fixed in the lower jaw.

The first and the third assumptions mean in particular that we neglect as we simulate normal chewing activity certain minor deviations that are known to appear in extreme situations, such as the mobility of teeth, mandibular deflection, and the possibility of the rotation of the lower jaw about the back-to-front axis. The second assumption means that we treat as inessential the position of the patient's head, the effect of gravity, and so on.

The above assumptions lead to the conclusion that the configuration space of the model is a three-dimensional manifold M with boundary ∂M, diffeomorphic to the three-dimensional ball (whose two-dimensional projections are known in dentistry as *Posselt figures* depicting boundary movements of the mandibula). The boundary ∂M consists of two overlapping parts, one of which is due to the mechanical limitations imposed by the structure of the jaw joints, and the other due to collision of the jaws. The second part is where the chewing occurs, and it and its vicinity are most interesting from the point of view of occlusion analysis.

As soon as we know the configuration space, we may derive various characteristics for evaluation of the articulation. The problem that arises here is to find the correspondence between a point in the configuration space (position of a point in the lower jaw) and the position of the whole jaw; in principle, the lower jaw is a rigid body and, as such, has six degrees of freedom. The position of a point in 3-dimensional space only provides three degrees of freedom, so the other three (rotation of the jaw) need to be restored.

We may represent contact between the elements of the joint as contacts between geometric surfaces, and derive the required relation between the translational and rotational parts of the position of the lower jaw. It should be noted that the assumption of contacts between two pairs of surfaces only binds two degrees of freedom, so an additional assumption about the possible positions is necessary. Our conjecture is that there is a linear relation between the elements of rotation matrices; this conjecture has been tested for several sets of real data, and the conclusion so far is that there is a linear relation that holds with accuracy below 0.3%, which is sufficient for practical purposes. Details of this kind of model may be found in [3]. The model that uses the approximation of the contact surfaces by quadratic surfaces produces a very complicated system of equations; simpler models may be used because, as observed from real data, rotation of the lower jaw near the contact points is very small (although it need not be small at the positions that are far from contact between the teeth; these are not interesting for the analysis).

2.   Another approach is *direct reconstruction* of the correspondence between the position of a point and the rotation of the jaw from measured data, using techniques of rotation interpolation. There are several techniques for the interpolation of rotation, using quaternions [10] or exponential mapping. In effect, this approach finds the configuration space described above by interpolation from measured points.

Interpolation is computationally cheap and provides sufficient accuracy; however, its application is limited to the cases where we have a sufficient number of measured points of the motion, so it cannot be directly applied to the virtual check of restoration for new articulation problems. This approach can be used for the initial check of articulation and the restoration of articulation motion after editing of occlusal surfaces.

At present we are mainly using the faster interpolation approach. Motion of the mandibular jaw is simulated using 6-DOF measurement data, obtained with the MM-JI-E system developed at Tokushima Bunri University and Tokushima University. The positions of three points in the lower jaw are sampled at a frequency in the range 30–200 Hz, while the accuracy of the measurement of positions is better than 150 μm. To decrease the granularity of the motion in the proximity of contacts between the jaws, we calculate inbetween positions using Catmull–Rom splines for the interpolation of rotation (quaternions) and translation [8].

The experimental data of the lower jaw motion are limited in their volume (20–40 full loops of mandibular movements for one patient), and may not cover all important positions of the jaw in real-life grinding. Therefore, even if our chewing characteristics are meaningful, some pathological situations may be overlooked. This risk can be significantly reduced when more valid positions in the proximity of contacts between jaws are generated. Also, the measurement device is expensive and complex in setting, so our intention is to limit its use to some pathological cases where computer simulation is unreliable. We are working on simulations of the lower jaw 'sliding' across the surface of the upper jaw, taking into account the geometry of teeth and a very simple model of constraints imposed by the mandibular joints.

The idea of this approach is based on the observation that the rotation of the lower jaw near contact positions is small (so the motion of the lower jaw is almost parallel translation); the basic conjecture is that the small rotations optimize contacts between the jaws. Thus, for each given position of the reference point in the lower jaw, we start from the position that is a translation of the occlusal position and find the rotation (within some fixed boundaries) that optimizes the contact. This approach, with some modifications, is currently under development.

24.3   Collision Detection

Checking and removing interferences between the restoration and existing teeth is an important function of our dental care system. The restoration must fit with the existing occlusion dynamically for lower jaw movements. If the motion data are acquired by measurements, collision detection can be limited to the restoration itself and the opposing teeth. If motion data are not available, collision detection for all teeth except the restoration is required to find valid positions of the lower jaw. These positions are then used to check interference between the restoration and the opposing teeth in a similar way as with measured motion data. Another application of collision detection techniques is tracing contact regions between teeth, which provides useful information for the diagnosis of occlusal disorders.

Fast and reliable collision detection is an important component of every animation, robot motion planning, and virtual reality system that does not allow interpenetration between objects in the virtual environment. However, in a typical situation, the geometry of objects is simple, and traditional collision detection techniques provide a binary response indicating whether or not the objects collide at their current configuration. If any interference region is found, further calculations are abandoned, and other collisions are ignored. In our application a collision detection technique must efficiently handle all (multipoint) contacts and collisions between very complex occlusal surfaces of jaws, modeled by 100 000–500 000 polygons. A short response time is required when the dentist interactively inspects occlusion for chosen lower jaw positions. This means that the efficiency of the algorithm cannot be based on the coherence of the jaw's positions implied by a priori known trajectories of its motion. Also, the penalty for the complexity of contacts between jaws should be negligible, i.e., the response time of the collision checking must be stable. The algorithm should run on standard graphics workstations or even personal computers equipped with a graphics accelerator.

24.3.1   Distance maps

The requirements imposed on the collision detection by jaw articulation cannot be met by a traditional algorithm running on sequential machines. General-purpose parallel computers which could provide sufficient computing power are too expensive. The natural choice is an architecture specialized in graphics calculations which can efficiently handle various geometrical calculations and is relatively cheap. Fortunately, the collision detection problem can be formulated in the framework of a hidden-surface removal algorithm. Intuitively we may say that two objects with closed surfaces do not collide if the observer located at an arbitrary point inside one 'empty' object cannot 'see' the surface of the second object. Of course, in a practical formulation, the number of observer positions and viewing directions must be limited. On the other hand, in many applications the configuration of the objects and constraints imposed on their motion provide information on where collisions can be expected. This is also the case in jaw articulation simulation, where collisions are only possible on occlusal and side surfaces of teeth. Our strategy of using hidden-surface removal techniques for collision detection seems to be justified by the rapid increase in the cost-performance of graphics hardware. It should be noted that advanced work on graphics processors has already brought powerful hidden-surface elimination techniques to the platform of personal computers equipped with an inexpensive graphics add-on board, e.g., Freedom Graphics from Evans & Sutherland with the OpenGL software application programming interface.

The practical problem is how to tailor the collision detection algorithm to the existing standard resources of hidden-surface techniques, such as z-buffer [5, 6, 9]. For simplicity, let us focus our attention on rendering applying orthogonal projection. The distances from a surface to an arbitrarily located screen plane are calculated along the projection direction orthogonal to this screen. The distances are compared for every element (pixel) of image and a surface positioned closer to the screen is qualified as visible. Consider a pair of objects with closed surfaces U and L. Let us call the *collision projection line* a line parallel to the projection direction that intersects both objects. A pair of objects does not collide if for every collision projection line i the maximal distance U_{max}^i for U will always be smaller than the minimal distance L_{min}^i for L:

$$\forall_i \quad U_{max}^i < L_{min}^i \tag{1}$$

If the two objects are convex, this is a necessary and sufficient condition for no interference. One may notice that this condition also holds for nonconvex objects if for every collision projection line i the surface of each object has only two intersection points. In [5] we show that if at least one object satisfies this requirement, then the collision detection problem can be solved efficiently using rasterizing graphics hardware. In general, for a pair of concave objects, relation (1) is sufficient but not necessary for the absence of collision. To exclude other noncollision configurations of the objects using hidden-surface removal techniques, depth-sorting of the surfaces is necessary [5]. Since the sorting is not supported by standard graphics hardware (there are few architectures that can handle sorting, see [2, 4]), real-time collision detection for complex objects cannot be achieved.

The jaws are concave objects; however, the constraints imposed on the motion of the lower jaw make the collision possible only for the occlusal and side surfaces of teeth. This means that the directions of the orthogonal projections for collision detection should be chosen in the proximity of the direction perpendicular to the occlusal plane of the upper jaw. It turns out that we can find a set P of projection directions for which every collision projection line has at most two intersections with the surface of the immobile upper jaw (section 24.3.2). The collision detection algorithm becomes a simple special case of our general technique handling the pair of convex and concave objects [5]. The necessary and sufficient condition for noncollision is the same as for a pair of convex objects, i.e., relation (1), because the structure of the jaw joints and the shape of the teeth do not allow configurations where the points of a tooth in an upper jaw lie between the points of teeth in the lower jaw in a projection direction from P. The algorithm is as follows:

1. For the screen located over the upper jaw and for a chosen projection direction from P, calculate the map of maximal distance to the surface of the upper jaw U (in practice, its occlusal surface).
2. For every step of the lower jaw motion:
   - Calculate the map of minimal distance to the surface of the lower jaw L.
   - Consider the corresponding pairs of elements (pixels) of the maps for U and L. Eliminate the pairs which represent background for at least one element.
   - For every remaining pair i calculate the difference of distance d^i between the upper and lower jaws ($d^i = L^i_{min} - U^i_{max}$). For the regions with $d^i < 0$ the collision is detected. Contact between the jaws is equivalent to $d^i = 0$.

As the result of collision detection, *distance maps* between upper and lower jaw are calculated for the current projection direction. The distance maps provide information about all possible collisions, which means that our algorithm can handle multipoint collisions. An additional benefit of the distance maps is information on the depth of interference for all regions of collision. The location and depth of collisions provides important data for the design of the restoration whose surface is corrected to avoid interferences with the existing teeth.

However, there are also some pitfalls of the technique presented, which are inherent to the sampling nature of algorithms applying rasterizing graphics hardware. First of all, the number of projection lines, along which the distance is measured, is limited by the resolution of the screen (raster grid). This means that collision status remains undetermined between sample points at the raster. The spatial frequency of sampling can be adjusted to the frequency of changes in the surface, but at the expense of increasing the cost of calculations (which exhibit linear increase with the number of pixels in the distance maps). If the surface still has some spikes with details over the sampling frequency we can afford, a collision check can be performed for the bounding volumes enclosing the spikes, which are enlarged adequately to the density of samples. If collision with the bounding volume is detected, then the spike itself can be processed using locally denser samples or an analytic solution. This discussion suggests that techniques of hierarchical (multiresolution) analysis are applicable to finding the best sampling strategy for particular application of the collision detection algorithm. It should be noted that the object itself may be represented at several levels of details to speed up its scan conversion by graphics hardware.

The accuracy of distance calculations is limited by the resolution of depth calculations, which is imposed by the graphics hardware. In our application this is not a problem, because the range of depth is very limited (usually 3–6 cm) while the number of the corresponding depth levels is equal to the depth resolution of z-buffer (usually 2^{24}). Finally, visibility/collision calculations are performed only for the surfaces or their regions projected onto the screen, which means that the robustness and performance of collision detection depends on the location and size of the screen and the choice of projection direction. The screen parameters are easy to determine in our application. The screen plane is located over the occlusal plane of the upper jaw, and the projection direction belongs to P. The size of the screen is determined by the size of the projection of the upper jaw on the screen plane. Because of the 'u-shaped' image of the jaw on the screen, many pixels (collision sample points) visualize background, and do not provide useful information about interferences. In order to decrease the number of such pixels, we use four screen locations, which correspond to the four clusters of teeth that cover the upper jaw: back-left, front-left, front-right and back-right. Each cluster can be efficiently projected on to a rectangular screen, minimizing the number of background pixels.

The time needed to calculate the distance maps for a jaw model composed of over 110 000 triangles is 0.22 seconds on SGI's Indigo^2 Extreme workstation (the map resolution is 512×512). Figure 24.2a shows an example of distance maps for the upper molar and premolar teeth, calculated for jaw position close to the centric occlusal position. Regions where the distance to the opposing teeth is below 1 mm are marked by yellow and red; zero distance, i.e., contact between jaws, is pure red. (On half-tone images, yellow corresponds to the brightest shade of gray, and red maps to dark gray in central parts of the occlusal surface.) We do not use color interpolation in the contact area here; borders between different tones of yellow and orange correspond to 0.2 mm intervals in distance.

A more detailed technical description and performance evaluation of our collision detection algorithm can be found in [5]. The algorithm is general-purpose, and can be efficiently used in other applications, especially if handling of multipoint collisions is required. The algorithm works well for both concave and convex objects modeled either by a polygonal mesh, NURBS surfaces, or other representations supported by the graphics accelerator.

24.3.2   Multiprojection distance maps

The best accuracy of collision detection can be expected when the projection plane is tangent to the contact points between objects. However, in practice this requirement is difficult to fulfill, because the number of contacts can be much higher than 3. Also, the projection direction should belong to the set P to simplify calculations (section 24.3.1). Of course, it is possible to optimize the orientation of the projection plane using a version of the least-squares method for all anticipated contact points. However, even for an 'optimal' projection direction, the angle between the projection direction and the normal to the surface can be quite big, which affects the accuracy of distance calculations for these regions of the surface. In our application the variation of the normal vectors to the occlusal surface of teeth is high, and the quality of collision detection should be at least comparable to the accuracy of the tooth surface scanning, which in our case is better than 10 μm.

We designed an experiment to evaluate errors of the presented collision detection technique, taking into account the orientation of the occlusal surface with respect to the projection direction. We used ray tracing as the reference method to validate the depth results provided by graphics hardware. The average distance based on 16 rays traced for every pixel was calculated. Generally, low errors were observed (RMS error = 0.9 μm), however, in the proximity of the boundary of the occlusal surface maximal error as high as 60 μm occurred. This means that the single projection direction, even 'optimally' chosen, cannot secure the required 10 μm accuracy of the distance measurement. The only solution is to increase the number of projection directions considered. This raises the following problems:

- A common framework for the analysis of the distance maps calculated for all projections is needed.
- The choice of projection directions should secure the required accuracy for every region of the occlusal surface in at least one projection. The results with poor accuracy for some regions should be discarded.
- All chosen projections must belong to P. In practice this means that the maximal angle between the projection direction perpendicular to the occlusal surface and other projections must be small (below 8–12 degrees).

We propose *multiprojection distance maps*, which accumulate in a single map the results contained in the distance maps for all projection directions. This requires matching the distance maps for some characteristic points of the surface of teeth to derive the minimum distance to the opposing teeth. We choose the vertices of the mesh describing the surface to project back the distance information from the 2D map space into the 3D object space. The mesh is recursively refined until the difference in distances for adjacent vertices is smaller than a threshold value or a mesh element becomes too small for further subdivision. Since the back-projection is a noninjective function, several vertices can be projected to the same pixel. The distance measure in the map is valid for one vertex only. We select the right vertex using the item buffer. (The item buffer stores for every pixel the unique identifier of the mesh element nearest to the observer and projected onto this pixel [11].) Application of the item buffer does not solve the problem of vertices belonging to the same mesh element and projected onto the same pixel. In our application we choose the vertex nearest to the occlusal surface, while for other vertices we add the length of the edge to the distance stored for the pixel. All these problems related to back-projection become less frequent as the resolution of the distance maps increases.

The multiprojection distance map is a compact framework for an analysis of the distribution of distances between the jaws with a meaningful accuracy for the whole occlusal surface. The minimal distance to the opposing teeth is calculated for all adaptively refined mesh vertices. Before the distance at the vertex is qualified as a valid minimal distance, the direction of the normal vector of the corresponding mesh element is compared with the projection direction for the current map. If the angle between these directions is bigger than the threshold value, the distance is marked as invalid, because of the previously discussed possibility of high errors in the distance measurement. The procedure of the distance validation is performed for vertices in the proximity of contact (usually a distance less than 200 µm is considered). For vertices located farther away, the accuracy of the distance calculations becomes less important. Information about the validity of the distance is used to choose subsequent projection directions until all vertices in the proximity of contact have valid distances or the number of projections used is bigger than the threshold value.

The projection directions used for multiprojection distance map calculations are predefined taking into account the morphological features of the surfaces of teeth. We start with the projection direction perpendicular to the occlusal plane. Then, the occlusal plane is rotated in positive and negative directions around the axis parallel to the main cusp located along the molar teeth (for back-left and back-right clusters). Subsequently, another rotation axis, perpendicular to the former one is chosen, and the rotations are applied again. For every iteration the bigger rotation angles (with a small random component to avoid too regular a distance sampling pattern for various maps) are used.

Every projection direction is checked for belonging to the set P; that is, each projection line intersecting the lower jaw must have at most two intersection points with a tooth in the upper jaw (section 24.3.1). In practice, all projection lines intersecting the upper jaw imposed by the screen resolution are checked because the position of the lower jaw changes in the course of articulation, while the validity of the projection direction is checked only once at the preprocessing stage. The stencil buffer is used to count intersection points for every pixel (projection line).

Calculations of the multiprojection distance maps for a model of jaws composed of 110 000 triangles takes 0.90 seconds per projection because of overhead due to back projection calculations and finding the minimum distance, operations that are not hardware-supported. Usually about nine projections are used to guarantee a distance calculation error below 10 μm. Figure 24.2b shows the distribution of the distance to the opposing teeth for multiprojection distance maps (9 projections) of the upper-left premolar and molar teeth. The color coding of the distance between jaws is the same as for Figure 24.2a. As expected, the use of multiple projections increases the area of the occlusal surface qualified as near contact area, and provides much better estimation of the distance to the opposing teeth.

During interaction with the dentist, the single projection map technique is chosen by default (for the same model of jaw only 0.22 seconds are needed; section 24.3.1). However, if high accuracy collision detection for the design of the restoration is needed, multiprojection distance maps are used. The multiprojection technique makes it

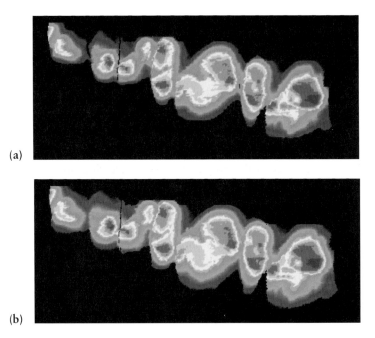

(a)

(b)

Figure 24.2 Distance maps calculated for (a) single, and (b) multiprojection directions.

possible to derive various advanced characteristics of contacts between jaws as discussed in the next section.

24.4 Characteristics of Grinding

Conventional methods of occlusal analysis are limited by their ignoring dynamics of occlusal relationship during mandibular motion. In traditional dental practice, a dentist evaluates occlusion using colored paper which leaves colored spots on the regions of teeth involved in contact during grinding ('tapping test'). More modern devices (e.g., the pressure-sensitive film sheet 'dental prescale' developed by Fuji Film Co.) allow the dentist to measure the distribution of load over teeth inside the patient's mouth. When similar characteristics are to be measured for restorations, a mechanical articulator and a mold of the jaws are needed. The articulator can reproduce some static positional relations between the jaws, but the actual functional mandibular movements and occlusal loading cannot be checked. Also, when a restoration is ready, any correction of the shape of occlusal surface requires work with hard material. It should be noted that such corrections are destructive, and mistakes committed by the dentist are unrecoverable. The proposed technique eliminates the need to use a mechanical articulator to analyze the influence of restoration on the existing articulation, and changes of shape are easy to perform. Also, characteristics calculated by the computer are more accurate and meaningful, and provide immediate feedback to the dentist.

Our basic idea for the evaluation of occlusion is to estimate interaction between teeth using variations of the distance map technique (section 24.3). We have chosen this technique because of the speed of calculations and globality of information, which is provided for the whole occlusal surface of the jaws. In our work we focus on offering deeper insight into load distribution over the occlusal surface, identification of regions impairing jaw articulation (which are important for automatic design of dental restorations), and evaluation of the grinding ability of teeth.

The load on teeth can be approximated by the minimal distance modulated by the dot product of the normal vector at the vertex with the projection direction. The load reflects the distribution of the pressure over the occlusal surface of teeth, assuming uniform consistency of the ground food. Also, the directions of maximal load can be investigated taking into account the projection direction with a minimal distance and the normal vector to the surface. Loading in unphysiologic directions, such as tipping forces, can lead to the migration of teeth.

However, the minimal distance and the load on the teeth characteristics do not provide reliable information about the local features of the surfaces in the proximity of the contact. In particular, recognition of the wear facets and signs of abrasion (parafunctions) is difficult. Let us call the *contact area* the set M of all points in the distance maps for one jaw that are within the threshold distance δ from the opposite jaw. We found that a more appropriate estimate for the load on the tooth in the contact area is provided by the characteristic

$$F = \sum_{i=1}^{p} \max(0, \delta - d_i) \cos \alpha_i \qquad (2)$$

where p is the number of projection directions used and α_i is the angle between the ith projection direction and the normal to the surface. This characteristic is sensitive to the values of distance, but also to the number of projection directions where $d_i < \delta$. It changes more dynamically in response to the shape of the surface than just the average distance value. In the regions where the value of F is high and stable, wear facets can be recognized.

24.4.1 Static and dynamic characteristics

The proposed characteristics can be described as *static*, relevant to a particular position of the jaws, or *dynamic*, obtained for a particular motion of the jaws. Static characteristics are usually found for meaningful positions of the jaws, e.g., the centric occlusal position. Examples of the minimal distance characteristics for static jaws positions have been presented in Figure 24.2. The dentist can choose the accuracy of the color fringe scale of the distance (or load on the teeth). The scale can be continuous, with the color linearly interpolated, or equidistance (equiload) contours on the surface may be encoded by a discrete scale of colors (Figure 24.2). The minimal distance and the characteristics of load on the teeth are provided to the dentist as 2D images, which also can be mapped on the 3D surface of the teeth (Figure 24.3). In the latter case, a selected grinding characteristic can be inspected simultaneously with the corresponding shape of the occlusal surface. This helps the dentist to decide the proper treatment of the existing teeth or correction of the shape of the restoration. The dentist may walkthrough around virtual teeth and focus his attention on a particular region of a tooth.

Dynamic characteristics require meaningful motion data, which can be obtained by measurement or simulated by computer, e.g., by sliding of the lower jaw in the lateral direction. Dynamic changes of the load over the teeth provide extremely useful information for diagnosis of occlusal parafunctions (unphysiologic loading force and duration) and for simulation of various treatment schemata. The dentist can simultaneously inspect the motion of the lower jaw and the corresponding characteristics of grinding. Figure 24.4 presents the distribution of the load on the

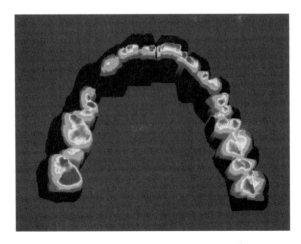

Figure 24.3 3D multiprojection distance maps projected on the teeth surface.

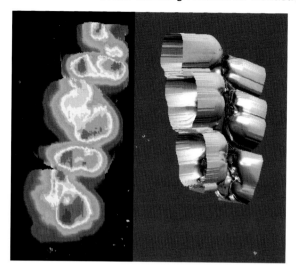

Figure 24.4 Dynamic load on the upper-left molar and premolar teeth for the lower jaw movement.

upper-left molar and premolar teeth and the corresponding position of the teeth in space. The load was calculated using the characteristic (2). Contact regions for $\delta <$ 1 mm are marked by yellow; red shows the highest load. (On half-tone images, yellow corresponds to the brightest shade of gray, and red maps to dark gray in central parts of the occlusal surface.) When single projection maps are used, 4–5 frames per second can be displayed. Even faster simulation is possible at the expense of a lower level of detail of the tooth model, which can be controlled by the dentist.

24.4.2   Cumulative distance maps

An attractive alternative to the dynamic characteristics of the chewing process are *cumulative* characteristics, obtained by the application of functions with a variable number of variables (such as max, or various averages) to characteristics obtained from sets of positions or motions. Cumulative characteristics can be used to derive the maximal load on teeth or minimal distance to opposing teeth found during movements of the lower jaw. An efficient tool to capture such information is required. We extend the notion of distance maps to *cumulative distance maps* (CDM). All discussed characteristics can be calculated not only for multiple projection directions, but also for multiple positions of the lower jaw motion. The CDM is a compact tool for representing depth and directions of all possible contacts/collisions encountered during the motion of the jaw. The CDM with the maximal load on the teeth provide the dentist with information on the worst-case pressure distribution over the teeth during the whole simulated jaw motion. Also, the total or maximal continuous duration of unphysiologic loading force on teeth can be measured. The dentist may decide on interactive adjustment of the designed restoration to avoid unbalanced load on the occlusal surface. Figure 24.5 presents the distribution of load on the upper-left first molar tooth. The load was calculated by finding the maximum over all positions in a

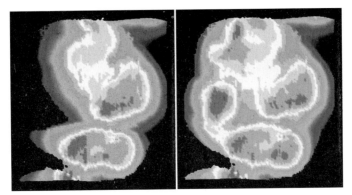

Figure 24.5   Distribution of load on the upper-left first molar tooth: static (left) and cumulative (right).

motion of the characteristic (2); the color coding is the same as in Figure 24.4. The left image was calculated for a single position, while the right image shows the cumulative distance maps for five loops of the motion of the lower jaw.

It should be noted that dynamic and cumulative characteristics of grinding are not available with traditional techniques used in dental practice.

24.4.3   Jaw motion trajectories

Mandibular border movements are recorded for accurate simulation of chewing. Animated chewing with visualization of contacts facilitates the understanding of this complex process. Diagnosis of dental, skeletal, or temporomandibular joint (TMJ) anomalies and functional disturbances [7] requires visualization of trajectories. *Posselt figures*, widely used in dentistry, describe the border movements, including the positions without contact. The *Posselt figures* show all movements of an incisal reference point between the two mandibular central incisors in sagittal, lateral, and horizontal directions. Such diagrams do not show the motion of the TMJs explicitly, and are usually only available in 2D. To overcome this problem and to give a better understanding of the lower jaw motion, we developed a motion visualization module. In 3D, it shows the path of the measured incisal reference point as in the Posselt figures, but additionally it shows the motion of the TMJs or two arbitrary points rigidly connected to the lower jaw. The correspondence between the different points is made visible by showing additional axes, which allow one to examine rotations easily. These axes depend on a visualization mode, selected by the user. In particular, selection between TMJ right and left or TMJ and incisal reference point is available. The axes are not drawn for all measured points because this would overload the visualization. An adjustable threshold determines whether or not the next axis should be drawn. Figure 24.6 shows the visualization of the lower jaw motion trajectories.

Velocity, which is another important motion parameter, is visualized by color. The calculation of velocity is easy because the measured data is obtained with a constant frame rate.

To understand the relation between motion and shape, the chewing animation is

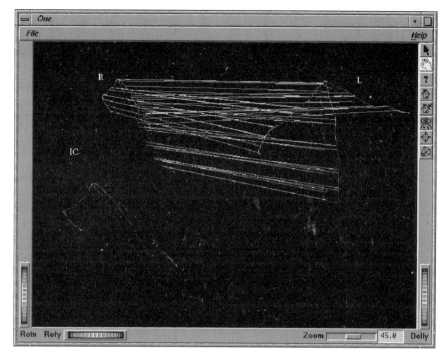

Figure 24.6   Lower jaw motion trajectories.

connected to the motion visualization. The current active frame (configuration of three points) is highlighted as the corresponding application runs.

24.5   Restoration Design

The CDM with the minimal distance calculated for restoration can be used to remove automatically all collisions of the restoration with existing teeth in the course of the habitual motions of the lower jaw. The CDMs store both the depth and location of collisions encountered during the whole motion. Also, the projection direction in which the minimal distance was calculated is available. Adjustment of the occlusal surface of restoration can be done by moving the vertices of the mesh (or control points) a specified number of units in the direction of the projection in which a collision is detected. This works well when collisions are small compared to distances between the vertices of the mesh, otherwise surface folding is possible. More secure is an iterative approach, in which the vertices are moved along the projection direction perpendicular to the occlusal plane a number of units equal to the minimal distance from the CDM projected in this direction. Usually, the sequence of CDM calculations followed by the adjustment of the surface must be repeated at least twice to remove all collisions.

Another problem is preserving morphological features of the occlusal surface of teeth, such as the main cusps. Our current approach is to use the CDM as a displacement map for a 3D warping algorithm. Constraints imposed on the smoothness of the occlusal surface are used to prevent discontinuities and abrupt changes. We present details of this algorithm in a forthcoming publication.

The automatic design of the occlusal surface of the restoration usually produces a 'reasonable' shape of the occlusal surface, i.e., main morphological features of teeth are preserved, the rules of aesthetic dentistry are respected, and all collisions are eliminated. However, in some cases, especially for patients with occlusion disorders, further adjustments are necessary. We provide the dentist with the possibility of interactive editing of the occlusal surface.

24.6   Handling Measurement Data

An important technical problem to be solved for successful articulation simulation is matching measurement data obtained from various measurement devices. This requires a common coordinate system for all movable elements that appear in the simulation. In practice, scanning the surfaces of teeth in the upper and lower jaws is performed separately, and the motion is measured using another device. Usually it is difficult to obtain explicit information about relations between the appropriate coordinate systems. In many cases the manufacturers do not provide information on coordinate systems used by the devices, which are treated as internal data. Our current approach is to measure the position of some reference points in the plaster mold of the jaws. An additional measurement using a mechanical scanner is needed to find the relative positions of the reference points for the jaws in the valid position. The centric occlusal position is used because it can easily be found by manual matching of plaster models of the jaws. A more rigorous approach requires the imprint of the occlusal position in the mouth of the patient using a thin bite record (e.g., silicon offers little resistance to closure and hardens quickly). This record is later used to match the plaster molds.

However, our observation is that the centric occlusal position can be found algorithmically, avoiding additional measurements. In the centric occlusal position, contact between the jaws is maximized. Both the area of contact and the number of contact regions matter. The initial guess of the lower jaw position based on physiological relations in matching opposing teeth is usually sufficiently good. In such a formulation, this is an optimization problem in multidimensional parameter space (6 DOF for the lower jaw positioning). Since such matching is performed once for each patient, the relatively long time of calculation is not critical.

Matching the motion data with the jaw surfaces measurement data is done by measuring the position of the three points in the teeth for which the motion measurement is recorded. Of course, the coordinate matching must be solved case by case, depending on the construction of the particular measurement devices.

24.7   User Interface

The user interface is the software and hardware that provides communication between the intelligent dental care system functions and the dentist, technician, and patient. An ideal system would not need a sophisticated user interface, because everything, including decision making, would be automated. But such a perfect system does not exist and is not expected to exist in the near future. Interaction of the dentist with the system is necessary for diagnosis, shape design, shape evaluation, machine operation, information retrieval, and so on. The IDCS development exploits metaphors that are familiar to dentists from everyday practice (pen, scalpel, mechanical articulator, tapping paper). A new input technique designed specifically for use with articulation simulation is under development.

The user interface of the intelligent dental care systems needs to provide textual, numeric and three-dimensional graphical input and output. For a two-dimensional graphical user interface, a lot of well-established tools are available. As for three-dimensional interactive user interfaces for various platforms, the choice is not so wide. The problems with three-dimensional graphics interfaces are the performance and the possibilities to customize or develop input devices based on software (manipulators) or hardware.

24.7.1   Structure of UI

The user interface may be structured in accordance with different abstraction levels. The user distinguishes the interface by what is in his perception and what he can modify. This is the text, numeric and graphical data. The application programmer's view is shown in Figure 24.7; here the emphasis lies on the various application programmer interfaces (API). The next viewpoint emphasizes the I/O devices, such as the screen, keyboard, mouse, and so on.

The requirements for the user interface of the IDCS are ease of use, fault tolerance, ease of learning, efficiency, and one-hand operation. A normal keyboard is inefficient from the point of view of these requirements. We recommend a touch screen, which allows operation by pen and finger to have a simulated keyboard, specialized menus, and easy drawing capabilities. Also, such a screen is needed for fast interactive visualization.

24.7.2   Visualization and animation

Visualization of the measured data based on the geometry of the teeth and the lower jaw motion allows the dentist to make a profound diagnosis. The animation capable of

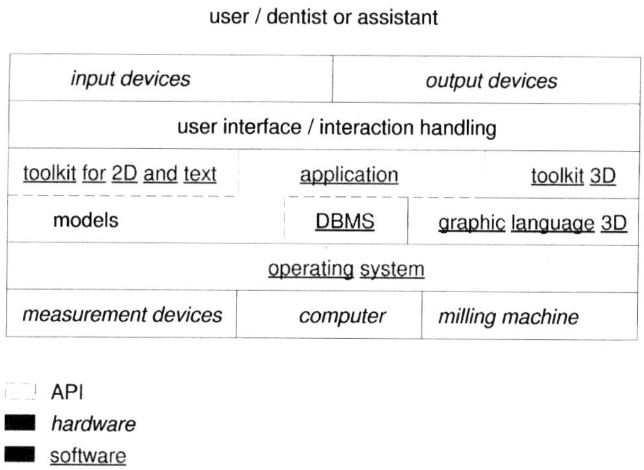

Figure 24.7   User interface structure.

providing a deeper understanding of the chewing process requires sophisticated computer graphics. But animation and initial diagnosis alone are not sufficient in themselves; also, the designed shape of the restoration needs to be visualized and evaluated. A simulation allows the dentist to evaluate the treatment beforehand, avoiding treatment errors. The user interface allows the dentist to visualize shapes, collision maps (section 24.3.1) and motion data (section 24.4.3) in various views and modes. Focusing on the point of examination by zooming or hiding other teeth is provided. Pseudocolors help to emphasize certain output properties.

Figure 24.8 shows the entry user interface with easy access to all functionality. Besides access to the simulation and visualization functions, it allows one to annotate each tooth in 3D. This information together with simulation results can be compiled to a hypertext (HTML) report, which also includes a reduced 3D model (VRML).

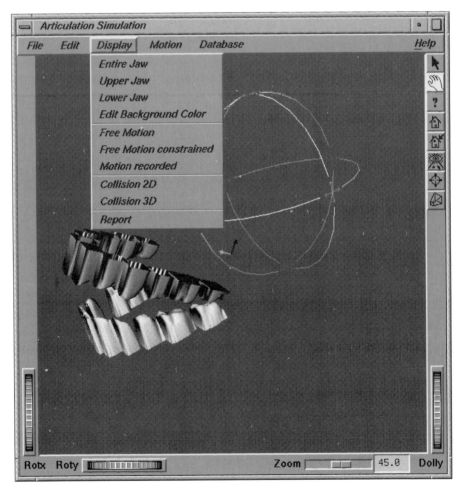

Figure 24.8 User interface entry.

24.7.3   Interaction in 3D

Simulation and visualization are dynamic processes which expect 3D control data from the user. Such data is also required for the modification of shapes. Traditionally, two-dimensional input devices, such as a mouse or trackball, have been used. For 3D simulation and editing, these devices are not adequate, and their use implies obvious inconveniences. We propose customized manipulators (also called 3D widgets [1]) which have an adequate hardware counterpart. A manipulator has a visual representation (e.g., sphere for manipulating object orientation) which has two purposes: describing the modes of active manipulation and actually controlling the manipulation. A manipulator can have different modes which constrain certain attributes (e.g., translation vs. rotation). A general manipulator has six DOFs and no limits. But the lower jaw does not actually have so much freedom. The implemented lower jaw manipulator allows only valid input configurations. A valid configuration is determined by measured shape and motion. If a constraint is violated (collision detected or motion set exceeded), the next valid configuration is chosen using a minimal distance algorithm. Another customized manipulator is deployed for shape modification. Here the wax modeling technique of a dental technician is emulated. Constraints here are the amount of selected wax (volume) and temperature (cooling time). This approach reduces the cognitive distance between the data and the user. The metaphor is based upon traditional methods using mechanical articulators and pen/scalpel, making all relevant operations easy to perform.

24.8   Implementation

The prototype is implemented on SGI workstations. Low-level graphic functionality, which needs to be fast, is implemented in OpenGL. Open Inventor is used for high-level interactive graphic operations. The Motif user interface is realized using ViewKit. ViewKit and Open Inventor are C++ class libraries.

24.9   Conclusion

The Intelligent Dental Care System is a system under development for the diagnosis and treatment of dental disorders using global articulation simulation and evaluation (that is, the articulation is evaluated across whole jaws rather than just the tooth under treatment). We have proposed a distance map technique to check multipoint collisions between opposing teeth. Distance maps provide necessary information for adjusting the shape of the designed restoration and can be used to derive several kinds of characteristics of contacts/clearances between opposing teeth, relevant to both particular positions of the lower jaw (static characteristics) and motions (dynamic and cumulative characteristics). The characteristics are calculated at interactive time rates on workstations equipped with standard graphics hardware, and enable meaningful visual representations via the user interface.

Acknowledgments

The IDCS project is funded by the Fukushima Prefectural Foundation for the Advancement of Science and Education. The authors thank Michael Cohen and Kiel Christianson from The University of Aizu for reviewing the manuscript. We also thank Yuko Kesen for her generous help in preparing this manuscript and her continuous support for the IDCS project.

References

[1] D. Brookshire Conner, Scott S. Snibbe, Kenneth P. Herndon, Daniel C. Robbins, Robert C. Zeleznik, Andries van Dam, Three-dimensional widgets, *Computer Graphics (1992 Symposium on Interactive 3D Graphics)*, 25: 183–188; March 1992.

[2] Michael Kelley, Kirk Gould, Brent Pease, Stephanie Winner, Alex Yen, Hardware accelerated rendering of CSG and transparency, *Computer Graphics Annual Conference Series, 1994*, 177–184; July 1994.

[3] Tosiyasu L. Kunii, Jens Herder, Karol Myszkowski, Oleg Okunev, Galina G. Okuneva, Articulation simulation for an Intelligent Dental Care System, *Displays*, 15(3): 181–188; 1994.

[4] Abraham Mammen, Transparency and antialiasing algorithms implemented with the virtual pixel maps technique, *IEEE Computer Graphics Appl.*, 9(4): 43–55; July 1989.

[5] Karol Myszkowski, Oleg Okunev, Tosiyasu L. Kunii, Fast collision detection between complex solids using rasterizing graphics hardware, *The Visual Computer*, 11(9): 497–511, 1995.

[6] Jarek Rossignac, Abe Megahed, Bengt-Olaf Schneider. Interactive inspection of solids: cross-sections and interferences. *Computer Graphics (SIGGRAPH '92 Proceedings)*, 26: 353–360; July 1992.

[7] Klaus H., Edith M. Rateitschak, Herbert F. Wolf, Thomas M. Hassell, *Color Atlas of Dental Medicine 1, Periodontology*, vol. 1. Georg Thieme Verlag, Stuttgart, New York, 2nd edn, 1989.

[8] John F. Schlag, Using geometric constructions to interpolate orientation with quaternions, *Graphics Gems II*, James R. Arvo, ed., pp. 377–380, Academic Press, 1991.

[9] Mikio Shinya, Marie-Claire Forgue, Interference detection through rasterization, *The Journal of Visualization and Computer Animation*, 2(4): 131–134, 1991.

[10] Ken Shoemake, Animating rotation with quaternion curves, *Computer Graphics (SIGGRAPH '85 Proceedings)*, 19: 245–254; July 1985.

[11] Hank Weghorst, Gary Hooper, Donald P. Greenberg. Improved computational methods for ray tracing. *ACM Transactions on Graphics*, 3(1): 52–69, 1984.

25
Visual User Interface – A Third-Generation GUI Paradigm

Mikael Jern

25.1 Introduction: The User Interface is the Gateway to Visualization

When people talk about the look and feel of computers, they are referring to the graphical user interface (GUI). The GUI improved enormously starting around 1971 with work at Xerox, and culminated in a real product a decade later when Steve Jobs had the wisdom and perseverance to introduce the Macintosh. The Mac was a major step forward in the marketplace and, by comparison, almost nothing has happened since. It took all the other computer companies more than five years to copy Apple and, in some cases, they have done so with inferior results even today.

The integration of modeling, visualization, client/server, and new interaction techniques will change and expand the paradigms of current work of humans using computers. One way to make visualization products easier to learn and use, and users more productive, is to improve the visual communication that takes place in all of the elements of the user interface, i.e., to provide decreased *'time-to-enlightenment'*. There is a clear need to take a long view of user interface design if we are to encourage evolution and not revolution of software for supporting information systems. The notion of 'interactive desktop data visualization' will prove itself to be more useful than traditional 'menu driven' techniques.

It is important to understand at the outset that a 'user interface' is not only a screen design but also a *method of interacting with the application and its data*. The combination is often referred to as 'look-and-feel'. 'Look' refers to the physical appearance of an application screen to a user, whereas 'feel' refers to the way the user interacts with the screen and hence the underlying application and its data model. The 'look' makes the applications more attractive and easier to use, but it does not change the basic way users work with numerical data. As information threatens to overwhelm them, corporations must be able to call upon the computer to help them visualize the meanings hidden behind numerical data. This chapter will focus on the 'feeling' of the GUI concept.

The rapid success of the desktop 'point & click' metaphor running under Macintosh and Windows environments has been driving the development of graphical user interfaces (GUI). These GUIs use icons, toolbars, browsers, multiple windows, navigation and coaching techniques, and direct manipulation of graphical objects, and reflect the easy comprehension of the combination of metaphors – the clarity of a cognitive model and the ease of navigation.

Visualization and Modeling
ISBN 0-12-227738-4

As graphics display adapters, high-resolution color monitors, and pointing devices have become generally affordable, users of these applications have been able to realize the benefits of intuitive human–computer interaction. Pointing devices allow users to interact with graphic objects on the display, while high-resolution graphics monitors allow efficient presentation of graphical information.

The industry is now moving toward a third-generation GUI with a 'picture-centric' focus emphasizing direct-interaction with graphical objects and data. This new paradigm, the *visual user interface* (VUI, pronounced *view-ee*) puts into practice the adage 'a visual user interface is worth a thousand commands.' The way a VUI improves on the capabilities of second-generation GUIs is to interpret text and numbers as pictures, showing their relative scales and various relationships. The most revolutionary difference of VUI technology is, however, that the users interact directly with graphics objects and the underlying data model instead of using menus and commands.

Reusable industry components and component-oriented visual programming, eclipsing object-oriented programming, has taken the software industry by storm. Visual Basic from Microsoft already has an installed base of several million users. Other component-oriented integration environments include Delphi from Borland, PowerSoft's PowerBuilder, Parts from Digitalk, Visual AppBuilder from Novell, XVT PowerObject from XVT Software, and NextStep Interface Builder from Next. This chapter will demonstrate visualization components and provide an example of a visual programming system (AVS/Express), for developing complete data visualization applications or building reusable visualization components (C++ classes or OLE) that can be used within larger applications. These 'visual' environments allow users to perform rapid prototyping and build components, connecting them together, with the compelling benefits of component-oriented application development and shielding the users from cross-platform and cross-protocol dependencies.

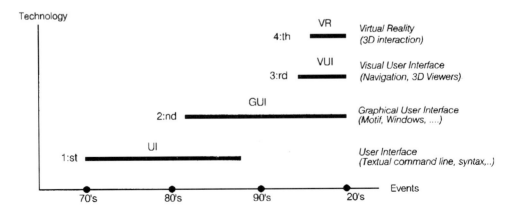

Figure 25.1   The visual user interface (VUI) represents a third-generation user interface paradigm and acts as the gap or 'missing link' between traditional GUI technology and advanced VR technology.

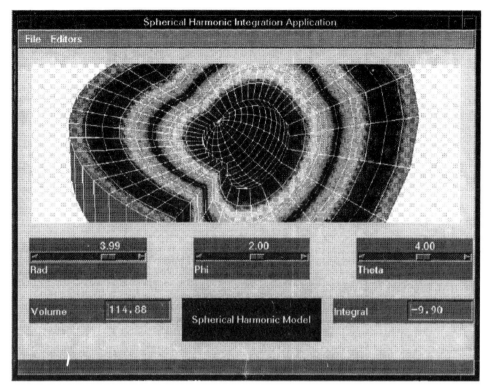

Figure 25.2 Example of a visual user interface (VUI) with direct manipulation 'steering' of the underlying 3D data model. The 3D data structure is parametrized so that a slider controls effect the angular sections and radius. Any time these are changed, the resulting 3D volume is calculated, and the spherical cosine function is integrated through this area. The demo shows an 'energy wave' originating from a single point in all directions, but blocked by some nearby walls. Colors (shades) indicate the spherical wave energy. This customized VUI example was produced with AVS/Express.

25.2 A Paradigm Shift to VUIs Based on Graphics Object-Oriented Technology

Computer science in particular feels the impact of shifts in technology and the future of industrial warfare. For example, many companies have suffered setbacks by recognizing too late the importance of the shift from character-oriented user interfaces (UI) to graphical user interfaces (GUI). Only a few years ago, these GUIs were never discussed in computer science literature, but now they constitute an entire field of study within computing. As the industry is now quickly moving toward the third-generation GUI – visual user interfaces (VUI) – the old models again risk being left behind.

There are four major trends in software development:

- Object-oriented technology
- Component software
- Visual programming
- Visual user interface (VUI)

Object-oriented has become the most widely used and abused buzzword in the software industry. Many so-called 'object-oriented' programs are only 'object-based,' meaning they provide some, but not all, of the benefits of object-oriented development. For instance, their objects can only inherit objects or methods from a single source and not multiple sources, or the code may not be entirely reusable, and so on. However, in the overall software engineering arena, the action is in object-oriented languages, object-oriented databases, object-oriented software engineering, object-oriented graphics, and object-oriented interaction techniques.

Object-oriented technology, however, is not new; it began at Xerox PARC already in the 1970s, but it has been held back by its need for powerful desktop computing. More than a buzzword, this is a paradigm shift at a serious level. Many billions of dollars have already been invested by Microsoft, IBM, Apple (joint venture in Taligent), and Hewlett-Packard in object-oriented software environments.

There are compelling reasons for object technology's current vogue. It solves three major problems facing software developers:

- The need for rapid, incremental, iterative development of new applications
- The need to capitalize software and thus encourage reuse of proven components
- The need to reduce maintenance cost

To drive down the cost of software development, one has to apply a principle that software theorists have known for years. The best programmers are not just a little better than average programmers. They are shockingly better – 10 times, maybe 100 times more productive. Visual programming and reusable component technology represent an important step toward a new paradigm in software engineering and will probably reduce our dependency on C++ gurus.

25.3   Visual User Interface (VUI) Technology

Key features of a UVI include:

- 'Picture-centric' user interface
- Direct interaction – 'Explore and navigate'
- Graphics object picking and data probing
- Close connection to data
- Object-oriented focused graphics
- Control of geometry resolution
- Direct engagement of the user

A well-designed VUI system generates enthusiasm and engagement from its users because of the following factors.

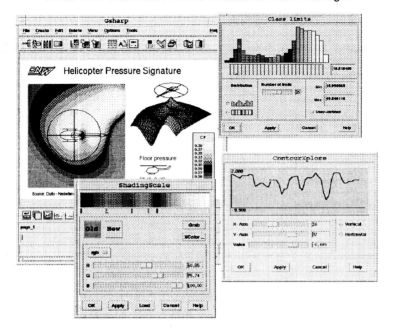

Figure 25.3   An example of a modern VUI interface, available in AVS/UNIRAS'
Gsharp product, with support of pickable graphics objects and data probing.

- Novices can learn the basic functionality quickly – the system immediately answers to a direct interaction with any graphics objects on the screen.
- Experienced users can work extremely rapidly to carry out a wide range of tasks.
- Users can immediately see whether their actions are furthering their goals and, if they are not, can simply change the direction of their activity.
- It interacts directly with the underlying data structure through the graphics objects – intimate connection to underlying data.
- Users gain confidence and mastery because they initiate an action, feel in control and can predict system responses.
- The large number of pop-up dialogs (typical for a GUI) is reduced.

25.3.1   'Look'-focused versus 'object'-focused interaction

The most revolutionary difference between a traditional GUI and VUI technology is that users interact directly with on screen graphics and the data behind the graphics without having to work with traditional GUI elements like pull-down menus and dialog boxes.

Most GUI environments are *'look'-focused*, i.e., the screen objects (graphics and data) are examined and manipulated through *intermediaries*. The screen objects feel distanced because they cannot be reached directly by the user, but must be 'looked at' or touched through GUI tools like pull-down menus, icons or dialogs, and controls.

The screen objects are therefore secondary because the GUI tools are manipulated as the primary action.

The *object-focused* VUI model eliminates the sense of an intermediary. The screen object in the user interface is intended to be concrete, immediate, and primary. The on-screen representation of the object is considered to represent the object itself, including its underlying data structure and properties, not merely a singular element through which the object shows itself. There will be limited needs for menus, browsers, dialogs, or other such GUI tools with which to identify, move, and manipulate the object, because the user can already see and interact with the screen objects themselves. We refer to this sense of immediacy with the screen objects of interest as *direct engagement*. The concreteness of direct engagement is achieved by making it seem as if the objects are physical, real-world things. Thus their concreteness is not only one of spatial localization and identity, but also one of image and behavior. The objects not only look like real things but they also move solidly.

Just seeing and moving an object is not enough to give a complete sense of identity. It must also have appropriate properties and data associated with it, just as real-world objects have properties. Since its properties, data structure, and behavior are properly owned by the object, the user must go to the object to get at them – the principle of primacy.

25.3.2   Object picking and data probing in VUI technology

Data visualization handles large and complex data sets which are presented on a 2D screen. Data exploration is much more comfortable when user interaction is supported for direct data selection and for direct object construction. The introduction of direct

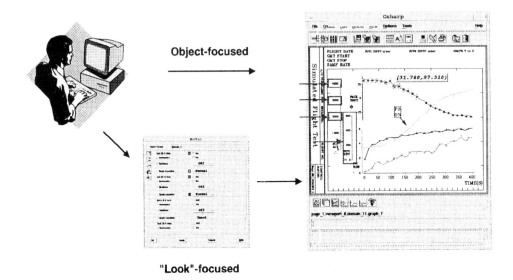

Figure 25.4   Graphics objects are manipulated through a dialog box in a 'look'-focused GUI, versus an object-focused direct interaction with the objects (gray arrows).

manipulation in data visualization has been viewed as part of a process which has seen the progressive lowering of the barriers that separate the users from their data, leading to faster, more direct interaction with it.

Examples of direct manipulation operations include the possibility for the user to pick any graph object and change its resources (attributes), modify viewing interactively, and drag-and-drop graphical objects. The user must also be able to explore an area of interest by direct 'pointing' into its domain. Direct manipulation, of course, demands a high image generation rate in order to offer an immediate and reversible feedback in interaction. It is important to understand at the outset that a 'user interface' is not only a screen design but also a *method of interacting with the application and its data.*

A VUI mimics what people do when they interpret information. When a person reads something containing many complex elements, he or she typically tries to visualize the relationships among those elements. With a VUI, those relationships are defined. A VUI remodels the data so that numerical values are hidden behind a picture that expresses these relationships as a graphical object. Information is automatically mapped into the graphics by the VUI application.

To change a graphics picture (bar chart, contour map, isosurface, etc.) in a traditional GUI-based visualization application, the numbers behind the picture must first be changed. To change the same picture in a VUI application, however, the user simply 'grabs' a bar or line in a graph and changes it directly. The numbers behind the picture change automatically to reflect the new picture.

The basis for this capability is object-oriented graphics technology. VUIs, as much as possible, represent information as physical objects. The information about the objects is stored in a 'database' as they exist in their own 2D or 3D 'world', not just as a 2D array of pixels drawn on the screen. The objects in a graph can be picked, highlighted, and manipulated as discrete entities.

The example in Figure 25.5, shows how the user can pick any graph objects such as an axis, curve, curve through a legend entry, etc. Closest data points are automatically identified. The resources (attributes) of an axis are interactively modified by pointing to the selected item. Upon selecting a component of an object, a user gets an immediate response.

The relationship of a visual object (curve, bar, pie, contour, vector, etc.) to its underlying data structure is instantaneous. If the user, for example, interactively 'drags' a curve, the underlying numerical data is immediately updated.

The use of a single window lets end users manipulate their data 'in place,' instead of having to switch between separate windows, for example, a graph window and a data editor window, to edit the underlying data. Synchronizing a data editor with a data probe operation could be a useful visual data operation and is illustrated in Figure 25.6. When the user moves the cursor across the selected graph, the corresponding numerical data value is both shown in a control above the cursor position and highlighted in the data editor. Selecting a cell in the data editor will highlight the position in the graph.

Why are VUIs valuable? Managers of all types must still make wise decisions despite being drowned with more and more data. Visualization technology eases the decision-making process by crunching the numbers and providing and providing meaningful pictures up front. Through the easy-to-use VUI, the managers can ask the 'what-if' questions, without any dependency on a graphics expert.

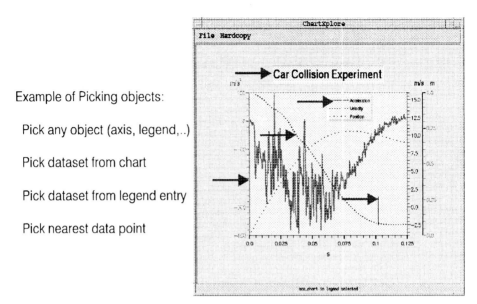

Example of Picking objects:

Pick any object (axis, legend,..)

Pick dataset from chart

Pick dataset from legend entry

Pick nearest data point

Figure 25.5 The basis for a VUI system is an object-oriented graphics technology. To change any item (graphics or data), the user simply points to the objcct and changes il directly.

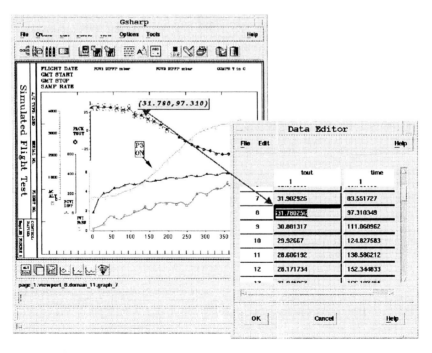

Figure 25.6 Data probing and synchronized data editor with probe.

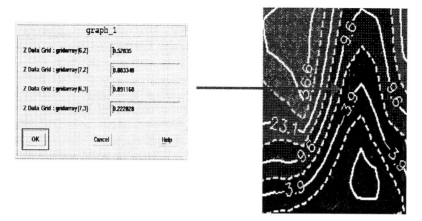

Figure 25.7 Data probing in contouring.

The challenge of the visualization environments is the graphical user interface. The ideal interface must be completely transparent to the user of the system, allowing interactive, intuitive, and creative exploration of data without previous knowledge of the system.

The rapid success of the desktop metaphor in the PC environment, which uses icons, toolbars, browsers, multiple windows, navigation technique, and direct manipulation of graphical objects, reflects the easy comprehension of the combination of metaphors – the clarity of a cognitive model and the ease of navigation.

User interfaces are now so important that, for many applications, the amount of code devoted to the user interface exceeds that for the application. An attractive look and feel and user interaction in a product is as important to its success as its functionality. For example, new releases of MS-Windows based products like WordPerfect, WORD, and CorelDRAW focus more on enhancing the user interaction methods and ease-of-use than adding new features.

The new VUI paradigm will foster direct visual comprehension that enables millions of users to manage complex visualization applications relatively easily. We need to improve the visual communication that takes place in all of the elements of the VUI.

While seeing high-quality images is still very important, the trend in visualization is on the graphical user interfaces.

UNIX workstations and power PCs are falling in price. This means that more and more people can now get access to systems that have the power to produce more sophisticated visualization. To spread the use of graphics throughout this widening community, we need to combine this power graphics with more intuitive user interface design. But visualization algorithms and the design of user interfaces have become much more sophisticated and these very different programming tasks can no longer be carried out by the same people.

Custom research has demonstrated that users working in a 'direct manipulation' graphical user interface environment are much more productive than those working in a classic menu-driven environment. The advanced VUI users also suffered less fatigue and could work longer at a given level of effort.

User interfaces are now becoming so important for developers that for many applications, the total amount of code and energy devoted to the user interface may exceed that for the application. It is actually common that the user interface design and usability testing represent more than 80% of the total development cycle.

25.4   ComponentWare – Standards for Visual Component Evolution

There is now a considerable pressure on developers to deliver VUI-based applications because end-user preference is increasingly for point&click, direct-manipulation user interfaces. User expectations are high, but developers are failing to keep pace. Point&click applications are not easy to develop. VUI models include object-oriented tools, event-driven processing, client/server technology and C++ programming, which are new and difficult topics to most developers.

A new software engineering industry based on the *open systems* paradigm, providing 'standard,' reusable components, is emerging to solve this dilemma. Developers want to purchase components of a complete solution from different vendors. A customer might like one vendor's database system, another's spreadsheet, another's GUI builder, and yet another's visualization software. For example, you can now benefit from and integrate into your application components from many sources, including graphics objects, spreadsheets, database (db) viewers, hypertext On-line Help systems, etc. These components are delivered in the form of custom Motif widgets, C++ classes or through the latest CORBA open standard, Windows Controls, VBXs and OCXs (Visual Basic) in the MS-Windows environment.

C++ classes provide mechanisms to build robust component technology, i.e., encapsulating code and data. But the complexity of C++ programming prohibits most programmers from accessing this object-oriented technology. The time to learn how to use a particular class interface can prevent novices from accessing this technology. C++ is powerful but hard to use. At a time when programming systems should be easier to use, development systems using C++ are becoming more powerful but much harder to use. This is not to say that the C++ language will not play a role in the future of software development environments. C++ is used by high-quality expert developers to build industry 'standard' components to be used in a large number of projects.

A major disadvantage with C++ classes is that they cannot reach across compiled language and CPU platforms and should be distributed as source code. In contrast, distributed 'standard' objects like CORBA (Common Object Request Broker Architecture) supported by the open UNIX-based OMG (Object Management Group) and Microsoft's OLE (Object Linking and Embedding) are packaged as binary components accessible to remote clients. Clients do not have to know which language or compiler built a server object (or where on the network the object physically resides). They only need to know its name and the interface it publishes.

The emerging world of software components is setting standards that set the rules of engagement among different types of components. Visual Basic has opened the component programming market. Hundreds of vendors have produced low- and high-level OCX visual components that you easily can add to the VB environment and integrate into your application.

25.4.1   Component reusability

An application will only survive if its developers have the means for rapidly adapting existing technology to improve the suitability of their application. For example, an application's old plotting system must be replaced with a modern interactive graphing system without the need to rewrite the entire application.

Two main attributes determine the adaptability of an application:

- The reusability of the components used to develop the application
- The number of developers that are attracted to use these components to adapt the application

Developers need access to both high-level and low-level components. An application composed of only high-level components could be more difficult to adjust to a targeted set of users. With only low-level components, much more work and expertise time is required to build an application. There is a tension here between 'breadth' and 'depth' of reusability. The ideal application is one where developers have access to all levels of granularity and can choose the appropriate level at which to begin the adaptation, modifying some combination of high-level components and low-level components. No one component can be too monolithic, all application components should be partitioned into a few lower-level components so that when a developer finds the components that require modification the reproduction of these components is as manageable as possible.

The ease-of-reuse is a major factor in determining software component survivability.

25.4.2   Custom VUI motif components

Any VUI component that is properly implemented according to the X Window and Motif standards and complies with the Motif Style Guide can be integrated into a software development environment. Programming languages, user interfaces, spreadsheets, graphics, databases, widgets, etc., are all part of this object paradigm in an open systems environment. These 'standard' components can therefore be integrated within a GUI builder tool, allowing developers to interactively access components, build, and test fully functional application programs. Because this approach also hides the complexity of X Window and Motif programming, it also enables application programmers to build sophisticated event-driven VUI applications without having to be experts in this new complex programming paradigm.

The Toolmaster Xplore VUI components from AVS/UNIRAS represent a higher level of graphics specialization than the standard Motif widget set. These 30 interactive VUI graphing 'custom' widgets are an extension of the standard Motif widget toolkit and encapsulate comprehensive graphics functionality, event handling, and data manipulation into object-oriented components. The Xplore widgets provide application builders with a 'programless' access to highly interactive methods. Specialized visualization widgets are included for exploring and analyzing numerical data based on the VUI paradigm, using 2D, 3D, and 4D contour maps, grid maps, X-Y-Z scatter maps and X-Y graph components (curve, area, bar), profiles, histogram, color legend and table data editor. A GUI builder can be extended and integrated with these components.

An increasing number of today's applications require event-driven interactive graphics operations, interacting directly with the underlying numerical data and the graphics objects. One of the more interesting ironies of Motif programming is that Motif, a toolkit designed for implementing 'graphical' user interfaces, provides no graphics drawing or events like pick and zoom functionality. The functionality of Motif is at a lower level.

The object-oriented architecture of X Toolkit (Xt) based widgets provides one possible industry standard for implementing reusable application and interface components in the UNIX environment. Specialized custom widgets inherit Xt functionality while providing their own specific functional extensions. For X-based visualization applications, they are an elegant but low-level solution to developing interactive graphical programming requirements.

'Custom Motif widgets' are available from many commercial software companies (see Figure 25.8). These widgets are general enough for the user to reuse throughout their custom environment, yet also specific enough to solve their needs readily, easily, and without a great deal of supporting code.

These higher level components provide a coherent set of useful graphics widgets that not only draw themselves but also support a wide range of interactive behavior and hardcopy rendering that is traditionally the responsibility of the application. Because these widgets manage themselves, application programmers can concentrate on developing the application code rather than visualization code.

Custom widgets offer benefits to both the program developer and the user:

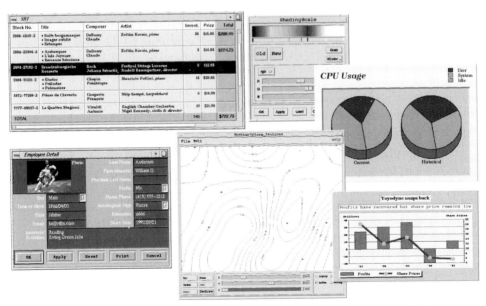

Figure 25.8 Example of commercial visual components from KL-Group and AVS/UNIRAS.

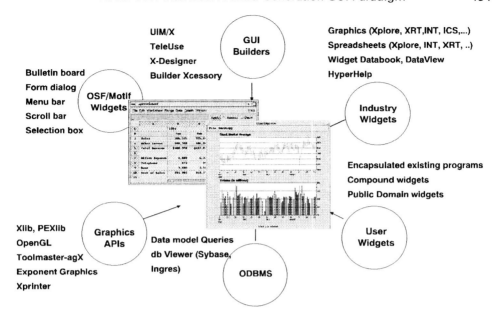

Figure 25.9 Applications including highly interactive visualization methods can be developed from commercial VUI components integrated into a GUI builder.

- Tedious and time consuming X event handling is removed from the developer.
- An object-oriented approach to data visualization is made possible, thus allowing. graphics objects to be directly manipulated.
- Motif Style Guide compliance ensures user acceptance and ease of use.
- They are accessible from most GUI builders.

An entirely new Motif manual, the *Widget Writer's Guide*, explains in detail the considerations involved in deciding whether you should spend your time writing a new Motif-derived widget, and if so, how to approach the task.

The 'Xplore' widgets include both low-level or 'atomic' graph widgets (Figure 25.10) for more experienced X and Motif developers and high-level 'compound graph' widgets for the application developers. An examples of a compound graph widget is the *ContourXplore* (Figure 25.11), combining functionality from the underlying graph widgets which together represent a complete encapsulated 'contour application.' The 'atomic' graph widgets can be used to build new compound widgets (see section 25.4.1 about component reusability).

25.5 Visual Programming Based on Components

Software development tools that support a visual form of programming are now in the introductory stages of their evolution and in many cases closely related to computer

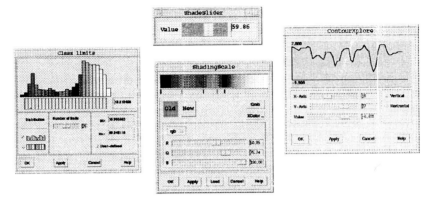

Figure 25.10   Example of low-level 'atomic' components.

graphics and visualization. For example, many of the GUI builders in use today include visual programming in the development process. Using visual technology, the GUI builders enable software developers to interactively, create, modify, test and automatically generate error-free C or C++ code for the user interface portion (dialogs, toolbars, tables, pull-down menus, etc.) of their applications. In addition, visual programming establishes user interface callbacks by providing visual connections between a UI widget and the associated function.

Perhaps the best-known visual programming tool is Microsoft's Visual Basic, introduced in 1991 and currently in Version 4. Visual Basic is used by several million developers as a high-level visual programming tool for creating custom applications. Visual Basic 4 offers a broad application development strategy and provides an easy-to-use programming paradigm that gets developers past their first major hurdle in application development.

AVS/Express is a multiplatform application development environment based on object-oriented visual programming. It provides state-of-the-art technology for advanced graphics, imaging, data visualization, and presentation graphics in an open and extensible environment. One uses visual programming to create and modify VUI components, and to combine them into higher-level application objects.

25.5.1   The strengths of visual programming

One of visual programming's greatest strengths is the ability to quickly examine an application's hierarchy of objects and their relationships. This is because a visual program provides a better representation of the mental model than a text file of C++ code. Visual programming promotes and encourages a structured approach to application construction. A complex application might have hundreds or even thousands of objects.

These 'visual programming' capabilities dramatically reduce the time required to construct a customized application. They also reduce the amount of new code that must be debugged and maintained. Rapid prototyping is another key area where visual programming has found acceptance. Developers are finding that visual programming gives them the ability to build applications by quickly and efficiently combining objects

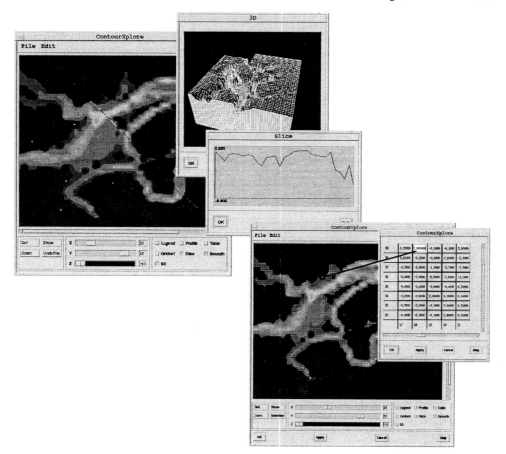

Figure 25.11 Example of a high-level custom Motif component 'ContourXplore' from AVS/UNIRAS. ContourXplore is a Compound graph widget (VUI component), which allows the display and direct interaction with a gridded data set. This VUI component is an example of an 'application' component, combining features from many underlying low-level graph 'atomic' widgets. Area selections, data editing, zoom, profile, and slice are supported. A Contour3D Graph widget is included for simultaneous viewing in both 2D and 3D. The profile in the 'slice widget' can be interactively edited, immediately updating the underlying data structure and the contour display. The picture above presents three views of profile data in a 2D gridded data set: a 2D contour, 3D surface, and a Slice graph. Constraints are used to keep the values consistent in all of its views. If either view of the profile values is edited, then all other views will be updated accordingly. In the lower right picture, a synchronized Data Editor is included. Moving the mouse over the 2D contour map will highlight the original data values from which the contour map was built, in the Data Editor widget. When the user is moving the mouse inside the Data Editor widget, the spatial location in the contour map is highlighted. ContourXplore is an example of a true VUI component supporting direct manipulation operations.

in ways that they would not have attempted with other development tools. End users are then able to provide immediate application design feedback to the developer.

Code reuse has many supporters in the software development community. The new category of visual programming environments constructs applications out of reusable objects, whether the objects are custom widgets/controls, C++ classes and distributed CORBA, or OLE objects. Existing old application code (C, Fortran, etc.) can be repackaged for the visual programming environment, thus providing the developer a path to bring proven technology into a modern application development environment. Once an object has been 'wrapped' for inclusion in the visual programming environment, the developer has a well-defined object that behaves by the rules. For example, rules automatically prevent connections between objects that do not process the same type of data.

These environments allow users to build components and connect them together with the compelling benefits of component-oriented application development and shielding the users from cross-platform and cross-protocol dependencies.

The advantages of using Visual Programming techniques can be summarized as:

- End user programming
- Object-oriented technology

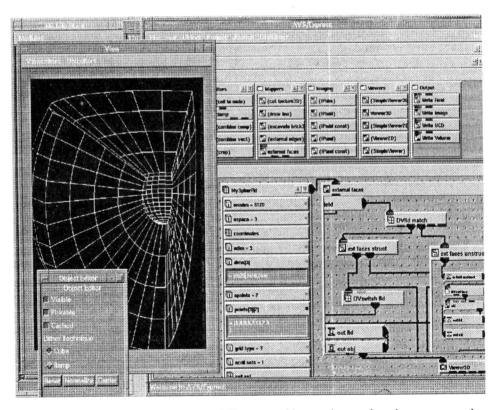

Figure 25.12 A view of the AVS/Express Network, a visual programming environment.

- Component software
- Rapid prototyping
- Design flexibility
- Encapsulation old code

25.5.2   The future development trend is visual programming

Future trends are always difficult to predict. However, it is clear that visual programming will become the dominant technology for application development. The transition to visual programming will not occur overnight, but its early successes have shown dramatic improvements in programmer productivity. The new class of desktop visual programming tools (Visual Basic 4, Delphi, etc.) Should bring overall awareness of this technology to a wider audience.

One of the most important driving forces behind the future success of visual programming will be growth in object-oriented software development, boosted by the emergence of distributed object standards such as OLE and CORBA. As more objects become available to application developers as components for inclusion in their applications, visual programming tools will become the preferred method for application construction. The next few years will present many opportunities for use of visual programming in the software development process. These new tools will provide us with the vision to rethink the way we develop new interaction techniques.

25.6   VUI Technology Used in VRML and the 3D World-Wide-Web (WWW)

3D interactive graphics on the network requires a 3D interactive format and an advanced VUI navigation system that combines 3D input and high-performance rendering capabilities. Using a '3D input technique,' the user wants to intuitively navigate inside the 3D data, while selecting 3D objects with the mouse triggers requests for access to remote media documents that can be text, still images, animations, or even other 3D objects. Time-critical rendering techniques in the 'navigation tools' allow the user to display complex 3D scenes at high and constant frame rates, making it possible to use it in the context of large-scale projects.

VRML (Virtual Reality Modeling Language) is the language for describing multiuser interactive simulations – virtual worlds networked via the global Internet and hyperlinked within the World Wide Web (WWW). VRML is an open, platform-independent file format for 3D graphics. Similar in concept to Web standard for text, HyperText Markup Language or HTML, VRML encodes computer-generated 3D graphics into a compact format for transportation over a network. As with HTML, a user can view the contents of a file – in this case an interactive 3D graphics file – as well as navigate to other VRML 'worlds' or HTML pages.

VRML is defined as a very compressed file format by nature of the fact that it is a high-level language which represents complex 3D graphics with minimal text. The real work is done by the browser in the local machine. The browser interprets the text, builds the appropriate geometry, and displays the motion. Nothing additional is required in the way of bandwidth to support 3D graphics on the WWW. The VRML files can also be compressed and then decompressed by the VRML browser.

Using the VUI technology with a VRML file, one can now fly through virtual 3D landscapes, visualize stock market trends in 3D, or inspect 3D models of products in on-line catalogs. Text, images, video, audio, and even other 3D models can be accessed directly from a true 3D environment, making information access as easy as browsing in a bookstore.

The visual cues provided by interactive 3D viewing with continuous control offer invaluable help in understanding the represented data. If images are rendered smoothly and quickly enough, an illusion of real-time exploration of a virtual environment can be achieved as the simulated observer moves through the model. For example, in scientific data visualization, large multidimensional data sets can be inspected and better understood by research colleagues by walking through their 3D virtual data projections.

To best perform its function, an interactive system for navigating a 3D VRML environment should combine time-critical rendering of the 3D scenes, interactive 3D navigation and viewing capabilities, level-of-detail selection to reduce the number of polyons rendered in each frame, and 'point-and-seek' functionality.

High feedback bandwidth and low response times are crucial for an interactive VRML session. In order to guarantee low response times when handling large datasets, the navigation tool must be able to adaptively trade rendering and computation quality with speed. For example, the special 'LevelOfDetail' feature of VRML is used to reduce the number of polygons rendered in each frame. The navigation tool should automatically simplify a scene if rendering performance begins to slow down while one is moving through the scene. As soon as one stops moving, the higher level of details returns. This is an important feature, which allow the user to navigate well on low-bandwidth networks. The user can always choose the most appropriate level of detail for graphics performance.

The 'point-and-click seek' navigation feature gives users an intuitive interface for 3D navigation. One simply points to a place in the world and the viewer takes you there. Authors can also build worlds in which the data defining the world is loaded only if the user 'navigates' closer to it and thus creates 'infinitely scalable' worlds.

25.7   Future Challenges

What does the future hold for data visualization systems and visual user interaction? Faster desktop computing will improve response time. We will see collaborative work by geographically separated teams of experts supported by the VRML standard and the effective use of networks. A major research effort is to provide effective analysis and visualization of very large data sets.

New models for interactive visualization are an important research topic and should include a more detailed study of the following areas:

- Foundations of visualization
- Simulation and integration of visualization with simulations
- Handling of multimodal interfaces

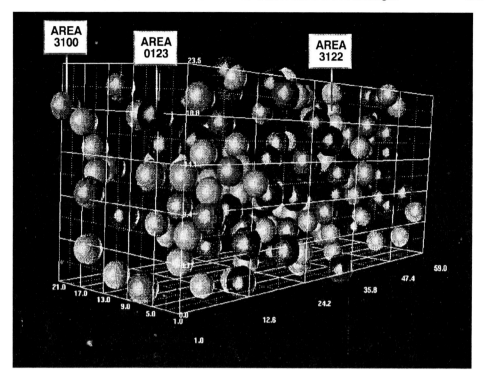

Figure 25.13 Example of a 3D VRML scene produced with AVS/Express to be viewed by a 3D browser. This annotated 3D scene is composed of spheres. Some spheres are associated with additional information that is accessed through HTTP. The signs help to guide the user. These media annotations link the spheres to other documents, thus allowing 'guided tours' within a world.

- Exploitation of virtual reality tools for interaction
- Exploration and interpretation of very large data sets in real time

25.7.1 Visualization of very large data sets

Direct-manipulation user interface applications allow the user to manipulate graphical objects directly. At the same time, these applications respond interactively to the user's input actions. Managing large data sets and interacting with them directly in real time and allowing more direct exploitation in the context of virtual reality input requires new visualization methods and is a challenging research topic. Below are some examples that have already been proven to solve the problem:

- Data reduction using wavelets
- Multiresolution models – interactive 'level-of-detail' selection, etc.
- Local rendering
- Data reference architecture (instead of 'data flow')

In order to deliver the maximum possible degree of interactivity and usability in a data exploration and interpretation system, there are the following key design objectives to be considered:

- Locally construct visualization objects – focus on specific details of interest.
- Interactive control of field value tolerance (grid size, etc.) – minimize the construction time.
- Interactive control of geometry tolerance – minimize the 'density' of low-level graphics primitives.
- Explore the 3D field data using navigation tools like the Spaceball, Glove, 3D mouse, etc.

In order to maximize user control of where features are to be extracted from, the visualization system needs to be able to very rapidly jump over entire regions of underlying field data, ignoring the underlying details while the user is steering the cursor around the field domain, and then slow down and interpolate local underlying field data when the user is carefully focusing interest on a localized region within the data.

Similarly, in order to minimize the density of low-level graphics primitives used to represent a given feature, a visualization system needs to be able to create only a few geometrically large primitives in regions where there is little or no variation in field values regardless of the way in which the field data is represented at the physical object layer. Conversely, in regions where there are sudden changes in field values, a system needs to be able to create many geometrically small primitives so as to adequately capture these changes and display them to the user.

25.7.2 3D Navigation tools

The computer industry and its large body of users are finally accepting the 20-year-old Xerox PARC User Interface technology as popularized by the Mac and publicized through Microsoft Windows. Is it not finally time to move on? These GUIs were based on low-power, bitmap graphics workstations, yet today we have available platforms with an order of magnitude greater computer power, high-resolution color graphics, 3D graphics accelerators, and a variety of input devices with more degrees of freedom than the mouse.

3D data visualization, for example, handles complex data sets which are presented on a 2D screen. Data exploration is much more comfortable when user interaction is supported for direct data selection and for direct object construction. Examples of direct manipulation operations include the possibility for the user to modify viewing and move the light sources interactively. The user must also be able to explore an area of interest by direct 'pointing' into the 3D domain. Direct manipulation, of course, demands a high image generation rate in order to offer an immediate and reversible feedback in interaction.

Traditional input devices (dials, a mouse, etc.) have only two degrees of freedom. Trying to compensate this drawback and enabling users to simulate 3D interaction with such devices using GUI software does not provide a suitable solution.

Experiments have shown that a 6D input device like the Spaceball will improve the interaction performance in 3D systems significantly, which is especially valuable to inexperienced scientists and engineers. This is also regarded as being closely related to the exploitation of virtual reality paradigms for the benefit of interactive visualization. The best-known attribute of virtual reality is the sense of presence or immersion. It is expensive to provide the latter, but the user's intuitive relationship with the data space can be enhanced by having more direct coupling with the attributes of the data. The sense of presence distinguishes virtual reality from multimedia systems or interactive computer graphics.

It is proposed that the more the application can persuade the user that the virtual data space is a natural extension of the user's space, the more productive will be the user's interaction with the data. Clearly, the validation of this claim will be the subject of work which is beyond the scope of this paper and which will include comparative studies of user efficiency and effectiveness using different interaction paradigms.

> Let us not limit our user interface vision with minor extension of the popular 2D metaphors of the past and present, but instead, explore the use of promising new technologies such as 6D input devices, direct manipulation, 4D real-time animation, and Virtual Reality.

Utilization of generalized interaction environments such as those using virtual reality tools and techniques will enable exploration of the appropriateness of the use of sound and gesture as a mode of direct interaction with the data. I believe that this could also be utilized to enhance the interactive visualization paradigm in the future.

Further Reading

Mikes and Keller, The fact and fictions about X Window System GUI development tools, *The X Journal* 2(1): 28-35; 1992.

M. Jern, Evolution of a visualization object component industry, *The X Journal* 2(1): 42–46; 1992.

M. Jern, Visual programming using higher level visualization Motif widgets, *Animation and Scientific Visualization*, R.A. Earnshaw, D. Watson, Academic Press, 1993.

ICS, *ICS Widget Databook*, ICS Cambridge, Mass., 1994.

S. Cunningham, *Computer Graphics Using Object-Oriented Programming*, Wiley, 1992.

F. Culwin, *An X/Motif Programmer's Primer*, Prentice Hall, 1993.

T. Berlage, *OSF/Motif – Concepts and Programming*, Addison-Wesley, 1992.

D.A. Young, *Object-oriented Programming with C++ and OSF/Motif*, Prentice Hall, 1992.

G. Lee, *Object-oriented GUI application development*, Prentice Hall, 1993.

Open Software Foundation, *The Widget Writer's Guide*, Prentice Hall, 1994.

G. Lee, *Object-oriented GUI Application Development*, Prentice Hall, 1993.

M. Burnett, A. Goldberg, G. Lewis, *Visual Object-oriented Programming*, Manning, 1995.

M. Jern, R.A. Earnshaw, Interactive real-time visualization systems using a virtual reality paradigm, *Visualization in Scientific Computing*, Springer-Verlag, 1995.

C. Upson, T. Fulhauber, D. Kamins, D. Laidlaw, D. Sclegel, J. Vroom, R. Gurwitz, A. van Dam, The Application Visualization System: A computational environment for scientific visualization, *IEEE Computer Graphics Appl.* 9(4): 30–42; 1989.

A. Parisi, M. Pesce, Virtual Reality Modeling Language (VRML), 1994. *URL: http://www.wired.com/vrml/*

Silicon Graphics WWW, 1995. *URL: http://www.sgi.com*

26
Multimedia Applications over Broadband ATM Networks

Wim Lamotte, Rae Earnshaw, Frank Van Reeth, and
Eddy Flerackers

26.1 Introduction

Within various classes of multimedia applications, advanced networking is becoming
an indispensible component. Given the intrinsic variation in the type of data (text,
video, sound, voice, images . . .) to be processed in multimedia systems on the one hand,
and the requirement of substantial bandwidth to communicate this multimedia data on
the other hand, an appropriate networking technology has to be utilised. Asynchronous
Transfer Mode (ATM) is such a technology allowing broadband communication of
various mixed forms of multimedia information. This chapter will elucidate how ATM
can be exploited to support multimedia applications requiring high communication
bandwidths.

The various scenarios we realised within the European RACE TEN-IBC project
VISINET ("3-dimensional visualisation over networks") will be discussed: it will be
shown how remote presentation, remote program execution and collaborative work
within 3D industrial design and architecture are implemented over ATM networks.

In addition to the VISINET results, we will discuss how a local MPEG-1 based Video
Retrieval trial is set up over the same ATM network. In the first part, we summarise the
VISINET experience, elaborating on the different scenarios, the network configuration,
the applications and some measurements. The second part will summarise the video
retrieval tests that we performed using a hybrid ATM-Ethernet network. And to finish,
we will draw some conclusions from the experiments described and show some future
directions for this research.

26.2 VISINET

26.2.1 Introduction

Computer-supported collaborative work over networks and networked multimedia has
become an important research topic over the past few years (see, e.g., [1–5]).

The participants in VISINET have conducted a trial of new working methods based
around the use of virtual representation and virtual reality techniques over trans-
European ATM networks. Designers, architects, city planners, and engineers have been

Visualization and Modeling
ISBN 0-12-227738-4

working collaboratively with virtual 3D models from a number of locations in the Netherlands, Belgium, the United Kingdom, and Portugal. The project started in August 1994 but, owing to delays in the availability of the trans-European ATM pilot network, user trials were only able to begin in January 1995.

The project is part of the TEN-IBC program, in which common-interest groups of users and application developers from different industry sectors have been working together to explore the potential for using ATM networks to allow people located in different parts of Europe to work together on the same design project.

VISINET connects partners in the Netherlands, Belgium, the United Kingdom, and Portugal via the European ATM network. Using these connections, different scenarios have been investigated, and the results are widely disseminated (see, e.g., [6, 7]). Let us first take a look at the overall objectives of VISINET.

26.2.2   Objectives

The main objectives of the trial were as follows:

- To demonstrate the use of broadband communications to provide advanced systems on an 'as required' basis, using off-the-shelf applications
- To evaluate the performance of new interactive tools such as virtual representation in a distributed environment
- To evaluate whether broadband will shorten the design to product lead times and increase quality by facilitating collaborative working
- To identify the commercial benefits of remote CAD working over broadband, and measure these benefits where possible
- To determine the potential size of the common interest group
- To increase awareness among potential users of remote CAD and virtual representation possibilities
- To identify obstacles to adoption of remote virtual representation
- To stimulate activity of CAD tool vendors and users in broadband communications

In the rest of this text we only elucidate the technical aspects of the project, we do not go into detail on the user-aspects.

26.2.3   Overview of scenarios

The trial scenarios can be classified under three different types:

Scenario 1: Remote presentation (Figure 26.1)
The design centre is asked by the client to perform 3D virtual representations and visualizations, which will be presented to the client by the design center over broadband networks. The results are discussed on-line, using voice and/or video.

Scenario 2: Remote program execution (Figure 26.2)
The remote execution scenario is similar to the remote presentation scenario, but the actions, i.e., 'treatment' of the virtual model/prototype, will now be performed by the users themselves, resulting in rendering on the machine of the computing center.

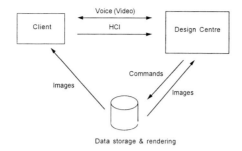

Figure 26.1   Remote presentation.

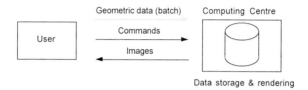

Figure 26.2   Remote program execution.

During the scenario there is no interaction of the designers at all.

Scenario 3: Collaborative work application (Figure 26.3)
Different sites are working together on the same database to reduce the time-to-market and cost of the projects by using the expertise of each other to intervene as soon as possible in the production design phase by having the comments of the partners involved in the different phases at the most appropriate moment.

26.2.4   Network connection diagram

In Figure 26.4, the network connections are depicted, with the respective line speeds for each interconnection. Note that these line speeds are the lines' maximum rates. In practice, a lower rate is usually allocated by the respective PNOs (ranging from 2 to 12

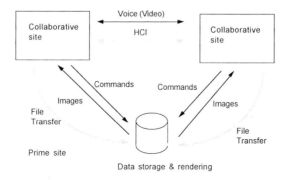

Figure 26.3   Collaborative work.

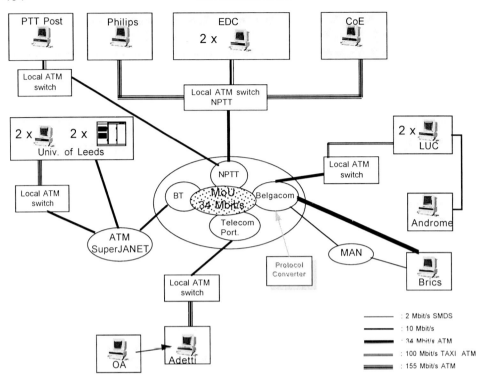

Figure 26.4   Network connection diagram.

Mbits/s, except between the Dutch sites, where a bandwidth of 155 Mbits/s is available). For more information on the SuperJANET network, which was used to connect the United Kingdom to the rest of the MoU network, see [8].

26.2.5   Applications

Since it was one of the objectives to use off-the-shelf technology and to investigate its effectiveness in supporting the different scenarios, we mostly used software that was already commercially available.

Videoconferencing with shared whiteboard : SGI's InPerson
InPerson is a commercially available videoconferencing tool, available for the Silicon Graphics platform. It allows users to communicate using voice and video, but additionally there is a shared whiteboard in which each participant can draw, sketch, paste images, or manipulate 3D models (based on the Open Inventor format). This is a very useful basic tool for the Remote Presentation scenario.

Sharing applications
XTeleScreen is being used as a means to transmit X-server calls over a network to a remote workstation. In this way, it is possible to use the same application with the same

data on more than one site. All participants see exactly the same interface. There are two modes of moderating such a session: In the 'polite' mode, there is one user in possession of the 'chalk.' Only when that user is explicitly handing over the chalk to another user can the latter take control of the program. The second mode is the 'anarchy' mode: In this mode, anyone can take the 'chalk' and start using the program at any time. Of course, for this method to work practically, there has to be another type of 'protocol' between the users (e.g., just by talking to each other).

Visualization

ElectroGIG's 3D-GO is an application for photorealistic images, 3D modeling, and animation. It contains a solid modeler, a ray tracer, an animation utility, and several modules for special effects such as particles. The X-windows version of 3D-GO, used in combination with XTeleScreen, provides a very interesting and powerful CSCW environment for joint editing and viewing, in the domains of product design, modeling, animation, and also as an aid for remote teaching and training of the 3D-GO product itself. This environment was extensively used in the Collaborative Work scenario of the project.

Another software tool, Alias Studio (from Alias) is a surface modeler which provides high-quality output of ray traced images and sophisticated animation. Since the ray tracer can be started as a shell-process, this allows the remote execution of rendering jobs, a useful feature for the Remote Execution scenario.

Pro Engineer is an engineering application devoted specially to highly technical product design, with a parametric modeler tool. Pro Engineer allows very easy changes in dimensions and features. Pro Engineer geometry can be translated to 3D-GO or Alias Studio to make photorealistic visualizations. This is one of the applications used for the Remote Presentation scenario.

Other CAD applications used during the VISINET project include AutoCAD, MicroStation, EMS, I/Design, and ComputerVision.

Virtual reality

With Division's dVS virtual reality distributed architecture and dVISE virtual reality visualization and authoring tool, 3D geometry can be transferred and interacted with in a virtual environment. The environment can be displayed on a monitor (SGI machines) or when running on appropriate hardware displayed in stereo mode, using a head mounted display (HMD) or shutter glasses (polarized LCD). As input devices, 2D or 3D mice or even more sophisticated 3D input devices (data-glove), can be used. In high-end SGI workstations, dVISE is capable of generating real-time animation sequences, with such characteristics as texture mapping, radiosity, or Phong lighting models and anti-aliasing.

dVISE, the virtual reality visualization and authoring tool that was used extensively, can convert 3D geometry in DXF format (produced, for example, in AutoCAD) into its own internal format (MAZ). This provides the possibility to make 'virtual walk-throughs' in 3D scenarios developed with third-party CAD systems. In dVISE's virtual environment, a set of tools can be used to change the properties of the geometry (material), change lighting conditions, and associate specific events (collision between the virtual user and the geometry) with sound sources. The system also provides a library with C programming language binding, for the development of special functionality.

dVS can be configured to work either in stand-alone or in group modes. In the latter mode, a group of users connected by means of a network is specified and each one is allowed to 'fly' in the virtual environment. While moving through the virtual 3D space, all users can see each others' virtual representations of a hand and face or body. A 'guided' tour around the scenario is made possible if all the users agree on some form of social protocol, where one of them is elected the Guide, and the others follow the Guide's virtual representation without bypassing him.

This application is used for the Collaborative Work as well as for the Remote Presentation Scenarios.

26.2.6   Bandwidth measurements

The total peak rate that was imposed on the international connections (typically between 8 and 12 Mbits/s) could be allocated in different ways to the different aspects of the application. The bandwidth used by the videoconferencing software InPerson greatly depends on the size of the video and the compression technique used. Table 26.1 gives the range within which the bandwidth resides. Furthermore, the impact of the collaborative work using XTeleScreen and 3D-GO is also measured. The figures given are the rates observed during a typical session: The minimum and maximum bandwidth are observed for operations requiring a lower or a higher bandwidth, respectively. For example, a low bandwidth is sufficient for just talking over the link, while a high bandwidth is required for communication-intensive 3D operations such as rotating a complex object or loading a complex image into the shared whiteboard. For the virtual reality applications, no detailed bandwidth measurements have been made yet.

Table 26.1   Collaborative work bandwidth measurements

Application	Minimum bandwidth (Kbits/s)	Maximum bandwidth (Mbits/s)
InPerson	345	8
XTeleScreen + 3D-GO	768	3.3
Collaborative work using InPerson, XTeleScreen, and 3D-GO	1113	11.3

26.3   Video Retrieval

26.3.1   Introduction

In this trial, tests have been performed to access a video server hosting several hundreds of megabytes of MPEG1-compressed video films. In order to enable multiple users, and access from a large distance (Europe-wide), the main communications channel uses the pan-European ATM network. The overall protocol used as basis is TCP/IP. But as we will point out in the following sections, the underlying medium is either ATM or Ethernet.

26.3.2   Generic configuration

The generic configuration is depicted in Figure 26.5. We use a UNIX-based video server and a PC as client workstation. The video server hosts the digital video films as well as an ATM interface board. The clients host an MPEG decoder board, allowing us to play an MPEG-1 compressed stream in real time.

The PC runs a sockets-based client program that connects to the video server. After requesting a certain movie, the MPEG data stream is sent by the server over the network to the PC. Here the client software transports the incoming data to the MPEG decoder card, where it is directly decoded and displayed.

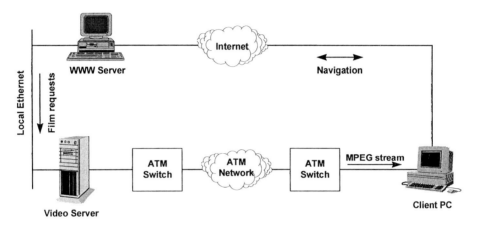

Figure 26.5   Generic client–server configuration.

Client PCs can be connected either directly to the ATM network or by using an ATM-to-Ethernet router (in practice, this function will be performed by a workstation that hosts both an ATM and an Ethernet interface), yielding the following hybrid configuration.

26.3.3   Hybrid configuration

In the hybrid ATM-Ethernet configuration (Figure 26.6), an SGI Indy workstation performs the routing from the ATM network to a local Ethernet and vice versa. This way, it is not necessary for the PC to have an ATM interface: Just by using the built-in routing mechanism of TCP/IP, the video stream is first sent via ATM to the router workstation and then over a local Ethernet to the PC.

26.3.4   Navigation

For navigational purposes, the World Wide Web is used (see Figure 26.7). By running a WWW-server on the video server or on any other Internet-linked machine (as in the case of Figure 26.5), the users of the Video Retrieval service can browse through the list

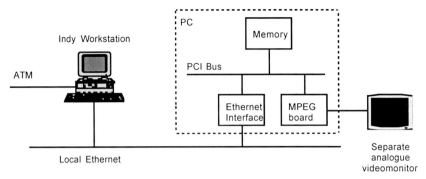

Figure 26.6   Hybrid client.

of available films. Just by clicking on a film's name, an identification of this film is sent to the video server, which responds by starting to send the video stream over the ATM connection to the client PC.

26.3.5   Tests

Within the framework of the INTERACT/SONAH European project, several inter-European tests have been conducted using different client configurations, with users in Portugal, Switzerland, and Sweden. During these tests, it turned out that the

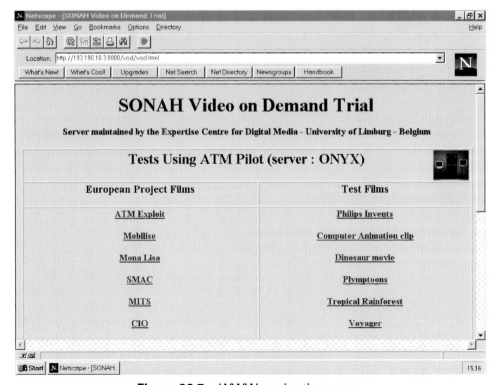

Figure 26.7   WWW navigation page.

performance depends very much on the TCP/IP stack used on the PC. The TCP/IP stack that is integrated in Windows 95 outperformed those that we used under Windows 3.1 or 3.11. Furthermore, in the hybrid ATM-Ethernet configuration, the performance also depends on the load of the local Ethernet. Another observation was that a sustained ATM data rate between 1.5 and 2.5 Mbits/s is sufficient for most MPEG-1 compressed video material.

In Table 26.2, we show some measurements for two different test films. In a hybrid ATM-Ethernet situation, we measured the actual data input at the client side, depending on different peak rates imposed on the ATM link. The data rates following the film names indicate the required display data rate, depending on the parameters that were imposed at compression time.

Note that the reported numbers are produced with a configuration in which the PC buffers the incoming video stream in a buffer of 64 Kbytes. A larger buffer could be used to cope with network fluctuations.

Table 26.2   Video retrieval bandwidth measurements

Film	ATM peak rate	Actual data rate	Perceived quality
Jurassic Park	2000	1765	Bad
(2040 Kbits/s)	2100	1797	Poor
	2200	1888	Poor
	2300	2029	Good
Philips Invents	1400	1262	Bad
(1500 Kbits/s)	1500	1278	Bad
	1600	1360	Poor
	1700	1521	Good

26.4   Conclusions – Future Research

In the collaborative work applications of VISINET, and the video retrieval experiments, we have shown that the use of (hybrid Ethernet-) ATM networks can provide a good network infrastructure for these kinds of applications, which require a substantial bandwidth.

Another important issue is the fact that the (mostly workstation-hosted) ATM infrastructure can be shared with other users in the local area network by letting a multi-homed (ATM + Ethernet) workstation perform IP routing between the Ethernet and the ATM network.

In the VISINET Extension, we incorporate new (non-SGI) platforms (e.g., PCs), investigate the integration of ISDN with the existing network, and incorporate compression techniques in order to lower the required bandwidth or to facilitate remote use of (graphical) supercomputers.

Regarding the video retrieval services, we will perform the migration to non-ATM networks (e.g., cable TV networks), which will also yield the incorporation of another type of client (e.g., a TV with a set-top box). At the server side, a distributed virtual server will be established on several ATM-linked machines.

Acknowledgments

We thank the staff of the Expertise Center for Digital Media for their support, and especially Kurt Dethier for most of the implementation of the Video Retrieval software. We moreover thank Belgacom (the Belgian telecom operator) and Alcatel Bell for their collaborative support. Part of this work has been funded by the European Commission, through the projects RACE TEN-IBC VISINET B2007 and RACE INTERACT/ SONAH R2085.

References

[1] R.L. Phillips, A network-based distributed, media-rich computing and information environment, (BCS Conference, Dec 94), to appear in *Digital Media and Electronic Publishing*, R.A. Earnshaw, H. Jones, J.A. Vince, eds., Academic Press, 1996.
[2] R.A. Earnshaw, Report on digital media and electronic publishing, *UK Graphics and Visualization Newsletter* (39): 8–9; Feb. 1995.
[3] R.A. Earnshaw, M. Jern, Fundamental approaches to interactive real-time visualization systems, *Scientific Visualization: Advances and Challenges*, L.J. Rosenblum et al., eds., pp. 223–238, Academic Press/IEEE Computer Society, 1994. (ISBN 0-12-227742-2).
[4] J. Schnepf, D. Du, E. Ritenour, A. Fahrmann, Building future medical education environments over ATM networks, *Commun. ACM*, 38(2): 54–69; 1995.
[5] C. Greenhalgh, S. Benford, MASSIVE: A collaborative virtual environment for teleconferencing, *ACM Trans. Computer–Human Interaction*, 2(3): 239–261; 1995.
[6] R.A. Earnshaw, VISINET and G7 Ministers' Meeting, *UK Graphics and Visualization Newsletter*, (40): 6; April 1995.
[7] R.A. Earnshaw, A.B. Haigh, Virtual reality trial over ATM, *UK Graphics and Visualization Newsletter* (39): 5–7: Feb. 1995.
[8] L. Clyne, SuperJANET ATM/Video Network – pilot service from 1 June 1994, *UK Graphics and Visualization Newsletter*, (37): 5–6; 1994.

Index